PISA 2012 Results: Creative Problem Solving

STUDENTS' SKILLS IN TACKLING REAL-LIFE PROBLEMS (VOLUME V)

OECD

BETTER POLICIES FOR BETTER LIVES

This work is published on the responsibility of the Secretary-General of the OECD. The opinions expressed and arguments employed herein do not necessarily reflect the official views of the Organisation or of the governments of its member countries.

This document and any map included herein are without prejudice to the status of or sovereignty over any territory, to the delimitation of international frontiers and boundaries and to the name of any territory, city or area.

Please cite this publication as:

OECD (2014), PISA 2012 Results: Creative Problem Solving: Students' Skills in Tackling Real-Life Problems (Volume V), PISA, OECD Publishing.
http://dx.doi.org/10.1787/9789264208070-en

ISBN 978-92-64-20806-3 (print)
ISBN 978-92-64-20807-0 (PDF)

Note by Turkey: The information in this document with reference to "Cyprus" relates to the southern part of the Island. There is no single authority representing both Turkish and Greek Cypriot people on the Island. Turkey recognises the Turkish Republic of Northern Cyprus (TRNC). Until a lasting and equitable solution is found within the context of the United Nations, Turkey shall preserve its position concerning the "Cyprus issue".

Note by all the European Union Member States of the OECD and the European Union: The Republic of Cyprus is recognised by all members of the United Nations with the exception of Turkey. The information in this document relates to the area under the effective control of the Government of the Republic of Cyprus.

The statistical data for Israel are supplied by and under the responsibility of the relevant Israeli authorities. The use of such data by the OECD is without prejudice to the status of the Golan Heights, East Jerusalem and Israeli settlements in the West Bank under the terms of international law.

Photo credits:
© Flying Colours Ltd/Getty Images
© Jacobs Stock Photography/Kzenon
© khoa vu/Flickr/Getty Images
© Mel Curtis/Corbis
© Shutterstock/Kzenon
© Simon Jarratt/Corbis

Corrigenda to OECD publications may be found on line at: www.oecd.org/publishing/corrigenda.
© OECD 2014

Foreword

Equipping citizens with the skills necessary to achieve their full potential, participate in an increasingly interconnected global economy, and ultimately convert better jobs into better lives is a central preoccupation of policy makers around the world. Results from the OECD's recent Survey of Adult Skills show that highly skilled adults are twice as likely to be employed and almost three times more likely to earn an above-median salary than poorly skilled adults. In other words, poor skills severely limit people's access to better-paying and more rewarding jobs. Highly skilled people are also more likely to volunteer, see themselves as actors rather than as objects of political processes, and are more likely to trust others. Fairness, integrity and inclusiveness in public policy thus all hinge on the skills of citizens.

The ongoing economic crisis has only increased the urgency of investing in the acquisition and development of citizens' skills – both through the education system and in the workplace. At a time when public budgets are tight and there is little room for further monetary and fiscal stimulus, investing in structural reforms to boost productivity, such as education and skills development, is key to future growth. Indeed, investment in these areas is essential to support the recovery, as well as to address long-standing issues such as youth unemployment and gender inequality.

In this context, more and more countries are looking beyond their own borders for evidence of the most successful and efficient policies and practices. Indeed, in a global economy, success is no longer measured against national standards alone, but against the best-performing and most rapidly improving education systems. Over the past decade, the OECD Programme for International Student Assessment, PISA, has become the world's premier yardstick for evaluating the quality, equity and efficiency of school systems. But the evidence base that PISA has produced goes well beyond statistical benchmarking. By identifying the characteristics of high-performing education systems PISA allows governments and educators to identify effective policies that they can then adapt to their local contexts.

The results from the PISA 2012 assessment, which was conducted at a time when many of the 65 participating countries and economies were grappling with the effects of the crisis, reveal wide differences in education outcomes, both within and across countries. Using the data collected in previous PISA rounds, we have been able to track the evolution of student performance over time and across subjects. Of the 64 countries and economies with comparable data, 40 improved their average performance in at least one subject. Top performers such as Shanghai in China or Singapore were able to further extend their lead, while countries like Brazil, Mexico, Tunisia and Turkey achieved major improvements from previously low levels of performance.

Some education systems have demonstrated that it is possible to secure strong and equitable learning outcomes at the same time as achieving rapid improvements. Of the 13 countries and economies that significantly improved their mathematics performance between 2003 and 2012, three also show improvements in equity in education during the same period, and another nine improved their performance while maintaining an already high level of equity – proving that countries do not have to sacrifice high performance to achieve equity in education opportunities.

Nonetheless, PISA 2012 results show wide differences between countries in mathematics performance. The equivalent of almost six years of schooling, 245 score points, separates the highest and lowest average performances

of the countries that took part in the PISA 2012 mathematics assessment. The difference in mathematics performances within countries is even greater, with over 300 points – the equivalent of more than seven years of schooling – often separating the highest- and the lowest-achieving students in a country. Clearly, all countries and economies have excellent students, but few have enabled all students to excel.

The report also reveals worrying gender differences in students' attitudes towards mathematics: even when girls perform as well as boys in mathematics, they report less perseverance, less motivation to learn mathematics, less belief in their own mathematics skills, and higher levels of anxiety about mathematics. While the average girl underperforms in mathematics compared with the average boy, the gender gap in favour of boys is even wider among the highest-achieving students. These findings have serious implications not only for higher education, where young women are already under-represented in the science, technology, engineering and mathematics fields of study, but also later on, when these young women enter the labour market. This confirms the findings of the OECD Gender Strategy, which identifies some of the factors that create – and widen – the gender gap in education, labour and entrepreneurship. Supporting girls' positive attitudes towards and investment in learning mathematics will go a long way towards narrowing this gap.

PISA 2012 also finds that the highest-performing school systems are those that allocate educational resources more equitably among advantaged and disadvantaged schools and that grant more autonomy over curricula and assessments to individual schools. A belief that all students can achieve at a high level and a willingness to engage all stakeholders in education – including students, through such channels as seeking student feedback on teaching practices – are hallmarks of successful school systems.

PISA is not only an accurate indicator of students' abilities to participate fully in society after compulsory school, but also a powerful tool that countries and economies can use to fine-tune their education policies. There is no single combination of policies and practices that will work for everyone, everywhere. Every country has room for improvement, even the top performers. That's why the OECD produces this triennial report on the state of education across the globe: to share evidence of the best policies and practices and to offer our timely and targeted support to help countries provide the best education possible for all of their students. With high levels of youth unemployment, rising inequality, a significant gender gap, and an urgent need to boost growth in many countries, we have no time to lose. The OECD stands ready to support policy makers in this challenging and crucial endeavour.

Angel Gurría
OECD Secretary-General

Acknowledgements

This report is the product of a collaborative effort between the countries participating in PISA, the experts and institutions working within the framework of the PISA Consortium, and the OECD Secretariat. The report was drafted by Andreas Schleicher, Francesco Avvisati, Francesca Borgonovi, Miyako Ikeda, Hiromichi Katayama, Flore-Anne Messy, Chiara Monticone, Guillermo Montt, Sophie Vayssettes and Pablo Zoido of the OECD Directorate for Education and Skills and the Directorate for Financial Affairs, with statistical support from Simone Bloem and Giannina Rech and editorial oversight by Marilyn Achiron. Additional analytical and editorial support was provided by Adele Atkinson, Jonas Bertling, Marika Boiron, Célia Braga-Schich, Tracey Burns, Michael Davidson, Cassandra Davis, Elizabeth Del Bourgo, John A. Dossey, Joachim Funke, Samuel Greiff, Tue Halgreen, Ben Jensen, Eckhard Klieme, André Laboul, Henry Levin, Barry McCrae, Juliette Mendelovits, Tadakazu Miki, Christian Monseur, Simon Normandeau, Lorena Ortega, Mathilde Overduin, Elodie Pools, Dara Ramalingam, William H. Schmidt (whose work was supported by the Thomas J. Alexander fellowship programme), Kaye Stacey, Lazar Stankov, Ross Turner, Elisabeth Villoutreix and Allan Wigfield. The system-level data collection was conducted by the OECD NESLI (INES Network for the Collection and Adjudication of System-Level Descriptive Information on Educational Structures, Policies and Practices) team: Bonifacio Agapin, Estelle Herbaut and Jean Yip. Volume II also draws on the analytic work undertaken by Jaap Scheerens and Douglas Willms in the context of PISA 2000. Administrative support was provided by Claire Chetcuti, Juliet Evans, Jennah Huxley and Diana Tramontano.

The OECD contracted the Australian Council for Educational Research (ACER) to manage the development of the mathematics, problem solving and financial literacy frameworks for PISA 2012. Achieve was also contracted by the OECD to develop the mathematics framework with ACER. The expert group that guided the preparation of the mathematics assessment framework and instruments was chaired by Kaye Stacey; Joachim Funke chaired the expert group that guided the preparation of the problem-solving assessment framework and instruments; and Annamaria Lusardi led the expert group that guided the preparation of the financial literacy assessment framework and instruments. The PISA assessment instruments and the data underlying the report were prepared by the PISA Consortium, under the direction of Raymond Adams at ACER.

The development of the report was steered by the PISA Governing Board, which is chaired by Lorna Bertrand (United Kingdom), with Benő Csapó (Hungary), Daniel McGrath (United States) and Ryo Watanabe (Japan) as vice chairs. Annex C of the volumes lists the members of the various PISA bodies, as well as the individual experts and consultants who have contributed to this report and to PISA in general.

Table of Contents

BOXES

FIGURES

TABLES

This book has...

StatLinkS

A service that delivers Excel® files from the printed page!

Look for the *StatLinks* at the bottom left-hand corner of the tables or graphs in this book.
To download the matching Excel® spreadsheet, just type the link into your Internet browser, starting with the ***http://dx.doi.org*** prefix.
If you're reading the PDF e-book edition, and your PC is connected to the Internet, simply click on the link. You'll find *StatLinks* appearing in more OECD books.

Executive Summary

In modern societies, all of life is problem solving. Changes in society, the environment, and in technology mean that the content of applicable knowledge evolves rapidly. Adapting, learning, daring to try out new things and always being ready to learn from mistakes are among the keys to resilience and success in an unpredictable world.

Few workers today, whether in manual or knowledge-based occupations, use repetitive actions to perform their job tasks. What's more, as the new Survey of Adult Skills (PIAAC) finds, one in ten workers is confronted every day with more complex problems that require at least 30 minutes to solve. Complex problem-solving skills are particularly in demand in fast-growing, highly skilled managerial, professional and technical occupations.

Are today's 15-year-olds acquiring the problem-solving skills needed in the 21st century? This volume reports the results from the PISA 2012 assessment of problem solving, which was administered, on computer, to about 85 000 students in 44 countries and economies.

Students in Singapore and Korea, followed by students in Japan, score higher in problem solving than students in all other participating countries and economies.

Four more East Asian partner economies score between 530 and 540 points on the PISA problem-solving scale: Macao-China (with a mean score of 540 points), Hong Kong-China (540 points), Shanghai-China (536 points) and Chinese Taipei (534 points); and Canada, Australia, Finland, England (United Kingdom), Estonia, France, the Netherlands, Italy, the Czech Republic, Germany, the United States and Belgium all score above the OECD average, but below the former group of countries.

Across OECD countries, 11.4% of 15-year-old students are top performers in problem solving.

Top performers attain proficiency Level 5 or 6 in problem solving, meaning that they can systematically explore a complex problem scenario, devise multi-step solutions that take into account all constraints, and adjust their plans in light of the feedback received. In Singapore, Korea and Japan, more than one in five students achieve this level, while more than one in six students perform at Level 5 or above in Hong Kong-China (19.3%), Chinese Taipei and Shanghai-China (18.3%), Canada (17.5%) and Australia (16.7%). By contrast, in Montenegro, Malaysia, Colombia, Uruguay, Bulgaria and Brazil, fewer than 2% of students perform at Level 5 or 6; and all of these countries perform well below the OECD average.

On average across OECD countries, about one in five students is able to solve only straightforward problems – if any – provided that they refer to familiar situations.

By contrast, fewer than one in ten students in Japan, Korea, Macao-China and Singapore are low-achievers in problem solving.

In Australia, Brazil, Italy, Japan, Korea, Macao-China, Serbia, England (United Kingdom) and the United States, students perform significantly better in problem solving, on average, than students in other countries who show similar performance in mathematics, reading and science.

In Australia, England (United Kingdom) and the United States, this is particularly true among strong and top performers in mathematics; in Italy, Japan and Korea, this is particularly true among moderate and low performers in mathematics.

Students in Hong Kong-China, Korea, Macao-China, Shanghai-China, Singapore and Chinese Taipei perform strongest on problems that require understanding, formulating or representing new knowledge, compared to other types of problems.

Many of the best-performing countries and economies in problem solving are those with better-than-expected performance on tasks related to acquiring knowledge, such as "exploring and understanding" and "representing and formulating" tasks, and relatively weaker performance on tasks involving only the use of knowledge, such as "planning and executing" tasks that do not require substantial understanding or representation of the problem situation. Meanwhile, students in Brazil, Ireland, Korea and the United States perform strongest on interactive problems (those that require the student to uncover some of the information needed to solve the problem) compared to static problems (those that have all information disclosed at the outset).

In Malaysia, Shanghai-China and Turkey, more than one in eight students attend a vocational study programme, and these students show significantly better performance in problem solving, on average, than students with comparable performance in mathematics, reading and science but who are in general study programmes.

This finding can be interpreted in two ways. On the one hand, the curriculum and teaching practices in these vocational programmes may equip students better for tackling complex, real-life problems in contexts that they do not usually encounter at school. On the other hand, better-than-expected performance in problem solving may be an indication that in these programmes, students' ability to solve problems is not nurtured within the core academic subjects.

Boys outperform girls in problem solving in 23 countries/economies, girls outperform boys in five countries/ economies, and in 16 countries/economies, there is no significant difference in average performance between boys and girls.

Gender differences are often larger among top performers. On average across OECD countries, there are three top-performing boys for every two top-performing girls in problem solving. In Croatia, Italy and the Slovak Republic, boys are as likely as girls to be low-achievers, but are more than twice as likely to be top performers as girls. In no country or economy are there more girls than boys among the top performers in problem solving. Girls appear to be stronger in performing the "planning and executing" tasks that measure how students use knowledge, compared to other tasks; and weaker in performing the more abstract "representing and formulating" tasks, which relate to how students acquire knowledge.

The impact of socio-economic status on problem-solving performance is weaker than it is on performance in mathematics, reading or science.

Students from disadvantaged backgrounds are more likely to score higher than expected in problem solving than in mathematics, perhaps because after-school opportunities to exercise their skills in problem solving arise in diverse social and cultural contexts. Still, the quality of schools matters: unequal access to high-quality schools means that, on average, disadvantaged students score below advantaged students in all subjects assessed, including problem solving.

■ Table V.A ■
SNAPSHOT OF PERFORMANCE IN PROBLEM SOLVING

	Countries/economies with mean score/share of top performers/relative performance/solution rate above the OECD average Countries/economies with share of low achievers below the OECD average
	Countries/economies with mean score/share of top performers/relative performance/share of low achievers/solution rate not statistically different from the OECD average
	Countries/economies with mean score/share of top performers/relative performance/solution rate below the OECD average Countries/economies with a share of low achievers above the OECD average

	Performance in problem solving				Relative performance in problem solving,	Performance in problem solving, by process		Performance in problem solving, by nature of the problem situation	
	Mean score in PISA 2012	Share of low achievers (below Level 2)	Share of top performers (Level 5 or 6)	Gender difference (boys - girls)	compared with students around the world with similar performance in mathematics, reading and science	Solution rate on tasks measuring **acquisition** of knowledge	Solution rate on tasks measuring **utilisation** of knowledge	Solution rate on items referring to a **static** problem situation	Solution rate on items referring to an **interactive** problem situation
	Mean score	%	%	Score dif.	Score dif.	Percent correct	Percent correct	Percent correct	Percent correct
OECD average	500	21.4	11.4	**7**	-7	45.5	46.4	47.1	43.8
Singapore	562	8.0	29.3	**9**	2	62.0	55.4	59.8	57.5
Korea	561	6.9	27.6	**13**	14	62.8	54.5	58.9	57.7
Japan	552	7.1	22.3	**19**	11	59.1	56.3	58.7	55.9
Macao-China	540	7.5	16.6	**10**	8	58.3	51.3	57.0	51.7
Hong Kong-China	540	10.4	19.3	**13**	-16	57.7	51.1	56.1	52.2
Shanghai-China	536	10.6	18.3	**25**	-51	56.9	49.8	56.7	50.3
Chinese Taipei	534	11.6	18.3	12	-9	56.9	50.1	56.3	50.1
Canada	526	14.7	17.5	**5**	0	52.6	52.1	52.7	50.5
Australia	523	15.5	16.7	2	7	52.3	51.5	52.8	49.9
Finland	523	14.3	15.0	**-6**	-8	50.2	51.0	52.1	47.7
England (United Kingdom)	517	16.4	14.3	6	8	49.6	49.1	49.5	47.9
Estonia	515	15.1	11.8	5	-15	46.8	49.5	49.7	45.6
France	511	16.5	12.0	5	5	49.6	49.4	50.3	47.6
Netherlands	511	18.5	13.6	5	-16	48.2	49.7	50.4	46.5
Italy	510	16.4	10.8	**18**	10	49.5	48.0	49.5	46.8
Czech Republic	509	18.4	11.9	8	1	45.0	46.9	46.2	44.4
Germany	509	19.2	12.8	**7**	-12	47.5	49.5	49.4	46.3
United States	508	18.2	11.6	3	10	46.5	47.1	46.6	45.9
Belgium	508	20.8	14.4	**8**	-10	47.0	47.5	48.3	45.4
Austria	506	18.4	10.9	**12**	-5	45.7	47.4	48.3	43.0
Norway	503	21.3	13.1	-3	1	47.7	48.1	49.4	44.5
Ireland	498	20.3	9.4	5	-18	44.6	45.5	44.4	44.6
Denmark	497	20.4	8.7	**10**	-11	44.2	48.1	47.9	42.3
Portugal	494	20.6	7.4	**16**	-3	41.6	45.7	44.0	42.0
Sweden	491	23.5	8.8	-4	-1	45.2	44.6	47.7	41.6
Russian Federation	489	22.1	7.3	**8**	-4	40.4	43.8	43.8	39.7
Slovak Republic	483	26.1	7.8	**22**	-5	40.5	43.2	44.2	38.8
Poland	481	25.7	6.9	0	-44	41.3	43.7	44.1	39.7
Spain	477	28.5	7.8	2	-20	40.0	42.3	42.3	39.8
Slovenia	476	28.5	6.6	-4	-34	37.8	42.3	42.9	36.7
Serbia	473	28.5	4.7	**15**	11	37.7	40.7	40.3	36.8
Croatia	466	32.3	4.7	**15**	-22	35.2	40.5	39.3	35.6
Hungary	459	35.0	5.6	3	-34	35.2	37.6	38.2	33.9
Turkey	454	35.8	2.2	**15**	-14	32.8	36.0	35.8	32.7
Israel	454	38.9	8.8	6	-28	38.7	37.0	39.7	35.6
Chile	448	38.3	2.1	**13**	1	30.9	35.2	34.9	31.8
Cyprus*	445	40.4	3.6	**-9**	-12	33.6	34.8	37.0	31.4
Brazil	428	47.3	1.8	**22**	7	28.0	32.0	29.8	29.1
Malaysia	422	50.5	0.9	8	-14	29.1	29.3	30.1	27.4
United Arab Emirates	411	54.8	2.5	**-26**	-43	28.4	29.0	29.9	27.1
Montenegro	407	56.8	0.8	**-6**	-24	25.6	30.0	30.3	25.1
Uruguay	403	57.9	1.2	**11**	-27	24.8	27.9	27.5	24.8
Bulgaria	402	56.7	1.6	**-17**	-54	23.7	26.7	28.4	22.3
Colombia	399	61.5	1.2	**31**	-7	21.8	27.7	26.3	23.7

Note: Countries/economies in which the performance difference between boys and girls is statistically significant are marked in bold.
Countries and economies are ranked in descending order of the mean score in problem solving in PISA 2012.
* See notes in the Reader's Guide.
Source: OECD, PISA 2012 Database, Tables V.2.1, V.2.2, V.2.6, V.3.1, V.3.6 and V.4.7.
StatLink 🔗 http://dx.doi.org/10.1787/888933003649

Reader's Guide

Data underlying the figures

The data referred to in this volume are presented in Annex B and, in greater detail, including some additional tables, on the PISA website (*www.pisa.oecd.org*).

Four symbols are used to denote missing data:

a   The category does not apply in the country concerned. Data are therefore missing.

c   There are too few observations or no observation to provide reliable estimates (i.e. there are fewer than 30 students or fewer than 5 schools with valid data).

m   Data are not available. These data were not submitted by the country or were collected but subsequently removed from the publication for technical reasons.

w   Data have been withdrawn or have not been collected at the request of the country concerned.

Country coverage

The PISA publications (*PISA 2012 Results*) feature data on 65 countries and economies, including all 34 OECD countries and 31 partner countries and economies (see map in the section *What is PISA?*).

This volume in particular contains data on 44 countries and economies that participated in the assessment of problem solving, including 28 OECD countries and 16 partner countries and economies.

The statistical data for Israel are supplied by and under the responsibility of the relevant Israeli authorities. The use of such data by the OECD is without prejudice to the status of the Golan Heights, East Jerusalem and Israeli settlements in the West Bank under the terms of international law.

Two notes were added to the statistical data related to Cyprus:

1. Note by Turkey: The information in this document with reference to "Cyprus" relates to the southern part of the Island. There is no single authority representing both Turkish and Greek Cypriot people on the Island. Turkey recognises the Turkish Republic of Northern Cyprus (TRNC). Until a lasting and equitable solution is found within the context of the United Nations, Turkey shall preserve its position concerning the "Cyprus issue".

2. Note by all the European Union Member States of the OECD and the European Union: The Republic of Cyprus is recognised by all members of the United Nations with the exception of Turkey. The information in this document relates to the area under the effective control of the Government of the Republic of Cyprus.

Calculating international averages

An OECD average corresponding to the arithmetic mean of the respective country estimates was calculated for most indicators presented in this report. The OECD average is used to compare performance across school systems. In the case of some countries, data may not be available for specific indicators, or specific categories may not apply. Readers should, therefore, keep in mind that the term "OECD average" refers to the OECD countries included in the respective comparisons.

Rounding figures

Because of rounding, some figures in tables may not exactly add up to the totals. Totals, differences and averages are always calculated on the basis of exact numbers and are rounded only after calculation.

All standard errors in this publication have been rounded to one or two decimal places. Where the value 0.0 or 0.00 is shown, this does not imply that the standard error is zero, but that it is smaller than 0.05 or 0.005, respectively.

Reporting student data

The report uses "15-year-olds" as shorthand for the PISA target population. PISA covers students who are aged between 15 years 3 months and 16 years 2 months at the time of assessment and who are enrolled in school and have completed at least 6 years of formal schooling, regardless of the type of institution in which they are enrolled and of whether they are in full-time or part-time education, of whether they attend academic or vocational programmes, and of whether they attend public or private schools or foreign schools within the country.

Focusing on statistically significant differences

This volume discusses only statistically significant differences or changes. These are denoted in darker colours in figures and in bold font in tables. See Annex A3 for further information.

Categorising student performance

This report uses a shorthand to describe students' levels of proficiency in the subjects assessed by PISA:

Top performers are those students proficient at Level 5 or 6 of the assessment.

Strong performers are those students proficient at Level 4 of the assessment.

Moderate performers are those students proficient at Level 2 or 3 of the assessment.

Lowest performers are those students proficient at or below Level 1 of the assessment.

Abbreviations used in this report

ESCS	PISA index of economic, social and cultural status	PPP	Purchasing power parity
GDP	Gross domestic product	S.D.	Standard deviation
ISCED	International Standard Classification of Education	S.E.	Standard error
ISCO	International Standard Classification of Occupations	STEM	Science, Technology, Engineering and Mathematics

Further documentation

For further information on the PISA assessment instruments and the methods used in PISA, see the *PISA 2012 Technical Report* (OECD, forthcoming). The reader should note that there are gaps in the numbering of tables because some tables appear on line only and are not included in this publication. To consult the set of web-only data tables, visit the PISA website (*www.pisa.oecd.org*).

This report uses the OECD StatLinks service. Below each table and chart is a url leading to a corresponding Excel™ workbook containing the underlying data. These urls are stable and will remain unchanged over time. In addition, readers of the e-books will be able to click directly on these links and the workbook will open in a separate window, if their internet browser is open and running.

What is PISA?

"What is important for citizens to know and be able to do?" That is the question that underlies the triennial survey of 15-year-old students around the world known as the Programme for International Student Assessment (PISA). PISA assesses the extent to which students near the end of compulsory education have acquired key knowledge and skills that are essential for full participation in modern societies. The assessment, which focuses on mathematics, reading, science and problem solving, does not just ascertain whether students can reproduce knowledge; it also examines how well students can extrapolate from what they have learned and apply that knowledge in unfamiliar settings, both in and outside of school. This approach reflects the fact that modern economies reward individuals not for what they know, but for what they can do with what they know.

PISA is an ongoing programme that offers insights for education policy and practice, and that helps monitor trends in students' acquisition of knowledge and skills across countries and economies and in different demographic subgroups within each country. PISA results reveal what is possible in education by showing what students in the highest-performing and most rapidly improving school systems can do. The findings allow policy makers around the world to gauge the knowledge and skills of students in their own countries in comparison with those in other countries, set policy targets against measurable goals achieved by other school systems, and learn from policies and practices applied elsewhere. While PISA cannot identify cause-and-effect relationships between policies/practices and student outcomes, it can show educators, policy makers and the interested public how education systems are similar and different – and what that means for students.

A test the whole world can take

PISA is now used as an assessment tool in many regions around the world. It was implemented in 43 countries and economies in the first assessment (32 in 2000 and 11 in 2002), 41 in the second assessment (2003), 57 in the third assessment (2006) and 75 in the fourth assessment (65 in 2009 and 10 in 2010). So far, 65 countries and economies have participated in PISA 2012.

In addition to OECD member countries, the survey has been or is being conducted in:

East, South and Southeast Asia: Himachal Pradesh-India, Hong Kong-China, Indonesia, Macao-China, Malaysia, Shanghai-China, Singapore, Chinese Taipei, Tamil Nadu-India, Thailand and Viet Nam.

Central, Mediterranean and Eastern Europe, and Central Asia: Albania, Azerbaijan, Bulgaria, Croatia, Georgia, Kazakhstan, Kyrgyzstan, Latvia, Liechtenstein, Lithuania, the former Yugoslav Republic of Macedonia, Malta, Moldova, Montenegro, Romania, the Russian Federation and Serbia.

The Middle East: Jordan, Qatar and the United Arab Emirates.

Central and South America: Argentina, Brazil, Colombia, Costa Rica, Netherlands-Antilles, Panama, Peru, Trinidad and Tobago, Uruguay and Miranda-Venezuela.

Africa: Mauritius and Tunisia.

Decisions about the scope and nature of the PISA assessments and the background information to be collected are made by participating countries based on recommendations from leading experts. Considerable efforts and resources are devoted to achieving cultural and linguistic breadth and balance in assessment materials. Since the design and translation of the test, as well as sampling and data collection, are subject to strict quality controls, PISA findings are considered to be highly valid and reliable.

...

Map of PISA countries and economies

OECD countries

Australia	Japan
Austria	Korea
Belgium	Luxembourg
Canada	Mexico
Chile	Netherlands
Czech Republic	New Zealand
Denmark	Norway
Estonia	Poland
Finland	Portugal
France	Slovak Republic
Germany	Slovenia
Greece	Spain
Hungary	Sweden
Iceland	Switzerland
Ireland	Turkey
Israel	United Kingdom
Italy	United States

Partner countries and economies in PISA 2012

Albania	Montenegro
Argentina	Peru
Brazil	Qatar
Bulgaria	Romania
Colombia	Russian Federation
Costa Rica	Serbia
Croatia	Shanghai-China
Cyprus[1,2]	Singapore
Hong Kong-China	Chinese Taipei
Indonesia	Thailand
Jordan	Tunisia
Kazakhstan	United Arab Emirates
Latvia	Uruguay
Liechtenstein	Viet Nam
Lithuania	
Macao-China	
Malaysia	

Partner countries and economies in previous cycles

Azerbaijan
Georgia
Himachal Pradesh-India
Kyrgyzstan
Former Yugoslav Republic of Macedonia
Malta
Mauritius
Miranda-Venezuela
Moldova
Panama
Tamil Nadu-India
Trinidad and Tobago

1. Note by Turkey: The information in this document with reference to "Cyprus" relates to the southern part of the Island. There is no single authority representing both Turkish and Greek Cypriot people on the Island. Turkey recognises the Turkish Republic of Northern Cyprus (TRNC). Until a lasting and equitable solution is found within the context of the United Nations, Turkey shall preserve its position concerning the "Cyprus issue".

2. Note by all the European Union Member States of the OECD and the European Union: The Republic of Cyprus is recognised by all members of the United Nations with the exception of Turkey. The information in this document relates to the area under the effective control of the Government of the Republic of Cyprus.

PISA's unique features include its:

- policy orientation, which links data on student learning outcomes with data on students' backgrounds and attitudes towards learning and on key factors that shape their learning, in and outside of school, in order to highlight differences in performance and identify the characteristics of students, schools and school systems that perform well;

- innovative concept of "literacy", which refers to students' capacity to apply knowledge and skills in key subjects, and to analyse, reason and communicate effectively as they identify, interpret and solve problems in a variety of situations;

- relevance to lifelong learning, as PISA asks students to report on their motivation to learn, their beliefs about themselves, and their learning strategies;

- regularity, which enables countries and economies to monitor their progress in meeting key learning objectives; and

- breadth of coverage, which, in PISA 2012, encompasses the 34 OECD member countries and 31 partner countries and economies.

Key features of PISA 2012

The content

- The PISA 2012 survey focused on mathematics, with reading, science and problem solving as minor areas of assessment. For the first time, PISA 2012 also included an assessment of the financial literacy of young people, which was optional for countries and economies.

- PISA assesses not only whether students can reproduce knowledge, but also whether they can extrapolate from what they have learned and apply their knowledge in new situations. It emphasises the mastery of processes, the understanding of concepts, and the ability to function in various types of situations.

The students

- Around 510 000 students completed the assessment in 2012, representing about 28 million 15-year-olds in the schools of the 65 participating countries and economies.

The assessment

- Paper-based tests were used, with assessments lasting a total of two hours for each student. In a range of countries and economies, an additional 40 minutes were devoted to the computer-based assessment of mathematics, reading and problem solving.

- Test items were a mixture of multiple-choice items and questions requiring students to construct their own responses. The items were organised in groups based on a passage setting out a real-life situation. A total of about 390 minutes of test items were covered, with different students taking different combinations of test items.

- Students answered a background questionnaire, which took 30 minutes to complete, that sought information about themselves, their homes and their school and learning experiences. School principals were given a questionnaire, to complete in 30 minutes, that covered the school system and the learning environment. In some countries and economies, optional questionnaires were distributed to parents, who were asked to provide information on their perceptions of and involvement in their child's school, their support for learning in the home, and their child's career expectations, particularly in mathematics. Countries and economies could choose two other optional questionnaires for students: one asked students about their familiarity with and use of information and communication technologies, and the second sought information about their education to date, including any interruptions in their schooling and whether and how they are preparing for a future career.

WHO ARE THE PISA STUDENTS?

Differences between countries in the nature and extent of pre-primary education and care, in the age of entry into formal schooling, in the structure of the school system, and in the prevalence of grade repetition mean that school grade levels are often not good indicators of where students are in their cognitive development. To better compare student performance internationally, PISA targets a specific age of students. PISA students are aged between 15 years 3 months and 16 years 2 months at the time of the assessment, and have completed at least 6 years of formal schooling. They can be enrolled in any type of institution, participate in full-time or part-time education, in academic or vocational programmes, and attend public or private schools or foreign schools within the country or economy. (For an operational definition of this target population, see Annex A2.) Using this age across countries and over time allows PISA to compare consistently the knowledge and skills of individuals born in the same year who are still in school at age 15, despite the diversity of their education histories in and outside of school.

The population of participating students is defined by strict technical standards, as are the students who are excluded from participating (see Annex A2). The overall exclusion rate within a country was required to be below 5% to ensure that, under reasonable assumptions, any distortions in national mean scores would remain within plus or minus 5 score points, i.e. typically within the order of magnitude of 2 standard errors of sampling. Exclusion could take place either through the schools that participated or the students who participated within schools (see Annex A2, Tables A2.1 and A2.2).

There are several reasons why a school or a student could be excluded from PISA. Schools might be excluded because they are situated in remote regions and are inaccessible, because they are very small, or because of organisational or operational factors that precluded participation. Students might be excluded because of intellectual disability or limited proficiency in the language of the assessment.

In 28 out of the 65 countries and economies participating in PISA 2012, the percentage of school-level exclusions amounted to less than 1%; it was less than 4% in all countries and economies. When the exclusion of students who met the internationally established exclusion criteria is also taken into account, the exclusion rates increase slightly. However, the overall exclusion rate remains below 2% in 30 participating countries and economies, below 5% in 57 participating countries and economies, and below 7% in all countries except Luxembourg (8.4%). In 11 out of the 34 OECD countries, the percentage of school-level exclusions amounted to less than 1% and was less than 3% in 31 OECD countries. When student exclusions within schools were also taken into account, there were 11 OECD countries below 2% and 26 OECD countries below 5%.

(For more detailed information about the restrictions on the level of exclusions in PISA 2012, see Annex A2.)

WHAT KINDS OF RESULTS DOES THE TEST PROVIDE?

The PISA assessment provides three main types of outcomes:

- basic indicators that provide a baseline profile of students' knowledge and skills;

- indicators that show how skills relate to important demographic, social, economic and educational variables; and

- indicators on trends that show changes in student performance and in the relationships between student-level and school-level variables and outcomes.

Although indicators can highlight important issues, they do not provide direct answers to policy questions. To respond to this, PISA also developed a policy-oriented analysis plan that uses the indicators as a basis for policy discussion.

WHERE CAN YOU FIND THE RESULTS?

This is the fifth of six volumes that presents the results from PISA 2012. It begins by providing the rationale for assessing problem-solving competence in PISA, and introduces the innovative features of the 2012 assessment. Chapter 2 introduces the problem-solving performance scale and proficiency levels, examines student performance in problem solving, and discusses the relationship between problem-solving performance and performance in mathematics, reading and science. Chapter 3 provides a nuanced look at student performance in problem solving by focusing on students' strengths and weaknesses in performing certain types of tasks. Chapter 4 looks at differences in problem-solving performance related to education tracks and to students' gender, socio-economic status and immigrant background. It also examines students' behaviours and attitudes related to problem solving, and students' familiarity with information and communication technology. The volume concludes with a chapter that discusses the implications of the PISA problem-solving assessment for education policy and practice.

The other five volumes cover the following issues:

Volume I, *What Students Know and Can Do: Student Performance in Mathematics, Reading and Science,* summarises the performance of students in PISA 2012. It describes how performance is defined, measured and reported, and then provides results from the assessment, showing what students are able to do in mathematics. After a summary of mathematics performance, it examines the ways in which this performance varies on subscales representing different aspects of mathematics literacy. Given that any comparison of the outcomes of education systems needs to take into consideration countries' social and economic circumstances, and the resources they devote to education, the volume also presents the results within countries' economic and social contexts. In addition, the volume examines the relationship between the frequency and intensity of students' exposure to subject content in school, what is known as "opportunity to learn", and student performance. The volume concludes with a description of student results in reading and science. Trends in student performance in mathematics between 2003 and 2012, in reading between 2000 and 2012, and in science between 2006 and 2012 are examined when comparable data are available. Throughout the volume, case studies examine in greater detail the policy reforms adopted by countries that have improved in PISA.

Volume II, *Excellence through Equity: Giving Every Student the Chance to Succeed,* defines and measures equity in education and analyses how equity in education has evolved across countries and economies between PISA 2003 and PISA 2012. The volume examines the relationship between student performance and socio-economic status, and describes how other individual student characteristics, such as immigrant background and family structure, and school characteristics, such as school location, are associated with socio-economic status and performance. The volume also reveals differences in how equitably countries allocate resources and opportunities to learn to schools with different

socio-economic profiles. Case studies, examining the policy reforms adopted by countries that have improved in PISA, are highlighted throughout the volume.

Volume III, *Ready to Learn: Students' Engagement, Drive and Self-Beliefs,* explores students' engagement with and at school, their drive and motivation to succeed, and the beliefs they hold about themselves as mathematics learners. The volume identifies the students who are at particular risk of having low levels of engagement in, and holding negative dispositions towards, school in general and mathematics in particular, and how engagement, drive, motivation and self-beliefs are related to mathematics performance. The volume identifies the roles schools can play in shaping the well-being of students and the role parents can play in promoting their children's engagement with and dispositions towards learning. Changes in students' engagement, drive, motivation and self-beliefs between 2003 and 2012, and how those dispositions have changed during the period among particular subgroups of students, notably socio-economically advantaged and disadvantaged students, boys and girls, and students at different levels of mathematics proficiency, are examined when comparable data are available. Throughout the volume, case studies examine in greater detail the policy reforms adopted by countries that have improved in PISA.

Volume IV, *What Makes Schools Successful? Resources, Policies and Practices,* examines how student performance is associated with various characteristics of individual schools and of concerned school systems. It discusses how 15-year-old students are selected and grouped into different schools, programmes, and education levels, and how human, financial, educational and time resources are allocated to different schools. The volume also examines how school systems balance autonomy with collaboration, and how the learning environment in school shapes student performance. Trends in these variables between 2003 and 2012 are examined when comparable data are available, and case studies, examining the policy reforms adopted by countries that have improved in PISA, are presented throughout the volume.

Volume VI, *Students and Money: Financial Literacy Skills for the 21st Century,* examines 15-year-old students' performance in financial literacy in the 18 countries and economies that participated in this optional assessment. It also discusses the relationship of financial literacy to students' and their families' background and to students' mathematics and reading skills. The volume also explores students' access to money and their experience with financial matters. In addition, it provides an overview of the current status of financial education in schools and highlights relevant case studies.

The frameworks for assessing mathematics, reading and science in 2012 are described in *PISA 2012 Assessment and Analytical Framework: Mathematics, Reading, Science, Problem Solving and Financial Literacy* (OECD, 2013). They are also summarised in this volume.

Technical annexes at the end of this report describe how questionnaire indices were constructed and discuss sampling issues, quality-assurance procedures, the reliability of coding, and the process followed for developing the assessment instruments. Many of the issues covered in the technical annexes are elaborated in greater detail in the *PISA 2012 Technical Report* (OECD, forthcoming).

All data tables referred to in the analysis are included at the end of the respective volume in Annex B1, and a set of additional data tables is available on line (*www.pisa.oecd.org*). A Reader's Guide is also provided in each volume to aid in interpreting the tables and figures that accompany the report. Data from regions within the participating countries are included in Annex B2.

References

OECD (forthcoming), *PISA 2012 Technical Report*, PISA, OECD Publishing.

OECD (2013), *PISA 2012 Assessment and Analytical Framework: Mathematics, Reading, Science, Problem Solving and Financial Literacy*, PISA, OECD Publishing.
http://dx.doi.org/10.1787/9789264190511-en

Assessing Problem-Solving Skills in PISA 2012

This chapter introduces the PISA 2012 assessment of problem solving. It provides the rationale for assessing problem-solving competence in PISA, and introduces the innovative features of the 2012 assessment. The framework for the assessment is presented, and sample items are discussed.

Non vitae, sed scholae discimus
[Too often,] we don't learn for life, but only for the lecture room
Seneca, *Ad Lucilium*, c. 65 AD

In Daniel Defoe's novel, Robinson Crusoe is stranded on a desert island. He first needs to secure food for himself. To solve this problem, he re-invents agriculture and tames a flock of wild goats. Then, he returns to his true longing: "My desire to venture over for the main[land] increased, rather than decreased, as the means for it seemed impossible. This at length put me upon thinking whether it was not possible to make myself a canoe […], even without tools, […] of the trunk of a great tree. This I not only thought possible, but easy" (Defoe, 1919).

Problems are situations with no obvious solution, and solving problems requires thinking and learning in action. Problem solving "involves initiating, usually on the basis of hunches or feelings, experimental interactions with the environment to clarify the nature of a problem and potential solutions", so that the problem-solver "can learn more […] about the nature of the problem and the effectiveness of their strategies", "modify their behaviour and launch a further round of experimental interactions with the environment" (Raven, 2000, p. 54). (Robinson Crusoe's first strategy to escape from his island in a canoe fails, for, as he explains, "my thoughts were so intent upon my voyage over the sea in [the canoe], that I never once considered how I should get it off the land".)

Just like Robinson Crusoe, we solve small problems every day: "My mobile phone has stopped working; how do I tell my friends that I'm running late for our appointment?"; "This meeting room is so cold; are these the switches to control the air conditioning?"; "I don't speak the local language, and my connecting flight leaves from a different airport in the same city. I just hope I can get there in time."

In modern societies, all of life is problem solving. Changes in society, the environment and in technology mean that the content of applicable knowledge evolves rapidly. Today's 15-year-olds are the Robinson Crusoes of a future that remains largely unknown to us. Adapting, learning, daring to try out new things, and always being ready to learn from mistakes are among the keys to resilience and success in an unpredictable world.

This chapter begins with a discussion of the rationale for including a separate assessment of problem solving in PISA. It then introduces what is new and distinctive about the PISA 2012 approach to assessing problem solving, and describes the main dimensions covered in the problem-solving framework. The chapter concludes by presenting the test interface and sample items from the PISA computer-based assessment of problem solving.

WHY PISA ASSESSES PROBLEM-SOLVING COMPETENCE

Today's workplaces demand people who can solve non-routine problems. Few workers, whether in manual or knowledge-based occupations, use repetitive actions to perform their job tasks. The Survey of Adult Skills (PIAAC), for instance, measured how often workers are faced with a new or difficult situation in their jobs that requires some thinking before taking action (OECD, 2013a). On average across countries, a large majority of workers are confronted at least once per week in their job with simple problems (those requiring less than 30 minutes to find a solution). Meanwhile, one in ten workers is confronted every day with more complex problems that require at least 30 minutes to find a good solution. Complex problem-solving skills are particularly in demand in fast-growing, highly skilled managerial, professional and technical occupations.

One possible explanation for this shift to non-routine tasks in the workplace is that, as computers and computerised machines were introduced in greater numbers, workers were needed less often to perform routine manual or analytical tasks. Instead, they were required to deal with the unexpected and the unfamiliar, and to bring the best out of the machines and computers working alongside them (Autor, Levy and Murnane, 2003). There is clear evidence of this change in the demand for skills in Germany, Japan and the United States (Box V.1.1 and Figure V.1.1).

Acknowledging these changes, the emphasis in education is shifting too, from equipping students with highly codified, routine skills to empowering them to confront and overcome complex, non-routine cognitive challenges. Indeed, the skills that are easiest to teach and test are also the skills that are easiest to digitise, automate and outsource. For students to be prepared for tomorrow's world, they need more than mastery of a repertoire of facts and procedures; students need to become lifelong learners who can handle unfamiliar situations where the effect of their interventions is not predictable. When asked to solve problems for which they have no ready-made strategy, they need to be able to think flexibly and creatively about how to overcome the barriers that stand in the way of a solution.

■ Figure V.1.1 ■

Trends in the demand for skills: Germany, United States and Japan

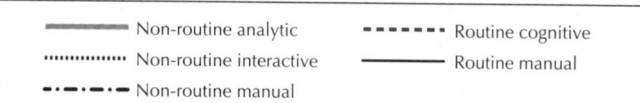

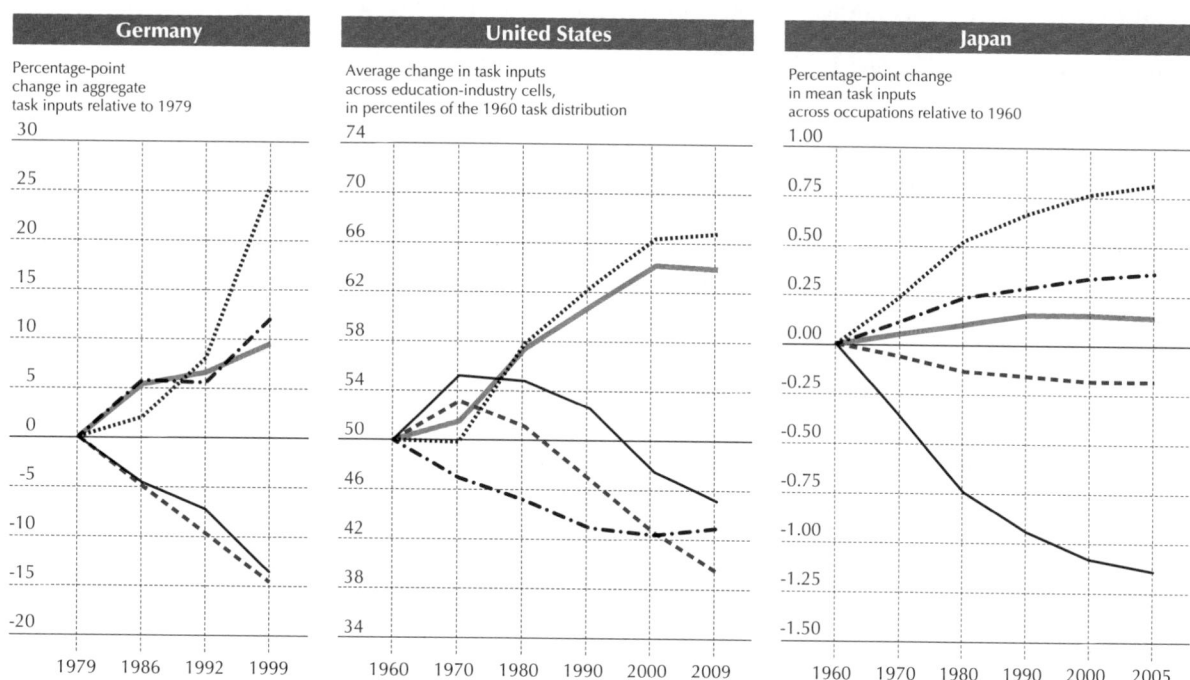

Note: The scale of the vertical axis is not directly comparable across countries due to different methodologies.
Sources: Germany: based on Spitz-Oener (2003), Table 3; United States: based on Autor and Price (2013), Table 1; Japan: based on Ikenaga and Kambayashi (2010), Figure 1.
StatLink ⟦▨⟧ http://dx.doi.org/10.1787/888933003554

Box V.1.1. **Long-term trends in the demand for problem-solving skills**

Trends in the demand for skills can be inferred from aggregate measures of workers' job requirements, repeated over time. Figure V.1.1 presents the observed evolution of job requirements in three major OECD countries: Germany, Japan and the United States. Across all three countries, there has been a marked increase in the demand for problem-solving skills.

According to Autor, Levy and Murnane (2003), job requirements can be classified into five major skill categories. A first distinction is between "routine" and "non-routine" tasks and skills. "Routine" skills correspond to tasks that "require methodical repetition of an unwavering procedure" (p. 1283), i.e. those tasks in which machines and computers can fairly easily replace human beings. They can be cognitive (such as data entry) or manual (such as repetitive production). "Non-routine" skills correspond to tasks that require tacit knowledge and are only imperfectly described in terms of a set of rules.

A further distinction, within non-routine skills, is between "manual" and "abstract" skills. Manual non-routine tasks, such as preparing a meal, demand situational adaptability, visual and language recognition, and interaction with other people. They are difficult to automate, but from the human perspective, they are straightforward, requiring primarily abilities that are hardwired into humans' evolutionary endowments. Abstract tasks are based on the processing of information and require problem-solving skills, intuition, persuasion and creativity. Among abstract skills, there are "analytic" and "interpersonal" skills: "interpersonal" tasks (such as managing teams or persuading potential buyers) require complex interpersonal communication, while "analytic" tasks require the transformation of data and information.

...

Problem-solving competence is an essential component of the skills required to perform interpersonal and non-routine analytic tasks successfully. In both kinds of tasks, workers need to think about how to engage with the situation, monitor the effect of their actions systematically, and adjust to feedback.

In Germany, a representative sample of workers has consistently reported on job requirements over more than 20 years, providing direct evidence of an increase in the use of non-routine analytic and interactive skills in the workplace during the 1980s and 1990s (Spitz-Oener, 2006). This increase has been accompanied by declines in the importance of routine skills, both analytic (such as skills needed for bookkeeping) and manual (such as sorting).

In the United States and Japan, the evolution of aggregate skill requirements has been estimated by matching job titles reported to the national population census with precise job descriptions in the dictionary of occupational titles, for the United States (Autor, Levy and Murnane, 2003; Autor and Price, 2013), or in the career matrix constructed by the Institute for Labour Policy and Training in Japan (Ikenaga and Kambayashi, 2010). Changes in the occupational shares for precisely defined occupations can then be translated into changes in the economy's skill requirements. This methodology has yielded strikingly similar results as found in Germany, over a longer period of time, i.e. since 1960.

While problem-solving skills are increasingly needed in today's economies, the ability to adapt to new circumstances, learn throughout life, and turn knowledge into action has always been important for full participation in society. The best educators have always aimed to foster the skills needed to perform non-routine tasks, i.e. to teach for life, not for school.

Recent evidence confirms that the generic skills examined in a problem-solving assessment such as PISA are strongly associated with academic success and are distinct from reasoning or intelligence, as traditionally measured (Wüstenberg et al., 2012; Greiff et al., 2013a; Funke and Frensch, 2007). In addition, other research strongly supports the view that good teachers and schools can develop students' overall problem-solving skills through and in addition to their competence in regular curricular subjects (Csapó and Funke, forthcoming).

Yet all too often teachers find that while their students may excel on routine exercises (those that they have already seen and practiced), they fail to solve problems that are unlike those they have previously encountered. Clearly, mastering the simple steps that are required to reach a solution is not enough. Students need to be able to know not only what to do, but also when to do it; and they need to feel motivated and interested. Mayer (1998) summarises these three components of successful problem solving in all domains as "skill", "metaskill" and "will".

The problem-solving assessment in PISA 2012 focuses on students' general reasoning skills, their ability to regulate problem-solving processes, and their willingness to do so, by confronting students with problems that do not require expert knowledge to solve. Individual problem solving was assessed as a separate domain for the first time in 2003 (OECD, 2005). The advances in our understanding of problem solving since then and the opportunities afforded by computers to improve the assessment of problem-solving skills led to the inclusion of problem solving as a core component of the PISA 2012 assessment.[1]

The regular assessments of mathematics, reading and science in PISA all include problem-solving tasks that assess students' ability to use their curricular knowledge to meet real-life challenges. Indeed, problem-solving competence need not be developed independently of expertise in curricular subjects; in fact, the literature on the development of general cognitive abilities suggests that content-based methods can be equally effective and may be preferable: "If you teach the specifics with abstraction in mind, the general is learned, but if you try to teach the general directly, the specifics are often not learned" (Adey et al., 2007, p. 92).

While schools are not the only environment in which problem-solving competence is nurtured, high-quality education, in a wide range of subjects, certainly helps to develop these skills. Progressive teaching methods, like problem-based learning, inquiry-based learning, and individual and group project work, can be used to foster deep understanding and prepare students to apply their knowledge in novel situations. Good teaching promotes self-regulated learning and metacognition – particularly knowledge about when and how to use certain strategies for learning or for problem solving – and develops cognitive dispositions that underpin problem solving. It prepares students to reason effectively in unfamiliar situations, and to fill gaps in their knowledge by observing, exploring and interacting with unknown systems.

All teachers can create opportunities to develop problem-solving competence. For instance, thinking habits, such as careful observation, awareness about one's working process, or critical self-evaluation, can be instilled in students as they learn techniques in the visual arts (Winner et al., 2013; see Box V.5.5) – and indeed, in any other subject in the school curriculum. Because the skills and dispositions that underpin successful problem solving in real life are not specific to particular subjects, students who learn to master them in several curricular contexts will be better equipped to use them outside of school as well.

Thus, by measuring 15-year-olds' problem-solving skills, PISA provides evidence about the comparative success of education systems in equipping students for success in life, evidence that can, in turn, inform education policies and practices.

THE PISA 2012 APPROACH TO ASSESSING STUDENT PERFORMANCE IN PROBLEM SOLVING

The problem-solving assessment in PISA 2012 focuses on general cognitive processes involved in problem solving, rather than on the ability to solve problems in particular school subjects. Given the advances in understanding the cognitive processes involved in problem solving and the possibility of using computer-based simulated scenarios,[2] the assessment also assigns a central place to so-called interactive problems.

A focus on general cognitive processes involved in solving problems

Research findings suggest that outside of artificial laboratory conditions, the situation in which a problem is embedded influences the strategies used to solve it (Kotovsky, Hayes and Simon, 1985; Funke, 1992). In real life, highly proficient problem-solvers in one context may act as novices when confronted with problems outside of their field of expertise.

In the context of a particular subject, trade or occupation, experts will use domain-specific knowledge and strategies to solve the problems. Meanwhile, those who solve problems efficiently, even when they arise outside of their field of expertise, have mastered general reasoning skills, can apply those skills where appropriate, and are motivated to engage with unfamiliar problems.

A glimpse at some of the names of problem-solving units included in the PISA assessment reveals the typical contexts included in the assessment: technology devices (e.g. *REMOTE CONTROL, CLOCK, LIGHTS*), unfamiliar spaces (e.g. *TRAFFIC, LOST*), food or drink (e.g. *VITAMINS, DRINK MACHINE*), etc. These contexts refer to situations that students may encounter outside of school as part of their everyday experience.

While including authentic scenarios related to real-life problems, the PISA 2012 problem-solving assessment avoids the need for specific, curricular knowledge as much as possible. Texts are short and use plain language. If arithmetic operations are required, calculators are embedded in the scenario. In contrast, when problem-solving tasks are incorporated in the assessment of the regular PISA domains of mathematics, reading and science, expert knowledge in these areas is needed in order to reach a solution.

By using authentic problem situations, the assessment also reduces the influence of affective factors related to school, or to specific subjects, on results. The student's familiarity with the context may still influence how he or she approaches the problem. Because the assessment tasks are embedded in real-life settings, in practice some students may be more familiar than others with the concrete contexts. However, since a wide range of contexts is included in the different assessment units, the degree of familiarity with the setting will vary, so that prior knowledge will not systematically influence performance. In addition, applying prior knowledge is never sufficient for solving new problems, even in familiar situations.

The centrality of interactive problem solving

In most problems that students practice in class or when studying for an exam, the information needed to solve the problem is provided at the outset. By contrast, solving real-life problems often requires identifying the pieces of information available in the environment/context that would be most useful for solving the problem.

Problems that require students to uncover useful information by exploring the problem situation are called *interactive problems*. These kinds of problems are encountered when using unfamiliar everyday devices, such as a new mobile phone, home appliance or vending machine. Outside of technological contexts, similar situations also arise in social interactions and in other settings as varied as cultivating plants or raising animals. A majority of PISA 2012 problem-solving tasks correspond to interactive problems. The prevalence of interactive problems in the PISA 2012 assessment reflects their importance in the real world.

The inclusion of interactive tasks, made possible by computer delivery, represents the main innovation over the PISA 2003 assessment of problem solving. PISA 2012 therefore provides a broader measure of problem-solving competency than previous assessments of problem solving.

The PISA definition of problem-solving competence

PISA 2012 defines problem-solving competence as:

…an individual's capacity to engage in cognitive processing to understand and resolve problem situations where a method of solution is not immediately obvious. It includes the willingness to engage with such situations in order to achieve one's potential as a constructive and reflective citizen.

The PISA 2012 framework publication (OECD, 2013b) discusses the definition in full. Among the key elements:

… an individual's capacity to engage in cognitive processing to understand and resolve problem situations…

Problem solving begins with recognising that a problem situation exists and establishing an understanding of the nature of the situation. It requires the solver to identify the specific problem(s) to be solved, plan and carry out a solution, and monitor and evaluate progress throughout the activity.

The verbs *engage, understand* and *resolve* underline that, in addition to the explicit responses to items, the assessment measures individuals' progress towards solving a problem, including the strategies they employ. Where appropriate, these strategies are tracked through behavioural data captured by the computer.

… where a method of solution is not immediately obvious…

This part of the definition corresponds to the definition of "problem" as a situation in which the goal cannot be achieved by merely applying previously learned procedures (Mayer, 1990). The PISA assessment of problem solving is only concerned with such non-routine tasks.

In many real-life situations, the same task may be considered a novel problem by some and a routine problem by others. With learning and practice, some activities that were initially experienced as problem solving may become routine activities. The problems included in the PISA assessment of problem solving involve tasks that are non-routine for 15-year-old students. Although some students may be familiar with the context or the goal of a problem situation that refers to a plausible real-world scenario, the particular problem faced is novel and the ways of achieving the goal are not immediately obvious.

For example, consider the problem of determining whether a lamp is not working because *a)* the switch is malfunctioning, *b)* there is no power, or *c)* the light bulb needs to be changed. Although the situation might be familiar to many 15-year-olds, few students, if any, have had the opportunity to develop expertise in this class of problems, and the unique design of a test unit around this problem situation makes sure that at least some adaptation of ready-made strategies is needed.

Even in non-routine problems, however, the knowledge of general strategies, including those learned at school, can be of help. The lamp problem described above is a case in point. As in many problems where the solver needs to develop an understanding of cause-effect relationships, an effective approach is to "vary one thing at a time". This strategy is at the heart of the experimental method in the natural sciences and is taught as such in school curricula throughout the world. Several problem-solving units included in the PISA assessment indirectly require students to apply a particular strategy in non-curricular contexts, without being prompted to do so.

… it includes the willingness to engage with such situations…

The last sentence of the definition underscores that the use of knowledge and skills to solve a problem depends on motivational and affective factors as well (Mayer, 1998; Funke, 2010). Students' willingness to engage with novel situations is an integral part of problem-solving competence. Motivational and affective factors are a distinct focus of the background questionnaire, which uses students' answers to measure their perseverance (whether they agree or not with the statement "When confronted with a problem, I give up easily", and other similar statements) and openness to problem solving ("I like to solve complex problems").

THE PISA 2012 FRAMEWORK FOR ASSESSING PROBLEM-SOLVING COMPETENCE

The PISA framework for assessing problem-solving competence guided the development of the assessment and sets the parameters for reporting results. The framework identifies three distinct aspects: the *nature of the problem situation*, the *problem-solving processes* involved in each task, and the *problem context*. The main elements of the problem-solving framework are summarised in Figure V.1.2.

▪ Figure V.1.2 ▪
Main features of the PISA problem-solving framework

NATURE OF THE PROBLEM SITUATION Is all the information needed to solve the problem disclosed at the outset?	▪ *Interactive:* not all information is disclosed; some information has to be uncovered by exploring the problem situation.
	▪ *Static:* all relevant information for solving the problem is disclosed at the outset.
PROBLEM-SOLVING PROCESS What are the main cognitive processes involved in the particular task?	▪ *Exploring and understanding* the information provided with the problem.
	▪ *Representing and formulating:* constructing graphical, tabular, symbolic or verbal representations of the problem situation and formulating hypotheses about the relevant factors and relationships between them.
	▪ *Planning and executing:* devising a plan by setting goals and sub-goals, and executing the sequential steps identified in the plan.
	▪ *Monitoring and reflecting:* monitoring progress, reacting to feedback, and reflecting on the solution, the information provided with the problem, or the strategy adopted.

PROBLEM CONTEXT In what everyday scenario is the problem embedded?	▪ *Setting:* does the scenario involve a technological device?	– *Technology* (involves a technological device)
		– *Non-technology*
	▪ *Focus:* what environment does the problem relate to?	– *Personal* (the student, family or close peers)
		– *Social* (the community or society in general)

The *nature of the problem situation* is determined by whether the information disclosed to the student at the outset is sufficient to solve the problem (*static problems*), or whether interaction with the problem situation is a necessary part of the solving activity (*interactive problems*). Examples of interactive problems include problems commonly faced when using unfamiliar devices, such as a new mobile phone or a ticket-vending machine.

For the purpose of the PISA assessment, the cognitive processes involved in problem solving are grouped into four *problem-solving processes*:

▪ *Exploring and understanding.* This involves exploring the problem situation by observing it, interacting with it, searching for information and finding limitations or obstacles; and demonstrating understanding of the information given and the information discovered while interacting with the problem situation.

▪ *Representing and formulating.* This involves using tables, graphs, symbols or words to represent aspects of the problem situation; and formulating hypotheses about the relevant factors in a problem and the relationships between them, to build a coherent mental representation of the problem situation.

▪ *Planning and executing.* This involves devising a plan or strategy to solve the problem, and executing it. It may involve clarifying the overall goal, setting subgoals, etc.

▪ *Monitoring and reflecting.* This involves monitoring progress, reacting to feedback, and reflecting on the solution, the information provided with the problem, or the strategy adopted.

No assumption is made that the processes involved in solving a particular problem are sequential or that all of the processes listed are involved in solving a particular problem. As individuals confront, represent and solve problems, they may move to a solution in a way that transcends the boundaries of a linear, step-by-step model. Nevertheless, single items were intended to have one of these processes as their main focus.

Although reasoning skills were not explicitly used to organise the domain, each of the problem-solving processes draws upon one or more of them. In understanding a problem situation, the solvers may need to distinguish between facts and

opinion; in formulating a solution, they may need to identify relationships between variables; in selecting a strategy, they may need to consider cause and effect; and, in reflecting on results, they may need to critically evaluate assumptions and alternative solutions. Deductive, inductive, analogical, combinatorial, and other types of reasoning are embedded within problem-solving tasks in PISA. It is important to note that these types of thinking can be taught and honed in classroom instruction (e.g. Adey et al., 2007; Klauer and Phye, 2008).

The *problem context* is classified according to two dimensions: technology or non-technology, and personal or social. Problems in technology settings involve a technological device, such as a digital clock, an air conditioner, or a ticket machine; problems in non-technology settings do not, and include problems such as task scheduling or decision making. Problems with a personal focus refer to situations involving only the student, the student's family or close peers; problems with a social focus relate to situations encountered more broadly in the community or society in general.

Items were developed to measure how well students perform when the various problem-solving processes are exercised within the two different types of problem situations across a range of contexts. Each of these key aspects is discussed and illustrated in Chapter 3.

THE DESIGN AND DELIVERY OF THE PISA 2012 COMPUTER-BASED ASSESSMENT OF PROBLEM SOLVING

The development of items for the assessment

As in all other domains, the items for the PISA 2012 problem-solving assessment came from two sources: the PISA Consortium and national submissions. The problem solving expert group that developed the PISA 2012 framework reviewed all materials to ensure that they reflected the defined construct of problem-solving competence. The items were then reviewed by national centres and field tested. If the national review indicated significant concern that an item would advantage a particular country or language group, it was not considered for inclusion in the main assessment. The procedures to ensure that no group would be consistently advantaged (or disadvantaged) by a particular item are described in greater detail in the *PISA 2012 Technical Report* (OECD, forthcoming).

A variety of response formats were used, including many that were only possible because the assessment was delivered by computer, such as the use of drop-down menus for selected response formats, or constructed responses coded automatically.

As usual in PISA, items are arranged in units grouped around a common stimulus. The survey included 16 units, with a total of 42 items. Sample units from the PISA assessment of problem solving are introduced and described at the end of this chapter.

The structure and delivery of the assessment

In the 28 OECD countries and 16 partner countries and economies that participated in the assessment of problem solving, the survey was conducted after the paper-based assessment of mathematics, reading and science. In countries that also assessed mathematics and reading on computers, these computer-based tests were administered at the same time as the problem-solving assessment. The 16 units of the problem-solving assessment were grouped into four clusters, each of which was designed to be completed in 20 minutes. Each student assessed was given either one or two clusters, depending on whether the student was also participating in the computer-based assessment of mathematics or reading. In all cases, the total time allocated to computer-based tests was 40 minutes.

The appearance of the test interface was consistent across items (see Figure V.1.3 for an example). For each item the stimulus material appeared in the top part of the screen. The item appeared in the lower part of the screen, and was separated visually from the stimulus by borders. The points at which the screen was divided varied from item to item so that scrolling was never required.

Test units within clusters and single items within units were delivered in a fixed order, with no possibility of returning to a previous item once students had begun the next item. Each test item, with its associated stimulus material, occupied a single computer screen. Students were asked to confirm that they wanted to proceed to the next item when they pressed the next item icon (arrow) in the bottom right corner of the test interface.

■ Figure V.1.3 ■
The test interface

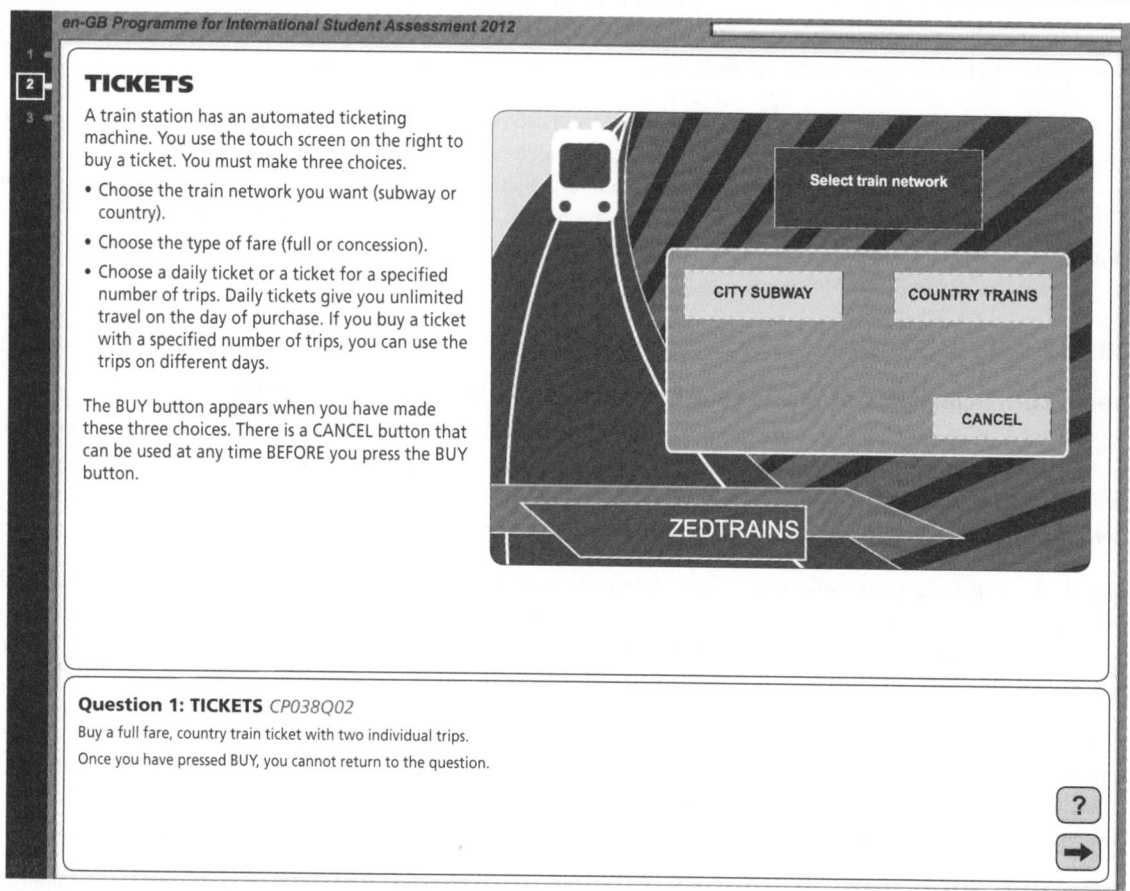

Question 1: TICKETS *CP038Q02*

Buy a full fare, country train ticket with two individual trips.

Once you have pressed BUY, you cannot return to the question.

The opportunities afforded by computer delivery

PISA 2012 marks the second time that individual problem-solving competence was assessed in PISA. In 2003, a paper and pencil test of cross-disciplinary problem solving was part of the assessment (OECD, 2005). In PISA 2012, computer delivery was fundamental to the conception of problem solving. A paper-and-pencil assessment of problem solving could not have measured the same construct. The inclusion of interactive problems, in which students need to explore the (simulated) environment and gather feedback on the effect of their interventions in order to obtain all the information needed to solve a problem, was only possible by asking students to use a computer to complete the assessment.

In addition, information about how students interact with the material as they progressed through the assessment was stored on the computer. This information includes the types of actions a student completes (e.g. mouse click, drag and drop, keystrokes), the frequency of interaction between the student and the material, the sequence of actions, the state of the system at any given point, and the timing of specific interactions.

The computer delivery made it possible to include authentic response formats, where the observed behaviour corresponds to the answer. This is a major step towards evaluating authentic problem-solving performance. For instance, Question 1 from the unit *TICKETS* asks students to use a machine that they have never seen before to buy a ticket (Figure V.1.3); students earn credit if they succeed in buying the ticket. Students do not need to describe the process in a text or drawing field, or by ticking boxes. Various selected response formats, such as drop-down menus, were also included that would not have been possible in a paper-based test.

In several items the score reflects not only the explicit response given by students, but also the sequence of actions that they perform before giving the response. For example, in a hypothetical item that required students to troubleshoot a malfunctioning device, where students would need to explore the device in order to uncover information, students

would not get credit for selecting the broken element from a number of given possibilities unless the data logged by the computer indicated that the student had taken the necessary steps to rule out other plausible alternatives. One of the innovative features of the problem-solving assessment is that information contained in log files about the sequence of actions performed by students was used to inform scoring of items where appropriate. For example, when it could be established that students had guessed an answer, they received no credit for that answer.

Given that the assessment was delivered on computers, familiarity with information and communication technologies (ICT) may have influenced students' performance. The ICT competence needed to navigate the test interface was limited to such basic skills as using a keyboard, a mouse or a touchpad, clicking radio buttons, dragging-and-dropping, scrolling and using pull-down menus and hyperlinks. In a further attempt to remove any advantage to students who were more familiar with computers, all students completed, before the assessment, a practice unit that contained examples of each of the response formats required.

PROBLEM-SOLVING TASKS

General characteristics of static and interactive problem-solving tasks

As in PISA 2003, static tasks include decision-making problems, where the student has to choose among alternatives under constraints, and system-analysis problems, where the student needs to identify relationships between parts of a system. The unit *TRAFFIC* is an example of a decision-making problem, and the unit *ROBOT CLEANER* is an example of a system-analysis problem (see the section on sample tasks below for more details on each unit).

In general, the five units with static items present analytical problems similar to those included in the PISA 2003 assessment of problem solving. However, since these items were delivered on a computer in 2012, PISA used new formats for the stimulus information (such as animations; see the unit *ROBOT CLEANER*) and new response formats (such as drag-and-drop).

Most interactive units included in the PISA 2012 assessment of problem solving belong to one of two classes of problems studied in the literature, "MicroDYN" systems and "finite-state automata". In both cases, exploration and control of an unknown system are the two main tasks for the student. The single exception is a resource-allocation problem, in which experimental interaction with the test scenario is needed to uncover important information about the available resources.

Four units are MicroDYN units, based on small dynamic systems of causal relationships (Greiff et al., 2013b; Wüstenberg et al., 2012). The unit *CLIMATE CONTROL* provides an illustration. MicroDYN units share a common structure. They consist of a system of causal relations involving only a few variables that have to be explored and controlled in order to reach assigned goal states. In the first, "knowledge-generation" phase, the student has to control up to three input variables; a graph illustrates the effect of inputs on up to three output variables. Students typically have to demonstrate rule knowledge after this first phase. Students are then asked to control the system to reach a certain target by choosing the appropriate input levels. MicroDYN units vary in the way inputs and outputs are connected in a system, in the number of variables that the system comprises, and in the fictitious scenario in which interactions with the variables take place.

Six interactive units are based on finite-state automata (Buchner and Funke, 1993; Funke, 2001), including the unit *TICKETS*. The field trial unit *MP3 PLAYER* also belongs to this group. In contrast to MycroDYN units, the outcome of an intervention is not represented by a quantity, but by a new state of the system. Many of these units are based on everyday technological devices, and the behaviour of the device depends on both the current state and on the input command received from the user. The context need not be technological, however; a simulated navigation task, where students need to orient themselves by exploring an unfamiliar neighbourhood, is similar in form. What students see in the next step depends both on where they are and what action they take.

The distinctive characteristic of finite-state automata is that there are only a finite number of possible states (not all of which are known at the outset), and a limited number of input commands (whose effect may or may not be transparent at the outset). The effect of the interventions may, or may not, depend on the current state of the system. The amount of relevant information that needs to be discovered, the number of possible actions, and the number of possible states all contribute to the level of difficulty of the item.

In these problems, students typically need to explore the system or device in order to understand the effect of their interventions, explain the functioning of the device, bring the device into some desired state, or propose improvements to the device.

Sample tasks from the PISA 2012 problem-solving assessment

Items from one unit included in the PISA 2012 field trial, and from four units that were included in the PISA 2012 main survey, are described below. For each unit, a screenshot of the stimulus information is provided, together with a brief description of the context of the unit. This is followed by a screenshot and description of each item from that unit. The test units described below are also available for viewing on the web at *http://cbasq.acer.edu.au*. The interactive nature of the units *MP3 PLAYER*, *CLIMATE CONTROL* and *TICKET MACHINE* can be best appreciated by trying to solve the items.

Sample unit 1: MP3 PLAYER (field trial)

■ Figure V.1.4 ■
MP3 PLAYER: Stimulus information

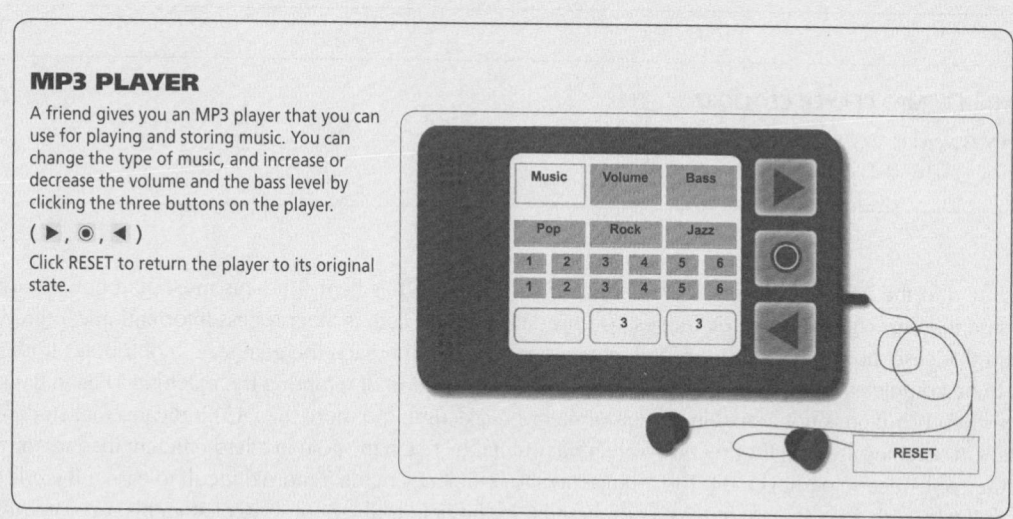

In the unit *MP3 PLAYER*, students are told that they have been given an MP3 player by a friend. They do not know how it works and must interact with it to find out, so the *nature of the problem situation* for each item in this unit is *interactive*. Since the focus of the unit is on discovering the rules that govern a device intended for use by an individual, the *context* of each item in the unit is *technology* and *personal*.

MP3 PLAYER: Item 1

■ Figure V.1.5 ■
MP3 PLAYER: Item 1

Question 1: MP3 PLAYER *CP043Q03*

The bottom row of the MP3 player shows the settings that you have chosen. Decide whether each of the following statements about the MP3 player is true or false.

Select "True" or "False" for each statement to show your answer.

Statement	True	False
You need to use the middle button (◉) to change the type of music.	○	○
You have to set the volume before you can set the bass level.	○	○
Once you have increased the volume, you can only decrease it if you change the type of music you are listening to.	○	○

In the first item in the unit, students are given a series of statements about how the system works and are asked to identify whether the statements are true or false. The statements offer scaffolding for students to explore the system. The problem-solving *process* for this item is *exploring and understanding,* and the exploration is guided but unrestricted. A "Reset" button is available that allows students to return the player to its initial state at any time and start their exploration again if desired. There is no restriction on the number of times this can be done. In the field trial this was a somewhat harder-than-average item, with 38% of students gaining full credit (True, False, False), due probably to the requirement that all three answers must be correct and the degree to which information has to be uncovered (no information is known about the system at the outset and so all knowledge of the rules of the system must come from interacting with it). Partial credit was not available for this item.

MP3 PLAYER: Item 2

■ Figure V.1.6 ■
MP3 PLAYER: Item 2

Question 2: MP3 PLAYER *CP043Q02*

Set the MP3 player to Rock, Volume 4, Bass 2.
Do this using as few clicks as possible. There is no RESET button.

The second item in the unit is classified as *planning and executing*. In this item, students must plan how to achieve a given goal and then execute this plan. Of interest for this partial-credit item is that process information captured by the computer (in this case, how many steps the student takes to successfully reach the goal state) contributes to the score. The task is to be completed using as few clicks as possible and the option of returning the machine to its initial state by pressing the "Reset" button is not available. If the number of clicks used (no more than 13) indicates that students have been efficient in reaching the goal they receive full credit; but if they reach the goal in a less-efficient manner (more than 13 clicks), they only receive partial credit. The requirement for efficiency made it more difficult to earn full credit for this item, though it was fairly easy to earn at least partial credit. In the field trial, about 39% of students received full credit and about 33% received partial credit.

MP3 PLAYER: Item 3

■ Figure V.1.7 ■
MP3 PLAYER: Item 3

Question 3: MP3 PLAYER *CP043Q01*

Shown below are four pictures of the MP3 player's screen. Three of the screens cannot happen if the MP3 player is working properly.
The remaining screen shows the MP3 player when it is working properly.

Which screen shows the MP3 player working properly?

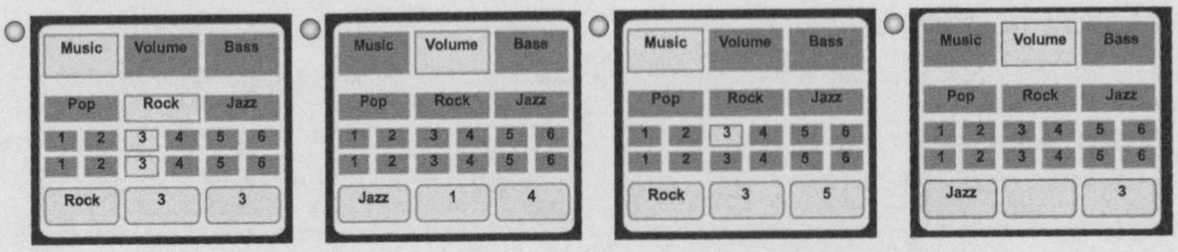

The third item in the unit is classified as *representing and formulating* since it requires students to form a mental representation of the way the whole system works in order to identify which of four given pictures shows the MP3 player when it is working properly. Returning the player to its initial state, which was possible in the first item, but absent in the second item of the unit, is again possible, so the student may interact with the system as much or as little as needed. Partial credit was not available for this item. In the field trial it was as difficult as the first item in the unit, with 39% of students selecting the correct response (the second option from the left).

MP3 PLAYER: Item 4

■ Figure V.1.8 ■
MP3 PLAYER: Item 4

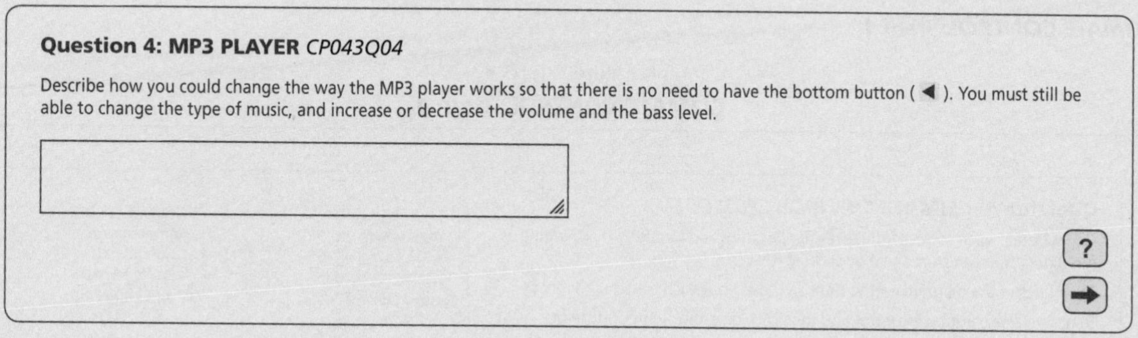

Question 4: MP3 PLAYER *CP043Q04*

Describe how you could change the way the MP3 player works so that there is no need to have the bottom button (◄). You must still be able to change the type of music, and increase or decrease the volume and the bass level.

?

➡️

The final item in this unit is classified as *monitoring and reflecting*, and asks students to reconceptualise the way the device works. This item is a constructed-response item and requires expert scoring. Full-credit answers are those that suggest how the MP3 player might operate with only two buttons instead of the original three. There is no single correct answer. Students may think creatively in devising a solution, but the most obvious solution is to suggest changing the way the top button works so that once you reach the right side of the display, one more click takes you back to the left of the display. In the field trial, this was by far the hardest item in the unit, likely because of the requirement of providing a constructed response and the item's degree of abstraction: students must imagine a hypothetical scenario and link it to their mental representation of how the system currently works, in order to describe a possible alternative functioning. Only 25% of students earned credit; partial credit was not available for this item.

Sample unit 2: CLIMATE CONTROL

■ Figure V.1.9 ■
CLIMATE CONTROL: Stimulus information

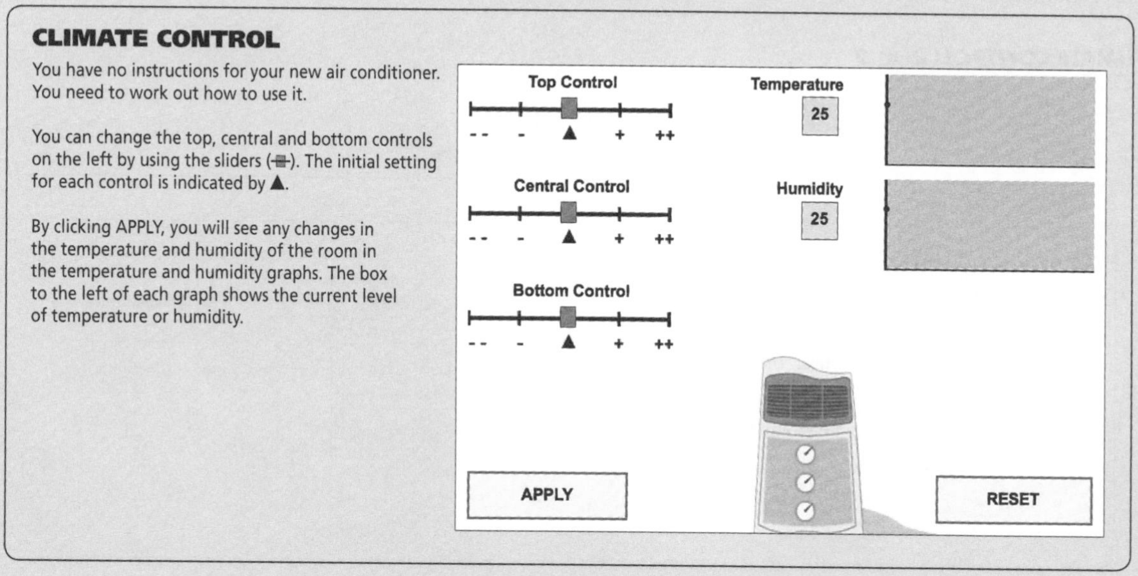

CLIMATE CONTROL

You have no instructions for your new air conditioner. You need to work out how to use it.

You can change the top, central and bottom controls on the left by using the sliders (▬). The initial setting for each control is indicated by ▲.

By clicking APPLY, you will see any changes in the temperature and humidity of the room in the temperature and humidity graphs. The box to the left of each graph shows the current level of temperature or humidity.

Top Control
-- - ▲ + ++

Central Control
-- - ▲ + ++

Bottom Control
-- - ▲ + ++

Temperature
25

Humidity
25

APPLY

RESET

In the unit *CLIMATE CONTROL*, students are told that they have a new air conditioner but no instructions for it. Students can use three controls (sliders) to vary temperature and humidity levels, but first they need to understand which control does what. A measure of temperature and humidity in the room appears in the top-right part of the screen, both in numeric and in graphical form. All items in this unit present an *interactive* problem situation, with context classified as *personal* and *technological*.

The unit *CLIMATE CONTROL* is a typical MicroDYN unit, with a first "knowledge-generation" task and a second "knowledge-application" task. Knowledge generation in the MicroDYN environment requires students to carefully monitor the effects of their interventions. The increase in the level of an input variable leads either to an increase, a decrease, a mixed effect (increase and decrease for different variables), or to no effect in one or more output variables.

CLIMATE CONTROL: Item 1

■ Figure V.1.10 ■

CLIMATE CONTROL: Item 1

Question 1: CLIMATE CONTROL *CP025Q01*

Find whether each control influences temperature and humidity by changing the sliders. You can start again by clicking RESET.

Draw lines in the diagram on the right to show what each control influences.

To draw a line, click on a control and then click on either Temperature or Humidity. You can remove any line by clicking on it.

Top Control	Temperature
Central Control	Humidity
Bottom Control	

`?`

`➡`

In the first item in the unit, students are invited to change the sliders to find out whether each control influences the temperature or the humidity level. The problem-solving *process* for this item is *representing and formulating*: the student must experiment to determine which controls have an impact on temperature and which on humidity, then represent the causal relations by drawing arrows between the three controls and the two outputs (temperature and humidity). There is no restriction on the number of rounds of exploration that the student is allowed. Full credit for this question requires that the causal diagram is correctly completed. Partial credit for this question is given if the student explores the relationships among variables efficiently, by varying only one input at a time, but fails to correctly represent them in a diagram.

CLIMATE CONTROL: Item 2

■ Figure V.1.11 ■

CLIMATE CONTROL: Item 2

Question 2: CLIMATE CONTROL *CP025Q02*

The correct relationship between the three controls, Temperature and Humidity is shown on the right.

Use the controls to set the temperature and humidity to the target levels. **Do this in a maximum of four steps.** The target levels are shown by the red bands across the Temperature and Humidity graphs. The range of values for each target level is 18-20 and is shown to the left of each red band. **You can only click APPLY four times and there is no RESET button.**

Top Control	→	Temperature
Central Control	→	Humidity
Bottom Control		

`?`

`➡`

The second item in the unit asks students to apply their new knowledge of how the air conditioner works to set temperature and humidity at specified target levels (lower than the initial state). This is a *planning and executing* item. To ensure that no further exploration is needed beyond the one conducted in the previous item, a diagram shows how the controls are related to temperature and humidity levels (students could not return to any previous item during the test). Because only four rounds of manipulation are permitted, students need to plan a few steps ahead and use a systematic, if simple, strategy to succeed in this task. Nevertheless, the target levels of temperature and humidity provided can be reached in several ways within four steps – the minimum number of steps needed is two – and a mistake can often be corrected, if immediate remedial action is taken. A possible strategy, for instance, is to set separate subgoals and to focus on temperature and humidity in successive steps. If the student is able to bring temperature and humidity both closer to their target levels within the four rounds of manipulation permitted, but does not reach the target for both, partial credit is given.

Sample unit 3: TICKETS

In the unit *TICKETS*, students are invited to imagine that they have just arrived at a train station that has an automated ticketing machine. The *context* for the items in these units is classified as *social* and *technological*.

■ Figure V.1.12 ■
TICKETS: Stimulus information

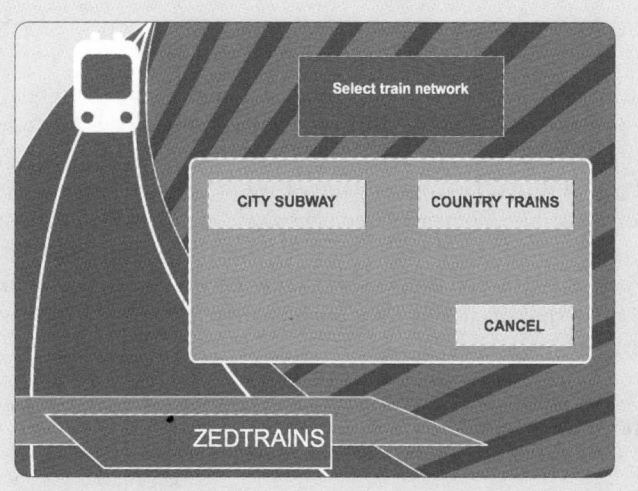

At the machine, students can buy subway or country train tickets, with full or concession fares; they can choose daily tickets or a ticket for a specified number of trips. All items in this unit present an *interactive* problem situation: students are required to engage with the unfamiliar machine and to use the machine to satisfy their needs.

TICKETS: Item 1

■ Figure V.1.13 ■
TICKETS: Item 1

Question 1: TICKETS *CP038Q02*
Buy a full fare, country train ticket with two individual trips.
Once you have pressed BUY, you cannot return to the question.

In the first item in the unit, students are invited to buy a full fare, country train ticket with two individual trips. This item measures the process of *planning and executing*. Students first have to select the network ("country trains"), then the fare type ("full fare"), then choose between a daily ticket and one for multiple individual trips, and finally indicate the number of trips (two). The solution requires multiple steps, and instructions are not given in the same order as they need to be applied. This is a relatively linear problem, compared to the following ones, but it is the first encounter with this new machine, which increases its level of difficulty relative to the following ones.

TICKETS: Item 2

■ Figure V.1.14 ■
TICKETS: Item 2

Question 2: TICKETS *CP038Q01*

You plan to take four trips around the city on the subway today. You are a student, so you can use concession fares.

Use the ticketing machine to find the cheapest ticket and press BUY.

Once you have pressed BUY, you cannot return to the question.

In the second item in the unit, students are asked to find and buy the cheapest ticket that allows them to take four trips around the city on the subway, within a single day. As students, they can use concession fares. This item is classified as *exploring and understanding* because this is the most crucial problem-solving process involved. Indeed, to accomplish the task, students must use a targeted exploration strategy, first generating at least the two most obvious possible alternatives (a daily subway tickets with concession fares, or an individual concession fare ticket with four trips), then verifying which of these is the cheapest ticket. If students visit both screens before buying the cheapest ticket (which happens to be the individual ticket with four trips) they are given full credit. Students who buy one of the two tickets without comparing the prices for the two only earn partial credit. Solving this problem involves multiple steps.

TICKETS: Item 3

■ Figure V.1.15 ■
TICKETS: Item 3

Question 3: TICKETS *CP038Q03*

You want to buy a ticket with two individual trips for the city subway. You are a student, so you can use concession fares.

Use the ticketing machine to purchase the best ticket available.

In the third item, students are asked to buy a ticket for two individual trips on the subway. They are told that they are eligible for concession fares. The third item in the unit is classified as *monitoring and reflecting,* since it requires them to modify their initial plan (to buy concession-fare tickets for the subway). When concession fares are selected, the machine says that "there are no tickets of this type available". In this task, students must realise that it is not possible to carry through their initial plan, and so must adjust this plan by buying a full fare ticket for the subway instead.

Sample unit 4: TRAFFIC

■ Figure V.1.16 ■
TRAFFIC: Stimulus information

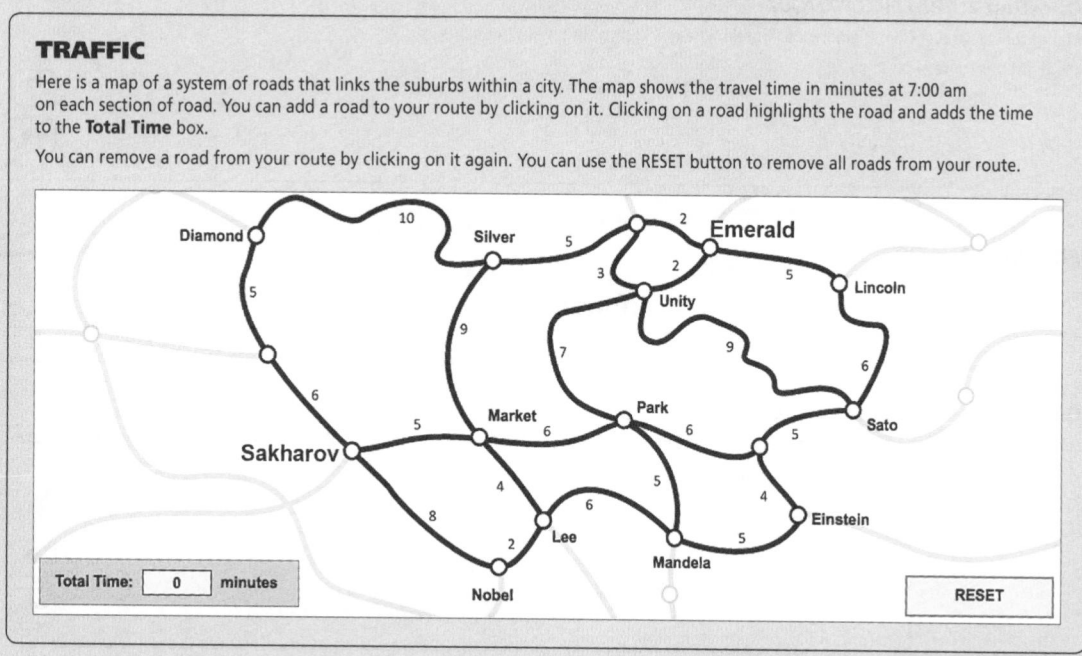

TRAFFIC

Here is a map of a system of roads that links the suburbs within a city. The map shows the travel time in minutes at 7:00 am on each section of road. You can add a road to your route by clicking on it. Clicking on a road highlights the road and adds the time to the **Total Time** box.

You can remove a road from your route by clicking on it again. You can use the RESET button to remove all roads from your route.

In the unit *TRAFFIC*, students are given a map of a road network with travel times indicated. While this is a unit with *static* items, because all the information about travel times is provided at the outset, it still exploits the advantages of computer delivery. Students can click on the map to highlight a route, with a calculator in the bottom left corner adding up travel times for the selected route. The *context* for the items in this unit is classified as *social* and *non-technological*.

TRAFFIC: Item 1

■ Figure V.1.17 ■
TRAFFIC: Item 1

Question 1: TRAFFIC *CP007Q01*

Pepe is at Sakharov and wants to travel to Emerald. He wants to complete his trip as quickly as possible. What is the shortest time for his trip?

○ 20 minutes
○ 21 minutes
○ 24 minutes
○ 28 minutes

?
➡

In the first item in the unit, a *planning and executing* item, students are asked about the shortest time to travel from "Sakharov" to "Emerald", two relatively close points shown on the map. Four response options are provided.

TRAFFIC: Item 2

The second item in the unit *TRAFFIC* is a similar *planning and executing* item. It asks students to find the quickest route between "Diamond" and "Einstein", two distant points on the map. This time, students must provide their answer by highlighting this route. Students can use the indication that the quickest route takes 31 minutes to avoid generating all possible alternatives systematically; instead, they can explore the network in a targeted way to find the route that takes 31 minutes.

■ Figure V.1.18 ■
TRAFFIC: Item 2

Question 2: TRAFFIC *CP007Q02*

Maria wants to travel from Diamond to Einstein. The quickest route takes 31 minutes.
Highlight this route.

TRAFFIC: Item 3

■ Figure V.1.19 ■
TRAFFIC: Item 3

Question 3: TRAFFIC *CP007Q03*

Julio lives in Silver, Maria lives in Lincoln and Don lives in Nobel. They want to meet in a suburb on the map. No-one wants to travel for more than 15 minutes.

Where could they meet?

--- ▼

In the third item, students have to use a drop-down menu to select the meeting point that satisfies a condition on travel times for all three participants in a meeting. The demand in this third item is classified as a *monitoring and reflecting* task, because students have to evaluate possible solutions against a given condition.

Sample unit 5: ROBOT CLEANER

■ Figure V.1.20 ■
ROBOT CLEANER: Stimulus information

ROBOT CLEANER

The animation shows the movement of a new robotic vacuum cleaner. It is being tested.

Click the START button to see what the vacuum cleaner does when it meets different types of objects.

You can use the RESET button to place the vacuum cleaner back in its starting position at any time.

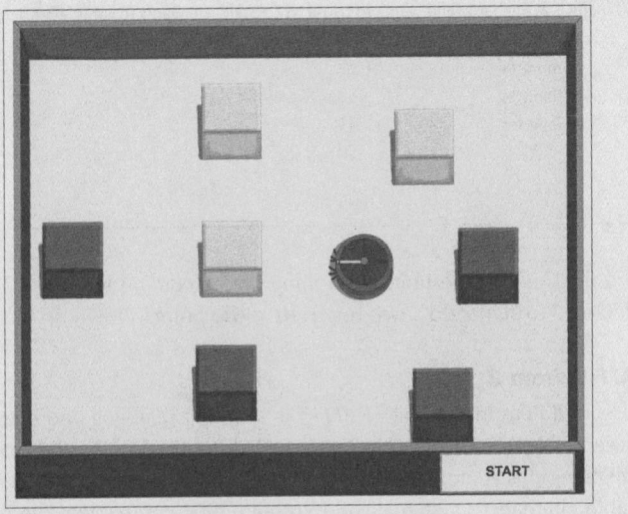

The unit *ROBOT CLEANER* presents students with an animation showing the behaviour of a robot cleaner in a room. The robotic vacuum cleaner moves forward until it meets an obstacle, then behaves according to a few, deterministic rules, depending on the kind of obstacle. Students can run the animation as many times as they wish to observe this behaviour. Despite the animated task prompt, the problem situations in this unit are *static*, because the student cannot intervene to change the behaviour of the vacuum cleaner or aspects of the environment. The *context* for the items in these units is classified as *social* and *non-technological*.

ROBOT CLEANER: Item 1

■ Figure V.1.21 ■
ROBOT CLEANER: Item 1

Question 1: ROBOT CLEANER *CP002Q08*

What does the vacuum cleaner do when it meets a red block?

○ It immediately moves to another red block.

○ It turns and moves to the nearest yellow block.

○ It turns a quarter circle (90 degrees) and moves forward until it meets something else.

○ It turns a half circle (180 degrees) and moves forward until it meets something else.

⟨?⟩
⟨➡⟩

In the first item, students must understand the behaviour of the vacuum cleaner when it meets a red block. The item is classified as *exploring and understanding*. To show their understanding, they are invited to select, among a list of four options and based on observation, the description that corresponds to the behaviour of the robot cleaner in this situation: "It turns a quarter circle (90 degrees) and moves forward until it meets something else."

ROBOT CLEANER: Item 2

■ Figure V.1.22 ■
ROBOT CLEANER: Item 2

Question 2: ROBOT CLEANER *CP002Q07*

At the beginning of the animation, the vacuum cleaner is facing the left wall. By the end of the animation it has pushed two yellow blocks.

If, instead of facing the left wall at the beginning of the animation, the vacuum cleaner was facing the right wall, how many yellow blocks would it have pushed by the end of the animation?

○ 0 ○ 1
○ 2 ○ 3

⟨?⟩
⟨➡⟩

In the second item in this unit, students must predict the behaviour of the vacuum cleaner using spatial reasoning. How many obstacles would the vacuum cleaner encounter if it started in a different position? This item is also an *exploring and understanding* item, because the correct prediction of the robot's behaviour requires at least a partial understanding of the rules and careful observation of the animation to grasp the information needed. It is made easier if the student notes that the new starting position corresponds to an intermediate state of the robot's trajectory in the animation. Response options are provided.

ROBOT CLEANER: Item 3

The final item in this unit is classified as *representing and formulating*, and asks students to describe the behaviour of the robot cleaner when it meets a yellow block. In contrast to the first task, students must formulate the answer themselves

by entering it in a text box. This item requires expert scoring for credit. Full-credit answers are those that describe both of the rules that govern the robot's behaviour (e.g. "it pushes the yellow block as far as it can and then turns around"). Partial credit was available for answers that only partially describe the behaviour, e.g. by listing only one of the two rules. Only a small percentage of students across participating countries obtained full credit for this item.

■ Figure V.1.23 ■
ROBOT CLEANER: Item 3

Question 3: ROBOT CLEANER *CP002Q06*

The vacuum cleaner's behaviour follows a set of rules. Based on the animation, write a rule that describes what the vacuum cleaner does when it meets a yellow block.

[?]

[→]

Notes

1. An assessment of collaborative problem-solving skills, which will be included in PISA 2015, will enrich the understanding of young people's ability to solve problems.

2. Ramalingam, McCrae and Philpot (forthcoming) trace the history of how the PISA assessment of problem solving was developed and discuss its relationship with the psychological literature on problem solving and how it is measured.

References

Adey, P. et al. (2007), "Can we be intelligent about intelligence? Why education needs the concept of plastic general ability", *Educational Research Review,* Vol. 2, pp. 75-97.

Autor, D.H., F. Levy and **R.J. Murnane** (2003), "The Skill Content of Recent Technological Change: An Empirical Exploration", *The Quarterly Journal of Economics,* Vol. 118, pp. 1278-1333.

Autor, D.H. and **B. Price** (2013), *The Changing Task Composition of the US Labor Market: An Update of Autor, Levy and Murnane (2003)*, mimeo, June 21, 2013.

Buchner, A. and **J. Funke** (1993), "Finite-State Automata: Dynamic Task Environments in Problem-Solving Research", *The Quarterly Journal of Experimental Psychology,* Vol. 46A, pp. 83-118.

Csapó, B. and **J. Funke** (forthcoming), "Developing and Assessing Problem Solving", Chapter 1 in Csapó, B. and J. Funke (eds.), *The Nature of Problem Solving*, OECD Publishing.

Defoe, D. (1919), *The Life and Adventures of Robinson Crusoe*, Seeley, Service & Co., London (Chapter IX).

Funke, J. (2010), "Complex problem solving: A case for complex cognition?", *Cognitive Processing,* Vol. 11, pp. 133-142.

Funke, J. (2001), "Dynamic systems as tools for analysing human judgement", *Thinking and Reasoning,* Vol. 7, pp. 69-79.

Funke, J. (1992), "Dealing with Dynamic Systems: Research Strategy, Diagnostic Approach and Experimental Results", *The German Journal of Psychology*, Vol. 16, pp. 24-43.

Funke, J. and **P.A. Frensch** (2007), "Complex problem solving: The European perspective – 10 years after", in D.H. Johannessen (ed.), *Learning to Solve Complex Scientific Problems,* Lawrence Erlbaum, New York, pp. 25-47.

Greiff, S. et al. (2013a), "Complex problem solving in educational settings – Something beyond g: Concept, assessment, measurement invariance, and construct validity", *Journal of Educational Psychology*, Vol. 105(2), pp. 364-379.

Greiff, S. et al. (2013b), "Computer-based assessment of complex problem solving: Concept, implementation, and application", *Educational Technology Research & Development*, Vol. 61, pp. 407-421.

Ikenaga, T. and **R. Kambayashi** (2010), *Long-term Trends in the Polarization of the Japanese Labor Market: The Increase of Non-routine Task Input and Its Valuation in the Labor Market,* Hitotsubashi University Institute of Economic Research Working Paper.

Klauer, K. and **G. Phye** (2008), "Inductive reasoning: A training approach", *Review of Educational Research,* Vol. 78, No. 1, pp. 85-123.

Kotovsky, K., J.R. Hayes and **H.A. Simon** (1985), "Why are some problems hard? Evidence from Tower of Hanoi", *Cognitive psychology*, Vol. 17, pp. 248-294.

Mayer, R.E. (1998), "Cognitive, metacognitive, and motivational aspects of problem solving", *Instructional Science*, Vol. 26, pp. 49-63.

Mayer, R.E. (1990), "Problem solving", in M.W. Eysenck (ed.), *The Blackwell Dictionary of Cognitive Psychology*, Basil Blackwell, Oxford, pp. 284-288.

OECD (forthcoming), *PISA 2012 Technical Report,* PISA, OECD Publishing.

OECD (2013a), *OECD Skills Outlook 2013: First Results from the Survey of Adult Skills*, OECD Publishing. *http://dx.doi.org/10.1787/9789264204256-en*

OECD (2013b), *PISA 2012 Assessment and Analytical Framework: Mathematics, Reading, Science, Problem Solving and Financial Literacy*, PISA, OECD Publishing. *http://dx.doi.org/10.1787/9789264190511-en*

OECD (2005), *Problem Solving for Tomorrow's World: First Measures of Cross-Curricular Competencies from PISA 2003*, PISA, OECD Publishing.
http://dx.doi.org/10.1787/9789264006430-en

Ramalingam, D., B. McCrae and **R. Philpot** (forthcoming), "The PISA 2012 Assessment of Problem Solving", Chapter 7 in Csapó, B. and J. Funke (eds.), *The Nature of Problem Solving*, OECD Publishing.

Raven, J. (2000), "Psychometrics, cognitive ability, and occupational performance", *Review of Psychology,* Vol. 7, pp. 51-74.

Spitz-Oener, A. (2006), "Technical Change, Job Tasks, and Rising Educational Demands: Looking outside the Wage Structure", *Journal of Labor Economics,* Vol. 24, pp. 235-270.

Winner, E., T. Goldstein and **S. Vincent-Lancrin** (2013), *Art for Art's Sake?: The Impact of Arts Education*, Educational Research and Innovation, OECD Publishing.
http://dx.doi.org/10.1787/9789264180789-en

Wüstenberg, S., S. Greiff and **J. Funke** (2012), "Complex problem solving – More than reasoning?", *Intelligence,* Vol. 40, pp. 1-14.

2

Student Performance in Problem Solving

This chapter examines student performance in problem solving. It introduces the problem-solving performance scale and proficiency levels, describes performance within and across countries and economies, and reports mean performance levels. It also discusses the relationship between problem-solving performance and performance in mathematics, reading and science.

How well prepared are 15-year-olds to solve problems that they have never encountered before, for which a routine solution has not been learned? The PISA 2012 computer-based assessment of problem solving uses scenarios that students may encounter in real life, outside of school, in order to measure the skills that students use to solve novel problems. As far as possible, these test problems do not require any expert knowledge to solve. As such, they offer a way of measuring the cognitive processes fundamental to problem solving in general.

What the data tell us

- Students in Singapore and Korea, followed by students in Japan, score higher in problem solving than students in all other participating countries and economies.

- On average across OECD countries, about one in five students is only able to solve very straightforward problems – if any – provided that they refer to familiar situations. By contrast, fewer than one in ten students in Japan, Korea, Macao-China and Singapore are low-achievers in problem solving.

- Across OECD countries, 11.4% of 15-year-old students are top performers in problem solving, meaning that they can systematically explore a complex problem scenario, devise multi-step solutions that take into account all constraints, and adjust their plans in light of the feedback received.

- Problem-solving performance is positively related to performance in other assessed subjects, but the relationship is weaker than that observed between performance in mathematics and reading or between performance in mathematics and science.

- In Australia, Brazil, Italy, Japan, Korea, Macao-China, Serbia, England (United Kingdom) and the United States, students perform significantly better in problem solving, on average, than students in other countries who show similar performance in mathematics, reading and science. In Australia, England (United Kingdom) and the United States, this is particularly true among strong and top performers in mathematics; in Italy, Japan and Korea, it is particularly true among moderate and low performers in mathematics.

HOW THE PISA 2012 PROBLEM-SOLVING RESULTS ARE REPORTED

The previous chapter introduced the concept of problem-solving competence that underlies this assessment. This section discusses how an overall measure of problem-solving competence was derived from students' answers to questions that measure different aspects of problem-solving competence, and how 15-year-olds were classified into seven proficiency levels, one of which comprises only those students who perform below the first, and lowest, described level of proficiency.

How the PISA 2012 problem-solving tests were analysed and scaled

The relative difficulty of each task included in the assessment of problem solving can be estimated based on student responses. Tasks are ordered by increasing levels of difficulty along a single dimension. The difficulty of tasks is estimated by considering the proportion of students who answer each question correctly, with smaller proportions of correct answers indicating growing difficulty. By this measure, the 42 problem-solving tasks included in the PISA 2012 assessment span a wide range of difficulties.

Conversely, the relative proficiency of students taking a particular test can be estimated by considering the proportion of test questions they answer correctly. Students' proficiency on the test can then be reported on the same scale that measures the difficulty of questions.

Estimates of student proficiency reflect the kinds of tasks students would be expected to perform successfully. This means that students are likely to be able to complete questions successfully at or below the difficulty level associated with their own position on the scale, although they may not always do so.[1] Conversely, they are unlikely to be able to complete questions above the difficulty level associated with their position on the scale, although they may sometimes do so. Figure V.2.1 illustrates how this probabilistic model works.

The further a student's performance is located above a given question on the proficiency scale, the more likely he or she is to successfully complete the question, and other questions of similar difficulty; the further the student's performance is located below a given question, the lower the probability that the student will be able to successfully complete the question, and other similarly difficult questions.

■ Figure V.2.1 ■
Relationship between questions and student performance on a scale

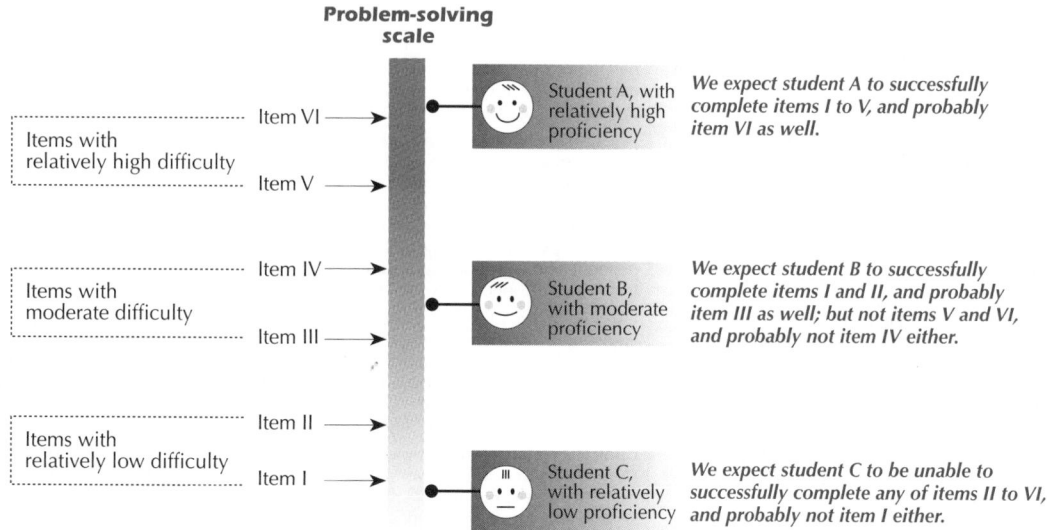

The location of student proficiency on this scale is set in relation to the particular group of questions included in the assessment; but just as the sample of students who participated in PISA in 2012 is drawn to represent all 15-year-olds in the participating countries and economies, the individual questions used in the assessment are selected so that their solutions provide a broad representation of the PISA 2012 definition of problem-solving competence.

How problem-solving proficiency levels are defined in PISA 2012

PISA 2012 provides an overall problem-solving proficiency scale, drawing on all the questions in the problem-solving assessment. The problem-solving scale was constructed to have a mean score among OECD countries of 500, with about two-thirds of students across OECD countries scoring between 400 and 600.[2] To help interpret what students' scores mean in substantive terms, the scale is divided into seven proficiency levels. Six of these are described based on the skills needed to successfully complete the tasks that are located within them.

The range of problem-solving tasks included in the PISA 2012 assessment allows for describing six levels of problem-solving proficiency. Level 1 is the lowest described level, and corresponds to an elementary level of problem-solving skills; Level 6 corresponds to the highest level of problem-solving skills. Students with a proficiency score within the range of Level 1 are expected to complete most Level 1 tasks successfully, but are unlikely to be able to complete tasks at higher levels. Students with scores in the Level 6 range are likely to be able to successfully complete all tasks included in the PISA assessment of problem solving.

A profile of PISA problem-solving questions

Several questions from the PISA 2012 assessment of problem solving were released to the public after the survey to illustrate the ways in which performance was measured. These items are presented at the end of Chapter 1.

Figure V.2.2 shows how these items map onto the described proficiency scale and presents a brief description of each task. Tasks included in the same unit can represent a range of difficulties. The unit *TICKETS*, for example, comprises questions at all levels between 2 and 5. Thus a single unit may cover a broad section of the PISA problem-solving scale.

A few tasks included in the test are associated with difficulty levels below Level 1. Among the released items, one task – Question 1 in unit *TRAFFIC* – is located below the lowest level of proficiency described. Although the number of items that falls below Level 1 is not sufficient to adequately describe the skills that students who perform below Level 1 possess, including tasks that most students, even in the lowest-performing countries, can complete is a way of ensuring that all countries can learn from the assessment results. This indicates that the PISA 2012 assessment of problem solving can measure not only proficiency in problem solving at different levels, but can also capture some of the elementary components of problem-solving skills.

■ Figure V.2.2 ■

Map of selected problem-solving questions, illustrating the proficiency levels

Level	Score range	Tasks	Task score	Nature of the task
6	Equal to or higher than 683 points	ROBOT CLEANER Task 3 (CP002Q06) Full credit	701	Fully describe the logic governing an unfamiliar system. After observing the behaviour of a (simulated) robot cleaner, the student identifies and writes down the two rules that, together, completely describe what the robot cleaner does when it meets with a certain type of obstacle.
5	618 to less than 683 points	CLIMATE CONTROL Task 2 (CP025Q02) Full credit	672	Efficiently control a system with multiple dependencies to achieve a given outcome. A diagram shows which controls of an air conditioner can be used to vary temperature and humidity levels. The student is only allowed four rounds of manipulation, but the target levels of temperature and humidity provided can be reached in several ways within these four steps and a mistake can often be corrected if immediate remedial action is taken. However, the student must use the information provided about causal dependencies to plan a few steps ahead, consistently monitor progress towards the target, and respond quickly to feedback.
5		TICKETS Task 2 (CP038Q01) Full credit	638	Use targeted exploration to accomplish a task. Buy tickets with a ticket machine, adjusting to feedback gathered over the course of the task to comply with all constraints: the ticket bought not only complies with three explicit instructions, but the student compared prices between the two possible options before making a selection, thus checking the constraint to buy the cheapest ticket. Execution of the solution involves multiple steps.
4	553 to less than 618 points	CLIMATE CONTROL Task 2 (CP025Q02) Partial credit	592	Control a system with multiple dependencies to achieve a given outcome. A diagram shows which controls of an air conditioner can be used to vary temperature and humidity levels. For partial credit, the student is able to bring the two outputs closer to their target levels, without actually reaching them for both, within the four rounds of manipulation permitted.
4		TICKETS Task 3 (CP038Q03)	579	Execute a plan for working around an unexpected impasse: a malfunction of the ticket machine that is only discovered after multiple steps. The student wants to buy subway tickets at the ticket machine and is eligible to concession fares, but when concession fares are selected, the machine says that "there are no tickets of this type available". The student instead buys a full fare ticket for the subway.
4		ROBOT CLEANER Task 2 (CP002Q07)	559	Predict the behaviour of a simple unfamiliar system using spatial reasoning. The task prompt shows the behaviour of a robot cleaner in a room, and the student is asked to predict the behaviour of the robot cleaner if it were in a different starting position. The new starting position corresponds to an intermediate state of the robot's trajectory shown to students: the correct prediction of the robot's behaviour does not necessarily require a full understanding of the rules governing it. A partial understanding of the rules and careful observation are sufficient.
3	488 to less than 553 points	TICKETS Task 1 (CP038Q02)	526	Use an unfamiliar ticketing machine to buy a ticket. The student follows explicit instructions to make the appropriate selection at each step. Instructions, however, are not given in the order in which they must be used, and multiple steps are needed to execute the solution.
3		CLIMATE CONTROL Task 1 (CP025Q01) Full credit	523	Explore and represent the relationships between variables in a system with multiple dependencies. An unfamiliar air conditioner has three controls that determine its effect on air temperature and humidity. The student must experiment with the controls to determine which controls have an impact on temperature and which on humidity, then represent the causal relations by drawing arrows between the three inputs (the controls) and the two outputs (temperature and humidity) (full credit).
3		Task 1 (CP025Q01) Partial credit	492	Partial credit for this question is given if the student explores the relationships between variables in an efficient way, by varying only one input at a time, but fails to correctly represent them in a diagram.
3		ROBOT CLEANER Task 1 (CP002Q08)	490	Understand behaviour of an unfamiliar system. Select, among a list of four options and based on observation, the description that corresponds to the behaviour of the robot cleaner in a specific situation: "What does the vacuum cleaner do when it meets a red block?" "It turns a quarter circle (90 degrees) and moves forward until it meets something else."
2	423 to less than 488 points	TICKETS Task 2 (CP038Q01) Partial credit	453	Use a machine to buy tickets for a given situation, without checking that the solution satisfies a condition (cheapest ticket). To obtain partial credit, the student buys either a daily ticket or four single tickets for the subway, with concession fares, but does not compare the two options to determine the best choice as requested. The student had the opportunity to learn how to use the basic functions of the machine in the previous task (TICKETS, Task 1). Buying a ticket involves multiple steps.
2		TRAFFIC Task 2 (CP007Q02)	446	Highlight the shortest route between two distant points on a map. An indication in the task prompt can be used to verify that the solution found corresponds to the shortest route.
1	358 to less than 423 points	ROBOT CLEANER Task 3 (CP002Q06) Partial credit	414	Partially describe the logic governing an unfamiliar system after observing its behaviour in an animation: recognise and formulate, at least partially, a rule governing the behaviour of the robot cleaner in a specific situation (e.g. "it turns").
1		TRAFFIC Task 3 (CP007Q03)	408	Evaluate different possibilities using a network diagram to find a meeting point that satisfies a condition on travel times for all three participants in a meeting.
Below 1	Below 358 points	TRAFFIC Task 1 (CP007Q01)	340	Read travel times on a simple network diagram to find the shortest route between two close points on a map. All necessary information is disclosed at the outset and response options are provided. The correct solution can be found with a few simple trial-and-error iterations.

Box V.2.1 presents the major differences between difficult and easy tasks, and links them to students' progress in problem solving.

Box V.2.1. **How students progress in problem solving**

As students acquire proficiency in problem solving, they learn to handle increasingly complex demands. What these demands are, and what it means for students to become better problem-solvers, can be inferred by comparing the easier tasks at the bottom of Figure V.2.2 to the harder tasks shown above them.

An analysis of the entire problem set used in PISA 2012 (Philpot et al., forthcoming) identified several characteristics that are associated with task difficulty:

1) Distance from goal and reasoning skills required: In problems at the bottom of the scale, there are generally few barriers to overcome in order to reach the solution; the goal is at most one or two steps away. In addition, overcoming the barriers does not require logical or combinatorial reasoning. In harder problems, the distance from the goal increases, and each step may require high levels of reasoning (such as combinatorial reasoning to identify all possible alternatives, deductive reasoning to eliminate possibilities, etc.).

2) Number of constraints and conditions: The easiest tasks involve at most one condition to be satisfied. In more difficult problems, the student often needs to monitor several conditions, and restrictions on actions, such as limits on the number of experimental rounds, are introduced. It thus becomes necessary to plan ahead, especially if the constraints cannot be addressed successively.

3) Amount of information: To solve the easiest problems, all that is required is understanding a small amount of information that is explicitly provided in a simple format. As the problems become more difficult, the amount of information required increases. Often, information has to be integrated from several sources and in several formats (e.g. graphs, tables and texts), including feedback received while solving the problem (as in the units *TICKETS* and *CLIMATE CONTROL*).

4) Unfamiliarity and system complexity: The easiest tasks are cast in familiar settings, such as those involving a public transport map (e.g. *TRAFFIC*). Tasks that use more abstract scenarios or that refer to less familiar objects (such as *ROBOT CLEANER*) are generally more difficult. In addition, the simplest problems have few possible actions, clear causal linkages, and no unexpected impasses. Tasks that are harder to solve usually involve a larger number of possible actions and consequences to monitor; and the components of the problem form a more interrelated system.

Initially, students may be able to solve only problems cast in familiar settings that require one simple condition to be satisfied and where the goal is only one or two steps away, as is the case in Tasks 1 and 3 of the unit *TRAFFIC*. As students develop their problem-solving proficiency (i.e. their capacity to understand and resolve problems whose solution is not immediately obvious), the complexity of problems that they can solve grows. At Level 3 on the problem-solving scale, students can handle information presented in several different formats, infer elementary relationships between the components of a simple system or device, and engage in experimental manipulation to confirm or refute a hypothesis. They are confident in solving problems such as Task 1 in unit *CLIMATE CONTROL* and Task 1 in unit *ROBOT CLEANER*. At Level 5, students fully grasp the underlying structure of a moderately complex problem, which allows them to think ahead, detect unexpected difficulties or mistakes, and adjust their plans accordingly – all of which are required to achieve the goal in *CLIMATE CONTROL* (Task 2) and *TICKETS* (Task 2).

WHAT STUDENTS CAN DO IN PROBLEM SOLVING

PISA summarises student performance in problem solving on a single scale that provides an overall assessment of students' problem-solving competence at age 15. Results for this overall performance measure are presented below, covering both the average level of performance in problem solving in each country/economy and the distribution of problem-solving proficiency. Chapter 3 analyses these results in more detail, covering the various components of proficiency in problem solving.

Average level of proficiency in problem solving

This section uses students' average scores to summarise the performance of countries and economies in problem solving, both relative to each other and to the OECD mean. Since problem solving is a new domain in PISA 2012, the OECD average performance was set at 500 score points, and the standard deviation across OECD countries at 100 score points. This establishes the benchmark against which each country's problem-solving performance in PISA 2012 is compared.

■ Figure V.2.3 ■

Comparing countries' and economies' performance in problem solving

	Statistically significantly **above** the OECD average
	Not statistically significantly different from the OECD average
	Statistically significantly **below** the OECD average

Mean score	Comparison country/economy	Countries and economies whose mean score is NOT statistically significantly different from the comparison country's/economy's score
562	Singapore	Korea
561	Korea	Singapore, Japan
552	Japan	Korea
540	Macao-China	Hong Kong-China, Shanghai-China
540	Hong Kong-China	Macao-China, Shanghai-China, Chinese Taipei
536	Shanghai-China	Macao-China, Hong Kong-China, Chinese Taipei
534	Chinese Taipei	Hong Kong-China, Shanghai-China
526	Canada	Australia, Finland, England (UK)
523	Australia	Canada, Finland, England (UK)
523	Finland	Canada, Australia, England (UK)
517	England (UK)	Canada, Australia, Finland, Estonia, France, Netherlands, Italy, Czech Republic, Germany, United States, Belgium, Austria
515	Estonia	England (UK), France, Netherlands, Italy, Czech Republic, Germany, United States
511	France	England (UK), Estonia, Netherlands, Italy, Czech Republic, Germany, United States, Belgium, Austria, Norway
511	Netherlands	England (UK), Estonia, France, Italy, Czech Republic, Germany, United States, Belgium, Austria, Norway
510	Italy	England (UK), Estonia, France, Netherlands, Czech Republic, Germany, United States, Belgium, Austria, Norway
509	Czech Republic	England (UK), Estonia, France, Netherlands, Italy, Germany, United States, Belgium, Austria, Norway
509	Germany	England (UK), Estonia, France, Netherlands, Italy, Czech Republic, United States, Belgium, Austria, Norway
508	United States	England (UK), Estonia, France, Netherlands, Italy, Czech Republic, Germany, Belgium, Austria, Norway, Ireland
508	Belgium	England (UK), France, Netherlands, Italy, Czech Republic, Germany, United States, Austria, Norway
506	Austria	England (UK), France, Netherlands, Italy, Czech Republic, Germany, United States, Belgium, Norway, Ireland
503	Norway	France, Netherlands, Italy, Czech Republic, Germany, United States, Belgium, Austria, Ireland, Denmark, Portugal
498	Ireland	United States, Austria, Norway, Denmark, Portugal, Sweden
497	Denmark	Norway, Ireland, Portugal, Sweden, Russian Federation
494	Portugal	Norway, Ireland, Denmark, Sweden, Russian Federation
491	Sweden	Ireland, Denmark, Portugal, Russian Federation, Slovak Republic, Poland
489	Russian Federation	Denmark, Portugal, Sweden, Slovak Republic, Poland
483	Slovak Republic	Sweden, Russian Federation, Poland, Spain, Slovenia
481	Poland	Sweden, Russian Federation, Slovak Republic, Spain, Slovenia, Serbia
477	Spain	Slovak Republic, Poland, Slovenia, Serbia, Croatia
476	Slovenia	Slovak Republic, Poland, Spain, Serbia
473	Serbia	Poland, Spain, Slovenia, Croatia
466	Croatia	Spain, Serbia, Hungary, Israel
459	Hungary	Croatia, Turkey, Israel
454	Turkey	Hungary, Israel, Chile
454	Israel	Croatia, Hungary, Turkey, Chile, Cyprus[1, 2]
448	Chile	Turkey, Israel, Cyprus[1, 2]
445	Cyprus[1, 2]	Israel, Chile
428	Brazil	Malaysia
422	Malaysia	Brazil
411	United Arab Emirates	Montenegro, Uruguay, Bulgaria
407	Montenegro	United Arab Emirates, Uruguay, Bulgaria
403	Uruguay	United Arab Emirates, Montenegro, Bulgaria, Colombia
402	Bulgaria	United Arab Emirates, Montenegro, Uruguay, Colombia
399	Colombia	Uruguay, Bulgaria

1. Footnote by Turkey: The information in this document with reference to "Cyprus" relates to the southern part of the Island. There is no single authority representing both Turkish and Greek Cypriot people on the Island. Turkey recognises the Turkish Republic of Northern Cyprus (TRNC). Until a lasting and equitable solution is found within the context of the United Nations, Turkey shall preserve its position concerning the "Cyprus issue".
2. Footnote by all the European Union Member States of the OECD and the European Union: The Republic of Cyprus is recognised by all members of the United Nations with the exception of Turkey. The information in this document relates to the area under the effective control of the Government of the Republic of Cyprus.

Source: OECD, PISA 2012 Database.
StatLink ᵐˢᵖ http://dx.doi.org/10.1787/888933003573

When interpreting mean performance, only those differences among countries and economies that are statistically significant should be taken into account (Box V.2.2). Figure V.2.3 shows each country's/economy's mean score, and allows readers to see for which pairs of countries/economies the differences between the means shown are statistically similar. The data on which Figure V.2.3 is based are presented in Annex B. For each country/economy shown in the middle column, the countries/economies listed in the column on the right are those whose mean scores are not sufficiently different to be distinguished with confidence.[3] For all other cases, Country A scores higher than Country B if Country A is above Country B in the list in the middle column, and scores lower if Country A is shown below Country B. For example, while Finland clearly ranks above the United States, the performance of England (United Kingdom) cannot be distinguished with confidence from either Finland or the United States.

Box V.2.2. **What is a statistically significant difference?**

A difference is called statistically significant if it is very unlikely that such a difference could be observed in the estimates based on samples, when in fact no true difference exists in the populations.

The results of the PISA assessments for countries and economies are estimates because they are obtained from samples of students, rather than a census of all students, and they are obtained using a limited set of assessment tasks, not the universe of all possible assessment tasks. When the sampling of students and assessment tasks are done with scientific rigour, it is possible to determine the magnitude of the uncertainty associated with the estimate. This uncertainty needs to be taken into account when making comparisons so that differences that could reasonably arise simply due to the sampling of students and tasks are not interpreted as differences that actually hold for the populations.

Figure V.2.3 lists each participating country and economy in descending order of its mean problem-solving score (left column). The values range from a high of 562 points for the partner country Singapore to a low of 399 points for the partner country Colombia. Countries and economies are also divided into three broad groups: those whose mean scores are statistically around the OECD mean (highlighted in dark blue), those whose mean scores are above the OECD mean (highlighted in pale blue), and those whose mean scores are below the OECD mean (highlighted in medium blue). Box V.2.3 provides guidance to gauge the magnitude of score differences.

Because the figures are derived from samples, it is not possible to determine a country's precise rank among the participating countries. However, it is possible to determine, with confidence, a range of ranks in which the country's performance lies (Figure V.2.4).

Singapore and Korea are the highest-performing countries in problem solving, with mean scores of 562 points and 561 points, respectively. Fifteen-year-olds in these two countries perform about a full proficiency level above the level of students in other OECD countries, on average. Japan ranks third among all participating countries, and second among OECD countries, with a mean score of 552 points. Four more East Asian partner economies score between 530 and 540 points on the PISA problem-solving scale: Macao-China (with a mean score of 540 points), Hong Kong-China (540 points), Shanghai-China (536 points) and Chinese Taipei (534 points). Twelve OECD countries perform above the OECD average, but below the former group of countries: Canada (526 points), Australia (523 points), Finland (523 points), England (United Kingdom) (517 points), Estonia (515 points), France (511 points), the Netherlands (511 points), Italy (510 points), the Czech Republic (509 points), Germany (509 points), the United States (508 points) and Belgium (508 points).

Five countries, Austria, Norway, Ireland, Denmark and Portugal, score around the OECD mean.

There are clear and substantial differences in mean country performance on the problem-solving assessment. Box V.2.3 illustrates how the differences in mean performance compare to differences in problem-solving proficiency within countries/economies. Among OECD countries, the lowest-performing country, Chile, has an average score of 448. This means that the gap between the highest- and lowest-performing OECD country is 113 score points – well above one standard deviation. About 90% of students from Korea perform above Chile's mean score; conversely, only about 10% of students from Chile perform above Korea's mean score (Table V.2.2). Overall, more than two proficiency levels (163 score points) separate the highest-performing (Singapore) and lowest-performing (Colombia) countries in problem solving. Only about one in 20 students in the four best-performing countries and economies performs at or below the mean of the lowest-performing country.

■ Figure V.2.4 [Part 1/2] ■

Problem-solving performance among participating countries/economies

			Problem-solving scale			
			Range of ranks			
			OECD countries		All countries/economies	
	Mean score	S.E.	Upper rank	Lower rank	Upper rank	Lower rank
Singapore	562	(1.2)			1	2
Korea	561	(4.3)	1	1	1	2
Japan	552	(3.1)	2	2	3	3
Macao-China	540	(1.0)			4	6
Hong Kong-China	540	(3.9)			4	7
Shanghai-China	536	(3.3)			4	7
Chinese Taipei	534	(2.9)			5	7
North West (Italy)	533	(8.6)				
Western Australia (Australia)	528	(4.0)				
North East (Italy)	527	(6.4)				
Canada	526	(2.4)	3	5	8	10
Australian Capital Territory (Australia)	526	(3.7)				
New South Wales (Australia)	525	(3.5)				
Flemish Community (Belgium)	525	(3.3)				
Victoria (Australia)	523	(4.1)				
Australia	523	(1.9)	3	6	8	11
Finland	523	(2.3)	3	6	8	11
Queensland (Australia)	522	(3.4)				
German-speaking Community (Belgium)	520	(2.6)				
South Australia (Australia)	520	(4.1)				
England (United Kingdom)	517	(4.2)	4	11	9	16
Estonia	515	(2.5)	6	10	11	15
Centre (Italy)	514	(10.8)				
Northern Territory (Australia)	513	(7.9)				
France	511	(3.4)	6	14	11	19
Netherlands	511	(4.4)	6	16	11	21
Italy	510	(4.0)	7	16	12	21
Czech Republic	509	(3.1)	7	15	12	20
Germany	509	(3.6)	7	16	12	21
United States	508	(3.9)	7	16	12	21
Belgium	508	(2.5)	9	16	14	21
Madrid (Spain)	507	(13.0)				
Austria	506	(3.6)	8	17	13	22
Alentejo (Portugal)	506	(13.4)				
Norway	503	(3.3)	11	18	16	23
Ireland	498	(3.2)	15	19	20	24
Denmark	497	(2.9)	16	20	21	25
Basque Country (Spain)	496	(3.9)				
Portugal	494	(3.6)	17	20	22	26
Sweden	491	(2.9)	18	21	23	27
Tasmania (Australia)	490	(4.0)				
Russian Federation	489	(3.4)			23	27
Catalonia (Spain)	488	(8.4)				
South Islands (Italy)	486	(8.5)				
French Community (Belgium)	485	(4.4)				
Slovak Republic	483	(3.6)	20	23	25	29
Poland	481	(4.4)	21	24	26	31
Spain	477	(4.1)	21	24	27	31
Slovenia	476	(1.5)	22	24	28	31

Notes: OECD countries are shown in bold black. Partner countries and economies are shown in bold blue. Regions are shown in black italics (OECD countries) or blue italics (partner countries).

Italian administrative regions are grouped into larger geographical units: Centre (*Lazio, Marche, Toscana, Umbria*), North East (*Bolzano, Emilia Romagna, Friuli Venezia Giulia, Trento, Veneto*), North West (*Liguria, Lombardia, Piemonte, Valle d'Aosta*), South (*Abruzzo, Campania, Molise, Puglia*), South Islands (*Basilicata, Calabria, Sardegna, Sicilia*).

Brazilian states are grouped into larger geographical units: Central-West Region (*Federal District, Goiás, Mato Grosso, Mato Grosso do Sul*), Northeast Region (*Alagoas, Bahia, Ceará, Maranhão, Paraíba, Pernambuco, Piauí, Rio Grande do Norte, Sergipe*), North Region (*Acre, Amapá, Amazonas, Pará, Rondônia, Roraima, Tocantins*), Southeast Region (*Espírito Santo, Minas Gerais, Rio de Janeiro, São Paulo*), South Region (*Paraná, Rio Grande do Sul, Santa Catarina*).

1. Footnote by Turkey: The information in this document with reference to "Cyprus" relates to the southern part of the Island. There is no single authority representing both Turkish and Greek Cypriot people on the Island. Turkey recognises the Turkish Republic of Northern Cyprus (TRNC). Until a lasting and equitable solution is found within the context of the United Nations, Turkey shall preserve its position concerning the "Cyprus issue".

2. Footnote by all the European Union Member States of the OECD and the European Union: The Republic of Cyprus is recognised by all members of the United Nations with the exception of Turkey. The information in this document relates to the area under the effective control of the Government of the Republic of Cyprus.

Countries, economies and subnational entities are ranked in descending order of mean problem-solving performance.

Source: OECD, PISA 2012 Database.

StatLink ▦豐➩ http://dx.doi.org/10.1787/888933003573

■ Figure V.2.4 [Part 2/2] ■

Problem-solving performance among participating countries/economies

	Mean score	S.E.	Problem-solving scale			
			Range of ranks			
			OECD countries		All countries/economies	
			Upper rank	Lower rank	Upper rank	Lower rank
South (Italy)	474	(8.4)				
Serbia	473	(3.1)			29	32
Croatia	466	(3.9)			31	33
Hungary	459	(4.0)	25	27	32	35
Dubai (United Arab Emirates)	457	(1.3)				
Turkey	454	(4.0)	25	28	33	36
Israel	454	(5.5)	25	28	33	37
Chile	448	(3.7)	26	28	34	37
Southeast Region (Brazil)	447	(6.3)				
Cyprus[1,2]	445	(1.4)			36	37
Central-West Region (Brazil)	441	(11.9)				
South Region (Brazil)	435	(7.8)				
Brazil	428	(4.7)			38	39
Medellín (Colombia)	424	(7.6)				
Manizales (Colombia)	423	(5.3)				
Malaysia	422	(3.5)			38	39
Sharjah (United Arab Emirates)	416	(8.6)				
United Arab Emirates	411	(2.8)			40	41
Bogotá (Colombia)	411	(5.7)				
Montenegro	407	(1.2)			40	42
Uruguay	403	(3.5)			41	44
Bulgaria	402	(5.1)			41	44
Colombia	399	(3.5)			42	44
Cali (Colombia)	398	(9.0)				
Fujairah (United Arab Emirates)	395	(4.0)				
Northeast Region (Brazil)	393	(11.0)				
Abu Dhabi (United Arab Emirates)	391	(5.3)				
North Region (Brazil)	383	(10.9)				
Ajman (United Arab Emirates)	375	(8.0)				
Ras al-Khaimah (United Arab Emirates)	373	(11.9)				
Umm al-Quwain (United Arab Emirates)	372	(3.5)				

Notes: OECD countries are shown in bold black. Partner countries and economies are shown in bold blue. Regions are shown in black italics (OECD countries) or blue italics (partner countries).

Italian administrative regions are grouped into larger geographical units: Centre (*Lazio, Marche, Toscana, Umbria*), North East (*Bolzano, Emilia Romagna, Friuli Venezia Giulia, Trento, Veneto*), North West (*Liguria, Lombardia, Piemonte, Valle d'Aosta*), South (*Abruzzo, Campania, Molise, Puglia*), South Islands (*Basilicata, Calabria, Sardegna, Sicilia*).

Brazilian states are grouped into larger geographical units: Central-West Region (*Federal District, Goiás, Mato Grosso, Mato Grosso do Sul*), Northeast Region (*Alagoas, Bahia, Ceará, Maranhão, Paraíba, Pernambuco, Piauí, Rio Grande do Norte, Sergipe*), North Region (*Acre, Amapá, Amazonas, Pará, Rondônia, Roraima, Tocantins*), Southeast Region (*Espírito Santo, Minas Gerais, Rio de Janeiro, São Paulo*), South Region (*Paraná, Rio Grande do Sul, Santa Catarina*).

1. Footnote by Turkey: The information in this document with reference to "Cyprus" relates to the southern part of the Island. There is no single authority representing both Turkish and Greek Cypriot people on the Island. Turkey recognises the Turkish Republic of Northern Cyprus (TRNC). Until a lasting and equitable solution is found within the context of the United Nations, Turkey shall preserve its position concerning the "Cyprus issue".

2. Footnote by all the European Union Member States of the OECD and the European Union: The Republic of Cyprus is recognised by all members of the United Nations with the exception of Turkey. The information in this document relates to the area under the effective control of the Government of the Republic of Cyprus.

Countries, economies and subnational entities are ranked in descending order of mean problem-solving performance.
Source: OECD, PISA 2012 Database.
StatLink ᔥᔊᔊ http://dx.doi.org/10.1787/888933003573

Box V.2.3. **Interpreting differences in PISA problem-solving scores: How large a gap?**

In PISA 2012, student performance in problem solving is described through six levels of proficiency, each of which represents 65 score points. Thus, a difference in performance of one proficiency level represents a comparatively large disparity in performance. For example, students proficient at Level 2 on the problem-solving scale are only starting to demonstrate problem-solving competence. They engage with unfamiliar problem situations, but need extensive guidance in order to progress towards a solution. They can perform only one task at a time, and can only test a simple hypothesis that is given to them. Meanwhile, students proficient at Level 3 are more self-directed in their problem solving. They can devise hypotheses to test themselves, and can handle multiple constraints by planning a few steps ahead, provided that the constraints can be addressed sequentially.

...

The difference in average performance between the highest- and lowest-performing countries is 163 score points. The difference between the highest- and lowest-performing OECD countries is 113 score points.

Within countries and economies, even larger gaps separate the highest- and lowest-performing students (Table V.2.2). On average across OECD countries, the distance between the highest-performing 10% of students and the lowest-performing 10% of students is equal to 245 score points; but half of all students in OECD countries score within 129 points of each other.

Treating all OECD countries as a single unit, one standard deviation in the distribution of student performance on the PISA problem-solving scale corresponds to 100 points; this means that, on average within OECD countries, two-thirds of the student population have scores within 100 points of the OECD mean, set at 500 score points.

Students at the different levels of proficiency in problem solving

This section describes performance in terms of the six levels of proficiency that have been constructed for reporting the PISA 2012 problem-solving assessment. A seventh proficiency level, below Level 1, includes those students who cannot successfully complete many of the items of Level 1 difficulty.

Figure V.2.5 shows what students can typically do at each of the six levels of proficiency in problem solving. These summary descriptions are based on the detailed analysis of task demands within each level. The task demands for released items are described in Figure V.2.2. The distribution of student performance across proficiency levels is shown in Figure V.2.6.

Proficiency at Level 6

Students proficient at Level 6 on the problem-solving scale are highly efficient problem-solvers. They can develop complete, coherent mental models of diverse problem scenarios, enabling them to solve complex problems efficiently.

Across OECD countries, only one in 40 students (2.5%) performs at this level, but student proficiency varies among countries. In Singapore and Korea, the proportion is more than three times as large (9.6% and 7.6%, respectively). In Singapore, almost one in ten students is a highly skilled problem-solver. These two countries also top the overall rankings in average performance (Figure V.2.4). In contrast, some countries and economies with above-average overall performance do not have many students at the highest level of problem-solving proficiency. Among these are Italy (mean score of 510 points) and France (511 points), both with smaller-than-average proportions of students reaching Level 6 (1.8% in Italy, 2.1% in France) (Figure V.2.6 and Table V.2.1).

The fact that such a small proportion of students performs at Level 6 indicates that the PISA scale can distinguish problem-solving proficiency up to the highest levels that 15-year-olds are capable of attaining. Indeed, in two OECD countries and seven partner countries and economies, fewer than one in 200 students perform at the top level.

Proficiency at Level 5

Students proficient at Level 5 on the problem-solving scale can systematically explore a complex problem scenario to gain an understanding of how relevant information is structured. When faced with a complex problem involving multiple constraints or unknowns, students whose highest level of proficiency is Level 5 try to solve them through targeted exploration, methodical execution of multi-step plans, and attentive monitoring of progress. In contrast, Level 6 problem-solvers are able to start by developing an overall strategic plan based on a complete mental model of the problem.

Since students proficient at Level 6 can also complete Level 5 tasks, the following descriptions use "proficient at Level 5" to mean those whose highest level of performance is either Level 5 or Level 6. The same terminology is used to refer to the cumulative proportions at lower levels. Students performing at Level 5 or 6 are also referred to as "top performers" in the rest of this report.

Across OECD countries, 11.4% of 15-year-old students are proficient at Level 5 or higher. In Singapore, Korea and Japan, more than one in five students are capable of Level 5 tasks. More than one in six students perform at Level 5 or above in Hong Kong-China (19.3%), Chinese Taipei and Shanghai-China (18.3%), Canada (17.5%) and Australia (16.7%).

All of these countries/economies also show relatively high mean proficiency. Conversely, countries with lower average performance also tend to have the smallest proportions of students who can complete Level 5 tasks. In Montenegro, Malaysia, Colombia, Uruguay, Bulgaria and Brazil, fewer than 2% of students perform at Level 5 or 6. All of these countries perform well below the OECD average.

■ Figure V.2.5 ■

Summary descriptions of the six levels of proficiency in problem solving

Level	Score range	Percentage of students able to perform tasks at this level or above (OECD average)	What students can typically do
1	358 to less than 423 points	91.8%	At Level 1, students can explore a problem scenario only in a limited way, but tend to do so only when they have encountered very similar situations before. Based on their observations of familiar scenarios, these students are able only to partially describe the behaviour of a simple, everyday device. In general, students at Level 1 can solve straightforward problems provided there is a simple condition to be satisfied and there are only one or two steps to be performed to reach the goal. Level 1 students tend not to be able to plan ahead or set subgoals.
2	423 to less than 488 points	78.6%	At Level 2, students can explore an unfamiliar problem scenario and understand a small part of it. They try, but only partially succeed, to understand and control digital devices with unfamiliar controls, such as home appliances and vending machines. Level 2 problem-solvers can test a simple hypothesis that is given to them and can solve a problem that has a single, specific constraint. They can plan and carry out one step at a time to achieve a subgoal, and have some capacity to monitor overall progress towards a solution.
3	488 to less than 553 points	56.6%	At Level 3, students can handle information presented in several different formats. They can explore a problem scenario and infer simple relationships among its components. They can control simple digital devices, but have trouble with more complex devices. Problem-solvers at Level 3 can fully deal with one condition, for example, by generating several solutions and checking to see whether these satisfy the condition. When there are multiple conditions or inter-related features, they can hold one variable constant to see the effect of change on the other variables. They can devise and execute tests to confirm or refute a given hypothesis. They understand the need to plan ahead and monitor progress, and are able to try a different option if necessary.
4	553 to less than 618 points	31.0%	At Level 4, students can explore a moderately complex problem scenario in a focused way. They grasp the links among the components of the scenario that are required to solve the problem. They can control moderately complex digital devices, such as unfamiliar vending machines or home appliances, but they don't always do so efficiently. These students can plan a few steps ahead and monitor the progress of their plans. They are usually able to adjust these plans or reformulate a goal in light of feedback. They can systematically try out different possibilities and check whether multiple conditions have been satisfied. They can form an hypothesis about why a system is malfunctioning and describe how to test it.
5	618 to less than 683 points	11.4%	At Level 5, students can systematically explore a complex problem scenario to gain an understanding of how relevant information is structured. When faced with unfamiliar, moderately complex devices, such as vending machines or home appliances, they respond quickly to feedback in order to control the device. In order to reach a solution, Level 5 problem-solvers think ahead to find the best strategy that addresses all the given constraints. They can immediately adjust their plans or backtrack when they detect unexpected difficulties or when they make mistakes that take them off course.
6	Equal to or higher than 683 points	2.5%	At Level 6, students can develop complete, coherent mental models of diverse problem scenarios, enabling them to solve complex problems efficiently. They can explore a scenario in a highly strategic manner to understand all information pertaining to the problem. The information may be presented in different formats, requiring interpretation and integration of related parts. When confronted with very complex devices, such as home appliances that work in an unusual or unexpected manner, they quickly learn how to control the devices to achieve a goal in an optimal way. Level 6 problem-solvers can set up general hypotheses about a system and thoroughly test them. They can follow a premise through to a logical conclusion or recognise when there is not enough information available to reach one. In order to reach a solution, these highly proficient problem-solvers can create complex, flexible, multi-step plans that they continually monitor during execution. Where necessary, they modify their strategies, taking all constraints into account, both explicit and implicit.

■ Figure V.2.6 ■

Proficiency in problem solving

Percentage of students at the different levels of problem-solving proficiency

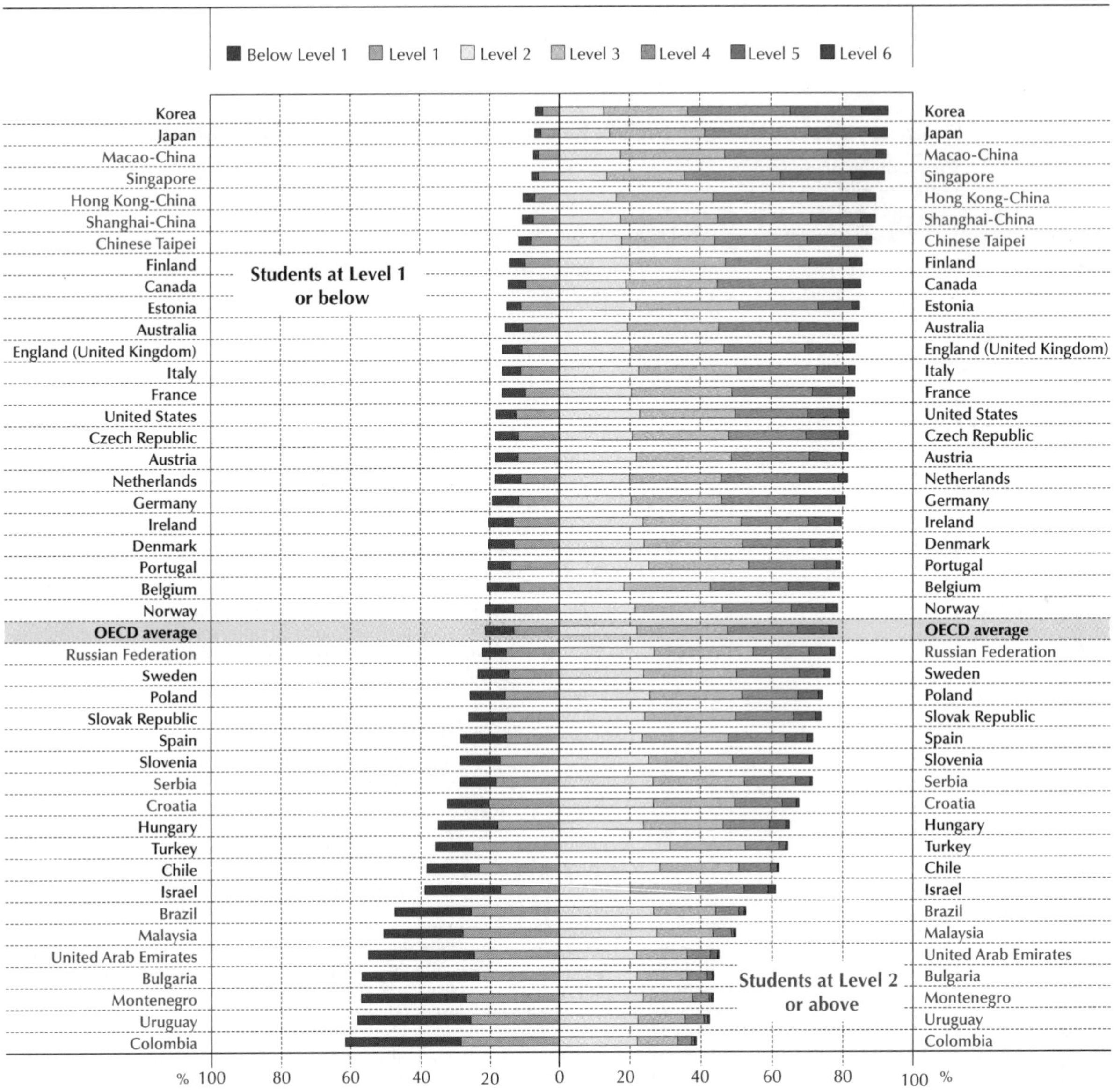

■ Below Level 1   ■ Level 1   □ Level 2   □ Level 3   ■ Level 4   ■ Level 5   ■ Level 6

Korea
Japan
Macao-China
Singapore
Hong Kong-China
Shanghai-China
Chinese Taipei
Finland
Canada
Estonia
Australia
England (United Kingdom)
Italy
France
United States
Czech Republic
Austria
Netherlands
Germany
Ireland
Denmark
Portugal
Belgium
Norway
OECD average
Russian Federation
Sweden
Poland
Slovak Republic
Spain
Slovenia
Serbia
Croatia
Hungary
Turkey
Chile
Israel
Brazil
Malaysia
United Arab Emirates
Bulgaria
Montenegro
Uruguay
Colombia

Students at Level 1 or below

Students at Level 2 or above

% 100   80   60   40   20   0   20   40   60   80   100 %

Countries and economies are ranked in descending order of the percentage of students at Levels 2, 3, 4, 5 and 6 in problem solving.
Source: OECD, PISA 2012 Database, Table V.2.1.
StatLink ᵐˢ⁴ http://dx.doi.org/10.1787/888933003573

In general, a ranking of countries and economies by the proportion of top-performing students (students at Level 5 or above) matches the ranking of countries/economies by mean performance, but there are a number of exceptions (Box V.2.4 and Figure V.2.7). In Belgium, the proportion of students proficient at Level 5 (14.4%) is larger than that in Estonia (11.8%), while overall, Estonia has higher average performance (515 points) than Belgium (508 points). Similarly, in Israel the proportion of top performers is large (8.8%) compared with countries of similar average performance (454 points), such as Turkey, where only 2.2% of students are top performers (Figure V.2.6 and Table V.2.1).

Proficiency at Level 4

Students proficient at Level 4 on the problem-solving scale can explore a problem scenario in a focused way, grasp the links among the components of the scenario that are required to solve the problem, plan a few steps ahead, and monitor

the progress of their plans. They can control moderately complex devices, such as unfamiliar vending machines or home appliances, but they don't always do so efficiently. In the sample task *CLIMATE CONTROL* (Task 2), for instance, they try to reach the target levels for humidity and temperature by addressing each of them in succession, rather than simultaneously.

Across OECD countries, 31% of students are proficient at Level 4 or higher. In Korea, Singapore and Japan, most 15-year-old students can complete tasks at Level 4; and in all of these countries, the highest proficiency attained by the largest proportion of students is Level 4. The mean performance of Singapore (562 points) and Korea (561 points) also falls within this level. By contrast, in Colombia, Montenegro, Malaysia, Uruguay, Bulgaria, Brazil and the United Arab Emirates fewer than one in ten students reaches Level 4. These are also the countries with the lowest mean scores in problem solving (Figure V.2.6 and Table V.2.1).

Proficiency at Level 3

Students proficient at Level 3 can handle information presented in several different formats. They can explore a problem scenario and infer simple relationships among its components. Problem-solvers at Level 3 can fully deal with one condition, for example, by generating several solutions and checking to see whether these satisfy the condition. When there are multiple conditions or inter-related features, they can hold one variable constant to see the effect of change on the other variables. They can devise and execute tests to confirm or refute a given hypothesis. They understand the need to plan ahead and monitor progress.

Across OECD countries, the majority (57%) of 15-year-old students are proficient at least at Level 3. For about one in four students (26%), Level 3 is the highest level reached. Level 3 is the most common level of proficiency in problem solving attained by students in 26 of the 44 countries and economies that assessed problem-solving skills in PISA 2012.

Three out of four students in Korea, Japan and Singapore attain at least Level 3 in problem solving. By contrast, in 18 countries, including eight OECD countries, fewer than one in two students can complete tasks at Level 3 successfully (Figure V.2.6 and Table V.2.1).

Proficiency at Level 2

Students proficient at Level 2 on the problem-solving scale can explore an unfamiliar problem scenario and understand a small part of it, can test a simple hypothesis that is given to them, and can solve a problem that has a single, specific constraint. They can plan and carry out one step at a time to achieve a subgoal, and have some capacity to monitor overall progress towards a solution.

Level 2 can be considered a baseline level of proficiency, at which students begin to demonstrate the problem-solving competencies that will enable them to participate effectively and productively in 21st-century societies. At this level of proficiency, students engage with an everyday problem, make progress towards a goal, and sometimes achieve it.

Figure V.2.6 ranks countries and economies by the proportion of 15-year-olds who can complete tasks at least at Level 2 difficulty. Across OECD countries, almost four in five students (79%) are proficient at Level 2 or higher. In Korea, Japan, Macao-China and Singapore, more than nine out of ten students perform at least at this level. By contrast, in six countries, only a minority of 15-year-old students reaches this baseline level of problem-solving performance. In eight countries/economies, Level 2 is the most common level of proficiency among students (Figure V.2.6 and Table V.2.1).

Proficiency at Level 1

Students proficient at Level 1 can explore a problem scenario only in a limited way; but in contrast with Level 2 problem-solvers, they tend to do so only when they have encountered very similar situations before. Based on their observations of familiar scenarios, these students are able only to partially describe the behaviour of a simple, everyday device.

In general, students at Level 1 can solve straightforward problems provided there is only a simple condition to be satisfied and there are only one or two steps to be performed to reach the goal. In contrast to students proficient at Level 2, Level 1 students tend not to be able to plan ahead or set subgoals.

Across OECD countries, 92% of 15-year-olds are proficient at Level 1 or higher. However, in Bulgaria and Colombia, around one in three students does not reach this elementary level of problem-solving proficiency; and in Uruguay, the United Arab Emirates, Montenegro, Malaysia, Brazil and Israel, more than one in five students do not reach this level.

Proficiency below Level 1

Given that the PISA 2012 problem-solving assessment was not designed to assess elementary problem-solving skills, there were insufficient items to fully describe performance that falls below Level 1 on the problem-solving scale. However, it was observed that some students with proficiency below Level 1 can use an unsystematic strategy to solve a simple problem set in a familiar context, such as Task 1 in sample unit *TRAFFIC*. They may even find the solution, provided there are a limited number of well-defined possibilities. On the whole, though, students who are below Level 1 show limited problem-solving skills, at best.

Across OECD countries, only 8% of students score below 358 points on the PISA scale, below Level 1. In Bulgaria, Colombia, Uruguay, the United Arab Emirates, Montenegro and Israel the proportion of students scoring below Level 1 is larger than the proportion of students scoring at any higher level of proficiency – making below Level 1 the most common level of proficiency in these six countries. Interestingly, in Israel, the proportion of students scoring at Level 1 (but not higher) is smaller than both the proportion of students who score below Level 1 and the proportion of students who score at Level 2. This indicates a strong polarisation of results. While in most countries, measures aimed at raising the general level of proficiency will likely benefit students at all levels of the performance distribution, in Israel, more targeted measures may be required for students who perform below Level 1 (Figure V.2.6 and Table V.2.1).

Box V.2.4. **Top performers in problem solving**

As machines and computers are increasingly replacing humans for performing routine tasks, highly skilled workers, who are capable of applying their unique skills flexibly in a variety of contexts, regulating their own learning, and handling novel situations, are more and more in demand. Knowing the proportion of 15-year-old students who perform at the highest levels in problem solving allows countries to estimate how well they can respond to this demand. Of particular interest is the proportion of students who, in addition to performing at the highest levels in problem solving, also show excellent mastery of specific subjects.

In analyses of PISA data, the phrase "top performers" refers to students who attain Level 5 or 6 in a domain. In problem solving, this corresponds to a performance above 618 score points.

Figure V.2.7 shows the proportion of top performers in problem solving in each country/economy, as well as the proportion of students who reach a comparable level of proficiency in at least one of the three assessment subjects: mathematics, reading and science. As noted earlier, the ranking of countries and economies by the percentage of top performers in problem solving substantially matches a ranking by mean performance levels. Notable exceptions are Belgium and Israel, which have larger proportions of top performers than other countries of similar or higher mean performance in problem solving.

In most countries and economies, most top performers in problem solving are also top performers in other domains. Most frequently, top performers in problem solving are also top performers in mathematics. In fact, across OECD countries, 64% of top performers in problem solving are also top performers in mathematics (Table V.2.3).

The proportion of students who reach the highest levels of proficiency in at least one domain (problem solving, mathematics, reading or science) can be considered a measure of the breadth of a country's/economy's pool of top performers. By this measure, the largest pool of top performers is found in Shanghai-China, where more than half of all students (56%) perform at the highest levels in at least one domain, followed by Singapore (46%), Hong Kong-China (40%), Korea and Chinese Taipei (39%) (Table V.2.3). Only one OECD country, Korea, is found among the five countries/economies with the largest proportion of top performers. On average across OECD countries, 20% of students are top performers in at least one assessment domain.

The proportion of students performing at the top in problem solving and in either mathematics, reading or science, too can be considered a measure of the depth of this pool. These are top performers who combine the mastery of a specific domain of knowledge with the ability to apply their unique skills flexibly, in a variety of contexts. By this measure, the deepest pools of top performers can be found in Singapore (25% of students), Korea (21%), Shanghai-China (18%) and Chinese Taipei (17%). On average across OECD countries, only 8% of students are top performers in both a core subject and in problem solving.

■ Figure V.2.7 ■

Top performers in problem solving

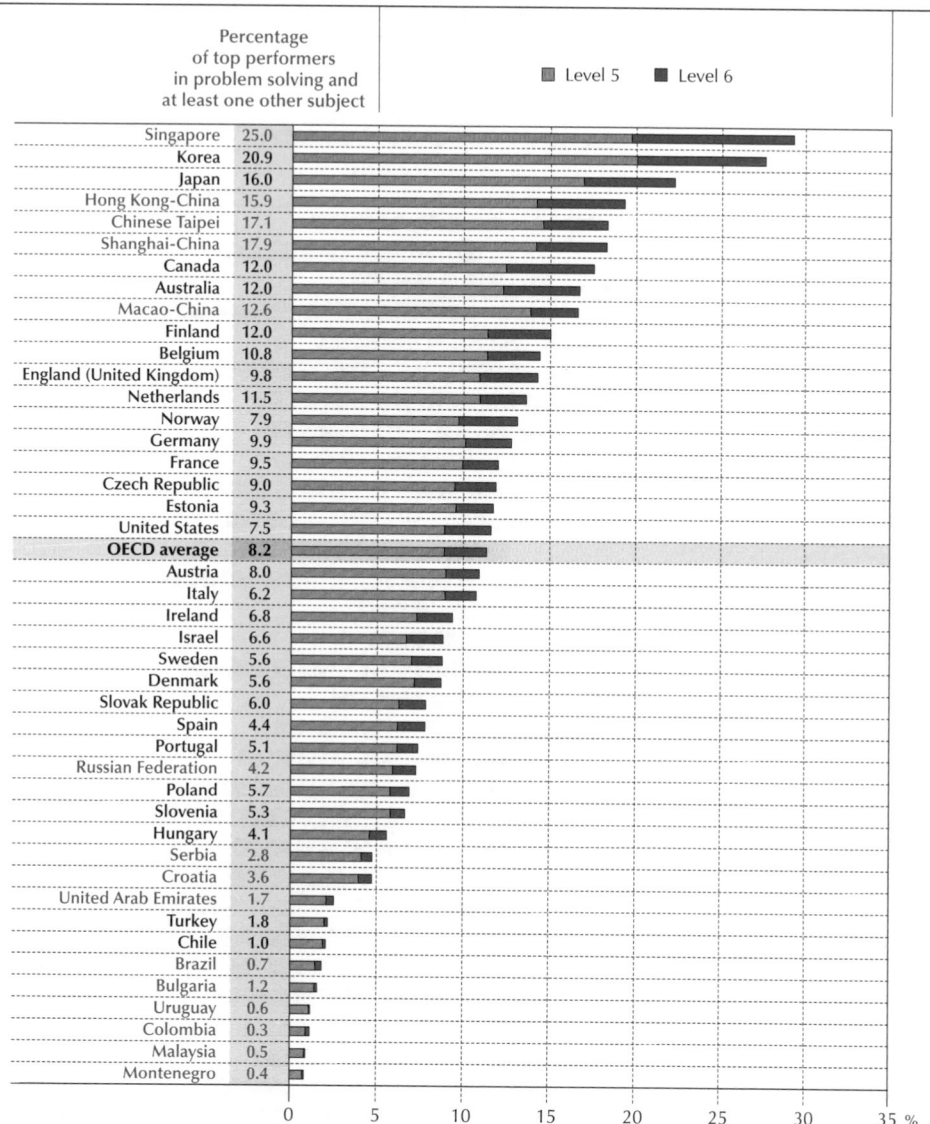

	Percentage of top performers in problem solving and at least one other subject	Level 5	Level 6
Singapore	25.0		
Korea	20.9		
Japan	16.0		
Hong Kong-China	15.9		
Chinese Taipei	17.1		
Shanghai-China	17.9		
Canada	12.0		
Australia	12.0		
Macao-China	12.6		
Finland	12.0		
Belgium	10.8		
England (United Kingdom)	9.8		
Netherlands	11.5		
Norway	7.9		
Germany	9.9		
France	9.5		
Czech Republic	9.0		
Estonia	9.3		
United States	7.5		
OECD average	8.2		
Austria	8.0		
Italy	6.2		
Ireland	6.8		
Israel	6.6		
Sweden	5.6		
Denmark	5.6		
Slovak Republic	6.0		
Spain	4.4		
Portugal	5.1		
Russian Federation	4.2		
Poland	5.7		
Slovenia	5.3		
Hungary	4.1		
Serbia	2.8		
Croatia	3.6		
United Arab Emirates	1.7		
Turkey	1.8		
Chile	1.0		
Brazil	0.7		
Bulgaria	1.2		
Uruguay	0.6		
Colombia	0.3		
Malaysia	0.5		
Montenegro	0.4		

Countries and economies are ranked in descending order of the percentage of top performers (Levels 5 and 6) in problem solving.
Source: OECD, PISA 2012 Database, Tables V.2.1 and V.2.3.
StatLink ᴍꜱ▟ http://dx.doi.org/10.1787/888933003573

VARIATION IN PROBLEM-SOLVING PROFICIENCY

When looking at how performance within each country/economy is distributed across the proficiency levels (Figure V.2.6), it becomes apparent that the variation observed between students from the same country/economy is, in general, much wider than the variation observed between countries/economies.

The standard deviation summarises the distribution of performance among 15-year-olds within each country/economy in a single figure. By this measure, the smallest variation in problem-solving proficiency is found in Turkey and Macao-China, with standard deviations below 80 score points (Figure V.2.8). Among top-performing countries, Japan also has a narrow spread of performance (the standard deviation is 85 score points). At the other extreme, Israel, Bulgaria, Belgium and the United Arab Emirates have the largest variations in problem-solving proficiency, with standard deviations well above 100 score points. The diversity in performance within Israel, Bulgaria, Belgium and the United Arab Emirates is therefore larger than the diversity that one would expect to find when sampling a diverse population of students across the 28 OECD countries that participated in the assessment.

■ Figure V.2.8 ■

Variation in problem-solving performance within countries and economies

Standard deviation and percentiles on the problem-solving scale

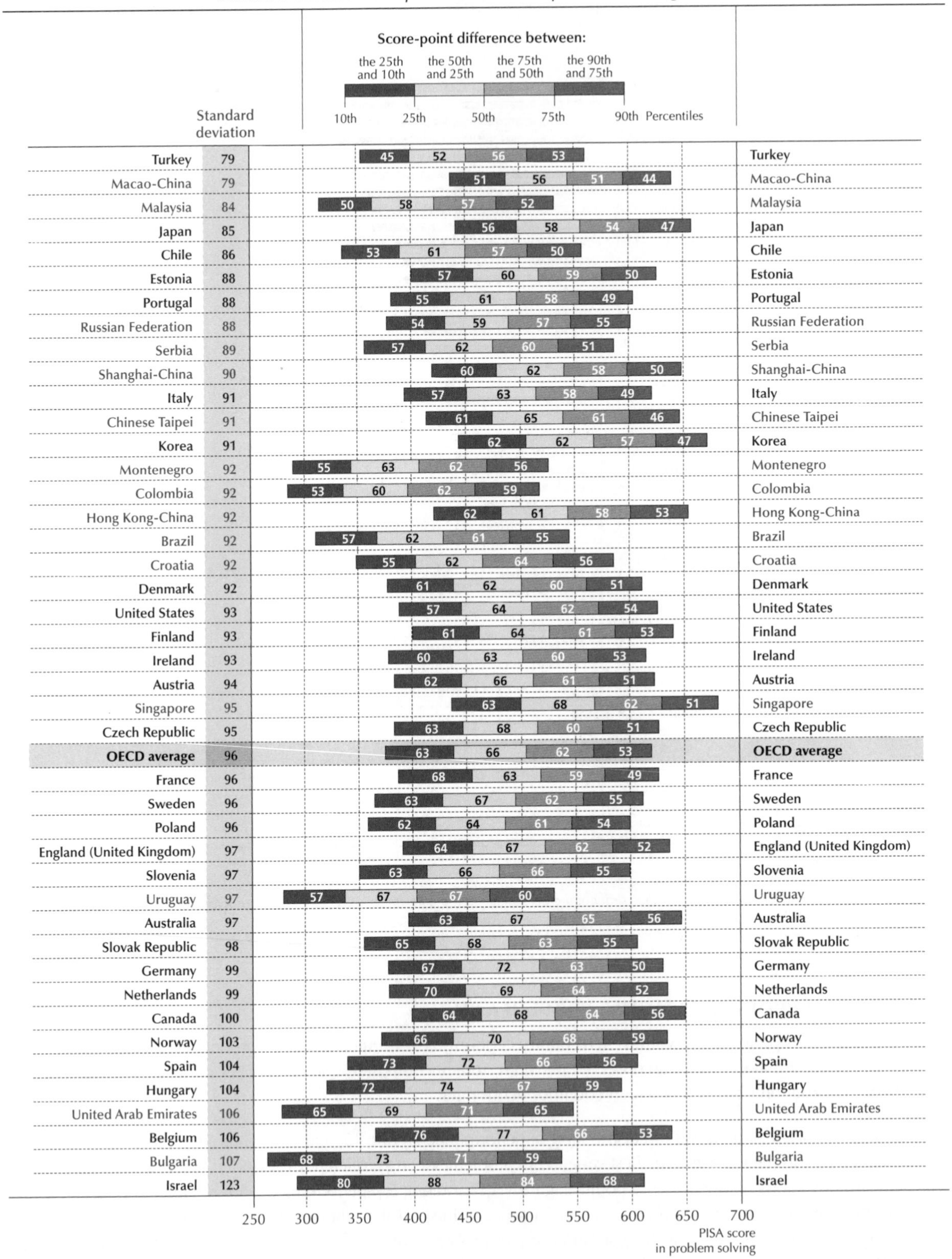

Score-point difference between:

	the 25th and 10th	the 50th and 25th	the 75th and 50th	the 90th and 75th

Country	Standard deviation	10th ... 25th ... 50th ... 75th ... 90th Percentiles	Country
Turkey	79	45 / 52 / 56 / 53	Turkey
Macao-China	79	51 / 56 / 51 / 44	Macao-China
Malaysia	84	50 / 58 / 57 / 52	Malaysia
Japan	85	56 / 58 / 54 / 47	Japan
Chile	86	53 / 61 / 57 / 50	Chile
Estonia	88	57 / 60 / 59 / 50	Estonia
Portugal	88	55 / 61 / 58 / 49	Portugal
Russian Federation	88	54 / 59 / 57 / 55	Russian Federation
Serbia	89	57 / 62 / 60 / 51	Serbia
Shanghai-China	90	60 / 62 / 58 / 50	Shanghai-China
Italy	91	57 / 63 / 58 / 49	Italy
Chinese Taipei	91	61 / 65 / 61 / 46	Chinese Taipei
Korea	91	62 / 62 / 57 / 47	Korea
Montenegro	92	55 / 63 / 62 / 56	Montenegro
Colombia	92	53 / 60 / 62 / 59	Colombia
Hong Kong-China	92	62 / 61 / 58 / 53	Hong Kong-China
Brazil	92	57 / 62 / 61 / 55	Brazil
Croatia	92	55 / 62 / 64 / 56	Croatia
Denmark	92	61 / 62 / 60 / 51	Denmark
United States	93	57 / 64 / 62 / 54	United States
Finland	93	61 / 64 / 61 / 53	Finland
Ireland	93	60 / 63 / 60 / 53	Ireland
Austria	94	62 / 66 / 61 / 51	Austria
Singapore	95	63 / 68 / 62 / 51	Singapore
Czech Republic	95	63 / 68 / 60 / 51	Czech Republic
OECD average	**96**	63 / 66 / 62 / 53	**OECD average**
France	96	68 / 63 / 59 / 49	France
Sweden	96	63 / 67 / 62 / 55	Sweden
Poland	96	62 / 64 / 61 / 54	Poland
England (United Kingdom)	97	64 / 67 / 62 / 52	England (United Kingdom)
Slovenia	97	63 / 66 / 66 / 55	Slovenia
Uruguay	97	57 / 67 / 67 / 60	Uruguay
Australia	97	63 / 67 / 65 / 56	Australia
Slovak Republic	98	65 / 68 / 63 / 55	Slovak Republic
Germany	99	67 / 72 / 63 / 50	Germany
Netherlands	99	70 / 69 / 64 / 52	Netherlands
Canada	100	64 / 68 / 64 / 56	Canada
Norway	103	66 / 70 / 68 / 59	Norway
Spain	104	73 / 72 / 66 / 56	Spain
Hungary	104	72 / 74 / 67 / 59	Hungary
United Arab Emirates	106	65 / 69 / 71 / 65	United Arab Emirates
Belgium	106	76 / 77 / 66 / 53	Belgium
Bulgaria	107	68 / 73 / 71 / 59	Bulgaria
Israel	123	80 / 88 / 84 / 68	Israel

250   300   350   400   450   500   550   600   650   700
PISA score in problem solving

Countries and economies are ranked in ascending order of the standard deviation in problem solving.
Source: OECD, PISA 2012 Database, Table V.2.2.
StatLink ⬛📊 http://dx.doi.org/10.1787/888933003573

Figure V.2.8 also shows how different parts of the performance distribution compare within and across countries and economies. The inter-quartile range – the gap between the top and bottom quarters of the performance distribution – provides another way of measuring differences in performance. On average across OECD countries, the inter-quartile range is equal to 129 score points. In the countries with the largest variations in problem-solving proficiency (Israel, Bulgaria and Belgium), the gap between the top and bottom quarters of students is more than 14 score points wider than the average gap in OECD countries (Table V.2.2).

In many countries, the higher-performing students score closer to the median level of performance than do the lower-performing students (Figure V.2.9). This means that most of the variation is concentrated among low-performing students. In Belgium, Germany, the Netherlands, Spain, France, the Czech Republic and Korea, the difference between the lowest-performing 10% of students and the median is more than 20 score points larger than the difference between the highest-performing 10% of students and the median. In these countries, many students perform well below the level achieved by a majority of students in the country and drag the mean performance down.

■ Figure V.2.9 ■

Performance differences among high- and low-achieving students

Gaps at the top and bottom end of the distribution of problem-solving performance

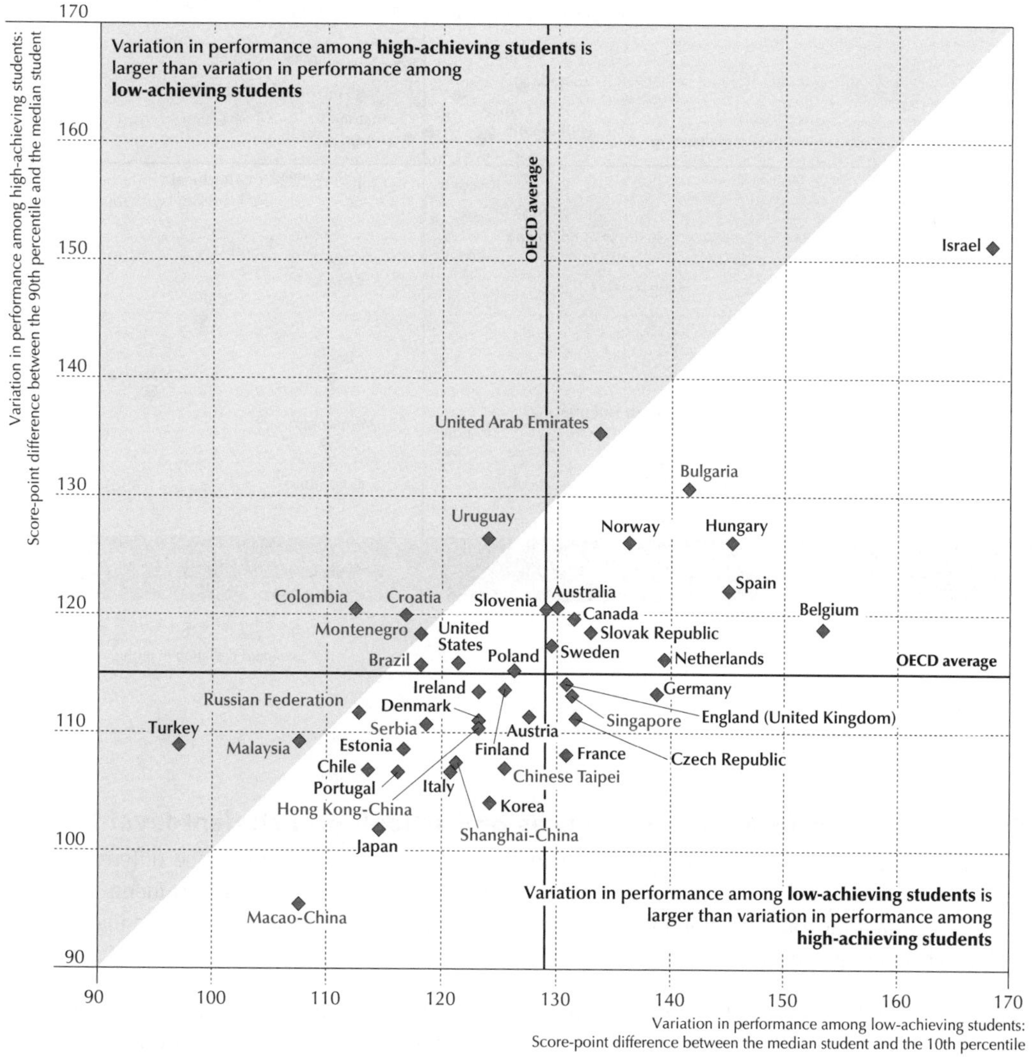

Variation in performance among high-achieving students:
Score-point difference between the 90th percentile and the median student (y-axis, 90 to 170)

Variation in performance among low-achieving students:
Score-point difference between the median student and the 10th percentile (x-axis, 90 to 170)

Variation in performance among **high-achieving students** is larger than variation in performance among **low-achieving students**

OECD average

Variation in performance among **low-achieving students** is larger than variation in performance among **high-achieving students**

Israel, United Arab Emirates, Bulgaria, Norway, Hungary, Uruguay, Colombia, Croatia, Slovenia, Australia, Spain, Belgium, Canada, Montenegro, United States, Slovak Republic, Brazil, Poland, Sweden, Netherlands, Ireland, Germany, Russian Federation, Denmark, Singapore, England (United Kingdom), Turkey, Serbia, Austria, Malaysia, Estonia, Finland, France, Czech Republic, Chile, Chinese Taipei, Portugal, Italy, Hong Kong-China, Korea, Shanghai-China, Japan, Macao-China

Source: OECD, PISA 2012 Database, Table V.2.2.
StatLink http://dx.doi.org/10.1787/888933003573

The performance variation in problem solving is not strongly related to mean performance (Figure V.2.10). Among countries and economies that perform above the OECD average, Canada and Belgium have a wider variation in performance than the OECD average. By contrast, Japan and Macao-China, among the top-performing countries and economies, show a narrow variation in student performance, as do Turkey and Malaysia, both of whose mean scores are well below the OECD average. This shows that narrowing differences in performance and fostering excellence are not necessarily conflicting objectives. It is possible to combine high average levels of performance with small variations in performance.

■ Figure V.2.10 ■

Average performance in problem solving and variation in performance

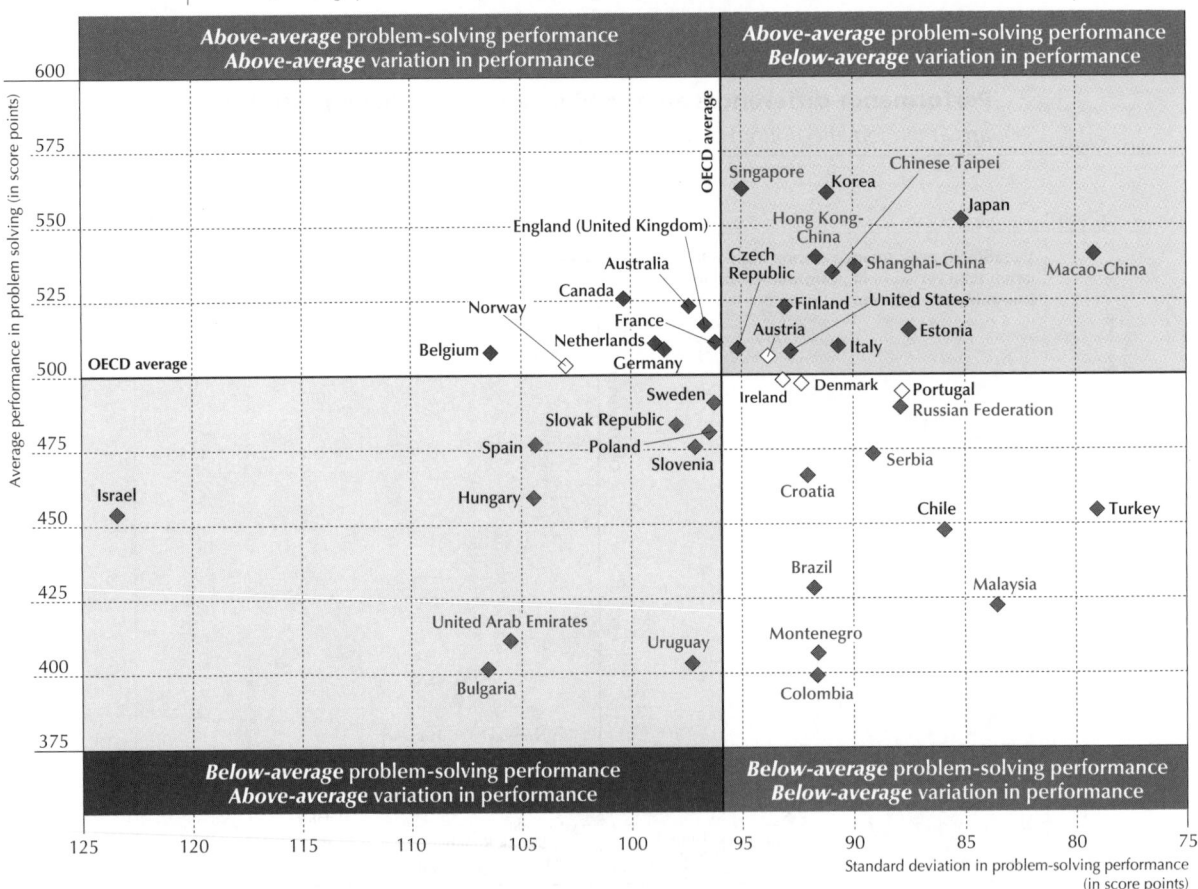

Source: OECD, PISA 2012 Database, Table V.2.2.

StatLink ⬛ http://dx.doi.org/10.1787/888933003573

Relationship between performance differences and school- and student-level factors

The variation in performance within countries can be divided into a measure of performance differences between students from the same school, and a measure of performance differences between groups of students from different schools. Figure V.2.11 shows the total variation in performance within each country/economy divided into its between-school and within-school components.

The data show that there is substantial variation in problem-solving results across schools. On average across OECD countries, the variation in student performance that is observed within schools amounts to 61% of the OECD average variation in student performance. The remaining variation (38%) is due to differences in student performance between schools (Table V.2.4).

■ Figure V.2.11 ■

Total variation in problem-solving performance and variation between and within schools

Expressed as a percentage of the average variation in student performance across OECD countries

	Total variation as a proportion of the OECD variation	Variation within schools (as a proportion of total)	Variation between schools (as a proportion of total)
Israel	164		
Hungary	118		
Bulgaria	123		
Netherlands	106		
United Arab Emirates	120		
Belgium	122		
Germany	105		
Slovenia	102		
Slovak Republic	104		
Czech Republic	98		
Austria	95		
Uruguay	102		
Brazil	91		
OECD average	**100**		
Italy	89		
Croatia	91		
Poland	100		
Shanghai-China	87		
Turkey	67		
Chinese Taipei	89		
Montenegro	91		
Chile	80		
Spain	118		
Colombia	91		
Singapore	97		
Hong Kong-China	91		
Serbia	86		
Russian Federation	83		
England (United Kingdom)	101		
Malaysia	75		
Korea	90		
Australia	102		
United States	93		
Japan	78		
Denmark	92		
Portugal	83		
Canada	109		
Norway	114		
Ireland	94		
Macao-China	68		
Estonia	83		
Sweden	100		
Finland	94		

OECD average 61 %

OECD average 38 %

100   80   60   40   20   0   20   40   60   80   100

Percentage of variation within and between schools

Countries and economies are ranked in descending order of the between-school variation in problem-solving performance as a proportion of the between-school variation in performance across OECD countries.
Source: OECD, PISA 2012 Database, Table V.2.4.
StatLink http://dx.doi.org/10.1787/888933003573

The variation in performance between schools is a measure of how big "school effects" are. These school effects may have three distinct explanations: first, they may reflect selection mechanisms that assign students to schools; in addition, they may be the result of differences in policies and practices across schools; finally, they may be the traces of local school cultures that originate from interactions among local communities.

The between-school variation in student results is therefore not a direct measure of the importance of school policies and practices for student performance in problem solving. However, if the between-school variation is compared across different student characteristics – some sensitive to differences in education policy and practices, such as performance in mathematics, others not, such as socio-economic status – one may infer the extent to which problem-solving results are related to instructional policies and practices.

Comparing between-school variations

Figure V.2.12 shows how much of the variation in student performance lies between schools in each country and economy. It shows that problem-solving proficiency, in general, is as closely related to school policies, practices, contextual factors (such as neighbourhood influences) and peer influences as is performance in the mathematics assessment. On average across OECD countries, 38% of the overall variation in problem-solving performance is observed between schools (Table V.2.4). This proportion is very similar across assessment domains: it ranges from 36% in science to 38% in reading.[4]

■ Figure V.2.12 ■

Between-school differences in problem-solving performance, mathematics performance and socio-economic status

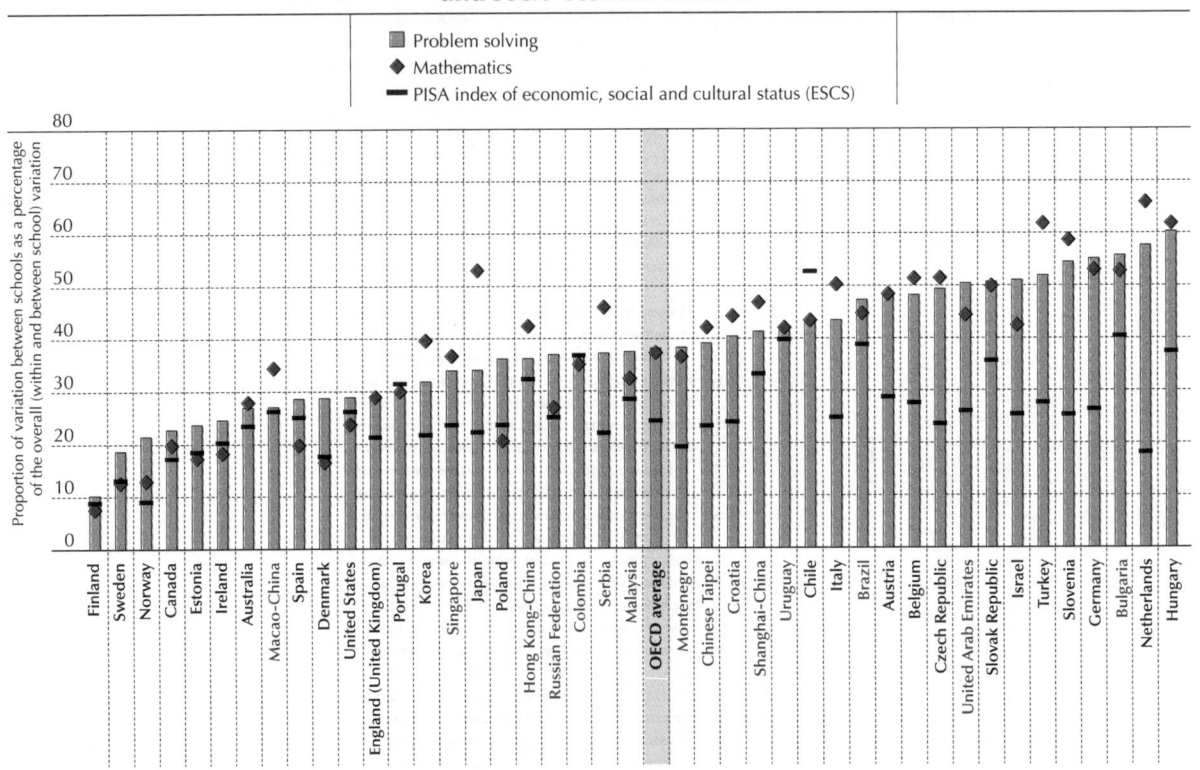

Countries and economies are ranked in ascending order of the proportion of variation in problem-solving performance that lies between schools.
Source: OECD, PISA 2012 Database, Table V.2.4.
StatLink ⛁ http://dx.doi.org/10.1787/888933003573

One might expect the proportion of variation in performance observed between schools to be smaller in problem solving than in mathematics, reading and science. First, the skills required in the PISA assessment of problem solving are not taught as a specific school subject in most countries, in contrast to those required in mathematics, reading and science. Second, assessments of problem solving are not explicitly used in high-stakes examinations that influence decisions about selecting students for different classes or schools, where these exist. Yet the association between differences in instruction and selection mechanisms and performance in problem solving is as strong as the association between instruction and selection and performance in mathematics, reading and science.

To compare the between-school variation across subjects and student characteristics the ratio of the between-school variation to the sum of the between- and within-school variation is computed. The within-school variation estimates how diverse students are within each school, on average. The between-school variation estimates how far the grouping of students across schools is from a random allocation of students to schools. Low levels of between-school variation (relative to the overall within- and between-school variation) indicate inclusion: within the limits given by its size, each school's diversity mirrors the level of diversity that exists in the country overall. Large proportions of variation between schools signal segregation: students tend to be grouped together only with students who are similar to them in the characteristic being examined.

While, in general, the influence of schools is as strong on performance in problem solving as for performance in curricular subjects, in some countries, the school seems to matter *more* for problem solving. In Denmark, Israel, Norway, Poland, the Russian Federation and Spain, for instance, performance in problem solving is more strongly associated with schools than performance in mathematics. In these countries, strong performers and poor performers in problem solving are more clearly sorted across different schools than strong and poor performers in mathematics. Conversely, in Japan, the Netherlands, Serbia and Turkey, students tend to be sorted across schools according to their mathematics level, but less so according to their performance in problem solving. All four of these countries have below-average levels of academic inclusion (as indicated by large variations in mathematics performance between schools). In these countries, however, problem-solving results are more similar between schools than are results in mathematics.

The between-school variation, on the other hand, is much larger in student outcome measures – such as reading, mathematics, or indeed problem solving – than in student background factors that influence performance, such as the *PISA index of economic, social and cultural status* (ESCS). Only 24% of the socio-economic variation lies between schools, on average across OECD countries. This means that in most countries, students within the same school tend to be more diverse in their socio-economic status than in their performance (Table V.2.4).

By comparing the variation between schools in the socio-economic status of students with the between-school variation in performance, one can gauge the importance of classroom interactions between teachers and students, or among students themselves, in shaping performance. Indeed, one could argue that the proportion of socio-economic variation between schools reflects residential segregation and school selection practices, and is not influenced by teacher-student or student-student relations. Over the course of a school year, this proportion will remain fixed. Performance, in addition to being influenced by these factors, will evolve over time. In particular, even if the allocation of pupils to schools remains the same, it is expected that over the course of schooling, differences in the quality of teaching create additional between-school variation in student performance.

The fact that the proportion of variation between schools is, in most countries, larger in problem-solving performance than in socio-economic status, is evidence that school-level factors are as important in explaining problem-solving performance as they are in explaining performance in mathematics or reading. There is only one exception: in Chile, the between-school variation in student performance (in all subjects) is smaller than the between-school variation in socio-economic status. This means that the school that a student attends says more about his or her socio-economic status than about his or her performance. In other countries and economies, such as Finland, Portugal and the United States, the pattern is less clear: the observed between-school variation in problem-solving performance is similar to the between-school variation in students' socio-economic status (Figure V.2.12 and Table V.2.4).

STUDENT PERFORMANCE IN PROBLEM SOLVING COMPARED WITH PERFORMANCE IN MATHEMATICS, READING AND SCIENCE

A key distinction between the PISA 2012 assessment of problem solving and the regular assessments of mathematics, reading and science is that the problem-solving assessment does not measure domain-specific knowledge; rather, it focuses as much as possible on the cognitive processes fundamental to problem solving. However, these processes can also be used and taught in the other subjects assessed. For this reason, problem-solving tasks are also included among the test units for mathematics, reading and science, where their solution requires expert knowledge specific to these domains, in addition to general problem-solving skills.

It is therefore expected that student performance in problem solving is positively correlated with student performance in mathematics, reading and science. This correlation hinges mostly on generic skills, and should thus be about the same magnitude as between any two regular assessment subjects.

The following sections examine the correlations between problem-solving performance and performance in mathematics, reading, and science. They then identify countries whose students' performance in problem solving is better than that of students around the world who share their level of proficiency in mathematics, reading and science. The chapter concludes with a discussion of the effects of computer delivery of the assessment on performance differences within and between countries.

Correlation between performance in mathematics, reading and science, and performance in problem solving

Students who do well in problem solving are likely to do well in other areas as well, and students who have poor problem-solving skills are likely to do poorly in other subjects assessed. Figure V.2.13 shows the strength of the relationship

between the three regular PISA domains and student performance in problem solving. The largest correlation is between mathematics and problem solving (0.81); the smallest is between reading and problem solving (0.75). These correlations may appear large, but they are smaller than the correlation observed among mathematics, reading and science.[5]

■ Figure V.2.13 ■

Relationship among problem-solving, mathematics, reading and science performance

OECD average latent correlation, where 0.00 signifies no relationship and 1.00 signifies the strongest positive relationship

Latent correlation between:			
Mathematics	**Reading**	**Science**	**and...**
0.81	0.75	0.78	**Problem solving**
	0.85	0.90	**Mathematics**
		0.88	**Reading**

Source: OECD, PISA 2012 Database, Table V.2.5.
StatLink http://dx.doi.org/10.1787/888933003573

■ Figure V.2.14 ■

Variation in problem-solving performance associated with performance in mathematics, reading and science

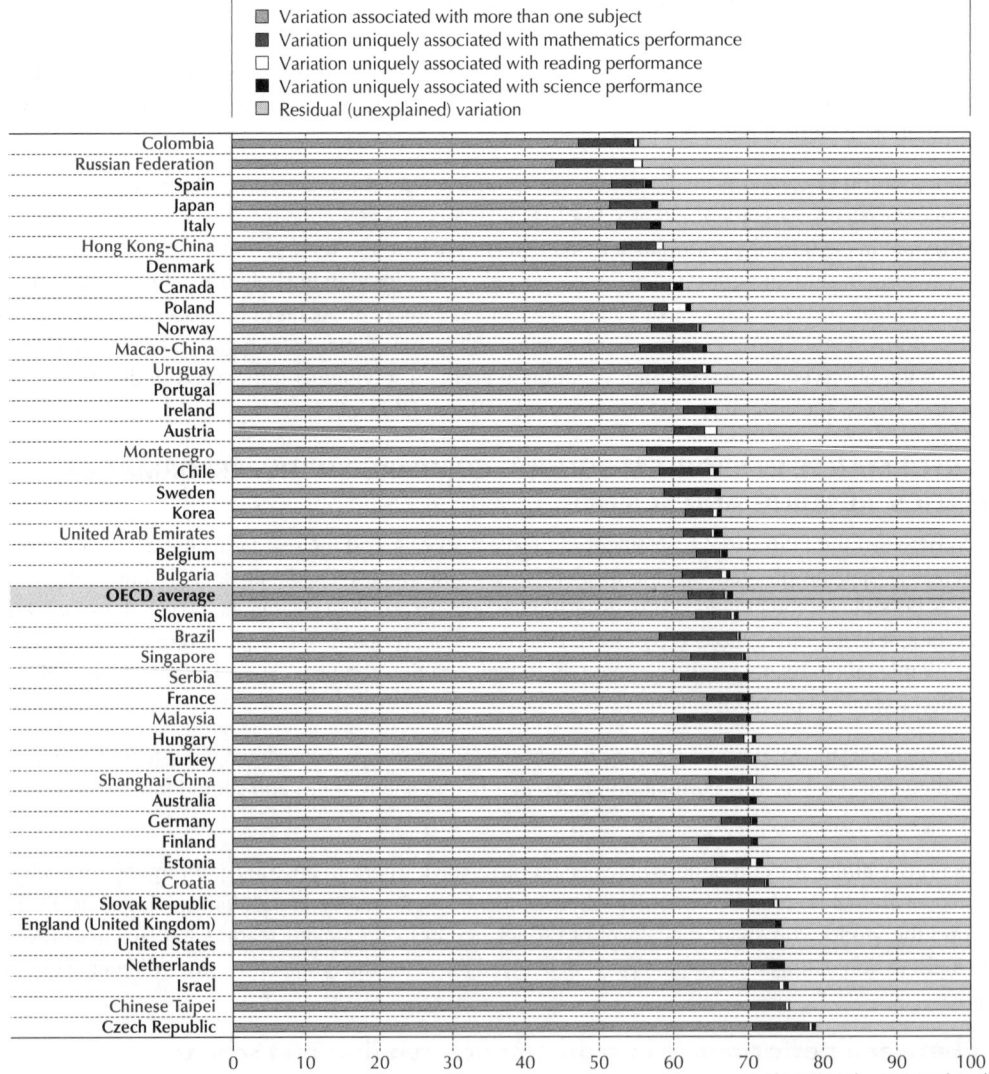

Countries and economies are ranked in ascending order of the total percentage of variance explained in problem solving.
Source: OECD, PISA 2012 Database, Table V.2.5.
StatLink http://dx.doi.org/10.1787/888933003573

Comparing the strength of the association among the skills measured in PISA clearly proves that problem solving constitutes a separate domain from mathematics, reading and science.

That the skills measured in the problem-solving assessment are those that are used in a wide range of contexts is confirmed by an analysis that relates the variation in problem-solving performance jointly to the variation in performance in mathematics, reading and science (Figure V.2.14). On average, about 68% of the problem-solving score reflects skills that are also measured in one of the three regular assessment domains.[6] The remaining 32% reflects skills that are uniquely captured by the assessment of problem solving. Of the 68% of variation that problem-solving performance shares with other domains, the overwhelming part is shared with all three regular assessment domains (62% of the total variation); about 5% is uniquely shared between problem solving and mathematics only; and about 1% of the variation in problem solving performance hinges on skills that are specifically measured in the assessments of reading or science (Table V.2.5).

Figure V.2.14 also shows that the association of problem-solving skills with performance in mathematics, reading and science is, in general, of similar strength across countries and economies. Comparatively weak associations between the skills measured in the problem-solving assessment and performance in mathematics, reading and science are found in Colombia, the Russian Federation, Spain, Japan, Italy and Hong Kong-China. In these countries and economies, more than in others, performance differences in problem solving do not necessarily match performance differences in core domains: some students who rank highly in, say, mathematics or reading, perform poorly in problem solving; conversely, some students who perform poorly in the core subjects still demonstrate high problem-solving proficiency.

Students' performance in problem solving relative to students with similar mathematics, reading and science skills

The strong positive correlations across domains indicate that, in general, students who perform at higher levels in mathematics, reading or science also perform well in problem solving. There are, however, wide variations in problem-solving performance for any given level of performance in the core domains assessed by PISA. This section uses this variation to assess country performance by comparing students from each country with students in other countries who have similar scores in mathematics, reading and science.[7]

■ Figure V.2.15 ■
Relative performance in problem solving

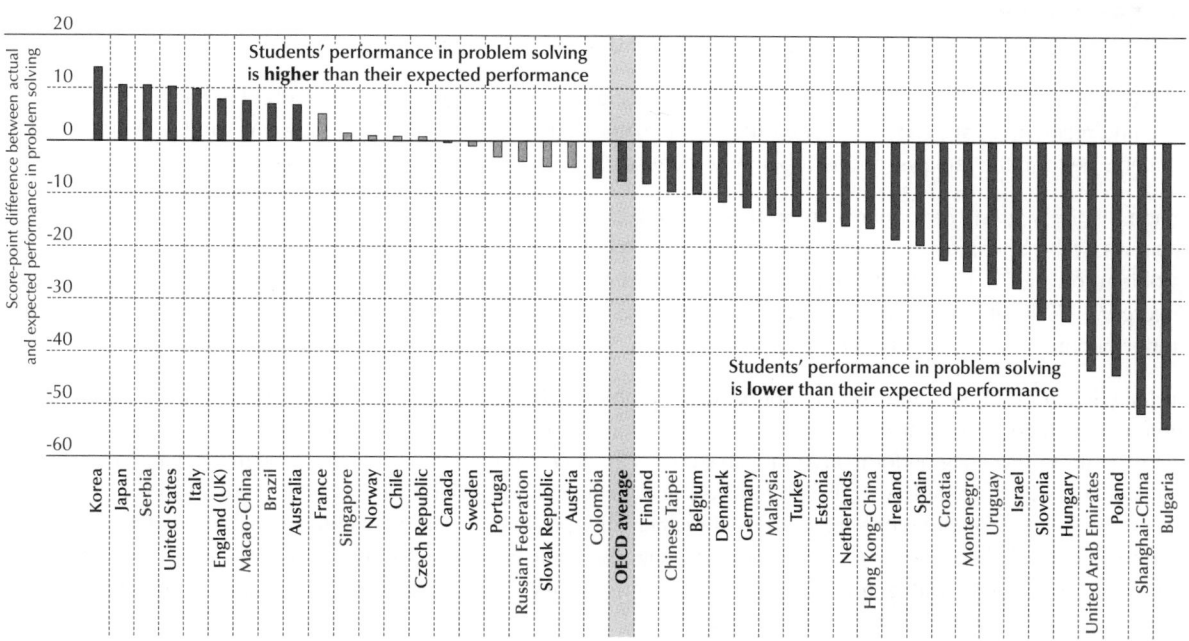

Notes: Significant differences are shown in a darker tone (see Annex A3).
Each student's expected performance is estimated, using a regression model, as the predicted performance in problem solving given his or her score in mathematics, reading and science.
Countries and economies are ranked in descending order of the score-point difference between actual and expected performance.
Source: OECD, PISA 2012 Database, Table V.2.6.
StatLink ᴍᴉˢᴸ http://dx.doi.org/10.1787/888933003573

Relative performance in problem solving is estimated by comparing students' actual performance to the performance predicted by a regression model that estimates, for each student, the expected performance in problem solving depending on the performance in the three core domains. Figure V.2.15 shows a ranking of countries/economies in relative performance.

In nine countries and economies, students perform significantly better, on average, in problem solving than students in other countries with similar skills in mathematics, reading and science. Of the 19 countries and economies whose mean performance is above the OECD average, Korea, Japan, the United States, Italy, England (United Kingdom), Macao-China and Australia have a specific strength in problem solving. In Brazil and in Serbia, students perform above the level attained by students of similar strength in the core assessment domains, on average; but this above-average relative performance in problem solving is not sufficient to raise the countries' mean absolute performance above the OECD average. In Korea, Japan, Serbia and the United States, the difference between students' scores in problem solving and their expected performance given their scores in mathematics, reading and science, exceeds 10 score points. In Korea, 61% of students outperform other students assessed in PISA with similar performance in core subjects on the problem-solving assessment (Figure V.2.15 and Table V.2.6).

In more than 20 countries and economies, students perform below par in problem solving, on average, when compared to students in the other participating countries and economies who display the same level of proficiency in mathematics, reading and science. In Bulgaria, Shanghai-China, Poland and the United Arab Emirates, the difference exceeds 40 score points. In Shanghai-China, 86% of students perform below the expected level in problem solving, given their performance in mathematics, reading and science. Students in these countries/economies struggle to use all the skills that they demonstrate in the other domains when asked to perform problem-solving tasks. In six other countries/economies, problem-solving performance falls short of its expected level, given students' performance in mathematics, reading and science, by between 20 and 40 score points: Hungary (34 score points), Slovenia (34 points), Israel (28 points), Uruguay (27 points), Montenegro (24 points) and Croatia (22 points). Spain, Ireland, Hong Kong-China, the Netherlands, Estonia, Turkey, Malaysia, Germany, Denmark, Belgium, Chinese Taipei, Finland and Colombia show smaller gaps. All these countries/economies could improve their performance in problem solving if their students performed at the same level as students in other countries/economies who demonstrate similar skills in mathematics, reading and science (Figure V.2.15 and Table V.2.6).

Students' performance in problem solving at different levels of performance in mathematics

Figure V.2.16 shows the average problem-solving performance of students at different levels of mathematics proficiency.

By comparing the performance of students from one country to the average performance observed across participating countries/economies at a given level of proficiency in mathematics, shown in Figure V.2.16, one can infer whether these students perform the same as, above or below students with similar proficiency in mathematics.

Is the relatively strong performance in problem solving observed in some countries mainly due to the ability of some students at the bottom of the class to perform above expectations in problem solving, or to the good performance in problem solving among students who perform at or above Level 4 in mathematics? The answer varies greatly by country. Figure V.2.17 illustrates nine possible patterns and shows which pattern prevails in each of the participating countries and economies, based on results reported in Table V.2.6.

In Italy, Japan and Korea, the good performance in problem solving is, to a large extent, due to the fact that lower-performing students score beyond expectations in the problem-solving assessment. In Italy and Japan, students with strong mathematics skills perform on a par with students in other countries that share the same mathematics proficiency; but students who score at low or moderate levels in mathematics have significantly better problem-solving skills than students in other countries with similar levels of mathematics proficiency. This may indicate that some of these students perform below their potential in mathematics; it may also indicate, more positively, that students at the bottom of the class who struggle with some subjects in school are remarkably resilient when it comes to confronting real-life challenges in non-curricular contexts (Figure V.2.17).

In contrast, in Australia, England (United Kingdom) and the United States, the best students in mathematics also have excellent problem-solving skills. These countries' good performance in problem solving is mainly due to strong performers in mathematics. This may suggest that in these countries, high performers in mathematics have access to – and take advantage of – the kinds of learning opportunities that are also useful for improving their problem-solving skills.

■ Figure V.2.16 ■
Expected performance in problem solving, by mathematics performance

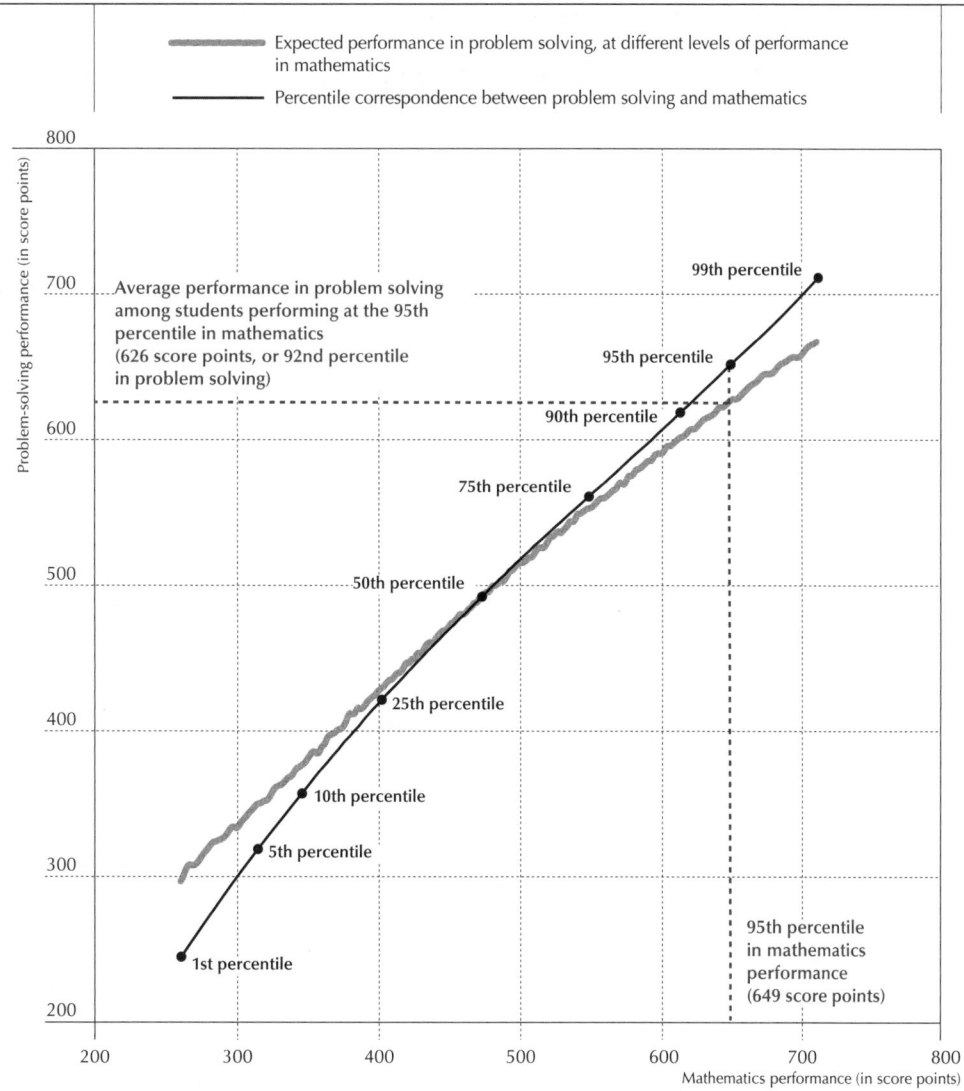

Notes: The blue line shows students' expected problem-solving performance at each level of proficiency in mathematics. This conditional expectation line is estimated with local linear regression on the pooled international sample of students (see Annex A3).
The black line shows the correspondence between percentiles of performance in problem solving and percentiles of performance in mathematics. Percentiles are estimated on the pooled international sample of students.
The comparison of the two lines indicates a certain amount of "mean reversion". For instance, students performing at the 95th percentile in mathematics perform at the 92nd percentile in problem solving, on average, and thus closer to the international mean. This observed mean reversion is as expected for two partially independent skills.
Source: OECD, PISA 2012 Database.
StatLink ⧉ http://dx.doi.org/10.1787/888933003573

There are similar differences among countries with overall weak performance in problem solving, relative to their students' performance in mathematics. In several of these countries, specific difficulties in problem solving are most apparent among students with poor mathematics skills, and students with strong mathematics skills often perform on or close to par with students in other countries/economies. These countries are shown in the top-right cell in Figure V.2.17. In other countries, weak performance in problem solving, relative to mathematics performance, is mainly due to strong performers in mathematics who demonstrate lower proficiency in problem solving than do similarly proficient students in other countries/economies. This may indicate that in these countries and economies, high performers in mathematics are not exposed to the learning opportunities that could also help them to develop their problem-solving skills. They are shown in the bottom-right cell in Figure V.2.17.

■ Figure V.2.17 ■

Patterns of relative performance in problem solving

Average performance compared to students with similar scores in mathematics

| Stronger | In line with | Weaker |

Higher among strong performers in mathematics

Australia, England (United Kingdom), United States

Canada, Czech Republic, Finland, Norway

Bulgaria, Colombia, Croatia, Denmark, Estonia, Germany, Hungary, Ireland, Israel, Netherlands, Slovenia, Spain, United Arab Emirates

Similar at all levels of mathematics performance

Brazil, Serbia

Chile, France, Sweden

Austria, Belgium, Malaysia, Montenegro, **Poland,** Shanghai-China, Singapore, **Slovak Republic,** Uruguay

Lower among strong performers in mathematics

Italy, Japan, Korea

Macao-China, **Portugal**

Hong Kong-China, Russian Federation, Chinese Taipei, **Turkey**

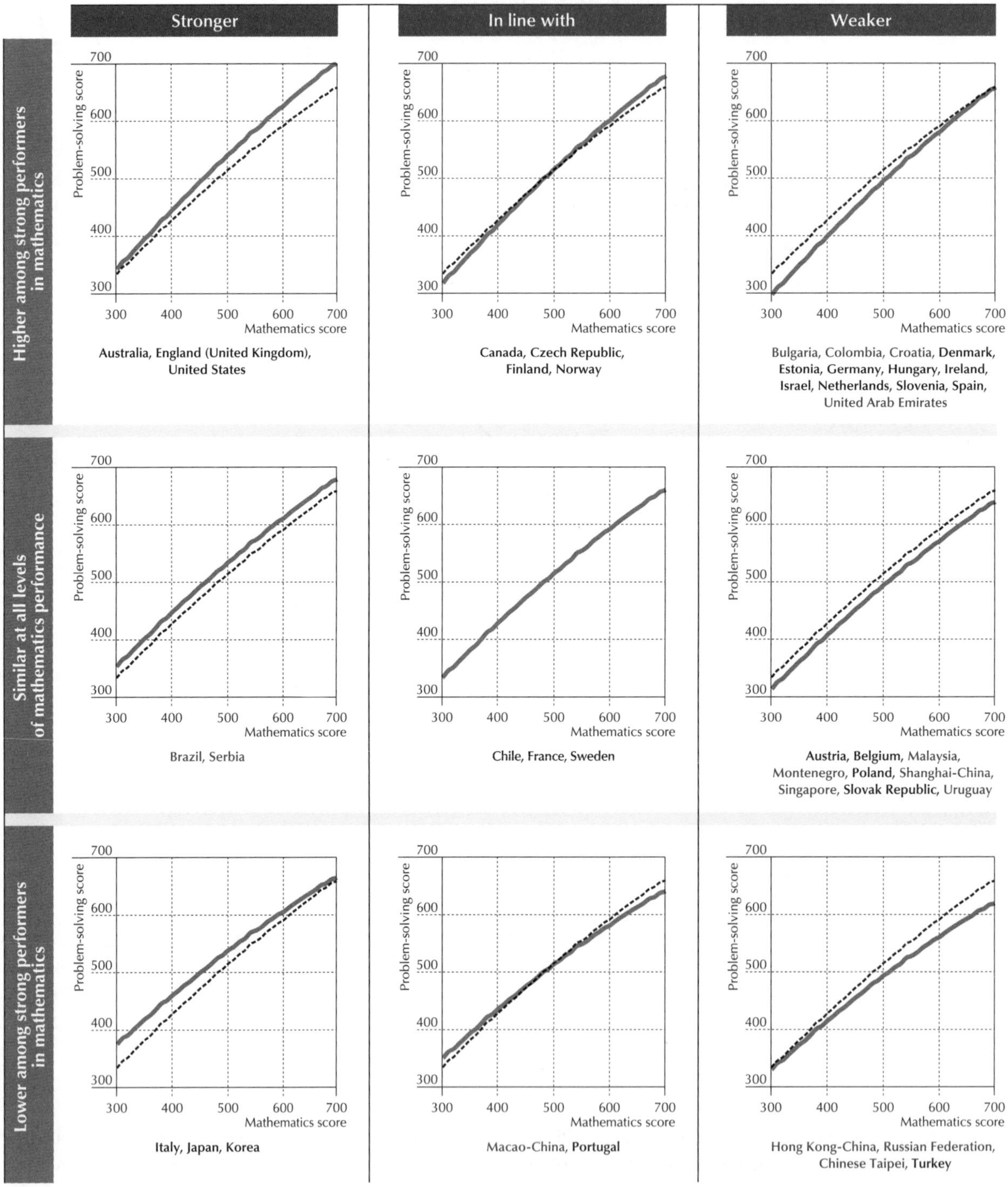

Notes: The dotted line is repeated across all graphs and shows the average performance in problem solving, across students from all participating countries/economies, at different levels of performance in mathematics (see Figure V.2.16). The continuous line illustrates nine possible patterns of relative performance in problem solving. Numbers on the axes refer to score points in the respective assessment domains.

Figures are for illustrative purposes only. Countries and economies are grouped according to the direction and significance of their relative performance in problem solving, compared with students around the world with similar scores in mathematics, and of their difference in relative performance between students performing at or above Level 4 and students performing below Level 4 in mathematics.

Source: OECD, PISA 2012 Database, Table V.2.6.

StatLink ᔐᕴᔏ http://dx.doi.org/10.1787/888933003573

The influence of computer delivery on performance in problem solving

The assessment of problem solving in PISA 2012 was designed and delivered on a computer platform. As explained in Chapter 1, this allowed for a wider definition of problem-solving competency – one that includes the willingness and capacity to explore an unknown environment to gather information about it.

Students participating in the PISA assessment of problem solving differ by how familiar they are with computers and with using computers as an assessment instrument. For some students, using computers may have increased test anxiety; for others, the use of computers may have had the opposite effect. For some, a lack of basic familiarity with a keyboard or mouse might have hindered their ability to complete the assessment in the time allotted. In part, variation in performance on the problem-solving test may result from differences in computer skills.

These differences may have influenced both the performance rankings within countries and the rankings among countries. How strong is this influence? It can be gauged by comparing results in problem solving with results on the computer-based test of mathematics, on the one hand, and with results on the paper-based tests in mathematics, on the other hand. Students who perform below their expected level across all computer-based tests may have a generic difficulty with basic computer skills, rather than a particular weakness in problem solving.

The proportion of variation in problem solving that is uniquely explained by performance differences in computer-based assessments, after accounting for differences in paper-based assessments, is a measure of the importance of the mode of delivery for rankings of students and schools within countries and economies. By this measure, the influence of the computer delivery on within-country/economy rankings appears to vary markedly across countries and economies. In Japan, the Russian Federation, Denmark, Norway, France and Poland more than 5% of the variation in performance on the problem-solving test can be explained by the mode of delivery. In contrast, in Chile, Ireland, Singapore, Chinese Taipei and the United States, less than 1% of the variation in performance in problem solving across students is explained by differences in computer skills (Figure V.2.18).

■ Figure V.2.18 ■

Influence of computer skills on the ranking of students within countries/economies

Variation in problem-solving performance uniquely associated with performance on computer-based assessments, after accounting for performance on paper-based assessments

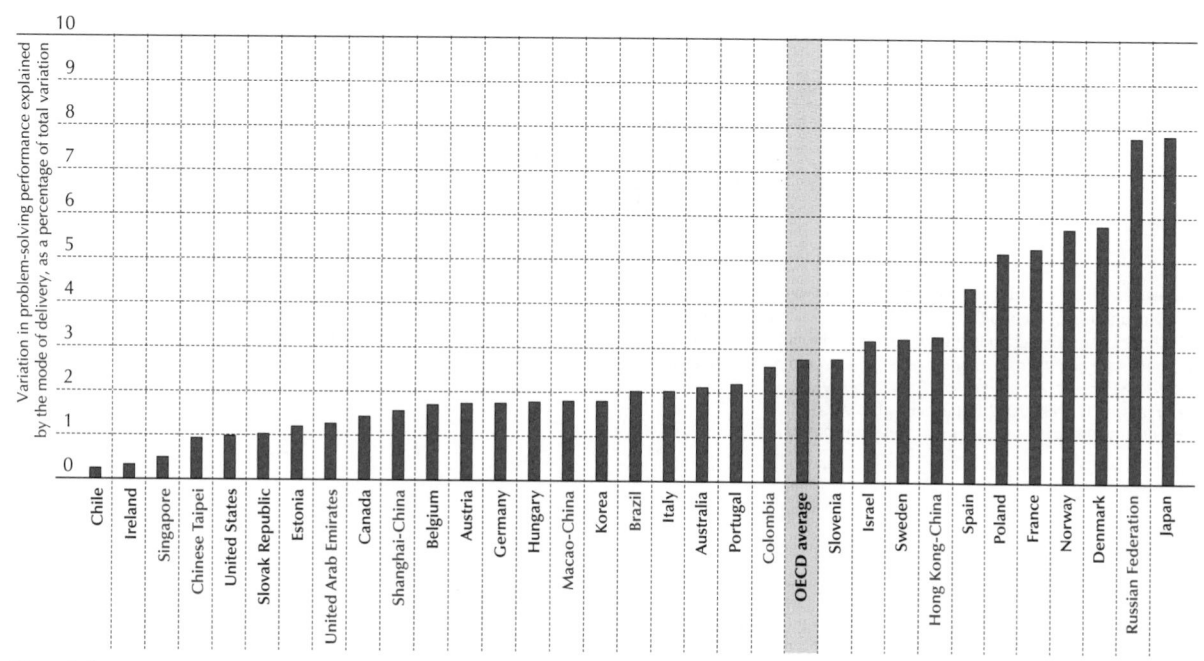

Note: Only countries/economies that participated in the computer-based assessment of mathematics are included in this figure.
Countries and economies are ranked in ascending order of the variation in problem-solving performance explained by computer skills.
Source: OECD, PISA 2012 Database, Table V.2.5.
StatLink ᘯᔞ http://dx.doi.org/10.1787/888933003573

The mode of delivery also bears an influence on between-country comparisons. Figure V.2.19 shows that in most countries with a relative weakness in problem-solving performance, this weakness is compounded by a more general weakness on computer-based assessments, which can be ascribed to the mode of delivery. Indeed, almost all of the country-level gaps between students' actual performance and their expected performance shrink when the comparison accounts for scores on the computer-based assessment of mathematics, rather than on the paper-based assessment of mathematics.

Nevertheless, in most cases, whether the country shows a relative strength or weakness in problem solving after accounting for performance in mathematics does not depend on whether the comparison is with students' performance on the paper-based test or on the computer-based test. This indicates that country-level computer mode effects are only part of the relative performance in problem solving discussed earlier in this chapter. One may even argue that the computer skills signalled by mode effects are related to actual problem-solving skills, such as the willingness and capacity to interact with unknown devices.

■ Figure V.2.19 ■
Influence of computer skills on relative performance in problem solving

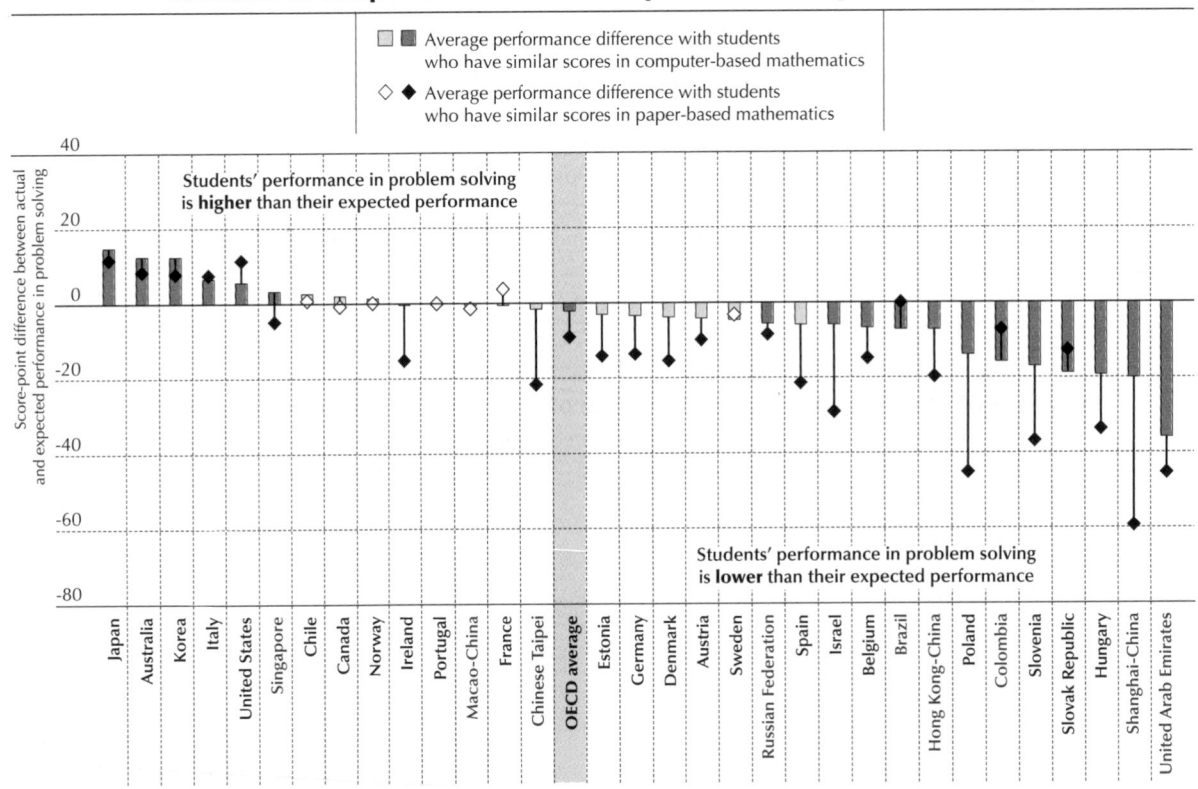

Notes: Statistically significant differences are shown in darker tones (see Annex A3).

Only countries/economies that participated in the computer-based assessment of mathematics are included in this figure.

The lines connecting diamonds and bars show the influence of computer skills on relative performance in problem solving.

Countries are ranked in descending order of the score-point difference between actual and expected performance, given students' scores on the computer-based assessment of mathematics.

Source: OECD, PISA 2012 Database, Table V.2.6.

StatLink ⟨⟨⟨⟨ http://dx.doi.org/10.1787/888933003573

Notes

1. In particular, a student has a probability of 0.62 of correctly answering an item at the same point on the scale. The width of each proficiency level described below is set so that, for a test composed entirely of questions spread uniformly across a level, all students whose scores fall within that level would be expected to get at least 50% of the questions correct. In particular, students who are at the lower score limit for a level are expected to get exactly 50% of the questions of this level correct.

2. Technically, the mean score for student performance in problem solving across OECD countries was set at 500 score points and the standard deviation at 100 score points, with the data weighted so that each OECD country contributed equally. The average standard deviation of the problem-solving scale across OECD countries, reported in the Appendix tables, is less than 100 score points, because it is computed as the arithmetic average of the countries' individual standard deviations. This reported measure is based only on variation of performance within countries, and does not include the performance variation across countries. The standard deviation of 100 used for standardising scores, on the other hand, is a measure of overall variation within and between OECD countries.

3. Confidence level of 95% for pairwise comparisons.

4. This proportion is known as the *intra-class correlation coefficient* in multi-level analyses and relates to the "index of inclusion" reported in Table V.2.4.

5. Note also that the correlations reported are latent correlations, which are not attenuated by measurement error.

6. Correlation and explained variance are strictly related concepts. A correlation of around 0.81 between problem solving and mathematics implies, for instance, that about two-thirds of the variation in problem-solving performance ($0.81 \times 0.81 = 0.66$) is common across the two domains of mathematics and problem solving.

7. "Students in other countries" refers to all 15-year-old students in countries that participated in the PISA assessment of problem solving. Most (54%) of these students are in just five countries: the United States (21%), Brazil (14%), the Russian Federation (7%), Japan (7%) and Turkey (5%).

References

Philpot, R. et al. (forthcoming), "Factors that influence the difficulty of problem solving items", Chapter 8 in Csapó, B. and J. Funke (eds.), *The Nature of Problem Solving*, OECD Publishing.

3

Students' Strengths and Weaknesses in Problem Solving

This chapter provides a nuanced look at student performance in problem solving by focusing on students' strengths and weaknesses in performing certain types of tasks. The items in the PISA problem-solving assessment are categorised by the nature of the problem (interactive or static items) and by the main cognitive processes involved in solving the problem (exploring and understanding; representing and formulating; planning and executing; monitoring and reflecting). The analysis in this chapter identifies the tasks and skills that students master better than students in other countries do, after taking into account overall differences in performance.

This chapter takes a more nuanced look at problem-solving performance by analysing how students interact with the test items. It focuses on performance profiles, rather than on performance levels, in order to identify each country's/economy's comparative strengths and weaknesses.

The PISA problem-solving framework defines a broad construct. Problem-solving competence in PISA encompasses success with different types of problems and the mastery of several distinct cognitive processes. This chapter analyses strengths and weaknesses in problem-solving by breaking down overall performance into success rates according to broad types of tasks (Box V.3.1).[1]

Why are students from certain countries particularly good at problem solving? The analysis in this chapter identifies the tasks and skills that these students master better than students in other countries. In doing so, it highlights, for each country/economy, the specific areas of problem solving with the greatest margin for improvement, thus suggesting priorities for improving curricula and teaching practices to foster students' capacity to solve problems in real life.

What the data tell us

- Students in Hong Kong-China, Korea, Macao-China, Shanghai-China, Singapore and Chinese Taipei perform strongest on problems that require understanding, formulating or representing new knowledge, compared to other types of problems.

- Students in Brazil, Ireland, Korea and the United States perform strongest on interactive problems (those that require the student to uncover some of the information needed to solve the problem) compared to static problems (those that have all information disclosed at the outset).

Box V.3.1. **How item-level success is reported**

PISA reports the performance of all students on the problem-solving assessment on a common scale, despite the fact that different subsets of students are administered different items, depending on the test booklet they receive. The item-response model that underlies the scaling of students' answers makes it possible to aggregate students' answers into an overall score even if each student sees only a subset of the entire PISA item pool (see Annex A5 and OECD, forthcoming).

While this approach has many advantages, it can potentially hide interesting differences in patterns of performance at lower levels of aggregation, i.e. on single items or on subsets of items. To explore these patterns, one must use the unscaled responses of the students who answered each item.

In this chapter, average percentages of correct responses are computed at the country/economy level. For each item, the percentage of correct responses is simply the number of correct (full credit) answers divided by the number of students who encountered the question (non-reached questions are counted as incorrect answers). The average percentage of correct responses on a particular group of items, or on the complete pool of problem-solving items, is then the simple average of item-by-country/economy percentages of correct responses.

On average across countries, the percentage of correct responses is a measure of the difficulty of items. By comparing the percentage of correct responses across two distinct sets of items, one can identify the relative difficulty of each set. By further comparing the percentage of correct responses across two sets of items and across countries, one can identify where the relative strengths and weaknesses of each country lie. For each subset of items and for each country/economy, the result of this comparison is reported as an odds ratio. Ratios equal to 1 for Country A, for instance, indicate that the pattern of performance across items is in line with the average OECD pattern of performance. Ratios above the value of 1 indicate that the items in this subset were easier for students in Country A than, on average, for students across OECD countries, after accounting for overall differences in performance across the test. A ratio of 1.2, for instance, indicates that full-credit answers within this subset were 1.2 times more prevalent than on average across OECD countries, after accounting for overall performance differences. Ratios below the value of 1 indicate that the items in this subset were, on average, harder than expected for students in Country A: the pattern of performance corresponds to a country-specific weakness on this subset of items.

The remainder of this chapter discusses in more detail the two main framework aspects (the nature of the problem situation, and problem-solving processes), and compares the performance profiles of countries within each aspect. It also links the framework aspects to skill demands and derives implications for teachers and curriculum developers.

FRAMEWORK ASPECTS AND RELATIVE SUCCESS OF STUDENTS IN EACH AREA

The PISA problem-solving framework provides the basis for the analyses in this chapter. The framework was used to develop items that vary by the *nature of the problem situation* and by the particular *problem-solving process* targeted (see Chapter 1 and OECD, 2013). Together, the 42 items included in the test, which also vary by *problem context*, by difficulty and by response format, are representative of the problem-solving domain as defined in PISA. The problem-solving proficiency scale summarises overall performance on the test. Instead of focusing on the overall proficiency in problem solving, this chapter analyses performance on subsets of items in order to identify systematic differences, across countries, in students' success in handling different families of tasks.

The PISA 2012 problem-solving framework organises the domain around two main aspects. A first important distinction among problem-solving items is between *interactive* and *static* items; this is referred to as the *nature of the problem situation*. A second important distinction between items is related to the main *cognitive processes* involved in problem solving. Each process is defined by a pair of verbs: *exploring and understanding; representing and formulating; planning and executing; monitoring and reflecting.*

Figure V.3.1 presents an overview of the classification of items according to their characteristics. A statistical analysis[2] confirms that the test was constructed so that there is no strong association between the main cognitive process involved in the task and the static or interactive nature of the problem situation. As a consequence, strengths and weaknesses in particular cognitive processes are unlikely to influence strengths and weaknesses that are found in interactive or static tasks.

■ Figure V.3.1 ■
Number of tasks, by framework aspect

Nature of the problem situation	Problem-solving process			
	Exploring and understanding (10 items)	Representing and formulating (9 items)	Planning and executing (16 items)	Monitoring and reflecting (7 items)
Static (15 items)	5	2	6	2
Interactive (27 items)	5	7	10	5

Source: OECD, PISA 2012 Database.

In addition to these two aspects, each assessment unit is also characterised, on a more superficial level, by the particular context in which the problem situation occurs. The framework distinguishes problems with a *social focus* from problems with a *personal focus*, as well as problems cast in a *technological setting* from problems cast in a *non-technological setting*.

Items in the problem-solving test can also be classified according to their response format. A major distinction is between selected-response formats, which ask respondents to choose one or more answers from a closed list of possible responses, and constructed-response formats, where students produce a self-constructed response.

Nature of the problem situation

How a problem is presented has important consequences for how it can be solved. Of crucial importance is whether the information about the problem disclosed at the outset is complete. These problem situations are considered *static*. Question 3 in the problem-solving unit *TRAFFIC*, described in the sample tasks section at the end of Chapter 1, is an example of a *static* unit: students are given all information about travel times and have to determine the best location for a meeting.

By contrast, problem situations may be *interactive*, meaning that students can explore the situation to uncover additional relevant information. Real-time navigation using a GPS system, where traffic congestion may be reported in response to a query, is an example of such a situation.

Interactive problem situations

Interactive problem situations often arise when encountering technological devices, such as ticket-vending machines, air-conditioning systems or mobile telephones for the first time, especially if the instructions for using them are not clear or are not available. Individuals often confront these types of problems in daily life. In these situations, some relevant information is often not apparent at the outset. For example, the effect of performing an operation (say, pushing a button on a remote control) may not be known and cannot be deduced, but rather must be inferred by actually performing the operation (pushing the button) and forming a hypothesis about its function based on the outcome. In general, some exploration or experimentation is needed to acquire the knowledge necessary to control the device. Another common scenario is when a person must troubleshoot a fault or malfunction in a device. Here a certain amount of strategic experimentation – generating and testing hypotheses – must take place in order to collect data on the circumstances under which the device fails.

Interactive problem situations can be simulated in a test setting by a computer. Including interactive problem situations in the computer-based PISA 2012 problem-solving assessment allows for a wider range of authentic, real-life scenarios to be presented than would otherwise be possible using pen-and-paper tests. Problems where the student explores and controls a simulated environment are a distinctive feature of the assessment.

Static problem situations

In *static* problems all relevant information is disclosed at the outset and the problem situation is not dynamic, i.e. it does not change during the course of solving the problem.

Examples of static problems are traditional *logic puzzles*, such as the Tower of Hanoi and the water jars problems ("How would you use three jars with the indicated capacities to measure out the desired amount of water?"); *decision-making problems*, where the student is required to understand a situation involving a number of well-defined alternatives and constraints so as to make a decision that satisfies the constraints (e.g. choosing the right pain killer given sufficient details about the patient, the complaint and the available pain killers); and *scheduling problems* for projects, such as building a house or generating a flight schedule for an airline, where a list of tasks with durations and relationships between tasks is given.

Figure V.3.2 illustrates how the nature of the problem situation varies across the PISA 2012 problem-solving items that were made public. While all of the interactive units shown in Figure V.3.2 are set in technology contexts, the assessment also included interactive problems in non-technology contexts; for instance, some items ask students to orient themselves in a maze. Overall, a majority of items – 27 of 42 – are *interactive*.

■ Figure V.3.2 ■
Examples of problem-solving tasks, by nature of the problem

Nature of the problem situation	Sample questions
Interactive	MP3 PLAYER – Items 1, 2, 3 and 4 (field trial)
	CLIMATE CONTROL – Items 1 and 2
	TICKETS – Items 1, 2 and 3
Static	TRAFFIC – Items 1, 2 and 3
	ROBOT CLEANER – Items 1, 2 and 3

Source: OECD, PISA 2012 Database.

What success on interactive tasks implies for education policy and practice

The static or interactive nature of the problem situation is related to how information is presented. Static problems, where all relevant information is disclosed at the outset, are the typical textbook problems encountered in schools, whereas in most contexts outside of schools, the relevant information to solve the problem has to be obtained by interacting with the environment. Static problems can be regarded as a special case of interactive problems. This highlights the fact that the set of skills that are required to solve static tasks is a subset of the skills required for interactive tasks.

To excel in interactive tasks, it is not sufficient to hold the problem-solving skills required by static, analytical problems; students must also be open to novelty, tolerate doubt and uncertainty, and dare to use intuitions ("hunches and feelings") to initiate a solution. A relatively weak performance on interactive items, compared to performance on static items, may indicate that students may benefit from greater opportunities to develop and exercise these traits, which are related to curiosity, perseverance and creativity.

Success on interactive and static tasks

Figure V.3.3 plots average success rates for interactive items against average success rates for static items. The figure immediately reveals that, in general, country rankings are similar across the two types of items. Performance on interactive items is strongly related to performance on static items. However, as Figure V.3.3 shows, performance is not always perfectly aligned. Countries that share similar levels of success on static items do not necessarily share the same performance on interactive items. Often, when considering two countries with similar performance on static items, one country is significantly stronger on interactive items than the other.

■ Figure V.3.3 ■

Differences in countries'/economies' success on problem-solving tasks, by nature of the problem

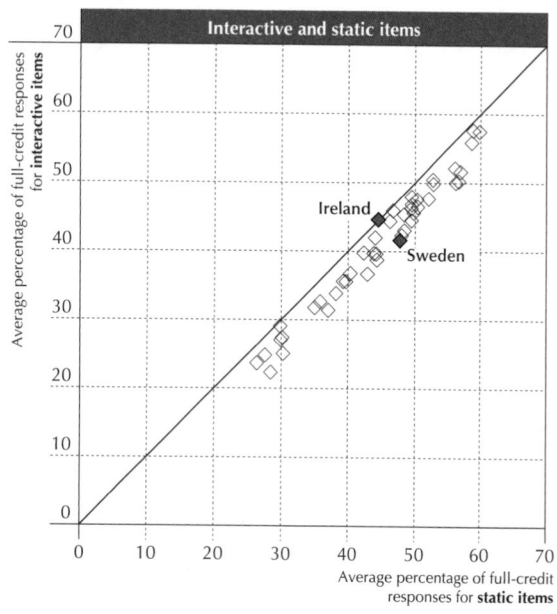

Note: Ireland and Sweden share similar levels of performance overall, but illustrate different patterns of performance across interactive and static items; this example is discussed in the text.
Source: OECD, PISA 2012 Database, Table V.3.1.
StatLink ▬▬▬ http://dx.doi.org/10.1787/888933003592

In Ireland, for instance, the percentage of full-credit answers was, on average, 44.6% across all items. This resulted from a 44.4% success rate on static items and a 44.6% success rate on interactive items. Because interactive items were found to be slightly harder than static items, on average across OECD countries, it can be deduced that performance on interactive items was stronger than expected in Ireland. In comparison, the success rate of students in Sweden (43.8%) was similar to that of students in Ireland overall, but this resulted from a higher success rate on static items (47.7%) and a lower success rate on interactive items (41.6%). While the former is in line with the OECD average, the latter is significantly below the OECD average (Figure V.3.3 and Table V.3.1).

Figure V.3.4 ranks countries and economies according to whether their students had greater success on interactive or on static tasks, after accounting for overall differences in performance. This analysis accounts for the relative difficulty of static and interactive tasks by comparing relative success in each country/economy to the average relative success across OECD countries. It also adjusts for country/economy-specific response format effects (Figure V.3.9). To continue with the same example used above, the measure of relative success on interactive items is 1.16 in Ireland – and thus significantly above 1, indicating stronger-than-expected performance on interactive items. Relative success is only 0.91 in Sweden (significantly below par), indicating weaker-than-expected performance on interactive items (Table V.3.1).

■ Figure V.3.4 ■

Relative success on problem-solving tasks, by nature of the problem

Success on interactive items, relative to static items, compared to the OECD average, after accounting for booklet and country/economy-specific response-format effects

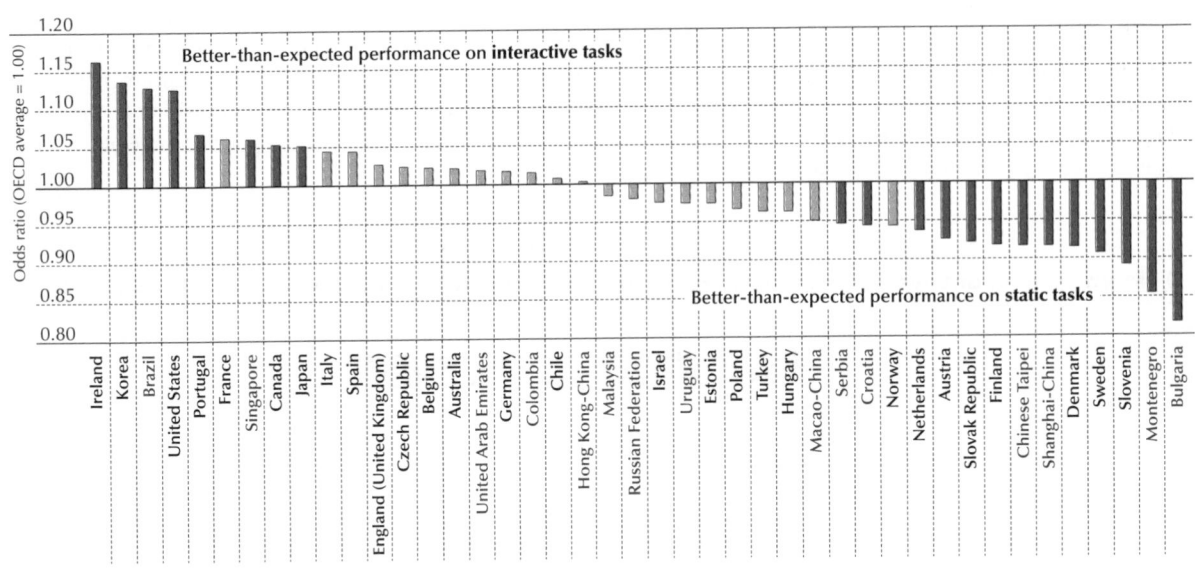

Notes: Values that are statistically significant are marked in a darker tone (see Annex A3).

This figure shows that students in Ireland are 1.16 times more likely than students across OECD countries, on average, to succeed on interactive items, given their success on static items.

Countries and economies are ranked in descending order of the relative likelihood of success on interactive tasks, based on success in performing static tasks.

Source: OECD, PISA 2012 Database, Table V.3.1.

StatLink ⣿⤓ http://dx.doi.org/10.1787/888933003592

Compared with students in other OECD countries, students in Ireland, Korea, Brazil, the United States, Portugal, Singapore, Canada and Japan were more successful on interactive tasks than expected, given their overall performance. In contrast, students in Bulgaria, Montenegro, Slovenia, Sweden, Denmark, Shanghai-China, Chinese Taipei, Finland, the Slovak Republic, Austria, the Netherlands, Croatia and Serbia had more facility with static tasks than with interactive tasks, as compared to the relative success of students in other OECD countries. This may indicate a difficulty related to the specific skills used uniquely to solve interactive tasks.

Problem-solving processes

Each item in the PISA 2012 assessment of problem solving was designed to focus on measuring one distinct problem-solving process. For the purposes of the PISA 2012 problem-solving assessment, the processes involved are:

- Exploring and understanding
- Representing and formulating
- Planning and executing
- Monitoring and reflecting

Each of these broad processes applies to both static and interactive problems.

Exploring and understanding. The objective is to build mental representations of each of the pieces of information presented in the problem. This involves:

- *exploring* the problem situation: observing it, interacting with it, searching for information and finding limitations or obstacles; and
- *understanding* given information and, in interactive problems, information discovered while interacting with the problem situation; and demonstrating understanding of relevant concepts.

Representing and formulating. The objective is to build a coherent mental representation of the problem situation (i.e. a situation model or a problem model). To do this, relevant information must be selected, mentally organised and integrated with relevant prior knowledge. This may involve:

- *representing* the problem by constructing tabular, graphic, symbolic or verbal representations, and shifting between representational formats; and
- *formulating* hypotheses by identifying the relevant factors in the problem and their inter-relationships; and organising and critically evaluating information.

Planning and executing. The objective is to use one's knowledge about the problem situation to devise a plan and execute it. Tasks where "planning and executing" is the main cognitive demand do not require any substantial prior understanding or representation of the problem situation, either because the situation is straightforward or because these aspects were previously solved. "Planning and executing" includes:

- *planning*, which consists of goal setting, including clarifying the overall goal, and setting subgoals, where necessary; and devising a plan or strategy to reach the goal state, including the steps to be undertaken; and
- *executing*, which consists of carrying out a plan.

Monitoring and reflecting. The objective is to regulate the distinct processes involved in problem solving, and to critically evaluate the solution, the information provided with the problem, or the strategy adopted. This includes:

- *monitoring* progress towards the goal at each stage, including checking intermediate and final results, detecting unexpected events, and taking remedial action when required; and
- *reflecting* on solutions from different perspectives, critically evaluating assumptions and alternative solutions, identifying the need for additional information or clarification and communicating progress in a suitable manner.

Figure V.3.5 uses the released items to illustrate how PISA 2012 targeted the four problem-solving processes. In general, items were not equally spread across the processes (Figure V.3.1). The assessment included a larger number of items tapping into *planning and executing*, and fewer items tapping into *monitoring and reflecting*, in recognition of the importance of being able to carry through a solution to a successful conclusion, and of the fact that monitoring progress is part of the three other processes as well.

■ Figure V.3.5 ■
Examples of problem-solving tasks, by process

Main problem-solving process	Sample questions
Exploring and understanding	MP3 PLAYER – Item 1 (field trial)
	ROBOT CLEANER – Items 1 and 2
	TICKETS – Item 2
Representing and formulating	MP3 PLAYER – Item 3 (field trial)
	CLIMATE CONTROL – Item 1
	ROBOT CLEANER – Item 3
Planning and executing	MP3 PLAYER – Item 2 (field trial)
	CLIMATE CONTROL – Item 2
	TICKETS – Item 1
	TRAFFIC – Items 1 and 2
Monitoring and reflecting	MP3 PLAYER – Item 4 (field trial)
	TICKETS – Item 3
	TRAFFIC – Item 3

Source: OECD, PISA 2012 Database.

What success on different problem-solving processes implies for education policy and practice

Strengths and weaknesses on items measuring particular problem-solving processes can be directly related to students' skills. Indeed, the classification by problem-solving process reflects the main demand of each item, although often several processes occur simultaneously, or in succession, while solving a particular item.

A major distinction among tasks is between acquisition and use of knowledge.

In knowledge-acquisition tasks, the goal is for students to develop or refine their mental representation of the problem space. Students need to generate and manipulate the information in a mental representation. The movement is from concrete to abstract, from information to knowledge. In the context of the PISA assessment of problem solving, knowledge-acquisition tasks may be classified either as "exploring and understanding" tasks or as "representing and formulating" tasks. The distinction within knowledge-acquisition tasks between the two processes is sometimes small, and may relate to the amount of scaffolding provided for exploring and representing the problem space. "Exploring and understanding" items often come with response options provided (as in *ROBOT CLEANER*, Item 1), which can guide the exploration phase, while "representing and formulating" items more often require constructed responses (as in *ROBOT CLEANER*, Item 3).

In knowledge-utilisation tasks, the goal is for students to solve a concrete problem. The movement is from abstract to concrete, from knowledge to action. Knowledge-utilisation tasks correspond to the process of "planning and executing". Within the PISA assessment of problem solving, tasks would only be classified as "planning and executing" if the execution of a plan is the dominant cognitive demand of the item (and likewise for other problem-solving processes). For instance, while all the items in unit *TICKETS* are introduced by a superficially similar demand ("buy a ticket", "find the cheapest ticket and press buy", "purchase the best ticket available"), only the first is classified as planning and executing. To ensure that no additional generation or refinement of knowledge about the problem is needed, items targeting "planning and executing" often had the results of "representing and formulating" tasks available, as is the case in Item 2 of unit *CLIMATE CONTROL*.

"Monitoring and reflecting" tasks are intentionally left out of this distinction, because they often combine both knowledge-acquisition and knowledge-utilisation aspects.

From an education perspective, the most insightful contrast is between performance on "planning and executing" tasks and performance on tasks requiring knowledge acquisition and abstract information processing. This contrast highlights a distinction that runs throughout school curricula. In the teaching of mathematics, for instance, there may be a trade-off between a focus on higher-order activities, such as mathematical modelling (understanding real-world situations and transferring them into mathematical models), and a focus on the mastery of basic concepts, facts, procedures and reasoning.

Students who are good at tasks whose main cognitive demand is "planning and executing" are good at using the knowledge they have; they can be characterised as goal-driven and persistent. Students who are strong on tasks measuring "exploring and understanding" or "representing and formulating" processes are good at generating new knowledge; they can be characterised as quick learners, who are highly inquisitive (questioning their own knowledge, challenging assumptions), generating and experimenting with alternatives, and good at abstract information processing. In practice, proficient problem-solvers are good at all sorts of tasks, and there is a strong positive relationship between success rates on any two sets of items. In the following sections, the focus is not on absolute levels of proficiency, but on areas of relative strength and weakness, compared with the skills observed among students with similar overall proficiency.

Success on items by problem-solving process involved

Figures V.3.6 and V.3.7 present national performance by problem-solving process – first, using percent-correct figures to illustrate absolute strength, then, adjusting for country/economy-specific response-format effects and accounting for overall differences in performance, to show areas where performance is unexpectedly strong or weak. Figure V.3.8 summarises countries'/economies' relative strengths and weaknesses revealed by the comparison of performance on items measuring different problem-solving processes to the average performance of students across OECD countries.

"Exploring and understanding" items, as a set, were found easier by students in Singapore, Norway, Hong Kong-China, Korea, Australia, Austria, Chinese Taipei, Japan, Macao-China, Sweden and Finland than by students in OECD countries, on average.

Items with "representing and formulating" tasks, as a set, were easier than expected in Macao-China, Chinese Taipei, Shanghai-China, Korea, Singapore, Hong Kong-China, Canada, Italy, Japan, France, Australia and Belgium.

Items assessing the process of "planning and executing", as a set, were easier than expected in Bulgaria, Montenegro, Croatia, Colombia, Uruguay, Serbia, Turkey, Slovenia, Brazil, Malaysia, Denmark, the Czech Republic, the Netherlands, Chile, Hungary, Finland, the Russian Federation, Portugal and Poland.

■ Figure V.3.6 ■

Differences in countries'/economies' success on problem-solving tasks, by process

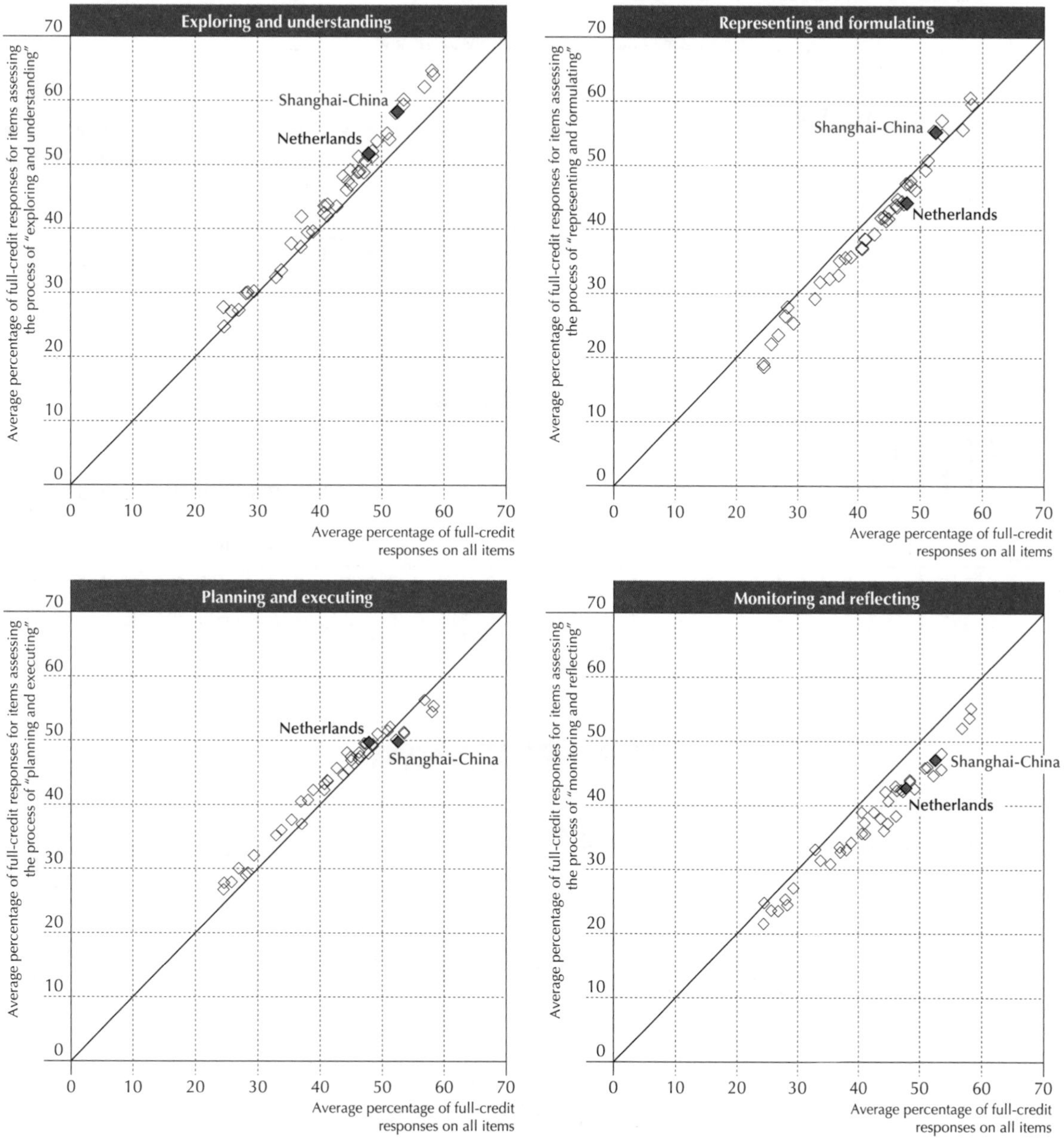

Exploring and understanding

Average percentage of full-credit responses for items assessing the process of "exploring and understanding"

Shanghai-China

Netherlands

Average percentage of full-credit responses on all items

Representing and formulating

Average percentage of full-credit responses for items assessing the process of "representing and formulating"

Shanghai-China

Netherlands

Average percentage of full-credit responses on all items

Planning and executing

Average percentage of full-credit responses for items assessing the process of "planning and executing"

Netherlands

Shanghai-China

Average percentage of full-credit responses on all items

Monitoring and reflecting

Average percentage of full-credit responses for items assessing the process of "monitoring and reflecting"

Shanghai-China

Netherlands

Average percentage of full-credit responses on all items

Note: The Netherlands and Shanghai-China share similar levels of performance on items assessing the process of "planning and executing", but have different levels of performance on all remaining items; this example is discussed in the text.
Source: OECD, PISA 2012 Database, Table V.3.2.
StatLink ᴹˢ▇ http://dx.doi.org/10.1787/888933003592

Finally, "monitoring and reflecting" items, taken together, were easier than expected in Colombia, Chile, Turkey, Spain, Uruguay, Ireland, Brazil, Croatia, Bulgaria, Singapore, the United States, the United Arab Emirates, Montenegro, the Czech Republic and England (United Kingdom).

To illustrate strengths and weaknesses on specific problem-solving processes, one can compare the performance of students in the Netherlands and Shanghai-China. Overall, students in Shanghai-China performed better on the problem-solving scale than students in the Netherlands. The average success rate on all assessment items is 52.6% for Shanghai-China and 47.9% for the Netherlands. However, student performance on planning and executing items in the Netherlands, with a success rate of 49.7%, on average, was comparable to that of students in Shanghai-China on these same items (49.8%).

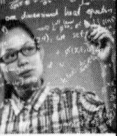

■ Figure V.3.7 ■

Relative success on problem-solving tasks, by process

After accounting for booklet and country/economy-specific response-format effects

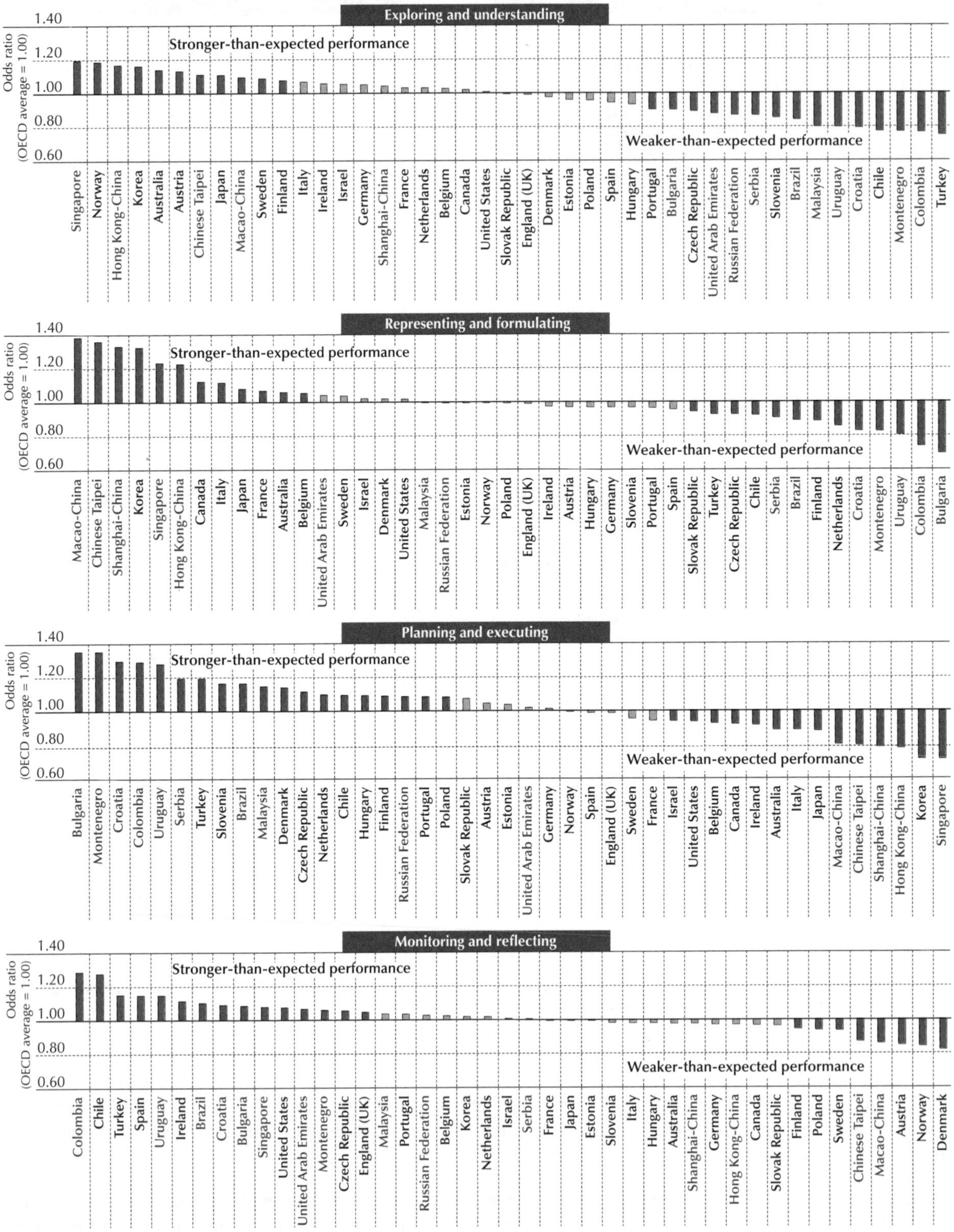
Exploring and understanding
Odds ratio (OECD average = 1.00)
1.40
1.20
1.00
0.80
0.60
Stronger-than-expected performance
Weaker-than-expected performance
Singapore
Norway
Hong Kong-China
Korea
Australia
Austria
Chinese Taipei
Japan
Macao-China
Sweden
Finland
Italy
Ireland
Israel
Germany
Shanghai-China
France
Netherlands
Belgium
Canada
United States
Slovak Republic
England (UK)
Denmark
Estonia
Poland
Spain
Hungary
Portugal
Bulgaria
Czech Republic
United Arab Emirates
Russian Federation
Serbia
Slovenia
Brazil
Malaysia
Uruguay
Croatia
Chile
Montenegro
Colombia
Turkey
Representing and formulating
Odds ratio (OECD average = 1.00)
1.40
1.20
1.00
0.80
0.60
Stronger-than-expected performance
Weaker-than-expected performance
Macao-China
Chinese Taipei
Shanghai-China
Korea
Singapore
Hong Kong-China
Canada
Italy
Japan
France
Australia
Belgium
United Arab Emirates
Sweden
Israel
Denmark
United States
Malaysia
Russian Federation
Estonia
Norway
Poland
England (UK)
Ireland
Austria
Hungary
Germany
Slovenia
Portugal
Spain
Slovak Republic
Turkey
Czech Republic
Chile
Serbia
Brazil
Finland
Netherlands
Croatia
Montenegro
Uruguay
Colombia
Bulgaria
Planning and executing
Odds ratio (OECD average = 1.00)
1.40
1.20
1.00
0.80
0.60
Stronger-than-expected performance
Weaker-than-expected performance
Bulgaria
Montenegro
Croatia
Colombia
Uruguay
Serbia
Turkey
Slovenia
Brazil
Malaysia
Denmark
Czech Republic
Netherlands
Chile
Hungary
Finland
Russian Federation
Portugal
Poland
Slovak Republic
Austria
Estonia
United Arab Emirates
Germany
Norway
Spain
England (UK)
Sweden
France
Israel
United States
Belgium
Canada
Ireland
Australia
Italy
Japan
Macao-China
Chinese Taipei
Shanghai-China
Hong Kong-China
Korea
Singapore
Monitoring and reflecting
Odds ratio (OECD average = 1.00)
1.40
1.20
1.00
0.80
0.60
Stronger-than-expected performance
Weaker-than-expected performance
Colombia
Chile
Turkey
Spain
Uruguay
Ireland
Brazil
Croatia
Bulgaria
Singapore
United States
United Arab Emirates
Montenegro
Czech Republic
England (UK)
Malaysia
Portugal
Russian Federation
Belgium
Korea
Netherlands
Israel
Serbia
France
Japan
Estonia
Slovenia
Italy
Hungary
Australia
Shanghai-China
Germany
Hong Kong-China
Canada
Slovak Republic
Finland
Poland
Sweden
Chinese Taipei
Macao-China
Austria
Norway
Denmark

Note: Values that are statistically significant are marked in a darker tone (see Annex A3).
Countries and economies are ranked in each chart in descending order of the relative success on tasks related to the respective problem-solving processes.
Source: OECD, PISA 2012 Database, Table V.3.2.
StatLink http://dx.doi.org/10.1787/888933003592

Thus, the main area for improving the performance of students in the Netherlands so that it is closer to the performance of students in Shanghai-China appears to be in the remaining items, while students in Shanghai-China could have scored higher on the problem-solving scale if their performance on planning and executing items were not significantly weaker than their performance on the remaining items (Figure V.3.6 and Table V.3.2).

■ Figure V.3.8 ■

Relative strengths and weaknesses in problem-solving processes

Stronger-than-expected performance on the problem-solving process
Non-significant strength or weakness
Weaker-than-expected performance on the problem-solving process

	Mean score in problem solving	Difference between observed and expected performance, by problem-solving process			
		Exploring and understanding	Representing and formulating	Planning and executing	Monitoring and reflecting
Singapore	562	Stronger	Stronger	Weaker	Stronger
Korea	561	Stronger	Stronger	Weaker	
Japan	552	Stronger	Stronger	Weaker	
Macao-China	540	Stronger	Stronger	Weaker	Weaker
Hong Kong-China	540	Stronger	Stronger	Weaker	
Shanghai-China	536		Stronger	Weaker	
Chinese Taipei	534	Stronger	Stronger	Weaker	Weaker
Canada	526		Stronger	Weaker	
Australia	523	Stronger	Stronger	Weaker	
Finland	523	Stronger	Weaker	Stronger	Weaker
England (United Kingdom)	517				Stronger
Estonia	515				
France	511		Stronger		
Netherlands	511		Weaker	Stronger	
Italy	510		Stronger	Weaker	
Czech Republic	509	Weaker	Weaker	Stronger	Stronger
Germany	509				
United States	508			Weaker	Stronger
Belgium	508		Stronger	Weaker	
Austria	506	Stronger			Weaker
Norway	503	Stronger			Weaker
Ireland	498			Weaker	Stronger
Denmark	497			Stronger	Weaker
Portugal	494	Weaker		Stronger	
Sweden	491	Stronger			Weaker
Russian Federation	489	Weaker		Stronger	
Slovak Republic	483		Weaker		
Poland	481			Stronger	Weaker
Spain	477				Stronger
Slovenia	476	Weaker		Stronger	
Serbia	473	Weaker	Weaker	Stronger	
Croatia	466	Weaker	Weaker	Stronger	Stronger
Hungary	459	Weaker	Weaker	Stronger	
Turkey	454	Weaker	Weaker	Stronger	Stronger
Israel	454			Weaker	
Chile	448	Weaker	Weaker	Stronger	Stronger
Brazil	428	Weaker	Weaker	Stronger	Stronger
Malaysia	422	Weaker		Stronger	
United Arab Emirates	411	Weaker			Stronger
Montenegro	407	Weaker	Weaker	Stronger	Stronger
Uruguay	403	Weaker	Weaker	Stronger	Stronger
Bulgaria	402	Weaker	Weaker	Stronger	Stronger
Colombia	399	Weaker	Weaker	Stronger	Stronger

Note: Countries/economies with stronger-(weaker-)than-expected performance are countries/economies whose students' relative likelihood of success in one group of tasks, based on their success in performing all other tasks, is significantly larger (smaller) than in the OECD average, after accounting for item difficulty and country/economy-specific response-format effects.

Countries and economies are ranked in descending order of the mean score in problem solving.

Source: OECD, PISA 2012 Database, Tables V.2.2 and V.3.2.

StatLink http://dx.doi.org/10.1787/888933003592

Figure V.3.8 summarises countries' and economies' strengths and weaknesses in problem-solving processes. Two patterns emerging from Figure V.3.8 are worth noting. First, there is substantial overlap between the countries/economies that are strong on "exploring and understanding" items and the countries/economies that are strong on "representing and formulating" items. Many of these same countries/economies, in turn, have weaker-than-expected performance on

"planning and executing" items. Conversely, there is also overlap between countries/economies that are strong on "planning and executing" items, but weak on "exploring and understanding" and "representing and formulating" items.

This overlap confirms the assumption that, from the point of view of skills development, the main contrast is between "knowledge-acquisition" processes and "knowledge-utilisation" processes. The observed difference in students' proficiency between these two major sets of skills may be traced back to differences in curricula and teaching practices.

Second, many of the best-performing countries and economies in problem solving are those with better-than-expected performance on knowledge-acquisition tasks ("exploring and understanding", "representing and formulating"), and relatively weaker performance on knowledge-utilisation tasks ("planning and executing" tasks that do not require substantial prior understanding or representation of the problem situation). This is observed despite the fact that the analysis adjusts for overall performance differences between countries and economies.

This pattern reflects the fact that performance differences across countries/economies are much more pronounced on knowledge-acquisition tasks than on knowledge-utilisation tasks (Figure V.3.6 and Table V.3.2). Around 40 percentage points separate the country with the highest percentage of correct answers from the country with the lowest percentage of correct answers on "exploring and understanding" tasks (64.7% success in Korea, 24.7% in Colombia) and on "representing and formulating" tasks (60.7% success in Korea, 18.7% in Colombia). In contrast, only about 30 percentage points separate the top and bottom percent-correct on "planning and executing" tasks (56.3% in Japan, 26.7% in Bulgaria). Similarly, there is a 30-percentage-point gap between the five best-performing systems and the five lowest-performing systems on knowledge-acquisition tasks, while the gap shrinks to about 20 percentage points on knowledge-utilisation tasks (Table V.3.6). While in absolute terms, top-performing countries/economies perform above-average on all problem-solving processes, the difference with lower-performing countries/economies narrows on "planning and executing" tasks.

This analysis shows that, in general, what differentiates high-performing systems, and particularly East Asian education systems, such as those in Hong Kong-China, Japan, Korea, Macao-China, Shanghai-China, Singapore and Chinese Taipei, from lower-performing ones, is their students' high level of proficiency on "exploring and understanding" and "representing and formulating" tasks.

Problem contexts and response formats

The problems in the PISA assessment can also be classified according to their context and response format. Solution rates and relative success on items by problem context are presented in Annex B (Tables V.3.3 and V.3.4). Figure V.3.9 shows the difference in relative success rates according to response formats.

The classification of problems by their context refers to the fictional frame (scenario) of the assessment problems and has no implications in terms of task demands. In contrast to the classification by nature of the problem situation or by problem-solving process, all items within a given unit share the same context.

Still, an individual's familiarity with and understanding of the problem context will affect his or her ability to solve the problem. Two dimensions were identified to ensure that assessment tasks reflect a range of contexts that are authentic and of interest to 15-year-olds: the setting (technology or not) and the focus (personal or social).

Problems set in a technology context are based on the functionality of a technological device, such as a mobile phone, a remote control for appliances and a ticket-vending machine. Knowledge of the inner workings of these devices is not required. Typically, students are led to explore and understand the functionality of a device as preparation for controlling the device or for troubleshooting its malfunction. Problems set in a non-technology context include tasks such as route planning, task scheduling and decision making.

Personal contexts include those relating primarily to the student, family and close peers. Social contexts typically do not involve the student directly and relate to situations encountered more broadly in the community or society in general.

Response formats also vary across items. One-third of the items (14 of 42 items) require students to select their response(s) by clicking a radio button or by selecting from a drop-down menu. This includes simple multiple-choice items, where there is one correct response to be selected, complex multiple-choice items, where two or three separate multiple-choice selections must be made, and variations of these (such as when there is more than one correct response to be selected). All of these items are automatically coded.

The remaining 28 items require students to construct their response, e.g. by entering text, dragging shapes, drawing lines between points, highlighting part of a diagram or interacting with the simulated device. Most of these items were also automatically coded. However, where it was considered important to ask students to explain their method or justify a selected response, a trained expert coded correct and incorrect answers, giving partial credit where appropriate. Six constructed response items required expert coding (Question 3 in the unit *ROBOT CLEANER* provides an example).

Students in many countries and economies, particularly in Asia, perform better, on average, on selected-response items than on constructed-response items. In the PISA problem-solving test, a pattern of relatively strong performance on selected-response items (and weak performance on constructed-response items) was found in Bulgaria, Shanghai-China, Malaysia, Korea, Macao-China, Uruguay, Hong Kong-China and Chinese Taipei. In these countries and economies, the success ratio on constructed-response items was at most 0.85 times as high as one could have expected, given performance on selected-response items and the relative difficulty of items as measured among OECD students. Several other countries, namely Israel, the United Arab Emirates, Colombia, Japan, Montenegro, Brazil, Turkey, Hungary and Croatia, had ratios of success significantly below one, also indicating unexpectedly weak performance on constructed-response items (Figure V.3.9 and Table V.3.5).

■ Figure V.3.9 ■

Relative success on problem-solving tasks, by response format

Success on constructed-response items, relative to selected-response items, compared to the OECD average, after accounting for booklet effects

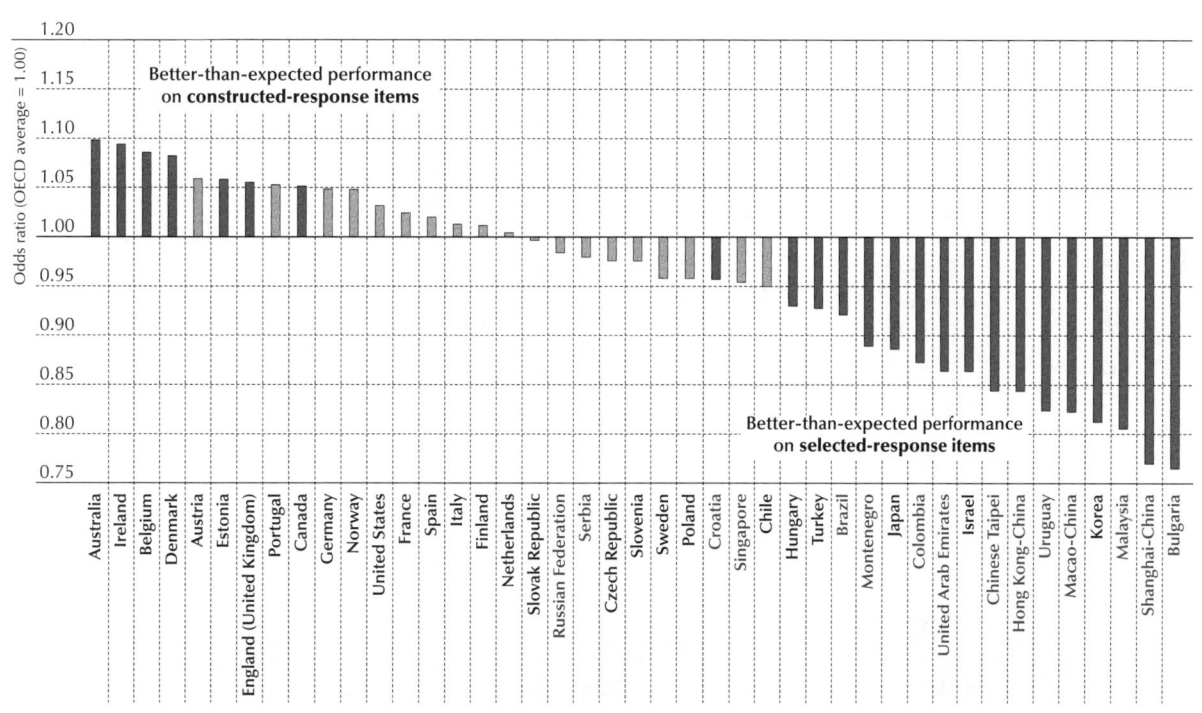

Note: Values that are statistically significant are marked in a darker tone (see Annex A3).
Countries and economies are ranked in descending order of the relative likelihood of success on constructed-response items, based on success in performing selected-response items.
Source: OECD, PISA 2012 Database, Table V.3.5.
StatLink ◤◢◣ http://dx.doi.org/10.1787/888933003592

The response format, however, is strongly associated with the particular process targeted by the item. Items that focus on measuring students' competence at "exploring and understanding" are mostly presented in a selected-response format. Items that focus on measuring students' competence at "planning and executing" are mostly presented in a constructed-response format. Nevertheless, within each set of items defined by a problem-solving process, there are both selected- and constructed-response items, so that one can control for the (country-specific) influence of the response format when comparing success ratios across item families involving different processes.

A GROUPING OF COUNTRIES BY THEIR STRENGTHS AND WEAKNESSES IN PROBLEM SOLVING

The analysis in this chapter identifies differences in the performance patterns of students across item types. The analysis has shown that two major dimensions along which performances of countries/economies differ are related to whether interaction with the problem situation is needed in order to uncover relevant information, and depending on whether the task primarily corresponds to knowledge-acquisition or to knowledge-utilisation processes.

Together, the differences in performance according to the nature of the problem situation and the major problem-solving process targeted identify several groups of countries/economies (Figure V.3.10). Interestingly, these groups often overlap with historical and geographical groupings.

■ Figure V.3.10 ■

Joint analysis of strengths and weaknesses, by nature of the problem and by process

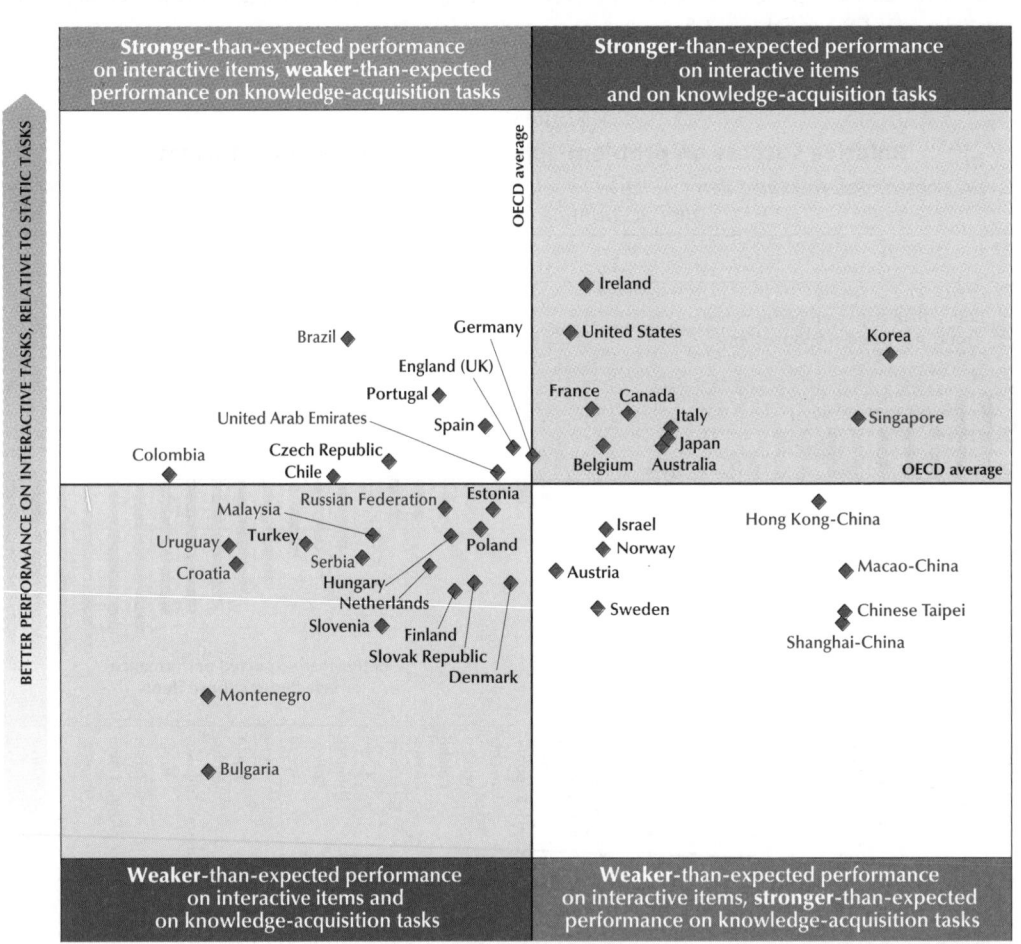

Note: This figure plots the odds ratios for success on interactive items, compared to static items, on the vertical axis, and the odds ratios for success on knowledge-acquisition tasks ("exploring and understanding" or "representing and formulating"), compared to knowledge-utilisation tasks ("planning and executing"), on the horizontal axis. Both axes are in logarithmic scale.
Source: OECD, PISA 2012 Database, Tables V.3.1 and V.3.6.
StatLink ᵐˢ■ http://dx.doi.org/10.1787/888933003592

Six East Asian countries and economies, namely Korea, Singapore, Hong Kong-China, Macao-China, Chinese Taipei and Shanghai-China, stand out for their very high success rates on knowledge-acquisition tasks, compared to their success rates on planning and executing tasks. Within this group, however, there are relatively stark differences in their performance on interactive problems. Students in Korea and Singapore are significantly more at ease with these problems than students in Shanghai-China, Chinese Taipei and Macao-China. Students from Hong Kong-China are in a middle position.

While all of these countries and economies rank in the top positions for overall performance, this analysis suggests that in Shanghai-China, Chinese Taipei and Macao-China, a focus on students' skills at dealing with interactive problem situations is required in order to improve further and close the performance gap with Korea and Singapore. In reviewing their curricula, teachers and curriculum developers may want to introduce more opportunities for students to develop and exercise the traits that are linked to success on interactive items, such as curiosity, perseverance and creativity. They may find inspiration in the curricula and teaching practices of their regional neighbours.

Among lower-performing countries and economies in problem solving, the low performance of Latin American countries (Brazil, Colombia, Chile and Uruguay) appears to be mainly due to a large performance gap on knowledge-acquisition tasks. These countries have no particular difficulty with interactive tasks – and Brazil even shows a relative strength on such tasks.

In these countries, efforts to raise problem-solving competency should concentrate mainly on improving students' performance on "exploring and understanding" and on "representing and formulating" tasks. These tasks require students to build mental representations of the problem situation from the pieces of information with which they are presented. Moving from the concrete problem scenario to an abstract representation and understanding of it often demands inductive or deductive reasoning skills. Teachers and curriculum experts may question whether current curricula include sufficient opportunities to model these abstract reasoning skills and whether these opportunities are offered in the classroom.

In contrast, several countries in Southern and Eastern Europe, namely Bulgaria, Montenegro, Slovenia, Croatia and Serbia, show relatively weak performance both on knowledge-acquisition tasks and on interactive tasks, compared to their performance on "planning and executing" and on static tasks. In these countries, students seem to find it particularly difficult to understand, elaborate on, and integrate information that is not explicitly given to them (in a verbal or visual format), but has to be inferred from experimental manipulation of the environment and careful observation of the effects of that manipulation. Students in these countries may benefit from greater opportunities to learn from hands-on experience.

The performance gap between OECD countries in Europe and North America and the top-performing countries in problem solving mainly originates from differences in students' performance on knowledge-acquisition tasks. In general, the PISA problem-solving assessment shows that there is significant room for improving students' ability to turn information into useful knowledge, as measured by performance differences on the dimensions of "exploring and understanding" and "representing and formulating" problem situations.

Within this group, Ireland and the United States stand out for their strong performance on interactive items, compared, for instance, to the Nordic countries (Sweden, Finland, Norway and Denmark), the Netherlands, and some countries in Central Europe (in particular, Poland, Hungary and the Slovak Republic). Therefore, the analysis also identifies a strong potential for the Nordic and Central European countries to improve on their students' ability to cope with interactive problem situations. To do so, educators may need to foster such dispositions as being open to novelty, tolerating doubt and uncertainty, and daring to use intuition to initiate a solution.

Finally, several countries, while performing at different levels, show a similar balance of skill when compared to each other, and one that is close to the OECD average pattern of performance. Italy and Australia, for instance, have a very similar pattern of performance to that observed in Japan, although in terms of overall performance, Japan ranks significantly above Australia, which, in turn, performs better than Italy. These three countries all perform close to their expected level on interactive items (based on the OECD average pattern of performance), and slightly above their expected level on knowledge-acquisition tasks (although the example of Korea and Singapore shows that significant gains are still possible for them). In other countries, such as Spain, England (United Kingdom) and Germany, performance across tasks reflects the balance observed across OECD countries, on average.

For students in this group of countries, as a whole, there are no clear indications as to which aspects of problem-solving competence deserve particular attention. Nevertheless, the profile of performance may differ across particular groups of students. Such differences across groups of students will be analysed in the next chapter.

Two notes of caution: First, throughout this chapter, patterns of performance within countries and economies have been compared to the OECD average patterns in order to identify comparative strengths and weaknesses. Implications drawn from this analysis tacitly assume that this international benchmark corresponds to a desirable balance between the various aspects of problem-solving competence. The OECD average was selected for pragmatic reasons only. Therefore, the normative interpretation of the benchmark can be challenged, and alternative comparisons (for instance, to the pattern observed in the top-performing country) are equally possible.

Second, although this analysis can provide interesting indications, any conclusion that is drawn from subsets of the PISA problem-solving test must be carefully checked against evidence collected independently in each system on the strengths of the respective curriculum and teaching practices. Lacking supporting evidence, the conclusions should be interpreted with caution. Indeed, the PISA problem-solving assessment comprises a total of 42 items. When success is analysed on subsets of items that share common characteristics, the number of items inevitably drops. While the 42 items together reflect a consensus view of what problem-solving competence is, when this item set is split into smaller sets to analyse the individual components of problem-solving competence, the resulting picture is necessarily less sharp.[3] The results of analyses based on small sets of items may sometimes be driven by idiosyncratic features of one or two items in the pool rather than by their common traits.

Notes

1. A complementary analysis that can diagnose more detailed strengths and weaknesses will be made possible by the availability of behavioural sequences recorded by the computer interface (process data). After having identified the elementary task demands of each assessment item, the data recording students' interactions with items can be used, for instance, to identify patterns in terms of frequent stumbling blocks that hinder students from reaching the solution.

2. Fisher's exact test of independence of rows and columns was performed. The null hypothesis of independence of rows and columns for the contingency tables pairing the cognitive processes with the nature of the problem situation cannot be rejected (p-value: 0.69).

3. This is a problem of external validity that is not reflected in the standard errors provided with the statistical analysis in this chapter. While the inference about strengths and weaknesses is internally valid for the particular test of problem solving analysed, the question of external validity is whether a different test, constructed according to the same definition and framework, would give exactly the same results: i.e. to what extent one can generalise from performance on a dozen items to competence on the unobserved construct underlying these items.

References

OECD (2013), *PISA 2012 Assessment and Analytical Framework: Mathematics, Reading, Science, Problem Solving and Financial Literacy*, OECD Publishing.
http://dx.doi.org/10.1787/9789264190511-en

OECD (forthcoming), *PISA 2012 Technical Report*, OECD Publishing.

4

How Problem-Solving Performance Varies within Countries

This chapter looks at differences in problem-solving performance related to education tracks within countries and to students' gender, socio-economic status and immigrant background. It also examines students' behaviours and attitudes related to problem solving, and their familiarity with information and communication technology. In addition, the chapter identifies particular groups of students who perform better in problem solving than expected, given their performance in mathematics, reading and science.

This chapter looks at performance differences across students and schools within countries. How does performance in problem solving relate to student characteristics, such as gender, socio-economic status, and immigrant background? Do students in certain study programmes perform better in problem solving than in the core curricular subjects? The chapter also looks at student behaviours and attitudes related to problem solving, as well as at indicators of familiarity with information and communication technology (ICT), as they were measured through background questionnaires in PISA 2012.

The aim of this chapter is to understand how differences between countries and economies that are presented in Chapters 2 and 3 are related to differences in performance among various groups of students. The chapter focuses on identifying particular groups of students who perform better in problem solving than could be expected, given their performance in mathematics, reading and science; and on understanding whether the strengths and weaknesses of systems stem from the strengths and weaknesses of certain groups of students.

What the data tell us

- In Malaysia, Shanghai-China and Turkey, more than one in eight students attend a vocational study programme, and these students show significantly better performance in problem solving, on average, than students with comparable performance in mathematics, reading and science but who are in general study programmes.

- On average across OECD countries, there are three top-performing boys for every two top-performing girls in problem solving. In Croatia, Italy and the Slovak Republic, boys are as likely as girls to be low-achievers, but are more than twice as likely as girls to be top performers. In no country or economy are there more girls than boys among the top performers in problem solving.

- Girls appear to be stronger in performing the "planning and executing" tasks that measure how students use knowledge, compared to other types of problems; and weaker in performing the more abstract "representing and formulating" tasks, which relate to how students acquire knowledge. This is particularly true among girls in Hong Kong-China, Korea and Chinese Taipei.

- The impact of socio-economic status on problem-solving performance is weaker than it is on performance in mathematics, reading or science.

- Not using a computer at home is negatively related to problem-solving performance in 29 of 33 participating countries and economies, even after accounting for socio-economic status. A similarly strong relationship is observed between lack of computer use at home and performance on the paper-based assessments of mathematics and reading.

PERFORMANCE DIFFERENCES UNIQUE TO PROBLEM SOLVING

The overall variation in problem-solving proficiency can be split into two components – one that is also observed in mathematics, reading and science (about two-thirds), and one that is unique to problem solving (about one-third) (see Chapter 2). This chapter will mainly explore the factors that are related to the unique aspects of problem-solving performance.

How much of the variation in performance that is unique to problem solving lies between schools, and what part is related to differences between students attending the same school? Figure V.4.1 shows that, on average, a similar proportion – about one-third – of the within-school and between-school variations in problem solving performance is not accounted for by differences in mathematics performance between and within schools, and can be considered unique to problem solving.

Therefore, not only do school policies and practices have a significant influence on the problem-solving performance of students (see Chapter 2, Figure V.2.12), but a large proportion of the between-school variation in performance is unique to problem solving. This means that the differences in problem-solving performance between schools do not stem solely from differences in mathematics performance.

School rankings based on problem solving will differ from school rankings based on mathematics. Among schools with similar results in mathematics, a significant proportion of the between-school differences in problem-solving performance likely reflects differences in schools' emphases on and approaches towards fostering students' problem-solving skills.

■ Figure V.4.1 ■
Performance variation unique to problem solving

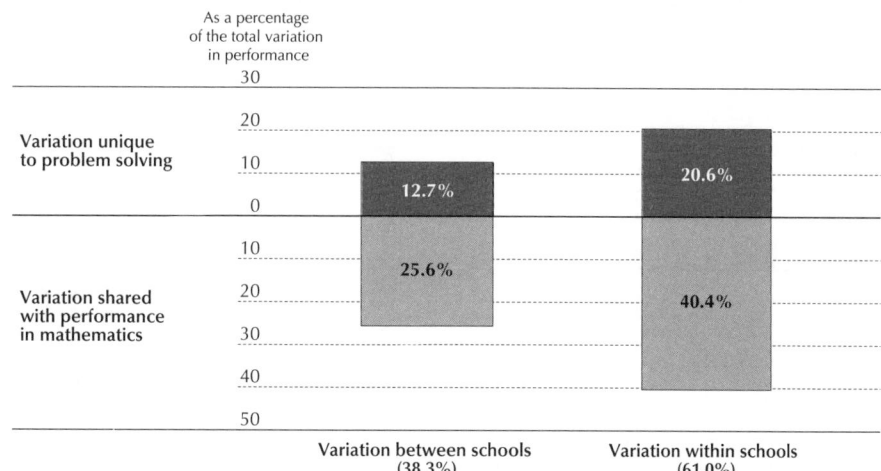

Note: The figure shows the components of the performance variation in problem solving for the OECD average.
Source: OECD, PISA 2012 Database, Table V.4.1.
StatLink http://dx.doi.org/10.1787/888933003611

Similarly, the differences across students within schools only partly reflect general academic proficiency. To the extent that performance differences in problem solving are unique to problem solving, their origins also differ from those of performance variations in curricular subjects.

PERFORMANCE DIFFERENCES ACROSS STUDY PROGRAMMES

Performance differences across schools can be at least partly related to differences in curricula. However, it is impossible to determine a causal impact of the curriculum on performance using only PISA data. The comparison between two study programmes will always be confounded by differences between students, teachers and schools that cannot be captured by questionnaires; even figures that account for socio-economic background or gender cannot be interpreted causally.

In most countries, there is a major distinction between vocational or pre-vocational study programmes and general study programmes. Generally, only a minority of 15-year-olds in each country is enrolled in vocational study programmes; the exceptions are Serbia, Croatia, Austria, Montenegro, Slovenia and Italy, where a majority of 15-year-olds students is enrolled in such programmes (Table V.4.2).

How are study programmes related to the unique aspects of problem-solving performance? This "relative performance in problem solving" of each study programme can be estimated by comparing the performance of students in each study programme only to students who share their same proficiency in mathematics, reading and science. Such a comparison can show whether good or poor performance in a subject is reflected in equally good or poor performance in problem solving; or, conversely, whether there is a specific advantage in problem solving for students in a particular type of study programme.

Figure V.4.2 shows that, in 4 of 31 countries and economies, namely Shanghai-China, Turkey, the United Arab Emirates and Malaysia, students in vocational study programmes have significantly better performance in problem solving than students with comparable performance in mathematics, reading and science who are in general study programmes. In all of these cases, the advantage of students in vocational programmes corresponds to at least 12 score points on the problem-solving scale. In all of these countries and economies, with the exception of the United Arab Emirates, more than one in eight students (more than 12.5%) attend vocational study programmes. Meanwhile, in the Russian Federation and Germany, students in vocational study programmes have significantly lower performance in problem solving than students with comparable performance in mathematics, reading and science. The gap between the two groups of students exceeds 24 score points on the problem-solving scale. In both countries, however, fewer than 5% of students are enrolled in a vocational study programme (Tables V.4.2 and V.4.4).

■ Figure V.4.2 ■

Relative performance in problem solving among students in vocational and pre-vocational tracks

Difference in problem-solving performance between students in vocational or pre-vocational programmes and students in general programmes with similar performance in mathematics, reading and science

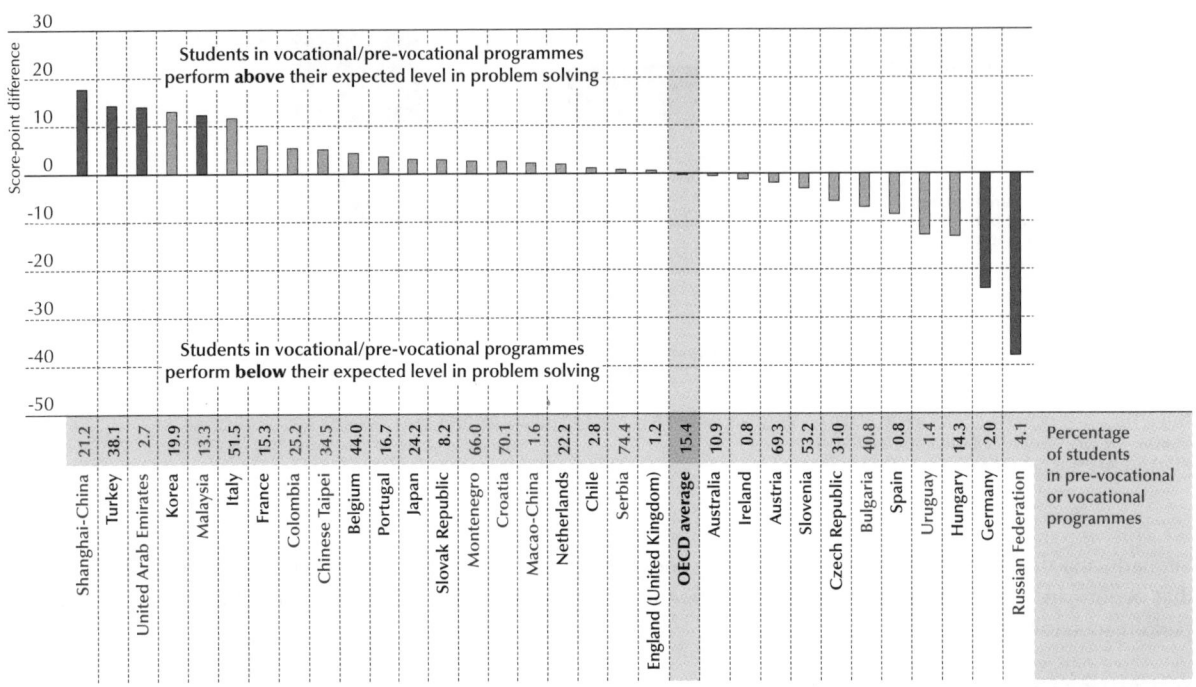

Note: Statistically significant differences are marked in a darker tone (see Annex A3).

Countries and economies are ranked in descending order of the score-point difference between students in vocational/pre-vocational programmes and those in general programmes with similar performance in mathematics, reading and science.

Source: OECD, PISA 2012 Database, Tables V.4.2 and V.4.4.

StatLink 🔢📊 http://dx.doi.org/10.1787/888933003611

Figure V.4.3 uses the national classification of study programmes to highlight education tracks where students have significantly better performance in problem solving than students with comparable performance in mathematics, reading and science in their country who are enrolled in different study programmes.

Many of the differences in relative performance across study programmes concern countries or economies with overall weaker-than-expected performance in problem solving (see Figure V.2.15 and Table V.2.6); in these cases, a "relatively strong" programme may constitute an exception to the overall weakness. Students enrolled in general study tracks that prepare for higher education in Germany (*Gymnasium*) and in Hungary (*Gimnázium*), for instance, show stronger performance in problem solving, on average, than other German or Hungarian students with similar scores in mathematics, reading and science. While, overall, students in Germany and Hungary perform below students from other countries with similar performance in core subjects, this finding suggest that students outside of these general study tracks account for most of this negative result. In other countries, students from specific vocational programmes score higher than other students in their country who are similarly proficient in mathematics, reading and science. Such is the case for students in the vocational upper secondary programmes in the Flemish and German-speaking Communities of Belgium: they tend to score 8 and 25 points, respectively, above their expected level when compared to all Belgian students of similar proficiency in core subjects. Similarly, in Portugal, students in the professional upper secondary track score 17 points above their expected level. The performance gap in problem solving between students in the professional track and students in the general track is in this case smaller in problem solving than in mathematics, reading and science (Table V.4.5).

Fewer significant differences can be observed among countries whose students, overall, are relatively strong in problem solving when compared with students in other countries with similar proficiency in mathematics, reading and science.

■ Figure V.4.3 [Part 1/2] ■

Relative performance in problem solving, by education track

	Education tracks with a relative strength in problem solving	Education tracks whose students' performance in problem solving is in line with their performance in mathematics, reading and science	Education tracks with a relative weakness in problem solving
		Numbers in parentheses indicate the proportion of 15-year-olds in the study programme	
Australia		General lower secondary (75.4%); Lower secondary with some vocational subjects (5.3%); General upper secondary (13.5%); Upper secondary with some vocational subjects (4.1%); Vocational upper secondary (1.5%)	
Austria	Charter schools (*Statutschulen*) (0.3%)	Pre-vocational transition year (*Polytechnische Schule*) and lower secondary (*Hauptschule*) (14.6%); General lower and upper secondary leading to university entrance qualifications (AHS) (25.7%); Vocational school for apprentices (*Berufsschule*) (15.4%); Intermediate technical and vocational school (BMS) (11.7%); College for higher vocational education (BHS) (32.4%)	
Belgium	Vocational upper secondary (Fl: TSO, KSO, BSO) (29.1%); Lower secondary (Ger.) (0.1%); Vocational upper secondary (Ger.) (0.2%)	Lower secondary (Fl.) (1.5%); General upper secondary (Fl.: ASO) (24.3%); Lower secondary (Fr.) (5.3%); General upper secondary (Fr.) (24.9%); Vocational upper secondary (Fr.) (10.5%); General upper secondary (Ger.) (0.4%); Vocational upper secondary, part-time programmes (Fl.,Fr.,Ger.) (0.5%); Special education (Fl.,Fr.,Ger.) (3.1%)	
Chile		Lower secondary (5.5%); Upper secondary, first cycle (87.8%); General upper secondary, second cycle (3.9%); Vocational upper secondary, second cycle (2.8%)	
Czech Republic	Basic school (47.1%)	General lower and upper secondary (Gymnasium) (19.3%); Vocational upper secondary with school-leaving exam (21.9%); Vocational upper secondary without school-leaving exam (8.4%); Special education (2.8%)	
Denmark	Upper secondary (0.5%)	Primary and lower secondary (88.3%); Continuation school (11.2%)	
Estonia	Lower secondary (98.1%)	General upper secondary (1.5%)	
France		Lower secondary (27.3%); Special education (lower secondary) (2.5%); General upper secondary (57.4%); Technical upper secondary (11.0%); Professional upper secondary (1.8%)	
Germany	General lower secondary with access to general upper secondary (*Gymnasium*) (36.1%)	Special education (2.8%); General lower secondary without access to general upper secondary (*Hauptschule*) (15.5%); General lower secondary without access to general upper secondary (*Realschule*) (33.5%); General upper secondary (*Gymnasium*) (0.8%); Comprehensive lower secondary (*Integrative Gesamtschule*) (9.3%)	Pre-vocational and vocational (*Übergangsjahr, Berufsschule, Berufsfachschule*) (2.0%)
Hungary	General upper secondary (*Gimnázium*) (38.2%)	Vocational upper secondary with access to post-secondary and tertiary (36.2%); Vocational upper secondary without access to post-secondary and tertiary (14.3%)	Primary school (11.3%)
Ireland	Transition year programme (24.3%)	Applied upper secondary (Leaving certificate applied) (0.8%); General upper secondary (Leaving certificate) (7.4%); Vocational upper secondary (Leaving certificate vocational) (5.1%)	Lower secondary (Junior certificate) (62.4%)
Italy		Scientific, classical, social science, scientific-technological, linguistic, artistic, music and performing arts high schools (45.9%); Technical institute (29.0%); Vocational institutes (service industry, industry, arts and crafts workers) (17.0%); Vocational training, vocational schools of Bolzano and Trento provinces (5.5%)	Lower secondary (2.6%)
Japan		General upper secondary (74.4%); Vocational upper secondary (24.2%)	
Korea		Lower secondary (5.9%); General upper secondary (74.2%); Vocational upper secondary (19.9%)	
Netherlands		Practical preparation for labour market (PRO) (2.5%); Pre-vocational secondary, years 1 and 2 (VMBO 1 & 2) (2.4%); Pre-vocational secondary, years 3 and 4, basic track (VMBO BB) (8.4%); Pre-vocational secondary, years 3 and 4, middle management track (VMBO KB) (11.4%); Pre-vocational secondary, years 3 and 4, theoretical and mixed track (VMBO GL/TL) (24.4%); Senior general secondary education (HAVO), leading to university of applied sciences (25.9%); Pre-university (VWO) (25.1%)	
Portugal	Professional upper secondary (7.2%)	Lower secondary (35.6%); General upper secondary (47.7%); Vocational training (CEF - *Curso de Educação e Formação*) (9.3%)	
Slovak Republic	Specialised upper secondary with school-leaving exam (26.1%)	General lower secondary (41.6%); Special education (1.2%); General lower and upper secondary (Gymnasium) (22.9%); Specialised upper secondary without school-leaving exam (ISCED 3C) (8.2%)	

Note: Numbers in parentheses indicate the proportion of 15-year-olds in the study programme; percentages may not add up to 100 within each country/economy because of rounding and of rare programmes for which results are not reported. Only countries/economies with results reported for more than one study programme are included in this figure. The middle column includes all programmes for which relative performance in problem solving is not statistically different from 0 (see Annex A3). In Belgium, the information about study programmes in variable PROGN was combined with information about regions to identify education tracks: "Fl." refers to the Flemish Community, "Fr." to the French Community, and "Ger." to the German-speaking Community; results for "Part-time vocational" programmes and "Special education" programmes are reported at the national level. In Germany, students in schools with multiple study programmes are classified according to their specific education track.

Source: OECD, PISA 2012 Database, Table V.4.5.
StatLink ⓘ http://dx.doi.org/10.1787/888933003611

■ Figure V.4.3 [Part 2/2] ■

Relative performance in problem solving, by education track

		Education tracks with a relative strength in problem solving	Education tracks whose students' performance in problem solving is in line with their performance in mathematics, reading and science	Education tracks with a relative weakness in problem solving
			Numbers in parentheses indicate the proportion of 15-year-olds in the study programme	
OECD	Slovenia	Technical upper secondary (38.3%)	General upper secondary (technical gymnasiums) (7.6%); Basic (elementary) education (5.4%)	General upper secondary (general and classical gymnasiums) (33.8%); Vocational programmes of medium duration (13.8%); Vocational programmes of short duration (1.1%)
	Spain		Lower secondary (99.2%); Initial vocational qualification programme (0.8%)	
	Sweden		General, compulsory basic (97.8%); General upper secondary (1.8%)	
	Turkey	Anatolian vocational high school (5.7%); Technical high school (1.5%); Anatolian technical high school (2.5%)	Primary school (2.7%); General, science, and social sciences high school (32.2%); Anatolian high school (22.5%); Vocational high school (24.7%); Multi programme high school (3.7%)	Anatolian teacher training high school (4.5%)
	England (United Kingdom)		General upper secondary, compulsory (Students studying mostly toward GCSE) (97.7%); Vocational upper secondary, compulsory (Students studying mostly towards a level 1 Diploma) (0.9%)	General upper secondary, post-compulsory (Students studying mostly for AS or A Levels) (1.1%)
Partners	Bulgaria	General upper secondary, specialised (47.6%)	General upper secondary, non-specialised (6.7%); Vocational upper secondary (40.8%)	Lower secondary (4.8%)
	Colombia		General upper secondary (35.7%); Vocational upper secondary (25.2%)	Lower secondary (39.1%)
	Croatia		Gymnasium (29.9%); Four year vocational programmes (46.7%); Vocational programmes for industry (6.5%); Vocational programmes for crafts (15.2%); Lower qualification vocational programmes (0.8%)	
	Macao-China		Lower secondary (54.9%); General upper secondary (43.5%); Pre-vocational or vocational upper secondary (1.6%)	
	Malaysia	Vocational upper secondary (13.3%)	Arts upper secondary (44.8%); Religious secondary (3.3%); Lower secondary (4.0%)	Science upper secondary (34.6%)
	Montenegro		General upper secondary school or gymnasium (33.6%); Four-year vocational secondary (60.0%); Three-year vocational secondary (6.0%);	
	Russian Federation	General upper secondary (13.4%)	Lower secondary (82.5%); Vocational upper secondary (technikum, college, etc.) (2.2%)	Vocational upper secondary (professional schools, etc.) (1.9%)
	Serbia	Arts upper secondary (1.6%)	General upper secondary (Gymnasium) (24.0%); Technical upper secondary (30.3%); Vocational technical upper secondary (6.5%); Medical upper secondary (9.3%); Economic upper secondary (18.8%); Vocational economic upper secondary (3.0%); Agricultural upper secondary (4.2%)	
	Shanghai-China	Vocational upper secondary (19.8%)	General upper secondary (34.3%)	General lower secondary (44.4%)
	Chinese Taipei		Junior high school (36.4%); Senior high school (29.1%); Vocational senior high school (30.6%); Five-year college (not including the last two years) (4.0%)	
	United Arab Emirates	Vocational secondary (2.7%)	General lower secondary (15.0%); General upper secondary (82.3%)	
	Uruguay		General lower secondary (31.4%); Lower secondary with a technological component (5.3%); Lower Secondary with a very important technological component (2.9%); Vocational lower secondary (1.3%); General upper secondary (50.2%); Vocational upper secondary (more than one year) (1.3%)	Technical upper secondary (6.2%)

Note: Numbers in parentheses indicate the proportion of 15-year-olds in the study programme; percentages may not add up to 100 within each country/economy because of rounding and of rare programmes for which results are not reported. Only countries/economies with results reported for more than one study programme are included in this figure. The middle column includes all programmes for which relative performance in problem solving is not statistically different from 0 (see Annex A3). In Belgium, the information about study programmes in variable PROGN was combined with information about regions to identify education tracks: "Fl." refers to the Flemish Community, "Fr." to the French Community, and "Ger." to the German-speaking Community; results for "Part-time vocational" programmes and "Special education" programmes are reported at the national level. In Germany, students in schools with multiple study programmes are classified according to their specific education track.

Source: OECD, PISA 2012 Database, Table V.4.5.
StatLink ⟶ http://dx.doi.org/10.1787/888933003611

Students in arts upper secondary programmes in Serbia seem to beat expectations by an even greater margin than other students in that country, but fewer than 2% of all 15-year-olds are in these programmes. In Italy, students who are held back in lower secondary education (about 2.6% of all 15-year-olds) are relatively weak in problem solving, even after accounting for differences in mathematics, reading and science performance. These students, therefore, do not seem to contribute to the overall (relative) strength of Italy's students in problem solving.

Strong performance in problem solving among students in certain education tracks, relative to their performance in the other subjects assessed by PISA, can be interpreted in two ways. On the one hand, the curriculum and teaching practices in these programmes may promote authentic learning, and equip students for tackling complex, real-life problems in contexts that they do not usually encounter at school. On the other hand, better-than-expected performance in problem solving may be an indication that in these programmes, students' potential is not nurtured as much as it could be within the core academic subjects.

GENDER DIFFERENCES IN PROBLEM SOLVING

Differences between boys and girls can be analysed in terms of overall proficiency in problem solving, in relation to performance differences observed in other domains, and in terms of the distinct cognitive abilities that are emphasised by different families of assessment tasks.

Boys score seven points higher than girls in problem solving, on average across OECD countries (Figure V.4.4). The variation observed among boys is also larger than the variation observed among girls. The standard deviation among boys is 100 score points, while the standard deviation among girls is only 91 score points. Similarly, the distance between the top (95th percentile) and the bottom (5th percentile) of the performance distribution is significantly larger among boys than among girls (Table V.4.7).

■ Figure V.4.4 ■
Gender differences in problem-solving performance

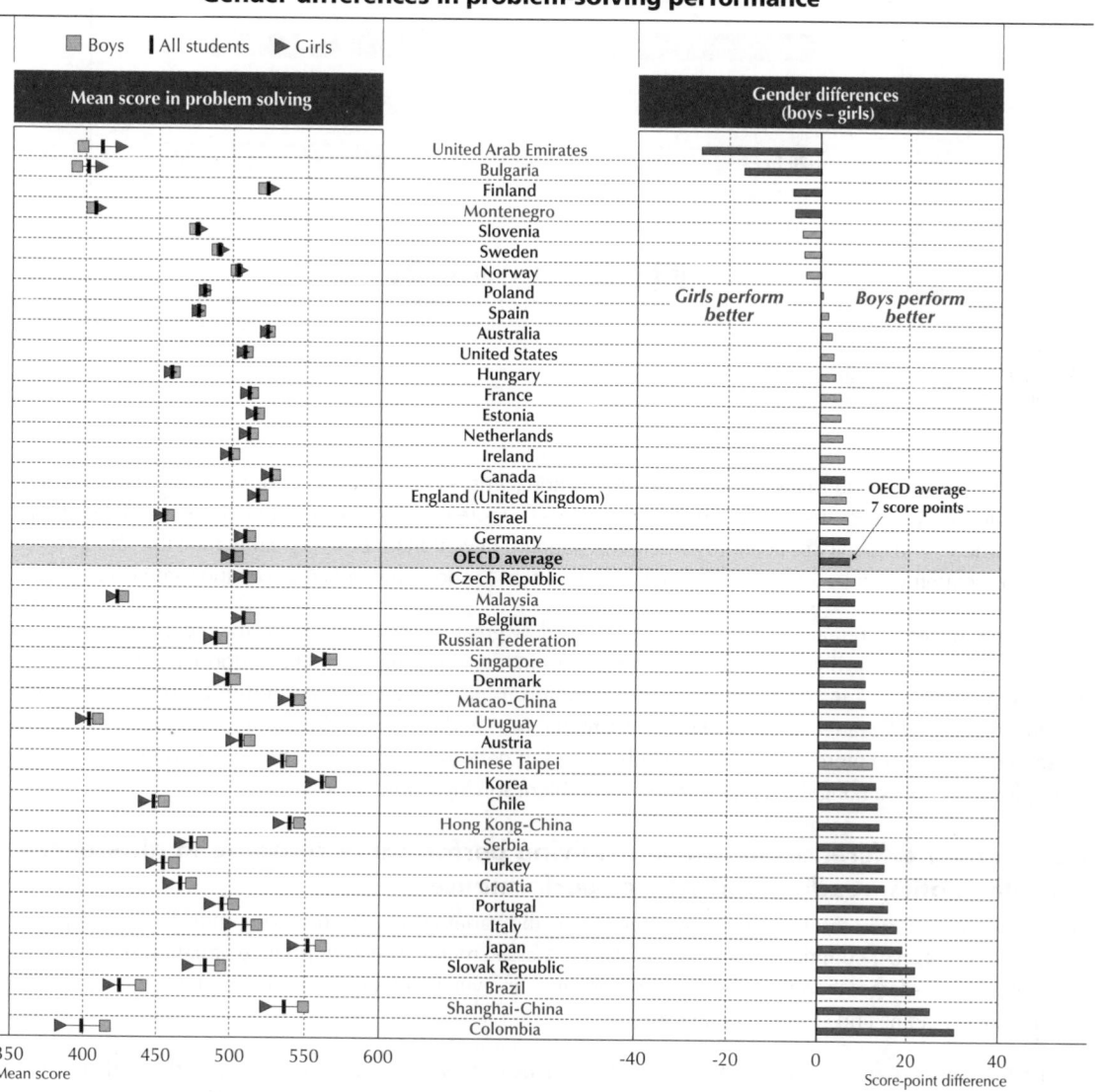

Note: Statistically significant gender differences are marked in a darker tone (see Annex A3).
Countries and economies are ranked in ascending order of the score-point difference (boys - girls).
Source: OECD, PISA 2012 Database, Tables V.2.2 and V.4.7.
StatLink ⬛🖵🖳 http://dx.doi.org/10.1787/888933003611

On average across OECD countries, boys are more likely than girls to perform at the highest levels in problem solving. The proportion of top-performing boys is 1.50 times larger than the proportion of top-performing girls. Girls and boys are equally represented at the lowest levels of performance (below Level 2) (Figure V.4.5 and Table V.4.6).

In more than half of the countries and economies that participated in the assessment of problem solving, boys outperform girls, on average. The largest advantage in favour of boys is found in Colombia, Shanghai-China, Brazil and the Slovak Republic, where the difference exceeds 20 score points. Among the exceptions are the United Arab Emirates, Bulgaria, Finland and Montenegro, where girls outperform boys, on average. In 16 countries/economies, the difference in performance between boys and girls is not statistically significant (Figure V.4.4 and Table V.4.7).

■ Figure V.4.5 ■

Proficiency in problem solving among girls and boys

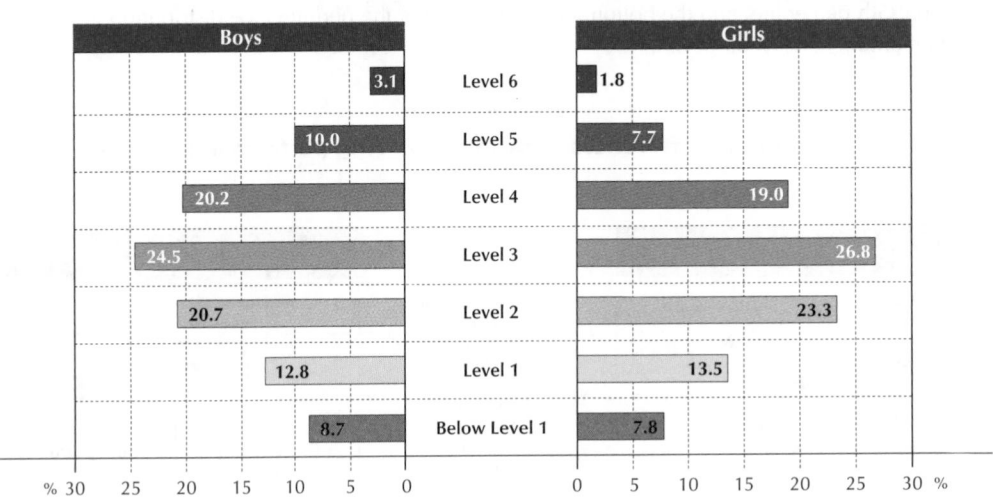

Source: OECD, PISA 2012 Database, Table V.4.6.

StatLink ᴍᴤ᛭ http://dx.doi.org/10.1787/888933003611

A greater variation in performance among boys than among girls is found in nearly every country/economy. The standard deviation for boys exceeds the standard deviation for girls by more than 15 score points in Israel, the United Arab Emirates and Italy. There is no country or economy where the standard deviation for boys is smaller than the standard deviation for girls. In ten countries and economies, the standard deviation for boys and girls is about the same (Table V.4.7).

Because the better performance of boys is accompanied by greater variation in performance, in several countries there are more boys at both the highest levels of performance – in line with higher average performance levels – and the lowest levels of performance – in line with the greater variation in performance. Boys tend to be under-represented among students in the middle range of performance. In Croatia, Italy and the Slovak Republic, boys are as likely as girls to be low-achievers, but are more than twice as likely to be top performers as girls. In no single country/economy are there more girls than boys among the top performers in problem solving (Table V.4.6).

How gender differences in problem-solving performance compare to differences in mathematics, reading and science performance

The greater variation in the results of boys, relative to the variation observed among girls, is not unique to problem solving. It is, in fact, a common finding across the PISA assessments. The performance variation observed among boys is about 1.2 times larger than that observed among girls, on average across countries – similar to the ratio observed in mathematics, reading and science (Table V.4.9).

Across the subjects assessed by PISA, gender differences in mean performance vary greatly. Girls outperform boys in reading; but boys outperform girls in mathematics. The advantage of girls in reading is as large as 40% of a standard deviation, on average, across OECD countries participating in the assessment of problem solving; while the advantage of boys in mathematics is equivalent to 11% of a standard deviation. In science, no clear advantage

for either boys or girls is found. Boys' advantage in problem solving (7% of a standard deviation on average across OECD countries) is thus lower than the advantage for boys in mathematics, but larger than the gender gap observed in science (Figure V.4.6).

It is not clear whether one should expect there to be a gender gap in problem solving. On the one hand, the questions posed in the PISA problem-solving assessment were not grounded in content knowledge, so boys' or girls' advantage in having mastered a particular subject area should not have influenced results. On the other hand, as shown in Chapter 2 (Figure V.2.13), performance in problem solving is more closely related to performance in mathematics than to performance in reading. One could therefore expect the gender difference in performance to be closer to that observed in mathematics – a modest advantage for boys, in most countries – than to that observed in reading – a large advantage for girls.

■ Figure V.4.6 ■

Difference between boys and girls in problem-solving, mathematics, reading and science performance

Expressed as a percentage of the overall variation in performance

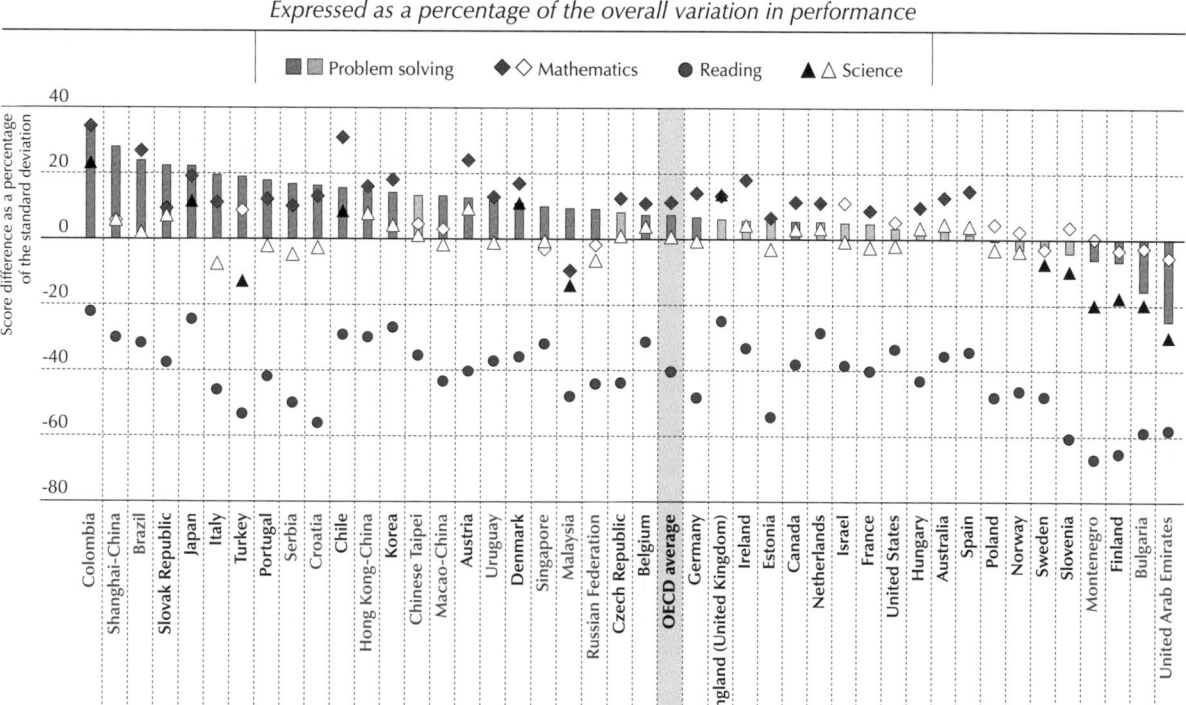

Notes: Gender differences that are statistically significant are marked in a darker tone (see Annex A3). All gender differences in reading performance are statistically significant.

Countries and economies are ranked in descending order of the gender difference in problem solving (boys - girls).

Source: OECD, PISA 2012 Database, Table V.4.8.

StatLink ⟨ms⟩ http://dx.doi.org/10.1787/888933003611

An analysis accounting for performance differences in curricular subjects shows that the gender gap in problem solving is largely the result of boys' strengths in the skills that are uniquely measured by the problem-solving assessment. Indeed, because the small disadvantage of girls in mathematics is counterbalanced by a large advantage in reading, when the analysis accounts for performance across all three subjects (mathematics, reading and science) – as shown in Figure V.4.7 – the resulting gender gap in the relative performance in problem solving (8 score points, in favour of boys) is not much different from the actual gender gap in problem solving.

There are few studies that focus on gender differences in problem solving (see Hyde, 2005; Wüstenberg et al., 2014). The results of the PISA 2003 assessment of problem solving showed very few countries in which there were significant gender differences in performance (OECD, 2005). However, the PISA 2003 assessment was limited to static problem situations, and its results cannot be compared with those of the PISA 2012 assessment. Moreover, the PISA 2003 assessment was a paper-based assessment, whereas the PISA 2012 assessment of problem solving was delivered by computer.

■ Figure V.4.7 ■

Relative performance in problem solving among girls

*Difference in problem-solving performance between girls and boys with similar performance
in mathematics, reading and science*

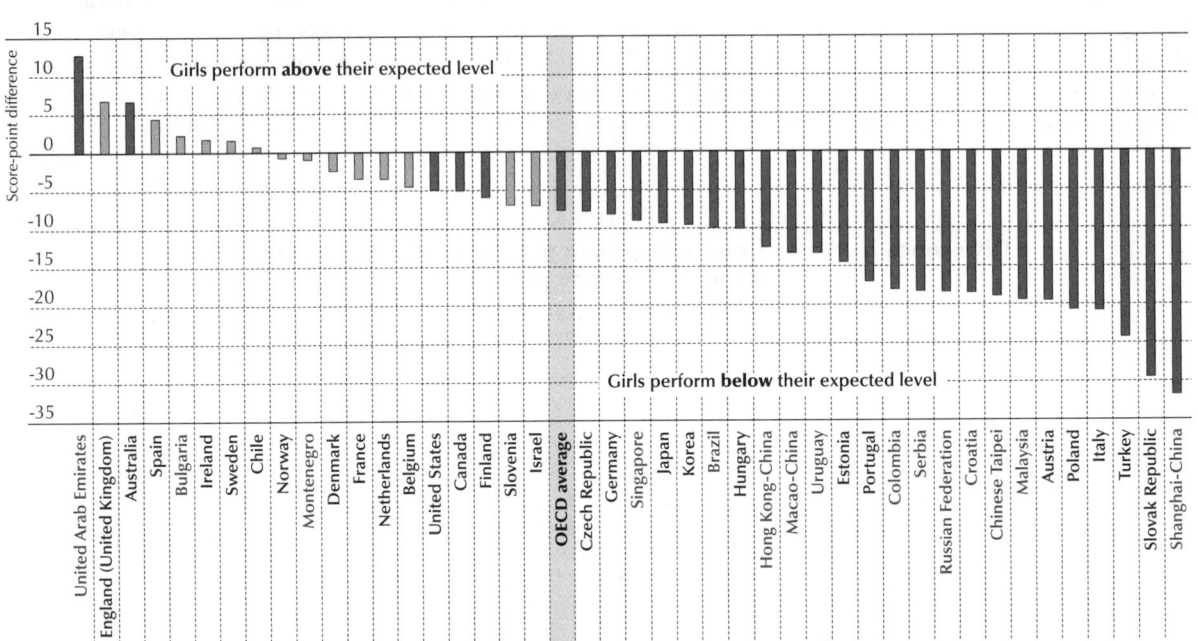

Note: Statistically significant differences are marked in a darker tone (see Annex A3).
*Countries and economies are ranked in descending order of the score-point difference in problem solving between girls and boys with similar performance
in mathematics, reading and science.*
Source: OECD, PISA 2012 Database, Table V.4.10.
StatLink ⬛⬛ http://dx.doi.org/10.1787/888933003611

In countries that also used computer-based instruments to assess mathematics and reading, boys perform better, relative to girls, in the computer test than in the paper test. In mathematics, the computer-based assessment shows a larger advantage for boys than girls; in reading, a smaller disadvantage for boys relative to girls (Table V.4.8). One can therefore speculate that the computer delivery of the problem-solving assessment contributed to the better performance of boys over girls in the assessment.

Differences in performance patterns across items

Performance differences between boys and girls vary across the problem-solving assessment, depending on the type of task involved. For example, a comparison of success rates for boys and girls across items representing the four major problem-solving processes identified in the framework – "exploring and understanding", "representing and formulating", "planning and executing", and "monitoring and reflecting" – reveals sharp contrasts.

Figure V.4.8 shows that girls perform better – and thus, in most cases, at similar levels as boys – on items measuring the "planning and executing" aspect. Table V.4.11b shows that, on average across OECD countries, the success ratio (i.e. the ratio of full-credit over no-credit and partial-credit answers) on these items for girls is 0.96 times the success ratio for boys – i.e. only slightly below that of boys. In contrast, girls' performance is lower on items measuring the "representing and formulating" aspect. Here, the success ratio among girls is only 0.84 times as high as that among boys. After accounting for their lower overall success on the assessment, as in Figure V.4.8, the "planning and executing" tasks that measure knowledge-utilisation processes appear to be a strong point for girls, while the more abstract "representing and formulating" tasks, which relate to knowledge-acquisition processes, appear to be a weak point for girls.

Based on the existing psychometric literature (see, for a review, Halpern and LaMay, 2000), a difference, in favour of boys, on items that require a greater amount of abstract information processing could be expected. This literature finds consistent gender differences on some tests of cognitive abilities. The most frequently cited difference is in the ability to transform a visual-spatial image in working memory. According to the literature, males often perform better than females on cognitive tasks requiring the ability to generate and manipulate the information in a mental representation. In the PISA assessment of problem solving, this ability is particularly important for success on "representing and formulating" tasks.

■ Figure V.4.8 ■
Girls' strengths and weaknesses, by problem-solving process
Relative likelihood of success in favour of girls, accounting for overall performance differences on the test

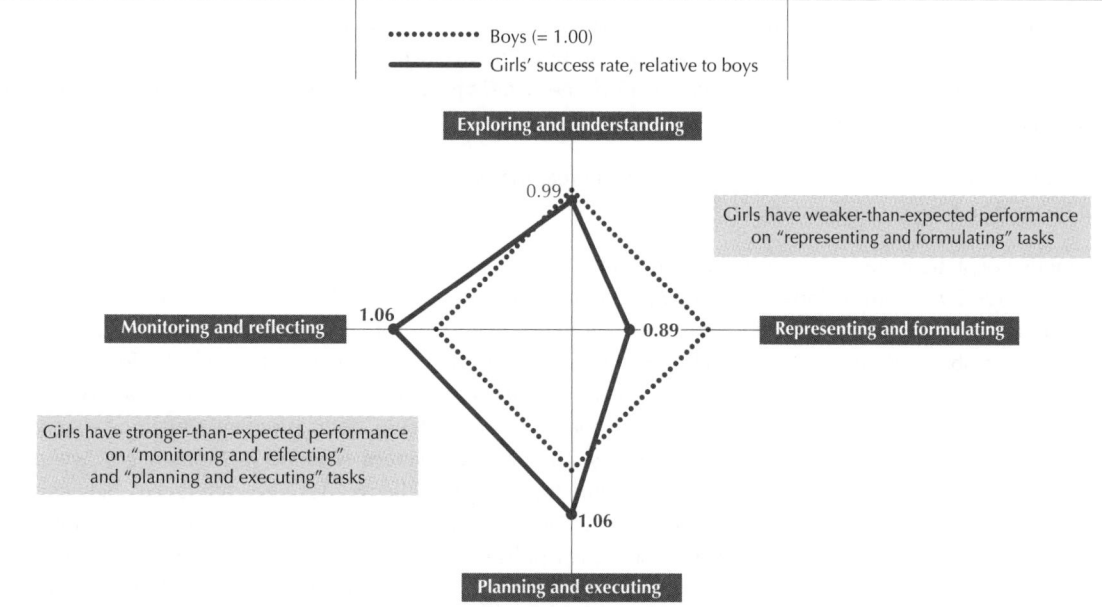

Notes: Gender differences that are statistically significant are marked in bold (see Annex A3).
This figure shows that girls' success rate on items measuring the processes of "representing and formulating" is only 0.89 times as large as that of boys, after accounting for overall performance differences on the test and on average across OECD countries.
Source: OECD, PISA 2012 Database, Table V.4.11b.
StatLink 🔗 http://dx.doi.org/10.1787/888933003611

The profile of performance across problem-solving processes differs significantly between boys and girls in 27 of the 44 countries and economies participating in the assessment.[1] In all but three of these countries/economies, girls perform below their expected level of performance in particular on items measuring "representing and formulating" processes (Table V.4.11b).

In Korea, girls score lower than boys on the overall problem-solving scale. An analysis by families of items shows that girls' performance is much weaker than boys' on items measuring "exploring and understanding" and "representing and formulating" processes, but is close to boys' performance (and thus stronger than expected) on "planning and executing" and "monitoring and reflecting" tasks. Therefore, the good performance of Korea on the problem-solving assessment, which is mainly attributed to the stronger-than-expected performance of its students on items measuring knowledge acquisition (see Chapter 3), results in part from boys' strong performance on these items. A similar pattern applies to Hong Kong-China and Macao-China as well: in both, boys outperform girls overall, and on knowledge-acquisition tasks in particular, but not on knowledge-utilisation tasks (Table V.4.11b).

In contrast, in many European countries, including those with above-average performance in problem solving, such as France, the Netherlands, Italy and Germany, the performance patterns for boys and girls are similar across the various problem-solving processes.

In Spain, Hong Kong-China, Korea and Macao-China, girls' performance is weaker than boys' performance on items measuring "exploring and understanding" processes, after accounting for overall differences in performance between boys and girls. In the remaining countries/economies, the evidence is not strong enough to identify different patterns for boys and girls.

On items measuring "representing and formulating" processes, girls' performance is weaker than boys' in 24 countries and economies, after accounting for overall differences in performance between boys and girls. The performance difference on these items, relative to the remaining test items, is largest in Shanghai-China, Colombia, Korea and Hong Kong-China, where girls perform only 0.8 times (at best) as well as expected. In the remaining 20 countries/economies, the evidence is not strong enough to identify different patterns for boys and girls (Table V.4.11b).

Girls' performance is stronger than boys' on "planning and executing" items in Hong Kong-China, Korea, Chinese Taipei, Brazil, Japan, Portugal, Singapore, Macao-China, England (United Kingdom), Australia, Serbia and Finland, after accounting for overall differences in performance between boys and girls. In all these countries and economies except Finland, girls perform at lower levels than boys, on average (but not significantly so in Chinese Taipei, England (United Kingdom) and Australia). In contrast, in Finland girls perform better than boys, on average; and this analysis shows that girls' strong performance overall stems mainly from their better performance on tasks measuring the process of "planning and executing" compared to boys (Table V.4.11b).

Finally, in Colombia, Shanghai-China, Denmark, Chile, Korea, Malaysia, England (United Kingdom) and Australia, girls perform better than boys on "monitoring and reflecting" items (Table V.4.11b).

The interactive or static nature of the problem situation is not associated with gender differences in performance, on average across OECD countries (Table V.4.11a): girls' performance on interactive items is similar to their performance on static items. The relative success ratio (odds ratio) on interactive items for girls compared to boys (0.92) is about the same ratio as observed on static items (0.93). Large differences in performance are found in Chile and Hungary, where girls perform more than 1.2 times worse on interactive items than on static items. Compared to boys in these two countries, girls seem to be particularly good at analysing and solving static problem situations – and weak at analysing and solving interactive problem situations. The opposite pattern is found in Montenegro, where girls perform more than 1.2 times better on interactive items than on static items. Because differences between girls' performance on static and their performance on interactive items are not systematic, the inclusion of interactive items in the PISA 2012 assessment cannot explain why the results of the PISA 2012 assessment indicate larger gender differences in problem-solving skills than the results of the PISA 2003 assessment, which found no difference, on average across OECD countries.

Similarly, in the PISA assessment of problem solving, there are no large gender differences in the patterns of performance that are related to the context of the problem. On average, girls' success rates are similar to those of boys – after accounting for overall differences across the test – on items situated in "personal" contexts, involving close relations, and on items that are cast in wider, impersonal contexts ("social" contexts). Girls tend to have slightly better performance on items involving technology devices than on those in non-technology settings. The overwhelming use of problem contexts that come from male-dominated fields (such as sports, weapons or cars) has been proposed as one reason behind gender differences in assessments of mathematical problem solving (Fennema, 2000), but does not seem to explain the performance differences found in PISA 2012 (Tables V.4.11c and V.4.11d).

There are no differences in the pattern of performance according to the response format: success rates for boys and girls are, in general, similarly balanced on selected-response and constructed-response items (Table V.4.11e).

THE RELATIONSHIP BETWEEN SOCIO-ECONOMIC STATUS, IMMIGRANT BACKGROUND AND PROBLEM-SOLVING PERFORMANCE

Performance differences related to socio-economic status

Unsurprisingly, socio-economic status – as measured, for instance, by the *PISA index of economic, social and cultural status* (ESCS) – relates positively to performance in problem solving, as it does indeed to performance in all domains assessed in PISA. But how do differences in performance by socio-economic status compare across domains?

In general, the strength of the association between performance and socio-economic status, measured as the percentage of variation in performance explained by socio-economic disparities, is similar for mathematics (the OECD average is 14.9%), reading (13.2%) and science (14.0%). Interestingly, Figure V.4.9a shows that this relationship is weaker in problem solving than in the three other domains. Still, even in problem solving, about 10.6% of the variation in performance can be explained by differences in socio-economic status; and on average, a one-unit increase in the ESCS index is associated with a score difference of 35 points in problem solving (Table V.4.13).

■ Figure V.4.9a ■

**Strength of the relationship between socio-economic status and performance
in problem solving, mathematics, reading and science**

Percentage of variation in performance explained by socio-economic status

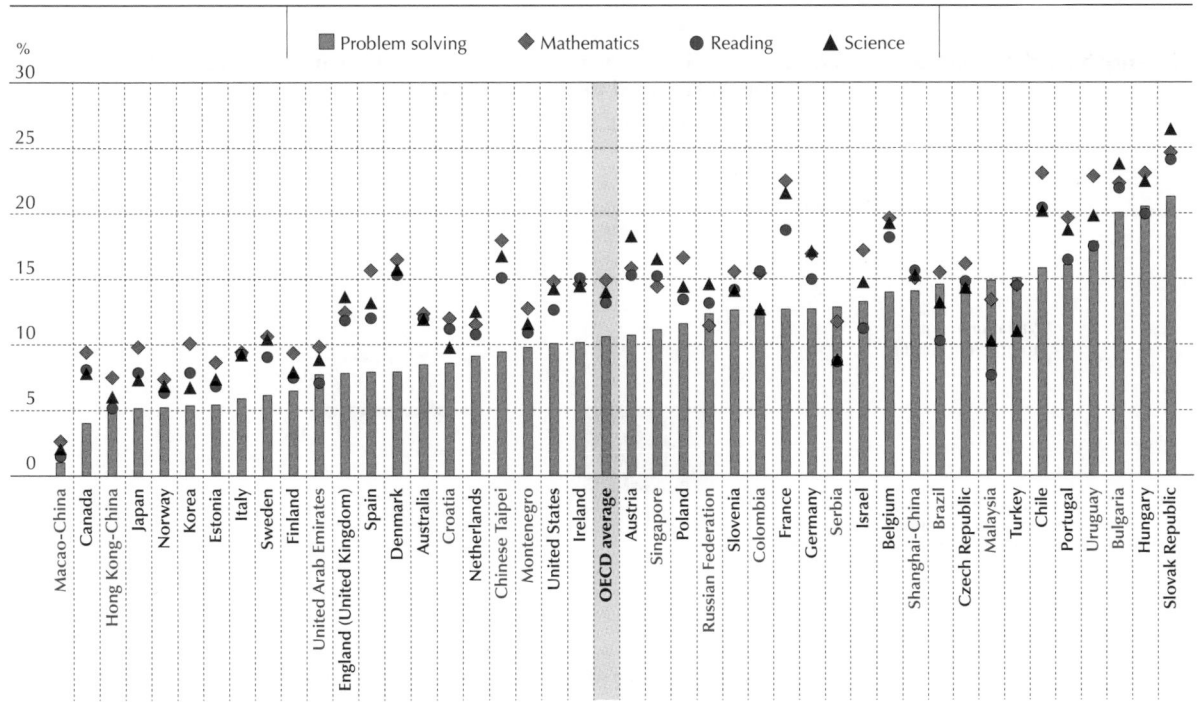

Note: All values are statistically significant (see Annex A3).
Countries and economies are ranked in ascending order of the strength of the relationship between performance in problem solving and the PISA index of economic, social and cultural status (ESCS).
Source: OECD, PISA 2012 Database, Table V.4.13.
StatLink http://dx.doi.org/10.1787/888933003611

As exceptions to this pattern, in the Czech Republic and Turkey, as well as in partner countries/economies Brazil, Malaysia, the Russian Federation, Serbia and Shanghai-China, the impact of socio-economic status on performance is as strong in problem solving as in mathematics. In no country, however, is the impact of socio-economic status stronger on problem solving than on mathematics performance (Figure V.4.9a and Table V.4.13).

Figure V.4.9b further explores the mechanisms through which socio-economic status is related to problem-solving performance. It shows that within the same school, students' performance in problem solving is almost unrelated to their socio-economic status. However, at the school level, schools with more advantaged student populations often perform better in problem solving, while schools with more disadvantaged student populations often perform poorly in problem solving. This school-level association, however, is not distinct from the one observed in mathematics: the schools that have more disadvantaged student populations and poor results in mathematics tend to perform poorly in problem solving too. The variation in performance between schools that is unique to problem solving and can be accounted for by differences in students' and schools' socio-economic status represents only 0.2% of the total variation in performance in problem solving (Table V.4.14).

Thus, the socio-economic status of students does not appear to have a direct association with their performance in problem solving. Instead, socio-economic disparities in problem-solving performance reflect, to a large part, unequal access to good teachers and schools, not a domain-specific disadvantage.

A simpler measure of socio-economic advantage yields the same conclusion: socio-economic differences have a weaker influence on problem-solving performance than on performance in curricular domains, and this influence is not due to a specific association between problem-solving performance and socio-economic disadvantage, but rather to the poorer performance, overall, observed among disadvantaged students. This simpler measure classifies students according to the highest occupational status of their father or mother. The higher-status group includes the children of managers, professionals,

technicians and associate professionals, such as teachers. On average across OECD countries, 51% of students are in this higher-status group; 43% are in the lower-status group, with their parents in semi-skilled or elementary occupations; and 6% have missing or incomplete information on both parents' occupation, and are therefore excluded from this analysis.

■ Figure V.4.9b ■

Strength of the relationship between socio-economic status and performance in problem solving, between and within schools

Percentage of variation in performance explained by socio-economic status of students and schools

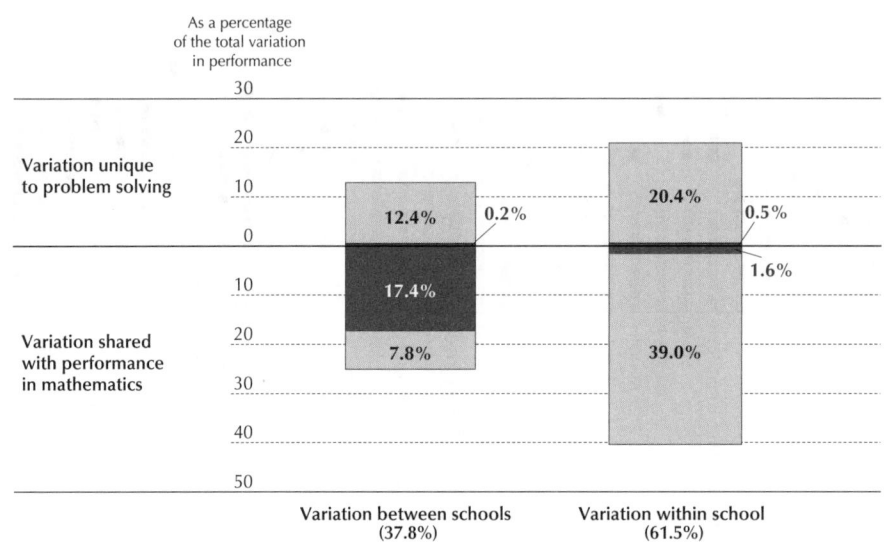

Notes: The figure shows the components of the performance variation in problem solving for the OECD average.
The variation in performance accounted for by the *PISA index of economic, social and cultural status* (ESCS) of students and schools is marked in blue. Estimates shown in this figure exclude students with missing information on the ESCS.
Source: OECD, PISA 2012 Database, Table V.4.14.
StatLink ⚊ http://dx.doi.org/10.1787/888933003611

Students who have at least one parent in highly skilled occupation score 45 points higher than students whose parents work in semi-skilled occupations or in elementary occupations, on average across OECD countries.

The performance gap in problem solving related to parents' highest occupational status amounts to almost half a standard deviation (48%) (Figure V.4.10). However, this gap is smaller than that observed in performance in mathematics (57%) reading and science (both 56%). In Norway, Hungary and the Russian Federation, the performance gap related to parents' highest occupational status is of the same magnitude in problem solving as in mathematics, reading and science; in Shanghai-China, Ireland and Italy, the gap is as large as in mathematics, but smaller than in reading; and in Serbia, the United Arab Emirates and Malaysia, it is as large in problem solving as in mathematics and larger than in reading. In all other countries and economies, the performance gap in problem solving related to parents' occupational status is smaller than that observed in mathematics, and often in the remaining domains as well. In France, Spain and Chinese Taipei, the gap observed in mathematics performance exceeds that observed in problem solving by more than one-sixth of a standard deviation (Table V.4.16).

The differences in problem solving performance related to parents' occupational status can be decomposed into two components. The first is poorer performance overall: students from lower-status families tend to perform less well in PISA than high-status students, irrespective of the school subject. The second is specific to problem solving. It reflects differences, across groups, in how academic potential translates into performance in problem solving, as well as differences in the skills uniquely measured by problem solving. In Chapter 2, the overall variation in problem-solving proficiency was similarly split into two components – one that is common to mathematics, reading and science (68%), and a residual component that is unique to problem solving (32%) (Table V.2.5). If the performance gap related to parents' occupational status reflected only poorer performance overall, it would not affect this residual component, and the size of the gap in problem-solving proficiency would be smaller than that in curricular subjects assessed by PISA.[2]

■ Figure V.4.10 ■

**Difference related to parents' occupational status
in problem-solving, mathematics, reading and science performance**

*Score difference between students whose parents' highest occupation is skilled and students
whose parents' highest occupation is semi-skilled or elementary expressed as a percentage
of the overall variation in performance*

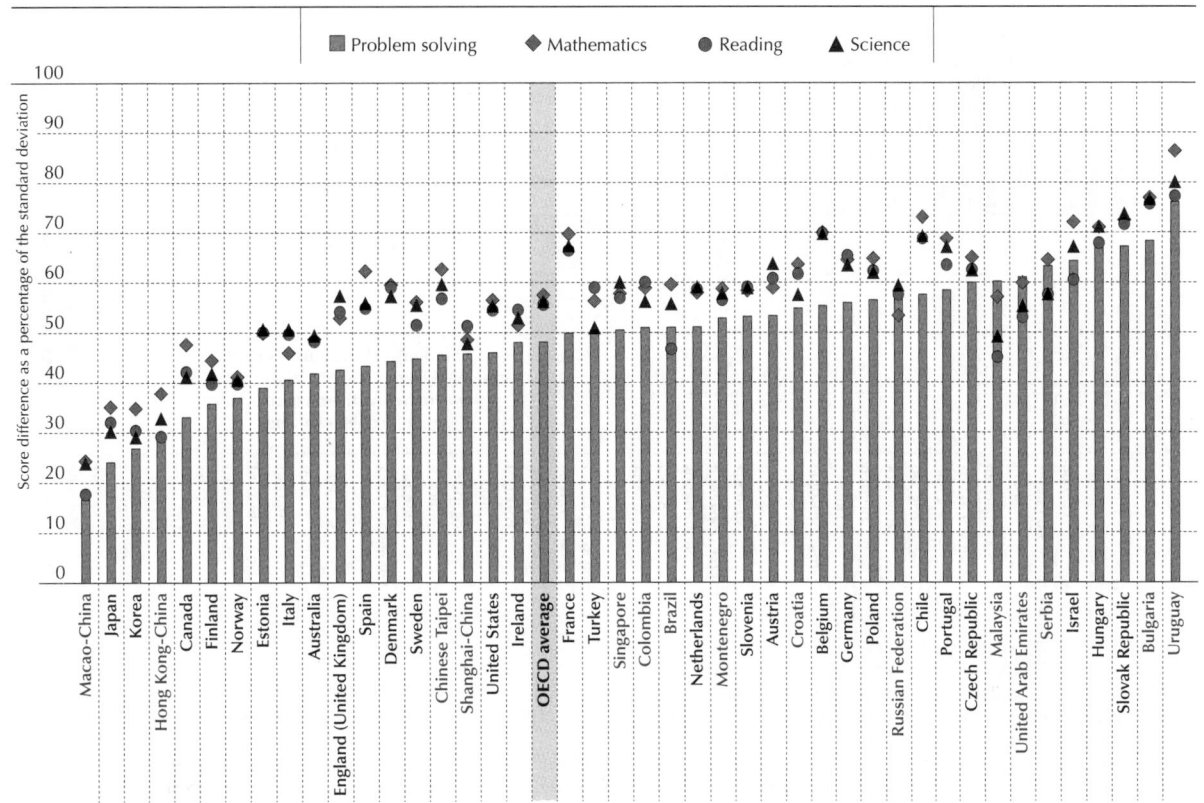

Notes: All values are statistically significant (see Annex A3).
Semi-skilled or elementary occupations include major ISCO groups 4, 5, 6, 7, 8 and 9. Skilled occupations include major ISCO groups 1, 2 and 3.
Countries and economies are ranked in ascending order of the difference in problem-solving performance between students whose parents' highest occupation is skilled and students whose parents' highest occupation is semi-skilled or elementary.
Source: OECD, PISA 2012 Database, Table V.4.16.
StatLink ⫸ http://dx.doi.org/10.1787/888933003611

To what extent does the performance gap related to parents' occupational status reflect a specific difficulty with problem solving rather than poorer performance overall? To identify specific difficulties with problem solving, the performance of lower-status students is compared with that of higher-status students who share similar performance in mathematics, reading and science.

On average across OECD countries, students whose parents work in semi-skilled and elementary occupations perform close to their expected level in problem solving, given their performance in mathematics, reading and science. The analysis of PISA data indicates that the poorer performance in problem solving observed among more disadvantaged students is not related to a specific difficulty with the skills assessed in this domain, but with poorer performance, in general, that is observed across the subjects assessed. In France, Chinese Taipei, Estonia and Canada, however, students whose parents work in occupations considered as semi-skilled or elementary tend to perform better in problem solving than students with the same mathematics, reading and science scores, but at least one of whose parents works in an occupation considered as skilled. One interpretation of this result is that, in these countries/economies, the potential of students from more disadvantaged families is not realised in curricular subjects. As a result, these students appear weaker in mathematics, reading and science than they do in problem solving. In contrast, in the Russian Federation, the United Arab Emirates, Malaysia, Serbia and the Slovak Republic, more disadvantaged students score lower in problem solving than students of similar performance in core academic subjects. In these countries, poor proficiency in the skills specific to problem solving contributes to disadvantaged students' low performance in problem solving (Figure V.4.11 and Table V.4.17).

■ Figure V.4.11 ■

Relative performance in problem solving among students whose parents work in semi-skilled or elementary occupations

Difference in problem-solving performance between lower-status students and higher-status students with similar performance in mathematics, reading and science

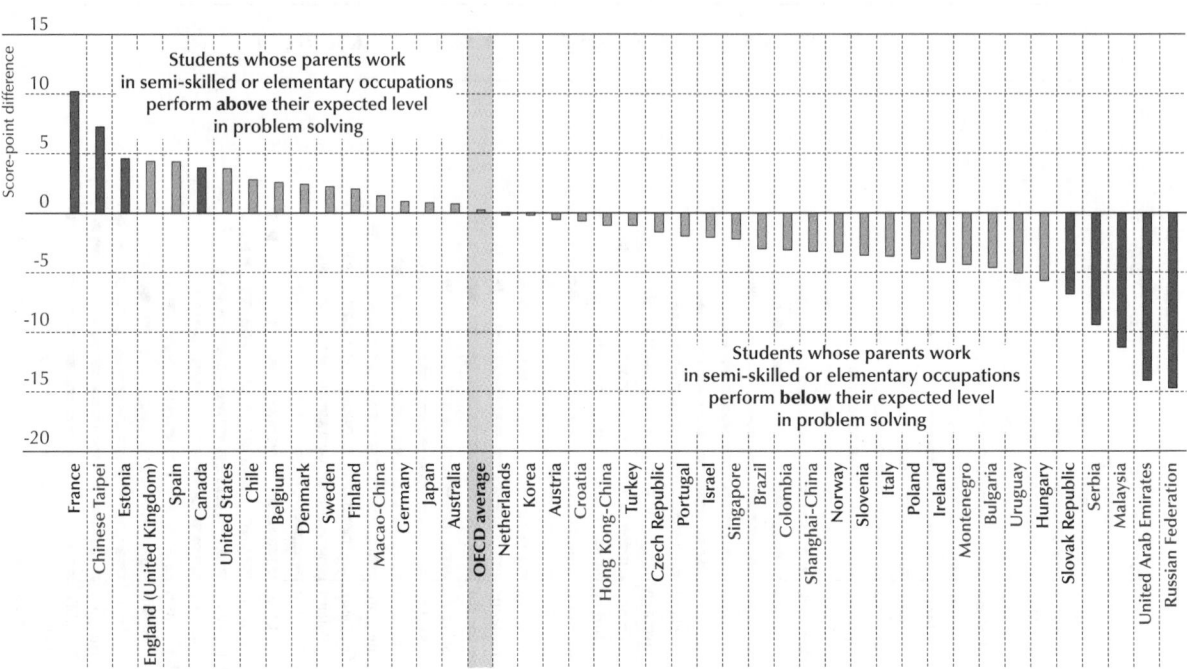

Notes: Statistically significant differences are marked in a darker tone (see Annex A3).

Lower-status students refers to students whose parents' highest occupation is semi-skilled or elementary; semi-skilled or elementary occupations include major ISCO groups 4, 5, 6, 7, 8 and 9.

Higher-status students refers to students whose parent's highest occupation is skilled; skilled occupations include major ISCO groups 1, 2 and 3.

Countries and economies are ranked in descending order of the score-point difference in problem solving between students whose parents' highest occupation is semi-skilled or elementary and students with similar performance in mathematics, reading and science whose parents' highest occupation is skilled.

Source: OECD, PISA 2012 Database, Table V.4.17.

StatLink ᕗ᠍᠍᠍ http://dx.doi.org/10.1787/888933003611

Performance patterns among advantaged and disadvantaged students

Do students from socio-economically disadvantaged backgrounds have different strengths and weaknesses in problem solving than students from more advantaged backgrounds, once their overall performance differences have been accounted for?

In general, students with at least one parent who works in a skilled occupation have the same pattern of performance on static and interactive items as students with parents who work in semi-skilled or elementary occupations; and the pattern of performance, by problem context, is also similar across the two groups. There are slight differences according to response format, in that students from more advantaged backgrounds have relatively more ease with items requiring constructed responses, while more disadvantaged students perform better on selected-response items. All these analyses adjust for the difficulty of items (Tables V.4.18a, V.4.18c, V.4.18d and V.4.18e).

Looking at the performance profile across items measuring the four problem-solving processes, the largest differences in performance related to parents' occupational status are found in items measuring "exploring and understanding" and "representing and formulating" processes (Figure V.4.12 and Table V.4.18b). These are the tasks related to knowledge acquisition and abstract information-processing. In contrast, performance differences are narrower in "planning and executing" and "monitoring and reflecting" tasks.

On "exploring and understanding" items, a larger-than-expected performance gap between higher- and lower-status students is observed, particularly in Italy, Singapore, Austria, Canada and the United States. In these countries, the odds ratio for exploring and understanding items (a measure of the likelihood of success on these items, relative to all other items) is more than 1.2 times larger for higher-status students than for lower-status students. By the same measure, in Chile, Brazil, Sweden and Uruguay, the performance gap in "representing and formulating" items is significantly wider than on other items, on average.

On "planning and executing" items, the performance gap between higher- and lower-status students in Shanghai-China, Turkey, Austria, Hong Kong-China, Canada, Singapore, Italy and Chile is between 1.15 and 1.20 times smaller than (or between 0.83 and 0.87 times as large as) on the remaining items. In these countries/economies, lower-status students reduce the performance gap substantially in items requiring them to set goals, devise a plan, and carry it out. These tasks are often introduced by concrete action verbs, such as "buy", "go to", and others that explicitly invite the student to interact with the system or device, in contrast to "representing and formulating" items, where the task is more abstract (e.g. "complete the diagram").

■ Figure V.4.12 ■

**Strengths and weaknesses in problem solving among students
with at least one parent working in skilled occupations, by process**

*Relative likelihood of success in favour of students whose parents' highest occupation is skilled,
accounting for overall performance differences on the test*

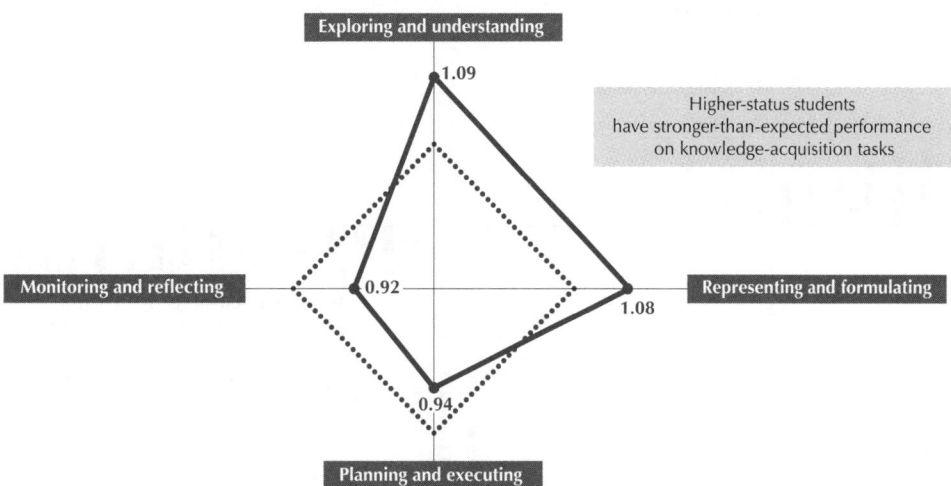

Students whose parents' highest occupation is semi-skilled or elementary (= 1.00)

Success rate of students whose parents' highest occupation is skilled, relative to students whose parents' highest occupation is semi-skilled or elementary

Exploring and understanding

1.09

Higher-status students have stronger-than-expected performance on knowledge-acquisition tasks

Monitoring and reflecting

0.92

Representing and formulating

1.08

Planning and executing

0.94

Notes: All differences between students with parents in skilled occupations and those with parents in semi-skilled or elementary occupations are statistically significant (see Annex A3).

Higher-status students refers to students whose parents' highest occupation is skilled. Knowledge-acquisition tasks refers to tasks measuring the processes of "exploring and understanding" or "representing and formulating".

This figure shows that the success rate on items measuring the processes of "representing and formulating" is 1.08 times larger among students with at least one parent working in a skilled occupation, compared to students whose parents' highest occupation is semi-skilled or elementary, after accounting for overall performance differences on the test and on average across OECD countries.

Source: OECD, PISA 2012 Database, Table V.4.18b.

StatLink ⦿🖹⬛ http://dx.doi.org/10.1787/888933003611

In Colombia and England (United Kingdom), the performance gap is substantially narrower on "monitoring and reflecting" items (more than 1.2 times smaller, or less than 0.83 times as large). In contrast, in Shanghai-China, the gap in performance on "monitoring and reflecting" items is larger than that on all remaining items, on average (Table V.4.18b).

Differences in performance profiles related to parents' highest occupational status may stem from greater access to opportunities for developing problem-solving skills both in and outside of school. Data from the OECD Survey of Adult Skills (OECD, 2013a) show that workers in occupations considered as skilled encounter abstract information-processing tasks and problems that require at least 30 minutes to solve much more frequently in their job than workers in semi-skilled or elementary occupations. These adults are more familiar with complex problem-solving tasks, and may be particularly good at them, thus they may value their children's success on abstract problem-solving tasks to a greater extent.

Immigrant background and student performance

In many countries and economies, children of immigrants are more at risk of low performance in education than the children of parents who were born in the country. A gap in problem-solving performance between immigrant and non-immigrant students is observed as well: children of immigrants tend to perform significantly below non-immigrant students (by 32 score points, on average across the OECD), and immigrant students are 1.77 times more likely than non-immigrant students to score below Level 2. This is not always the case, however: in the United Arab Emirates, Israel, Montenegro, Singapore, Australia and Macao-China, immigrant students score better than non-immigrant students in problem solving (Table V.4.19).

When performance differences between immigrant and non-immigrant students are compared across domains, the difference observed in problem-solving performance appears similar to that observed in mathematics and reading, but smaller than that observed in science, on average (Table V.4.20).

■ Figure V.4.13 ■

Relative performance in problem solving among immigrant students

Difference in problem-solving performance between immigrant students and non-immigrant students with similar performance in mathematics, reading, and science

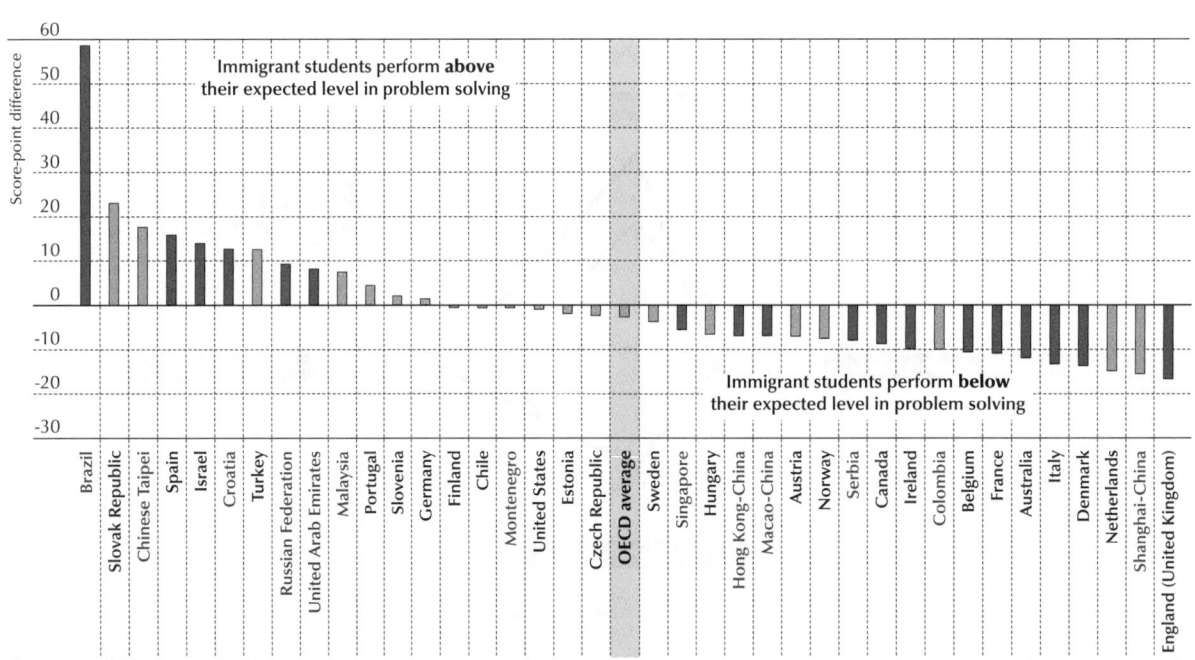

Note: Statistically significant differences are marked in a darker tone (see Annex A3).
Countries and economies are ranked in descending order of the score-point difference in problem solving between immigrant students and non-immigrant students with similar performance in mathematics, reading and science.
Source: OECD, PISA 2012 Database, Table V.4.21.
StatLink ⬛🖼⬛ http://dx.doi.org/10.1787/888933003611

Figure V.4.13 compares immigrant students' performance in problem solving with the performance of non-immigrant students who perform similarly in mathematics, reading and science. On average across OECD countries, there is no difference in the problem-solving performance between the two groups. Significant differences are found in 18 of the 39 countries/economies with sufficient data. This implies that, in many countries/economies, immigrant students' poorer (or sometimes, better) performance in problem solving is related to differences that affect academic performance, in general, rather than problem-solving performance in particular.

When it comes to problem solving, immigrant students in Brazil, Spain, Israel, Croatia, the Russian Federation and the United Arab Emirates perform better than non-immigrant students with similar mathematics, reading and science scores. In these countries, immigrant students are either particularly good at problem solving – or perform below their potential in the assessments of curricular subjects. In contrast, in England (United Kingdom), Denmark, Italy, Australia,

France, Belgium, Ireland, Canada, Serbia, Macao-China, Hong Kong-China and Singapore, immigrant students perform worse in problem solving than a comparison group of non-immigrant students who have similar scores in mathematics, reading and science. In these countries/economies, the poorer performance of immigrant students indicates a specific difficulty in the skills uniquely measured by the assessment of problem solving (Figure V.4.13).

HOW STUDENTS' SELF-REPORTED DISPOSITIONS TOWARDS PROBLEM SOLVING RELATE TO PERFORMANCE

A recurrent theme in the literature about problem solving is that problem solving is personal and directed; that is, the problem-solver's processing of the problem situation is guided by his or her personal goals (Mayer and Wittrock, 2006). Motivational and affective factors at work in a specific problem situation may be influenced by the context (whether it is familiar or not), the constraints and resources available, the pay-offs attached to the eventual outcomes, and the incentives related to the possible actions.

There is no doubt that performance on the PISA test of problem solving is influenced by affective and motivational factors in addition to cognitive potential. The willingness to engage with the problems is perhaps influenced by the assessment situation (e.g. the assessment has low stakes for students and takes place at school) or its mode of delivery (the computer-based interface).

To gauge differences in motivational and affective factors separately from differences in performance, the PISA student questionnaire includes questions measuring students' perseverance and openness to problem solving. Average levels of perseverance and openness to problem solving, and their relation to gender, socio-economic status and performance in mathematics, are presented in Chapter 3 of Volume III, *Ready to Learn*. Table V.4.23 analyses the relationship between students' perseverance and openness to problem solving and their performance in problem solving.

One of the main results of analyses in Chapter 3 of Volume III is that high achievement in mathematics almost always corresponds to high levels on the *index of openness to problem solving,* a measure of general drive and motivation (not related to mathematics contexts) (OECD, 2013b). High levels of openness to problem solving are no guarantee of high performance; in fact, the lowest-performing students among those with low levels of motivation show similar performance on the PISA assessment as the lowest-performing students among those with high levels of motivation. But at the top of the performance distribution, openness to problem solving is associated with large performance differences. The association between perseverance and performance in mathematics is also stronger among high-achieving students than among low-achieving students, although the difference is less marked than that related to openness to problem solving. Everything in the PISA data indicates that high levels of perseverance and openness to problem solving work as a catalyst for ever-higher performance among the most talented students.

When the same analyses are repeated using performance in problem solving instead of performance in mathematics, the same conclusion emerges: perseverance and, even more so, openness to problem solving are strongly associated with performance, particularly at the highest levels of proficiency.

This shows that students' ability to perform at high levels is not only a function of their aptitude and talent; if students do not cultivate their intelligence with hard work and perseverance, they will not achieve mastery in any field. Moreover, general drive and motivation appear to spur high performance in all situations in which students encounter cognitive challenges, not just in an assessment of mathematics.

HOW PROBLEM-SOLVING PERFORMANCE RELATES TO DIFFERENCES IN ICT USE ACROSS STUDENTS

Since problem-solving skills were assessed with a computer-based test in PISA 2012, familiarity with computers may have contributed to students' performance on the test.

PISA data show that access to a home computer is now nearly universal for students in all countries and economies participating in PISA. On average across OECD countries that participated in the problem-solving assessment, 94% of students have at least one computer at home to use for schoolwork. Only in Colombia, Turkey, Malaysia, Japan, Brazil, Shanghai-China, Chile, Uruguay and Estonia is this proportion smaller than 90%. Accordingly, use of computers at home is also nearly universal (Table V.4.24). Across the OECD countries that distributed the optional questionnaire on familiarity with information and communication technology (ICT) and participated in the problem-solving assessment, 95% of students, on average, use a desktop, laptop or tablet computer at home. In all countries except Turkey, Japan,

Korea, Uruguay, Shanghai-China and Chile, more than 90% of students do (Table V.4.25). The few students who do not use a computer at home tend to come from socio-economically disadvantaged families. But even among disadvantaged students, some level of familiarity with computers is now universal in some countries. In Germany, Denmark, Finland, the Netherlands, Norway, Sweden and Austria, more than 98% of students whose parents work in semi-skilled or elementary occupations have and use a home computer.

In all of the 33 countries and economies that both distributed the optional questionnaire on ICT familiarity and administered the computer-based assessment of problem solving, students who use computers at home perform significantly better than students who do not (Figure V.4.14). Because socio-economically advantaged students are more likely than disadvantaged students to use a computer at home, the performance advantage among students who use a computer at home tends to be smaller after accounting for students' socio-economic status, gender and immigrant background. Still, in all 33 countries and economies, students who use a computer at home perform better than those who do not, even after accounting for these characteristics (a similarly strong relationship is observed between lack of computer use at home and performance on the paper-based assessments of mathematics and reading, as discussed at the end of this section); only in Ireland, Finland, Italy and Germany is the difference not statistically significant, possibly because the small sample of non-users results in imprecise estimates of their performance.

■ Figure V.4.14 ■
Difference in problem-solving performance related to the use of computers at home

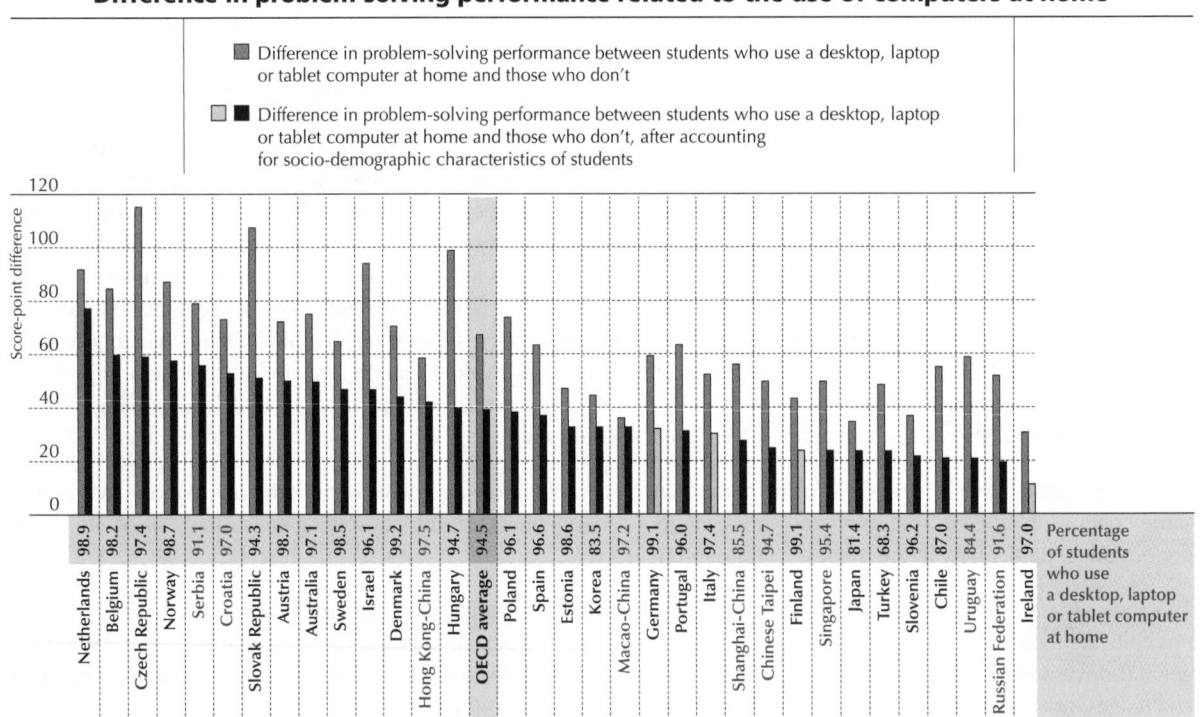

Notes: Statistically significant differences are marked in a darker tone (see Annex A3).
Only countries/economies that participated in the questionnaire on ICT familiarity and in the assessment of problem solving are shown in this figure.
Countries are ranked in descending order of the score-point difference in problem-solving performance between students who use a desktop, laptop or tablet computer at home and those who don't, after accounting for socio-demographic characteristics of students.
Source: OECD, PISA 2012 Database, Table V.4.25.
StatLink ⌧ http://dx.doi.org/10.1787/888933003611

Using computers at school (whether desktop, laptop or tablet computers) is part of the school experience for 15-year-olds in most countries, but is not nearly as common as the use of computers at home. On average across OECD countries, 72% of students reported that they use computers at school. In Shanghai-China, Korea, Turkey and Uruguay, fewer than 50% of students reported that they use computers at school (in Uruguay, 15-year-olds were too old to benefit from the Plan Ceibal, an initiative that began in 2007 and equips all children in primary school with a laptop computer). By contrast, in the Netherlands, Australia and Norway, more than 90% of students use a computer at school (Table V.4.26).

There is no consistent pattern across countries in the performance difference between students who reported that they use computers at school and students who reported that they do not use computers or had no access to computers at school. In the Netherlands, Australia, Norway, the Slovak Republic, Sweden, Serbia, Shanghai-China, Chinese Taipei, Macao-China, Spain and Belgium, students who use computers at school outperform those who do not, even after accounting for socio-demographic disparities across the two groups. In Israel, Uruguay, Singapore, Portugal, Denmark and Estonia, the opposite is true: students who do not use computers at school perform better in problem solving than students who do, after accounting for differences in socio-economic status, gender and immigrant background. In the remaining countries, there is no significant performance difference between these two groups of students (Figure V.4.15).

■ Figure V.4.15 ■

Difference in problem-solving performance related to the use of computers at school

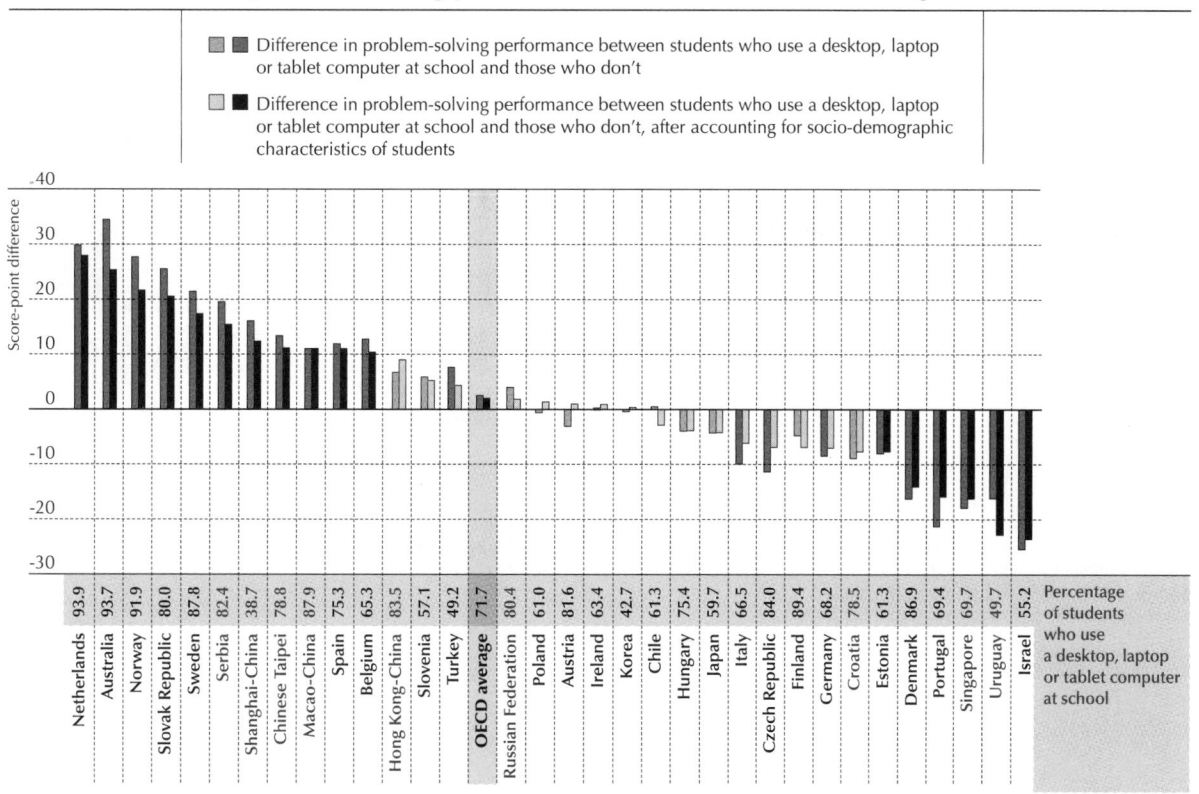

Notes: Statistically significant differences are marked in a darker tone (see Annex A3).
Only countries/economies that participated in the questionnaire on ICT familiarity and in the assessment of problem solving are shown in this figure.
Countries are ranked in descending order of the score-point difference in problem-solving performance between students who use a desktop, laptop or tablet computer at school and those who don't, after accounting for socio-demographic characteristics of students.
Source: OECD, PISA 2012 Database, Table V.4.26.
StatLink ⌨☐ http://dx.doi.org/10.1787/888933003611

In sum, using a computer at home is strongly related to problem-solving performance in 29 of 33 participating countries and economies; but in most countries only a small minority of students do not use a computer at home. In contrast, the relationship between using a computer at school and problem-solving performance varies across countries. It is positive in 11 countries and economies, negative in six countries, and makes no difference in 16 (Figures V.4.14 and V.4.15).

While it makes intuitive sense to link performance on a computer-based assessment with an indicator of computer familiarity, such as the use of computers at home, PISA data show that differences in performance on computer-based assessments are not larger than differences in performance on paper-based assessments, across students of varying familiarity with computers (Figure V.4.16). If students who do not use computers at home perform poorly, then, it is not because these students are at an unfair disadvantage; rather, the fact that these students lack familiarity with computers is indicative of a wider disadvantage in education that manifests itself on paper-and-pencil tests as well as on computer-based assessments.

■ Figure V.4.16 ■

Difference in problem-solving, mathematics, reading and science performance related to computer use at home

Score difference between students who use computers at home and students who don't, after accounting for socio-demographic characteristics, expressed as a percentage of the overall variation in performance

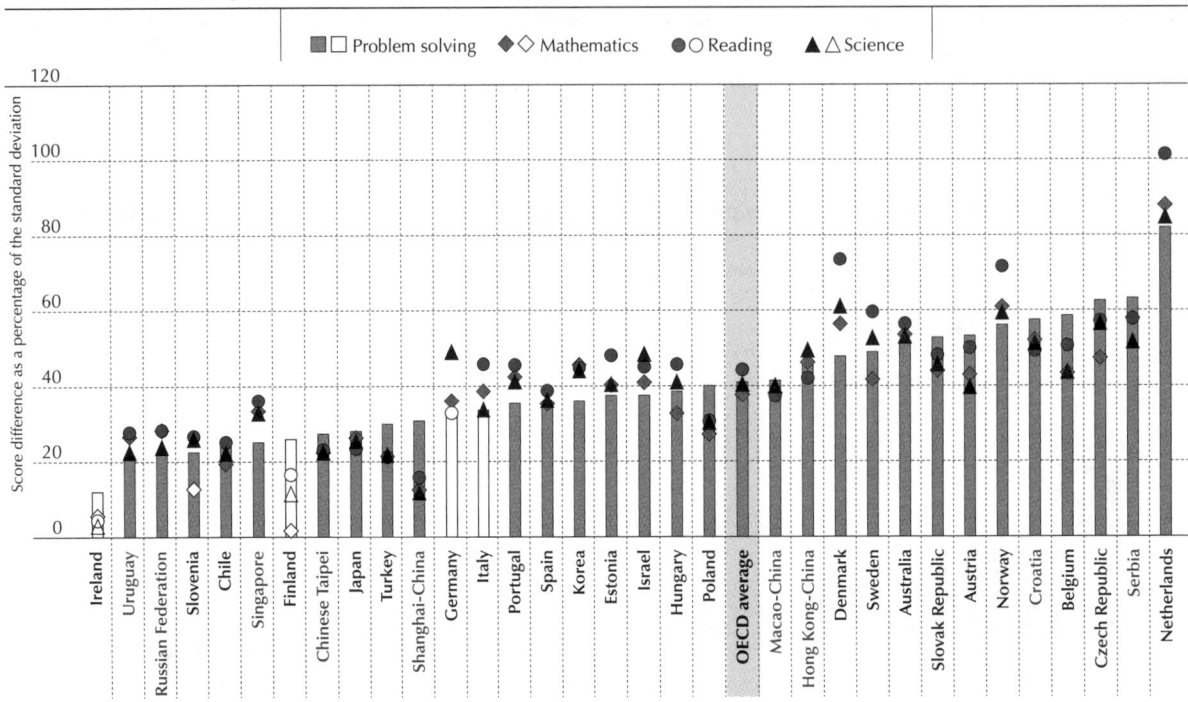

Notes: Statistically significant differences are marked in a darker tone (see Annex A3).

Only countries/economies that participated in the questionnaire on ICT familiarity and in the assessment of problem solving are shown in this figure.

Countries and economies are ranked in ascending order of the difference in problem-solving performance associated with the use of computers at home, after accounting for socio-demographic characteristics of students.

Source: OECD, PISA 2012 Database, Table V.4.27.

StatLink ᵃᵍᵖᵖ http://dx.doi.org/10.1787/888933003611

Notes

1. Based on pair-wise comparisons of national patterns to OECD average patterns. Note that p-values have not been adjusted for the joint testing of multiple hypotheses.

2. Specifically, the fact that problem-solving proficiency shares about 2/3 of its overall variation with mathematics, reading or science implies that one can expect, by virtue of this common variation alone, the socio-economic effect size in problem solving to be at least 82% as large as the socio-economic effect size in mathematics, reading or science ($\sqrt{2/3} = 0.82$).

References

Fennema, E. (2000), *Gender and Mathematics: What is Known and What Do I Wish Was Known?*, paper presented at the Fifth Annual Forum of the National Institute for Science Education, 22-23 May, 2000, Detroit Michigan, *http://www.wcer.wisc.edu/archive/nise/news_Activities/Forums/Fennemapaper.htm*.

Halpern, D.F. and **M.L LaMay** (2000), "The Smarter Sex: A Critical Review of Sex Differences in Intelligence", *Educational Psychology Review*, Vol. 12, No. 2, pp. 229-246.

Hyde, J.S. (2005), "The Gender Similarities Hypothesis", *American Psychologist*, Vol. 60, No. 6, pp. 581-592. *http://dx.doi.org/10.1037/0003-066X.60.6.581*

Mayer, R.E. and **M.C. Wittrock** (2006), "Problem Solving" in P.A. Alexander and P.H. Winne (eds.), *Handbook of Educational Psychology*, 2nd Edition, Lawrence Erlbaum Associates, Mahwah, New Jersey, Chapter 13.

OECD (2005), *Problem Solving for Tomorrow's World: First Measures of Cross-Curricular Competencies from PISA 2003*, PISA, OECD Publishing. *http://dx.doi.org/10.1787/9789264006430-en*

OECD (2013a), *OECD Skills Outlook 2013: First Results from the Survey of Adult Skills*, OECD Publishing. *http://dx.doi.org/10.1787/9789264204256-en*

OECD (2013b), *PISA 2012 Results: Ready to Learn: Students' Engagement, Drive and Self-Beliefs (Volume III)*, PISA, OECD Publishing. *http://dx.doi.org/10.1787/9789264201170-en*

Wüstenberg, S. et al. (2014), "Cross-national gender differences in complex problem solving and their determinants", *Learning and Individual Differences*, Vol. 29, pp. 18-29.

5

Implications of the Problem-Solving Assessment for Policy and Practice

In order to succeed in life, students must be able to apply the problem-solving strategies that they learn at school beyond the curricular contexts in which they are usually cast. This chapter discusses the implications of the PISA problem-solving assessment for education policy and practice.

In a rapidly changing world, individuals are constantly faced with novel situations and unexpected problems that they had never encountered at school, and for which they cannot find specific guidance in prior experience. The ability to handle such situations and solve these problems as they arise is associated with greater opportunities for employment and with the ability to participate fully in society.

Recent evidence from the Survey of Adult Skills (PIAAC) shows that adults who reach the highest level of proficiency in problem solving have access to those occupations where most new jobs were created over the past 15 years (Figure V.5.1).[1] What's more, this trend is related to shifts in the demand for skills that have been observed, over a longer period of time, across the most advanced economies (Box V.1.1). This implies that today's 15-year-olds who lack advanced problem-solving skills face high risks of economic disadvantage as adults. They must compete for jobs in occupations where opportunities are becoming rare; and if they are unable to adapt to new circumstances and learn in unfamiliar contexts, they may find it particularly difficult to move to better jobs as economic and technological conditions evolve.

■ Figure V.5.1 ■

Employment growth across occupations, grouped by workers' level of problem-solving skills

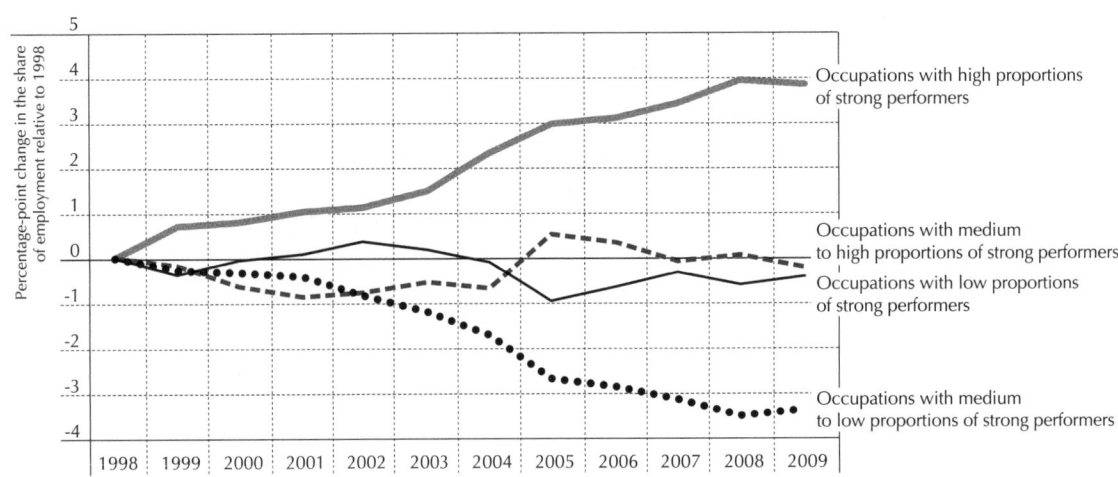

Notes: Results from the Survey of Adult Skills (PIAAC) are used to identify occupations associated with high levels of proficiency in problem solving (proficiency Level 2 or 3 on the PIAAC scale), and then time-series data available from the Labour Force Survey (LFS) database are used to track changes in those occupations over time. Only the 24 OECD countries available in the 1998 LFS database are included in the analysis.
Occupations with high proportions (more than 45%) of workers who are strong performers in problem solving include managers and professionals. Occupations with medium to high proportions (40-45%) of strong performers include technicians and associate professionals (excluding health associate professionals) as well as office clerks. Occupations with medium to low proportions (25-40%) of strong performers include health associate professionals, such as nurses, customer services clerks, sales workers, as well as craft and related trades workers (excluding building workers). Occupations with low proportions (less than 25%) of strong performers include building workers, plant and machine operators and assemblers, and elementary occupations.
Source: Eurostat, LFS database; Survey of Adults Skills (PIAAC) (2012).
StatLink ⟨≡⟩ http://dx.doi.org/10.1787/888933003630

IMPROVE ASSESSMENTS TO MAKE LEARNING MORE RELEVANT

While it is notoriously difficult to teach and to assess skills that are not easily codified in a set of rules or procedures (Box V.5.1), the importance of problem-solving skills in the 21st century is now widely recognised. In many regions of the world, such as Alberta (Canada) (Box V.5.2), employers and parents ask schools and teachers to develop these skills in young people, in order to equip them for success in life.

The PISA 2012 assessment of problem-solving skills represents a major advance towards making learning more relevant. It helps to identify how students can learn better, teachers can teach better, and schools can operate more effectively in the 21st century. Built on a deep understanding of what constitutes individual problem-solving competence, it provides educators around the world, as well as parents, employers and policy makers, with first-of-its-kind evidence on how well prepared today's 15-year-olds are to solve complex, unfamiliar problems that they may encounter outside of curricular contexts.

Box V.5.1. **When solutions are taught, problem solving is not learned**

Every teacher knows that rules and procedures to solve routine problems are relatively easy both to teach and to test. But skills that can be codified in rules can also be performed by a computer. By their nature, the skills needed to solve complex, non-routine problems cannot be reduced to rules, and so they are relatively difficult to both teach and assess.

While everyone agrees that children need problem-solving skills, in practice, these skills have largely been taught by focusing only on rules-based solutions, like the rules of algebra. The rules of algebra are important, but applying algebraic rules is just the second step of a two-step problem-solving process. The first step – the step computers can't do – involves examining the messy set of facts in a real-world problem to determine which set of algebraic rules to apply.

For example, the labour market today values a mechanical engineer's ability to formulate a problem as a particular mathematical model. Once the model is formulated, a computer – not the engineer – will apply rules to calculate the actual solution. How do engineers choose the correct mathematical model? They likely rely on analogies with problems they have solved in the past.

It follows that to develop the expertise and flexibility required by non-routine problems, education in any subject, trade or occupation must include exposure to numerous real-world problems on which to draw.

Source: Levy (2010).

Box V.5.2. **Developing a curriculum for the 21st century in Alberta (Canada)**

Canada is a relative latecomer to the top of the international education rankings. Unlike Japan or Singapore, Canada found itself among the best-performing countries only after the release of the PISA rankings in 2000. Since then, Canada has consistently performed above the OECD average in PISA, although performance declined in 2012 relative to the previous assessments. At the regional level, when compared to the other nine Canadian provinces, Alberta, along with British Columbia, stands outs for its strong performance. In PISA 2012, Alberta students scored 517 points, on average, in mathematics and 539 points in science. With 531 points in problem solving, their performance is in line with Canada's average performance.

Canadian education is governed at a provincial level; thus education systems in each of the ten provinces and three territories have their own history, governance structure, and education strategy.

The Government of Alberta recently decided to develop a new vision for the future of teaching and learning, one that will inspire the curriculum for the 21st century. Through a series of province-wide consultations starting in 2009, the government developed a curriculum redesign project (Alberta Education, 2010). While Albertans expressed pride in their schools and universities, they also voiced the need for a transformation of the education system in order to help students engage in a rapidly changing knowledge-based society. These participatory dialogues inspired and informed the project, an ongoing initiative that involves revising the curriculum with the aim of developing engaged thinkers and ethical citizens with an entrepreneurial spirit.

In this context, a framework for student learning was developed that identifies critical thinking, problem solving and decision making as key cross-curriculum competencies (Alberta Education, 2013a, 2013b). This involves, for example, developing the confidence and skills in students to solve different types of problems, including novel and ill-defined tasks and tasks related to their learning, work and personal lives; stimulating the use of multiple approaches to solving problems; and modelling students' ability to transfer knowledge and experience gained in the past to solve problems and make decisions in the future. Proposals for further collaborative curriculum development are under review and the new curriculum is expected to be launched by 2016.

...

> The open consultation leading to the formulation of the 21st Century Skills Curriculum in Alberta proves that problem-solving skills are valued by the economy and society at large. It also shows how curriculum reforms can provide opportunities to involve stakeholders – including parents, employers, and students themselves – in education, so that learning becomes a common goal and a shared responsibility.
>
> **Sources:** Alberta Education (2010); Alberta Education (2013a); Alberta Education (2013b).

The assessment of problem-solving skills in PISA 2012 recognises that, in order to succeed in life, students must be able to apply the problem-solving strategies that they learn at school beyond the curricular contexts in which they are usually cast. While most problem-solving activities in schools are compartmentalised by subject, such as problem solving in mathematics or in science, success in the PISA problem-solving assessment hinges on skills that are useful in a broad spectrum of contexts, in and out of school. Students who perform well in problem solving are able to examine the problem situation to collect useful information; build a coherent mental representation of the relevant parts involved and of the relationships between them, and communicate this representation; plan a strategy for overcoming the obstacles to resolving the problem and execute the plan while monitoring its progress; and critically review each step and reflect on possible alternatives and missing pieces.

EMPOWER STUDENTS TO SOLVE PROBLEMS

The analysis of results from the problem-solving assessment shows that, on average across OECD countries, about one in five students is only able to solve very straightforward problems – if any – provided they refer to familiar situations, such as choosing from a catalogue of furniture, showing different brands and prices, the cheapest models to furnish a room (Level 1 tasks). In six partner countries, fewer than half the students are able to perform beyond this baseline level of problem-solving proficiency. In contrast, in Korea, Japan, Macao-China and Singapore, more than nine out of ten students can complete tasks at Level 2 at least. These countries/economies are close to the goal of giving each student the basic tools needed to meet the challenges that arise in daily life.

As in other assessment areas, there are wide differences between countries in the ability of 15-year-olds to fully engage with and solve non-routine problems in real-life contexts. Over 160 score points separate the mean performance of the best- and lowest-performing countries – the equivalent of between two and three proficiency levels (on a scale going from "below Level 1" to "Level 6 and above"). In the best-performing countries – Singapore and Korea – 15-year-old students, on average, are able to engage with moderately complex situations in a systematic way. For example, they can troubleshoot an unfamiliar device that is malfunctioning: they grasp the links among the elements of the problem situation, they can plan a few steps ahead and adjust their plans in light of feedback, and they can form a hypothesis about why a device is malfunctioning and describe how to test it (Level 4 tasks). By contrast, in the lowest-performing countries, students, on average, are only able to solve very simple problems that do not require to think ahead and that are cast in familiar settings, such as determining which solution, among a limited set of alternatives, best meets a single constraint by using a "trial-and-error" strategy (Level 1 tasks). Mean performance differences between countries, however, represent only a fraction of overall variation in student performance. Within countries, about 245 score points (or four proficiency levels), on average, separate the highest-performing 10% of students from the lowest-performing 10% of students. Thus, even within the best-performing countries, significant numbers of 15-year-olds do not possess the basic problem-solving skills considered necessary to succeed in today's world, such as the ability to think just one step ahead or to engage with unfamiliar problem situations.

But how can teachers and schools foster students' competence in solving problems across domains? Research shows that training problem-solving skills out of context is not the solution (Box V.5.3). One promising approach is to encourage teachers and students to reflect on solution strategies when dealing with subject-specific problems in the classroom. This metacognitive reflection might support students' own reflection, and expand their repertoire of generic principles applicable to different contexts (Box V.5.4). In addition, such strategies can be applied within all areas of instruction – from reading and mathematics to biology, history, and the visual arts (Box V.5.5). Students who recognise, for instance, a systematic exploration strategy when it occurs in history or science class may use it with more ease when confronted with unfamiliar problems. When teachers ask students to describe the steps they took to solve a problem, they encourage students' metacognition, which, in turn, improves general problem-solving skills.

Box V.5.3. **Problem-solving skills are best developed within meaningful contexts**

Decades of intense research have shown that direct training approaches for domain-general competencies (e.g. intelligence, working memory capacity, or brain efficiency) do not lead to greater capacity to solve problems independently of their domain. Domain-general competencies, such as intelligence, are extremely difficult and costly to train. They can be increased only within narrow limits, and the increases are usually not stable over time. Even more important, domain-general competencies do not help to solve a problem when a person lacks knowledge about the problem at hand and its solution. The highest intelligence, largest working memory capacity, or the most efficient brain cannot help to solve a problem if the person has no meaningful knowledge to process.

A more effective alternative for broadening competencies is to teach concrete content knowledge in ways that aid subsequent transfer to new situations, problem types and content. This flexible kind of expertise, however, does not develop on its own.

One important precondition for transfer is that students must focus on the common, deep structure underlying two problem situations rather than on their superficial differences. Only then will they apply the knowledge acquired in one situation to solve a problem in another. This can be accomplished by pointing out to students that two problem solutions require similar actions; by using diagrams to visualise the deep structures of different problems; by fostering comparisons between examples that highlight their structural similarities or differences; and by the use of analogies between phenomena arising in different domains.

People are less likely to transfer isolated pieces of knowledge than they are to transfer parts of well-integrated hierarchical knowledge structures. The more connections a learner sees between the learning environment and the outside world, the easier the transfer will be.

Source: Schneider and Stern (2010).

Box V.5.4. **What is metacognitive instruction?**

An important component of the problem-solving skill of students is the ability to monitor and regulate their own thinking and learning. Metacognition – thinking about and regulating thinking – is the "engine" that starts, regulates and evaluates the cognitive processes. The learning environments with the greatest potential to enhance these processes are those centred on metacognitive teaching methods.

Various models have been developed to help students regulate their behaviour during learning, in all kinds of disciplines. In general, metacognitive instruction relies on teachers' ability to help students become aware and consciously reflect on their own thought. It is characterised by frequent questioning by teachers or self-questioning by students themselves ("Have I solved problems like this before? Am I on the right track? What information do I need?"). This questioning may take place in classroom dialogue and "thinking aloud" sequences that make the reasoning explicit and model the solution strategies of other students. Metacognitive instruction can be successfully embedded in co-operative learning settings, where students work in small groups with assigned roles.

The problems or inquiries that students work on must have room enough to allow students not only to learn routine procedures that are useful for their solution, but also to practice the questioning and dialogue and to experience some struggle before the goal is reached. In metacognitive instruction, students often work on challenging tasks that require them to think for an extended time. Such tasks also offer many opportunities for teachers to help students learn from their mistakes.

By focusing attention on learning as a process, metacognitive instruction further conveys the message that success comes from hard work; it therefore positively influences dispositions towards learning across the ability spectrum and reduces anxiety.

...

Studies have shown that metacognitive pedagogies can be effective across kindergartens, primary and secondary schools, and in higher education. In mathematics, students exposed to metacognitive pedagogies outperformed their counterparts in the control groups on routine textbook problems as well as on complex, unfamiliar and non-routine mathematics tasks.

Source: Mevarech and Kramarski (forthcoming).

Box V.5.5. **Teaching problem-solving skills through the visual arts**

If you ask someone what students learn in visual arts classes, you are likely to hear that they learn how to paint, or draw, or throw a pot. Of course students learn arts techniques in arts classes. But what else do they learn? Are there any kinds of general thinking dispositions that are instilled as students study arts techniques?

An ethnographic study, based on video observations and interviews conducted in two prestigious art schools in the Boston area (Hetland et al., 2013), identified several habits of mind and working styles – all of which are applicable in contexts beyond the visual arts – taught in arts classes at the same time as students were learning the craft of painting and drawing. For example, through frequent dialogue with their teachers, all of whom are practicing artists, these highly motivated students are taught to *envision* what they cannot observe directly with their eyes, to *observe* carefully, to *reflect* on their work process and product, to *engage and persist* in their efforts, and to *stretch and explore* creative possibilities:

- Envision: Students in the visual arts classes observed in this study are constantly asked to envision what they cannot observe directly with their eyes – e.g. to detect the underlying structure of a form they were drawing and then envision how that structure could be shown in their work.

- Observe: The skill of careful observation is taught all the time in visual arts classes and is not restricted to drawing classes where students draw from a model. Students are taught to look more closely than they ordinarily do and to see with "new" eyes.

- Reflect: Students are asked to become reflective about their art making. Teachers frequently ask open-ended questions that prompt students to reflect and explain, whether aloud or even silently to themselves. Students are thus stimulated to develop metacognitive awareness about their work and working process. Students are also asked to talk about what works and what does not work in their own pieces and in those by their peers. Thus students are trained to make critical judgements and to justify these judgements.

- Engage and persist. Teachers in visual arts classes present their students with projects that engage them, and they teach their students to stick to a task for a sustained period of time. Thus they are teaching their students to focus and develop inner-directedness. As one of the teachers said, she teaches them to learn "how to work through frustration."

- Stretch and explore. Students are asked to try new things and thereby to extend beyond what they have done before – to explore and take risks. As one painting teacher said, "You ask kids to play, and then in one-on-one conversation you name what they've stumbled on."

Source: Hetland et al. (2013); Winner et al. (2013).

REVISE SCHOOL PRACTICES AND EDUCATION POLICIES

Within all countries and economies, problem-solving results vary greatly between schools: differences in problem-solving performance between schools are as large as differences in mathematics performance, indicating that schools have an important role to play in building these skills. Several high-performing countries, such as Singapore, have recognised the importance of schools in developing problem-solving skills and have prioritised problem-solving skills throughout the curriculum (Box V.5.6).

Box V.5.6. **Developing and assessing problem-solving skills in Singapore**

Singapore ranks at the top in problem-solving performance, with students scoring on average 562 points on the PISA scale. The strong performance of Singapore students in problem solving may be related to several aspects of teaching and learning in Singapore.

In addition to the country's emphasis on providing a strong grounding in literacy and numeracy, a sharper focus on developing thinking skills in schools was launched in 1997 with the project "Thinking Schools, Learning Nation" (MOE, 1997). A fundamental review of the curriculum and assessment system was subsequently undertaken, and related revisions to subject syllabi were introduced (MOE, 2014a). National examinations were revised in tandem, giving greater importance to assessing higher-order thinking and problem-solving skills (SEAB, 2014a).

In 2009, Singapore undertook another review that identified the 21st century competencies considered important: critical and inventive thinking; communication, collaboration and information skills; and civic literacy, global awareness and cross-cultural skills. The 21st century competencies framework (MOE, 2014b) now guides the development of the national curriculum as well as school-based programmes to nurture these competencies.

Closely linked to the development of 21st century competencies is a wider effort across schools to harness information and communication technology (ICT) for teaching and learning. Provisions from three waves of the ICT Masterplan since 1997 have enabled teachers to use ICT tools that help students learn and work independently and collaboratively (MOE, 2011a; MOE, 2011b).

At the subject level, the curriculum is reviewed in regular cycles to ensure alignment with developments in the discipline and national educational goals. The mathematics curriculum, for example, has an explicit focus on problem solving and details the teaching, learning and assessment of problem-solving skills. Students are guided to apply mathematical models and thinking to real-world contexts (MOE, 2014c). The science curriculum places scientific inquiry at the heart of teaching and learning science. Students are provided with opportunities to engage with a scientific phenomenon or problem, collect and interpret the evidence, reason, conduct investigations and make inferences or decisions (MOE, 2014d). Social studies reinforce the inquiry mindset, requiring students to examine evidence to support points of view (SEAB, 2014b). Collectively, these approaches help students become more adept at inquiring, culling relevant information to create new knowledge, experimenting with alternatives, and working with uncertainty when dealing with unfamiliar problems.

Teachers are key to ensuring implementation, and there is strong support for teachers' professional learning throughout their careers. The Academy of Singapore Teachers and the specialised teacher academies lead in developing teacher capacity across all schools. Professional learning activities include mentoring beginning teachers, in-service teacher training, and the establishment of teacher-learning communities to promote teacher collaboration (MOE, 2012). In addition, the Ministry's curriculum officers and subject specialists work closely with Master Teachers in the academies to support teachers in developing classroom resources and teaching strategies.

Sources: Ministry of Education, Academy of Singapore Teachers (2012); Ministry of Education, Educational Technology Division (2011a); Ministry of Education, Educational Technology Division (2011b); MOE (2014a); MOE (2014b); MOE (2014c); MOE (2014d); MOE (1997), Singapore Examinations and Assessment Board (2014a); Singapore Examinations and Assessment Board (2014b).

The association between performance in problem solving and performance in the core PISA domains of mathematics, reading and science is strong and positive at the individual, the school and the country levels. In general among students, high performers in mathematics, reading or science also show the highest levels of problem-solving competence when confronted with unfamiliar problems in non-curricular contexts. They can develop coherent mental representations of the problem situation, plan ahead in a focused way, and show flexibility in incorporating feedback and in reflecting on the problem and its solution. Similarly, at the system level, the countries in which students are most prepared to use their mathematics, reading and science skills in real-life contexts are also those where students are most at ease with the cognitive processes that are required to solve everyday problems, such as interacting with unfamiliar technological devices.

Nevertheless, the strength of association between problem-solving skills and domain-specific skills that are explicitly taught in school subjects is weaker than the association between, say, mathematics and reading skills. And while better results in problem solving are associated with better results in mathematics, reading and science, the pattern is not without exceptions. Performance in problem solving, among both students and school systems, is not identical to that in other assessed subjects. In nine countries and economies (Australia, Brazil, Italy, Japan, Korea, Macao-China, Serbia, England [United Kingdom] and the United States), students perform significantly better in problem solving than students in other countries/economies who show similar performance in mathematics, reading and science. Countries where students perform worse in problem-solving than students with similar proficiency in curricular domains in other countries may look more closely at the features of the curricula and instructional styles in the more successful countries to determine how to equip students better for tackling complex, real-life problems in contexts that they do not usually encounter at school.

A closer analysis reveals interesting differences within this set of nine countries. In some, such as the United States, England (United Kingdom) and Australia, the good performance in problem solving at the system level stems mainly from the students with the strongest performance in mathematics. This alignment suggests that, in these countries, high performers in mathematics have greater access to the kinds of learning opportunities that build problem-solving skills. In others, such as Japan, Korea and Italy, the good performance in problem solving at the system level can be attributed to the resilience of many low achievers in mathematics. These countries, more than others, seem to offer students who struggle to master the basic curriculum second chances to develop the problem-solving skills that are required to fully participate in today's societies (Box V.5.7).

Box V.5.7. **Developing and assessing problem-solving skills in Japan: Cross-curricular project-based learning**

Japan ranks at or near the top in all subjects assessed in PISA 2012, and performance in problem solving is no exception. What's more, Japanese students, who score 552 points, on average, show better performance in problem solving than students with similar performance in mathematics, reading and science in other countries and economies, particularly among moderate and low performers in core subjects. On the problem-solving scale, at least 20 points separate Japanese students who perform below Level 4 in mathematics, reading or science from similarly proficient students in other countries (Table V.2.6). One plausible explanation for this is Japan's focus on developing every student's problem-solving skills through his or her participation in cross-curricular, student-led projects, both within the subjects and through integrated learning activities.

In the late 1990's, the "zest for living" approach was introduced by the Japanese government through a reform to the Course of Study, Japan's national curriculum standards. The aim of the approach was to strengthen students' ability to think critically and creatively, and to identify and solve problems independently. This reform prompted substantial changes towards an inquiry-based, student-centred model of learning. The need for improving students' engagement and motivation was at the heart of these transformations.

The new approach led to a revision of subject-matter curricula. The new curricula reduced the content load by about 30%. For example, the number of English words that students had to memorise in junior high school was reduced from 1 000 to 900. The intention was to create space, within each subject, for deepening learning through classroom activities that cultivate introspection, the desire to learn and think, independent decision-making, and problem-solving skills. In 2007, new national assessments that focus on the ability of students to apply their knowledge in real-world contexts were introduced in sixth and ninth grades.

The reform also allocated more time for elective offerings and introduced a new class period in all schools, called "Integrated Learning". In these classes, students engage in cross-curricular projects related to international understanding, social welfare and health, or environmental issues, that provide opportunities to practise observation and experimentation and to discover multiple solutions to problems and draw connections to their own lives (MEXT, 2002; Aranil and Fukaya, 2010). The homeroom teacher is responsible for this class period, and topics are often decided in collaboration with other teachers in the same school. The Ministry of Education, as well as local school boards, produce guidelines and scripted examples for the integrated study lesson, often in collaboration with other agencies and with private-sector employers (see *www.mext.go.jp/a_menu/shotou/sougou/syokatsu.htm*).

...

Students' work is recorded in portfolios and qualitative feedback is provided to students and families, but the work is not formally assessed.

The implementation of this reform sparked some controversy. In practice, the guidelines for teaching the "Integrated Learning" course gave a great deal of freedom to schools and teachers for deciding how to implement the programme, but not all teachers, particularly at the secondary level, felt that they were adequately prepared to do so. This resulted in changes to the curriculum standards, implemented in 2011 and 2012, involving a reduction of the time allocated to "Integrated Learning" in favour of teaching academic subjects (OECD, 2012). Nonetheless, the "zest for living" approach is still promoted throughout the curriculum and the national standards continue to recommend that schools increase the amount of learning activities, in all subjects, that involve the application of knowledge through observation and experimentation.

Japan's constant effort to improve the curriculum and instruction to promote more relevant learning has resulted not only in good results on the PISA test, but also in remarkable improvements, between 2003 and 2012, in students' sense of belonging at school and in their dispositions towards learning (see Volume III, *Ready to Learn: Students' Engagement, Drive and Self-Beliefs*) (OECD, 2013a).

Sources: Aranil and Fukaya (2010); MEXT (2002); OECD (2013a); OECD (2012).

It seems that problem solving is a distinct skill with similar attributes as proficiency in specific school subjects. While influenced by differences in individuals' cognitive abilities, its development depends on the opportunities offered by good teaching. Ensuring opportunities to develop problem-solving skills for all students and in all subjects, including those not assessed in PISA, in turn, depends on school- and system-level policies.

LEARN FROM CURRICULAR DIVERSITY AND PERFORMANCE DIFFERENCES IN PROBLEM SOLVING

Improving the curriculum and instruction to promote learning for life is a huge challenge. It is, to some extent, reassuring to know that students with good results in mathematics, reading and science also have, by and large, good results in problem solving. At the very least, this is consistent with the idea that better instruction in the core subjects corresponds to a greater capacity of students to meet the challenges they will encounter in life beyond school.

Further indications about how to improve the curriculum and instruction may come from the strengths and weaknesses in problem solving that are observed within and across countries. The analysis in Chapter 3, for instance, identifies interesting differences in performance across different types of problem-solving tasks. These differences are likely a reflection of how well students learn, through the content of the various school subjects and the way in which it is taught, to handle unexpected obstacles and deal with novelty.

In some countries and economies, such as Finland, Shanghai-China and Sweden, students master the skills needed to solve static, analytical problems similar to those that textbooks and exam sheets typically contain as well or better than 15-year-olds, on average, across OECD countries. But the same 15-year-olds are less successful when not all information that is needed to solve the problem is disclosed, and the information provided must be completed by interacting with the problem situation. A specific difficulty with items that require students to be open to novelty, tolerate doubt and uncertainty, and dare to use intuitions ("hunches and feelings") to initiate a solution suggests that opportunities to develop and exercise these traits, which are related to curiosity, perseverance and creativity, need to be prioritised.

In yet other countries and economies, such as Portugal and Slovenia, students are better at using their knowledge to plan and execute a solution than they are at acquiring such useful knowledge themselves, questioning their own knowledge, and generating and experimenting with alternatives. While these students appear to be goal-driven, motivated and persistent, their relatively weak performance on problems that require abstract information processing suggests that opportunities to develop the reasoning skills and habits of self-directed learners and effective problem-solvers need to be prioritised.

The analysis in Chapter 4 also identifies, within many countries and economies, certain study programmes whose students perform significantly better in problem solving, on average, than students in the same country/economy with

similar proficiency in mathematics, reading and science. In Shanghai-China and Turkey, for instance, students in certain vocational study programmes have significantly better performance in problem solving than students with comparable performance in mathematics, reading and science in the remaining study programmes. By contrast, in Germany, it is students in the education tracks with the strongest emphasis on academic learning (*Gymnasium*) who score higher than expected in problem solving, given their performance in core subjects. This may be because the instructional practices in the sciences and the arts in these programmes equip students for tackling complex, real-life problems in contexts that they do not usually encounter at school. If this is the case, students in these programmes not only learn the curriculum, they also learn how to enrich their knowledge and use that knowledge outside of school contexts. Alternatively, better-than-expected performance in problem solving may have a less positive interpretation, particularly if it coincides with low performance overall: it may indicate that in these programmes, students' cognitive potential is not realised within the core academic subjects.

Whether it signals strong performance in problem solving or weak performance in the core subjects, the variation across programmes in their relative performance may have profound implications for policy, and invites further investigation. Reducing this variation could involve revising the curriculum and instructional practices within each programme by borrowing the best elements of other programmes, while preserving the diversity in curricula needed to make the most of each student's talents. Even within school systems that encourage diversity of curricula, the acquisition of critical reasoning and problem-solving skills can be promoted as a common aim, as these skills are applicable – and essential – in all pursuits.

REDUCE GENDER DISPARITIES AMONG TOP PERFORMERS

Gender differences in school performance tend to vary across school subjects. In most countries and economies, boys perform better than girls in mathematics, while girls perform better than boys in reading. These gender differences, however, vary substantially across countries. This suggests that the observed differences are not inherent, but are largely the result of the opportunities provided by parents, schools and society in general for boys and girls to cultivate their individual talents.

Gender stereotypes about what boys and girls are good at, and what kind of occupations are suitable for them reinforce and crystallise performance differences between boys and girls, even if they initially reflect only the random variation among students. Because problem-solving skills are required in all kinds of occupations, and are not taught as such in school, but rather are nurtured by good instructional practices in every subject, performance in problem solving should not be strongly influenced by such gender-based stereotypes. Problem-solving performance could then be regarded as an overall indicator of gender biases in a country's education system.

The good news is that in most countries/economies, there are no large differences in boys' and girls' average performance in problem solving. However, countries that do show significant gender differences in problem-solving performance, such as the United Arab Emirates (where girls outperform boys), Colombia and Japan (where boys outperform girls), may not be offering boys and girls equitable opportunities in education, particularly if these differences are also apparent in other subjects. Unless countries invest as much in the development of girls' skills as they do in boys' skills, they may lose out in the global competition for talent.

While boys and girls do not differ markedly in their average performance, the variation in problem-solving performance is larger among boys than among girls. At lower levels of proficiency, there are, in general, equal proportions of boys and girls. But the highest-performing students in problem solving are largely boys – with a few notable exceptions, such as Australia, Finland and Norway, where the proportion of top-performing girls is about the same as the proportion of top-performing boys. Similarly, among adults, top-performers in problem solving are mostly men (OECD, 2013b).[2] Increasing the number of girls at the highest performance levels in problem solving, and improving their ability to handle complex, unfamiliar problems, may help more women attain leadership positions in the future.

REDUCE INEQUITIES IN EDUCATION RELATED TO SOCIO-ECONOMIC STATUS

While large and significant, the impact of socio-economic disadvantage on problem-solving skills is weaker than it is on performance in mathematics, reading or science. At all levels of the socio-economic ladder, there is more variation in performance in problem solving than there is in mathematics, perhaps because after-school opportunities to develop problem-solving skills are more evenly distributed than opportunities to develop proficiency in mathematics or reading.

Still, unequal access to high-quality education means that the risk of not reaching the baseline level of performance in problem solving is about twice as large for disadvantaged students as it is for their more advantaged peers, on average. The fact that inequities in education opportunities extend beyond the boundaries of individual school subjects to performance in problem solving underscores the importance of promoting equal learning opportunities for all. Because current inequities have such significant consequences over the long term, the policies that aim to reduce socio-economic disparities in education can be expected to benefit the lives of students well beyond their school days.

Notes

1. The Survey of Adult Skills (PIAAC) is based on a different assessment framework. PIAAC defines "problem solving in technology-rich environments" as the ability to use digital technology, communication tools and networks to acquire and evaluate information, communicate with others and perform practical tasks. The PIAAC assessment focuses on the abilities to solve problems for personal, work and civic purposes by setting up appropriate goals and plans, and accessing and making use of information through computers and computer networks (PIAAC Expert Group in Problem Solving in Technology-Rich Environments, 2009; OECD, 2013b).

2. The Survey of Adult Skills (PIAAC) similarly finds that there are about three men for every two women performing at the highest level of proficiency (Level 3) in "problem solving in technology-rich environments". On average across countries, 6.9% of men perform at this level, but only 4.7% of all women aged 16-65 do. More equal shares of men and women performing at the top are found in Australia, Canada and Finland (Table A3.5 in OECD, 2013b).

References

Alberta Education (2013a), Ministerial Order on Student Learning (#001/2013), *http://education.alberta.ca/department/policy/ standards/goals.aspx.*

Alberta Education (2013b), Curriculum Redesign, *http://education.alberta.ca/department/ipr/curriculum.aspx.*

Alberta Education (2010), Inspiring Education: A Dialogue with Albertans, retrieved from *http://www.inspiringeducation.alberta.ca/ LinkClick.aspx?fileticket=BjGiTVRiuD8%3d&tabid=37.*

Aranil, M. and **Fukaya, K.** (2010), "Japanese National Curriculum Standards Reform: Integrated Study and Its Challenges", in Joseph I. Zajda (ed.), *Globalisation, Ideology and Education Policy Reforms, Globalisation, Comparative Education and Policy Research*, Volume 11, pp. 63-77.

Hetland, L. et al. (2013), *Studio thinking 2: The real benefits of visual arts education*, 2nd edition (first edition: 2007), Teachers College Press, New York.

Levy, F. (2010), "How Technology Changes Demands for Human Skills", *OECD Education Working Papers*, No. 45, OECD Publishing. *http://dx.doi.org/10.1787/5kmhds6czqzq-en*

Mevarech Z. and **B. Kramarski** (forthcoming), *Critical Maths for Innovation: The Role of Metacognitive Pedagogies*, OECD Publishing.

MEXT (Ministry of Education, Culture, Sports, Science and Technology) (2002), Japanese Government Policies in Education, Culture, Sports, Science and Technology 2001: Educational Reform for the 21st Century, Ministry of Education, Culture, Sports, Science and Technology, Japan.

Ministry of Education, Academy of Singapore Teachers (2012), Professional Networks, *http://www.academyofsingaporeteachers. moe.gov.sg/professional-networks* (accessed 5 February 2014).

Ministry of Education, Educational Technology Division (2011a), The ICT Connection, *http://ictconnection.moe.edu.sg/our-ict-masterplan-journey/our-ict-in-education-journey* (accessed 5 February 2014).

Ministry of Education, Educational Technology Division (2011b), The ICT Connection, *http://ictconnection.moe.edu.sg/masterplan-3/ mp3-towards-21cc* (accessed 5 February 2014).

MOE (Ministry of Education), Singapore (2014a), MOE Subject Syllabuses, *http://www.moe.gov.sg/education/syllabuses/* (accessed 5 February 2014).

MOE (Ministry of Education), Singapore (2014b), Singapore (2014b), 21st Century Competencies, *http://www.moe.gov.sg/education/21cc/* (accessed 17 March 2014).

MOE (Ministry of Education), Singapore (2014c), O- & N(A)-Level Mathematics Teaching and Learning syllabus, *http://www.moe.gov. sg/education/syllabuses/sciences/files/ordinary-and-normal-academic-level-maths-2013.pdf* (accessed 5 February 2014).

MOE (Ministry of Education), Singapore (2014d), Primary Science Syllabus 2014, *http://www.moe.gov.sg/education/syllabuses/sciences/ files/science-primary-2014.pdf* (accessed 5 February 2014).

MOE (Ministry of Education), Singapore (1997), *Shaping our Future: Thinking Schools, Learning Nation,* speech by Prime Minister Goh Chok Tong at the 7th International Conference on Thinking on 2 June 1997, *http://www.moe.gov.sg/media/speeches/1997/020697.htm* (accessed 5 February 2014).

Singapore Examinations and Assessment Board (SEAB), Singapore (2014a), Singapore-Cambridge GCE O-Level examination syllabuses, *http://www.seab.gov.sg/oLevel/syllabusSchool.html* (accessed 5 February 2014).

Singapore Examinations and Assessment Board (SEAB), Singapore (2014b), Singapore-Cambridge GCE O-Level Combined Humanities (Social Studies Elective) examination syllabus, *http://www.seab.gov.sg/oLevel/2015Syllabus/2204_2015.pdf* (accessed 5 February 2014).

OECD (2013a), *PISA 2012 Results: Ready to Learn: Students' Engagement, Drive and Self-Beliefs (Volume III),* PISA, OECD Publishing, *http://dx.doi.org/10.1787/9789264201170-en.*

OECD (2013b), *OECD Skills Outlook 2013: First Results from the Survey of Adult Skills,* OECD Publishing. *http://dx.doi.org/10.1787/9789264204256-en*

OECD (2012), *Lessons from PISA for Japan, Strong Performers and Successful Reformers in Education,* OECD Publishing. *http://dx.doi.org/10.1787/9789264118539-en*

PIAAC Expert Group in Problem Solving in Technology-Rich Environments (2009), "PIAAC Problem Solving in Technology-Rich Environments: A Conceptual Framework", *OECD Education Working Papers,* No. 36, OECD Publishing. *http://dx.doi.org/10.1787/220262483674*

Schneider M. and **E. Stern** (2010), *The cognitive perspective on learning: Ten cornerstone findings,* Chapter 3 in H. Dumont, D. Istance and F. Benavides, *The Nature of Learning: Using Research to Inspire Practice,* OECD Publishing. *http://dx.doi.org/10.1787/9789264086487-en*

Singapore Examinations and Assessment Board (SEAB), Singapore (2014a), Singapore-Cambridge GCE O-Level examination syllabuses, *http://www.seab.gov.sg/oLevel/syllabusSchool.html* (accessed 5 February 2014).

Singapore Examinations and Assessment Board (SEAB), Singapore (2014b), Singapore-Cambridge GCE O-Level Combined Humanities (Social Studies Elective) examination syllabus, *http://www.seab.gov.sg/oLevel/2015Syllabus/2204_2015.pdf* (accessed 5 February 2014).

Winner, E., T. Goldstein and **S. Vincent-Lancrin** (2013), *Art for Art's Sake?: The Impact of Arts Education,* Educational Research and Innovation, OECD Publishing. *http://dx.doi.org/10.1787/9789264180789-en*

Annex A

PISA 2012 TECHNICAL BACKGROUND

All figures and tables in Annex A are available on line

Notes regarding Cyprus

Note by Turkey: The information in this document with reference to "Cyprus" relates to the southern part of the Island. There is no single authority representing both Turkish and Greek Cypriot people on the Island. Turkey recognises the Turkish Republic of Northern Cyprus (TRNC). Until a lasting and equitable solution is found within the context of the United Nations, Turkey shall preserve its position concerning the "Cyprus issue".

Note by all the European Union Member States of the OECD and the European Union: The Republic of Cyprus is recognised by all members of the United Nations with the exception of Turkey. The information in this document relates to the area under the effective control of the Government of the Republic of Cyprus.

A note regarding Israel

The statistical data for Israel are supplied by and under the responsibility of the relevant Israeli authorities. The use of such data by the OECD is without prejudice to the status of the Golan Heights, East Jerusalem and Israeli settlements in the West Bank under the terms of international law.

ANNEX A1

INDICES FROM THE STUDENT CONTEXT QUESTIONNAIRES

Explanation of the indices

This section explains the indices derived from the student context questionnaires used in PISA 2012.

Several PISA measures reflect indices that summarise responses from students, their parents or school representatives (typically principals) to a series of related questions. The questions were selected from a larger pool of questions on the basis of theoretical considerations and previous research. The *PISA 2012 Assessment and Analytical Framework* (OECD, 2013a) provides an in-depth description of this conceptual framework. Structural equation modelling was used to confirm the theoretically expected behaviour of the indices and to validate their comparability across countries. For this purpose, a model was estimated separately for each country and collectively for all OECD countries. For a detailed description of other PISA indices and details on the methods, see the *PISA 2012 Technical Report* (OECD, forthcoming).

There are two types of indices: simple indices and scale indices.

Simple indices are the variables that are constructed through the arithmetic transformation or recoding of one or more items, in exactly the same way across assessments. Here, item responses are used to calculate meaningful variables, such as the recoding of the four-digit ISCO-08 codes into "Highest parents' socio-economic index (HISEI)" or, teacher-student ratio based on information from the school questionnaire.

Scale indices are the variables constructed through the scaling of multiple items. Unless otherwise indicated, the index was scaled using a weighted likelihood estimate (WLE) (Warm, 1989), using a one-parameter item response model (a partial credit model was used in the case of items with more than two categories). For details on how each scale index was constructed see the *PISA 2012 Technical Report* (OECD, forthcoming). In general, the scaling was done in three stages:

- The item parameters were estimated from equal-sized subsamples of students from all participating countries and economies.

- The estimates were computed for all students and all schools by anchoring the item parameters obtained in the preceding step.

- The indices were then standardised so that the mean of the index value for the OECD student population was zero and the standard deviation was one (countries being given equal weight in the standardisation process).

Sequential codes were assigned to the different response categories of the questions in the sequence in which the latter appeared in the student, school or parent questionnaires. Where indicated in this section, these codes were inverted for the purpose of constructing indices or scales. Negative values for an index do not necessarily imply that students responded negatively to the underlying questions. A negative value merely indicates that the respondents answered less positively than all respondents did on average across OECD countries. Likewise, a positive value on an index indicates that the respondents answered more favourably, or more positively, than respondents did, on average, across OECD countries. Terms enclosed in brackets < > in the following descriptions were replaced in the national versions of the student, school and parent questionnaires by the appropriate national equivalent. For example, the term <qualification at ISCED level 5A> was translated in the United States into "Bachelor's degree, post-graduate certificate program, Master's degree program or first professional degree program". Similarly the term <classes in the language of assessment> in Luxembourg was translated into "German classes" or "French classes" depending on whether students received the German or French version of the assessment instruments.

In addition to simple and scaled indices described in this annex, there are a number of variables from the questionnaires that correspond to single items not used to construct indices. These non-recoded variables have prefix of "ST" for the questionnaire items in the student background questionnaire, and "IC" for the items in the information and communication technology familiarity questionnaire. All the context questionnaires as well as the PISA international database, including all variables, are available through *www.pisa.oecd.org*.

Student-level simple indices

Study programme

In PISA 2012, study programmes available to 15-year-old students in each country were collected both through the student tracking form and the student questionnaire. All study programmes were classified using ISCED (OECD, 1999). In the PISA international database, all national programmes are indicated in a variable (PROGN) where the first six digits refer to the national centre code and the last two digits to the national study programme code.

The following internationally comparable indices were derived from the data on study programmes:

- Programme level (ISCEDL) indicates whether students are (1) primary education level (ISCED 1); (2) lower-secondary education level (ISCED 2); or (3) upper secondary education level (ISCED 3).

- Programme designation (ISCEDD) indicates the designation of the study programme: (1) = "A" (general programmes designed to give access to the next programme level); (2) = "B" (programmes designed to give access to vocational studies at the next programme level); (3) = "C" (programmes designed to give direct access to the labour market); or (4) = "M" (modular programmes that combine any or all of these characteristics).

- Programme orientation (ISCEDO) indicates whether the programme's curricular content is (1) general; (2) pre-vocational; (3) vocational; or (4) modular programmes that combine any or all of these characteristics.

Occupational status of parents

Occupational data for both a student's father and a student's mother were obtained by asking open-ended questions in the student questionnaire. The responses were coded to four-digit ISCO codes (ILO, 1990) and then mapped to the SEI index of Ganzeboom et al. (1992). Higher scores of SEI indicate higher levels of occupational status. The following three indices are obtained:

- Mother's occupational status (OCOD1).

- Father's occupational status (OCOD2).

- The highest occupational level of parents (HISEI) corresponds to the higher SEI score of either parent or to the only available parent's SEI score.

Some of the analyses distinguish between four different categories of occupations by the major groups identified by the ISCO coding of the highest parental occupation: Elementary (ISCO 9), semi-skilled blue-collar (ISCO 6, 7 and 8), semi-skilled white-collar (ISCO 4 and 5), skilled (ISCO 1, 2 and 3). This classification follows the same methodology used in other OECD publications such as *Education at a Glance* (OECD, 2013b) and the *OECD Skills Outlook* (OECD, 2013c).[1]

Education level of parents

The education level of parents is classified using ISCED (OECD, 1999) based on students' responses in the student questionnaire.

As in PISA 2000, 2003, 2006 and 2009, indices were constructed by selecting the highest level for each parent and then assigning them to the following categories: (0) None, (1) ISCED 1 (primary education), (2) ISCED 2 (lower secondary), (3) ISCED 3B or 3C (vocational/pre-vocational upper secondary), (4) ISCED 3A (upper secondary) and/or ISCED 4 (non-tertiary post-secondary), (5) ISCED 5B (vocational tertiary), (6) ISCED 5A, 6 (theoretically oriented tertiary and post-graduate). The following three indices with these categories are developed:

- Mother's education level (MISCED).

- Father's education level (FISCED).

- Highest education level of parents (HISCED) corresponds to the higher ISCED level of either parent.

Highest education level of parents was also converted into the number of years of schooling (PARED). For the conversion of level of education into years of schooling, see Table A1.1 in Volume I (OECD, 2013d).

Immigration background

Information on the country of birth of students and their parents is collected in a similar manner as in PISA 2000, PISA 2003 and PISA 2006 by using nationally specific ISO coded variables. The ISO codes of the country of birth for students and their parents are available in the PISA international database (COBN_S, COBN_M, and COBN_F).

The index on immigrant background (IMMIG) has the following categories: (1) native students (those students born in the country of assessment, or those with at least one parent born in that country; students who were born abroad with at least one parent born in the country of assessment are also classified as native students), (2) second-generation students (those born in the country of assessment but whose parents were born in another country) and (3) first-generation students (those born outside the country of assessment and whose parents were also born in another country). Students with missing responses for either the student or for both parents, or for all three questions have been given missing values for this variable.

Use of computers at home

An indicator about students' use of desktop, laptop or tablet computers at home was derived using their responses to the questionnaire on students' familiarity with information and communication. Three items in question IC01 ("Are any of these devices available for you to use at home?") were used: Desktop computer; Portable laptop or notebook; <Tablet computer> (e.g. <iPad®>, <BlackBerry® PlayBookTM>). Students who answered "Yes, and I use it" to at least one of these questions have a value of 1 for this indicator.

Use of computers at school

An indicator about students' use of desktop, laptop or tablet computers at school was derived using their responses to the questionnaire on students' familiarity with information and communication technology (ICT). Three items in question IC02 ("Are any of these devices available for you to use at school?") were used: Desktop computer; Portable laptop or notebook; <Tablet computer> (e.g. <iPad®>, <BlackBerry® PlayBookTM>). Students who answered "Yes, and I use it" to at least one of these questions have a value of 1 for this indicator.

. . . .

1. Note that for ISCO coding 0 "Arm forces", the following recoding was followed: "Officers" were coded as "Managers" (ISCO 1), and "Other armed forces occupations" (drivers, gunners, seaman, generic armed forces) as "Plant and Machine operators" (ISCO 8). In addition, all answers starting with "97" (housewives, students, and "vague occupations") were coded into missing.

Student-level scale indices

In order to obtain trends for socio-economic scale indices from 2000 to 2012, the scaling of the indices WEALTH, HEDRES, CULTPOSS, HOMEPOS and ESCS was based on data from all cycles from 2000 to 2012.

Family wealth

The *index of family wealth* (WEALTH) is based on students' responses on whether they had the following at home: a room of their own, a link to the Internet, a dishwasher (treated as a country-specific item), a DVD player, and three other country-specific items; and their responses on the number of cellular phones, televisions, computers, cars and the number of rooms with a bath or shower.

Home educational resources

The *index of home educational resources* (HEDRES) is based on the items measuring the existence of educational resources at home including a desk and a quiet place to study, a computer that students can use for schoolwork, educational software, books to help with students' school work, technical reference books and a dictionary.

Cultural possessions

The *index of cultural possessions* (CULTPOSS) is based on the students' responses to whether they had the following at home: classic literature, books of poetry and works of art.

Economic, social and cultural status

The *PISA index of economic, social and cultural status* (ESCS) was derived from the following three indices: *highest occupational status of parents* (HISEI), *highest education level of parents* in years of education according to ISCED (PARED), and *home possessions* (HOMEPOS). The *index of home possessions* (HOMEPOS) comprises all items on the indices of WEALTH, CULTPOSS and HEDRES, as well as books in the home recoded into a four-level categorical variable (0-10 books, 11-25 or 26-100 books, 101-200 or 201-500 books, more than 500 books).

The *PISA index of economic, social and cultural status* (ESCS) was derived from a principal component analysis of standardised variables (each variable has an OECD mean of zero and a standard deviation of one), taking the factor scores for the first principal component as measures of the *PISA index of economic, social and cultural status*.

Principal component analysis was also performed for each participating country to determine to what extent the components of the index operate in similar ways across countries. The analysis revealed that patterns of factor loading were very similar across countries, with all three components contributing to a similar extent to the index (for details on reliability and factor loadings, see the *PISA 2012 Technical Report* (OECD, forthcoming).

The imputation of components for students with missing data on one component was done on the basis of a regression on the other two variables, with an additional random error component. The final values on the *PISA index of economic, social and cultural status* (ESCS) for PISA 2012 have an OECD mean of zero and a standard deviation of one.

Perseverance

The *index of perseverance* (PERSEV) was constructed using student responses (ST93) over whether they report that the following statements describe them very much, mostly, somewhat, not much, not at all: When confronted with a problem, I give up easily; I put off difficult problems; I remain interested in the tasks that I start; I continue working on tasks until everything is perfect; When confronted with a problem, I do more than what is expected of me.

Openness to problem solving

The *index of openness to problem solving* (OPENPS) was constructed using student responses (ST94) over whether they report that the following statements describe them very much, mostly, somewhat, not much, not at all: I can handle a lot of information; I am quick to understand things; I seek explanations of things; I can easily link facts together; I like to solve complex problems.

The rotated design of the student questionnaire

A major innovation in PISA 2012 is the rotated design of the student questionnaire. One of the main reasons for a rotated design, which has previously been implemented for the cognitive assessment, was to extend the content coverage of the student questionnaire. Table A1.1 provides an overview of the rotation design and content of questionnaire forms for the main survey.

The *PISA 2012 Technical Report* (OECD, forthcoming) provides all details regarding the rotated design of the student questionnaire in PISA 2012, including its implications in terms of (a) proficiency estimates, (b) international reports and trends, (c) further analyses, (d) structure and documentation of the international database, and (e) logistics have been discussed elsewhere. The rotated design has negligible implications for proficiency estimates and correlations of proficiency estimates with context constructs. The international database (available at *www.pisa.oecd.org*) includes all background variables for each student. The variables based on questions that students answered reflect their responses; those that are based on questions that were not administered show a distinctive missing code. Rotation allows the estimation of a full co-variance matrix which means that all variables can be correlated with all other variables. It does not affect conclusions in terms of whether or not an effect would be considered significant in multilevel models.

Table A1.1 **Student questionnaire rotation design**

Form A	Common Question Set (all forms)	Question Set 1 – Mathematics Attitudes / Problem Solving	Question Set 3 – Opportunity to Learn / Learning Strategies
Form B	Common Question Set (all forms)	Question Set 2 – School Climate / Attitudes towards School / Anxiety	Question Set 1 – Mathematics Attitudes / Problem Solving
Form C	Common Question Set (all forms)	Question Set 3 – Opportunity to Learn / Learning Strategies	Question Set 2 – School Climate / Attitudes towards School / Anxiety

Note: For details regarding the questions in each question set, please refer to the *PISA 2012 Technical Report* (OECD, forthcoming).

References

Ganzeboom, H.B.G., P. De Graaf, and D.J. Treiman (with J. De Leeuw) (1992), "A Standard International Socio-Economic Index of Occupational Status", *Social Science Research* (21-1), pp. 1-56.

ILO (1990), *ISCO-88: International Standard Classification of Occupations,* International Labour Office, Geneva.

OECD (forthcoming), *PISA 2012 Technical Report*, PISA, OECD Publishing.

OECD (2013a), *PISA 2012 Assessment and Analytical Framework: Mathematics, Reading, Science, Problem Solving and Financial Literacy*, PISA, OECD Publishing.
http://dx.doi.org/10.1787/9789264190511-en

OECD (2013b), *Education at a Glance 2013: OECD Indicators,* OECD Publishing.
http://dx.doi.org/10.1787/eag-2013-en

OECD (2013c), *OECD Skills Outlook 2013: First Results from the Survey of Adult Skills,* OECD Publishing.
http://dx.doi.org/10.1787/9789264204256-en

OECD (2013d), *PISA 2012 Results: What Students Know and Can Do: Student Performance in Mathematics, Reading and Science (Volume I)*, PISA, OECD Publishing.
http://dx.doi.org/10.1787/9789264201118-en

OECD (2004), *Learning for Tomorrow's World: First Results from PISA 2003*, PISA, OECD Publishing.
http://dx.doi.org/10.1787/9789264006416-en

OECD (1999), *Classifying Educational Programmes: Manual for ISCED-97 Implementation in OECD Countries.*
http://www.oecd.org/education/skills-beyond-school/1962350.pdf

Warm, T.A. (1989), "Weighted likelihood estimation of ability in item response theory", Psychometrika, Volume 54, Issue 3, pp 427-450.
http://dx.doi.org/10.1007/BF02294627

ANNEX A2

THE PISA TARGET POPULATION, THE PISA SAMPLES AND THE DEFINITION OF SCHOOLS

Definition of the PISA target population

PISA 2012 provides an assessment of the cumulative yield of education and learning at a point at which most young adults are still enrolled in initial education.

A major challenge for an international survey is to ensure that international comparability of national target populations is guaranteed in such a venture.

Differences between countries in the nature and extent of pre-primary education and care, the age of entry into formal schooling and the institutional structure of education systems do not allow the definition of internationally comparable grade levels of schooling. Consequently, international comparisons of education performance typically define their populations with reference to a target age group. Some previous international assessments have defined their target population on the basis of the grade level that provides maximum coverage of a particular age cohort. A disadvantage of this approach is that slight variations in the age distribution of students across grade levels often lead to the selection of different target grades in different countries, or between education systems within countries, raising serious questions about the comparability of results across, and at times within, countries. In addition, because not all students of the desired age are usually represented in grade-based samples, there may be a more serious potential bias in the results if the unrepresented students are typically enrolled in the next higher grade in some countries and the next lower grade in others. This would exclude students with potentially higher levels of performance in the former countries and students with potentially lower levels of performance in the latter.

In order to address this problem, PISA uses an age-based definition for its target population, i.e. a definition that is not tied to the institutional structures of national education systems. PISA assesses students who were aged between 15 years and 3 (complete) months and 16 years and 2 (complete) months at the beginning of the assessment period, plus or minus a 1 month allowable variation, and who were enrolled in an educational institution with Grade 7 or higher, regardless of the grade levels or type of institution in which they were enrolled, and regardless of whether they were in full-time or part-time education. Educational institutions are generally referred to as schools in this publication, although some educational institutions (in particular, some types of vocational education establishments) may not be termed schools in certain countries. As expected from this definition, the average age of students across OECD countries was 15 years and 9 months. The range in country means was 2 months and 5 days (0.18 years), from the minimum country mean of 15 years and 8 months to the maximum country mean of 15 years and 10 months.

Given this definition of population, PISA makes statements about the knowledge and skills of a group of individuals who were born within a comparable reference period, but who may have undergone different educational experiences both in and outside of schools. In PISA, these knowledge and skills are referred to as the yield of education at an age that is common across countries. Depending on countries' policies on school entry, selection and promotion, these students may be distributed over a narrower or a wider range of grades across different education systems, tracks or streams. It is important to consider these differences when comparing PISA results across countries, as observed differences between students at age 15 may no longer appear as students' educational experiences converge later on.

If a country's scale scores in reading, scientific or mathematical literacy are significantly higher than those in another country, it cannot automatically be inferred that the schools or particular parts of the education system in the first country are more effective than those in the second. However, one can legitimately conclude that the cumulative impact of learning experiences in the first country, starting in early childhood and up to the age of 15, and embracing experiences both in school, home and beyond, have resulted in higher outcomes in the literacy domains that PISA measures.

The PISA target population did not include residents attending schools in a foreign country. It does, however, include foreign nationals attending schools in the country of assessment.

To accommodate countries that desired grade-based results for the purpose of national analyses, PISA 2012 provided a sampling option to supplement age-based sampling with grade-based sampling.

Population coverage

All countries attempted to maximise the coverage of 15-year-olds enrolled in education in their national samples, including students enrolled in special educational institutions. As a result, PISA 2012 reached standards of population coverage that are unprecedented in international surveys of this kind.

The sampling standards used in PISA permitted countries to exclude up to a total of 5% of the relevant population either by excluding schools or by excluding students within schools. All but eight countries, Luxembourg (8.40%), Canada (6.38%), Denmark (6.18%), Norway (6.11%), Estonia (5.80%), Sweden (5.44%), the United Kingdom (5.43%) and the United States (5.35%), achieved this standard, and in 30 countries and economies, the overall exclusion rate was less than 2%. When language exclusions were accounted for (i.e. removed from the overall exclusion rate), Norway , Sweden, the United Kingdom and the United States no longer had an exclusion rate greater than 5%. For details, see *www.pisa.oecd.org*.

Exclusions within the above limits include:

- At the school level: *i)* schools that were geographically inaccessible or where the administration of the PISA assessment was not considered feasible; and *ii)* schools that provided teaching only for students in the categories defined under "within-school exclusions", such as schools for the blind. The percentage of 15-year-olds enrolled in such schools had to be less than 2.5% of the nationally desired target population [0.5% maximum for *i)* and 2% maximum for *ii)*]. The magnitude, nature and justification of school-level exclusions are documented in the *PISA 2012 Technical Report* (OECD, forthcoming).

- At the student level: *i)* students with an intellectual disability; *ii)* students with a functional disability; *iii)* students with limited assessment language proficiency; *iv)* other – a category defined by the national centres and approved by the international centre; and *v)* students taught in a language of instruction for the main domain for which no materials were available. Students could not be excluded solely because of low proficiency or common discipline problems. The percentage of 15-year-olds excluded within schools had to be less than 2.5% of the nationally desired target population.

Table A2.1 describes the target population of the countries participating in PISA 2012. Further information on the target population and the implementation of PISA sampling standards can be found in the *PISA 2012 Technical Report* (OECD, forthcoming).

- *Column 1* shows the *total number of 15-year-olds* according to the most recent available information, which in most countries meant the year 2011 as the year before the assessment.

- *Column 2* shows the number of 15-year-olds enrolled in schools in Grade 7 or above (as defined above), which is referred to as the *eligible population*.

- *Column 3* shows the *national desired target population*. Countries were allowed to exclude up to 0.5% of students a priori from the eligible population, essentially for practical reasons. The following a priori exclusions exceed this limit but were agreed with the PISA Consortium: Belgium excluded 0.23% of its population for a particular type of student educated while working; Canada excluded 1.14% of its population from Territories and Aboriginal reserves; Chile excluded 0.04% of its students who live in Easter Island, Juan Fernandez Archipelago and Antarctica; Indonesia excluded 1.55% of its students from two provinces because of operational reasons; Ireland excluded 0.05% of its students in three island schools off the west coast; Latvia excluded 0.08% of its students in distance learning schools; and Serbia excluded 2.11% of its students taught in Serbian in Kosovo.

- *Column 4* shows the *number of students enrolled in schools that were excluded from the national desired target population* either from the sampling frame or later in the field during data collection.

- *Column 5* shows the *size of the national desired target population after subtracting the students enrolled in excluded schools*. This is obtained by subtracting Column 4 from Column 3.

- *Column 6* shows the *percentage of students enrolled in excluded schools*. This is obtained by dividing Column 4 by Column 3 and multiplying by 100.

- *Column 7* shows the *number of students participating in PISA 2012*. Note that in some cases this number does not account for 15-year-olds assessed as part of additional national options.

- *Column 8* shows the *weighted number of participating students*, i.e. the number of students in the nationally defined target population that the PISA sample represents.

- Each country attempted to maximise the coverage of the PISA target population within the sampled schools. In the case of each sampled school, all eligible students, namely those 15 years of age, regardless of grade, were first listed. Sampled students who were to be excluded had still to be included in the sampling documentation, and a list drawn up stating the reason for their exclusion. *Column 9* indicates the *total number of excluded students*, which is further described and classified into specific categories in Table A2.2.

- *Column 10* indicates the *weighted number of excluded students*, i.e. the overall number of students in the nationally defined target population represented by the number of students excluded from the sample, which is also described and classified by exclusion categories in Table A2.2. Excluded students were excluded based on five categories: *i)* students with an intellectual disability – the student has a mental or emotional disability and is cognitively delayed such that he/she cannot perform in the PISA testing situation; *ii)* students with a functional disability – the student has a moderate to severe permanent physical disability such that he/she cannot perform in the PISA testing situation; *iii)* students with a limited assessment language proficiency – the student is unable to read or speak any of the languages of the assessment in the country and would be unable to overcome the language barrier in the testing situation (typically a student who has received less than one year of instruction in the languages of the assessment may be excluded); *iv)* other – a category defined by the national centres and approved by the international centre; and *v)* students taught in a language of instruction for the main domain for which no materials were available.

- *Column 11* shows the *percentage of students excluded within schools*. This is calculated as the weighted number of excluded students (Column 10), divided by the weighted number of excluded and participating students (Column 8 plus Column 10), then multiplied by 100.

- *Column 12* shows the *overall exclusion rate*, which represents the weighted percentage of the national desired target population excluded from PISA either through school-level exclusions or through the exclusion of students within schools. It is calculated as the school-level exclusion rate (Column 6 divided by 100) plus within-school exclusion rate (Column 11 divided by 100) multiplied by 1 minus the school-level exclusion rate (Column 6 divided by 100). This result is then multiplied by 100. Eight countries, Canada, Denmark, Estonia, Luxembourg, Norway, Sweden, the United Kingdom and the United States, had exclusion rates higher than 5%. When language exclusions were accounted for (i.e. removed from the overall exclusion rate), Norway, Sweden, the United Kingdom and the United States no longer had an exclusion rate greater than 5%".

[Part 1/2]
Table A2.1 PISA target populations and samples

		Population and sample information						
		Total population of 15-year-olds	Total enrolled population of 15-year-olds at Grade 7 or above	Total in national desired target population	Total school-level exclusions	Total in national desired target population after all school exclusions and before within-school exclusions	School-level exclusion rate (%)	Number of participating students	Weighted number of participating students
		(1)	(2)	(3)	(4)	(5)	(6)	(7)	(8)
OECD	Australia	291 967	288 159	288 159	5 702	282 457	1.98	17 774	250 779
	Austria	93 537	89 073	89 073	106	88 967	0.12	4 756	82 242
	Belgium	123 469	121 493	121 209	1 324	119 885	1.09	9 690	117 912
	Canada	417 873	409 453	404 767	2 936	401 831	0.73	21 548	348 070
	Chile	274 803	252 733	252 625	2 687	249 938	1.06	6 857	229 199
	Czech Republic	96 946	93 214	93 214	1 577	91 637	1.69	6 535	82 101
	Denmark	72 310	70 854	70 854	1 965	68 889	2.77	7 481	65 642
	Estonia	12 649	12 438	12 438	442	11 996	3.55	5 867	11 634
	Finland	62 523	62 195	62 195	523	61 672	0.84	8 829	60 047
	France	792 983	755 447	755 447	27 403	728 044	3.63	5 682	701 399
	Germany	798 136	798 136	798 136	10 914	787 222	1.37	5 001	756 907
	Greece	110 521	105 096	105 096	1 364	103 732	1.30	5 125	96 640
	Hungary	111 761	108 816	108 816	1 725	107 091	1.59	4 810	91 179
	Iceland	4 505	4 491	4 491	10	4 481	0.22	3 508	4 169
	Ireland	59 296	57 979	57 952	0	57 952	0.00	5 016	54 010
	Israel	118 953	113 278	113 278	2 784	110 494	2.46	6 061	107 745
	Italy	605 490	566 973	566 973	8 498	558 475	1.50	38 142	521 288
	Japan	1 241 786	1 214 756	1 214 756	26 099	1 188 657	2.15	6 351	1 128 179
	Korea	687 104	672 101	672 101	3 053	669 048	0.45	5 033	603 632
	Luxembourg	6 187	6 082	6 082	151	5 931	2.48	5 260	5 523
	Mexico	2 114 745	1 472 875	1 472 875	7 307	1 465 568	0.50	33 806	1 326 025
	Netherlands	194 000	193 190	193 190	7 546	185 644	3.91	4 460	196 262
	New Zealand	60 940	59 118	59 118	579	58 539	0.98	5 248	53 414
	Norway	64 917	64 777	64 777	750	64 027	1.16	4 686	59 432
	Poland	425 597	410 700	410 700	6 900	403 800	1.68	5 662	379 275
	Portugal	108 728	127 537	127 537	0	127 537	0.00	5 722	96 034
	Slovak Republic	59 723	59 367	59 367	1 480	57 887	2.49	5 737	54 486
	Slovenia	19 471	18 935	18 935	115	18 820	0.61	7 229	18 303
	Spain	423 444	404 374	404 374	2 031	402 343	0.50	25 335	374 266
	Sweden	102 087	102 027	102 027	1 705	100 322	1.67	4 739	94 988
	Switzerland	87 200	85 239	85 239	2 479	82 760	2.91	11 234	79 679
	Turkey	1 266 638	965 736	965 736	10 387	955 349	1.08	4 848	866 681
	United Kingdom	738 066	745 581	745 581	19 820	725 761	2.66	12 659	688 236
	United States	3 985 714	4 074 457	4 074 457	41 142	4 033 315	1.01	6 111	3 536 153
Partners	Albania	76 910	50 157	50 157	56	50 101	0.11	4 743	42 466
	Argentina	684 879	637 603	637 603	3 995	633 608	0.63	5 908	545 942
	Brazil	3 574 928	2 786 064	2 786 064	34 932	2 751 132	1.25	20 091	2 470 804
	Bulgaria	70 188	59 684	59 684	1 437	58 247	2.41	5 282	54 255
	Colombia	889 729	620 422	620 422	4	620 418	0.00	11 173	560 805
	Costa Rica	81 489	64 326	64 326	0	64 326	0.00	4 602	40 384
	Croatia	48 155	46 550	46 550	417	46 133	0.90	6 153	45 502
	Cyprus*	9 956	9 956	9 955	128	9 827	1.29	5 078	9 650
	Hong Kong-China	84 200	77 864	77 864	813	77 051	1.04	4 670	70 636
	Indonesia	4 174 217	3 599 844	3 544 028	8 039	3 535 989	0.23	5 622	2 645 155
	Jordan	129 492	125 333	125 333	141	125 192	0.11	7 038	111 098
	Kazakhstan	258 716	247 048	247 048	7 374	239 674	2.98	5 808	208 411
	Latvia	18 789	18 389	18 375	655	17 720	3.56	5 276	16 054
	Liechtenstein	417	383	383	1	382	0.26	293	314
	Lithuania	38 524	35 567	35 567	526	35 041	1.48	4 618	33 042
	Macao-China	6 600	5 416	5 416	6	5 410	0.11	5 335	5 366
	Malaysia	544 302	457 999	457 999	225	457 774	0.05	5 197	432 080
	Montenegro	8 600	8 600	8 600	18	8 582	0.21	4 744	7 714
	Peru	584 294	508 969	508 969	263	508 706	0.05	6 035	419 945
	Qatar	11 667	11 532	11 532	202	11 330	1.75	10 966	11 003
	Romania	146 243	146 243	146 243	5 091	141 152	3.48	5 074	140 915
	Russian Federation	1 272 632	1 268 814	1 268 814	17 800	1 251 014	1.40	6 418	1 172 539
	Serbia	80 089	75 870	74 272	1 987	72 285	2.67	4 684	67 934
	Shanghai-China	108 056	90 796	90 796	1 252	89 544	1.38	6 374	85 127
	Singapore	53 637	52 163	52 163	293	51 870	0.56	5 546	51 088
	Chinese Taipei	328 356	328 336	328 336	1 747	326 589	0.53	6 046	292 542
	Thailand	982 080	784 897	784 897	9 123	775 774	1.16	6 606	703 012
	Tunisia	132 313	132 313	132 313	169	132 144	0.13	4 407	120 784
	United Arab Emirates	48 824	48 446	48 446	971	47 475	2.00	11 500	40 612
	Uruguay	54 638	46 442	46 442	14	46 428	0.03	5 315	39 771
	Viet Nam	1 717 996	1 091 462	1 091 462	7 729	1 083 733	0.71	4 959	956 517

Notes: For a full explanation of the details in this table please refer to the *PISA 2012 Technical Report* (OECD, forthcoming). The figure for total national population of 15-year-olds enrolled in Column 2 may occasionally be larger than the total number of 15-year-olds in Column 1 due to differing data sources.
Information for the adjudicated regions is available on line.
* See notes at the beginning of this Annex.
StatLink ⟡⟡⟡ http://dx.doi.org/10.1787/888933003725

[Part 2/2]

Table A2.1 **PISA target populations and samples**

		Population and sample information				Coverage indices		
		Number of excluded students	Weighted number of excluded students	Within-school exclusion rate (%)	Overall exclusion rate (%)	Coverage index 1: Coverage of national desired population	Coverage index 2: Coverage of national enrolled population	Coverage index 3: Coverage of 15-year-old population
		(9)	(10)	(11)	(12)	(13)	(14)	(15)
OECD	Australia	505	5 282	2.06	4.00	0.960	0.960	0.859
	Austria	46	1 011	1.21	1.33	0.987	0.987	0.879
	Belgium	39	367	0.31	1.40	0.986	0.984	0.955
	Canada	1 796	21 013	5.69	6.38	0.936	0.926	0.833
	Chile	18	548	0.24	1.30	0.987	0.987	0.834
	Czech Republic	15	118	0.14	1.83	0.982	0.982	0.847
	Denmark	368	2 381	3.50	6.18	0.938	0.938	0.908
	Estonia	143	277	2.33	5.80	0.942	0.942	0.920
	Finland	225	653	1.08	1.91	0.981	0.981	0.960
	France	52	5 828	0.82	4.42	0.956	0.956	0.885
	Germany	8	1 302	0.17	1.54	0.985	0.985	0.948
	Greece	136	2 304	2.33	3.60	0.964	0.964	0.874
	Hungary	27	928	1.01	2.58	0.974	0.974	0.816
	Iceland	155	156	3.60	3.81	0.962	0.962	0.925
	Ireland	271	2 524	4.47	4.47	0.955	0.955	0.911
	Israel	114	1 884	1.72	4.13	0.959	0.959	0.906
	Italy	741	9 855	1.86	3.33	0.967	0.967	0.861
	Japan	0	0	0.00	2.15	0.979	0.979	0.909
	Korea	17	2 238	0.37	0.82	0.992	0.992	0.879
	Luxembourg	357	357	6.07	8.40	0.872	0.916	0.893
	Mexico	58	3 247	0.24	0.74	0.993	0.993	0.627
	Netherlands	27	1 056	0.54	4.42	0.956	0.956	1.012
	New Zealand	255	2 030	3.66	4.61	0.954	0.954	0.876
	Norway	278	3 133	5.01	6.11	0.939	0.939	0.916
	Poland	212	11 566	2.96	4.59	0.954	0.954	0.891
	Portugal	124	1 560	1.60	1.60	0.984	0.984	0.883
	Slovak Republic	29	246	0.45	2.93	0.971	0.971	0.912
	Slovenia	84	181	0.98	1.58	0.984	0.984	0.940
	Spain	959	14 931	3.84	4.32	0.957	0.957	0.884
	Sweden	201	3 789	3.84	5.44	0.946	0.946	0.930
	Switzerland	256	1 093	1.35	4.22	0.958	0.958	0.914
	Turkey	21	3 684	0.42	1.49	0.985	0.985	0.684
	United Kingdom	486	20 173	2.85	5.43	0.946	0.946	0.932
	United States	319	162 194	4.39	5.35	0.946	0.946	0.887
Partners	Albania	1	10	0.02	0.14	0.999	0.999	0.552
	Argentina	12	641	0.12	0.74	0.993	0.993	0.797
	Brazil	44	4 900	0.20	1.45	0.986	0.986	0.691
	Bulgaria	6	80	0.15	2.55	0.974	0.974	0.773
	Colombia	23	789	0.14	0.14	0.999	0.999	0.630
	Costa Rica	2	12	0.03	0.03	1.000	1.000	0.496
	Croatia	91	627	1.36	2.24	0.978	0.978	0.945
	Cyprus*	157	200	2.03	3.29	0.967	0.967	0.969
	Hong Kong-China	38	518	0.73	1.76	0.982	0.982	0.839
	Indonesia	2	860	0.03	0.26	0.997	0.982	0.634
	Jordan	19	304	0.27	0.39	0.996	0.996	0.858
	Kazakhstan	25	951	0.45	3.43	0.966	0.966	0.806
	Latvia	14	76	0.47	4.02	0.960	0.959	0.854
	Liechtenstein	13	13	3.97	4.22	0.958	0.958	0.753
	Lithuania	130	867	2.56	4.00	0.960	0.960	0.858
	Macao-China	3	3	0.06	0.17	0.998	0.998	0.813
	Malaysia	7	554	0.13	0.18	0.998	0.998	0.794
	Montenegro	4	8	0.10	0.31	0.997	0.997	0.897
	Peru	8	549	0.13	0.18	0.998	0.998	0.719
	Qatar	85	85	0.77	2.51	0.975	0.975	0.943
	Romania	0	0	0.00	3.48	0.965	0.965	0.964
	Russian Federation	69	11 940	1.01	2.40	0.976	0.976	0.921
	Serbia	10	136	0.20	2.87	0.971	0.951	0.848
	Shanghai-China	8	107	0.13	1.50	0.985	0.985	0.788
	Singapore	33	315	0.61	1.17	0.988	0.988	0.952
	Chinese Taipei	44	2 029	0.69	1.22	0.988	0.988	0.891
	Thailand	12	1 144	0.16	1.32	0.987	0.987	0.716
	Tunisia	5	130	0.11	0.24	0.998	0.998	0.913
	United Arab Emirates	11	37	0.09	2.09	0.979	0.979	0.832
	Uruguay	15	99	0.25	0.28	0.997	0.997	0.728
	Viet Nam	1	198	0.02	0.73	0.993	0.993	0.557

Notes: For a full explanation of the details in this table please refer to the *PISA 2012 Technical Report* (OECD, forthcoming). The figure for total national population of 15-year-olds enrolled in Column 2 may occasionally be larger than the total number of 15-year-olds in Column 1 due to differing data sources.
Information for the adjudicated regions is available on line.
* See notes at the beginning of this Annex.
StatLink ᴬᵐˢᴸ http://dx.doi.org/10.1787/888933003725

[Part 1/1]

Table A2.2 Exclusions

	Student exclusions (unweighted)						Student exclusions (weighted)					
	Number of excluded students with functional disability (Code 1)	Number of excluded students with intellectual disability (Code 2)	Number of excluded students because of language (Code 3)	Number of excluded students for other reasons (Code 4)	Number of excluded students because of no materials available in the language of instruction (Code 5)	Total number of excluded students	Weighted number of excluded students with functional disability (Code 1)	Weighted number of excluded students with intellectual disability (Code 2)	Weighted number of excluded students because of language (Code 3)	Weighted number of excluded students for other reasons (Code 4)	Weighted number of excluded students because of no materials available in the language of instruction (Code 5)	Total weighted number of excluded students
	(1)	(2)	(3)	(4)	(5)	(6)	(7)	(8)	(9)	(10)	(11)	(12)
OECD												
Australia	39	395	71	0	0	505	471	3 925	886	0	0	5 282
Austria	11	24	11	0	0	46	332	438	241	0	0	1 011
Belgium	5	22	12	0	0	39	24	154	189	0	0	367
Canada	82	1 593	121	0	0	1 796	981	18 682	1 350	0	0	21 013
Chile	3	15	0	0	0	18	74	474	0	0	0	548
Czech Republic	1	8	6	0	0	15	1	84	34	0	0	118
Denmark	10	204	112	42	0	368	44	1 469	559	310	0	2 381
Estonia	7	134	2	0	0	143	14	260	3	0	0	277
Finland	5	80	101	15	24	225	43	363	166	47	35	653
France	52	0	0	0	0	52	5 828	0	0	0	0	5 828
Germany	0	4	4	0	0	8	0	705	597	0	0	1 302
Greece	3	18	4	111	0	136	49	348	91	1 816	0	2 304
Hungary	1	15	2	9	0	27	36	568	27	296	0	928
Iceland	5	105	27	18	0	155	5	105	27	18	0	156
Ireland	13	159	33	66	0	271	121	1 521	283	599	0	2 524
Israel	9	91	14	0	0	114	133	1 492	260	0	0	1 884
Italy	64	566	111	0	0	741	596	7 899	1 361	0	0	9 855
Japan	0	0	0	0	0	0	0	0	0	0	0	0
Luxembourg	6	261	90	0	0	357	6	261	90	0	0	357
Mexico	21	36	1	0	0	58	812	2 390	45	0	0	3 247
Netherlands	5	21	1	0	0	27	188	819	50	0	0	1 056
New Zealand	27	118	99	0	11	255	235	926	813	0	57	2 030
Norway	11	192	75	0	0	278	120	2 180	832	0	0	3 133
Poland	23	89	6	88	6	212	1 470	5 187	177	4 644	89	11 566
Portugal	69	48	7	0	0	124	860	605	94	0	0	1 560
Korea	2	15	0	0	0	17	223	2 015	0	0	0	2 238
Slovak Republic	2	14	0	13	0	29	22	135	0	89	0	246
Slovenia	13	27	44	0	0	84	23	76	81	0	0	181
Spain	56	679	224	0	0	959	618	11 330	2 984	0	0	14 931
Sweden	120	0	81	0	0	201	2 218	0	1 571	0	0	3 789
Switzerland	7	99	150	0	0	256	41	346	706	0	0	1 093
Turkey	5	14	2	0	0	21	757	2 556	371	0	0	3 684
United Kingdom	40	405	41	0	0	486	1 468	15 514	3 191	0	0	20 173
United States	37	219	63	0	0	319	18 399	113 965	29 830	0	0	162 194
Partners												
Albania	0	0	1	0	0	1	0	0	10	0	0	10
Argentina	1	11	0	0	0	12	84	557	0	0	0	641
Brazil	17	27	0	0	0	44	1 792	3 108	0	0	0	4 900
Bulgaria	6	0	0	0	0	6	80	0	0	0	0	80
Colombia	12	10	1	0	0	23	397	378	14	0	0	789
Costa Rica	0	2	0	0	0	2	0	12	0	0	0	12
Croatia	10	78	3	0	0	91	69	539	19	0	0	627
Cyprus*	8	54	60	35	0	157	9	64	72	55	0	200
Hong Kong-China	4	33	1	0	0	38	57	446	15	0	0	518
Indonesia	1	0	1	0	0	2	426	0	434	0	0	860
Jordan	8	6	5	0	0	19	109	72	122	0	0	304
Kazakhstan	9	16	0	0	0	25	317	634	0	0	0	951
Latvia	3	7	4	0	0	14	8	45	24	0	0	76
Liechtenstein	1	7	5	0	0	13	1	7	5	0	0	13
Lithuania	10	120	0	0	0	130	66	801	0	0	0	867
Macao-China	0	1	2	0	0	3	0	1	2	0	0	3
Malaysia	3	4	0	0	0	7	274	279	0	0	0	554
Montenegro	3	1	0	0	0	4	7	1	0	0	0	8
Peru	3	5	0	0	0	8	269	280	0	0	0	549
Qatar	23	43	19	0	0	85	23	43	19	0	0	85
Romania	0	0	0	0	0	0	0	0	0	0	0	0
Russian Federation	25	40	4	0	0	69	4 345	6 934	660	0	0	11 940
Serbia	4	4	2	0	0	10	53	55	28	0	0	136
Shanghai-China	1	6	1	0	0	8	14	80	14	0	0	107
Singapore	5	17	11	0	0	33	50	157	109	0	0	315
Chinese Taipei	6	36	2	0	0	44	296	1 664	70	0	0	2 029
Thailand	2	10	0	0	0	12	13	1 131	0	0	0	1 144
Tunisia	4	1	0	0	0	5	104	26	0	0	0	130
United Arab Emirates	3	7	1	0	0	11	26	9	2	0	0	37
Uruguay	9	6	0	0	0	15	66	33	0	0	0	99
Viet Nam	0	1	0	0	0	1	0	198	0	0	0	198

Exclusion codes:
Code 1 Functional disability – student has a moderate to severe permanent physical disability.
Code 2 Intellectual disability – student has a mental or emotional disability and has either been tested as cognitively delayed or is considered in the professional opinion of qualified staff to be cognitively delayed.
Code 3 Limited assessment language proficiency – student is not a native speaker of any of the languages of the assessment in the country and has been resident in the country for less than one year.
Code 4 Other reasons defined by the national centres and approved by the international centre.
Code 5 No materials available in the language of instruction.
Note: For a full explanation of the details in this table please refer to the *PISA 2012 Technical Report* (OECD, forthcoming).
Information for the adjudicated regions is available on line.
* See notes at the beginning of this Annex.
StatLink ᵐˢᵖ http://dx.doi.org/10.1787/888933003725

- **Column 13** presents an *index of the extent to which the national desired target population is covered by the PISA sample*. Canada, Denmark, Estonia, Luxembourg, Norway, Sweden, the United Kingdom and the United States were the only countries where the coverage is below 95%.

- **Column 14** presents an *index of the extent to which 15-year-olds enrolled in schools are covered by the PISA sample*. The index measures the overall proportion of the national enrolled population that is covered by the non-excluded portion of the student sample. The index takes into account both school-level and student-level exclusions. Values close to 100 indicate that the PISA sample represents the entire education system as defined for PISA 2012. The index is the weighted number of participating students (Column 8) divided by the weighted number of participating and excluded students (Column 8 plus Column 10), times the nationally defined target population (Column 5) divided by the eligible population (Column 2).

- **Column 15** presents an *index of the coverage of the 15-year-old population*. This index is the weighted number of participating students (Column 8) divided by the total population of 15-year-old students (Column 1).

This high level of coverage contributes to the comparability of the assessment results. For example, even assuming that the excluded students would have systematically scored worse than those who participated, and that this relationship is moderately strong, an exclusion rate in the order of 5% would likely lead to an overestimation of national mean scores of less than 5 score points (on a scale with an international mean of 500 score points and a standard deviation of 100 score points). This assessment is based on the following calculations: if the correlation between the propensity of exclusions and student performance is 0.3, resulting mean scores would likely be overestimated by 1 score point if the exclusion rate is 1%, by 3 score points if the exclusion rate is 5%, and by 6 score points if the exclusion rate is 10%. If the correlation between the propensity of exclusions and student performance is 0.5, resulting mean scores would be overestimated by 1 score point if the exclusion rate is 1%, by 5 score points if the exclusion rate is 5%, and by 10 score points if the exclusion rate is 10%. For this calculation, a model was employed that assumes a bivariate normal distribution for performance and the propensity to participate. For details, see the *PISA 2012 Technical Report* (OECD, forthcoming).

Sampling procedures and response rates

The accuracy of any survey results depends on the quality of the information on which national samples are based as well as on the sampling procedures. Quality standards, procedures, instruments and verification mechanisms were developed for PISA that ensured that national samples yielded comparable data and that the results could be compared with confidence.

Most PISA samples were designed as two-stage stratified samples (where countries applied different sampling designs, these are documented in the *PISA 2012 Technical Report* [OECD, forthcoming]). The first stage consisted of sampling individual schools in which 15-year-old students could be enrolled. Schools were sampled systematically with probabilities proportional to size, the measure of size being a function of the estimated number of eligible (15-year-old) students enrolled. A minimum of 150 schools were selected in each country (where this number existed), although the requirements for national analyses often required a somewhat larger sample. As the schools were sampled, replacement schools were simultaneously identified, in case a sampled school chose not to participate in PISA 2012.

In the case of Iceland, Liechtenstein, Luxembourg, Macao-China and Qatar, all schools and all eligible students within schools were included in the sample.

Experts from the PISA Consortium performed the sample selection process for most participating countries and monitored it closely in those countries that selected their own samples. The second stage of the selection process sampled students within sampled schools. Once schools were selected, a list of each sampled school's 15-year-old students was prepared. From this list, 35 students were then selected with equal probability (all 15-year-old students were selected if fewer than 35 were enrolled). The number of students to be sampled per school could deviate from 35, but could not be less than 20.

Data-quality standards in PISA required minimum participation rates for schools as well as for students. These standards were established to minimise the potential for response biases. In the case of countries meeting these standards, it was likely that any bias resulting from non-response would be negligible, i.e. typically smaller than the sampling error.

A minimum response rate of 85% was required for the schools initially selected. Where the initial response rate of schools was between 65% and 85%, however, an acceptable school response rate could still be achieved through the use of replacement schools. This procedure brought with it a risk of increased response bias. Participating countries were, therefore, encouraged to persuade as many of the schools in the original sample as possible to participate. Schools with a student participation rate between 25% and 50% were not regarded as participating schools, but data from these schools were included in the database and contributed to the various estimations. Data from schools with a student participation rate of less than 25% were excluded from the database.

PISA 2012 also required a minimum participation rate of 80% of students within participating schools. This minimum participation rate had to be met at the national level, not necessarily by each participating school. Follow-up sessions were required in schools in which too few students had participated in the original assessment sessions. Student participation rates were calculated over all original schools, and also over all schools, whether original sample or replacement schools, and from the participation of students in both the original assessment and any follow-up sessions. A student who participated in the original or follow-up cognitive sessions was regarded as a participant. Those who attended only the questionnaire session were included in the international database and contributed to the statistics presented in this publication if they provided at least a description of their father's or mother's occupation.

[Part 1/2]

Table A2.3 **Response rates**

		Initial sample – before school replacement					Final sample – after school replacement		
		Weighted school participation rate before replacement (%)	Weighted number of responding schools (weighted also by enrolment)	Weighted number of schools sampled (responding and non-responding) (weighted also by enrolment)	Number of responding schools (unweighted)	Number of responding and non-responding schools (unweighted)	Weighted school participation rate after replacement (%)	Weighted number of responding schools (weighted also by enrolment)	Weighted number of schools sampled (responding and non-responding) (weighted also by enrolment)
		(1)	(2)	(3)	(4)	(5)	(6)	(7)	(8)
OECD	Australia	98	268 631	274 432	757	790	98	268 631	274 432
	Austria	100	88 967	88 967	191	191	100	88 967	88 967
	Belgium	84	100 482	119 019	246	294	97	115 004	119 006
	Canada	91	362 178	396 757	828	907	93	368 600	396 757
	Chile	92	220 009	239 429	200	224	99	236 576	239 370
	Czech Republic	98	87 238	88 884	292	297	100	88 447	88 797
	Denmark	87	61 749	71 015	311	366	96	67 709	70 892
	Estonia	100	12 046	12 046	206	206	100	12 046	12 046
	Finland	99	59 740	60 323	310	313	99	59 912	60 323
	France	97	703 458	728 401	223	231	97	703 458	728 401
	Germany	98	735 944	753 179	227	233	98	737 778	753 179
	Greece	93	95 107	102 087	176	192	99	100 892	102 053
	Hungary	98	99 317	101 751	198	208	99	101 187	101 751
	Iceland	99	4 395	4 424	133	140	99	4 395	4 424
	Ireland	99	56 962	57 711	182	185	99	57 316	57 711
	Israel	91	99 543	109 326	166	186	94	103 075	109 895
	Italy	89	478 317	536 921	1 104	1 232	97	522 686	536 821
	Japan	86	1 015 198	1 175 794	173	200	96	1 123 211	1 175 794
	Korea	100	661 575	662 510	156	157	100	661 575	662 510
	Luxembourg	100	5 931	5 931	42	42	100	5 931	5 931
	Mexico	92	1 323 816	1 442 242	1 431	1 562	95	1 374 615	1 442 234
	Netherlands	75	139 709	185 468	148	199	89	165 635	185 320
	New Zealand	81	47 441	58 676	156	197	89	52 360	58 616
	Norway	85	54 201	63 653	177	208	95	60 270	63 642
	Poland	85	343 344	402 116	159	188	98	393 872	402 116
	Portugal	95	122 238	128 129	186	195	96	122 713	128 050
	Slovak Republic	87	50 182	57 353	202	236	99	57 599	58 201
	Slovenia	98	18 329	18 680	335	353	98	18 329	18 680
	Spain	100	402 604	403 999	902	904	100	402 604	403 999
	Sweden	99	98 645	99 726	207	211	100	99 536	99 767
	Switzerland	94	78 825	83 450	397	422	98	82 032	83 424
	Turkey	97	921 643	945 357	165	170	100	944 807	945 357
	United Kingdom	80	564 438	705 011	477	550	89	624 499	699 839
	United States	67	2 647 253	3 945 575	139	207	77	3 040 661	3 938 077
Partners	Albania	100	49 632	49 632	204	204	100	49 632	49 632
	Argentina	95	578 723	606 069	218	229	96	580 989	606 069
	Brazil	93	2 545 863	2 745 045	803	886	95	2 622 293	2 747 688
	Bulgaria	99	57 101	57 574	186	188	100	57 464	57 574
	Colombia	87	530 553	612 605	323	363	97	596 557	612 261
	Costa Rica	99	64 235	64 920	191	193	99	64 235	64 920
	Croatia	99	45 037	45 636	161	164	100	45 608	45 636
	Cyprus*	97	9 485	9 821	117	131	97	9 485	9 821
	Hong Kong-China	79	60 277	76 589	123	156	94	72 064	76 567
	Indonesia	95	2 799 943	2 950 696	199	210	98	2 892 365	2 951 028
	Jordan	100	119 147	119 147	233	233	100	119 147	119 147
	Kazakhstan	100	239 767	239 767	218	218	100	239 767	239 767
	Latvia	88	15 371	17 488	186	213	100	17 428	17 448
	Liechtenstein	100	382	382	12	12	100	382	382
	Lithuania	98	33 989	34 614	211	216	100	34 604	34 604
	Macao-China	100	5 410	5 410	45	45	100	5 410	5 410
	Malaysia	100	455 543	455 543	164	164	100	455 543	455 543
	Montenegro	100	8 540	8 540	51	51	100	8 540	8 540
	Peru	98	503 915	514 574	238	243	99	507 602	514 574
	Qatar	100	11 333	11 340	157	164	100	11 333	11 340
	Romania	100	139 597	139 597	178	178	100	139 597	139 597
	Russian Federation	100	1 243 564	1 243 564	227	227	100	1 243 564	1 243 564
	Serbia	90	65 537	72 819	143	160	95	69 433	72 752
	Shanghai-China	100	89 832	89 832	155	155	100	89 832	89 832
	Singapore	98	50 415	51 687	170	176	98	50 945	51 896
	Chinese Taipei	100	324 667	324 667	163	163	100	324 667	324 667
	Thailand	98	757 516	772 654	235	240	100	772 452	772 654
	Tunisia	99	129 229	130 141	152	153	99	129 229	130 141
	United Arab Emirates	99	46 469	46 748	453	460	99	46 469	46 748
	Uruguay	99	45 736	46 009	179	180	100	46 009	46 009
	Viet Nam	100	1 068 462	1 068 462	162	162	100	1 068 462	1 068 462

Information for the adjudicated regions is available on line.
* See notes at the beginning of this Annex.
StatLink http://dx.doi.org/10.1787/888933003725

[Part 2/2]

Table A2.3 **Response rates**

		Final sample – after school replacement			Final sample – students within schools after school replacement			
		Number of responding schools (unweighted)	Number of responding and non-responding schools (unweighted)	Weighted student participation rate after replacement (%)	Number of students assessed (weighted)	Number of students sampled (assessed and absent) (weighted)	Number of students assessed (unweighted)	Number of students sampled (assessed and absent) (unweighted)
		(9)	(10)	(11)	(12)	(13)	(14)	(15)
OECD	Australia	757	790	87	213 495	246 012	17 491	20 799
	Austria	191	191	92	75 393	82 242	4 756	5 318
	Belgium	282	294	91	103 914	114 360	9 649	10 595
	Canada	840	907	81	261 928	324 328	20 994	25 835
	Chile	221	224	95	214 558	226 689	6 857	7 246
	Czech Republic	295	297	90	73 536	81 642	6 528	7 222
	Denmark	339	366	89	56 096	62 988	7 463	8 496
	Estonia	206	206	93	10 807	11 634	5 867	6 316
	Finland	311	313	91	54 126	59 653	8 829	9 789
	France	223	231	89	605 371	676 730	5 641	6 308
	Germany	228	233	93	692 226	742 416	4 990	5 355
	Greece	188	192	97	92 444	95 580	5 125	5 301
	Hungary	204	208	93	84 032	90 652	4 810	5 184
	Iceland	133	140	85	3 503	4 135	3 503	4 135
	Ireland	183	185	84	45 115	53 644	5 016	5 977
	Israel	172	186	90	91 181	101 288	6 061	6 727
	Italy	1 186	1 232	93	473 104	510 005	38 084	41 003
	Japan	191	200	96	1 034 803	1 076 786	6 351	6 609
	Korea	156	157	99	595 461	603 004	5 033	5 101
	Luxembourg	42	42	95	5 260	5 523	5 260	5 523
	Mexico	1 468	1 562	94	1 193 866	1 271 639	33 786	35 972
	Netherlands	177	199	85	148 432	174 697	4 434	5 215
	New Zealand	177	197	85	40 397	47 703	5 248	6 206
	Norway	197	208	91	51 155	56 286	4 686	5 156
	Poland	182	188	88	325 389	371 434	5 629	6 452
	Portugal	187	195	87	80 719	92 395	5 608	6 426
	Slovak Republic	231	236	94	50 544	53 912	5 737	6 106
	Slovenia	335	353	90	16 146	17 849	7 211	7 921
	Spain	902	904	90	334 382	372 042	26 443	29 027
	Sweden	209	211	92	87 359	94 784	4 739	5 141
	Switzerland	410	422	92	72 116	78 424	11 218	12 138
	Turkey	169	170	98	850 830	866 269	4 847	4 939
	United Kingdom	505	550	86	528 231	613 736	12 638	14 649
	United States	161	207	89	2 429 718	2 734 268	6 094	6 848
Partners	Albania	204	204	92	39 275	42 466	4 743	5 102
	Argentina	219	229	88	457 294	519 733	5 804	6 680
	Brazil	837	886	90	2 133 035	2 368 438	19 877	22 326
	Bulgaria	187	188	96	51 819	54 145	5 280	5 508
	Colombia	352	363	93	507 178	544 862	11 164	12 045
	Costa Rica	191	193	89	35 525	39 930	4 582	5 187
	Croatia	163	164	92	41 912	45 473	6 153	6 675
	Cyprus*	117	131	93	8 719	9 344	5 078	5 458
	Hong Kong-China	147	156	93	62 059	66 665	4 659	5 004
	Indonesia	206	210	95	2 478 961	2 605 254	5 579	5 885
	Jordan	233	233	95	105 493	111 098	7 038	7 402
	Kazakhstan	218	218	99	206 053	208 411	5 808	5 874
	Latvia	211	213	91	14 579	16 039	5 276	5 785
	Liechtenstein	12	12	93	293	314	293	314
	Lithuania	216	216	92	30 429	33 042	4 618	5 018
	Macao-China	45	45	99	5 335	5 366	5 335	5 366
	Malaysia	164	164	94	405 983	432 080	5 197	5 529
	Montenegro	51	51	94	7 233	7 714	4 799	5 117
	Peru	240	243	96	398 193	414 728	6 035	6 291
	Qatar	157	164	100	10 966	10 996	10 966	10 996
	Romania	178	178	98	137 860	140 915	5 074	5 188
	Russian Federation	227	227	97	1 141 317	1 172 539	6 418	6 602
	Serbia	152	160	93	60 366	64 658	4 681	5 017
	Shanghai-China	155	155	98	83 821	85 127	6 374	6 467
	Singapore	172	176	94	47 465	50 330	5 546	5 887
	Chinese Taipei	163	163	96	281 799	292 542	6 046	6 279
	Thailand	239	240	99	695 088	702 818	6 606	6 681
	Tunisia	152	153	90	108 342	119 917	4 391	4 857
	United Arab Emirates	453	460	95	38 228	40 384	11 460	12 148
	Uruguay	180	180	90	35 800	39 771	5 315	5 904
	Viet Nam	162	162	100	955 222	956 517	4 959	4 966

Information for the adjudicated regions is available on line.
* See notes at the beginning of this Annex.
StatLink http://dx.doi.org/10.1787/888933003725

Table A2.3 shows the response rates for students and schools, before and after replacement.

- *Column 1* shows the *weighted participation rate of schools before replacement*. This is obtained by dividing Column 2 by Column 3, multiply by 100.

- *Column 2* shows the *weighted number of responding schools before school replacement* (weighted by student enrolment).

- *Column 3* shows the *weighted number of sampled schools before school replacement* (including both responding and non-responding schools, weighted by student enrolment).

- *Column 4* shows the *unweighted number of responding schools before school replacement*.

- *Column 5* shows the *unweighted number of responding and non-responding schools before school replacement*.

- *Column 6* shows the *weighted participation rate of schools after replacement*. This is obtained by dividing Column 7 by Column 8, multiply by 100.

- *Column 7* shows the *weighted number of responding schools after school replacement (weighted by student enrolment)*.

- *Column 8* shows the *weighted number of schools sampled after school replacement* (including both responding and non-responding schools, weighted by student enrolment).

- *Column 9* shows the *unweighted number of responding schools after school replacement*.

- *Column 10* shows the *unweighted number of responding and non-responding schools after school replacement*.

- *Column 11* shows the *weighted student participation rate after replacement*. This is obtained by dividing Column 12 by Column 13, multiply by 100.

- *Column 12* shows the *weighted number of students assessed*.

- *Column 13* shows the *weighted number of students sampled* (including both students who were assessed and students who were absent on the day of the assessment).

- *Column 14* shows the *unweighted number of students assessed*. Note that any students in schools with student-response rates less than 50% were not included in these rates (both weighted and unweighted).

- *Column 15* shows the *unweighted number of students sampled* (including both students that were assessed and students who were absent on the day of the assessment). Note that any students in schools where fewer than half of the eligible students were assessed were not included in these rates (neither weighted nor unweighted).

Differences between the problem-solving sample and the main PISA student sample

Out of the 65 countries and economies that participated in PISA 2012, 44 also implemented the computer-based assessment (CBA) of problem solving. Of these, 12 countries and economies only assessed problem solving, while 32 also assessed mathematics and (digital) reading on computers.

In all 44 countries/economies, only a random sub-sample of students who participated in the paper-based assessment (PBA) of mathematics were sampled to be administered the assessment of problem solving. However, as long at least one student in a participating school was sampled for the computer-based assessment, all students in the PISA sample from that school received multiple imputations (plausible values) of performance in problem solving, This is similar to the procedure used to impute plausible values for minor domains in PISA (for instance, not all test booklets in 2012 included reading questions; but all students received imputed values for reading performance).

Table A2.4 compares the final samples (after school replacement) for mathematics and problem solving.

- *Column 1* shows the overall number of schools with valid data in the PISA 2012 database.

- *Column 2* shows the students with valid data in mathematics. This is the number of students with data included in the main database. All these students have imputed values for performance in mathematics, reading and science. Students are considered as participating in the assessment of mathematics if they were sampled to sit the paper-based assessment (all booklets included mathematics questions) and attended a test session. Those who only attended the questionnaire session but provided at least a description of their father's or mother's occupation are also regarded as participants.

- *Column 3* shows the number of schools with valid data in the PISA 2012 computer-based assessments database.

- *Column 4* shows the number of students with valid data in problem solving. This corresponds to all participating students (Column 2) within schools who were sampled for the computer-based assessments in PISA 2012 and were included in the database (Column 3). For all these students, performance in problem solving could be imputed. All these students contributed to the statistics presented in this publication (with the exception of statistics based on item-level performance).

- *Column 5* shows the number of students included in the database who were sampled for the assessment of problem solving. These are the students with valid data who were sampled to sit the computer-based assessment and assigned a form (the computer equivalent of a paper booklet) containing at least one cluster of problem-solving questions.

- *Column 6* shows the number of students who were actually assessed in problem solving. These are the students sampled for the assessment of problem solving who actually attended the computer-based assessment session and were administered the test. All these students contributed to statistics based on item-level performance in this volume. Differences between the number of students in Columns 5 and 6 can occur for several reasons: students who skipped the computer-based session; students who did not reach any of the problem-solving questions in their test form; technical problems with the computer; etc.

[Part 1/1]

Table A2.4 **Sample size for performance in mathematics and problem solving**

	Mathematics		Problem solving			
	Number of schools with valid data (unweighted)	Number of students with valid data (unweighted)	Number of schools with valid data (unweighted)	Number of students with valid data (unweighted)	Number of students with valid data sampled for the assessment of problem solving (unweighted)	Number of students who were administered the assessment of problem solving (unweighted)
	(1)	(2)	(3)	(4)	(5)	(6)
OECD Australia	775	14 481	775	14 481	5 922	5 612
Austria	191	4 755	191	4 755	1 376	1 331
Belgium	287	8 597	287	8 597	2 309	2 147
Canada	885	21 544	885	21 544	5 415	4 602
Chile	221	6 856	221	6 856	1 674	1 578
Czech Republic	297	5 327	297	5 327	3 229	3 076
Denmark	341	7 481	341	7 481	2 104	1 948
Estonia	206	4 779	206	4 779	1 412	1 367
Finland	311	8 829	311	8 829	3 685	3 531
France	226	4 613	226	4 613	1 509	1 345
Germany	230	5 001	230	5 001	1 426	1 350
Greece	188	5 125	0	0	0	0
Hungary	204	4 810	204	4 810	1 355	1 300
Iceland	134	3 508	0	0	0	0
Ireland	183	5 016	183	5 016	1 303	1 190
Israel	172	5 055	172	5 055	1 445	1 346
Italy	1 194	31 073	208	5 495	1 554	1 371
Japan	191	6 351	191	6 351	3 178	3 014
Korea	156	5 033	156	5 033	1 351	1 336
Luxembourg	42	5 258	0	0	0	0
Mexico	1 471	33 806	0	0	0	0
Netherlands	179	4 460	179	4 460	2 258	1 752
New Zealand	177	4 291	0	0	0	0
Norway	197	4 686	197	4 686	1 463	1 240
Poland	184	4 607	184	4 607	1 256	1 227
Portugal	195	5 722	195	5 722	1 631	1 446
Slovak Republic	231	4 678	231	4 678	1 589	1 465
Slovenia	338	5 911	338	5 911	2 179	2 065
Spain	902	25 313	368	10 175	2 866	2 709
Sweden	209	4 736	209	4 736	1 337	1 258
Switzerland	411	11 229	0	0	0	0
Turkey	170	4 848	170	4 848	2 022	1 995
United Kingdom	507	12 659	170	4 185	1 963	1 458
United States	162	4 978	162	4 978	1 300	1 273
Partners Albania	204	4 743	0	0	0	0
Argentina	226	5 908	0	0	0	0
Brazil	839	19 204	241	5 506	1 590	1 463
Bulgaria	188	5 282	188	5 282	2 333	2 145
Colombia	352	9 073	352	9 073	2 595	2 307
Costa Rica	193	4 602	0	0	0	0
Croatia	163	5 008	163	5 008	2 016	1 924
Cyprus*	117	5 078	117	5 078	2 630	2 503
Hong Kong-China	148	4 670	148	4 670	1 367	1 325
Indonesia	209	5 622	0	0	0	0
Jordan	233	7 038	0	0	0	0
Kazakhstan	218	5 808	0	0	0	0
Latvia	211	4 306	0	0	0	0
Liechtenstein	12	293	0	0	0	0
Lithuania	216	4 618	0	0	0	0
Macao-China	45	5 335	45	5 335	1 577	1 565
Malaysia	164	5 197	164	5 197	2 072	1 929
Montenegro	51	4 744	51	4 744	2 101	1 845
Peru	240	6 035	0	0	0	0
Qatar	157	10 966	0	0	0	0
Romania	178	5 074	0	0	0	0
Russian Federation	227	5 231	227	5 231	1 574	1 543
Serbia	153	4 684	153	4 684	1 930	1 777
Shanghai-China	155	5 177	155	5 177	1 213	1 203
Singapore	172	5 546	172	5 546	1 438	1 394
Chinese Taipei	163	6 046	163	6 046	1 512	1 484
Thailand	239	6 606	0	0	0	0
Tunisia	153	4 407	0	0	0	0
United Arab Emirates	458	11 500	458	11 500	3 418	3 262
Uruguay	180	5 315	180	5 315	2 048	2 013
Viet Nam	162	4 959	0	0	0	0

* See notes at the beginning of this Annex.

StatLink ⫘⫘ http://dx.doi.org/10.1787/888933003725

In all but four of the 44 countries/economies that assessed problem solving, the school samples for CBA and PBA coincide. As a consequence, in 40 countries/economies the main student dataset, containing the results of paper-based assessments, and the CBA dataset have the same number of observations. In Brazil, Italy, Spain and the United Kingdom, in contrast, the CBA school sample is smaller than the main sample. Brazil and Italy did not over-sample students for CBA to provide results at regional level. In Spain, students were over-sampled only in the Basque Country and in Catalonia, but not in the remaining adjudicated regions. In the United Kingdom, only schools in England participated in the computer-based assessment of problem solving.

Definition of schools

In some countries, sub-units within schools were sampled instead of schools and this may affect the estimation of the between-school variance components. In Austria, the Czech Republic, Germany, Hungary, Japan, Romania and Slovenia, schools with more than one study programme were split into the units delivering these programmes. In the Netherlands, for schools with both lower and upper secondary programmes, schools were split into units delivering each programme level. In the Flemish Community of Belgium, in the case of multi-campus schools, implantations (campuses) were sampled, whereas in the French Community, in the case of multi-campus schools, the larger administrative units were sampled. In Australia, for schools with more than one campus, the individual campuses were listed for sampling. In Argentina, Croatia and Dubai (United Arab Emirates), schools that had more than one campus had the locations listed for sampling. In Spain, the schools in the Basque region with multi-linguistic models were split into linguistic models for sampling.

ANNEX A3

TECHNICAL NOTES ON ANALYSES IN THIS VOLUME

Methods and definitions

Relative performance in problem solving

Relative performance in problem solving is defined as the difference between a student's actual performance in problem solving and his or her expected performance, based on performance in other domains:

$$RP_i^{ps} = y_i^{ps} - E(y_i^{ps}|y_i^{mrs})$$

where y_i^{ps} represents student i's performance in problem solving, and y_i^{mrs} is a vector of student i's performance in other domains (such as mathematics, reading and science).

A student's (conditionally) expected performance is estimated using regression models; relative performance is therefore based on residuals from regression models. All analyses of relative performance in this volume derive residuals from parametric regression models that allow for curvilinear shapes and, when more than one domain enters the conditioning arguments, for interaction terms (second- or third-degree polynomials). However, different regression methods can be used, including non-parametric ones. Figure V.2.16, for instance, graphically displays a non-parametric regression of problem-solving performance on mathematics performance.

In some analyses, the regression model is calibrated only on a subsample of comparison students (e.g. on boys, when the relative performance of girls is analysed). In others, where the comparison group is less well defined and the focus is on comparisons to the national or international average, the regression model is calibrated on all students. In all cases, five distinct regression models are estimated to compute five plausible values of relative performance.

Relative risk or increased likelihood

The relative risk is a measure of the association between an antecedent factor and an outcome factor. The relative risk is simply the ratio of two risks, i.e. the risk of observing the outcome when the antecedent is present and the risk of observing the outcome when the antecedent is not present. Figure A3.1 presents the notation that is used in the following.

■ Figure A3.1 ■
Labels used in a two-way table

p_{11}	p_{12}	$p_{1.}$
p_{21}	p_{22}	$p_{2.}$
$p_{.1}$	$p_{.2}$	$p_{..}$

$p_{..}$ is equal to $\frac{n_{..}}{n_{..}}$, with $n_{..}$ the total number of students and $p_{..}$ is therefore equal to 1, $p_{i.}$, $p_{.j}$ respectively represent the marginal probabilities for each row and for each column. The marginal probabilities are equal to the marginal frequencies divided by the total number of students. Finally, the p_{ij} represents the probabilities for each cell and are equal to the number of observations in a particular cell divided by the total number of observations.

In PISA, the rows represent the antecedent factor, with the first row for "having the antecedent" and the second row for "not having the antecedent". The columns represent the outcome: the first column for "having the outcome" and the second column for "not having the outcome". The relative risk is then equal to:

$$RR = \frac{(p_{11}/p_{1.})}{(p_{21}/p_{2.})}$$

Statistics based on multilevel models

Statistics based on multilevel models include variance components (between- and within-school variance), the *index of inclusion* derived from these components, and regression coefficients where this has been indicated. Multilevel models are generally specified as two-level regression models (the student and school levels), with normally distributed residuals, and estimated with maximum likelihood estimation. Where the dependent variable is mathematics performance, the estimation uses five plausible values for each student's performance on the mathematics scale. Models were estimated using Mplus® software.

In multilevel models, weights are used at both the student and school levels. The purpose of these weights is to account for differences in the probabilities of students being selected in the sample. Since PISA applies a two-stage sampling procedure, these differences are due to factors at both the school and the student levels. For the multilevel models, student final weights (W_FSTUWT) were used.

Within-school-weights correspond to student final weights, rescaled to sum up within each school to the school sample size. Between-school weights correspond to the sum of student final weights (W_FSTUWT) within each school. The definition of between-school weights has changed with respect to PISA 2009.

The *index of inclusion* is defined and estimated as:

$$100 * \frac{\sigma_w^2}{\sigma_w^2 + \sigma_b^2}$$

where σ_w^2 and σ_b^2, respectively, represent the within- and between-variance estimates.

The results in multilevel models, and the between-school variance estimate in particular, depend on how schools are defined and organised within countries and by the units that were chosen for sampling purposes. For example, in some countries, some of the schools in the PISA sample were defined as administrative units (even if they spanned several geographically separate institutions, as in Italy); in others they were defined as those parts of larger educational institutions that serve 15-year-olds; in still others they were defined as physical school buildings; and in others they were defined from a management perspective (e.g. entities having a principal). The *PISA 2012 Technical Report* (OECD, forthcoming) and Annex A2 provide an overview of how schools were defined. In Slovenia, the primary sampling unit is defined as a group of students who follow the same study programme within a school (an educational track within a school). So in this particular case the between-school variance is actually the within-school, between-track variation. The use of stratification variables in the selection of schools may also affect the estimate of the between-school variance, particularly if stratification variables are associated with between-school differences.

Because of the manner in which students were sampled, the within-school variation includes variation between classes as well as between students.

Effect sizes

An effect size is a measure of the strength of the relationship between two variables. The term effect size is commonly used to refer to standardised differences. Standardising a difference is useful when a metric has no intrinsic meaning – as is the case with PISA performance scales or scale indices. Indeed, a standardised difference allows comparisons of the strength of between-group differences across measures that vary in their metric.

A standardised difference is obtained by dividing the raw difference between two groups, such as boys and girls, by a measure of the variation in the underlying data. In this volume, the pooled standard deviation was used to standardise differences. The effect size between two subgroups is thus calculated as:

$$\frac{m_1 - m_2}{\sqrt{\sigma_{1,2}^2}}$$

where m_1 and m_2, respectively, represent the mean values for the subgroups 1 and 2, and $\sigma_{1,2}^2$ represents the variance for the population pooling subgroups 1 and 2.

Relative success ratios on subsets of items

The relative likelihood of success on a subset of items is computed as follows.

First, a country-specific measure of success on each item is computed by converting the percentage of correct answers into the logit scale (the logarithm of odds is used instead of the percentage; odds are also referred to as success ratios, because they correspond to the number of full-credit answers over the number of no- and partial-credit answers). This success measure can also be interpreted as an item-difficulty parameter: lower success measures indicate more difficult items.

Next, a relative success measure for a given subset of items is derived as the difference between the average success on items in the subset and the average success on items outside of the subset. Again, this measure can also be interpreted as a relative difficulty of items in the two subsets.

Finally, a relative likelihood of success is derived that takes into account differences in item difficulty by subtracting the average relative success in OECD countries (i.e. the average difficulty of items) from country-specific figures (or similarly, the relative success in a comparison group – e.g. boys – from the relative success in the focus group – e.g. girls). This difference is used as a basis for computing odds ratios (the difference of logits being the logarithm of the odds ratio).

By design, each item carries the same weight in these analyses. However, the probability of success on a given item is also influenced by its position within the test booklet. While *ex ante*, booklets are assigned so that they are present in equal proportions within any subsample, in practice given the finite number of students taking the test small differences remain. To control for these differences, booklet dummies are included in the model and generalised odds ratios are estimated with logistic regression. Similarly, in some analyses country- or group-specific dummies are included for the response format to ensure that inferences about strengths and weaknesses on the items measuring the various framework aspects are not driven by the association of selected- and constructed-response formats with specific item families.

Standard errors and significance tests

The statistics in this report represent estimates of national performance based on samples of students, rather than values that could be calculated if every student in every country had answered every question. Consequently, it is important to measure the degree of uncertainty of the estimates. In PISA, each estimate has an associated degree of uncertainty, which is expressed through a standard error. The use of confidence intervals provides a way to make inferences about the population means and proportions in a manner that reflects the uncertainty associated with the sample estimates. From an observed sample statistic and assuming a normal distribution, it can be inferred that the corresponding population result would lie within the confidence interval in 95 out of 100 replications of the measurement on different samples drawn from the same population.

In many cases, readers are primarily interested in whether a given value in a particular country is different from a second value in the same or another country, e.g. whether girls in a country perform better than boys in the same country. In the tables and charts used in this report, differences are labelled as statistically significant when a difference of that size, smaller or larger, would be observed less than 5% of the time, if there were actually no difference in corresponding population values. Similarly, the risk of reporting a correlation as significant if there is, in fact, no correlation between two measures, is contained at 5%.

Throughout the report, significance tests were undertaken to assess the statistical significance of the comparisons made.

Gender differences and differences between subgroup means

Gender differences in student performance or other indices were tested for statistical significance. Positive differences indicate higher scores for boys while negative differences indicate higher scores for girls. Generally, differences marked in bold in the tables in this volume are statistically significant at the 95% confidence level.

Similarly, differences between other groups of students (e.g. native students and students with an immigrant background) were tested for statistical significance. The definitions of the subgroups can in general be found in the tables and the text accompanying the analysis. All differences marked in bold in the tables presented in Annex B of this report are statistically significant at the 95% level.

Differences between subgroup means, after accounting for other variables

For many tables, subgroup comparisons were performed both on the observed difference ("before accounting for other variables") and after accounting for other variables, such as the *PISA index of economic, social and cultural status of students* (ESCS). The adjusted differences were estimated using linear regression and tested for significance at the 95% confidence level. Significant differences are marked in bold.

Performance differences between the top and bottom quartiles of PISA indices and scales

Differences in average performance between the top and bottom quarters of the PISA indices and scales were tested for statistical significance. Figures marked in bold indicate that performance between the top and bottom quarters of students on the respective index is statistically significantly different at the 95% confidence level.

Change in the performance per unit of the index

For many tables, the difference in student performance per unit of the index shown was calculated. Figures in bold indicate that the differences are statistically significantly different from zero at the 95% confidence level.

Relative risk or increased likelihood

Figures in bold in the data tables presented in Annex B of this report indicate that the relative risk is statistically significantly different from 1 at the 95% confidence level. To compute statistical significance around the value of 1 (the null hypothesis), the relative-risk statistic is assumed to follow a log-normal distribution, rather than a normal distribution, under the null hypothesis.

Range of ranks

To calculate the range of ranks for countries, data are simulated using the mean and standard error of the mean for each relevant country to generate a distribution of possible values. Some 10 000 simulations are implemented and, based on these values, 10 000 possible rankings for each country are produced. For each country, the counts for each rank are aggregated from largest to smallest until they equal 9 500 or more. Then the range of ranks per country is reported, including all the ranks that have been aggregated. This means that there is at least 95% confidence about the range of ranks, and it is safe to assume unimodality in this distribution of ranks. This method has been used in all cycles of PISA since 2003, including PISA 2012.

The main difference between the range of ranks (e.g. Figure V.2.4) and the comparison of countries' mean performance (e.g. Figure V.2.3) is that the former takes account of the multiple comparisons involved in determining ranks and the asymmetry of the distribution of rank estimates, while the latter does not. Therefore, sometimes there is a slight difference between the range of ranks and counting the number of countries above a given country, based on pairwise comparisons of the selected countries' performance. For instance, the difference in average performance between England (United Kingdom), which is listed in eleventh place in Figure V.2.3, and Canada, which is listed in eighth place, is not statistically significant. However, because it is highly unlikely that all three countries/economies listed between eight and tenth place in reality have lower performance than England (United Kingdom), the rank for England (United Kingdom)

among all countries can be restricted to be, with 95% confidence, at best ninth (Figure V.2.4). Since it is safe to assume that the distribution of rank estimates for each country has a single mode (unimodality), the results of range of ranks for countries should be used when examining countries' rankings.

Standard errors in statistics estimated from multilevel models

For statistics based on multilevel models (such as the estimates of variance components and regression coefficients from two-level regression models) the standard errors are not estimated with the usual replication method which accounts for stratification and sampling rates from finite populations. Instead, standard errors are "model-based": their computation assumes that schools, and students within schools, are sampled at random (with sampling probabilities reflected in school and student weights) from a theoretical, infinite population of schools and students which complies with the model's parametric assumptions.

The standard error for the estimated *index of inclusion* is calculated by deriving an approximate distribution for it from the (model-based) standard errors for the variance components, using the delta-method.

Differences between rankings based on proficiency scales and average percent-correct rankings

PISA international results are based on a scaling of students' item scores with an item response model (see the *PISA 2012 Technical Report*, OECD, forthcoming). This scaling is undertaken for a number of reasons. First, it supports the construction of described proficiency scales. Second, this approach summarises students' responses to many items with few indices. In doing so, it ensures that the indices are comparable across students who respond to different test booklets that are composed of different subsets of items (Adams et al., 2010). The scaling of students' scores reflects the PISA approach, which consists in building internationally supported assessment frameworks and then developing items pools that sample widely from those frameworks in an agreed fashion.

The average percent-correct approach used in Chapter 3 in this volume provides an alternative way of comparing country performance on the assessment. The advantage of the average percent-correct approach is that it can be easily replicated on arbitrary subsets of items.

When rankings based on the percent-correct approach, using all items, are compared to rankings based on the usual scaling approach, small differences will occur for six reasons. First, the percent-correct methodology assigns an arbitrary value (typically, either 0 or 0.5) to all partial-credit answers; percent-correct figures are therefore based on a smaller set of information about students' performance on the test than scaled results, where each partial credit value is scaled to its specific difficulty. Second, the percent-correct methodology ignores students who did not answer any problem-solving item, despite being assigned to a problem-solving booklet and having answered, at least partially, the student questionnaire. Because it is impossible to know why they did not answer problem-solving questions (e.g. a technical failure of the computer system or a deliberate absence from the test), their answers are coded as "not administered" rather than as incorrect, and treated as missing. The usual scaling approach, in contrast, corrects for possible self-selection in taking the test by imputing performance from the available information about these students, including their performance on other tests. Third, the percent-correct methodology weights all items equally, whereas in the scaling approach the items are weighted according to the number of booklets in which they were included. Fourth, the percent-correct approach does not address the booklet effect that was observed in PISA. Fifth, the scaling methodology transforms percentage values that are bounded at zero and 100 into the logit scale. This transformation has the effect of "stretching out" very low and very high percentages in comparison to percentages that are close to 50%. Sixth, when a problem such as a translation error affecting one item in one country is detected after the test has been administered, this item is coded as missing for all students in the country; the percent-correct rankings may therefore be based on fewer items than the scaled results. In the PISA 2012 assessment of problem solving, one item (CP018Q05) was withdrawn after the test in France, because by mistake a crucial direction to students had not been included in the national version.

References

Adams, R., A. Berezner and **M. Jakubowski** (2010), "Analysis of PISA 2006 Preferred Items Ranking Using the Percent-Correct Method", *OECD Education Working Papers*, No. 46, OECD Publishing.
http://dx.doi.org/10.1787/5km4psmntkq5-e

OECD (forthcoming), *PISA 2012 Technical Report*, PISA, OECD Publishing.

ANNEX A4
QUALITY ASSURANCE

Quality assurance procedures were implemented in all parts of PISA 2012, as was done for all previous PISA surveys.

The consistent quality and linguistic equivalence of the PISA 2012 assessment instruments were facilitated by providing countries with equivalent source versions of the assessment instruments in English and French and requiring countries (other than those assessing students in English and French) to prepare and consolidate two independent translations using both source versions. Precise translation and adaptation guidelines were supplied, also including instructions for selecting and training the translators. For each country, the translation and format of the assessment instruments (including test materials, marking guides, questionnaires and manuals) were verified by expert translators appointed by the PISA Consortium before they were used in the PISA 2012 field trial and main study. These translators' mother tongue was the language of instruction in the country concerned and they were knowledgeable about education systems. For further information on the PISA translation procedures, see the *PISA 2012 Technical Report* (OECD, forthcoming).

The survey was implemented through standardised procedures. The PISA Consortium provided comprehensive manuals that explained the implementation of the survey, including precise instructions for the work of School Co-ordinators and scripts for Test Administrators to use during the assessment sessions. Proposed adaptations to survey procedures, or proposed modifications to the assessment session script, were submitted to the PISA Consortium for approval prior to verification. The PISA Consortium then verified the national translation and adaptation of these manuals.

To establish the credibility of PISA as valid and unbiased and to encourage uniformity in administering the assessment sessions, Test Administrators in participating countries were selected using the following criteria: it was required that the Test Administrator not be the mathematics, reading or science instructor of any students in the sessions he or she would administer for PISA; it was recommended that the Test Administrator not be a member of the staff of any school where he or she would administer for PISA; and it was considered preferable that the Test Administrator not be a member of the staff of any school in the PISA sample. Participating countries organised an in-person training session for Test Administrators.

Participating countries and economies were required to ensure that: Test Administrators worked with the School Co-ordinator to prepare the assessment session, including updating student tracking forms and identifying excluded students; no extra time was given for the cognitive items (while it was permissible to give extra time for the student questionnaire); no instrument was administered before the two one-hour parts of the cognitive session; Test Administrators recorded the student participation status on the student tracking forms and filled in a Session Report Form; no cognitive instrument was permitted to be photocopied; no cognitive instrument could be viewed by school staff before the assessment session; and Test Administrators returned the material to the national centre immediately after the assessment sessions.

National Project Managers were encouraged to organise a follow-up session when more than 15% of the PISA sample was not able to attend the original assessment session.

National Quality Monitors from the PISA Consortium visited all national centres to review data-collection procedures. Finally, School Quality Monitors from the PISA Consortium visited a sample of seven schools during the assessment. For further information on the field operations, see the *PISA 2012 Technical Report* (OECD, forthcoming).

Marking procedures were designed to ensure consistent and accurate application of the marking guides outlined in the PISA Operations Manuals. National Project Managers were required to submit proposed modifications to these procedures to the Consortium for approval. Reliability studies to analyse the consistency of marking were implemented.

Software specially designed for PISA facilitated data entry, detected common errors during data entry, and facilitated the process of data cleaning. Training sessions familiarised National Project Managers with these procedures.

For a description of the quality assurance procedures applied in PISA and in the results, see the *PISA 2012 Technical Report* (OECD, forthcoming).

The results of adjudication showed that the PISA Technical Standards were fully met in all countries and economies that participated in PISA 2012, with the exception of Albania. Albania submitted parental occupation data that were incomplete and appeared inaccurate, since there was over-use of a narrow range of occupations. It was not possible to resolve these issues during the course of data cleaning, and as a result neither parental occupation data nor any indices which depend on this data are included in the international dataset. Results for Albania are omitted from any analyses which depend on these indices.

ANNEX A5
THE PROBLEM-SOLVING ASSESSMENT DESIGN

How the PISA 2012 assessments of problem-solving was designed

The development of the PISA 2012 problem-solving tasks was co-ordinated by an international consortium of educational research institutions contracted by the OECD, under the guidance of a group of problem-solving experts from participating countries (members of the problem solving expert group are listed in Annex C of this Volume). Participating countries contributed stimulus material and questions, which were reviewed, tried out and refined iteratively over the three years leading up to the administration of the assessment in 2012. The development process involved provisions for several rounds of commentary from participating countries, as well as small-scale piloting and a formal field trial in which samples of 15-year-olds (about 1 000 students) from participating countries took part. The problem-solving expert group recommended the final selection of tasks, which included material submitted by participating countries. The selection was made with regard to both their technical quality, assessed on the basis of their performance in the field trial, and their cultural appropriateness and interest level for 15-year-olds, as judged by the participating countries. Another essential criterion for selecting the set of material as a whole was its fit to the framework described in Chapter 1 of this volume, in order to maintain the balance across various aspect categories. Finally, it was carefully ensured that the set of questions covered a range of difficulty, allowing good measurement and description of the problem-solving competence of all 15-year-old students, from the least proficient to the highly able.

Forty-two problem-solving questions arranged in 16 units were used in PISA 2012, but each student in the sample only saw a fraction of the total pool because different sets of questions were given to different students. The problem-solving questions selected for inclusion in PISA 2012 were organised into four 20-minutes clusters. In countries that also assessed mathematics and reading on computers, computer-based mathematics and digital reading questions were similarly arranged in 20-minutes clusters, and assembled together with problem-solving clusters to form test forms (the computer equivalent of paper booklets). In all cases, the total time allocated to computer-based tests was 40 minutes.

In countries that assessed only problem-solving on computers, the four clusters of problem-solving units (CP1-CP4) were rotated so that each cluster appeared twice in each of the two possible positions in the form and every cluster formed two pairs with two other clusters. Eight test forms were built according to the scheme illustrated in Figure A5.1: According to this scheme, each problem-solving item was administered to about one half of all students assessed in problem solving (see Table A2.4).

In those countries that assessed problem solving, mathematics and reading on computers, the four clusters of problem-solving units, the four clusters of mathematics units (CM1-CM4) and the two clusters of reading units (CR1, CR2) were combined into 24 test forms as illustrated in Figure A5.2. One form was chosen at random for administration to each student.

■ Figure A5.1 ■
PISA 2012 computer-based test design:
Problem solving only

Form ID	Cluster	
31	CP1	CP2
32	CP2	CP3
33	CP3	CP4
34	CP4	CP1
35	CP2	CP1
36	CP3	CP2
37	CP4	CP3
38	CP1	CP4

■ Figure A5.2 ■
PISA 2012 computer-based test design:
Problem solving, mathematics and reading

Form ID	Cluster	
41	CP1	CP2
42	CR1	CR2
43	CM3	CM4
44	CP3	CR1
45	CR2	CM2
46	CM1	CP4
47	CR2	CR1
48	CM2	CM1
49	CP3	CP4
50	CM4	CR2
51	CP1	CM3
52	CR1	CP2
53	CM1	CM3
54	CP4	CP1
55	CR1	CR2
56	CP2	CM4
57	CR2	CP3
58	CM2	CR1
59	CP2	CP3
60	CM4	CM2
61	CR2	CR1
62	CM3	CP1
63	CR1	CM1
64	CP4	CR2

This scheme ensured that every cluster appeared twice in each position for problem solving and computer-based mathematics and four times for digital reading. Moreover, every cluster appeared twice with clusters from a different domain – once in the first and once in the second position within the form. Each of the three domains got the same number of appearances within the 24 forms and therefore an equal proportion of the student sample was assessed in each domain. According to this scheme, each problem-solving item was administered to about one third of all students assessed in problem solving (see Table A2.4), or one sixth of all students assessed on computer.

This design made it possible to construct a single scale of problem-solving proficiency, in which each question is associated with a particular point on the scale that indicates its difficulty, whereby each student's performance is associated with a particular point on the same scale that indicates his or her estimated proficiency. A description of the modelling technique used to construct this scale can be found in the *PISA 2012 Technical Report* (OECD, forthcoming).

References

OECD (forthcoming), *PISA 2012 Technical Report,* PISA, OECD Publishing.

ANNEX A6
TECHNICAL NOTE ON BRAZIL

In 2006, the education system in Brazil was revised to include one more year at the beginning of primary school, with the compulsory school age being lowered from seven to six years old. This change has been implemented in stages and will be completed in 2016. At the time the PISA 2012 survey took place, many of the 15-year-olds in Grade 7 had started their education under the previous system. They were therefore equivalent to Grade 6 students in the previous system. Since students below Grade 7 are not eligible for participation in PISA, the Grade 7 students in the sample were not included in the database.

Brazil also has many rural "multigrade" schools where it is difficult to identify the exact grade of each student, so not possible to identify students who are at least in Grade 7. The results for Brazil have therefore been analysed both with and without these rural schools. The results reported in the main chapters of this report are those of the Brazilian sample without the rural schools, while this annex gives the results for Brazil with the rural schools included.

[Part 1/1]

Table A6.1 **Percentage of Brazilian students at each proficiency level on the problem-solving scale**

		Percentage of students at each level												
		Below Level 1 (below 358.49 score points)		Level 1 (from 358.49 to less than 423.42 score points)		Level 2 (from 423.42 to less than 488.35 score points)		Level 3 (from 488.35 to less than 553.28 score points)		Level 4 (from 553.28 to less than 618.21 score points)		Level 5 (from 618.21 to less than 683.14 score points)		Level 6 (above 683.14 score points)	
		%	S.E.	%	S.E.	%	S.E.	%	S.E.	%	S.E.	%	S.E.	%	S.E.
Problem-solving scale	All	23.5	(1.6)	25.5	(1.4)	26.1	(1.3)	16.8	(1.4)	6.3	(0.8)	1.4	(0.3)	0.4	(0.1)
	Boys	20.8	(1.8)	23.8	(1.5)	25.9	(1.5)	18.3	(1.7)	8.5	(1.2)	2.0	(0.4)	0.6	(0.3)
	Girls	26.0	(1.9)	27.1	(1.9)	26.2	(1.5)	15.3	(1.7)	4.3	(0.7)	0.9	(0.3)	0.1	(0.1)

StatLink ᵃᵢˢᵖ http://dx.doi.org/10.1787/888933003744

[Part 1/1]

Table A6.2 **Mean score, variation and gender differences in student performance in Brazil**

	All students				Gender differences						Percentiles															
	Mean score		Standard deviation		Boys		Girls		Difference (B - G)		5th		10th		25th		50th (median)		75th		90th		95th	
	Mean	S.E.	S.D.	S.E.	Mean score	S.E.	Mean score	S.E.	Score dif.	S.E.	Score	S.E.	Score	S.E.	Score	S.E.	Score	S.E.	Score	S.E.	Score	S.E.	Score	S.E.
Problem-solving scale	425	(4.5)	92	(2.3)	436	(5.2)	415	(4.4)	**21**	(3.3)	273	(5.8)	307	(4.7)	363	(4.8)	426	(5.2)	487	(6.1)	543	(5.7)	573	(5.7)

Note: Values that are statistically significant are indicated in bold (see Annex A3).
StatLink ᵃᵢˢᵖ http://dx.doi.org/10.1787/888933003744

Annex B

PISA 2012 DATA

All tables in Annex B are available on line

Annex B1: Results for countries and economies
http://dx.doi.org/10.1787/888933003668
http://dx.doi.org/10.1787/888933003687
http://dx.doi.org/10.1787/888933003706

Annex B2: Results for regions within countries
http://dx.doi.org/10.1787/888933003763

Annex B3: List of tables available on line

The reader should note that there are gaps
in the numbering of tables because some tables
appear on line only and are not included in this publication.

ANNEX B1

RESULTS FOR COUNTRIES AND ECONOMIES

[Part 1/2]

Table V.2.1   **Percentage of students at each proficiency level in problem solving**

		Percentage of students at each level												
		Below Level 1 (below 358.49 score points)		Level 1 (from 358.49 to less than 423.42 score points)		Level 2 (from 423.42 to less than 488.35 score points)		Level 3 (from 488.35 to less than 553.28 score points)		Level 4 (from 553.28 to less than 618.21 score points)		Level 5 (from 618.21 to less than 683.14 score points)		Level 6 (above 683.14 score points)	
		%	S.E.	%	S.E.	%	S.E.	%	S.E.	%	S.E.	%	S.E.	%	S.E.
OECD	Australia	5.0	(0.3)	10.5	(0.5)	19.4	(0.5)	25.8	(0.7)	22.6	(0.5)	12.3	(0.5)	4.4	(0.3)
	Austria	6.5	(0.9)	11.9	(0.8)	21.8	(1.1)	26.9	(1.2)	21.9	(1.0)	9.0	(0.8)	2.0	(0.4)
	Belgium	9.2	(0.6)	11.6	(0.6)	18.3	(0.7)	24.5	(0.6)	22.0	(0.7)	11.4	(0.7)	3.0	(0.3)
	Canada	5.1	(0.4)	9.6	(0.4)	19.0	(0.6)	25.8	(0.7)	22.9	(0.6)	12.4	(0.6)	5.1	(0.4)
	Chile	15.1	(1.3)	23.1	(1.1)	28.6	(1.0)	22.2	(1.0)	8.8	(0.7)	1.9	(0.3)	0.2	(0.1)
	Czech Republic	6.5	(0.7)	11.9	(0.9)	20.7	(1.0)	27.2	(0.9)	21.8	(0.9)	9.5	(0.7)	2.4	(0.3)
	Denmark	7.3	(0.7)	13.1	(0.7)	24.1	(0.8)	27.8	(0.9)	19.0	(1.1)	7.2	(0.7)	1.6	(0.3)
	Estonia	4.0	(0.5)	11.1	(0.8)	21.8	(0.7)	29.2	(1.0)	22.2	(0.8)	9.5	(0.7)	2.2	(0.3)
	Finland	4.5	(0.4)	9.9	(0.5)	20.0	(0.9)	27.1	(1.1)	23.5	(0.8)	11.4	(0.6)	3.6	(0.5)
	France	6.6	(0.9)	9.8	(0.7)	20.5	(1.0)	28.4	(1.1)	22.6	(0.9)	9.9	(0.7)	2.1	(0.3)
	Germany	7.5	(0.8)	11.8	(0.9)	20.3	(0.9)	25.6	(1.0)	22.0	(1.0)	10.1	(1.0)	2.7	(0.4)
	Hungary	17.2	(1.3)	17.8	(0.9)	23.9	(1.2)	22.4	(0.9)	13.0	(1.0)	4.6	(0.7)	1.0	(0.2)
	Ireland	7.0	(0.8)	13.3	(0.9)	23.8	(0.9)	27.8	(0.9)	18.8	(0.8)	7.3	(0.6)	2.1	(0.3)
	Israel	21.9	(1.4)	17.0	(0.9)	20.1	(0.8)	18.5	(0.9)	13.7	(0.9)	6.7	(0.8)	2.1	(0.4)
	Italy	5.2	(0.7)	11.2	(1.1)	22.5	(1.0)	28.0	(1.1)	22.3	(1.1)	8.9	(0.9)	1.8	(0.3)
	Japan	1.8	(0.4)	5.3	(0.6)	14.6	(0.9)	26.9	(1.1)	29.2	(1.0)	16.9	(1.0)	5.3	(0.7)
	Korea	2.1	(0.3)	4.8	(0.6)	12.9	(0.9)	23.7	(1.0)	28.8	(0.9)	20.0	(1.2)	7.6	(0.9)
	Netherlands	7.4	(1.0)	11.2	(1.0)	19.9	(1.2)	26.0	(1.3)	22.0	(1.2)	10.9	(1.0)	2.7	(0.5)
	Norway	8.1	(0.7)	13.2	(0.7)	21.5	(0.9)	24.7	(0.8)	19.4	(0.8)	9.7	(0.7)	3.4	(0.4)
	Poland	10.0	(1.1)	15.7	(1.0)	25.7	(0.9)	26.0	(1.0)	15.7	(1.0)	5.8	(0.7)	1.1	(0.2)
	Portugal	6.5	(0.6)	14.1	(1.0)	25.5	(0.9)	28.1	(1.0)	18.4	(0.9)	6.2	(0.6)	1.2	(0.3)
	Slovak Republic	10.7	(1.1)	15.4	(1.1)	24.3	(1.0)	25.6	(1.3)	16.2	(1.2)	6.3	(0.6)	1.6	(0.5)
	Slovenia	11.4	(0.6)	17.1	(1.0)	25.4	(1.2)	23.7	(0.8)	15.8	(0.8)	5.8	(0.5)	0.9	(0.2)
	Spain	13.1	(1.2)	15.3	(0.8)	23.6	(0.9)	24.2	(1.0)	15.9	(0.8)	6.2	(0.6)	1.6	(0.3)
	Sweden	8.8	(0.7)	14.6	(0.8)	23.9	(0.9)	26.3	(0.8)	17.6	(0.7)	7.0	(0.5)	1.8	(0.3)
	Turkey	11.0	(1.1)	24.8	(1.3)	31.4	(1.4)	21.2	(1.2)	9.4	(1.1)	2.0	(0.5)	0.2	(0.1)
	England (United Kingdom)	5.5	(0.8)	10.8	(0.8)	20.2	(1.3)	26.5	(0.9)	22.7	(1.1)	10.9	(0.8)	3.3	(0.6)
	United States	5.7	(0.8)	12.5	(0.9)	22.8	(1.0)	27.0	(1.0)	20.4	(0.9)	8.9	(0.7)	2.7	(0.5)
	OECD average	8.2	(0.2)	13.2	(0.2)	22.0	(0.2)	25.6	(0.2)	19.6	(0.2)	8.9	(0.1)	2.5	(0.1)
Partners	Brazil	21.9	(1.6)	25.4	(1.4)	26.9	(1.3)	17.4	(1.4)	6.6	(0.8)	1.5	(0.3)	0.4	(0.2)
	Bulgaria	33.3	(1.9)	23.3	(1.1)	22.1	(1.0)	14.1	(0.8)	5.6	(0.7)	1.4	(0.3)	0.2	(0.1)
	Colombia	33.2	(1.7)	28.3	(1.1)	22.2	(0.9)	11.3	(0.8)	3.9	(0.5)	0.9	(0.2)	0.2	(0.1)
	Croatia	12.0	(1.0)	20.2	(1.0)	26.8	(1.2)	22.9	(1.1)	13.2	(1.1)	4.0	(0.6)	0.8	(0.2)
	Cyprus*	19.6	(0.6)	20.9	(0.6)	25.5	(0.8)	20.4	(0.9)	10.1	(0.6)	3.0	(0.3)	0.5	(0.2)
	Hong Kong-China	3.3	(0.5)	7.1	(0.7)	16.3	(1.0)	27.4	(1.4)	26.5	(1.0)	14.2	(1.1)	5.1	(0.6)
	Macao-China	1.6	(0.2)	6.0	(0.4)	17.5	(0.6)	29.5	(0.8)	28.9	(0.9)	13.8	(0.6)	2.8	(0.3)
	Malaysia	22.7	(1.5)	27.8	(1.2)	27.8	(1.2)	15.7	(0.9)	5.2	(0.6)	0.8	(0.2)	0.1	(0.0)
	Montenegro	30.0	(0.8)	26.8	(0.8)	23.9	(1.0)	13.8	(0.7)	4.6	(0.4)	0.7	(0.2)	0.1	(0.1)
	Russian Federation	6.8	(0.7)	15.4	(1.1)	27.0	(0.9)	27.9	(1.2)	15.7	(0.9)	5.9	(0.7)	1.4	(0.3)
	Serbia	10.3	(1.0)	18.3	(0.8)	26.7	(1.4)	25.8	(1.1)	14.3	(0.8)	4.1	(0.4)	0.6	(0.2)
	Shanghai-China	3.1	(0.5)	7.5	(0.6)	17.5	(0.8)	27.4	(1.1)	26.2	(1.0)	14.1	(0.9)	4.1	(0.6)
	Singapore	2.0	(0.2)	6.0	(0.4)	13.8	(0.6)	21.9	(0.7)	27.0	(1.0)	19.7	(0.7)	9.6	(0.4)
	Chinese Taipei	3.4	(0.6)	8.2	(0.6)	17.8	(0.8)	26.3	(1.0)	25.9	(1.0)	14.6	(0.7)	3.8	(0.4)
	United Arab Emirates	30.3	(1.2)	24.6	(0.8)	22.0	(0.7)	14.2	(0.6)	6.4	(0.4)	2.1	(0.2)	0.4	(0.1)
	Uruguay	32.4	(1.6)	25.6	(1.0)	22.4	(1.0)	13.2	(0.7)	5.3	(0.5)	1.1	(0.2)	0.1	(0.1)

* See notes at the beginning of this Annex.

StatLink ᴍᴤ️ http://dx.doi.org/10.1787/888933003668

[Part 2/2]
Table V.2.1 **Percentage of students at each proficiency level in problem solving**

		Percentage of students at or above each proficiency level										
		Level 1 or above (above 358.49 score points)		Level 2 or above (above 423.42 score points)		Level 3 or above (above 488.35 score points)		Level 4 or above (above 553.28 score points)		Level 5 or above (above 618.21 score points)		Level 6 (above 683.14 score points)	
		%	S.E.	%	S.E.	%	S.E.	%	S.E.	%	S.E.	%	S.E.
OECD	Australia	95.0	(0.3)	84.5	(0.6)	65.1	(0.8)	39.3	(0.8)	16.7	(0.6)	4.4	(0.3)
	Austria	93.5	(0.9)	81.6	(1.3)	59.7	(1.6)	32.9	(1.5)	10.9	(1.0)	2.0	(0.4)
	Belgium	90.8	(0.6)	79.2	(0.9)	60.9	(1.0)	36.4	(1.0)	14.4	(0.8)	3.0	(0.3)
	Canada	94.9	(0.4)	85.3	(0.7)	66.3	(0.9)	40.5	(1.0)	17.5	(0.8)	5.1	(0.4)
	Chile	84.9	(1.3)	61.7	(1.8)	33.1	(1.6)	10.9	(0.9)	2.1	(0.3)	0.2	(0.1)
	Czech Republic	93.5	(0.7)	81.6	(1.1)	60.9	(1.5)	33.7	(1.3)	11.9	(0.8)	2.4	(0.3)
	Denmark	92.7	(0.7)	79.6	(1.1)	55.6	(1.3)	27.7	(1.2)	8.7	(0.8)	1.6	(0.3)
	Estonia	96.0	(0.5)	84.9	(1.0)	63.1	(1.2)	34.0	(1.1)	11.8	(0.8)	2.2	(0.3)
	Finland	95.5	(0.4)	85.7	(0.7)	65.6	(1.1)	38.5	(1.1)	15.0	(0.8)	3.6	(0.5)
	France	93.4	(0.9)	83.5	(1.1)	63.1	(1.3)	34.6	(1.4)	12.0	(0.9)	2.1	(0.3)
	Germany	92.5	(0.8)	80.8	(1.4)	60.5	(1.5)	34.8	(1.4)	12.8	(1.1)	2.7	(0.4)
	Hungary	82.8	(1.3)	65.0	(1.5)	41.1	(1.6)	18.6	(1.4)	5.6	(0.8)	1.0	(0.2)
	Ireland	93.0	(0.8)	79.7	(1.1)	55.9	(1.4)	28.1	(1.2)	9.4	(0.7)	2.1	(0.3)
	Israel	78.1	(1.4)	61.1	(1.8)	41.0	(1.9)	22.5	(1.6)	8.8	(1.0)	2.1	(0.4)
	Italy	94.8	(0.7)	83.6	(1.5)	61.1	(1.9)	33.1	(1.8)	10.8	(1.1)	1.8	(0.3)
	Japan	98.2	(0.4)	92.9	(0.8)	78.3	(1.3)	51.5	(1.6)	22.3	(1.2)	5.3	(0.7)
	Korea	97.9	(0.3)	93.1	(0.8)	80.2	(1.5)	56.5	(2.0)	27.6	(1.7)	7.6	(0.9)
	Netherlands	92.6	(1.0)	81.5	(1.5)	61.6	(1.9)	35.6	(2.0)	13.6	(1.2)	2.7	(0.5)
	Norway	91.9	(0.7)	78.7	(1.1)	57.2	(1.3)	32.5	(1.3)	13.1	(0.9)	3.4	(0.4)
	Poland	90.0	(1.1)	74.3	(1.7)	48.5	(1.9)	22.5	(1.5)	6.9	(0.8)	1.1	(0.2)
	Portugal	93.5	(0.6)	79.4	(1.3)	54.0	(1.8)	25.8	(1.4)	7.4	(0.8)	1.2	(0.3)
	Slovak Republic	89.3	(1.1)	73.9	(1.6)	49.7	(1.6)	24.0	(1.4)	7.8	(0.9)	1.6	(0.5)
	Slovenia	88.6	(0.6)	71.5	(1.0)	46.1	(0.9)	22.4	(0.7)	6.6	(0.5)	0.9	(0.2)
	Spain	86.9	(1.2)	71.5	(1.4)	48.0	(1.5)	23.7	(1.3)	7.8	(0.7)	1.6	(0.3)
	Sweden	91.2	(0.7)	76.5	(1.1)	52.6	(1.3)	26.3	(1.0)	8.8	(0.6)	1.8	(0.3)
	Turkey	89.0	(1.1)	64.2	(1.9)	32.8	(2.2)	11.6	(1.5)	2.2	(0.5)	0.2	(0.1)
	England (United Kingdom)	94.5	(0.8)	83.6	(1.3)	63.5	(1.8)	37.0	(1.6)	14.3	(1.1)	3.3	(0.6)
	United States	94.3	(0.8)	81.8	(1.3)	59.0	(1.8)	32.0	(1.5)	11.6	(1.0)	2.7	(0.5)
	OECD average	91.8	(0.2)	78.6	(0.2)	56.6	(0.3)	31.0	(0.3)	11.4	(0.2)	2.5	(0.1)
Partners	Brazil	78.1	(1.6)	52.7	(2.3)	25.8	(2.2)	8.4	(1.0)	1.8	(0.4)	0.4	(0.2)
	Bulgaria	66.7	(1.9)	43.3	(1.9)	21.3	(1.5)	7.2	(1.0)	1.6	(0.4)	0.2	(0.1)
	Colombia	66.8	(1.7)	38.5	(1.6)	16.4	(1.2)	5.0	(0.6)	1.2	(0.3)	0.2	(0.1)
	Croatia	88.0	(1.0)	67.7	(1.6)	40.9	(1.9)	18.0	(1.5)	4.7	(0.7)	0.8	(0.2)
	Cyprus*	80.4	(0.6)	59.6	(0.8)	34.1	(0.9)	13.7	(0.6)	3.6	(0.3)	0.5	(0.2)
	Hong Kong-China	96.7	(0.5)	89.6	(1.1)	73.2	(1.7)	45.8	(1.8)	19.3	(1.3)	5.1	(0.6)
	Macao-China	98.4	(0.2)	92.5	(0.5)	75.0	(0.6)	45.5	(0.7)	16.6	(0.6)	2.8	(0.3)
	Malaysia	77.3	(1.5)	49.5	(1.8)	21.8	(1.4)	6.1	(0.8)	0.9	(0.2)	0.1	(0.0)
	Montenegro	70.0	(0.8)	43.2	(0.9)	19.3	(0.7)	5.5	(0.4)	0.8	(0.2)	0.1	(0.1)
	Russian Federation	93.2	(0.7)	77.9	(1.5)	50.9	(1.5)	23.0	(1.4)	7.3	(0.9)	1.4	(0.3)
	Serbia	89.7	(1.0)	71.5	(1.5)	44.8	(1.6)	19.0	(1.0)	4.7	(0.4)	0.6	(0.2)
	Shanghai-China	96.9	(0.5)	89.4	(0.9)	71.9	(1.4)	44.4	(1.6)	18.3	(1.3)	4.1	(0.6)
	Singapore	98.0	(0.2)	92.0	(0.4)	78.2	(0.6)	56.3	(0.8)	29.3	(0.9)	9.6	(0.4)
	Chinese Taipei	96.6	(0.6)	88.4	(0.9)	70.5	(1.3)	44.2	(1.3)	18.3	(0.9)	3.8	(0.4)
	United Arab Emirates	69.7	(1.2)	45.2	(1.1)	23.2	(0.9)	9.0	(0.5)	2.5	(0.2)	0.4	(0.1)
	Uruguay	67.6	(1.6)	42.1	(1.5)	19.7	(1.1)	6.5	(0.6)	1.2	(0.2)	0.1	(0.1)

* See notes at the beginning of this Annex.
StatLink ⍾ http://dx.doi.org/10.1787/888933003668

[Part 1/2]

Table V.2.2 **Mean score and variation in student performance in problem solving**

| | Mean score | | Standard deviation | | Percentiles | | | | | | | | | | | | |
| | | | | | 5th | | 10th | | 25th | | 50th (median) | | 75th | | 90th | | 95th | |
	Mean	S.E.	S.D.	S.E.	Score	S.E.	Score	S.E.	Score	S.E.	Score	S.E.	Score	S.E.	Score	S.E.	Score	S.E.
Australia	523	(1.9)	97	(1.0)	358	(3.5)	396	(2.7)	459	(2.4)	526	(2.3)	591	(2.2)	646	(2.3)	677	(2.8)
Austria	506	(3.6)	94	(2.9)	345	(8.7)	384	(6.8)	446	(4.6)	511	(3.8)	572	(3.7)	623	(4.4)	650	(4.9)
Belgium	508	(2.5)	106	(1.8)	317	(6.8)	364	(4.8)	441	(3.4)	518	(2.7)	583	(2.6)	637	(2.5)	665	(3.3)
Canada	526	(2.4)	100	(1.7)	357	(4.3)	398	(3.8)	462	(3.1)	530	(2.5)	594	(2.8)	649	(3.3)	684	(4.4)
Chile	448	(3.7)	86	(1.7)	304	(5.7)	337	(5.5)	390	(4.8)	450	(3.8)	507	(3.5)	557	(4.2)	587	(4.0)
Czech Republic	509	(3.1)	95	(2.0)	344	(6.6)	384	(5.7)	447	(4.5)	515	(3.7)	575	(2.9)	626	(4.0)	656	(3.8)
Denmark	497	(2.9)	92	(1.9)	339	(5.7)	377	(5.2)	438	(3.8)	500	(3.3)	560	(3.3)	611	(4.5)	641	(4.9)
Estonia	515	(2.5)	88	(1.5)	368	(4.2)	400	(4.6)	458	(3.4)	517	(2.8)	576	(3.1)	626	(3.7)	654	(4.0)
Finland	523	(2.3)	93	(1.2)	364	(4.8)	401	(3.1)	462	(3.5)	526	(2.6)	587	(3.1)	640	(3.6)	671	(3.9)
France	511	(3.4)	96	(4.1)	340	(10.5)	387	(6.8)	455	(4.1)	518	(3.4)	577	(3.5)	626	(3.8)	653	(4.8)
Germany	509	(3.6)	99	(2.5)	335	(7.0)	377	(6.9)	444	(5.3)	516	(3.6)	579	(4.0)	629	(4.3)	659	(5.8)
Hungary	459	(4.0)	104	(2.7)	277	(8.4)	319	(8.8)	391	(6.1)	465	(4.4)	532	(5.4)	591	(5.5)	622	(5.8)
Ireland	498	(3.2)	93	(2.0)	340	(6.5)	378	(5.0)	438	(4.0)	501	(3.1)	562	(3.5)	615	(3.8)	647	(4.6)
Israel	454	(5.5)	123	(3.2)	242	(10.6)	291	(7.8)	372	(6.2)	460	(6.4)	543	(6.2)	611	(6.7)	647	(7.5)
Italy	510	(4.0)	91	(2.1)	356	(7.2)	394	(5.8)	451	(5.2)	514	(4.9)	572	(4.5)	621	(4.6)	649	(5.5)
Japan	552	(3.1)	85	(1.9)	405	(6.5)	441	(5.5)	498	(3.8)	556	(3.4)	610	(3.4)	658	(3.7)	685	(4.4)
Korea	561	(4.3)	91	(1.8)	406	(6.6)	443	(5.9)	505	(5.1)	568	(4.5)	625	(4.6)	672	(4.4)	698	(5.1)
Netherlands	511	(4.4)	99	(3.0)	336	(8.6)	378	(8.5)	448	(5.9)	517	(4.9)	581	(4.8)	633	(4.8)	662	(5.1)
Norway	503	(3.3)	103	(1.9)	328	(6.7)	370	(4.9)	436	(3.9)	507	(3.5)	574	(3.8)	633	(4.3)	665	(6.0)
Poland	481	(4.4)	96	(3.4)	318	(8.9)	358	(6.3)	421	(5.4)	485	(4.3)	546	(4.6)	600	(4.8)	632	(6.0)
Portugal	494	(3.6)	88	(1.6)	345	(5.5)	381	(4.3)	436	(4.2)	497	(4.3)	555	(3.7)	604	(4.2)	633	(5.4)
Slovak Republic	483	(3.6)	98	(2.7)	314	(7.1)	354	(6.2)	420	(4.8)	487	(3.9)	550	(4.2)	606	(5.2)	639	(6.9)
Slovenia	476	(1.5)	97	(1.3)	310	(5.4)	350	(3.8)	413	(3.0)	479	(2.4)	545	(2.3)	599	(2.8)	628	(3.7)
Spain	477	(4.1)	104	(2.9)	292	(10.4)	338	(7.8)	411	(5.3)	483	(3.8)	549	(3.9)	605	(4.3)	638	(5.0)
Sweden	491	(2.9)	96	(1.8)	328	(7.6)	365	(4.0)	428	(3.7)	494	(3.2)	557	(2.9)	612	(3.7)	643	(4.4)
Turkey	454	(4.0)	79	(2.2)	328	(4.5)	354	(4.3)	399	(4.0)	451	(4.3)	508	(5.7)	560	(6.8)	590	(8.0)
England (United Kingdom)	517	(4.2)	97	(2.4)	352	(9.2)	391	(6.0)	455	(5.7)	522	(4.8)	584	(4.1)	636	(4.5)	667	(5.0)
United States	508	(3.9)	93	(2.3)	352	(7.1)	388	(6.0)	446	(4.9)	510	(4.2)	571	(4.1)	626	(4.4)	658	(5.3)
OECD average	500	(0.7)	96	(0.4)	336	(1.4)	375	(1.1)	438	(0.9)	504	(0.7)	567	(0.7)	620	(0.8)	650	(1.0)
Brazil	428	(4.7)	92	(2.4)	276	(7.1)	311	(5.7)	368	(5.5)	429	(5.2)	490	(6.3)	545	(5.6)	575	(5.6)
Bulgaria	402	(5.1)	107	(3.5)	220	(10.2)	263	(8.6)	331	(6.1)	405	(5.5)	476	(5.3)	535	(7.1)	571	(7.6)
Colombia	399	(3.5)	92	(2.0)	253	(5.4)	284	(4.9)	337	(4.3)	397	(3.7)	459	(4.1)	517	(5.2)	553	(5.6)
Croatia	466	(3.9)	92	(2.0)	314	(5.6)	349	(4.9)	404	(4.0)	465	(4.2)	530	(4.6)	585	(5.1)	616	(6.2)
Cyprus*	445	(1.4)	99	(1.0)	278	(4.3)	315	(2.8)	378	(2.4)	447	(1.8)	513	(2.7)	571	(2.8)	604	(3.5)
Hong Kong-China	540	(3.9)	92	(2.2)	379	(6.7)	421	(6.7)	483	(5.6)	544	(4.2)	601	(3.7)	654	(4.1)	684	(4.9)
Macao-China	540	(1.0)	79	(0.8)	405	(3.3)	437	(3.0)	488	(1.5)	544	(1.7)	595	(1.6)	640	(2.1)	664	(2.2)
Malaysia	422	(3.5)	84	(2.0)	287	(4.7)	315	(4.5)	364	(4.2)	422	(4.1)	479	(4.1)	531	(5.0)	561	(6.0)
Montenegro	407	(1.2)	92	(1.1)	256	(4.3)	289	(3.1)	344	(2.5)	407	(2.2)	470	(2.2)	526	(3.8)	556	(3.4)
Russian Federation	489	(3.4)	88	(2.0)	345	(4.7)	377	(4.8)	431	(4.0)	490	(3.5)	547	(4.1)	602	(6.1)	635	(5.9)
Serbia	473	(3.1)	89	(1.9)	322	(6.4)	357	(6.1)	414	(4.3)	476	(3.8)	535	(3.4)	586	(3.4)	616	(3.4)
Shanghai-China	536	(3.3)	90	(2.2)	381	(7.0)	419	(5.7)	479	(3.9)	541	(3.5)	599	(3.9)	648	(4.7)	676	(4.9)
Singapore	562	(1.2)	95	(1.0)	398	(3.0)	436	(2.9)	500	(2.0)	568	(2.1)	629	(1.9)	681	(2.1)	710	(3.4)
Chinese Taipei	534	(2.9)	91	(1.9)	377	(6.7)	414	(5.1)	475	(4.1)	540	(3.3)	601	(2.9)	646	(3.2)	674	(3.2)
United Arab Emirates	411	(2.8)	106	(1.8)	237	(5.9)	277	(5.3)	342	(3.6)	411	(2.9)	482	(3.1)	546	(3.3)	584	(3.8)
Uruguay	403	(3.5)	97	(2.0)	244	(5.9)	279	(5.1)	337	(4.7)	403	(3.9)	470	(3.9)	530	(4.3)	566	(6.0)

* See notes at the beginning of this Annex.

StatLink ᴍˢᴾ http://dx.doi.org/10.1787/888933003668

[Part 2/2]

Table V.2.2 **Mean score and variation in student performance in problem solving**

	Range of performance							
	Inter-quartile range (75th minus 25th percentile)		Inter-decile range (90th minus 10th percentile)		Top range (90th minus 50th percentile)		Bottom range (50th minus 10th percentile)	
	Range	S.E.	Range	S.E.	Range	S.E.	Range	S.E.
Australia	132	(2.1)	251	(3.0)	121	(2.2)	130	(2.8)
Austria	126	(4.5)	239	(7.3)	111	(4.0)	128	(5.7)
Belgium	143	(3.2)	272	(5.3)	119	(2.5)	153	(4.5)
Canada	132	(3.0)	251	(4.1)	120	(2.4)	131	(3.1)
Chile	118	(3.8)	220	(5.7)	107	(3.4)	114	(4.2)
Czech Republic	128	(4.0)	243	(6.6)	111	(3.8)	132	(5.0)
Denmark	122	(3.7)	234	(6.3)	111	(5.0)	123	(4.7)
Estonia	118	(3.5)	225	(4.7)	109	(4.2)	117	(4.1)
Finland	125	(3.8)	239	(3.8)	114	(3.6)	125	(3.1)
France	122	(4.4)	239	(7.4)	108	(3.4)	131	(6.6)
Germany	135	(4.8)	252	(7.3)	113	(3.6)	139	(5.9)
Hungary	141	(7.1)	272	(9.5)	126	(4.7)	145	(8.2)
Ireland	124	(3.6)	237	(5.1)	113	(2.7)	123	(4.0)
Israel	172	(5.0)	320	(8.8)	151	(5.3)	168	(6.9)
Italy	121	(4.3)	227	(6.6)	107	(3.5)	121	(4.9)
Japan	112	(3.2)	216	(5.7)	102	(3.1)	115	(4.2)
Korea	120	(3.6)	228	(5.6)	104	(3.5)	124	(4.5)
Netherlands	133	(6.0)	256	(9.0)	116	(4.0)	139	(7.6)
Norway	138	(3.5)	262	(5.8)	126	(3.3)	136	(4.8)
Poland	125	(4.1)	242	(6.6)	115	(3.7)	126	(4.9)
Portugal	119	(3.7)	223	(4.8)	107	(3.9)	116	(3.2)
Slovak Republic	131	(4.6)	251	(7.8)	118	(5.6)	133	(5.1)
Slovenia	132	(3.5)	249	(4.5)	120	(3.4)	129	(4.0)
Spain	138	(4.3)	267	(7.8)	122	(3.5)	145	(6.3)
Sweden	129	(3.1)	247	(4.7)	117	(4.0)	130	(3.6)
Turkey	109	(4.7)	206	(7.0)	109	(4.9)	97	(3.8)
England (United Kingdom)	129	(4.8)	245	(6.2)	114	(4.1)	131	(4.3)
United States	126	(4.2)	237	(6.3)	116	(3.6)	121	(5.0)
OECD average	129	(0.8)	245	(1.2)	115	(0.7)	129	(0.9)
Brazil	122	(4.1)	234	(6.1)	116	(4.0)	118	(5.0)
Bulgaria	145	(5.5)	272	(10.2)	131	(6.1)	142	(6.7)
Colombia	122	(3.8)	233	(6.3)	120	(4.4)	112	(3.9)
Croatia	126	(3.5)	237	(5.9)	120	(4.4)	117	(4.4)
Cyprus*	135	(3.1)	256	(4.0)	124	(3.1)	132	(3.3)
Hong Kong-China	119	(4.4)	234	(6.7)	110	(4.2)	123	(5.2)
Macao-China	107	(2.1)	203	(3.1)	95	(2.5)	108	(3.2)
Malaysia	115	(3.8)	217	(5.6)	109	(3.9)	108	(3.4)
Montenegro	126	(3.3)	237	(4.4)	118	(4.6)	118	(3.8)
Russian Federation	116	(3.8)	224	(6.6)	112	(4.6)	113	(4.0)
Serbia	122	(4.0)	229	(6.4)	111	(3.4)	119	(5.4)
Shanghai-China	120	(4.0)	229	(7.1)	107	(3.5)	121	(5.0)
Singapore	130	(2.4)	244	(3.5)	113	(2.9)	131	(3.4)
Chinese Taipei	126	(3.5)	232	(5.4)	107	(3.5)	125	(4.3)
United Arab Emirates	139	(3.5)	269	(5.7)	135	(3.4)	134	(4.4)
Uruguay	134	(4.3)	250	(6.3)	126	(4.0)	124	(4.1)

* See notes at the beginning of this Annex.
StatLink ᗰᔕᒪ http://dx.doi.org/10.1787/888933003668

[Part 1/1]

Table V.2.3 **Top performers in problem solving and other curricular subjects**

| | 15-year-old students who are: | | | | | | | | Percentage of top performers in problem solving who are also top performers in mathematics | | Percentage of top performers in problem solving who are also top performers in reading | | Percentage of top performers in problem solving who are also top performers in science | |
| | Not top performers in any of the four domains | | Top performers in at least one subject, but not in problem solving | | Top performers in problem solving, but not in any of the other subjects assessed | | Top performers in problem solving and in at least one other subject | | | | | | | |
	%	S.E.	%	S.E.	%	S.E.	%	S.E.	%	S.E.	%	S.E.	%	S.E.
Australia	75.6	(0.8)	7.7	(0.4)	4.7	(0.4)	12.0	(0.5)	61.3	(2.0)	47.1	(2.0)	54.9	(1.8)
Austria	80.8	(1.1)	8.2	(0.7)	3.0	(0.4)	8.0	(0.7)	66.8	(2.9)	31.8	(3.5)	42.8	(3.3)
Belgium	74.1	(0.7)	11.5	(0.6)	3.5	(0.4)	10.8	(0.6)	70.8	(2.5)	47.4	(2.7)	43.3	(2.5)
Canada	72.6	(0.9)	9.9	(0.4)	5.5	(0.4)	12.0	(0.6)	57.7	(2.1)	44.5	(1.8)	43.9	(2.0)
Chile	96.7	(0.4)	1.2	(0.2)	1.1	(0.2)	1.0	(0.2)	40.0	(5.3)	12.8	(3.4)	22.9	(4.5)
Czech Republic	81.9	(0.9)	6.2	(0.5)	2.9	(0.5)	9.0	(0.7)	70.3	(3.2)	34.9	(2.6)	45.0	(3.1)
Denmark	84.3	(0.9)	6.9	(0.7)	3.2	(0.5)	5.6	(0.6)	55.9	(4.7)	30.9	(3.1)	42.4	(4.3)
Estonia	78.4	(0.8)	9.9	(0.7)	2.5	(0.4)	9.3	(0.7)	69.8	(2.5)	41.5	(3.9)	62.1	(3.2)
Finland	73.1	(0.8)	11.9	(0.8)	3.0	(0.4)	12.0	(0.7)	66.1	(2.5)	49.5	(2.0)	65.4	(2.4)
France	78.8	(1.0)	9.2	(0.7)	2.5	(0.4)	9.5	(0.8)	67.4	(2.7)	55.3	(3.5)	44.9	(3.4)
Germany	76.6	(1.2)	10.6	(0.8)	2.9	(0.5)	9.9	(0.8)	72.2	(2.9)	39.0	(2.7)	53.3	(3.6)
Hungary	86.9	(1.2)	7.5	(0.8)	1.5	(0.4)	4.1	(0.6)	67.8	(5.8)	42.0	(5.3)	50.7	(4.7)
Ireland	80.5	(0.8)	10.1	(0.6)	2.6	(0.4)	6.8	(0.5)	59.0	(3.5)	52.0	(3.1)	57.2	(3.5)
Israel	83.6	(1.3)	7.6	(0.7)	2.2	(0.4)	6.6	(0.8)	63.5	(3.0)	51.7	(3.8)	44.3	(3.4)
Italy	81.7	(1.2)	7.6	(0.7)	4.6	(0.6)	6.2	(0.7)	49.4	(3.7)	27.3	(3.7)	34.3	(4.2)
Japan	63.7	(1.6)	14.1	(0.9)	6.3	(0.5)	16.0	(1.1)	62.9	(2.4)	47.0	(2.5)	50.7	(2.3)
Korea	61.0	(2.0)	11.3	(0.8)	6.7	(0.7)	20.9	(1.5)	73.5	(2.1)	40.3	(2.5)	34.1	(2.7)
Netherlands	75.4	(1.3)	11.0	(0.8)	2.1	(0.5)	11.5	(1.0)	79.1	(2.7)	45.1	(3.9)	57.3	(4.1)
Norway	79.9	(1.0)	7.0	(0.6)	5.2	(0.8)	7.9	(0.6)	46.9	(3.8)	42.5	(4.2)	36.9	(3.3)
Poland	78.7	(1.4)	14.4	(1.0)	1.1	(0.3)	5.7	(0.7)	75.8	(4.0)	57.3	(4.2)	61.9	(5.1)
Portugal	84.8	(1.0)	7.8	(0.6)	2.3	(0.5)	5.1	(0.6)	64.9	(4.5)	34.3	(4.8)	32.5	(4.0)
Slovak Republic	86.1	(1.0)	6.1	(0.7)	1.8	(0.4)	6.0	(0.8)	74.5	(4.8)	32.3	(5.4)	42.4	(6.4)
Slovenia	82.6	(0.6)	10.8	(0.5)	1.4	(0.2)	5.3	(0.5)	74.4	(3.1)	34.9	(3.8)	60.1	(3.4)
Spain	86.1	(0.8)	6.1	(0.6)	3.4	(0.4)	4.4	(0.4)	46.6	(3.3)	28.8	(3.3)	28.5	(2.8)
Sweden	84.4	(0.9)	6.8	(0.8)	3.2	(0.4)	5.6	(0.5)	52.3	(3.3)	41.3	(3.8)	38.6	(3.2)
Turkey	91.7	(1.4)	6.1	(1.0)	0.3	(0.2)	1.8	(0.5)	76.2	(7.2)	49.3	(9.9)	30.1	(5.6)
England (United Kingdom)	78.9	(1.3)	6.8	(0.6)	4.4	(0.5)	9.8	(0.9)	59.0	(3.1)	41.7	(3.6)	52.8	(3.2)
United States	83.9	(1.0)	4.5	(0.5)	4.1	(0.5)	7.5	(0.7)	54.6	(2.9)	45.1	(2.8)	46.9	(3.1)
OECD average	80.1	(0.2)	8.5	(0.1)	3.1	(0.1)	8.2	(0.1)	63.5	(0.7)	41.0	(0.7)	45.7	(0.7)
Brazil	97.6	(0.5)	0.6	(0.2)	1.1	(0.3)	0.7	(0.2)	34.1	(8.4)	14.5	(5.9)	12.0	(5.4)
Bulgaria	92.6	(0.9)	5.8	(0.7)	0.3	(0.2)	1.2	(0.3)	65.5	(8.2)	50.1	(8.8)	54.1	(12.0)
Colombia	98.6	(0.3)	0.3	(0.1)	0.9	(0.2)	0.3	(0.1)	17.6	(7.0)	9.3	(6.1)	6.8	(4.0)
Croatia	89.5	(1.3)	5.8	(0.7)	1.1	(0.2)	3.6	(0.6)	70.3	(5.5)	36.3	(4.8)	46.1	(6.7)
Cyprus*	92.4	(0.5)	4.0	(0.4)	1.4	(0.2)	2.2	(0.2)	49.4	(4.4)	36.4	(4.9)	28.5	(6.2)
Hong Kong-China	60.2	(1.5)	20.5	(1.1)	3.4	(0.4)	15.9	(1.1)	79.8	(2.2)	48.9	(3.2)	49.4	(3.1)
Macao-China	70.8	(0.6)	12.6	(0.5)	4.0	(0.4)	12.6	(0.4)	74.9	(2.3)	26.5	(1.7)	28.3	(1.8)
Malaysia	98.1	(0.4)	1.0	(0.2)	0.4	(0.1)	0.5	(0.2)	50.7	(9.5)	4.4	(3.3)	20.8	(8.3)
Montenegro	97.8	(0.3)	1.4	(0.2)	0.4	(0.1)	0.4	(0.1)	39.4	(11.9)	21.3	(11.1)	18.4	(9.7)
Russian Federation	86.8	(1.1)	5.9	(0.7)	3.0	(0.5)	4.2	(0.6)	50.0	(4.5)	32.1	(3.8)	31.3	(4.0)
Serbia	92.5	(0.7)	2.7	(0.5)	1.9	(0.3)	2.8	(0.4)	53.0	(6.9)	24.9	(4.8)	23.8	(4.6)
Shanghai-China	43.6	(1.4)	38.1	(1.5)	0.3	(0.1)	17.9	(1.3)	98.0	(0.7)	71.7	(2.3)	75.1	(2.0)
Singapore	54.2	(0.7)	16.5	(0.6)	4.3	(0.4)	25.0	(0.7)	84.1	(1.2)	50.2	(1.5)	57.0	(1.7)
Chinese Taipei	61.3	(1.3)	20.4	(1.0)	1.2	(0.2)	17.1	(0.9)	93.0	(1.2)	43.7	(2.6)	35.3	(2.2)
United Arab Emirates	94.3	(0.4)	3.2	(0.3)	0.8	(0.1)	1.7	(0.2)	54.9	(3.7)	36.8	(4.5)	46.6	(4.0)
Uruguay	97.2	(0.5)	1.6	(0.3)	0.5	(0.1)	0.6	(0.2)	44.7	(9.0)	23.8	(5.7)	28.0	(9.6)

OECD (left margin, top group); *Partners* (left margin, bottom group)

* See notes at the beginning of this Annex.

StatLink ᴍᶳᴾ http://dx.doi.org/10.1787/888933003668

[Part 1/2]

Table V.2.4 **Between- and within-school variation in problem-solving performance**

		Total variation in problem-solving performance[1]		Variation in problem-solving performance between schools[2]		Variation in problem-solving performance within schools[3]		As a percentage of the average total variation in problem-solving performance across OECD countries		
								Total variation	Between-school variation	Within-school variation
		Variance	S.E.	Variance	S.E.	Variance	S.E.	%	%	%
OECD	Australia	9 482	(209)	2 569	(178)	6 951	(106)	102.4	27.7	75.1
	Austria	8 801	(547)	4 183	(532)	4 505	(121)	95.1	45.2	48.7
	Belgium	11 314	(392)	5 412	(513)	5 804	(144)	122.2	58.4	62.7
	Canada	10 063	(343)	2 271	(236)	7 692	(168)	108.7	24.5	83.1
	Chile	7 382	(283)	3 153	(299)	4 123	(90)	79.7	34.1	44.5
	Czech Republic	9 056	(371)	4 366	(473)	4 474	(174)	97.8	47.1	48.3
	Denmark	8 522	(363)	2 441	(326)	6 048	(164)	92.0	26.4	65.3
	Estonia	7 658	(252)	1 826	(245)	5 868	(171)	82.7	19.7	63.4
	Finland	8 658	(218)	884	(120)	7 753	(183)	93.5	9.5	83.7
	France	9 250	(812)	w	w	w	w	99.9	w	w
	Germany	9 703	(475)	5 328	(471)	4 334	(111)	104.8	57.5	46.8
	Hungary	10 907	(573)	6 445	(683)	4 245	(113)	117.8	69.6	45.8
	Ireland	8 676	(338)	2 117	(272)	6 486	(162)	93.7	22.9	70.0
	Israel	15 230	(809)	7 751	(860)	7 429	(199)	164.5	83.7	80.2
	Italy	8 219	(363)	3 461	(360)	4 496	(131)	88.8	37.4	48.6
	Japan	7 251	(320)	2 459	(280)	4 768	(124)	78.3	26.6	51.5
	Korea	8 311	(331)	2 604	(288)	5 575	(197)	89.8	28.1	60.2
	Netherlands	9 783	(597)	5 649	(634)	4 147	(146)	105.7	61.0	44.8
	Norway	10 600	(401)	2 264	(340)	8 270	(237)	114.5	24.4	89.3
	Poland	9 303	(639)	3 357	(675)	5 930	(204)	100.5	36.3	64.0
	Portugal	7 712	(280)	2 314	(240)	5 420	(157)	83.3	25.0	58.5
	Slovak Republic	9 597	(526)	4 761	(569)	4 625	(161)	103.7	51.4	50.0
	Slovenia	9 428	(230)	5 114	(434)	4 272	(153)	101.8	55.2	46.1
	Spain	10 890	(613)	3 121	(470)	7 776	(213)	117.6	33.7	84.0
	Sweden	9 260	(348)	1 720	(321)	7 474	(182)	100.0	18.6	80.7
	Turkey	6 246	(367)	3 239	(385)	2 997	(89)	67.5	35.0	32.4
	England (United Kingdom)	9 342	(455)	2 735	(386)	6 606	(179)	100.9	29.5	71.3
	United States	8 610	(398)	2 485	(410)	6 106	(165)	93.0	26.8	65.9
	OECD average	9 259	(85)	3 548	(87)	5 646	(30)	100.0	38.3	61.0
Partners	Brazil	8 421	(448)	3 988	(491)	4 435	(153)	90.9	43.1	47.9
	Bulgaria	11 347	(776)	6 294	(750)	4 994	(125)	122.5	68.0	53.9
	Colombia	8 397	(343)	3 092	(332)	5 262	(156)	90.7	33.4	56.8
	Croatia	8 472	(346)	3 426	(403)	5 042	(137)	91.5	37.0	54.5
	Cyprus*	9 781	(194)	3 448	(1 455)	6 641	(167)	105.6	37.2	71.7
	Hong Kong-China	8 401	(397)	3 034	(365)	5 347	(160)	90.7	32.8	57.8
	Macao-China	6 269	(129)	1 871	(1 217)	5 035	(166)	67.7	20.2	54.4
	Malaysia	6 982	(320)	2 614	(306)	4 361	(162)	75.4	28.2	47.1
	Montenegro	8 390	(201)	3 212	(670)	5 178	(163)	90.6	34.7	55.9
	Russian Federation	7 725	(360)	2 857	(393)	4 872	(145)	83.4	30.9	52.6
	Serbia	7 942	(358)	2 935	(333)	4 949	(164)	85.8	31.7	53.4
	Shanghai-China	8 082	(413)	3 333	(362)	4 723	(151)	87.3	36.0	51.0
	Singapore	9 021	(181)	3 061	(362)	5 962	(159)	97.4	33.1	64.4
	Chinese Taipei	8 266	(363)	3 214	(374)	5 010	(150)	89.3	34.7	54.1
	United Arab Emirates	11 134	(390)	5 607	(477)	5 504	(150)	120.2	60.6	59.4
	Uruguay	9 457	(383)	4 000	(419)	5 446	(133)	102.1	43.2	58.8

1. The total variation in student performance is calculated from the square of the standard deviation for all students.
2. In some countries/economies, sub-units within schools were sampled instead of schools; this may affect the estimation of between-school variation components (see Annex A3).
3. Due to the unbalanced clustered nature of the data, the sum of the between- and within-school variation components, as an estimate from a sample, does not necessarily add up to the total.
4. The *index of academic inclusion* is calculated as 100 × (1-rho), where rho stands for the intra-class correlation of performance, i.e. the variation in student performance between schools, divided by the sum of the variation in student performance between schools and the variation in student performance within schools.
5. The *index of social inclusion* is calculated as 100 × (1-rho), where rho stands for the intra-class correlation of socio-economic status, i.e. the between-school variation in the *PISA index of economic, social and cultural status* (ESCS) of students, divided by the sum of the between-school variation in students' socio-economic status and the within-school variation in students' socio-economic status.
* See notes at the beginning of this Annex.
StatLink http://dx.doi.org/10.1787/888933003668

[Part 2/2]

Table V.2.4   **Between- and within-school variation in problem-solving performance**

| | Index of academic inclusion: Proportion of performance variation within schools[4] | | | | | | | | Index of social inclusion: Proportion of ESCS variation within schools[5] | |
| | Problem solving | | Mathematics | | Reading | | Science | | | |
	%	S.E.	%	S.E.	%	S.E.	%	S.E.	%	S.E.
Australia	73.0	(1.4)	72.1	(1.8)	73.1	(1.5)	75.6	(1.5)	76.5	(1.2)
Austria	51.9	(3.1)	51.6	(2.4)	46.7	(2.0)	52.0	(2.4)	71.2	(2.9)
Belgium	51.7	(2.5)	48.6	(2.3)	45.6	(2.6)	50.8	(2.4)	72.4	(2.1)
Canada	77.2	(1.8)	80.2	(1.4)	81.1	(1.3)	82.8	(1.4)	82.8	(1.3)
Chile	56.7	(2.4)	56.6	(2.2)	55.5	(2.3)	58.8	(2.2)	47.2	(2.4)
Czech Republic	50.6	(3.0)	48.5	(2.8)	50.0	(2.8)	52.6	(3.1)	76.4	(2.3)
Denmark	71.2	(2.7)	83.5	(2.0)	79.0	(3.8)	82.4	(2.5)	82.3	(1.7)
Estonia	76.3	(2.5)	82.7	(2.4)	78.8	(2.8)	81.1	(2.3)	81.5	(2.1)
Finland	89.8	(1.3)	92.5	(1.2)	90.9	(1.2)	92.3	(1.1)	91.1	(1.1)
France	w	w	w	w	w	w	w	w	w	w
Germany	44.9	(2.3)	47.0	(2.1)	42.7	(2.1)	47.2	(2.5)	73.6	(2.0)
Hungary	39.7	(2.7)	38.1	(2.5)	35.3	(2.2)	42.8	(2.6)	62.6	(2.8)
Ireland	75.4	(2.4)	81.8	(2.3)	77.5	(2.6)	81.7	(2.4)	79.7	(2.3)
Israel	48.9	(2.9)	57.6	(2.8)	54.6	(3.6)	56.6	(3.1)	74.6	(1.9)
Italy	56.5	(2.6)	49.7	(2.9)	49.5	(2.9)	50.6	(2.8)	75.1	(2.4)
Japan	66.0	(2.6)	47.0	(2.5)	55.3	(2.6)	56.6	(2.6)	77.8	(1.8)
Korea	68.2	(2.5)	60.4	(3.2)	63.7	(3.2)	63.7	(3.1)	78.3	(2.0)
Netherlands	42.3	(2.9)	34.1	(2.2)	34.4	(2.7)	38.8	(2.4)	81.8	(1.9)
Norway	78.5	(2.6)	87.1	(1.8)	86.2	(1.9)	86.9	(2.1)	91.0	(1.5)
Poland	63.9	(4.8)	79.5	(3.4)	79.6	(2.6)	82.0	(2.9)	76.4	(2.3)
Portugal	70.1	(2.3)	70.1	(2.5)	68.8	(2.4)	68.5	(2.6)	68.6	(3.6)
Slovak Republic	49.3	(3.1)	50.1	(2.9)	38.1	(2.7)	45.6	(3.0)	64.4	(3.0)
Slovenia	45.5	(2.3)	41.3	(2.5)	39.9	(2.2)	43.9	(2.6)	74.6	(2.0)
Spain	71.4	(3.1)	80.2	(1.8)	80.7	(2.1)	80.6	(2.2)	74.9	(2.3)
Sweden	81.3	(2.9)	87.5	(1.8)	83.5	(2.0)	83.3	(2.0)	86.9	(1.5)
Turkey	48.1	(3.2)	38.2	(3.3)	44.4	(3.2)	43.6	(3.1)	72.3	(3.0)
England (United Kingdom)	70.7	(3.0)	71.1	(2.9)	69.2	(3.1)	70.7	(2.7)	78.7	(2.5)
United States	71.1	(3.5)	76.3	(2.2)	76.3	(2.6)	76.0	(2.3)	73.8	(2.5)
OECD average	61.9	(0.5)	62.8	(0.5)	61.5	(0.5)	64.0	(0.5)	75.7	(0.4)
Brazil	52.7	(3.2)	55.3	(3.5)	58.7	(3.2)	57.2	(3.3)	61.2	(3.5)
Bulgaria	44.2	(3.1)	47.2	(2.7)	40.6	(2.4)	45.6	(2.6)	59.6	(2.9)
Colombia	63.0	(2.7)	64.9	(2.9)	61.2	(3.1)	67.0	(3.0)	63.2	(3.0)
Croatia	59.5	(3.0)	55.7	(3.9)	48.9	(2.9)	62.2	(3.3)	75.9	(2.2)
Cyprus*	66.1	(8.3)	67.6	(4.8)	65.5	(4.6)	60.1	(11.9)	76.6	(3.4)
Hong Kong-China	63.8	(2.8)	57.6	(2.2)	58.4	(2.4)	63.5	(2.3)	67.7	(3.6)
Macao-China	72.9	(12.8)	65.6	(22.0)	64.7	(17.2)	66.5	(36.7)	73.7	(4.7)
Malaysia	62.5	(2.9)	67.6	(3.2)	74.9	(2.7)	73.5	(2.7)	71.5	(2.5)
Montenegro	61.7	(5.1)	63.5	(7.3)	62.4	(5.3)	65.3	(5.9)	80.6	(5.6)
Russian Federation	63.0	(3.4)	73.2	(2.6)	67.3	(2.8)	70.5	(2.4)	75.0	(2.5)
Serbia	62.8	(2.7)	54.0	(3.3)	54.5	(2.9)	58.5	(3.0)	78.0	(2.4)
Shanghai-China	58.6	(2.7)	53.1	(2.7)	53.2	(2.7)	53.9	(2.6)	66.8	(2.6)
Singapore	66.1	(2.8)	63.3	(3.2)	64.3	(3.1)	63.0	(3.2)	76.4	(2.7)
Chinese Taipei	60.9	(3.0)	57.9	(3.2)	61.2	(2.9)	58.0	(3.3)	76.7	(2.1)
United Arab Emirates	49.5	(2.2)	55.6	(2.2)	51.0	(2.0)	56.6	(2.1)	73.9	(1.7)
Uruguay	57.7	(2.6)	58.0	(3.0)	54.7	(2.8)	60.8	(2.9)	60.2	(3.8)

OECD (rows Australia–United States); *Partners* (rows Brazil–Uruguay)

1. The total variation in student performance is calculated from the square of the standard deviation for all students.
2. In some countries/economies, sub-units within schools were sampled instead of schools; this may affect the estimation of between-school variation components (see Annex A3).
3. Due to the unbalanced clustered nature of the data, the sum of the between- and within-school variation components, as an estimate from a sample, does not necessarily add up to the total.
4. The *index of academic inclusion* is calculated as 100 × (1-rho), where rho stands for the intra-class correlation of performance, i.e. the variation in student performance between schools, divided by the sum of the variation in student performance between schools and the variation in student performance within schools.
5. The *index of social inclusion* is calculated as 100 × (1-rho), where rho stands for the intra-class correlation of socio-economic status, i.e. the between-school variation in the *PISA index of economic, social and cultural status* (ESCS) of students, divided by the sum of the between-school variation in students' socio-economic status and the within-school variation in students' socio-economic status.
* See notes at the beginning of this Annex.
StatLink http://dx.doi.org/10.1787/888933003668

[Part 1/2]

Table V.2.5 **Correlation of problem-solving performance with performance in mathematics, reading and science**

		Correlation[1] between performance in problem solving and performance in curricular domains						For comparison: Correlation[1] between performance in curricular domains					
		Problem solving and mathematics		Problem solving and reading		Problem solving and science		Mathematics and reading		Mathematics and science		Reading and science	
		Corr.	S.E.	Corr.	S.E.	Corr.	S.E.	Corr.	S.E.	Corr.	S.E.	Corr.	S.E.
OECD	Australia	0.83	(0.00)	0.77	(0.01)	0.81	(0.01)	0.87	(0.00)	0.91	(0.00)	0.90	(0.00)
	Austria	0.80	(0.01)	0.76	(0.01)	0.77	(0.02)	0.85	(0.01)	0.91	(0.00)	0.88	(0.01)
	Belgium	0.81	(0.01)	0.76	(0.01)	0.79	(0.01)	0.88	(0.01)	0.92	(0.00)	0.90	(0.00)
	Canada	0.76	(0.01)	0.71	(0.01)	0.75	(0.01)	0.82	(0.00)	0.87	(0.00)	0.87	(0.00)
	Chile	0.80	(0.01)	0.72	(0.01)	0.75	(0.01)	0.80	(0.01)	0.86	(0.01)	0.84	(0.01)
	Czech Republic	0.88	(0.01)	0.79	(0.01)	0.83	(0.01)	0.84	(0.01)	0.88	(0.01)	0.84	(0.01)
	Denmark	0.77	(0.01)	0.69	(0.02)	0.74	(0.02)	0.84	(0.01)	0.90	(0.00)	0.88	(0.01)
	Estonia	0.83	(0.01)	0.77	(0.01)	0.80	(0.01)	0.83	(0.01)	0.88	(0.00)	0.85	(0.01)
	Finland	0.83	(0.01)	0.74	(0.01)	0.79	(0.01)	0.82	(0.01)	0.89	(0.00)	0.87	(0.00)
	France	0.83	(0.02)	0.76	(0.02)	0.80	(0.02)	0.86	(0.01)	0.90	(0.01)	0.88	(0.01)
	Germany	0.83	(0.01)	0.77	(0.01)	0.81	(0.01)	0.87	(0.01)	0.92	(0.00)	0.90	(0.00)
	Hungary	0.83	(0.01)	0.79	(0.01)	0.81	(0.01)	0.87	(0.01)	0.93	(0.00)	0.88	(0.01)
	Ireland	0.80	(0.01)	0.74	(0.01)	0.79	(0.01)	0.87	(0.01)	0.91	(0.00)	0.90	(0.00)
	Israel	0.85	(0.01)	0.79	(0.01)	0.84	(0.01)	0.84	(0.01)	0.91	(0.00)	0.88	(0.01)
	Italy	0.75	(0.01)	0.67	(0.02)	0.73	(0.02)	0.84	(0.01)	0.88	(0.01)	0.85	(0.01)
	Japan	0.75	(0.01)	0.68	(0.02)	0.72	(0.01)	0.86	(0.01)	0.89	(0.01)	0.89	(0.01)
	Korea	0.80	(0.01)	0.76	(0.01)	0.77	(0.01)	0.88	(0.01)	0.90	(0.00)	0.88	(0.01)
	Netherlands	0.84	(0.01)	0.80	(0.02)	0.85	(0.01)	0.88	(0.01)	0.92	(0.00)	0.89	(0.01)
	Norway	0.79	(0.01)	0.71	(0.01)	0.75	(0.02)	0.84	(0.01)	0.90	(0.00)	0.86	(0.01)
	Poland	0.75	(0.02)	0.75	(0.02)	0.75	(0.02)	0.83	(0.01)	0.89	(0.00)	0.87	(0.01)
	Portugal	0.80	(0.01)	0.71	(0.02)	0.76	(0.01)	0.84	(0.01)	0.90	(0.00)	0.86	(0.01)
	Slovak Republic	0.85	(0.01)	0.78	(0.01)	0.82	(0.01)	0.85	(0.01)	0.92	(0.01)	0.89	(0.01)
	Slovenia	0.81	(0.01)	0.75	(0.01)	0.80	(0.01)	0.83	(0.01)	0.90	(0.00)	0.90	(0.00)
	Spain	0.75	(0.01)	0.67	(0.02)	0.71	(0.01)	0.83	(0.01)	0.89	(0.00)	0.83	(0.01)
	Sweden	0.81	(0.01)	0.71	(0.01)	0.76	(0.01)	0.85	(0.00)	0.89	(0.00)	0.87	(0.01)
	Turkey	0.84	(0.01)	0.73	(0.02)	0.77	(0.01)	0.81	(0.01)	0.87	(0.01)	0.84	(0.01)
	England (United Kingdom)	0.86	(0.01)	0.79	(0.01)	0.83	(0.01)	0.90	(0.01)	0.93	(0.00)	0.91	(0.00)
	United States	0.86	(0.01)	0.80	(0.01)	0.83	(0.01)	0.89	(0.01)	0.93	(0.00)	0.91	(0.00)
	OECD average	0.81	(0.00)	0.75	(0.00)	0.78	(0.00)	0.85	(0.00)	0.90	(0.00)	0.88	(0.00)
Partners	Brazil	0.83	(0.01)	0.70	(0.02)	0.75	(0.02)	0.80	(0.01)	0.86	(0.01)	0.82	(0.01)
	Bulgaria	0.81	(0.01)	0.75	(0.01)	0.78	(0.01)	0.83	(0.01)	0.89	(0.01)	0.88	(0.01)
	Colombia	0.74	(0.02)	0.65	(0.02)	0.67	(0.02)	0.81	(0.01)	0.86	(0.01)	0.81	(0.01)
	Croatia	0.85	(0.01)	0.74	(0.02)	0.79	(0.01)	0.83	(0.01)	0.89	(0.01)	0.84	(0.01)
	Cyprus*	0.80	(0.01)	0.71	(0.01)	0.76	(0.01)	0.82	(0.00)	0.89	(0.00)	0.85	(0.00)
	Hong Kong-China	0.76	(0.01)	0.72	(0.02)	0.71	(0.01)	0.86	(0.01)	0.89	(0.01)	0.90	(0.00)
	Macao-China	0.80	(0.01)	0.69	(0.01)	0.74	(0.01)	0.82	(0.01)	0.87	(0.00)	0.86	(0.01)
	Malaysia	0.83	(0.01)	0.70	(0.01)	0.78	(0.01)	0.80	(0.01)	0.88	(0.01)	0.85	(0.01)
	Montenegro	0.81	(0.01)	0.68	(0.01)	0.75	(0.01)	0.80	(0.01)	0.89	(0.00)	0.84	(0.01)
	Russian Federation	0.74	(0.01)	0.65	(0.02)	0.65	(0.02)	0.78	(0.01)	0.85	(0.01)	0.84	(0.01)
	Serbia	0.83	(0.01)	0.72	(0.01)	0.77	(0.01)	0.82	(0.01)	0.88	(0.01)	0.83	(0.01)
	Shanghai-China	0.84	(0.01)	0.79	(0.01)	0.79	(0.01)	0.89	(0.01)	0.92	(0.00)	0.90	(0.01)
	Singapore	0.83	(0.00)	0.74	(0.01)	0.79	(0.01)	0.90	(0.00)	0.94	(0.00)	0.92	(0.00)
	Chinese Taipei	0.86	(0.01)	0.81	(0.01)	0.83	(0.01)	0.89	(0.00)	0.93	(0.00)	0.91	(0.00)
	United Arab Emirates	0.80	(0.01)	0.75	(0.01)	0.78	(0.01)	0.85	(0.01)	0.89	(0.00)	0.89	(0.00)
	Uruguay	0.79	(0.01)	0.71	(0.01)	0.73	(0.01)	0.81	(0.01)	0.84	(0.01)	0.83	(0.01)

1. The reported correlations are pairwise correlations between the corresponding latent constructs.

2. Total explained variance is the R-squared coefficient from a regression of problem-solving performance on mathematics, reading and science performance. Variation uniquely associated with each domain is measured as the difference between the R-squared of the full regression and the R-squared of a regression of problem solving on the two remaining domains only. The residual variation is computed as: 100 - total explained variation.

3. The variation explained by the mode of delivery is measured as the difference between the R-squared of regression of problem-solving performance on mathematics, reading and science performance and the R-squared of the same regression augmented with computer-based mathematics performance.

* See notes at the beginning of this Annex.

StatLink ⟍ᴍ⟍ http://dx.doi.org/10.1787/888933003668

[Part 2/2]

Table V.2.5 Correlation of problem-solving performance with performance in mathematics, reading and science

| | Variation in problem-solving performance associated with mathematics, reading and science performance | | | | | | | | | | | | | Variation in problem-solving performance explained by the mode of delivery, as a percentage of total variation[3] | |
| | Total explained variation[2] | | Variation uniquely associated with mathematics performance[2] | | Variation uniquely associated with reading performance[2] | | Variation uniquely associated with science performance[2] | | Variation associated with more than one domain[2] | | Residual (unexplained) variation[2] | | | |
	%	S.E.	%	S.E.	%	S.E.	%	S.E.	%	S.E.	%	S.E.	%	S.E.
Australia	71.1	(0.8)	4.5	(0.4)	0.1	(0.1)	0.7	(0.2)	65.7	(0.8)	28.9	(0.8)	2.1	(0.4)
Austria	65.9	(2.3)	4.1	(0.7)	1.6	(0.5)	0.1	(0.1)	60.1	(2.5)	34.1	(2.3)	1.7	(0.7)
Belgium	67.2	(1.4)	3.1	(0.5)	0.2	(0.1)	0.8	(0.2)	63.1	(1.5)	32.8	(1.4)	1.7	(0.4)
Canada	61.3	(1.2)	3.8	(0.5)	0.5	(0.2)	1.2	(0.3)	55.8	(1.3)	38.7	(1.2)	1.4	(0.4)
Chile	66.1	(1.5)	6.7	(0.6)	0.6	(0.2)	0.6	(0.2)	58.2	(1.6)	33.9	(1.5)	0.2	(0.2)
Czech Republic	79.0	(1.2)	7.5	(0.7)	0.4	(0.2)	0.5	(0.2)	70.6	(1.4)	21.0	(1.2)	m	m
Denmark	60.0	(2.3)	4.7	(0.8)	0.1	(0.1)	0.6	(0.3)	54.6	(2.5)	40.0	(2.3)	5.8	(1.1)
Estonia	72.0	(1.4)	4.8	(0.6)	0.8	(0.3)	0.8	(0.3)	65.6	(1.4)	28.0	(1.4)	1.2	(0.6)
Finland	71.3	(1.0)	7.1	(0.6)	0.1	(0.1)	0.6	(0.2)	63.4	(1.0)	28.7	(1.0)	m	m
France	70.3	(3.3)	4.8	(0.6)	0.1	(0.1)	0.9	(0.3)	64.5	(3.1)	29.7	(3.3)	5.3	(2.8)
Germany	71.2	(1.6)	3.9	(0.6)	0.2	(0.1)	0.7	(0.2)	66.4	(1.7)	28.8	(1.6)	1.7	(0.6)
Hungary	71.0	(1.6)	2.5	(0.4)	1.1	(0.4)	0.4	(0.2)	66.9	(1.6)	29.0	(1.6)	1.8	(0.4)
Ireland	65.8	(1.3)	3.1	(0.5)	0.1	(0.1)	1.2	(0.4)	61.4	(1.3)	34.2	(1.3)	0.3	(0.3)
Israel	75.4	(1.3)	4.2	(0.5)	0.6	(0.2)	0.6	(0.2)	69.9	(1.3)	24.6	(1.3)	3.2	(0.6)
Italy	58.4	(2.0)	4.5	(0.8)	0.0	(0.1)	1.4	(0.5)	52.5	(2.0)	41.6	(2.0)	2.0	(0.6)
Japan	58.0	(1.9)	5.7	(0.8)	0.0	(0.0)	0.8	(0.3)	51.5	(1.9)	42.0	(1.9)	7.8	(0.9)
Korea	66.5	(1.6)	3.7	(0.6)	0.6	(0.2)	0.5	(0.2)	61.6	(1.6)	33.5	(1.6)	1.8	(0.4)
Netherlands	74.9	(2.0)	2.1	(0.4)	0.1	(0.1)	2.2	(0.5)	70.4	(2.1)	25.1	(2.0)	m	m
Norway	63.8	(2.1)	6.1	(0.8)	0.3	(0.2)	0.3	(0.2)	57.2	(2.2)	36.2	(2.1)	5.7	(1.0)
Poland	62.4	(2.5)	1.8	(0.5)	2.5	(0.6)	0.6	(0.3)	57.5	(2.4)	37.6	(2.5)	5.2	(1.5)
Portugal	65.5	(2.1)	6.8	(0.8)	0.2	(0.1)	0.2	(0.2)	58.2	(2.2)	34.5	(2.1)	2.2	(0.5)
Slovak Republic	74.1	(1.6)	5.8	(1.0)	0.5	(0.2)	0.1	(0.1)	67.6	(1.9)	25.9	(1.6)	1.0	(0.3)
Slovenia	68.7	(1.1)	4.7	(0.6)	0.4	(0.2)	0.5	(0.2)	63.0	(0.9)	31.3	(1.1)	2.8	(0.4)
Spain	57.1	(2.0)	4.3	(0.9)	0.2	(0.2)	0.8	(0.3)	51.7	(1.9)	42.9	(2.0)	4.4	(0.9)
Sweden	66.4	(1.4)	6.9	(0.8)	0.0	(0.0)	0.6	(0.3)	58.8	(1.3)	33.6	(1.4)	3.2	(0.7)
Turkey	71.0	(1.6)	9.6	(0.8)	0.3	(0.1)	0.2	(0.1)	60.9	(1.9)	29.0	(1.6)	m	m
England (United Kingdom)	74.4	(1.3)	4.5	(0.6)	0.0	(0.0)	0.7	(0.3)	69.1	(1.4)	25.6	(1.3)	m	m
United States	74.8	(1.5)	4.4	(0.6)	0.2	(0.2)	0.3	(0.2)	69.8	(1.6)	25.2	(1.5)	1.0	(0.4)
OECD average	68.0	(0.3)	4.9	(0.1)	0.4	(0.0)	0.7	(0.0)	62.0	(0.3)	32.0	(0.3)	2.8	(0.2)
Brazil	69.0	(2.1)	10.4	(1.2)	0.3	(0.2)	0.2	(0.2)	58.1	(2.4)	31.0	(2.1)	2.0	(0.7)
Bulgaria	67.6	(2.0)	5.2	(0.8)	0.7	(0.3)	0.4	(0.2)	61.2	(2.1)	32.4	(2.0)	m	m
Colombia	55.4	(2.5)	7.5	(0.9)	0.5	(0.2)	0.1	(0.1)	47.3	(2.4)	44.6	(2.5)	2.6	(0.7)
Croatia	72.7	(1.6)	8.2	(0.9)	0.2	(0.2)	0.3	(0.1)	64.0	(1.9)	27.3	(1.6)	m	m
Cyprus*	65.4	(1.1)	6.5	(0.5)	0.4	(0.1)	0.3	(0.1)	58.2	(1.1)	34.6	(1.1)	m	m
Hong Kong-China	58.7	(2.1)	4.8	(0.7)	0.9	(0.4)	0.0	(0.1)	52.9	(2.1)	41.3	(2.1)	3.3	(0.7)
Macao-China	64.5	(1.0)	8.5	(0.6)	0.1	(0.1)	0.4	(0.1)	55.6	(1.0)	35.5	(1.0)	1.8	(0.3)
Malaysia	70.4	(1.4)	9.3	(0.9)	0.0	(0.1)	0.5	(0.2)	60.6	(1.6)	29.6	(1.4)	m	m
Montenegro	66.0	(1.3)	9.2	(0.8)	0.1	(0.1)	0.2	(0.1)	56.5	(1.1)	34.0	(1.3)	m	m
Russian Federation	55.9	(2.0)	10.5	(1.1)	1.2	(0.3)	0.1	(0.1)	44.2	(2.6)	44.1	(2.0)	7.8	(1.4)
Serbia	70.0	(1.2)	8.3	(0.9)	0.1	(0.1)	0.6	(0.3)	61.0	(1.5)	30.0	(1.2)	m	m
Shanghai-China	71.1	(1.4)	5.8	(0.6)	0.4	(0.2)	0.0	(0.1)	64.8	(1.6)	28.9	(1.4)	1.6	(0.4)
Singapore	69.7	(0.6)	6.8	(0.7)	0.2	(0.1)	0.3	(0.1)	62.4	(0.9)	30.3	(0.6)	0.5	(0.2)
Chinese Taipei	75.5	(1.1)	4.7	(0.4)	0.4	(0.1)	0.1	(0.1)	70.3	(1.2)	24.5	(1.1)	0.9	(0.3)
United Arab Emirates	66.6	(1.2)	3.7	(0.5)	0.4	(0.2)	1.1	(0.2)	61.4	(1.2)	33.4	(1.2)	1.3	(0.4)
Uruguay	65.1	(1.7)	7.8	(0.8)	0.5	(0.3)	0.6	(0.2)	56.1	(1.8)	34.9	(1.7)	m	m

1. The reported correlations are pairwise correlations between the corresponding latent constructs.
2. Total explained variance is the R-squared coefficient from a regression of problem-solving performance on mathematics, reading and science performance. Variation uniquely associated with each domain is measured as the difference between the R-squared of the full regression and the R-squared of a regression of problem solving on the two remaining domains only. The residual variation is computed as: 100 - total explained variation.
3. The variation explained by the mode of delivery is measured as the difference between the R-squared of regression of problem-solving performance on mathematics, reading and science performance and the R-squared of the same regression augmented with computer-based mathematics performance.
* See notes at the beginning of this Annex.
StatLink ⭲ http://dx.doi.org/10.1787/888933003668

[Part 1/3]

Relative performance in problem solving compared with performance in mathematics, reading and science

Table V.2.6

	Relative performance in problem solving compared with students around the world[1] with similar scores in...											
	... Mathematics, reading and science (expected performance)				... Mathematics							
	Relative performance across all students[2] (actual minus expected score)		Percentage of students who perform above their expected score[3]		Relative performance across all students[4]		Relative performance among strong and top performers in mathematics (at or above Level 4)[4]		Relative performance among moderate and low performers in mathematics (at or below Level 3)[4]		Difference in relative performance: strong and top performers minus moderate and low performers	
	Score dif.	S.E.	%	S.E.	Score dif.	S.E.	Score dif.	S.E.	Score dif.	S.E.	Score dif.	S.E.
OECD												
Australia	7	(1.5)	56.0	(1.2)	10	(1.6)	14	(1.8)	8	(1.7)	6	(1.6)
Austria	-5	(2.7)	46.4	(2.1)	-8	(2.8)	-8	(3.5)	-9	(3.3)	1	(3.9)
Belgium	-10	(2.1)	43.0	(1.5)	-13	(2.1)	-10	(2.6)	-16	(2.7)	6	(3.2)
Canada	0	(1.9)	50.5	(1.2)	1	(2.0)	5	(2.1)	-2	(2.3)	7	(2.3)
Chile	1	(2.7)	51.6	(2.3)	3	(2.7)	-1	(3.8)	3	(2.8)	-4	(3.3)
Czech Republic	1	(2.4)	51.8	(2.3)	0	(2.5)	6	(2.7)	-3	(2.9)	9	(3.0)
Denmark	-11	(2.5)	41.7	(2.0)	-14	(2.5)	-8	(3.2)	-16	(2.9)	8	(3.3)
Estonia	-15	(1.9)	38.2	(1.6)	-13	(2.0)	-5	(2.2)	-17	(2.4)	12	(2.5)
Finland	-8	(2.0)	43.8	(1.7)	-3	(2.0)	7	(2.4)	-9	(2.2)	16	(2.1)
France	5	(2.7)	56.5	(1.8)	5	(2.8)	5	(2.8)	6	(3.4)	-1	(3.6)
Germany	-12	(2.6)	41.0	(2.0)	-12	(2.6)	-6	(3.0)	-16	(3.3)	10	(3.7)
Hungary	-34	(2.6)	26.7	(1.7)	-32	(2.8)	-22	(3.5)	-35	(3.2)	14	(4.1)
Ireland	-18	(2.9)	36.2	(2.1)	-14	(2.9)	-7	(3.1)	-17	(3.3)	10	(3.1)
Israel	-28	(2.8)	33.9	(1.8)	-28	(2.9)	-2	(3.4)	-35	(3.2)	33	(3.9)
Italy	10	(3.5)	56.8	(2.5)	9	(3.5)	0	(4.2)	13	(3.8)	-12	(4.0)
Japan	11	(2.0)	57.7	(1.6)	13	(2.1)	4	(2.4)	21	(2.6)	-17	(2.9)
Korea	14	(2.6)	61.1	(2.1)	9	(2.6)	6	(2.7)	13	(3.3)	-7	(2.9)
Netherlands	-16	(3.5)	39.2	(2.4)	-18	(3.8)	-8	(3.8)	-26	(5.0)	17	(5.0)
Norway	1	(3.1)	51.0	(2.1)	2	(3.1)	12	(3.1)	-2	(3.4)	14	(2.7)
Poland	-44	(3.5)	22.3	(1.8)	-44	(3.5)	-44	(3.4)	-43	(4.2)	-1	(3.5)
Portugal	-3	(2.7)	47.3	(2.1)	-5	(2.7)	-12	(3.4)	-2	(2.8)	-10	(3.1)
Slovak Republic	-5	(2.4)	45.7	(2.2)	-11	(2.5)	-11	(4.6)	-11	(2.7)	0	(4.8)
Slovenia	-34	(1.3)	27.4	(0.9)	-35	(1.3)	-30	(1.6)	-38	(1.8)	8	(2.5)
Spain	-20	(3.8)	39.7	(2.0)	-20	(3.8)	-12	(4.4)	-22	(4.1)	10	(3.8)
Sweden	-1	(2.8)	49.2	(2.1)	-2	(2.8)	1	(3.1)	-2	(3.0)	3	(2.7)
Turkey	-14	(1.9)	37.1	(1.8)	-12	(2.0)	-28	(3.4)	-9	(2.1)	-19	(3.6)
England (United Kingdom)	8	(2.4)	57.0	(1.9)	11	(2.5)	15	(2.6)	9	(3.0)	6	(3.2)
United States	10	(2.1)	59.4	(1.9)	13	(2.1)	20	(2.6)	11	(2.4)	9	(2.9)
OECD average	-7	(0.5)	45.3	(0.4)	-7	(0.5)	-4	(0.6)	-9	(0.6)	5	(0.6)
Partners												
Brazil	7	(2.9)	56.3	(2.4)	6	(3.0)	19	(7.9)	6	(3.0)	13	(7.4)
Bulgaria	-54	(3.0)	18.0	(1.2)	-57	(3.1)	-46	(4.4)	-59	(3.4)	13	(5.2)
Colombia	-7	(2.8)	45.6	(2.1)	-5	(2.8)	14	(7.4)	-6	(2.8)	20	(7.2)
Croatia	-22	(2.5)	32.3	(2.0)	-20	(2.5)	-13	(2.7)	-22	(2.8)	9	(3.1)
Cyprus*	-12	(1.3)	41.8	(1.2)	-15	(1.3)	-14	(2.9)	-15	(1.4)	1	(2.9)
Hong Kong-China	-16	(2.7)	39.2	(1.8)	-19	(2.7)	-23	(3.0)	-12	(3.8)	-11	(3.8)
Macao-China	8	(1.1)	56.7	(1.0)	0	(1.1)	-8	(1.3)	8	(1.8)	-16	(2.2)
Malaysia	-14	(2.2)	38.6	(2.0)	-21	(2.3)	-18	(3.9)	-21	(2.5)	3	(4.3)
Montenegro	-24	(1.4)	32.0	(1.0)	-27	(1.4)	-20	(5.9)	-28	(1.4)	7	(5.9)
Russian Federation	-4	(2.4)	47.4	(1.9)	-7	(2.6)	-12	(4.2)	-5	(2.5)	-7	(3.5)
Serbia	11	(2.4)	59.0	(2.2)	6	(2.4)	1	(2.9)	7	(2.5)	-5	(3.2)
Shanghai-China	-51	(2.5)	14.3	(1.3)	-59	(2.5)	-59	(2.6)	-57	(3.7)	-2	(3.4)
Singapore	2	(1.0)	51.3	(1.0)	-4	(1.0)	-5	(1.4)	-2	(1.3)	-3	(1.8)
Chinese Taipei	-9	(1.8)	41.7	(1.6)	-21	(1.9)	-29	(2.0)	-10	(2.5)	-19	(2.3)
United Arab Emirates	-43	(2.1)	24.2	(1.1)	-44	(2.2)	-28	(3.5)	-46	(2.4)	17	(3.8)
Uruguay	-27	(2.9)	32.6	(1.9)	-30	(3.0)	-24	(6.0)	-30	(3.1)	6	(5.8)

Note: Values that are statistically significant are indicated in bold (see Annex A3).

1. "Students around the world" refers to 15-year-old students in countries and economies that participated in the PISA 2012 assessment of problem solving. National samples are weighted according to the size of the target population using final student weights.
2. This column reports the difference between actual performance and the fitted value from a regression using a second-degree polynomial as regression function (math, math sq., read, read sq., scie, scie sq., math×read, math×scie, read×scie).
3. This column reports the percentage of students for whom the difference between actual performance and the fitted value from a regression is positive. Values that are indicated in bold are significantly larger or smaller than 50%.
4. This column reports the difference between actual performance and the fitted value from a regression using a cubic polynomial as regression function.
* See notes at the beginning of this Annex.

StatLink ᓂᔈᐧ http://dx.doi.org/10.1787/888933003668

[Part 2/3]
Relative performance in problem solving compared with performance in mathematics, reading and science

Table V.2.6

	Relative performance in problem solving compared with students around the world[1] with similar scores in...															
	... Reading								... Science							
	Relative performance across all students[2]		Relative performance among strong and top performers in mathematics (at or above Level 4)[4]		Relative performance among moderate and low performers in mathematics (at or below Level 3)[4]		Difference in relative performance: strong and top performers minus moderate and low performers		Relative performance across all students[2]		Relative performance among strong and top performers in mathematics (at or above Level 4)[4]		Relative performance among moderate and low performers in mathematics (at or below Level 3)[4]		Difference in relative performance: strong and top performers minus moderate and low performers	
	Score dif.	S.E.	Score dif.	S.E.	Score dif.	S.E.	Score dif.	S.E.	Score dif.	S.E.	Score dif.	S.E.	Score dif.	S.E.	Score dif.	S.E.
OECD																
Australia	**10**	(1.7)	**10**	(2.1)	**10**	(1.8)	0	(2.0)	**4**	(1.7)	2	(2.0)	**6**	(1.9)	-4	(1.9)
Austria	**11**	(3.0)	**11**	(4.0)	**11**	(3.3)	0	(4.2)	0	(2.9)	-2	(3.5)	1	(3.3)	-3	(3.9)
Belgium	-3	(2.3)	-2	(3.1)	-3	(2.7)	2	(3.4)	2	(1.9)	4	(2.3)	3	(2.1)	5	(3.1)
Canada	**4**	(1.9)	2	(2.6)	5	(2.4)	-3	(3.2)	3	(1.9)	4	(2.3)	3	(2.1)	1	(2.4)
Chile	**-9**	(2.7)	-8	(4.3)	**-9**	(2.8)	1	(4.4)	**-8**	(2.8)	**-15**	(4.1)	**-8**	(2.9)	-7	(3.8)
Czech Republic	**11**	(2.8)	**16**	(2.9)	**10**	(3.2)	5	(3.3)	0	(2.6)	4	(3.3)	-1	(3.0)	5	(3.6)
Denmark	-3	(2.6)	-6	(4.3)	-2	(3.0)	-3	(4.9)	-3	(2.7)	**-10**	(3.3)	-1	(3.0)	**-8**	(3.4)
Estonia	-1	(2.1)	3	(2.4)	-3	(2.5)	**6**	(2.5)	**-21**	(2.0)	**-16**	(2.2)	**-24**	(2.6)	**8**	(2.7)
Finland	1	(2.2)	-5	(3.0)	4	(2.6)	-9	(3.4)	**-16**	(2.2)	**-17**	(2.7)	**-15**	(2.3)	-2	(2.6)
France	3	(3.2)	-9	(3.4)	9	(4.0)	**-18**	(4.3)	**10**	(2.9)	5	(3.3)	**12**	(3.4)	-7	(3.8)
Germany	-1	(2.8)	4	(3.4)	-3	(3.2)	7	(3.7)	**-13**	(2.8)	-9	(3.3)	**-15**	(3.3)	7	(3.6)
Hungary	**-35**	(2.8)	**-23**	(4.5)	**-39**	(3.1)	**16**	(4.8)	**-38**	(2.6)	**-24**	(3.7)	**-43**	(2.9)	**19**	(4.2)
Ireland	**-23**	(2.8)	**-22**	(3.1)	**-24**	(3.2)	2	(3.1)	**-21**	(3.0)	**-22**	(3.4)	**-21**	(3.3)	-2	(3.1)
Israel	**-39**	(3.1)	**-26**	(3.8)	**-45**	(3.5)	**19**	(4.3)	**-23**	(2.9)	-1	(3.6)	**-30**	(3.2)	**29**	(4.2)
Italy	**16**	(3.7)	-2	(4.1)	**22**	(4.2)	**-24**	(4.3)	**11**	(3.6)	-4	(4.6)	**16**	(3.9)	**-20**	(4.5)
Japan	**19**	(1.9)	2	(2.5)	**34**	(2.5)	**-32**	(3.4)	**12**	(2.2)	-1	(2.3)	**25**	(2.9)	**-26**	(3.0)
Korea	**29**	(2.8)	**30**	(3.0)	**29**	(3.5)	1	(3.3)	**28**	(2.9)	**30**	(3.2)	**27**	(3.5)	4	(3.4)
Netherlands	-2	(3.4)	6	(3.5)	-6	(4.4)	12	(4.9)	**-9**	(3.1)	-3	(3.3)	**-13**	(4.0)	10	(4.5)
Norway	-3	(3.2)	-6	(3.7)	-2	(3.5)	-5	(3.3)	6	(3.2)	4	(3.5)	7	(3.4)	-4	(3.1)
Poland	**-37**	(3.5)	**-35**	(3.8)	**-38**	(4.0)	4	(3.5)	**-42**	(3.6)	**-41**	(3.5)	**-43**	(4.2)	2	(3.7)
Portugal	1	(2.7)	**-11**	(3.7)	4	(2.9)	**-15**	(3.5)	2	(2.9)	-5	(3.4)	4	(3.1)	**-9**	(2.9)
Slovak Republic	**8**	(2.6)	3	(5.2)	**10**	(2.9)	-6	(5.8)	5	(2.5)	2	(4.8)	6	(2.8)	-4	(5.3)
Slovenia	**-13**	(1.6)	**-13**	(2.3)	**-13**	(1.9)	0	(2.8)	**-37**	(1.5)	**-34**	(4.0)	**-39**	(2.1)	4	(2.9)
Spain	**-15**	(3.8)	**-19**	(4.7)	**-14**	(4.1)	-5	(4.2)	**-21**	(3.0)	**-16**	(3.8)	**-22**	(4.0)	6	(3.9)
Sweden	0	(3.0)	**-16**	(4.2)	6	(3.1)	**-22**	(4.0)	1	(3.0)	**-8**	(3.9)	4	(3.1)	**-13**	(3.2)
Turkey	**-29**	(2.3)	**-37**	(3.5)	**-27**	(2.6)	-10	(3.8)	**-17**	(2.1)	**-22**	(4.0)	**-16**	(2.2)	-6	(4.2)
England (United Kingdom)	**13**	(2.4)	**13**	(3.0)	**14**	(3.1)	0	(3.9)	2	(2.5)	0	(2.6)	4	(3.0)	-4	(3.0)
United States	**7**	(2.2)	**9**	(2.8)	**6**	(2.4)	3	(3.0)	**9**	(2.3)	**9**	(2.8)	**9**	(2.6)	0	(3.0)
OECD average	**-3**	(0.5)	**-5**	(0.7)	**-2**	(0.6)	**-3**	(0.7)	**-6**	(0.5)	**-7**	(0.6)	**-6**	(0.6)	-1	(0.7)
Partners																
Brazil	**-7**	(3.0)	-7	(7.6)	**-7**	(3.0)	0	(7.6)	2	(2.9)	12	(8.1)	1	(2.9)	10	(7.7)
Bulgaria	**-54**	(3.5)	**-68**	(4.6)	**-51**	(3.9)	**-16**	(5.3)	**-56**	(3.2)	**-56**	(4.4)	**-56**	(3.5)	0	(5.0)
Colombia	**-29**	(3.2)	**-22**	(6.8)	**-29**	(3.2)	7	(6.1)	**-19**	(3.0)	-2	(9.1)	**-20**	(3.0)	18	(8.7)
Croatia	**-25**	(2.8)	**-21**	(3.7)	**-26**	(3.0)	4	(4.0)	**-28**	(2.7)	**-23**	(3.7)	**-30**	(2.9)	7	(3.8)
Cyprus*	**-20**	(1.4)	**-36**	(3.0)	**-17**	(1.4)	**-19**	(3.0)	**-6**	(1.4)	**-13**	(2.9)	**-5**	(1.4)	**-8**	(3.0)
Hong Kong-China	1	(3.2)	-1	(3.7)	3	(4.0)	-4	(4.3)	**-7**	(2.9)	**-10**	(3.1)	-5	(3.7)	-5	(3.8)
Macao-China	**30**	(1.2)	**18**	(1.7)	**36**	(1.4)	**-18**	(2.1)	**22**	(1.2)	**15**	(1.7)	**25**	(1.6)	**-11**	(2.4)
Malaysia	-2	(2.6)	-7	(7.9)	-2	(2.6)	-6	(7.4)	**-13**	(2.6)	-8	(5.2)	**-13**	(2.6)	5	(5.1)
Montenegro	**-36**	(1.5)	**-50**	(4.3)	**-35**	(1.6)	**-15**	(4.7)	**-21**	(1.4)	**-22**	(5.7)	**-21**	(1.5)	-1	(6.1)
Russian Federation	**6**	(2.4)	**-10**	(4.7)	9	(2.5)	**-19**	(4.7)	-1	(2.5)	**-16**	(4.0)	2	(2.6)	**-18**	(4.0)
Serbia	**12**	(2.7)	1	(3.8)	**14**	(2.9)	**-14**	(4.4)	**17**	(2.9)	**11**	(4.0)	**18**	(3.0)	-7	(4.5)
Shanghai-China	**-22**	(2.6)	**-17**	(2.9)	**-29**	(3.4)	12	(3.4)	**-31**	(2.6)	**-28**	(2.9)	**-36**	(3.6)	8	(3.7)
Singapore	**26**	(1.1)	**18**	(1.7)	**33**	(1.5)	**-15**	(2.4)	**19**	(1.0)	**12**	(1.3)	**27**	(1.5)	**-14**	(2.1)
Chinese Taipei	**13**	(2.1)	**14**	(2.5)	**12**	(2.5)	2	(2.7)	**13**	(2.1)	**20**	(2.3)	**10**	(2.5)	**11**	(2.5)
United Arab Emirates	**-47**	(2.0)	**-32**	(3.7)	**-49**	(2.1)	**16**	(3.9)	**-48**	(2.1)	**-37**	(3.4)	**-50**	(2.3)	**13**	(3.5)
Uruguay	**-32**	(3.0)	**-35**	(7.2)	**-32**	(3.1)	-3	(7.7)	**-30**	(2.9)	**-37**	(6.2)	**-29**	(3.0)	-8	(6.4)

Note: Values that are statistically significant are indicated in bold (see Annex A3).
1. "Students around the world" refers to 15-year-old students in countries and economies that participated in the PISA 2012 assessment of problem solving. National samples are weighted according to the size of the target population using final student weights.
2. This column reports the difference between actual performance and the fitted value from a regression using a second-degree polynomial as regression function (math, math sq., read, read sq., scie, scie sq., math×read, math×scie, read×scie).
3. This column reports the percentage of students for whom the difference between actual performance and the fitted value from a regression is positive. Values that are indicated in bold are significantly larger or smaller than 50%.
4. This column reports the difference between actual performance and the fitted value from a regression using a cubic polynomial as regression function.
* See notes at the beginning of this Annex.
StatLink ᵐˢᵖ http://dx.doi.org/10.1787/888933003668

[Part 3/3]
Relative performance in problem solving compared with performance in mathematics, reading and science

Table V.2.6

	Relative performance in problem solving compared with students in countries/economies that also assessed mathematics on computers who have similar scores in...					
	...Paper-based mathematics (A)		...Computer-based mathematics (B)		Mode effects: Score-point difference attributed to computer delivery (A - B)	
	Relative performance across all students[4]		Relative performance across all students[4]			
	Score dif.	S.E.	Score dif.	S.E.	Score dif.	S.E.
OECD						
Australia	8	(1.6)	12	(1.7)	-4	(1.3)
Austria	-10	(2.8)	-4	(2.8)	-6	(2.4)
Belgium	-15	(2.2)	-7	(2.4)	-8	(1.6)
Canada	-1	(1.9)	2	(2.0)	-3	(1.4)
Chile	1	(2.8)	3	(3.6)	-2	(2.3)
Czech Republic	-2	(2.5)	m	m	m	m
Denmark	-15	(2.6)	-4	(2.4)	-12	(1.9)
Estonia	-14	(2.1)	-3	(2.6)	-11	(1.7)
Finland	-5	(2.1)	m	m	m	m
France	4	(2.7)	-1	(2.3)	4	(2.3)
Germany	-14	(2.6)	-3	(2.5)	-10	(2.0)
Hungary	-34	(2.8)	-19	(2.7)	-14	(2.2)
Ireland	-15	(3.0)	0	(3.5)	-15	(2.2)
Israel	-29	(3.0)	-6	(3.0)	-23	(2.5)
Italy	8	(3.5)	7	(3.2)	1	(2.7)
Japan	12	(2.1)	15	(2.1)	-3	(1.7)
Korea	8	(2.6)	12	(2.7)	-5	(2.0)
Netherlands	-19	(3.9)	m	m	m	m
Norway	0	(3.2)	1	(3.0)	-1	(2.2)
Poland	-45	(3.5)	-14	(3.1)	-31	(2.2)
Portugal	-7	(2.7)	0	(2.9)	-6	(2.1)
Slovak Republic	-13	(2.5)	-19	(2.8)	6	(1.8)
Slovenia	-37	(1.3)	-17	(1.3)	-20	(0.9)
Spain	-21	(3.8)	-6	(3.6)	-15	(2.6)
Sweden	-3	(2.8)	-5	(3.0)	1	(2.3)
Turkey	-14	(2.1)	m	m	m	m
England (United Kingdom)	9	(2.6)	m	m	m	m
United States	11	(2.1)	6	(2.2)	6	(1.6)
OECD average	-9	(0.5)	-2	(0.6)	-7	(0.4)
Partners						
Brazil	5	(2.9)	-7	(2.7)	12	(2.3)
Bulgaria	-59	(3.2)	m	m	m	m
Colombia	-7	(2.8)	-16	(3.0)	9	(2.3)
Croatia	-22	(2.6)	m	m	m	m
Cyprus*	-16	(1.4)	m	m	m	m
Hong Kong-China	-20	(2.8)	-7	(3.1)	-12	(2.1)
Macao-China	-1	(1.2)	-1	(1.4)	-1	(1.0)
Malaysia	-23	(2.5)	m	m	m	m
Montenegro	-29	(1.5)	m	m	m	m
Russian Federation	-8	(2.6)	-6	(2.4)	-3	(1.9)
Serbia	4	(2.4)	m	m	m	m
Shanghai-China	-59	(2.5)	-20	(2.7)	-39	(2.2)
Singapore	-5	(1.0)	3	(1.2)	-8	(1.0)
Chinese Taipei	-22	(2.0)	-2	(2.6)	-20	(2.0)
United Arab Emirates	-45	(2.2)	-36	(1.9)	-9	(1.7)
Uruguay	-32	(3.0)	m	m	m	m

Note: Values that are statistically significant are indicated in bold (see Annex A3).

1. "Students around the world" refers to 15-year-old students in countries and economies that participated in the PISA 2012 assessment of problem solving. National samples are weighted according to the size of the target population using final student weights.

2. This column reports the difference between actual performance and the fitted value from a regression using a second-degree polynomial as regression function (math, math sq., read, read sq., scie, scie sq., math×read, math×scie, read×scie).

3. This column reports the percentage of students for whom the difference between actual performance and the fitted value from a regression is positive. Values that are indicated in bold are significantly larger or smaller than 50%.

4. This column reports the difference between actual performance and the fitted value from a regression using a cubic polynomial as regression function.

* See notes at the beginning of this Annex.

StatLink http://dx.doi.org/10.1787/888933003668

[Part 1/1]
Table V.3.1 **Performance in problem solving, by nature of the problem situation**

| | Average proportion of full-credit responses | | | | | | Relative likelihood of success on interactive tasks, based on success in performing all other tasks (OECD average = 1.00) | | | |
| | All items (42 items) | | Items referring to a static problem situation (15 items) | | Items referring to an interactive problem situation (27 items) | | Accounting for booklet effects[1] | | Accounting for booklet and country/economy-specific response-format effects[2] | |
	%	S.E.	%	S.E.	%	S.E.	Odds ratio	S.E.	Odds ratio	S.E.
Australia	50.9	(0.4)	52.8	(0.5)	49.9	(0.5)	1.03	(0.02)	1.02	(0.02)
Austria	44.9	(0.8)	48.3	(1.0)	43.0	(0.8)	**0.93**	(0.03)	**0.93**	(0.03)
Belgium	46.4	(0.5)	48.3	(0.6)	45.4	(0.6)	1.03	(0.02)	1.02	(0.02)
Canada	51.3	(0.6)	52.7	(0.7)	50.5	(0.7)	**1.06**	(0.02)	**1.05**	(0.02)
Chile	32.9	(0.8)	34.9	(0.9)	31.8	(0.8)	1.01	(0.03)	1.01	(0.03)
Czech Republic	45.0	(0.7)	46.2	(0.7)	44.4	(0.7)	1.02	(0.02)	1.02	(0.02)
Denmark	44.3	(0.8)	47.9	(0.9)	42.3	(0.8)	**0.92**	(0.02)	**0.91**	(0.02)
Estonia	47.1	(0.7)	49.7	(0.8)	45.6	(0.8)	0.98	(0.03)	0.97	(0.03)
Finland	49.3	(0.5)	52.1	(0.6)	47.7	(0.6)	**0.92**	(0.01)	**0.92**	(0.01)
France	48.5	(0.7)	50.3	(0.8)	47.6	(0.7)	1.06	(0.03)	1.06	(0.03)
Germany	47.4	(0.7)	49.4	(0.8)	46.3	(0.8)	1.02	(0.03)	1.02	(0.03)
Hungary	35.4	(0.9)	38.2	(1.1)	33.9	(0.9)	0.96	(0.03)	0.96	(0.03)
Ireland	44.6	(0.8)	44.4	(0.9)	44.6	(0.9)	**1.17**	(0.04)	**1.16**	(0.03)
Israel	37.1	(1.3)	39.7	(1.4)	35.6	(1.3)	0.96	(0.03)	0.98	(0.03)
Italy	47.8	(0.9)	49.5	(1.0)	46.8	(0.9)	1.05	(0.03)	1.04	(0.03)
Japan	56.9	(0.7)	58.7	(0.8)	55.9	(0.7)	1.04	(0.02)	**1.05**	(0.02)
Korea	58.1	(0.9)	58.9	(1.0)	57.7	(1.0)	**1.11**	(0.03)	**1.14**	(0.03)
Netherlands	47.9	(1.1)	50.4	(1.2)	46.5	(1.2)	**0.94**	(0.02)	**0.94**	(0.02)
Norway	46.3	(0.9)	49.4	(1.0)	44.5	(0.9)	0.95	(0.03)	0.94	(0.03)
Poland	41.3	(1.0)	44.1	(1.0)	39.7	(1.1)	0.96	(0.03)	0.97	(0.03)
Portugal	42.7	(0.9)	44.0	(0.9)	42.0	(1.0)	**1.07**	(0.03)	**1.07**	(0.03)
Slovak Republic	40.7	(0.8)	44.2	(1.0)	38.8	(0.9)	**0.92**	(0.03)	**0.92**	(0.03)
Slovenia	38.9	(0.7)	42.9	(0.8)	36.7	(0.8)	**0.89**	(0.03)	**0.89**	(0.03)
Spain	40.7	(0.8)	42.3	(0.9)	39.8	(0.9)	1.05	(0.02)	1.04	(0.02)
Sweden	43.8	(0.7)	47.7	(0.9)	41.6	(0.7)	**0.90**	(0.02)	**0.91**	(0.02)
Turkey	33.8	(0.9)	35.8	(0.9)	32.7	(0.9)	0.95	(0.02)	0.96	(0.02)
England (United Kingdom)	48.5	(1.1)	49.5	(1.0)	47.9	(1.1)	1.03	(0.02)	1.03	(0.02)
United States	46.2	(1.0)	46.6	(1.1)	45.9	(1.0)	**1.13**	(0.04)	**1.13**	(0.04)
OECD average	45.0	(0.2)	47.1	(0.2)	43.8	(0.2)	1.00	(0.01)	1.00	(0.01)
Brazil	29.4	(0.9)	29.8	(1.0)	29.1	(1.0)	**1.12**	(0.04)	**1.13**	(0.04)
Bulgaria	24.5	(0.8)	28.4	(0.9)	22.3	(0.8)	**0.79**	(0.02)	**0.82**	(0.02)
Colombia	24.6	(0.7)	26.3	(0.8)	23.7	(0.7)	1.01	(0.03)	1.02	(0.03)
Croatia	36.9	(0.9)	39.3	(1.0)	35.6	(0.9)	**0.94**	(0.02)	**0.94**	(0.02)
Cyprus*	33.4	(0.4)	37.0	(0.5)	31.4	(0.5)	**0.85**	(0.02)	**0.87**	(0.02)
Hong Kong-China	53.6	(0.8)	56.1	(0.9)	52.2	(0.8)	0.99	(0.02)	1.00	(0.02)
Macao-China	53.6	(0.5)	57.0	(0.6)	51.7	(0.6)	**0.93**	(0.02)	**0.95**	(0.03)
Malaysia	28.4	(0.8)	30.1	(0.9)	27.4	(0.8)	0.96	(0.02)	0.98	(0.02)
Montenegro	26.9	(0.4)	30.3	(0.5)	25.1	(0.4)	**0.84**	(0.02)	**0.85**	(0.02)
Russian Federation	41.2	(0.8)	43.8	(0.9)	39.7	(0.8)	0.98	(0.02)	0.98	(0.02)
Serbia	38.1	(0.8)	40.3	(0.8)	36.8	(0.8)	**0.94**	(0.02)	**0.95**	(0.02)
Shanghai-China	52.6	(0.8)	56.7	(1.0)	50.3	(0.9)	**0.89**	(0.03)	**0.92**	(0.03)
Singapore	58.3	(0.7)	59.8	(0.8)	57.5	(0.7)	1.05	(0.03)	1.06	(0.03)
Chinese Taipei	52.3	(0.8)	56.3	(0.9)	50.1	(0.8)	**0.90**	(0.03)	**0.92**	(0.03)
United Arab Emirates	28.1	(0.5)	29.9	(0.6)	27.1	(0.6)	1.01	(0.03)	1.02	(0.03)
Uruguay	25.8	(0.6)	27.5	(0.7)	24.8	(0.6)	**0.95**	(0.02)	0.97	(0.02)

Note: Values that are statistically significant are indicated in bold (see Annex A3).
1. Generalised odds ratios estimated with logistic regression on the pooled PISA sample. The average logit coefficient on country dummies for OECD countries is set at 0; booklet dummies are added to the estimation.
2. Generalised odds ratios estimated with logistic regression on the pooled PISA sample. The average logit coefficient on country dummies for OECD countries is set at 0; booklet dummies and response-format dummies interacted with country/economy dummies are added to the estimation.
* See notes at the beginning of this Annex.
StatLink ᴖ█ᴨᴱ█▄ http://dx.doi.org/10.1787/888933003687

[Part 1/2]
Table V.3.2 **Performance in problem solving, by process**

		Average proportion of full-credit responses								
	All items (42 items)		Items assessing the process of "exploring and understanding" (10 items)		Items assessing the process of "representing and formulating" (8 items)		Items assessing the process of "planning and executing" (17 items)		Items assessing the process of "monitoring and reflecting" (7 items)	
	%	S.E.	%	S.E.	%	S.E.	%	S.E.	%	S.E.
Australia	50.9	(0.4)	54.9	(0.5)	49.3	(0.6)	51.5	(0.5)	45.9	(0.5)
Austria	44.9	(0.8)	49.2	(1.0)	41.8	(1.0)	47.4	(0.9)	37.2	(0.9)
Belgium	46.4	(0.5)	49.0	(0.7)	44.8	(0.8)	47.5	(0.6)	42.4	(0.7)
Canada	51.3	(0.6)	54.1	(0.7)	50.9	(0.9)	52.1	(0.6)	46.0	(0.8)
Chile	32.9	(0.8)	32.5	(1.0)	29.3	(0.9)	35.2	(0.8)	33.2	(0.8)
Czech Republic	45.0	(0.7)	46.9	(0.9)	42.9	(0.9)	46.9	(0.6)	40.7	(0.7)
Denmark	44.3	(0.8)	46.1	(1.0)	42.1	(1.2)	48.1	(0.8)	36.1	(0.9)
Estonia	47.1	(0.7)	48.9	(1.0)	44.4	(1.0)	49.5	(0.8)	42.5	(0.8)
Finland	49.3	(0.5)	53.7	(0.6)	46.3	(0.7)	51.0	(0.6)	42.7	(0.6)
France	48.5	(0.7)	52.2	(1.0)	46.9	(0.9)	49.4	(0.8)	43.8	(0.8)
Germany	47.4	(0.7)	50.6	(1.1)	44.1	(1.1)	49.5	(0.8)	42.2	(0.9)
Hungary	35.4	(0.9)	37.7	(1.1)	32.4	(1.1)	37.6	(0.9)	30.9	(1.1)
Ireland	44.6	(0.8)	47.5	(1.2)	41.4	(0.9)	45.5	(0.8)	42.2	(1.1)
Israel	37.1	(1.3)	41.9	(1.5)	35.2	(1.5)	37.0	(1.3)	32.7	(1.3)
Italy	47.8	(0.9)	51.5	(1.2)	47.2	(1.2)	48.0	(0.9)	42.8	(0.9)
Japan	56.9	(0.7)	62.2	(0.9)	55.7	(0.9)	56.3	(0.7)	52.1	(0.7)
Korea	58.1	(0.9)	64.7	(1.1)	60.7	(1.3)	54.5	(0.9)	53.7	(1.1)
Netherlands	47.9	(1.1)	51.8	(1.2)	44.2	(1.3)	49.7	(1.1)	42.8	(1.2)
Norway	46.3	(0.9)	51.3	(1.0)	43.6	(1.2)	48.1	(1.0)	38.4	(1.1)
Poland	41.3	(1.0)	43.8	(1.2)	38.5	(1.3)	43.7	(1.0)	35.6	(1.1)
Portugal	42.7	(0.9)	43.5	(1.3)	39.4	(1.3)	45.7	(1.0)	39.0	(1.1)
Slovak Republic	40.7	(0.8)	43.6	(1.2)	37.1	(1.1)	43.2	(0.9)	35.7	(0.9)
Slovenia	38.9	(0.7)	39.6	(1.0)	35.8	(1.0)	42.3	(0.7)	34.2	(0.8)
Spain	40.7	(0.8)	42.5	(1.0)	37.3	(0.9)	42.3	(0.9)	39.0	(1.0)
Sweden	43.8	(0.7)	48.3	(1.1)	41.9	(1.0)	44.6	(0.7)	38.0	(0.9)
Turkey	33.8	(0.9)	33.5	(1.0)	31.9	(1.1)	36.0	(0.9)	31.4	(1.0)
England (United Kingdom)	48.5	(1.1)	51.3	(1.3)	47.7	(1.3)	49.1	(1.0)	44.0	(1.0)
United States	46.2	(1.0)	48.9	(1.2)	43.9	(1.3)	47.1	(1.0)	43.1	(1.2)
OECD average	45.0	(0.2)	47.9	(0.2)	42.7	(0.2)	46.4	(0.2)	40.3	(0.2)
Brazil	29.4	(0.9)	30.2	(1.1)	25.4	(1.2)	32.0	(1.1)	27.1	(0.9)
Bulgaria	24.5	(0.8)	27.8	(0.9)	19.1	(0.9)	26.7	(0.8)	21.6	(0.9)
Colombia	24.6	(0.7)	24.7	(0.9)	18.7	(0.8)	27.7	(0.8)	24.9	(0.8)
Croatia	36.9	(0.9)	37.2	(1.0)	33.0	(1.1)	40.5	(0.9)	33.5	(0.9)
Cyprus*	33.4	(0.4)	36.2	(0.5)	30.7	(0.6)	34.8	(0.5)	29.8	(0.5)
Hong Kong-China	53.6	(0.8)	60.2	(1.2)	54.9	(1.0)	51.1	(0.8)	48.2	(1.1)
Macao-China	53.6	(0.5)	59.4	(0.9)	57.1	(0.9)	51.3	(0.5)	45.7	(0.8)
Malaysia	28.4	(0.8)	30.1	(0.9)	27.9	(1.0)	29.3	(0.7)	24.5	(0.8)
Montenegro	26.9	(0.4)	27.3	(0.6)	23.6	(0.5)	30.0	(0.5)	23.6	(0.5)
Russian Federation	41.2	(0.8)	42.0	(1.0)	38.6	(1.1)	43.8	(0.8)	37.3	(0.9)
Serbia	38.1	(0.8)	39.5	(0.9)	35.7	(0.9)	40.7	(0.8)	33.1	(0.9)
Shanghai-China	52.6	(0.8)	58.3	(1.1)	55.3	(1.2)	49.8	(0.7)	47.2	(1.1)
Singapore	58.3	(0.7)	64.1	(1.0)	59.7	(0.9)	55.4	(0.7)	55.2	(0.8)
Chinese Taipei	52.3	(0.8)	58.1	(1.0)	55.5	(1.2)	50.1	(0.8)	44.7	(1.0)
United Arab Emirates	28.1	(0.5)	30.0	(0.6)	26.6	(0.8)	29.0	(0.6)	25.4	(0.7)
Uruguay	25.8	(0.6)	27.1	(0.7)	22.2	(0.7)	27.9	(0.7)	23.7	(0.7)

Note: Values that are statistically significant are indicated in bold (see Annex A3).
1. Generalised odds ratios estimated with logistic regression on the pooled PISA sample. The average logit coefficient on country dummies for OECD countries is set at 0; booklet dummies are added to the estimation.
2. Generalised odds ratios estimated with logistic regression on the pooled PISA sample. The average logit coefficient on country dummies for OECD countries is set at 0; booklet dummies and response-format dummies interacted with country/economy dummies are added to the estimation.
* See notes at the beginning of this Annex.
StatLink ⫘ http://dx.doi.org/10.1787/888933003687

[Part 2/2]
Table V.3.2 **Performance in problem solving, by process**

	On items assessing the process of "exploring and understanding"				On items assessing the process of "representing and formulating"				On items assessing the process of "planning and executing"				On items assessing the process of "monitoring and reflecting"			
	Accounting for booklet effects[1]		Accounting for booklet and country/economy-specific response-format effects[2]		Accounting for booklet effects[1]		Accounting for booklet and country/economy-specific response-format effects[2]		Accounting for booklet effects[1]		Accounting for booklet and country/economy-specific response-format effects[2]		Accounting for booklet effects[1]		Accounting for booklet and country/economy-specific response-format effects[2]	
	Odds ratio	S.E.	Odds ratio	S.E.	Odds ratio	S.E.	Odds ratio	S.E.	Odds ratio	S.E.	Odds ratio	S.E.	Odds ratio	S.E.	Odds ratio	S.E.
OECD Australia	**1.06**	(0.02)	**1.14**	(0.02)	**1.06**	(0.02)	**1.06**	(0.02)	**0.93**	(0.02)	**0.89**	(0.02)	0.98	(0.02)	0.98	(0.02)
Austria	**1.08**	(0.03)	**1.13**	(0.04)	0.97	(0.04)	0.97	(0.04)	1.06	(0.03)	1.04	(0.03)	**0.85**	(0.03)	**0.85**	(0.03)
Belgium	0.98	(0.02)	1.03	(0.02)	**1.05**	(0.03)	**1.05**	(0.03)	**0.96**	(0.02)	**0.93**	(0.02)	1.03	(0.03)	1.03	(0.03)
Canada	0.99	(0.02)	1.02	(0.02)	**1.12**	(0.03)	**1.12**	(0.03)	**0.95**	(0.02)	**0.92**	(0.02)	0.97	(0.02)	0.97	(0.02)
Chile	**0.83**	(0.03)	**0.77**	(0.03)	**0.92**	(0.03)	**0.92**	(0.03)	1.06	(0.03)	**1.09**	(0.03)	**1.27**	(0.04)	**1.28**	(0.04)
Czech Republic	**0.92**	(0.02)	**0.89**	(0.02)	**0.92**	(0.02)	**0.92**	(0.02)	**1.09**	(0.02)	**1.11**	(0.02)	**1.05**	(0.02)	**1.06**	(0.02)
Denmark	**0.94**	(0.03)	0.97	(0.03)	1.02	(0.04)	1.02	(0.04)	**1.15**	(0.03)	**1.14**	(0.04)	**0.82**	(0.03)	**0.82**	(0.03)
Estonia	**0.94**	(0.03)	0.96	(0.03)	1.00	(0.03)	1.00	(0.03)	1.05	(0.03)	1.04	(0.03)	1.00	(0.03)	1.00	(0.03)
Finland	**1.06**	(0.02)	**1.08**	(0.02)	**0.88**	(0.02)	**0.89**	(0.02)	**1.09**	(0.02)	**1.09**	(0.02)	**0.94**	(0.02)	**0.95**	(0.02)
France	1.02	(0.03)	1.03	(0.04)	**1.07**	(0.03)	**1.07**	(0.03)	0.95	(0.03)	0.94	(0.03)	1.00	(0.04)	1.00	(0.04)
Germany	1.02	(0.03)	1.05	(0.04)	0.97	(0.03)	0.97	(0.03)	1.03	(0.03)	1.01	(0.03)	0.97	(0.03)	0.97	(0.03)
Hungary	0.98	(0.03)	0.93	(0.04)	0.97	(0.03)	0.97	(0.03)	1.05	(0.03)	**1.09**	(0.04)	0.98	(0.03)	0.98	(0.03)
Ireland	1.00	(0.04)	1.06	(0.04)	0.97	(0.03)	0.97	(0.03)	0.95	(0.03)	**0.91**	(0.03)	**1.12**	(0.04)	**1.11**	(0.04)
Israel	**1.12**	(0.03)	1.05	(0.03)	1.02	(0.03)	1.02	(0.03)	**0.90**	(0.02)	0.94	(0.03)	1.00	(0.03)	1.01	(0.03)
Italy	1.05	(0.03)	1.07	(0.04)	**1.12**	(0.03)	**1.12**	(0.03)	**0.90**	(0.02)	**0.89**	(0.03)	0.98	(0.03)	0.98	(0.03)
Japan	**1.15**	(0.03)	**1.11**	(0.03)	**1.08**	(0.02)	**1.08**	(0.02)	**0.86**	(0.02)	**0.88**	(0.02)	0.99	(0.02)	1.00	(0.02)
Korea	**1.25**	(0.04)	**1.16**	(0.04)	**1.33**	(0.05)	**1.32**	(0.05)	**0.69**	(0.02)	**0.71**	(0.02)	1.00	(0.03)	1.02	(0.03)
Netherlands	1.02	(0.02)	1.03	(0.03)	**0.85**	(0.02)	**0.85**	(0.02)	**1.09**	(0.02)	**1.10**	(0.02)	1.02	(0.02)	1.02	(0.02)
Norway	**1.12**	(0.04)	**1.19**	(0.04)	1.00	(0.03)	1.00	(0.03)	1.01	(0.03)	0.99	(0.03)	**0.84**	(0.03)	**0.84**	(0.03)
Poland	0.98	(0.03)	0.96	(0.03)	0.99	(0.03)	0.99	(0.03)	1.05	(0.03)	**1.08**	(0.03)	0.94	(0.03)	0.94	(0.03)
Portugal	**0.90**	(0.03)	**0.90**	(0.03)	0.96	(0.03)	0.96	(0.04)	**1.09**	(0.04)	**1.08**	(0.04)	1.04	(0.05)	1.04	(0.05)
Slovak Republic	1.00	(0.03)	1.00	(0.04)	**0.94**	(0.03)	**0.94**	(0.03)	**1.06**	(0.03)	1.07	(0.04)	0.97	(0.03)	0.96	(0.03)
Slovenia	**0.89**	(0.03)	**0.85**	(0.03)	0.97	(0.03)	0.97	(0.03)	**1.13**	(0.02)	**1.16**	(0.03)	**1.15**	(0.03)	**1.15**	(0.03)
Spain	0.94	(0.03)	0.94	(0.03)	0.96	(0.03)	0.95	(0.03)	0.99	(0.03)	0.99	(0.03)	**1.15**	(0.03)	**1.15**	(0.03)
Sweden	**1.09**	(0.04)	**1.09**	(0.04)	1.04	(0.03)	1.04	(0.03)	0.94	(0.03)	0.95	(0.04)	**0.94**	(0.03)	**0.94**	(0.03)
Turkey	**0.82**	(0.02)	**0.75**	(0.02)	**0.92**	(0.02)	0.93	(0.02)	**1.14**	(0.02)	**1.19**	(0.03)	**1.15**	(0.03)	**1.15**	(0.03)
England (United Kingdom)	0.97	(0.02)	0.99	(0.02)	0.98	(0.03)	0.99	(0.03)	1.01	(0.02)	0.99	(0.02)	**1.05**	(0.03)	**1.05**	(0.02)
United States	0.99	(0.03)	1.01	(0.03)	1.02	(0.04)	1.02	(0.04)	0.95	(0.03)	0.94	(0.03)	**1.08**	(0.04)	**1.08**	(0.04)
OECD average	1.00	(0.01)	1.00	(0.01)	1.00	(0.01)	1.00	(0.01)	1.00	(0.00)	1.00	(0.01)	1.00	(0.01)	1.00	(0.01)
Partners Brazil	**0.90**	(0.03)	**0.84**	(0.03)	**0.89**	(0.04)	**0.89**	(0.04)	**1.10**	(0.04)	**1.16**	(0.05)	**1.10**	(0.05)	**1.10**	(0.05)
Bulgaria	1.05	(0.03)	**0.90**	(0.02)	**0.69**	(0.02)	**0.69**	(0.02)	**1.17**	(0.03)	**1.35**	(0.04)	**1.07**	(0.03)	**1.09**	(0.03)
Colombia	**0.86**	(0.03)	**0.77**	(0.03)	**0.74**	(0.03)	**0.74**	(0.03)	**1.18**	(0.04)	**1.29**	(0.05)	**1.28**	(0.05)	**1.29**	(0.05)
Croatia	**0.85**	(0.02)	**0.79**	(0.02)	**0.82**	(0.02)	**0.83**	(0.02)	**1.24**	(0.03)	**1.30**	(0.03)	**1.09**	(0.03)	**1.09**	(0.03)
Cyprus*	0.98	(0.02)	**0.90**	(0.02)	**0.88**	(0.02)	**0.88**	(0.02)	**1.07**	(0.02)	**1.14**	(0.02)	**1.06**	(0.02)	**1.07**	(0.02)
Hong Kong-China	**1.23**	(0.04)	**1.17**	(0.05)	**1.23**	(0.04)	**1.23**	(0.04)	**0.76**	(0.02)	**0.78**	(0.03)	0.96	(0.03)	0.97	(0.03)
Macao-China	**1.18**	(0.04)	**1.09**	(0.04)	**1.38**	(0.04)	**1.38**	(0.04)	**0.77**	(0.02)	**0.80**	(0.02)	**0.85**	(0.02)	**0.86**	(0.03)
Malaysia	**0.93**	(0.03)	**0.80**	(0.02)	1.00	(0.03)	1.00	(0.03)	1.04	(0.02)	**1.15**	(0.03)	1.03	(0.03)	1.04	(0.03)
Montenegro	**0.86**	(0.02)	**0.77**	(0.02)	**0.82**	(0.02)	**0.82**	(0.02)	**1.24**	(0.03)	**1.35**	(0.03)	1.05	(0.03)	**1.06**	(0.03)
Russian Federation	**0.90**	(0.02)	**0.87**	(0.03)	1.00	(0.03)	1.00	(0.03)	**1.07**	(0.03)	**1.08**	(0.04)	1.03	(0.04)	1.03	(0.04)
Serbia	**0.90**	(0.02)	**0.87**	(0.02)	**0.90**	(0.02)	**0.90**	(0.02)	**1.16**	(0.02)	**1.19**	(0.03)	1.00	(0.03)	1.01	(0.02)
Shanghai-China	**1.17**	(0.04)	1.04	(0.03)	**1.33**	(0.05)	**1.33**	(0.05)	**0.74**	(0.02)	**0.78**	(0.03)	0.96	(0.03)	0.98	(0.03)
Singapore	**1.18**	(0.04)	**1.19**	(0.04)	**1.23**	(0.04)	**1.23**	(0.04)	**0.73**	(0.02)	**0.71**	(0.02)	**1.07**	(0.03)	**1.08**	(0.03)
Chinese Taipei	**1.18**	(0.03)	**1.11**	(0.04)	**1.36**	(0.04)	**1.36**	(0.04)	**0.77**	(0.02)	**0.79**	(0.02)	**0.86**	(0.03)	**0.87**	(0.03)
United Arab Emirates	0.97	(0.02)	**0.88**	(0.02)	1.04	(0.03)	1.04	(0.03)	0.96	(0.02)	1.02	(0.03)	**1.07**	(0.03)	**1.07**	(0.03)
Uruguay	**0.91**	(0.02)	**0.80**	(0.02)	**0.80**	(0.02)	**0.80**	(0.02)	**1.15**	(0.03)	**1.28**	(0.04)	**1.14**	(0.03)	**1.15**	(0.03)

Note: Values that are statistically significant are indicated in bold (see Annex A3).
1. Generalised odds ratios estimated with logistic regression on the pooled PISA sample. The average logit coefficient on country dummies for OECD countries is set at 0; booklet dummies are added to the estimation.
2. Generalised odds ratios estimated with logistic regression on the pooled PISA sample. The average logit coefficient on country dummies for OECD countries is set at 0; booklet dummies and response-format dummies interacted with country/economy dummies are added to the estimation.
* See notes at the beginning of this Annex.
StatLink ⟶ http://dx.doi.org/10.1787/888933003687

[Part 1/1]
Table V.3.3 Performance in problem solving, by technology setting

| | | Average proportion of full-credit responses | | | | | | Relative likelihood of success on tasks set in a technology context, based on success in performing all other tasks (OECD average = 1.00) | | | |
| | | All items (42 items) | | Items not involving a technological device (24 items) | | Items involving a technological device (18 items) | | Accounting for booklet effects[1] | | Accounting for booklet and country/economy-specific response-format effects[2] | |
		%	S.E.	%	S.E.	%	S.E.	Odds ratio	S.E.	Odds ratio	S.E.
OECD	Australia	50.9	(0.4)	49.1	(0.4)	52.7	(0.5)	**1.14**	(0.02)	**1.13**	(0.02)
	Austria	44.9	(0.8)	44.4	(0.9)	45.4	(0.8)	1.02	(0.03)	1.01	(0.03)
	Belgium	46.4	(0.5)	45.6	(0.6)	47.3	(0.6)	**1.05**	(0.02)	**1.04**	(0.02)
	Canada	51.3	(0.6)	50.3	(0.6)	52.3	(0.7)	**1.06**	(0.02)	**1.05**	(0.02)
	Chile	32.9	(0.8)	32.3	(0.8)	33.5	(0.8)	1.04	(0.03)	1.04	(0.03)
	Czech Republic	45.0	(0.7)	43.5	(0.7)	46.6	(0.8)	**0.96**	(0.01)	**0.97**	(0.01)
	Denmark	44.3	(0.8)	45.4	(0.9)	43.2	(0.8)	**0.89**	(0.02)	**0.88**	(0.02)
	Estonia	47.1	(0.7)	47.1	(0.8)	47.1	(0.8)	0.98	(0.03)	0.97	(0.03)
	Finland	49.3	(0.5)	49.7	(0.6)	48.8	(0.6)	**0.82**	(0.01)	**0.82**	(0.01)
	France	48.5	(0.7)	47.8	(0.8)	49.2	(0.7)	1.06	(0.03)	1.06	(0.03)
	Germany	47.4	(0.7)	46.9	(0.8)	47.8	(0.8)	1.02	(0.02)	1.02	(0.02)
	Hungary	35.4	(0.9)	35.3	(1.0)	35.5	(0.9)	0.98	(0.03)	0.99	(0.03)
	Ireland	44.6	(0.8)	42.6	(0.9)	46.5	(0.9)	**1.16**	(0.04)	**1.15**	(0.04)
	Israel	37.1	(1.3)	36.6	(1.4)	37.5	(1.3)	1.00	(0.04)	1.02	(0.04)
	Italy	47.8	(0.9)	47.3	(1.0)	48.3	(0.9)	1.03	(0.03)	1.03	(0.03)
	Japan	56.9	(0.7)	56.0	(0.8)	57.8	(0.7)	**1.05**	(0.03)	**1.07**	(0.03)
	Korea	58.1	(0.9)	57.8	(1.0)	58.4	(1.0)	1.01	(0.03)	1.03	(0.03)
	Netherlands	47.9	(1.1)	47.1	(1.2)	48.7	(1.1)	**0.90**	(0.02)	**0.91**	(0.02)
	Norway	46.3	(0.9)	46.4	(0.9)	46.2	(1.0)	0.97	(0.03)	0.97	(0.03)
	Poland	41.3	(1.0)	41.1	(1.1)	41.4	(1.1)	1.00	(0.03)	1.00	(0.03)
	Portugal	42.7	(0.9)	42.1	(0.9)	43.3	(1.0)	1.04	(0.03)	1.03	(0.03)
	Slovak Republic	40.7	(0.8)	41.1	(0.9)	40.3	(1.0)	0.95	(0.03)	0.95	(0.03)
	Slovenia	38.9	(0.7)	39.0	(0.9)	38.8	(0.8)	0.96	(0.04)	0.96	(0.04)
	Spain	40.7	(0.8)	40.3	(0.9)	41.1	(0.8)	1.02	(0.03)	1.01	(0.03)
	Sweden	43.8	(0.7)	43.8	(0.8)	43.8	(0.8)	0.98	(0.03)	0.98	(0.03)
	Turkey	33.8	(0.9)	34.0	(0.9)	33.6	(1.0)	**0.83**	(0.02)	**0.85**	(0.02)
	England (United Kingdom)	48.5	(1.1)	46.1	(1.0)	50.9	(1.2)	1.03	(0.02)	1.03	(0.02)
	United States	46.2	(1.0)	44.6	(1.2)	47.8	(0.9)	**1.12**	(0.04)	**1.11**	(0.04)
	OECD average	45.0	(0.2)	44.4	(0.2)	45.5	(0.2)	1.00	(0.01)	1.00	(0.01)
Partners	Brazil	29.4	(0.9)	28.9	(1.0)	29.8	(1.0)	1.03	(0.04)	1.03	(0.04)
	Bulgaria	24.5	(0.8)	25.2	(0.8)	23.7	(0.9)	**0.78**	(0.02)	**0.81**	(0.02)
	Colombia	24.6	(0.7)	24.6	(0.7)	24.5	(0.8)	0.98	(0.03)	0.99	(0.03)
	Croatia	36.9	(0.9)	36.9	(0.9)	36.9	(0.9)	**0.85**	(0.02)	**0.86**	(0.02)
	Cyprus*	33.4	(0.4)	33.0	(0.4)	33.9	(0.5)	**0.88**	(0.02)	**0.90**	(0.02)
	Hong Kong-China	53.6	(0.8)	52.2	(0.9)	55.0	(0.9)	**1.10**	(0.03)	**1.12**	(0.03)
	Macao-China	53.6	(0.5)	54.7	(0.6)	52.4	(0.6)	**0.89**	(0.02)	**0.90**	(0.02)
	Malaysia	28.4	(0.8)	28.8	(0.8)	28.0	(0.8)	**0.82**	(0.02)	**0.84**	(0.02)
	Montenegro	26.9	(0.4)	27.7	(0.5)	26.2	(0.4)	**0.79**	(OECD)	**0.80**	(0.02)
	Russian Federation	41.2	(0.8)	40.6	(0.9)	41.7	(0.8)	1.03	(0.02)	1.03	(0.02)
	Serbia	38.1	(0.8)	38.4	(0.8)	37.7	(0.8)	**0.82**	(0.02)	**0.83**	(0.02)
	Shanghai-China	52.6	(0.8)	54.3	(0.9)	50.8	(1.0)	**0.86**	(0.02)	**0.87**	(0.03)
	Singapore	58.3	(0.7)	56.3	(0.7)	60.4	(0.8)	**1.17**	(0.04)	**1.17**	(0.04)
	Chinese Taipei	52.3	(0.8)	52.1	(0.9)	52.5	(0.9)	1.00	(0.02)	1.01	(0.03)
	United Arab Emirates	28.1	(0.5)	27.4	(0.6)	28.8	(0.6)	**1.06**	(0.02)	**1.07**	(0.02)
	Uruguay	25.8	(0.6)	25.9	(0.7)	25.6	(0.7)	**0.83**	(0.02)	**0.86**	(0.02)

Note: Values that are statistically significant are indicated in bold (see Annex A3).
1. Generalised odds ratios estimated with logistic regression on the pooled PISA sample. The average logit coefficient on country dummies for OECD countries is set at 0; booklet dummies are added to the estimation.
2. Generalised odds ratios estimated with logistic regression on the pooled PISA sample. The average logit coefficient on country dummies for OECD countries is set at 0; booklet dummies and response-format dummies interacted with country/economy dummies are added to the estimation.
* See notes at the beginning of this Annex.
StatLink http://dx.doi.org/10.1787/888933003687

[Part 1/1]

Table V.3.4 **Performance in problem solving, by social focus**

		Average proportion of full-credit responses						Relative likelihood of success on tasks set in a social context, based on success in performing all other tasks (OECD average = 1.00)			
		All items (42 items)		Items relating primarily to the self, family, and peer groups (personal contexts) (29 items)		Items relating to the community or society in general (social contexts) (13 items)		Accounting for booklet effects[1]		Accounting for booklet and country/economy-specific response-format effects[2]	
		%	S.E.	%	S.E.	%	S.E.	Odds ratio	S.E.	Odds ratio	S.E.
OECD	Australia	50.9	(0.4)	47.1	(0.4)	55.6	(0.5)	1.02	(0.02)	**1.07**	(0.02)
	Austria	44.9	(0.8)	41.4	(0.9)	49.2	(0.8)	1.00	(0.02)	1.03	(0.03)
	Belgium	46.4	(0.5)	42.8	(0.6)	50.8	(0.6)	1.00	(0.02)	1.04	(0.02)
	Canada	51.3	(0.6)	47.8	(0.6)	55.5	(0.8)	0.99	(0.02)	1.01	(0.03)
	Chile	32.9	(0.8)	30.5	(0.8)	35.9	(0.9)	**0.93**	(0.03)	**0.90**	(0.03)
	Czech Republic	45.0	(0.7)	41.7	(0.7)	49.0	(0.8)	1.02	(0.01)	1.02	(0.02)
	Denmark	44.3	(0.8)	41.9	(0.8)	47.3	(0.8)	**0.90**	(0.02)	**0.92**	(0.02)
	Estonia	47.1	(0.7)	44.3	(0.8)	50.4	(0.8)	**0.93**	(0.03)	**0.94**	(0.03)
	Finland	49.3	(0.5)	46.2	(0.6)	53.0	(0.6)	1.00	(0.02)	1.01	(0.02)
	France	48.5	(0.7)	45.3	(0.6)	52.6	(0.9)	0.96	(0.03)	0.97	(0.03)
	Germany	47.4	(0.7)	44.1	(0.8)	51.4	(0.8)	0.98	(0.02)	0.99	(0.03)
	Hungary	35.4	(0.9)	32.5	(0.9)	39.0	(1.0)	0.97	(0.03)	**0.93**	(0.03)
	Ireland	44.6	(0.8)	40.4	(0.8)	49.6	(0.9)	**1.06**	(0.03)	**1.11**	(0.03)
	Israel	37.1	(1.3)	34.3	(1.3)	40.4	(1.4)	0.95	(0.03)	**0.89**	(0.03)
	Italy	47.8	(0.9)	44.1	(0.9)	52.2	(1.0)	1.01	(0.03)	1.02	(0.03)
	Japan	56.9	(0.7)	51.9	(0.7)	62.9	(0.8)	**1.15**	(0.02)	**1.12**	(0.02)
	Korea	58.1	(0.9)	53.9	(0.9)	63.2	(1.1)	**1.07**	(0.03)	0.99	(0.03)
	Netherlands	47.9	(1.1)	43.2	(1.2)	53.6	(1.1)	**1.16**	(0.02)	**1.19**	(0.03)
	Norway	46.3	(0.9)	43.2	(0.9)	50.0	(0.9)	0.96	(0.03)	0.97	(0.03)
	Poland	41.3	(1.0)	37.7	(1.0)	45.6	(1.1)	1.01	(0.02)	0.99	(0.03)
	Portugal	42.7	(0.9)	38.5	(0.9)	47.8	(1.0)	**1.06**	(0.03)	**1.10**	(0.03)
	Slovak Republic	40.7	(0.8)	37.9	(0.9)	44.1	(0.9)	**0.94**	(0.02)	**0.93**	(0.02)
	Slovenia	38.9	(0.7)	36.3	(0.8)	42.1	(0.8)	**0.92**	(0.02)	**0.90**	(0.03)
	Spain	40.7	(0.8)	37.6	(0.8)	44.4	(0.9)	0.96	(0.03)	0.96	(0.03)
	Sweden	43.8	(0.7)	40.0	(0.7)	48.4	(0.8)	1.02	(0.03)	1.01	(0.03)
	Turkey	33.8	(0.9)	31.4	(0.9)	36.6	(1.0)	**0.96**	(0.02)	**0.92**	(0.02)
	England (United Kingdom)	48.5	(1.1)	44.5	(1.1)	53.3	(1.1)	**1.09**	(0.02)	**1.13**	(0.03)
	United States	46.2	(1.0)	42.5	(1.0)	50.7	(1.1)	1.02	(0.02)	1.03	(0.03)
	OECD average	45.0	(0.2)	41.5	(0.2)	49.1	(0.2)	1.00	(0.00)	1.00	(0.01)
Partners	Brazil	29.4	(0.9)	26.5	(0.9)	32.9	(1.0)	1.00	(0.03)	0.96	(0.04)
	Bulgaria	24.5	(0.8)	21.1	(0.8)	28.6	(1.0)	**1.15**	(0.03)	1.05	(0.03)
	Colombia	24.6	(0.7)	21.9	(0.7)	27.9	(0.8)	1.01	(0.04)	0.95	(0.05)
	Croatia	36.9	(0.9)	33.6	(0.9)	41.0	(1.0)	**1.05**	(0.02)	1.04	(0.02)
	Cyprus*	33.4	(0.4)	30.6	(0.5)	36.9	(0.5)	1.01	(0.02)	**0.96**	(0.02)
	Hong Kong-China	53.6	(0.8)	49.5	(0.9)	58.5	(0.8)	**1.05**	(0.03)	0.99	(0.03)
	Macao-China	53.6	(0.5)	49.4	(0.5)	58.6	(0.7)	**1.06**	(0.02)	0.99	(0.03)
	Malaysia	28.4	(0.8)	25.8	(0.8)	31.6	(0.8)	1.01	(0.02)	**0.92**	(0.02)
	Montenegro	26.9	(0.4)	24.1	(0.4)	30.3	(0.5)	**1.05**	(0.02)	1.00	(0.02)
	Russian Federation	41.2	(0.8)	37.7	(0.8)	45.4	(0.9)	1.00	(0.04)	1.00	(0.04)
	Serbia	38.1	(0.8)	35.1	(0.8)	41.7	(0.8)	1.01	(0.02)	1.00	(0.02)
	Shanghai-China	52.6	(0.8)	48.3	(0.9)	57.7	(0.9)	**1.06**	(0.03)	0.97	(0.03)
	Singapore	58.3	(0.7)	53.8	(0.7)	63.8	(0.8)	**1.10**	(0.03)	**1.10**	(0.03)
	Chinese Taipei	52.3	(0.8)	47.1	(0.8)	58.5	(0.9)	**1.16**	(0.03)	**1.11**	(0.03)
	United Arab Emirates	28.1	(0.5)	24.4	(0.5)	32.5	(0.7)	**1.09**	(0.03)	1.04	(0.03)
	Uruguay	25.8	(0.6)	23.3	(0.6)	28.8	(0.7)	1.01	(0.02)	**0.93**	(0.02)

Note: Values that are statistically significant are indicated in bold (see Annex A3).

1. Generalised odds ratios estimated with logistic regression on the pooled PISA sample. The average logit coefficient on country dummies for OECD countries is set at 0; booklet dummies are added to the estimation.

2. Generalised odds ratios estimated with logistic regression on the pooled PISA sample. The average logit coefficient on country dummies for OECD countries is set at 0; booklet dummies and response-format dummies interacted with country/economy dummies are added to the estimation.

* See notes at the beginning of this Annex.

StatLink http://dx.doi.org/10.1787/888933003687

[Part 1/1]
Table V.3.5 **Performance in problem solving, by response format**

	Average proportion of full-credit responses						Relative likelihood of success on constructed response items, based on success in performing all other tasks, accounting for booklet effects (OECD average = 1.00)[1,2]	
	All items (42 items)		Items requiring simple or complex multiple-choice selections (14 items)		Items requiring constructed responses (28 items)			
	%	S.E.	%	S.E.	%	S.E.	Odds ratio	S.E.
OECD								
Australia	50.9	(0.4)	53.9	(0.5)	49.5	(0.5)	**1.10**	(0.02)
Austria	44.9	(0.8)	48.4	(0.9)	43.2	(0.9)	1.06	(0.03)
Belgium	46.4	(0.5)	49.5	(0.6)	44.9	(0.6)	**1.09**	(0.02)
Canada	51.3	(0.6)	54.9	(0.8)	49.5	(0.6)	**1.05**	(0.02)
Chile	32.9	(0.8)	37.7	(0.9)	30.5	(0.8)	0.95	(0.03)
Czech Republic	45.0	(0.7)	48.9	(0.7)	43.1	(0.7)	0.98	(0.02)
Denmark	44.3	(0.8)	47.4	(1.0)	42.8	(0.8)	**1.08**	(0.03)
Estonia	47.1	(0.7)	50.6	(0.8)	45.4	(0.8)	**1.06**	(0.03)
Finland	49.3	(0.5)	52.6	(0.6)	47.6	(0.6)	1.01	(0.02)
France	48.5	(0.7)	52.4	(0.9)	46.5	(0.7)	1.02	(0.03)
Germany	47.4	(0.7)	51.1	(0.8)	45.5	(0.8)	1.05	(0.03)
Hungary	35.4	(0.9)	40.6	(1.0)	32.8	(0.9)	**0.93**	(0.03)
Ireland	44.6	(0.8)	47.6	(1.0)	43.1	(0.8)	**1.09**	(0.04)
Israel	37.1	(1.3)	43.5	(1.3)	33.9	(1.4)	**0.86**	(0.03)
Italy	47.8	(0.9)	52.1	(1.1)	45.7	(0.9)	1.01	(0.03)
Japan	56.9	(0.7)	63.1	(0.8)	53.8	(0.7)	**0.89**	(0.02)
Korea	58.1	(0.9)	65.6	(1.0)	54.4	(1.0)	**0.81**	(0.02)
Netherlands	47.9	(1.1)	51.3	(1.0)	46.2	(1.3)	1.00	(0.02)
Norway	46.3	(0.9)	49.9	(0.9)	44.5	(1.0)	1.05	(0.04)
Poland	41.3	(1.0)	46.3	(1.1)	38.7	(1.1)	0.96	(0.03)
Portugal	42.7	(0.9)	46.3	(1.0)	40.9	(1.0)	1.05	(0.03)
Slovak Republic	40.7	(0.8)	45.1	(0.9)	38.5	(0.9)	1.00	(0.03)
Slovenia	38.9	(0.7)	43.5	(0.8)	36.6	(0.7)	0.98	(0.03)
Spain	40.7	(0.8)	44.7	(0.8)	38.7	(0.9)	1.02	(0.03)
Sweden	43.8	(0.7)	48.8	(0.9)	41.3	(0.7)	0.96	(0.03)
Turkey	33.8	(0.9)	38.1	(0.9)	31.6	(0.9)	**0.93**	(0.02)
England (United Kingdom)	48.5	(1.1)	51.1	(1.2)	47.2	(1.1)	**1.06**	(0.02)
United States	46.2	(1.0)	50.1	(1.0)	44.2	(1.0)	1.03	(0.03)
OECD average	45.0	(0.2)	49.1	(0.2)	42.9	(0.2)	1.00	(0.01)
Partners								
Brazil	29.4	(0.9)	34.3	(1.1)	26.9	(0.9)	**0.92**	(0.03)
Bulgaria	24.5	(0.8)	30.6	(0.9)	21.4	(0.8)	**0.76**	(0.02)
Colombia	24.6	(0.7)	29.8	(0.8)	22.0	(0.7)	**0.87**	(0.03)
Croatia	36.9	(0.9)	40.9	(0.8)	34.9	(0.9)	**0.96**	(0.02)
Cyprus*	33.4	(0.4)	38.6	(0.4)	30.9	(0.5)	**0.88**	(0.02)
Hong Kong-China	53.6	(0.8)	60.7	(0.9)	50.0	(0.8)	**0.84**	(0.02)
Macao-China	53.6	(0.5)	61.0	(0.7)	49.8	(0.6)	**0.82**	(0.02)
Malaysia	28.4	(0.8)	34.4	(0.8)	25.4	(0.8)	**0.81**	(0.02)
Montenegro	26.9	(0.4)	31.3	(0.5)	24.7	(0.4)	**0.89**	(0.02)
Russian Federation	41.2	(0.8)	45.8	(0.9)	38.9	(0.8)	0.98	(0.03)
Serbia	38.1	(0.8)	41.8	(0.8)	36.2	(0.8)	0.98	(0.02)
Shanghai-China	52.6	(0.8)	61.2	(0.9)	48.3	(0.9)	**0.77**	(0.02)
Singapore	58.3	(0.7)	63.3	(0.8)	55.8	(0.7)	0.95	(0.03)
Chinese Taipei	52.3	(0.8)	59.3	(0.8)	48.7	(0.9)	**0.84**	(0.02)
United Arab Emirates	28.1	(0.5)	33.8	(0.6)	25.2	(0.6)	**0.86**	(0.02)
Uruguay	25.8	(0.6)	31.1	(0.7)	23.1	(0.6)	**0.82**	(0.02)

Note: Values that are statistically significant are indicated in bold (see Annex A3).
1. This classification is not independent of the classification of items by process or context (personal/social). Items measuring the process of "exploring and understanding" and items related to social contexts are under-represented among constructed-response items.
2. Generalised odds ratios estimated with logistic regression on the pooled PISA sample. The average logit coefficient on country dummies for OECD countries is set at 0; booklet dummies and response-format dummies interacted with country/economy dummies are added to the estimation.
* See notes at the beginning of this Annex.
StatLink ⟐ http://dx.doi.org/10.1787/888933003687

[Part 1/1]

Table V.3.6   **Relative performance on knowledge-acquisition and knowledge-utilisation tasks**

	Average proportion of full-credit responses				Relative likelihood of success on knowledge-acquisition tasks, based on success on knowledge-utilisation tasks (OECD average = 1.00)			
	Knowledge-acquisition tasks[1] (18 items)		Knowledge-utilisation tasks[2] (17 items)		Accounting for booklet effects[3]		Accounting for booklet and country/economy-specific response-format effects[4]	
	%	S.E.	%	S.E.	Odds ratio	S.E.	Odds ratio	S.E.
OECD								
Australia	52.3	(0.5)	51.5	(0.5)	**1.11**	(0.02)	**1.16**	(0.02)
Austria	45.7	(0.9)	47.4	(0.9)	0.99	(0.03)	1.03	(0.03)
Belgium	47.0	(0.6)	47.5	(0.6)	**1.05**	(0.02)	**1.08**	(0.03)
Canada	52.6	(0.8)	52.1	(0.6)	**1.08**	(0.03)	**1.12**	(0.03)
Chile	30.9	(0.9)	35.2	(0.8)	**0.85**	(0.03)	**0.79**	(0.03)
Czech Republic	45.0	(0.8)	46.9	(0.6)	**0.87**	(0.02)	**0.85**	(0.02)
Denmark	44.2	(0.9)	48.1	(0.8)	**0.94**	(0.03)	0.98	(0.03)
Estonia	46.8	(0.9)	49.5	(0.8)	**0.94**	(0.03)	0.96	(0.03)
Finland	50.2	(0.6)	51.0	(0.6)	**0.91**	(0.02)	**0.91**	(0.02)
France	49.6	(0.8)	49.4	(0.8)	**1.07**	(0.03)	1.07	(0.04)
Germany	47.5	(1.0)	49.5	(0.8)	0.97	(0.03)	1.00	(0.04)
Hungary	35.2	(1.0)	37.6	(0.9)	0.95	(0.03)	**0.91**	(0.03)
Ireland	44.6	(1.0)	45.5	(0.8)	1.04	(0.03)	1.06	(0.04)
Israel	38.7	(1.4)	37.0	(1.3)	**1.13**	(0.03)	**1.09**	(0.04)
Italy	49.5	(1.1)	48.0	(0.9)	**1.15**	(0.03)	**1.17**	(0.04)
Japan	59.1	(0.8)	56.3	(0.7)	**1.20**	(0.03)	**1.17**	(0.03)
Korea	62.8	(1.1)	54.5	(0.9)	**1.53**	(0.05)	**1.51**	(0.05)
Netherlands	48.2	(1.2)	49.7	(1.1)	**0.89**	(0.02)	**0.89**	(0.02)
Norway	47.7	(1.0)	48.1	(1.0)	**1.05**	(0.03)	**1.09**	(0.04)
Poland	41.3	(1.2)	43.7	(1.0)	0.96	(0.03)	0.94	(0.03)
Portugal	41.6	(1.1)	45.7	(1.0)	**0.91**	(0.03)	**0.90**	(0.03)
Slovak Republic	40.5	(1.0)	43.2	(0.9)	0.94	(0.03)	0.94	(0.04)
Slovenia	37.8	(0.9)	42.3	(0.7)	**0.86**	(0.02)	**0.84**	(0.03)
Spain	40.0	(0.8)	42.3	(0.9)	0.96	(0.03)	0.95	(0.03)
Sweden	45.2	(1.0)	44.6	(0.7)	**1.08**	(0.04)	1.08	(0.04)
Turkey	32.8	(1.0)	36.0	(0.9)	**0.81**	(0.02)	**0.77**	(0.02)
England (United Kingdom)	49.6	(1.2)	49.1	(1.0)	0.96	(0.02)	0.98	(0.02)
United States	46.5	(1.1)	47.1	(1.0)	1.04	(0.03)	1.05	(0.04)
OECD average	45.5	(0.2)	46.4	(0.2)	1.00	(0.01)	1.00	(0.01)
Partners								
Brazil	28.0	(1.1)	32.0	(1.1)	**0.87**	(0.03)	**0.81**	(0.04)
Bulgaria	23.7	(0.9)	26.7	(0.8)	**0.80**	(0.02)	**0.68**	(0.02)
Colombia	21.8	(0.8)	27.7	(0.8)	**0.75**	(0.03)	**0.65**	(0.03)
Croatia	35.2	(1.0)	40.5	(0.9)	**0.75**	(0.02)	**0.71**	(0.02)
Cyprus*	33.6	(0.5)	34.8	(0.5)	**0.89**	(0.02)	**0.83**	(0.02)
Hong Kong-China	57.7	(1.0)	51.1	(0.8)	**1.41**	(0.04)	**1.39**	(0.05)
Macao-China	58.3	(0.7)	51.3	(0.5)	**1.44**	(0.05)	**1.44**	(0.05)
Malaysia	29.1	(0.9)	29.3	(0.7)	**0.92**	(0.02)	**0.83**	(0.02)
Montenegro	25.6	(0.5)	30.0	(0.5)	**0.75**	(0.02)	**0.68**	(0.02)
Russian Federation	40.4	(1.0)	43.8	(0.8)	**0.92**	(0.03)	**0.90**	(0.04)
Serbia	37.7	(0.9)	40.7	(0.8)	**0.84**	(0.02)	**0.82**	(0.02)
Shanghai-China	56.9	(1.0)	49.8	(0.7)	**1.45**	(0.04)	**1.43**	(0.05)
Singapore	62.0	(0.8)	55.4	(0.7)	**1.42**	(0.04)	**1.46**	(0.04)
Chinese Taipei	56.9	(1.0)	50.1	(0.8)	**1.43**	(0.04)	**1.43**	(0.05)
United Arab Emirates	28.4	(0.6)	29.0	(0.6)	1.02	(0.03)	0.96	(0.03)
Uruguay	24.8	(0.7)	27.9	(0.7)	**0.79**	(0.02)	**0.70**	(0.02)

Note: Values that are statistically significant are indicated in bold (see Annex A3).
1. "Knowledge-acquisition tasks" are tasks measuring the processes of "exploring and understanding" or "representing and formulating".
2. "Knowledge-utilisation tasks" are tasks measuring the process of "planning and executing".
3. Generalised odds ratios estimated with logistic regression on the pooled PISA sample. The average logit coefficient on country dummies for OECD countries is set at 0; booklet dummies are added to the estimation.
4. Generalised odds ratios estimated with logistic regression on the pooled PISA sample. The average logit coefficient on country dummies for OECD countries is set at 0; booklet dummies and response-format dummies interacted with country/economy dummies are added to the estimation.
* See notes at the beginning of this Annex.
StatLink ⟮⟯ http://dx.doi.org/10.1787/888933003687

[Part 1/2]

Strength of the relationship between problem-solving and mathematics performance, between and within schools[1]

Table V.4.1

		Variation in student performance in problem solving					Variation accounted for by students' performance in mathematics[4]		
		Total[2]		Between schools[3]		Within schools[3]		Total	Between schools	Within schools
		Variance	S.E.	Variance	S.E.	Variance	S.E.	%	%	%
OECD	Australia	9 482	(198)	2 569	(178)	6 951	(106)	69.4	53.8	75.4
	Austria	8 801	(550)	4 183	(532)	4 505	(121)	63.2	71.3	59.1
	Belgium	11 314	(393)	5 412	(513)	5 804	(144)	65.3	73.8	57.7
	Canada	10 063	(333)	2 271	(236)	7 692	(168)	57.8	32.7	63.8
	Chile	7 382	(289)	3 153	(299)	4 123	(90)	63.7	69.4	59.3
	Czech Republic	9 056	(389)	4 366	(473)	4 474	(174)	77.5	84.1	70.3
	Denmark	8 522	(354)	2 441	(326)	6 048	(164)	58.8	29.0	71.3
	Estonia	7 658	(267)	1 826	(245)	5 868	(171)	69.1	48.8	75.5
	Finland	8 658	(225)	884	(120)	7 753	(183)	69.7	27.0	74.6
	France	9 250	(786)	w	w	w	w	68.5	w	w
	Germany	9 703	(486)	5 328	(471)	4 334	(111)	69.6	73.1	64.9
	Hungary	10 907	(568)	6 445	(683)	4 245	(113)	68.5	80.2	48.9
	Ireland	8 676	(365)	2 117	(272)	6 486	(162)	63.5	46.8	68.9
	Israel	15 230	(792)	7 751	(860)	7 429	(199)	72.9	77.9	66.2
	Italy	8 219	(376)	3 461	(360)	4 496	(131)	56.6	65.8	49.1
	Japan	7 251	(325)	2 459	(280)	4 768	(124)	57.0	77.8	45.9
	Korea	8 311	(321)	2 604	(288)	5 575	(197)	64.4	75.1	59.1
	Netherlands	9 783	(592)	5 649	(634)	4 147	(146)	71.3	78.4	61.3
	Norway	10 600	(395)	2 264	(340)	8 270	(237)	62.8	22.9	73.7
	Poland	9 303	(645)	3 357	(675)	5 930	(204)	56.5	41.9	64.8
	Portugal	7 712	(281)	2 314	(240)	5 420	(157)	64.7	62.5	65.9
	Slovak Republic	9 597	(539)	4 761	(569)	4 625	(161)	72.9	76.6	68.9
	Slovenia	9 428	(251)	5 114	(434)	4 272	(153)	66.2	73.5	58.7
	Spain	10 890	(596)	3 121	(470)	7 776	(213)	55.6	32.8	64.7
	Sweden	9 260	(349)	1 720	(321)	7 474	(182)	65.5	35.7	72.0
	Turkey	6 246	(349)	3 239	(385)	2 997	(89)	70.0	83.4	55.6
	England (United Kingdom)	9 342	(459)	2 735	(386)	6 606	(179)	73.4	65.6	76.8
	United States	8 610	(419)	2 485	(410)	6 106	(165)	73.7	59.9	79.2
	OECD average	9 259	(85)	3 548	(87)	5 646	(30)	66.0	60.3	65.0
Partners	Brazil	8 421	(434)	3 988	(491)	4 435	(153)	68.2	68.6	68.3
	Bulgaria	11 347	(752)	6 294	(750)	4 994	(125)	65.1	73.8	51.9
	Colombia	8 397	(358)	3 092	(332)	5 262	(156)	54.4	58.0	53.0
	Croatia	8 472	(361)	3 426	(403)	5 042	(137)	71.9	78.8	67.2
	Cyprus*	9 781	(195)	3 448	(1 455)	6 641	(167)	64.0	70.7	62.0
	Hong Kong-China	8 401	(403)	3 034	(365)	5 347	(160)	57.0	70.8	49.2
	Macao-China	6 269	(129)	1 078	(237)	5 040	(167)	63.6	84.5	58.5
	Malaysia	6 982	(330)	2 614	(306)	4 361	(162)	69.4	72.0	67.6
	Montenegro	8 390	(200)	3 212	(670)	5 178	(163)	65.5	79.6	56.3
	Russian Federation	7 725	(353)	2 857	(393)	4 872	(145)	54.6	42.8	62.1
	Serbia	7 942	(342)	2 935	(333)	4 949	(164)	69.0	76.6	64.2
	Shanghai-China	8 082	(404)	3 333	(362)	4 723	(151)	70.4	76.9	65.6
	Singapore	9 021	(182)	3 061	(362)	5 962	(159)	69.3	65.9	71.0
	Chinese Taipei	8 266	(350)	3 214	(374)	5 010	(150)	74.6	82.6	69.4
	United Arab Emirates	11 134	(385)	5 607	(477)	5 504	(150)	63.5	68.4	57.3
	Uruguay	9 457	(388)	4 000	(419)	5 446	(133)	63.0	66.2	60.5

1. The total variation in student performance is calculated from the square of the standard deviation for all students.
2. In some countries/economies, sub-units within schools were sampled instead of schools; this may affect the estimation of between-school variance components (see Annex A3).
3. Due to the unbalanced clustered nature of the data, the sum of the between- and within-school variation components, as an estimate from a sample, does not necessarily add up to the total.
4. Based on the residual variation in a model with student performance in mathematics.
5. Based on the residual variation in a model with student performance in mathematics and school average performance in mathematics.
* See notes at the beginning of this Annex.

StatLink ᴍ�s┚ http://dx.doi.org/10.1787/888933003706

[Part 2/2]

Strength of the relationship between problem-solving and mathematics performance, between and within schools[1]

Table V.4.1

		Variation accounted for by students' and schools' performance in mathematics[5]		Variation in student performance unique to problem solving[5]					
		Total	Between schools	Within schools	Total		Between schools		Within schools	
		%	%	%	Variance	S.E.	Variance	S.E.	Variance	S.E.
OECD	Australia	69.7	55.4	75.4	2 868	(77)	1 145	(81)	1 712	(33)
	Austria	63.3	71.8	59.1	3 232	(230)	1 179	(221)	1 841	(63)
	Belgium	65.4	74.1	57.7	3 915	(160)	1 404	(169)	2 454	(69)
	Canada	58.0	34.2	63.8	4 223	(186)	1 494	(155)	2 781	(93)
	Chile	63.8	69.7	59.3	2 669	(115)	955	(106)	1 679	(42)
	Czech Republic	77.6	84.2	70.4	2 030	(112)	688	(112)	1 327	(51)
	Denmark	58.9	29.3	71.3	3 507	(221)	1 726	(226)	1 734	(61)
	Estonia	69.1	48.9	75.5	2 369	(132)	934	(141)	1 439	(37)
	Finland	70.1	29.4	74.6	2 592	(79)	624	(73)	1 967	(60)
	France	68.5	w	w	2 910	(494)	w	w	w	w
	Germany	69.8	73.7	65.0	2 932	(166)	1 400	(161)	1 519	(47)
	Hungary	69.2	82.9	48.9	3 357	(155)	1 103	(129)	2 169	(80)
	Ireland	63.5	46.8	68.9	3 164	(128)	1 127	(137)	2 017	(54)
	Israel	74.3	82.4	66.2	3 914	(192)	1 367	(166)	2 510	(109)
	Italy	56.6	65.8	49.1	3 568	(180)	1 183	(152)	2 290	(77)
	Japan	57.2	78.8	46.0	3 105	(99)	522	(75)	2 577	(64)
	Korea	64.5	75.3	59.1	2 954	(127)	644	(81)	2 278	(94)
	Netherlands	71.3	78.6	61.3	2 808	(227)	1 208	(215)	1 604	(47)
	Norway	63.0	24.4	73.7	3 917	(246)	1 711	(238)	2 175	(66)
	Poland	56.8	42.9	64.8	4 019	(445)	1 917	(436)	2 088	(80)
	Portugal	64.7	62.6	65.9	2 722	(162)	865	(125)	1 847	(58)
	Slovak Republic	73.0	76.9	68.9	2 593	(124)	1 098	(124)	1 437	(53)
	Slovenia	66.2	73.6	58.7	3 183	(97)	1 351	(140)	1 763	(69)
	Spain	55.6	33.0	64.7	4 835	(400)	2 092	(336)	2 743	(79)
	Sweden	65.6	36.2	72.0	3 186	(190)	1 098	(175)	2 092	(71)
	Turkey	70.0	83.4	55.6	1 873	(72)	538	(69)	1 330	(33)
	England (United Kingdom)	73.5	65.9	76.8	2 478	(132)	933	(126)	1 534	(41)
	United States	73.7	59.9	79.2	2 265	(173)	996	(181)	1 270	(38)
	OECD average	**66.2**	**61.0**	**65.0**	**3 114**	**(40)**	**1 177**	**(37)**	**1 907**	**(12)**
Partners	Brazil	68.2	68.8	68.3	2 674	(158)	1 244	(172)	1 406	(44)
	Bulgaria	66.1	77.2	51.9	3 845	(234)	1 432	(209)	2 400	(87)
	Colombia	54.5	58.3	53.0	3 817	(229)	1 289	(146)	2 474	(147)
	Croatia	71.9	78.8	67.2	2 384	(92)	727	(87)	1 653	(43)
	Cyprus*	64.0	70.7	62.0	3 518	(124)	1 010	(212)	2 523	(89)
	Hong Kong-China	57.1	70.9	49.2	3 606	(160)	882	(114)	2 719	(89)
	Macao-China	63.8	85.8	58.5	2 269	(60)	154	(51)	2 090	(69)
	Malaysia	69.8	73.4	67.6	2 111	(93)	696	(78)	1 412	(50)
	Montenegro	66.3	83.0	56.3	2 828	(109)	547	(114)	2 261	(84)
	Russian Federation	54.7	42.9	62.1	3 502	(199)	1 631	(193)	1 848	(63)
	Serbia	69.1	77.2	64.2	2 456	(111)	669	(99)	1 772	(50)
	Shanghai-China	70.4	77.0	65.6	2 395	(123)	766	(108)	1 626	(44)
	Singapore	69.4	66.5	71.0	2 756	(61)	1 026	(136)	1 729	(40)
	Chinese Taipei	74.6	82.6	69.4	2 101	(86)	558	(77)	1 534	(37)
	United Arab Emirates	64.3	71.2	57.3	3 978	(151)	1 614	(161)	2 350	(83)
	Uruguay	63.0	66.4	60.5	3 496	(176)	1 344	(169)	2 149	(58)

1. The total variation in student performance is calculated from the square of the standard deviation for all students.
2. In some countries/economies, sub-units within schools were sampled instead of schools; this may affect the estimation of between-school variance components (see Annex A3).
3. Due to the unbalanced clustered nature of the data, the sum of the between- and within-school variation components, as an estimate from a sample, does not necessarily add up to the total.
4. Based on the residual variation in a model with student performance in mathematics.
5. Based on the residual variation in a model with student performance in mathematics and school average performance in mathematics.
* See notes at the beginning of this Annex.

StatLink ⟨⟨⟨ http://dx.doi.org/10.1787/888933003706

[Part 1/1]
Table V.4.2 Performance in problem solving and programme orientation

	Percentage of students						Performance in problem solving						Difference in problem-solving performance: Students in vocational programmes minus students in general programmes (V - G)			
	General programmes (G)		Vocational (incl. pre-vocational) study programmes (V)		Modular programmes		General programmes (G)		Vocational (incl. pre-vocational) study programmes (V)		Modular programmes		Observed		After accounting for socio-demographic characteristics of students[1]	
	%	S.E.	%	S.E.	%	S.E.	Mean score	S.E.	Mean score	S.E.	Mean score	S.E.	Score dif.	S.E.	Score dif.	S.E.
OECD																
Australia	89.1	(0.5)	10.9	(0.5)	0.0	c	526	(2.0)	497	(3.3)	c	c	**-29**	(3.5)	**-22**	(3.3)
Austria	30.7	(0.9)	69.3	(0.9)	0.0	c	534	(7.9)	494	(3.6)	c	c	**-40**	(8.6)	**-28**	(7.9)
Belgium	56.0	(1.1)	44.0	(1.1)	0.0	c	541	(3.3)	465	(3.5)	c	c	**-76**	(5.0)	**-57**	(4.8)
Canada	0.0	c	0.0	c	100.0	c	c	c	c	c	526	(2.4)	c	c	c	c
Chile	97.2	(0.2)	2.8	(0.2)	0.0	c	448	(3.7)	446	(9.4)	c	c	-2	(8.7)	17	(8.2)
Czech Republic	69.0	(1.2)	31.0	(1.2)	0.0	c	515	(3.9)	496	(4.9)	c	c	-19	(6.1)	-13	(5.7)
Denmark	100.0	c	0.0	c	0.0	c	497	(2.9)	c	c	c	c	c	c	c	c
Estonia	99.6	(0.2)	0.4	(0.2)	0.0	c	515	(2.5)	c	c	c	c	c	c	c	c
Finland	100.0	c	0.0	c	0.0	c	523	(2.3)	c	c	c	c	c	c	c	c
France	84.7	(1.2)	15.3	(1.2)	0.0	c	518	(3.8)	474	(7.1)	c	c	**-44**	(8.1)	**-31**	(7.9)
Germany	98.0	(0.9)	2.0	(0.9)	0.0	c	510	(3.6)	446	(13.4)	c	c	**-64**	(14.1)	**-61**	(13.0)
Hungary	85.7	(1.1)	14.3	(1.1)	0.0	c	475	(4.1)	361	(10.2)	c	c	**-114**	(10.7)	**-83**	(11.8)
Ireland	99.2	(0.2)	0.8	(0.2)	0.0	c	499	(3.2)	400	(13.7)	c	c	**-99**	(13.7)	**-77**	(13.9)
Israel	96.9	(0.2)	3.1	(0.2)	0.0	c	w	w	w	w	c	c	w	w	w	w
Italy	48.5	(1.6)	51.5	(1.6)	0.0	c	530	(5.4)	490	(5.8)	c	c	**-40**	(8.2)	**-36**	(8.2)
Japan	75.8	(0.8)	24.2	(0.8)	0.0	c	560	(3.6)	529	(6.3)	c	c	**-31**	(7.2)	**-22**	(6.8)
Korea	80.1	(1.4)	19.9	(1.4)	0.0	c	572	(4.7)	518	(9.9)	c	c	**-54**	(11.0)	**-42**	(10.5)
Netherlands	77.8	(1.7)	22.2	(1.7)	0.0	c	538	(5.3)	417	(7.9)	c	c	**-121**	(9.3)	**-108**	(8.6)
Norway	100.0	c	0.0	c	0.0	c	503	(3.3)	c	c	c	c	c	c	c	c
Poland	99.9	(0.0)	0.1	(0.0)	0.0	c	481	(4.4)	c	c	c	c	c	c	c	c
Portugal	83.3	(2.0)	16.7	(2.0)	0.0	c	504	(3.4)	446	(7.4)	c	c	**-58**	(7.4)	**-38**	(7.2)
Slovak Republic	65.7	(1.5)	8.2	(1.4)	26.1	(1.3)	488	(4.2)	407	(11.1)	496	(5.8)	**-81**	(11.8)	**-60**	(10.2)
Slovenia	46.8	(0.5)	53.2	(0.5)	0.0	c	521	(2.7)	436	(1.7)	c	c	**-84**	(3.2)	**-70**	(3.8)
Spain	99.2	(0.2)	0.8	(0.2)	0.0	c	478	(4.1)	361	(21.8)	c	c	**-116**	(22.3)	**-100**	(19.5)
Sweden	99.6	(0.1)	0.4	(0.1)	0.0	c	491	(2.9)	c	c	c	c	c	c	c	c
Turkey	61.9	(0.5)	38.1	(0.5)	0.0	c	467	(5.8)	434	(4.1)	c	c	**-33**	(6.9)	**-25**	(5.9)
England (United Kingdom)	98.8	(0.2)	1.2	(0.2)	0.0	c	518	(4.2)	445	(14.8)	c	c	**-72**	(15.0)	**-70**	(15.5)
United States	100.0	c	0.0	c	0.0	c	508	(3.9)	c	c	c	c	c	c	c	c
OECD average	80.1	(0.2)	15.4	(0.2)	4.5	(0.0)	508	(0.8)	443	(2.3)	511	(3.1)	**-67**	(2.4)	**-59**	(2.3)
Partners																
Brazil	100.0	c	0.0	c	0.0	c	428	(4.7)	c	c	c	c	c	c	c	c
Bulgaria	59.2	(1.6)	40.8	(1.6)	0.0	c	420	(6.2)	375	(8.5)	c	c	**-45**	(10.6)	**-26**	(8.7)
Colombia	74.8	(2.3)	25.2	(2.3)	0.0	c	391	(3.8)	425	(5.5)	c	c	**34**	(6.1)	**31**	(5.2)
Croatia	29.9	(1.2)	70.1	(1.2)	0.0	c	531	(5.8)	439	(4.1)	c	c	**-93**	(6.9)	**-89**	(6.8)
Cyprus*	89.2	(0.1)	10.8	(0.1)	0.0	c	456	(1.5)	349	(3.1)	c	c	**-108**	(3.2)	**-92**	(4.0)
Hong Kong-China	100.0	c	0.0	c	0.0	c	540	(3.9)	c	c	c	c	c	c	c	c
Macao-China	98.4	(0.1)	1.6	(0.1)	0.0	c	541	(1.0)	531	(7.6)	c	c	-10	(7.6)	-9	(7.5)
Malaysia	86.7	(1.2)	13.3	(1.2)	0.0	c	423	(3.9)	422	(6.6)	c	c	-1	(7.6)	2	(6.7)
Montenegro	34.0	(0.2)	66.0	(0.2)	0.0	c	452	(2.5)	383	(1.4)	c	c	**-69**	(2.9)	**-56**	(3.3)
Russian Federation	95.9	(1.1)	4.1	(1.1)	0.0	c	491	(3.3)	436	(14.1)	c	c	**-55**	(13.9)	**-46**	(11.5)
Serbia	25.6	(1.0)	74.4	(1.0)	0.0	c	528	(6.2)	455	(3.8)	c	c	**-74**	(7.4)	**-56**	(8.0)
Shanghai-China	78.8	(0.6)	21.2	(0.6)	0.0	c	548	(4.0)	493	(4.8)	c	c	**-56**	(6.3)	**-42**	(6.4)
Singapore	100.0	c	0.0	c	0.0	c	562	(1.2)	c	c	c	c	c	c	c	c
Chinese Taipei	65.5	(1.4)	34.5	(1.4)	0.0	c	551	(3.1)	503	(4.5)	c	c	**-47**	(5.3)	**-35**	(5.2)
United Arab Emirates	97.3	(0.0)	2.7	(0.0)	0.0	c	410	(2.8)	435	(5.2)	c	c	**25**	(5.8)	**20**	(6.3)
Uruguay	97.3	(0.4)	1.4	(0.4)	1.3	(0.3)	405	(3.4)	365	(25.3)	318	(16.0)	-41	(25.0)	-25	(21.7)

Note: Values that are statistically significant are indicated in bold (see Annex A3).
1. The adjusted result corresponds to the coefficient from a regression where the *PISA index of economic, social and cultural status* (ESCS), ESCS squared, boy, and an immigrant (first-generation) dummy are introduced as further independent variables.
* See notes at the beginning of this Annex.

StatLink http://dx.doi.org/10.1787/888933003706

[Part 1/3]
Differences in problem-solving, mathematics, reading and science performance
Table V.4.3 **related to programme orientation**

| | Programme orientation effects: Mean score difference between students in vocational programmes and students in general programmes | | | | | | | | | | | |
| | Problem solving | | Mathematics | | Reading | | Science | | Computer-based mathematics | | Digital reading | |
	Score dif.	S.E.	Score dif.	S.E.	Score dif.	S.E.	Score dif.	S.E.	Score dif.	S.E.	Score dif.	S.E.
Australia	**-29**	(3.5)	**-34**	(3.5)	**-34**	(3.3)	**-31**	(3.7)	**-29**	(3.6)	**-34**	(3.8)
Austria	**-40**	(8.6)	**-38**	(6.7)	**-55**	(6.7)	**-42**	(6.2)	**-32**	(8.8)	**-27**	(9.7)
Belgium	**-76**	(5.0)	**-92**	(4.4)	**-98**	(4.3)	**-89**	(4.2)	**-79**	(4.5)	**-79**	(5.5)
Canada	c	c	c	c	c	c	c	c	c	c	c	c
Chile	-2	(8.7)	-2	(7.2)	-2	(7.8)	-9	(7.5)	-1	(6.9)	-10	(8.1)
Czech Republic	**-19**	(6.1)	**-15**	(5.5)	**-14**	(5.2)	**-16**	(5.6)	m	m	m	m
Denmark	c	c	c	c	c	c	c	c	c	c	c	c
Estonia	c	c	c	c	c	c	c	c	c	c	c	c
Finland	c	c	c	c	c	c	c	c	m	m	m	m
France	**-44**	(8.1)	**-56**	(7.2)	**-76**	(8.6)	**-61**	(9.5)	**-42**	(6.5)	**-56**	(9.9)
Germany	**-64**	(14.1)	**-37**	(13.9)	**-59**	(13.3)	**-57**	(12.5)	**-25**	(10.5)	**-38**	(18.5)
Hungary	**-114**	(10.7)	**-100**	(5.8)	**-108**	(7.8)	**-100**	(6.7)	**-104**	(11.3)	**-139**	(12.4)
Ireland	**-99**	(13.7)	**-106**	(11.6)	**-106**	(14.4)	**-119**	(13.5)	**-101**	(13.6)	**-86**	(14.4)
Israel	w	w	w	w	w	w	w	w	w	w	w	w
Italy	**-40**	(8.2)	**-59**	(7.1)	**-80**	(7.4)	**-64**	(7.6)	**-43**	(8.0)	**-63**	(8.2)
Japan	**-31**	(7.2)	**-52**	(7.9)	**-51**	(8.4)	**-43**	(8.2)	**-41**	(7.5)	**-31**	(7.5)
Korea	**-54**	(11.0)	**-88**	(10.3)	**-67**	(9.1)	**-67**	(8.3)	**-73**	(10.5)	**-50**	(8.6)
Netherlands	**-121**	(9.3)	**-132**	(5.3)	**-132**	(7.2)	**-133**	(6.1)	m	m	m	m
Norway	c	c	c	c	c	c	c	c	c	c	c	c
Poland	c	c	c	c	c	c	c	c	c	c	c	c
Portugal	**-58**	(7.4)	**-78**	(6.1)	**-91**	(6.0)	**-79**	(5.8)	**-52**	(5.7)	**-80**	(6.3)
Slovak Republic	**-81**	(11.8)	**-95**	(10.2)	**-106**	(14.1)	**-94**	(13.1)	**-73**	(11.4)	**-99**	(12.7)
Slovenia	**-84**	(3.2)	**-94**	(3.1)	**-99**	(2.9)	**-93**	(2.9)	**-86**	(2.5)	**-105**	(2.9)
Spain	**-116**	(22.3)	**-114**	(9.1)	**-134**	(12.6)	**-114**	(17.8)	**-88**	(14.2)	**-150**	(16.0)
Sweden	c	c	c	c	c	c	c	c	c	c	c	c
Turkey	**-33**	(6.9)	**-63**	(7.8)	**-50**	(7.1)	**-49**	(6.4)	m	m	m	m
England (United Kingdom)	**-72**	(15.0)	**-80**	(13.0)	**-83**	(13.9)	**-90**	(12.7)	m	m	m	m
United States	c	c	c	c	c	c	c	c	c	c	c	c
OECD average	**-67**	(2.4)	**-74**	(2.0)	**-83**	(2.2)	**-76**	(2.0)	**-63**	(2.4)	**-78**	(3.1)
Brazil	c	c	c	c	c	c	c	c	c	c	c	c
Bulgaria	**-45**	(10.6)	**-38**	(7.6)	**-57**	(11.1)	**-42**	(8.7)	m	m	m	m
Colombia	**34**	(6.1)	**31**	(5.5)	**34**	(5.8)	**29**	(5.2)	**23**	(5.8)	**36**	(7.1)
Croatia	**-93**	(6.9)	**-105**	(7.2)	**-105**	(5.7)	**-93**	(6.0)	m	m	m	m
Cyprus*	**-108**	(3.2)	**-106**	(3.0)	**-151**	(4.3)	**-111**	(3.4)	m	m	m	m
Hong Kong-China	c	c	c	c	c	c	c	c	c	c	c	c
Macao-China	**-10**	(7.6)	**-17**	(8.0)	0	(7.6)	**-15**	(7.5)	-4	(7.0)	5	(9.3)
Malaysia	-1	(7.6)	-16	(9.0)	-9	(9.7)	-12	(8.5)	m	m	m	m
Montenegro	**-69**	(2.9)	**-78**	(2.7)	**-85**	(3.0)	**-77**	(2.5)	m	m	m	m
Russian Federation	**-55**	(13.9)	**-21**	(8.9)	**-31**	(12.8)	**-31**	(11.2)	**-42**	(13.1)	-33	(19.8)
Serbia	**-74**	(7.4)	**-89**	(9.3)	**-85**	(9.4)	**-76**	(8.8)	m	m	m	m
Shanghai-China	**-56**	(6.3)	**-92**	(6.3)	**-69**	(5.2)	**-76**	(5.5)	**-75**	(7.0)	**-63**	(7.0)
Singapore	c	c	c	c	c	c	c	c	c	c	c	c
Chinese Taipei	**-47**	(5.3)	**-77**	(5.4)	**-55**	(5.3)	**-56**	(4.1)	**-57**	(5.1)	**-46**	(5.8)
United Arab Emirates	**25**	(5.8)	**14**	(5.4)	**11**	(5.5)	5	(6.3)	7	(5.3)	**14**	(6.0)
Uruguay	**-41**	(25.0)	-23	(17.2)	**-53**	(21.2)	-36	(22.2)	m	m	m	m

Note: Values that are statistically significant are indicated in bold (see Annex A3).
* See notes at the beginning of this Annex.
StatLink ⏷ http://dx.doi.org/10.1787/888933003706

[Part 2/3]
Differences in problem-solving, mathematics, reading and science performance related to programme orientation

Table V.4.3

| | Programme orientation effect size: Programme orientation effect divided by the variation in scores within each country/economy (standard deviation) | | | | | | | | | | | |
| | Problem solving | | Mathematics | | Reading | | Science | | Computer-based mathematics | | Digital reading | |
	Effect size	S.E.	Effect size	S.E.	Effect size	S.E.	Effect size	S.E.	Effect size	S.E.	Effect size	S.E.
Australia	-0.30	(0.04)	-0.35	(0.04)	-0.35	(0.03)	-0.31	(0.04)	-0.31	(0.04)	-0.35	(0.04)
Austria	-0.43	(0.09)	-0.41	(0.07)	-0.59	(0.07)	-0.46	(0.07)	-0.36	(0.10)	-0.26	(0.10)
Belgium	-0.72	(0.04)	-0.90	(0.04)	-0.96	(0.04)	-0.88	(0.04)	-0.80	(0.04)	-0.80	(0.05)
Canada	c	c	c	c	c	c	c	c	c	c	c	c
Chile	-0.02	(0.10)	-0.03	(0.09)	-0.02	(0.10)	-0.12	(0.09)	-0.01	(0.08)	-0.12	(0.10)
Czech Republic	-0.20	(0.06)	-0.16	(0.06)	-0.16	(0.06)	-0.17	(0.06)	m	m	m	m
Denmark	c	c	c	c	c	c	c	c	c	c	c	c
Estonia	c	c	c	c	c	c	c	c	c	c	c	c
Finland	c	c	c	c	c	c	c	c	m	m	m	m
France	-0.45	(0.09)	-0.58	(0.07)	-0.70	(0.07)	-0.61	(0.09)	-0.46	(0.07)	-0.57	(0.10)
Germany	-0.65	(0.15)	-0.38	(0.14)	-0.65	(0.14)	-0.59	(0.13)	-0.27	(0.11)	-0.38	(0.19)
Hungary	-1.09	(0.09)	-1.07	(0.06)	-1.18	(0.08)	-1.11	(0.07)	-1.13	(0.11)	-1.24	(0.09)
Ireland	-1.07	(0.14)	-1.26	(0.14)	-1.23	(0.17)	-1.31	(0.15)	-1.26	(0.17)	-1.05	(0.17)
Israel	w	w	w	w	w	w	w	w	w	w	w	w
Italy	-0.44	(0.09)	-0.63	(0.07)	-0.81	(0.06)	-0.67	(0.07)	-0.52	(0.09)	-0.66	(0.08)
Japan	-0.36	(0.08)	-0.55	(0.08)	-0.52	(0.08)	-0.45	(0.08)	-0.47	(0.08)	-0.40	(0.09)
Korea	-0.59	(0.12)	-0.88	(0.09)	-0.78	(0.10)	-0.82	(0.09)	-0.81	(0.11)	-0.62	(0.10)
Netherlands	-1.22	(0.08)	-1.44	(0.05)	-1.42	(0.06)	-1.40	(0.06)	m	m	m	m
Norway	c	c	c	c	c	c	c	c	c	c	c	c
Poland	c	c	c	c	c	c	c	c	c	c	c	c
Portugal	-0.65	(0.08)	-0.83	(0.06)	-0.97	(0.06)	-0.89	(0.06)	-0.61	(0.06)	-0.90	(0.06)
Slovak Republic	-0.78	(0.11)	-0.88	(0.09)	-0.95	(0.12)	-0.86	(0.11)	-0.80	(0.12)	-0.97	(0.12)
Slovenia	-0.87	(0.03)	-1.02	(0.03)	-1.08	(0.03)	-1.02	(0.03)	-0.98	(0.03)	-1.06	(0.03)
Spain	-1.12	(0.22)	-1.31	(0.11)	-1.45	(0.14)	-1.32	(0.20)	-1.07	(0.17)	-1.53	(0.16)
Sweden	c	c	c	c	c	c	c	c	c	c	c	c
Turkey	-0.42	(0.08)	-0.69	(0.07)	-0.59	(0.08)	-0.62	(0.07)	m	m	m	m
England (United Kingdom)	-0.75	(0.16)	-0.83	(0.14)	-0.84	(0.15)	-0.89	(0.13)	m	m	m	m
United States	c	c	c	c	c	c	c	c	c	c	c	c
OECD average	-0.67	(0.02)	-0.78	(0.02)	-0.85	(0.02)	-0.81	(0.02)	-0.69	(0.03)	-0.79	(0.03)
Brazil	c	c	c	c	c	c	c	c	c	c	c	c
Bulgaria	-0.43	(0.09)	-0.40	(0.08)	-0.48	(0.09)	-0.41	(0.08)	m	m	m	m
Colombia	0.37	(0.07)	0.41	(0.07)	0.41	(0.07)	0.39	(0.07)	0.31	(0.08)	0.39	(0.08)
Croatia	-1.01	(0.06)	-1.19	(0.06)	-1.22	(0.05)	-1.09	(0.05)	m	m	m	m
Cyprus*	-1.09	(0.03)	-1.14	(0.03)	-1.36	(0.03)	-1.15	(0.03)	m	m	m	m
Hong Kong-China	c	c	c	c	c	c	c	c	c	c	c	c
Macao-China	-0.13	(0.10)	-0.18	(0.08)	0.00	(0.09)	-0.20	(0.09)	-0.04	(0.08)	0.06	(0.13)
Malaysia	-0.01	(0.09)	-0.19	(0.11)	-0.10	(0.12)	-0.15	(0.11)	m	m	m	m
Montenegro	-0.76	(0.03)	-0.94	(0.03)	-0.92	(0.03)	-0.91	(0.03)	m	m	m	m
Russian Federation	-0.63	(0.15)	-0.24	(0.10)	-0.34	(0.14)	-0.36	(0.13)	-0.52	(0.16)	-0.39	(0.23)
Serbia	-0.83	(0.08)	-0.98	(0.09)	-0.92	(0.10)	-0.87	(0.09)	m	m	m	m
Shanghai-China	-0.62	(0.07)	-0.92	(0.06)	-0.86	(0.07)	-0.92	(0.07)	-0.80	(0.07)	-0.76	(0.08)
Singapore	c	c	c	c	c	c	c	c	c	c	c	c
Chinese Taipei	-0.52	(0.06)	-0.66	(0.04)	-0.60	(0.05)	-0.67	(0.05)	-0.65	(0.05)	-0.52	(0.06)
United Arab Emirates	0.23	(0.05)	0.15	(0.06)	0.12	(0.06)	0.05	(0.07)	0.08	(0.06)	0.13	(0.05)
Uruguay	-0.42	(0.26)	-0.27	(0.20)	-0.56	(0.22)	-0.38	(0.23)	m	m	m	m

Note: Values that are statistically significant are indicated in bold (see Annex A3).
* See notes at the beginning of this Annex.
StatLink ⌦ http://dx.doi.org/10.1787/888933003706

[Part 3/3]
Differences in problem-solving, mathematics, reading and science performance related to programme orientation

Table V.4.3

		Difference in programme orientation effect sizes between problem solving (PS) and...								
		... Mathematics (PS - M)		... Reading (PS - R)		... Science (PS - S)		... Computer-based mathematics (PS - CBM)		... Digital reading (PS - DR)	
		Effect size dif.	S.E.	Effect size dif.	S.E.	Effect size dif.	S.E.	Effect size dif.	S.E.	Effect size dif.	S.E.
OECD	Australia	**0.06**	(0.03)	**0.05**	(0.03)	0.01	(0.03)	0.02	(0.03)	0.05	(0.03)
	Austria	-0.02	(0.07)	**0.16**	(0.07)	0.03	(0.07)	-0.07	(0.06)	**-0.17**	(0.09)
	Belgium	**0.19**	(0.03)	**0.25**	(0.03)	**0.17**	(0.03)	**0.08**	(0.03)	**0.08**	(0.04)
	Canada	c	c	c	c	c	c	c	c	c	c
	Chile	0.01	(0.06)	0.00	(0.08)	0.10	(0.06)	-0.01	(0.09)	0.10	(0.08)
	Czech Republic	-0.04	(0.05)	-0.03	(0.06)	-0.02	(0.05)	m	m	m	m
	Denmark	c	c	c	c	c	c	c	c	c	c
	Estonia	c	c	c	c	c	c	c	c	c	c
	Finland	c	c	c	c	c	c	m	m	m	m
	France	0.12	(0.06)	**0.25**	(0.07)	**0.16**	(0.08)	0.01	(0.06)	0.12	(0.08)
	Germany	**-0.26**	(0.10)	0.00	(0.12)	-0.05	(0.11)	**-0.38**	(0.12)	-0.27	(0.16)
	Hungary	-0.03	(0.09)	0.08	(0.10)	0.01	(0.08)	0.03	(0.10)	0.15	(0.09)
	Ireland	0.19	(0.12)	0.16	(0.18)	0.24	(0.16)	0.19	(0.12)	-0.02	(0.15)
	Israel	w	w	w	w	w	w	w	w	w	w
	Italy	**0.20**	(0.07)	**0.37**	(0.07)	**0.24**	(0.07)	0.08	(0.06)	**0.23**	(0.08)
	Japan	**0.19**	(0.06)	**0.15**	(0.06)	0.09	(0.06)	**0.10**	(0.05)	0.04	(0.05)
	Korea	**0.30**	(0.07)	0.19	(0.10)	**0.23**	(0.10)	**0.22**	(0.09)	0.03	(0.09)
	Netherlands	**0.22**	(0.06)	**0.20**	(0.06)	**0.18**	(0.06)	m	m	m	m
	Norway	c	c	c	c	c	c	c	c	c	c
	Poland	c	c	c	c	c	c	c	c	c	c
	Portugal	**0.18**	(0.08)	**0.32**	(0.07)	**0.24**	(0.06)	-0.04	(0.07)	**0.24**	(0.09)
	Slovak Republic	0.10	(0.07)	0.17	(0.10)	0.08	(0.09)	0.02	(0.08)	**0.19**	(0.08)
	Slovenia	**0.16**	(0.03)	**0.21**	(0.03)	**0.16**	(0.02)	**0.11**	(0.02)	**0.20**	(0.02)
	Spain	0.20	(0.20)	**0.33**	(0.17)	0.20	(0.19)	-0.04	(0.29)	0.42	(0.30)
	Sweden	c	c	c	c	c	c	c	c	c	c
	Turkey	**0.27**	(0.05)	**0.17**	(0.07)	**0.20**	(0.06)	m	m	m	m
	England (United Kingdom)	0.08	(0.11)	0.10	(0.12)	0.14	(0.10)	m	m	m	m
	United States	c	c	c	c	c	c	c	c	c	c
	OECD average	**0.11**	(0.02)	**0.18**	(0.02)	**0.13**	(0.02)	0.01	(0.03)	**0.11**	(0.03)
Partners	Brazil	c	c	c	c	c	c	c	c	c	c
	Bulgaria	-0.02	(0.06)	0.05	(0.07)	-0.01	(0.07)	m	m	m	m
	Colombia	-0.04	(0.05)	-0.04	(0.06)	-0.02	(0.06)	0.06	(0.06)	-0.02	(0.06)
	Croatia	**0.18**	(0.03)	**0.21**	(0.04)	0.08	(0.05)	m	m	m	m
	Cyprus*	0.05	(0.03)	**0.27**	(0.04)	0.06	(0.04)	m	m	m	m
	Hong Kong-China	c	c	c	c	c	c	c	c	c	c
	Macao-China	0.05	(0.06)	-0.13	(0.08)	0.07	(0.08)	-0.08	(0.07)	-0.19	(0.10)
	Malaysia	**0.18**	(0.06)	0.09	(0.07)	**0.14**	(0.06)	m	m	m	m
	Montenegro	**0.18**	(0.02)	**0.16**	(0.02)	**0.15**	(0.02)	m	m	m	m
	Russian Federation	**-0.38**	(0.16)	-0.29	(0.19)	-0.27	(0.17)	-0.10	(0.10)	-0.24	(0.15)
	Serbia	**0.16**	(0.05)	0.10	(0.07)	0.05	(0.06)	m	m	m	m
	Shanghai-China	**0.30**	(0.06)	**0.24**	(0.06)	**0.31**	(0.07)	**0.18**	(0.07)	0.14	(0.08)
	Singapore	c	c	c	c	c	c	c	c	c	c
	Chinese Taipei	**0.14**	(0.04)	0.08	(0.04)	**0.15**	(0.04)	**0.13**	(0.05)	0.00	(0.05)
	United Arab Emirates	0.08	(0.04)	**0.12**	(0.05)	**0.18**	(0.05)	**0.15**	(0.05)	**0.10**	(0.04)
	Uruguay	-0.15	(0.11)	0.15	(0.10)	-0.04	(0.10)	m	m	m	m

Note: Values that are statistically significant are indicated in bold (see Annex A3).
* See notes at the beginning of this Annex.
StatLink ᵐˢᵖ http://dx.doi.org/10.1787/888933003706

[Part 1/1]

Table V.4.4 Relative performance in problem solving, by programme orientation

Problem-solving performance of students in vocational and pre-vocational programmes compared with that of students in general programmes with similar performance in mathematics, reading and science

	Average difference in problem solving compared with students in general programmes with similar performance in mathematics[1]		Percentage of students in vocational programmes who outperform students in general programmes with similar performance in mathematics[2]		Average difference in problem solving compared with students in general programmes with similar performance in reading[1]		Percentage of students in vocational programmes who outperform students in general programmes with similar performance in reading[2]		Average difference in problem solving compared with students in general programmes with similar performance in science[1]		Percentage of students in vocational programmes who outperform students in general programmes with similar performance in science[2]		Average difference in problem solving compared with students in general programmes with similar performance in mathematics, reading and science[3]		Percentage of students in vocational programmes who outperform students in general programmes with similar performance in mathematics, reading and science[2]	
	Score dif.	S.E.	%	S.E.	Score dif.	S.E.	%	S.E.	Score dif.	S.E.	%	S.E.	Score dif.	S.E.	%	S.E.
OECD																
Australia	-1	(2.4)	49.8	(1.9)	-2	(2.4)	49.3	(1.9)	-5	(2.5)	47.2	(2.0)	-1	(2.3)	49.9	(2.0)
Austria	-11	(7.8)	43.3	(6.1)	1	(8.4)	51.6	(5.8)	-8	(8.1)	45.8	(5.9)	-2	(8.2)	49.8	(6.4)
Belgium	1	(4.0)	51.1	(2.7)	3	(4.6)	53.3	(2.7)	-1	(4.3)	49.9	(2.9)	4	(4.1)	53.3	(2.9)
Canada	c	c	c	c	c	c	c	c	c	c	c	c	c	c	c	c
Chile	0	(4.9)	52.3	(5.2)	0	(6.5)	51.7	(6.1)	6	(5.3)	55.4	(5.3)	1	(4.7)	51.5	(5.1)
Czech Republic	-7	(4.6)	43.9	(4.4)	-7	(5.6)	45.5	(4.3)	-6	(4.8)	46.9	(3.9)	-6	(4.5)	44.8	(4.6)
Denmark	c	c	c	c	c	c	c	c	c	c	c	c	c	c	c	c
Estonia	c	c	c	c	c	c	c	c	c	c	c	c	c	c	c	c
Finland	c	c	c	c	c	c	c	c	c	c	c	c	c	c	c	c
France	2	(6.0)	52.9	(4.9)	9	(6.9)	55.4	(4.9)	5	(7.1)	54.0	(5.4)	6	(6.0)	56.0	(5.3)
Germany	**-32**	(9.1)	**22.7**	(7.3)	-14	(10.7)	38.7	(11.3)	-15	(10.5)	41.8	(8.8)	**-24**	(8.8)	**30.7**	(8.2)
Hungary	-22	(11.1)	37.8	(6.9)	-17	(11.1)	39.3	(6.2)	**-22**	(9.4)	**37.4**	(6.2)	-13	(11.0)	41.9	(6.9)
Ireland	-6	(10.4)	44.3	(9.0)	-14	(14.6)	42.8	(10.2)	-4	(13.6)	45.6	(10.0)	-1	(12.2)	48.0	(11.0)
Israel	w	w	w	w	w	w	w	w	w	w	w	w	w	w	w	w
Italy	5	(6.6)	54.4	(4.2)	**14**	(7.3)	**58.5**	(4.1)	8	(6.9)	56.4	(4.5)	12	(6.6)	**58.6**	(4.1)
Japan	4	(4.8)	53.6	(3.3)	-1	(4.7)	49.6	(3.2)	-3	(5.1)	48.1	(3.3)	3	(4.8)	53.4	(3.3)
Korea	13	(7.1)	59.2	(5.2)	2	(8.9)	50.5	(5.9)	5	(8.8)	51.7	(6.0)	13	(7.8)	58.4	(5.6)
Netherlands	-4	(9.6)	50.2	(5.9)	-14	(9.9)	42.8	(5.9)	-6	(10.0)	46.8	(6.7)	2	(10.5)	51.9	(7.6)
Norway	c	c	c	c	c	c	c	c	c	c	c	c	c	c	c	c
Poland	c	c	c	c	c	c	c	c	c	c	c	c	c	c	c	c
Portugal	0	(6.6)	50.5	(4.8)	0	(6.2)	50.9	(4.3)	-1	(5.8)	50.4	(4.1)	4	(6.4)	53.1	(4.7)
Slovak Republic	-1	(7.9)	50.3	(7.6)	0	(9.9)	52.3	(7.2)	-5	(9.5)	47.7	(7.2)	3	(8.6)	54.0	(8.1)
Slovenia	**-11**	(5.3)	45.1	(3.3)	-8	(6.1)	45.4	(3.6)	-6	(4.5)	47.7	(2.8)	-3	(5.0)	49.3	(3.3)
Spain	-14	(20.5)	43.9	(14.4)	-18	(19.7)	38.0	(13.7)	-23	(17.5)	37.1	(11.3)	-9	(19.2)	43.3	(13.4)
Sweden	c	c	c	c	c	c	c	c	c	c	c	c	c	c	c	c
Turkey	**14**	(4.1)	**62.9**	(3.8)	5	(5.7)	54.2	(4.5)	8	(5.2)	56.2	(4.2)	**14**	(4.2)	**62.9**	(4.1)
England (United Kingdom)	-2	(10.1)	45.6	(10.7)	-7	(10.9)	47.1	(11.5)	0	(9.5)	52.6	(10.0)	1	(9.5)	52.2	(11.6)
United States	c	c	c	c	c	c	c	c	c	c	c	c	c	c	c	c
OECD average	**-5**	(2.4)	47.5	(1.6)	-4	(2.2)	48.1	(1.7)	-4	(2.1)	48.0	(1.5)	0	(2.2)	50.3	(1.7)
Partners																
Brazil	c	c	c	c	c	c	c	c	c	c	c	c	c	c	c	c
Bulgaria	-11	(7.5)	45.4	(4.4)	-6	(8.0)	48.1	(4.4)	-10	(7.9)	46.2	(4.4)	-7	(7.5)	47.7	(4.6)
Colombia	6	(4.4)	55.4	(3.7)	**10**	(5.2)	56.7	(3.8)	**11**	(5.0)	57.9	(3.5)	5	(4.5)	55.0	(3.9)
Croatia	-2	(6.5)	49.3	(4.9)	-16	(12.3)	39.8	(6.5)	**-22**	(7.5)	35.5	(4.7)	3	(8.1)	52.5	(6.1)
Cyprus*	**-19**	(3.3)	38.4	(2.8)	**-20**	(3.8)	**40.6**	(2.5)	**-27**	(3.2)	35.8	(2.5)	**-14**	(3.7)	**42.6**	(3.3)
Hong Kong-China	c	c	c	c	c	c	c	c	c	c	c	c	c	c	c	c
Macao-China	2	(4.9)	51.7	(6.3)	-10	(5.7)	42.5	(7.6)	1	(5.6)	49.4	(7.2)	2	(4.8)	53.1	(5.3)
Malaysia	13	(4.4)	**62.8**	(4.4)	7	(4.9)	56.3	(4.2)	10	(4.1)	58.6	(3.7)	12	(4.3)	**62.4**	(4.5)
Montenegro	1	(2.4)	50.8	(1.8)	**-10**	(3.1)	**43.9**	(2.3)	-4	(2.6)	47.2	(1.8)	3	(2.7)	51.7	(2.0)
Russian Federation	-39	(13.4)	29.1	(6.9)	-35	(14.4)	30.7	(7.3)	-35	(13.1)	31.6	(7.1)	-38	(13.6)	29.4	(8.1)
Serbia	0	(6.3)	50.0	(4.7)	-13	(8.5)	42.4	(5.2)	-13	(8.3)	41.4	(5.7)	1	(6.4)	51.0	(5.0)
Shanghai-China	17	(5.5)	64.0	(4.5)	9	(6.0)	57.3	(4.7)	14	(6.5)	60.7	(4.5)	18	(5.7)	65.0	(4.6)
Singapore	c	c	c	c	c	c	c	c	c	c	c	c	c	c	c	c
Chinese Taipei	4	(3.8)	54.4	(3.5)	-3	(4.1)	47.7	(3.3)	4	(4.0)	53.2	(3.2)	5	(3.7)	54.7	(3.3)
United Arab Emirates	**11**	(4.1)	**58.8**	(4.2)	**17**	(4.4)	58.8	(5.6)	**21**	(4.7)	**64.6**	(4.3)	**14**	(4.1)	**60.7**	(4.6)
Uruguay	-20	(13.1)	37.1	(9.6)	-2	(13.3)	51.1	(9.6)	-14	(12.4)	43.6	(9.3)	-13	(11.1)	43.7	(10.6)

Note: Values that are statistically significant are indicated in bold (see Annex A3).

1. This column reports the difference between actual performance and the fitted value from a regression using a cubic polynomial as regression function.

2. This column reports the percentage of students for whom the difference between actual performance and the fitted value from a regression is positive. Values that are indicated in bold are significantly larger or smaller than 50%.

3. This column reports the difference between actual performance and the fitted value from a regression using a second-degree polynomial as regression function (math, math sq., read, read sq., scie, scie sq., math×read, math×scie, read×scie).

* See notes at the beginning of this Annex.

StatLink ⌦ http://dx.doi.org/10.1787/888933003706

[Part 1/2]
Table V.4.6 **Percentage of students at each proficiency level in problem solving, by gender**

	Boys													
	Below Level 1 (below 358.49 score points)		Level 1 (from 358.49 to less than 423.42 score points)		Level 2 (from 423.42 to less than 488.35 score points)		Level 3 (from 488.35 to less than 553.28 score points)		Level 4 (from 553.28 to less than 618.21 score points)		Level 5 (from 618.21 to less than 683.14 score points)		Level 6 (above 683.14 score points)	
	%	S.E.	%	S.E.	%	S.E.	%	S.E.	%	S.E.	%	S.E.	%	S.E.
Australia	5.3	(0.4)	10.8	(0.7)	18.8	(0.6)	24.9	(0.9)	22.5	(0.8)	12.6	(0.7)	5.1	(0.5)
Austria	6.4	(1.1)	11.1	(1.1)	20.6	(1.3)	25.8	(1.4)	22.9	(1.3)	10.3	(1.0)	2.9	(0.6)
Belgium	9.4	(0.8)	11.6	(0.8)	17.0	(0.8)	23.2	(0.9)	22.3	(1.0)	12.7	(0.8)	3.8	(0.5)
Canada	5.3	(0.6)	9.6	(0.5)	18.1	(0.7)	25.1	(0.8)	23.0	(0.7)	13.1	(0.7)	5.9	(0.6)
Chile	14.4	(1.5)	21.2	(1.5)	27.2	(1.4)	23.9	(1.2)	10.5	(1.0)	2.6	(0.4)	0.3	(0.1)
Czech Republic	7.2	(0.9)	10.6	(1.0)	19.7	(1.1)	26.3	(1.2)	22.8	(1.3)	10.6	(1.1)	2.8	(0.4)
Denmark	7.0	(0.9)	13.0	(1.0)	22.5	(1.0)	26.9	(1.3)	20.4	(1.5)	8.1	(1.0)	2.1	(0.4)
Estonia	4.3	(0.6)	11.0	(1.0)	21.1	(1.0)	28.1	(1.2)	22.2	(1.2)	10.5	(0.8)	2.8	(0.4)
Finland	5.2	(0.6)	10.8	(0.7)	20.5	(1.4)	26.1	(1.3)	22.1	(1.0)	11.2	(0.7)	4.1	(0.6)
France	7.1	(1.0)	9.6	(0.8)	20.0	(1.4)	26.6	(1.4)	23.0	(1.1)	11.3	(0.9)	2.6	(0.5)
Germany	7.9	(0.9)	12.1	(1.1)	18.7	(1.2)	24.2	(1.1)	22.2	(1.2)	11.4	(1.3)	3.5	(0.6)
Hungary	19.0	(1.8)	16.5	(1.2)	22.0	(1.5)	21.5	(1.4)	13.9	(1.2)	5.5	(0.8)	1.5	(0.4)
Ireland	7.5	(1.2)	13.1	(1.3)	22.7	(1.2)	27.2	(1.2)	18.6	(1.2)	8.0	(0.9)	3.0	(0.6)
Israel	24.0	(2.2)	15.2	(1.4)	17.0	(1.2)	17.1	(1.2)	14.9	(1.6)	8.6	(1.3)	3.2	(0.7)
Italy	5.6	(0.9)	10.7	(1.5)	19.4	(1.3)	25.7	(1.4)	24.0	(1.4)	11.9	(1.1)	2.7	(0.5)
Japan	1.9	(0.5)	4.9	(0.6)	13.2	(1.0)	23.8	(1.3)	28.9	(1.4)	20.0	(1.5)	7.3	(0.9)
Korea	2.3	(0.4)	4.8	(0.7)	11.6	(1.1)	21.8	(1.3)	28.6	(1.5)	21.5	(1.4)	9.4	(1.1)
Netherlands	7.7	(1.2)	11.0	(1.2)	19.0	(1.3)	24.7	(1.6)	22.5	(1.7)	12.1	(1.4)	3.1	(0.6)
Norway	9.0	(0.9)	13.1	(0.9)	21.4	(1.2)	24.0	(1.0)	18.8	(1.1)	9.9	(1.0)	3.8	(0.5)
Poland	11.8	(1.2)	15.5	(1.2)	23.4	(1.2)	24.2	(1.6)	16.9	(1.2)	6.6	(0.8)	1.5	(0.3)
Portugal	6.3	(0.8)	12.8	(1.2)	23.2	(1.5)	27.7	(1.3)	20.6	(1.2)	7.7	(0.8)	1.7	(0.4)
Slovak Republic	9.4	(1.1)	14.9	(1.2)	23.2	(1.3)	23.7	(1.3)	18.1	(1.6)	8.3	(0.9)	2.4	(0.8)
Slovenia	13.2	(0.8)	16.8	(1.3)	24.3	(1.6)	22.3	(1.2)	16.3	(1.0)	6.1	(0.7)	1.1	(0.4)
Spain	14.1	(1.4)	15.6	(0.9)	21.5	(1.3)	23.5	(1.5)	16.2	(1.2)	7.0	(0.8)	2.2	(0.4)
Sweden	10.2	(0.9)	14.8	(1.1)	23.1	(1.0)	24.8	(1.0)	17.6	(0.9)	7.3	(0.7)	2.2	(0.4)
Turkey	9.4	(1.2)	23.7	(1.6)	30.6	(1.8)	22.4	(1.4)	10.9	(1.3)	2.7	(0.6)	0.3	(0.1)
England (United Kingdom)	5.7	(1.1)	10.4	(1.0)	19.5	(1.3)	25.5	(1.3)	23.2	(1.3)	12.1	(1.3)	3.6	(0.9)
United States	6.6	(1.0)	12.4	(1.1)	21.4	(1.3)	25.8	(1.2)	20.8	(1.2)	9.8	(0.9)	3.2	(0.5)
OECD average	8.7	(0.2)	12.8	(0.2)	20.7	(0.2)	24.5	(0.2)	20.2	(0.2)	10.0	(0.2)	3.1	(0.1)
Brazil	19.1	(1.8)	23.5	(1.5)	26.7	(1.5)	19.0	(1.8)	8.9	(1.3)	2.1	(0.5)	0.6	(0.3)
Bulgaria	36.7	(2.1)	22.7	(1.2)	20.9	(1.3)	12.9	(1.1)	5.3	(0.8)	1.4	(0.4)	0.2	(0.1)
Colombia	27.1	(1.9)	27.6	(1.4)	23.8	(1.3)	14.1	(1.1)	5.7	(0.7)	1.3	(0.4)	0.3	(0.1)
Croatia	12.2	(1.4)	18.7	(1.4)	24.6	(1.5)	22.4	(1.4)	15.3	(1.4)	5.6	(0.8)	1.2	(0.3)
Cyprus*	22.9	(0.8)	19.7	(1.1)	23.4	(1.1)	19.2	(1.1)	10.3	(1.0)	3.7	(0.4)	0.7	(0.3)
Hong Kong-China	3.1	(0.6)	6.6	(0.8)	15.3	(1.0)	25.9	(1.5)	27.2	(1.2)	15.7	(1.3)	6.1	(0.8)
Macao-China	1.5	(0.3)	5.6	(0.7)	16.7	(0.9)	27.9	(1.2)	29.2	(1.1)	15.6	(0.8)	3.5	(0.5)
Malaysia	22.4	(1.7)	26.2	(1.5)	27.3	(1.5)	16.6	(1.2)	6.1	(0.9)	1.2	(0.4)	0.1	(0.1)
Montenegro	32.4	(1.0)	25.7	(1.1)	22.4	(1.0)	13.6	(0.8)	4.8	(0.7)	1.0	(0.3)	0.1	(0.1)
Russian Federation	6.4	(0.7)	14.6	(1.1)	26.0	(1.2)	28.6	(1.8)	16.2	(1.0)	6.7	(1.0)	1.5	(0.4)
Serbia	9.2	(1.2)	17.1	(1.2)	25.5	(2.0)	26.4	(1.6)	15.8	(1.1)	5.3	(0.6)	0.8	(0.3)
Shanghai-China	2.6	(0.5)	6.2	(0.7)	15.0	(1.2)	25.6	(1.3)	27.8	(1.8)	17.0	(1.2)	5.7	(0.7)
Singapore	2.3	(0.4)	6.3	(0.5)	13.0	(0.7)	20.1	(0.9)	25.8	(0.9)	20.4	(1.0)	12.0	(0.7)
Chinese Taipei	4.2	(0.8)	7.9	(0.8)	15.8	(1.2)	23.9	(1.3)	25.9	(1.7)	17.3	(1.2)	5.0	(0.8)
United Arab Emirates	37.1	(2.0)	22.4	(1.5)	18.5	(1.0)	12.7	(0.9)	6.7	(0.7)	2.2	(0.3)	0.5	(0.1)
Uruguay	31.5	(1.8)	23.6	(1.3)	22.0	(1.3)	14.6	(1.1)	6.5	(0.8)	1.6	(0.4)	0.1	(0.1)

Note: Values that are statistically significant are indicated in bold (see Annex A3).
* See notes at the beginning of this Annex.
StatLink ᵃˢᵖ http://dx.doi.org/10.1787/888933003706

[Part 2/2]
Table V.4.6 **Percentage of students at each proficiency level in problem solving, by gender**

		Girls													Increased likelihood of boys scoring below Level 2 (less than 423.42 score points)		Increased likelihood of boys scoring at or above Level 5 (above 618.21 score points)	
		Below Level 1 (below 358.49 score points)		Level 1 (from 358.49 to less than 423.42 score points)		Level 2 (from 423.42 to less than 488.35 score points)		Level 3 (from 488.35 to less than 553.28 score points)		Level 4 (from 553.28 to less than 618.21 score points)		Level 5 (from 618.21 to less than 683.14 score points)		Level 6 (above 683.14 score points)					
		%	S.E.	%	S.E.	%	S.E.	%	S.E.	%	S.E.	%	S.E.	%	S.E.	Relative risk	S.E.	Relative risk	S.E.
OECD	Australia	4.7	(0.4)	10.1	(0.5)	20.0	(0.8)	26.7	(1.0)	22.7	(0.7)	12.0	(0.6)	3.7	(0.3)	1.09	(0.06)	**1.13**	(0.07)
	Austria	6.5	(1.0)	12.8	(1.2)	23.1	(2.2)	28.0	(1.8)	20.9	(1.4)	7.6	(0.9)	1.1	(0.3)	0.91	(0.10)	**1.52**	(0.21)
	Belgium	9.0	(0.8)	11.6	(0.8)	19.7	(1.2)	25.8	(0.9)	21.8	(0.9)	10.0	(0.8)	2.2	(0.3)	1.02	(0.08)	**1.36**	(0.11)
	Canada	4.9	(0.4)	9.7	(0.6)	19.9	(1.0)	26.6	(1.0)	22.8	(0.8)	11.8	(0.7)	4.3	(0.4)	1.02	(0.05)	**1.18**	(0.06)
	Chile	15.9	(1.5)	25.0	(1.2)	30.0	(1.3)	20.6	(1.3)	7.2	(0.8)	1.3	(0.3)	0.1	(0.0)	**0.87**	(0.05)	**2.09**	(0.57)
	Czech Republic	5.9	(0.8)	13.2	(1.2)	21.8	(1.4)	28.2	(1.3)	20.6	(1.2)	8.3	(0.8)	2.0	(0.4)	0.93	(0.09)	**1.30**	(0.14)
	Denmark	7.6	(0.7)	13.1	(1.0)	25.6	(1.1)	28.8	(1.8)	17.7	(1.4)	6.2	(0.7)	1.0	(0.3)	0.96	(0.07)	**1.41**	(0.17)
	Estonia	3.8	(0.5)	11.1	(1.1)	22.4	(1.0)	30.2	(1.5)	22.2	(1.0)	8.6	(0.9)	1.6	(0.5)	1.03	(0.10)	**1.30**	(0.13)
	Finland	3.7	(0.4)	8.9	(0.6)	19.5	(1.3)	28.2	(1.6)	25.1	(1.2)	11.6	(0.8)	3.0	(0.5)	**1.27**	(0.10)	1.05	(0.08)
	France	6.2	(1.0)	10.1	(0.9)	20.9	(1.2)	30.2	(1.4)	22.3	(1.2)	8.6	(0.9)	1.7	(0.4)	1.03	(0.1)	**1.35**	(0.13)
	Germany	7.0	(0.9)	11.5	(1.0)	21.9	(1.1)	27.2	(1.4)	21.9	(1.2)	8.7	(0.9)	1.8	(0.4)	1.08	(0.08)	**1.41**	(0.17)
	Hungary	15.6	(1.5)	18.9	(1.2)	25.7	(1.4)	23.3	(1.2)	12.3	(1.2)	3.7	(0.7)	0.5	(0.2)	1.03	(0.07)	**1.67**	(0.22)
	Ireland	6.5	(0.7)	13.5	(1.0)	24.9	(1.2)	28.4	(1.1)	19.0	(1.0)	6.6	(0.7)	1.1	(0.3)	1.03	(0.10)	**1.41**	(0.20)
	Israel	19.8	(1.3)	18.8	(1.0)	23.1	(1.0)	19.8	(1.0)	12.5	(0.9)	4.8	(0.6)	1.1	(0.3)	1.02	(0.07)	**1.97**	(0.31)
	Italy	4.6	(0.8)	11.8	(1.2)	26.2	(1.6)	30.7	(1.5)	20.3	(1.6)	5.5	(1.0)	0.8	(0.3)	1.00	(0.14)	**2.31**	(0.37)
	Japan	1.7	(0.4)	5.8	(0.8)	16.1	(1.2)	30.3	(1.3)	29.5	(1.2)	13.6	(1.1)	3.2	(0.6)	0.92	(0.1)*	**1.63**	(0.13)
	Korea	2.0	(0.4)	4.7	(0.7)	14.5	(1.3)	25.9	(1.3)	29.1	(1.5)	18.3	(1.7)	5.5	(0.9)	1.06	(0.17)	**1.30**	(0.12)
	Netherlands	7.0	(1.0)	11.4	(1.1)	20.8	(1.4)	27.4	(1.6)	21.5	(1.6)	9.8	(1.0)	2.2	(0.6)	1.02	(0.07)	**1.26**	(0.13)
	Norway	7.2	(0.8)	13.3	(1.0)	21.5	(1.2)	25.4	(1.1)	20.1	(1.2)	9.5	(1.1)	3.0	(0.5)	1.08	(0.08)	1.09	(0.11)
	Poland	8.3	(1.2)	15.9	(1.4)	28.0	(1.4)	27.7	(1.3)	14.4	(1.2)	4.9	(0.8)	0.7	(0.3)	1.13	(0.1)	**1.44**	(0.20)
	Portugal	6.6	(0.7)	15.4	(1.1)	27.7	(1.2)	28.6	(1.6)	16.2	(1.0)	4.6	(0.6)	0.7	(0.3)	**0.87**	(0.05)	**1.76**	(0.21)
	Slovak Republic	12.2	(1.5)	15.9	(1.6)	25.5	(1.5)	27.7	(1.8)	14.1	(1.3)	4.1	(0.6)	0.6	(0.3)	0.86	(0.07)	**2.28**	(0.30)
	Slovenia	9.4	(0.8)	17.5	(1.0)	26.6	(1.6)	25.2	(1.3)	15.2	(1.1)	5.4	(0.9)	0.6	(0.2)	**1.11**	(0.06)	1.21	(0.24)
	Spain	12.1	(1.2)	15.0	(1.0)	25.7	(1.1)	25.0	(1.2)	15.7	(1.0)	5.4	(0.6)	1.0	(0.3)	1.09	(0.06)	**1.43**	(0.16)
	Sweden	7.4	(0.8)	14.4	(0.9)	24.8	(1.3)	27.8	(1.2)	17.5	(0.9)	6.7	(0.8)	1.4	(0.3)	**1.15**	(0.08)	1.17	(0.14)
	Turkey	12.6	(1.4)	25.9	(1.6)	32.3	(1.6)	20.0	(1.5)	7.9	(1.3)	1.3	(0.6)	0.0	(0.1)	**0.86**	(0.05)	2.36	(1.04)
	England (United Kingdom)	5.4	(1.0)	11.2	(1.1)	20.8	(1.7)	27.5	(1.3)	22.2	(1.5)	9.9	(1.0)	3.0	(0.6)	0.97	(0.10)	1.22	(0.14)
	United States	4.7	(0.7)	12.7	(1.2)	24.2	(1.3)	28.3	(1.3)	19.9	(1.2)	7.9	(0.8)	2.3	(0.5)	1.09	(0.1)	**1.27**	(0.12)
	OECD average	7.8	(0.2)	13.5	(0.2)	23.3	(0.3)	26.8	(0.3)	19.0	(0.2)	7.7	(0.2)	1.8	(0.1)	1.02	(0.02)	**1.50**	(0.05)
Partners	Brazil	24.5	(1.9)	27.2	(1.9)	27.0	(1.6)	15.8	(1.7)	4.5	(0.7)	0.9	(0.3)	0.1	(0.1)	**0.83**	(0.03)	**2.62**	(0.67)
	Bulgaria	29.8	(2.0)	24.0	(1.4)	23.3	(1.2)	15.3	(1.2)	6.0	(0.9)	1.4	(0.4)	0.2	(0.1)	**1.10**	(0.04)	1.00	(0.31)
	Colombia	38.5	(1.9)	29.0	(1.3)	20.7	(1.3)	8.9	(0.9)	2.2	(0.5)	0.5	(0.2)	0.2	(0.1)	**0.81**	(0.03)	**2.17**	(0.82)
	Croatia	11.9	(1.1)	21.9	(1.3)	29.2	(1.5)	23.4	(1.5)	11.1	(1.3)	2.2	(0.6)	0.3	(0.1)	0.92	(0.06)	**2.71**	(0.53)
	Cyprus*	16.0	(0.8)	22.1	(0.9)	27.7	(1.4)	21.7	(1.5)	9.8	(0.7)	2.3	(0.4)	0.4	(0.2)	**1.12**	(0.05)	**1.66**	(0.35)
	Hong Kong-China	3.6	(0.6)	7.7	(1.2)	17.6	(1.4)	29.1	(2.0)	25.8	(1.3)	12.4	(1.5)	3.9	(1.0)	0.87	(0.11)	**1.34**	(0.16)
	Macao-China	1.6	(0.3)	6.4	(0.6)	18.4	(0.8)	31.1	(1.1)	28.6	(1.2)	12.0	(0.8)	2.0	(0.3)	0.90	(0.11)	**1.37**	(0.10)
	Malaysia	22.9	(1.7)	29.3	(1.4)	28.2	(1.3)	14.8	(1.2)	4.4	(0.6)	0.4	(0.3)	0.0	(0.0)	0.93	(0.04)	3.29	(2.44)
	Montenegro	27.6	(1.1)	28.0	(1.2)	25.3	(1.5)	14.1	(1.0)	4.4	(0.6)	0.4	(0.2)	0.1	(0.1)	1.04	(0.03)	2.41	(1.50)
	Russian Federation	7.1	(0.9)	16.2	(1.5)	28.0	(1.2)	27.2	(1.5)	15.2	(1.2)	5.1	(0.7)	1.2	(0.4)	0.90	(0.06)	**1.31**	(0.16)
	Serbia	11.4	(1.1)	19.4	(1.1)	27.8	(2.0)	25.2	(1.5)	12.8	(0.9)	2.9	(0.5)	0.5	(0.2)	**0.85**	(0.06)	**1.80**	(0.35)
	Shanghai-China	3.5	(0.6)	8.8	(0.8)	19.9	(1.0)	29.2	(1.4)	24.6	(1.2)	11.4	(1.2)	2.6	(0.6)	**0.72**	(0.07)	**1.63**	(0.17)
	Singapore	1.7	(0.3)	5.5	(0.5)	14.6	(0.8)	23.8	(1.3)	28.3	(1.6)	19.0	(1.0)	7.1	(0.6)	1.20	(0.13)	**1.24**	(0.05)
	Chinese Taipei	2.7	(0.5)	8.5	(0.9)	19.8	(1.2)	28.6	(1.2)	25.9	(1.2)	12.0	(1.3)	2.5	(0.6)	1.07	(0.12)	**1.54**	(0.25)
	United Arab Emirates	23.7	(1.4)	26.6	(1.0)	25.3	(1.0)	15.7	(0.8)	6.2	(0.6)	2.0	(0.3)	0.4	(0.1)	**1.18**	(0.05)	1.14	(0.20)
	Uruguay	33.1	(1.9)	27.3	(1.6)	22.7	(1.2)	11.9	(0.9)	4.3	(0.6)	0.6	(0.2)	0.0	(0.0)	**0.91**	(0.03)	**2.88**	(0.99)

Note: Values that are statistically significant are indicated in bold (see Annex A3).
* See notes at the beginning of this Annex.
StatLink ᴧᴦᴘ http://dx.doi.org/10.1787/888933003706

[Part 1/3]

Table V.4.7   **Mean score and variation in student performance in problem solving, by gender**

		Mean score					Standard deviation						5th percentile					
		Boys		Girls		Difference (B - G)		Boys		Girls		Difference (B - G)		Boys		Girls		Difference (B - G)
		Mean	S.E.	Mean	S.E.	Score dif.	S.E.	S.D.	S.E.	S.D.	S.E.	Dif.	S.E.	Score	S.E.	Score	S.E.	Score dif.	S.E.
OECD	Australia	524	(2.4)	522	(2.2)	2	(2.6)	100	(1.3)	95	(1.3)	**5**	(1.6)	355	(3.9)	361	(4.8)	-5	(5.3)
	Austria	512	(4.4)	500	(4.1)	**12**	(4.8)	98	(4.0)	90	(2.7)	8	(3.3)	345	(11.3)	344	(9.8)	0	(12.7)
	Belgium	512	(3.1)	504	(3.1)	**8**	(3.7)	110	(2.4)	102	(2.1)	**8**	(2.6)	313	(8.7)	321	(8.7)	-8	(10.6)
	Canada	528	(2.8)	523	(2.5)	**5**	(2.2)	104	(2.6)	96	(1.3)	**8**	(2.4)	355	(5.4)	359	(5.0)	-5	(6.9)
	Chile	455	(4.5)	441	(3.7)	**13**	(3.8)	89	(2.2)	82	(1.9)	**7**	(2.3)	303	(7.1)	304	(6.2)	-1	(6.7)
	Czech Republic	513	(3.9)	505	(3.5)	8	(4.1)	98	(2.6)	92	(2.3)	6	(2.9)	334	(10.4)	351	(7.3)	-17	(9.9)
	Denmark	502	(3.7)	492	(2.9)	**10**	(3.1)	94	(2.3)	90	(2.1)	5	(2.2)	342	(7.6)	336	(6.4)	6	(8.4)
	Estonia	517	(3.3)	513	(2.6)	5	(3.1)	91	(2.0)	84	(1.7)	6	(2.1)	366	(6.5)	369	(5.5)	-3	(7.6)
	Finland	520	(2.8)	526	(2.6)	**-6**	(3.0)	96	(1.5)	89	(1.6)	**7**	(2.0)	355	(6.1)	373	(4.7)	**-18**	(7.5)
	France	513	(4.0)	509	(3.5)	5	(3.1)	100	(4.3)	93	(4.5)	7	(3.3)	335	(13.1)	344	(13.1)	-8	(13.8)
	Germany	512	(4.1)	505	(3.7)	**7**	(2.9)	103	(2.8)	94	(2.5)	**9**	(2.2)	333	(7.9)	338	(8.6)	-5	(8.1)
	Hungary	461	(5.0)	457	(4.3)	3	(4.8)	110	(3.3)	99	(3.3)	**12**	(3.8)	272	(10.1)	286	(14.2)	-14	(16.8)
	Ireland	501	(4.8)	496	(3.2)	5	(5.0)	97	(3.1)	89	(1.8)	**9**	(3.4)	336	(9.7)	343	(7.4)	-8	(11.5)
	Israel	457	(8.9)	451	(4.1)	6	(8.5)	134	(4.1)	112	(2.8)	**22**	(3.3)	227	(13.8)	259	(10.2)	**-32**	(13.3)
	Italy	518	(5.2)	500	(4.5)	**18**	(5.7)	97	(2.6)	82	(2.7)	**15**	(3.0)	351	(12.5)	362	(8.4)	-11	(13.1)
	Japan	561	(4.1)	542	(3.0)	**19**	(3.7)	89	(2.5)	79	(2.0)	**10**	(2.3)	406	(9.0)	405	(6.8)	1	(8.7)
	Korea	567	(5.1)	554	(5.1)	**13**	(5.5)	95	(2.5)	87	(2.0)	8	(2.9)	403	(8.7)	408	(6.9)	-6	(9.7)
	Netherlands	513	(4.9)	508	(4.5)	5	(3.3)	101	(3.5)	96	(3.3)	5	(3.2)	334	(10.4)	339	(9.6)	-5	(9.7)
	Norway	502	(3.6)	505	(3.8)	-3	(3.6)	106	(2.4)	99	(2.2)	7	(2.5)	318	(8.1)	340	(7.1)	**-22**	(8.4)
	Poland	481	(4.9)	481	(4.6)	0	(3.3)	103	(3.7)	90	(3.4)	**14**	(2.6)	306	(10.7)	331	(10.2)	**-25**	(9.5)
	Portugal	502	(4.0)	486	(3.6)	**16**	(2.6)	91	(1.9)	84	(1.8)	**7**	(1.8)	345	(7.2)	346	(5.5)	-1	(6.6)
	Slovak Republic	494	(4.2)	472	(4.1)	**22**	(4.4)	100	(3.4)	94	(2.8)	6	(3.2)	327	(7.4)	302	(9.7)	**24**	(9.2)
	Slovenia	474	(2.1)	478	(2.2)	-4	(3.0)	102	(1.6)	91	(2.0)	**11**	(2.6)	300	(4.3)	325	(6.9)	**-25**	(7.4)
	Spain	478	(4.8)	476	(4.1)	2	(3.4)	109	(3.3)	99	(3.1)	**10**	(2.7)	285	(12.9)	301	(10.0)	-16	(10.5)
	Sweden	489	(3.7)	493	(3.1)	-4	(3.6)	101	(2.4)	91	(2.0)	**9**	(2.7)	317	(7.4)	340	(8.1)	**-22**	(10.3)
	Turkey	462	(4.3)	447	(4.6)	**15**	(4.0)	81	(2.4)	77	(2.6)	4	(2.3)	334	(6.4)	324	(4.4)	10	(6.9)
	England (United Kingdom)	520	(5.4)	514	(4.6)	6	(5.5)	98	(3.0)	95	(2.9)	4	(3.4)	351	(11.8)	353	(10.5)	-2	(14.5)
	United States	509	(4.2)	506	(4.2)	3	(3.1)	97	(3.0)	88	(2.0)	**9**	(2.5)	345	(9.4)	361	(7.4)	-16	(8.8)
	OECD average	503	(0.8)	497	(0.7)	**7**	(0.8)	100	(0.5)	91	(0.5)	**8**	(0.5)	332	(1.7)	340	(1.6)	**-8**	(1.9)
Partners	Brazil	440	(5.4)	418	(4.6)	**22**	(3.3)	95	(3.1)	87	(2.2)	**8**	(2.5)	282	(9.7)	272	(6.7)	10	(8.6)
	Bulgaria	394	(5.8)	410	(5.3)	**-17**	(4.9)	110	(3.8)	102	(4.0)	8	(3.4)	205	(11.0)	237	(10.7)	**-32**	(10.8)
	Colombia	415	(4.1)	385	(3.9)	**31**	(3.8)	92	(2.3)	89	(2.3)	4	(2.5)	267	(6.6)	242	(6.3)	**25**	(6.2)
	Croatia	474	(4.8)	459	(4.0)	**15**	(4.4)	98	(2.4)	85	(2.3)	**13**	(2.5)	311	(7.3)	318	(7.2)	-7	(9.2)
	Cyprus*	440	(1.8)	449	(2.0)	**-9**	(2.5)	107	(1.5)	90	(1.3)	**17**	(1.9)	263	(6.4)	298	(5.8)	**-36**	(6.5)
	Hong Kong-China	546	(4.6)	532	(4.8)	**13**	(5.2)	93	(2.3)	90	(3.1)	3	(3.1)	384	(9.1)	376	(7.2)	7	(8.1)
	Macao-China	546	(1.5)	535	(1.3)	**10**	(2.0)	81	(1.3)	77	(1.3)	4	(2.0)	407	(4.6)	403	(4.5)	4	(5.6)
	Malaysia	427	(3.9)	419	(4.0)	**8**	(3.7)	86	(2.5)	81	(1.9)	6	(2.1)	289	(5.6)	285	(6.3)	3	(6.5)
	Montenegro	404	(1.8)	409	(1.8)	**-6**	(2.8)	95	(1.8)	88	(1.4)	7	(2.5)	251	(5.7)	263	(4.7)	-12	(6.9)
	Russian Federation	493	(3.9)	485	(3.7)	8	(3.1)	89	(2.2)	87	(2.5)	2	(2.6)	347	(6.0)	343	(6.0)	4	(7.9)
	Serbia	481	(3.8)	466	(3.2)	**15**	(3.5)	90	(2.5)	88	(2.2)	2	(2.6)	330	(7.5)	314	(6.5)	**16**	(6.8)
	Shanghai-China	549	(3.4)	524	(3.8)	**25**	(2.9)	90	(2.2)	88	(2.8)	3	(2.0)	390	(8.1)	373	(8.2)	17	(7.4)
	Singapore	567	(1.8)	558	(1.7)	**9**	(2.5)	100	(1.3)	89	(1.2)	**11**	(1.7)	394	(4.7)	402	(5.9)	-8	(8.0)
	Chinese Taipei	540	(4.5)	528	(4.1)	12	(6.3)	96	(2.9)	85	(2.1)	**11**	(3.1)	369	(10.7)	384	(5.8)	-16	(10.2)
	United Arab Emirates	398	(4.6)	424	(3.2)	**-26**	(5.6)	114	(2.9)	95	(2.2)	**20**	(3.8)	215	(9.0)	270	(6.3)	**-54**	(10.6)
	Uruguay	409	(4.0)	398	(3.8)	**11**	(3.4)	102	(2.2)	93	(2.2)	**9**	(1.8)	242	(7.6)	245	(6.7)	-3	(7.1)

Note: Values that are statistically significant are indicated in bold (see Annex A3).
* See notes at the beginning of this Annex.
StatLink ⫘ http://dx.doi.org/10.1787/888933003706

[Part 2/3]

Table V.4.7 **Mean score and variation in student performance in problem solving, by gender**

	10th percentile						25th percentile						50th percentile (median)					
	Boys		Girls		Difference (B - G)		Boys		Girls		Difference (B - G)		Boys		Girls		Difference (B - G)	
	Score	S.E.	Score	S.E.	Score dif.	S.E.	Score	S.E.	Score	S.E.	Score dif.	S.E.	Score	S.E.	Score	S.E.	Score dif.	S.E.
Australia	392	(3.1)	400	(3.2)	-8	(3.6)	457	(3.3)	460	(2.9)	-3	(3.6)	528	(3.0)	524	(2.6)	3	(3.3)
Austria	386	(8.9)	382	(7.1)	4	(8.4)	449	(5.6)	442	(5.7)	7	(6.9)	517	(4.7)	506	(4.9)	12	(6.1)
Belgium	363	(7.1)	365	(6.0)	-3	(8.6)	441	(5.0)	440	(4.1)	1	(5.9)	522	(3.5)	513	(3.5)	9	(4.5)
Canada	397	(4.0)	400	(4.6)	-3	(4.6)	464	(3.9)	460	(3.4)	3	(3.9)	533	(2.9)	526	(2.8)	7	(2.7)
Chile	338	(6.1)	335	(5.6)	4	(5.2)	395	(6.1)	385	(4.9)	9	(5.3)	458	(5.3)	443	(4.5)	15	(5.2)
Czech Republic	381	(8.4)	386	(6.0)	-5	(9.3)	452	(6.0)	443	(4.8)	9	(6.6)	521	(4.8)	510	(4.5)	11	(5.9)
Denmark	379	(6.6)	376	(5.7)	3	(6.0)	441	(5.0)	436	(3.7)	5	(4.8)	505	(4.5)	496	(3.4)	10	(4.9)
Estonia	399	(5.9)	402	(5.4)	-3	(6.8)	459	(4.6)	457	(4.0)	2	(5.2)	520	(4.1)	515	(3.1)	5	(4.5)
Finland	394	(4.9)	409	(4.7)	-15	(7.1)	456	(3.7)	469	(3.8)	-13	(4.0)	523	(3.3)	530	(3.2)	-7	(3.8)
France	384	(7.6)	391	(8.3)	-7	(8.2)	454	(5.5)	456	(4.3)	-2	(5.5)	521	(4.7)	516	(3.4)	5	(4.5)
Germany	373	(7.5)	382	(6.9)	-9	(5.5)	443	(6.8)	445	(5.1)	-2	(5.6)	519	(4.3)	512	(4.2)	7	(4.0)
Hungary	308	(10.2)	328	(8.9)	-20	(12.7)	384	(10.5)	396	(6.1)	-12	(10.8)	467	(5.5)	463	(4.9)	5	(6.3)
Ireland	377	(7.9)	380	(5.4)	-3	(9.6)	438	(6.2)	438	(4.1)	0	(7.0)	504	(4.4)	499	(3.7)	5	(5.3)
Israel	277	(11.5)	304	(7.9)	-28	(11.9)	362	(10.0)	379	(5.1)	-17	(9.9)	464	(11.4)	456	(5.3)	8	(11.3)
Italy	391	(7.4)	397	(7.3)	-6	(9.2)	455	(8.1)	448	(5.3)	7	(8.5)	526	(5.6)	503	(4.6)	23	(6.1)
Japan	445	(6.3)	438	(5.7)	6	(6.1)	504	(5.2)	492	(4.0)	12	(5.0)	567	(4.5)	546	(3.6)	22	(4.7)
Korea	444	(8.1)	443	(6.9)	1	(9.1)	510	(6.9)	501	(6.5)	10	(7.7)	575	(5.5)	559	(5.6)	16	(6.3)
Netherlands	377	(10.4)	379	(8.7)	-2	(8.6)	449	(7.2)	447	(6.2)	1	(6.2)	521	(5.7)	514	(5.0)	7	(4.2)
Norway	365	(5.9)	376	(5.9)	-11	(6.7)	433	(4.8)	439	(4.7)	-6	(5.4)	505	(3.8)	508	(4.1)	-3	(4.2)
Poland	347	(7.5)	368	(7.0)	-21	(6.8)	416	(5.7)	426	(6.1)	-10	(6.0)	486	(5.6)	483	(4.7)	3	(5.6)
Portugal	384	(5.7)	378	(5.1)	6	(5.0)	441	(5.3)	431	(4.3)	10	(3.8)	507	(5.2)	489	(4.4)	18	(4.7)
Slovak Republic	363	(7.3)	345	(8.7)	18	(7.5)	426	(5.8)	414	(6.4)	12	(6.6)	495	(5.4)	480	(4.9)	15	(6.1)
Slovenia	341	(4.3)	361	(4.6)	-21	(6.8)	408	(4.5)	417	(4.3)	-9	(5.5)	477	(3.5)	480	(3.4)	-4	(4.5)
Spain	334	(9.7)	344	(8.0)	-10	(8.0)	406	(6.0)	416	(5.1)	-10	(5.6)	485	(5.1)	482	(3.9)	3	(4.9)
Sweden	357	(6.4)	373	(5.7)	-17	(7.3)	423	(5.3)	432	(3.6)	-10	(5.2)	493	(4.1)	495	(3.9)	-2	(4.7)
Turkey	361	(5.6)	349	(4.3)	12	(5.8)	404	(5.0)	394	(4.7)	11	(5.2)	459	(4.7)	444	(5.0)	14	(5.0)
England (United Kingdom)	391	(8.2)	391	(7.2)	0	(9.3)	457	(6.7)	453	(6.2)	3	(6.5)	525	(6.2)	518	(5.2)	7	(6.8)
United States	383	(7.2)	394	(6.5)	-11	(6.4)	443	(6.0)	447	(4.9)	-4	(5.1)	513	(4.9)	507	(4.6)	6	(4.1)
OECD average	372	(1.4)	378	(1.2)	-5	(1.5)	438	(1.2)	438	(0.9)	0	(1.2)	508	(1.0)	501	(0.8)	8	(1.0)
Brazil	319	(8.4)	305	(5.7)	14	(8.4)	377	(6.5)	360	(5.1)	17	(5.2)	440	(6.6)	419	(5.9)	21	(4.6)
Bulgaria	250	(10.0)	278	(8.3)	-28	(9.5)	321	(7.2)	343	(6.4)	-22	(6.7)	396	(6.8)	413	(5.8)	-17	(6.4)
Colombia	300	(5.0)	273	(5.6)	27	(6.3)	353	(4.9)	326	(4.5)	27	(4.4)	413	(4.3)	384	(4.8)	29	(5.0)
Croatia	347	(6.8)	350	(5.0)	-3	(6.8)	406	(5.6)	402	(4.6)	5	(6.0)	473	(6.1)	459	(4.7)	14	(6.0)
Cyprus*	299	(4.8)	333	(4.5)	-34	(6.3)	366	(3.4)	388	(3.4)	-22	(4.9)	444	(2.7)	451	(2.4)	-7	(3.6)
Hong Kong-China	425	(7.1)	416	(8.1)	9	(7.8)	488	(5.9)	477	(5.9)	11	(6.3)	551	(5.0)	537	(5.1)	14	(5.7)
Macao-China	439	(3.9)	434	(3.4)	5	(5.4)	492	(2.8)	485	(2.1)	7	(3.7)	550	(2.7)	539	(2.3)	11	(4.0)
Malaysia	315	(4.6)	314	(6.0)	1	(5.6)	365	(5.0)	364	(4.7)	2	(5.0)	426	(4.6)	418	(4.7)	8	(4.5)
Montenegro	282	(4.0)	296	(4.8)	-14	(6.8)	338	(3.0)	351	(3.6)	-13	(4.3)	403	(2.9)	411	(3.2)	-9	(4.7)
Russian Federation	380	(4.8)	374	(5.8)	6	(5.3)	435	(4.6)	428	(4.7)	7	(4.6)	495	(4.0)	485	(4.1)	10	(4.7)
Serbia	363	(6.9)	350	(6.9)	13	(6.4)	420	(5.3)	408	(3.7)	11	(4.8)	484	(5.1)	469	(4.4)	15	(5.3)
Shanghai-China	431	(6.7)	411	(7.1)	21	(7.2)	491	(4.8)	468	(5.0)	23	(4.7)	554	(4.9)	528	(4.4)	26	(4.6)
Singapore	432	(4.1)	440	(4.2)	-8	(5.4)	501	(2.9)	498	(2.8)	2	(4.1)	573	(2.5)	562	(3.0)	11	(3.6)
Chinese Taipei	410	(8.0)	417	(4.4)	-7	(7.4)	479	(5.7)	471	(4.7)	8	(6.3)	548	(5.0)	532	(4.0)	17	(6.6)
United Arab Emirates	253	(6.7)	307	(5.6)	-53	(8.5)	319	(6.6)	362	(4.2)	-43	(7.8)	396	(5.2)	422	(3.7)	-26	(6.3)
Uruguay	279	(5.9)	280	(5.8)	-1	(5.5)	338	(5.4)	335	(5.2)	4	(5.1)	410	(4.7)	398	(4.7)	12	(4.9)

Note: Values that are statistically significant are indicated in bold (see Annex A3).
* See notes at the beginning of this Annex.
StatLink ⌗⌗ http://dx.doi.org/10.1787/888933003706

[Part 3/3]
Table V.4.7 **Mean score and variation in student performance in problem solving, by gender**

	75th percentile						90th percentile						95th percentile					
	Boys		Girls		Difference (B - G)		Boys		Girls		Difference (B - G)		Boys		Girls		Difference (B - G)	
	Score	S.E.	Score	S.E.	Score dif.	S.E.	Score	S.E.	Score	S.E.	Score dif.	S.E.	Score	S.E.	Score	S.E.	Score dif.	S.E.
OECD																		
Australia	594	(3.1)	588	(2.7)	6	(3.6)	651	(3.4)	641	(2.8)	**10**	(4.2)	684	(4.1)	671	(3.1)	**12**	(4.6)
Austria	581	(4.8)	564	(4.6)	17	(6.0)	631	(5.9)	612	(5.0)	**19**	(6.9)	661	(7.2)	639	(5.3)	**22**	(8.2)
Belgium	591	(2.9)	576	(3.0)	15	(3.3)	644	(3.3)	627	(3.9)	**17**	(4.3)	673	(4.0)	656	(4.6)	**18**	(5.2)
Canada	599	(3.4)	589	(2.9)	10	(3.1)	656	(3.9)	643	(3.4)	**13**	(4.0)	690	(5.0)	675	(4.1)	**15**	(5.2)
Chile	517	(4.5)	499	(4.0)	18	(4.5)	567	(5.3)	546	(4.4)	**21**	(5.6)	597	(5.9)	576	(5.7)	**21**	(7.2)
Czech Republic	582	(4.3)	568	(4.2)	13	(5.4)	632	(5.1)	620	(4.5)	12	(5.9)	662	(5.5)	650	(5.2)	12	(7.5)
Denmark	568	(4.4)	553	(4.1)	16	(5.8)	619	(5.6)	604	(4.8)	15	(6.4)	650	(6.3)	631	(5.0)	**19**	(5.9)
Estonia	580	(3.8)	571	(3.4)	9	(4.3)	632	(3.5)	619	(4.2)	12	(4.4)	661	(4.9)	647	(5.7)	14	(6.5)
Finland	586	(3.8)	588	(3.4)	-2	(4.3)	642	(5.0)	638	(4.1)	3	(5.5)	675	(6.4)	667	(3.9)	8	(6.8)
France	583	(4.1)	571	(3.9)	12	(4.3)	634	(4.3)	619	(4.8)	14	(4.8)	659	(5.6)	647	(4.9)	12	(5.8)
Germany	586	(5.1)	572	(4.6)	14	(4.8)	637	(4.9)	620	(5.3)	17	(5.3)	669	(6.0)	649	(6.8)	**20**	(7.3)
Hungary	540	(5.8)	525	(6.0)	15	(5.6)	600	(7.5)	581	(6.1)	19	(5.3)	633	(7.2)	611	(6.3)	**22**	(6.2)
Ireland	566	(5.9)	558	(3.7)	8	(6.7)	622	(7.6)	607	(4.1)	15	(8.3)	660	(7.1)	635	(4.0)	**25**	(8.1)
Israel	560	(10.3)	529	(4.8)	31	(10.4)	628	(8.2)	591	(4.9)	**37**	(7.5)	664	(8.1)	626	(5.4)	**38**	(9.0)
Italy	587	(5.1)	557	(5.3)	30	(6.4)	635	(4.3)	599	(6.2)	**36**	(6.5)	662	(5.2)	627	(6.9)	**36**	(7.3)
Japan	623	(4.2)	596	(3.5)	27	(4.6)	670	(4.7)	641	(3.9)	**29**	(5.4)	697	(6.0)	667	(5.1)	**30**	(5.8)
Korea	633	(5.0)	615	(5.6)	18	(6.1)	680	(5.4)	661	(5.9)	**19**	(6.2)	709	(6.5)	686	(6.1)	**23**	(7.1)
Netherlands	586	(5.3)	576	(5.8)	10	(4.6)	638	(5.2)	626	(6.3)	12	(5.6)	665	(5.0)	656	(7.4)	9	(6.9)
Norway	575	(4.8)	574	(4.0)	1	(4.5)	636	(5.4)	630	(4.9)	7	(6.4)	669	(8.5)	662	(5.8)	7	(7.8)
Poland	553	(5.2)	540	(4.8)	14	(4.8)	607	(5.1)	592	(6.0)	15	(5.6)	639	(6.5)	623	(6.6)	16	(6.7)
Portugal	565	(4.4)	544	(3.7)	21	(3.5)	615	(4.6)	591	(5.2)	24	(4.5)	644	(6.0)	622	(6.4)	**23**	(6.4)
Slovak Republic	564	(4.8)	536	(4.4)	28	(5.7)	622	(7.1)	585	(5.5)	**37**	(7.0)	654	(7.9)	615	(5.6)	**39**	(6.9)
Slovenia	548	(3.4)	542	(3.8)	6	(5.5)	602	(4.4)	596	(4.8)	6	(7.4)	631	(5.8)	624	(6.7)	6	(9.5)
Spain	554	(4.5)	545	(4.5)	9	(4.9)	613	(5.6)	597	(5.8)	16	(7.2)	647	(6.3)	628	(7.1)	**19**	(9.2)
Sweden	559	(3.6)	555	(3.7)	4	(4.3)	615	(5.3)	608	(4.2)	7	(6.4)	649	(6.3)	639	(4.2)	9	(6.6)
Turkey	517	(5.7)	498	(6.1)	18	(5.1)	570	(6.7)	549	(8.1)	21	(6.0)	599	(7.4)	579	(9.4)	21	(7.5)
England (United Kingdom)	589	(5.4)	579	(5.3)	10	(6.2)	640	(5.3)	630	(5.8)	9	(7.2)	671	(8.3)	663	(7.2)	9	(10.4)
United States	577	(4.6)	566	(4.4)	11	(4.7)	632	(4.9)	619	(5.7)	13	(5.6)	666	(6.3)	650	(7.2)	17	(7.1)
OECD average	574	(0.9)	560	(0.8)	14	(1.0)	627	(1.0)	610	(1.0)	17	(1.1)	659	(1.2)	640	(1.1)	19	(1.4)
Partners																		
Brazil	505	(7.0)	478	(6.1)	27	(4.6)	560	(6.8)	529	(5.6)	**31**	(5.8)	589	(7.1)	557	(6.3)	**31**	(6.6)
Bulgaria	470	(6.1)	481	(6.2)	-11	(6.5)	532	(8.5)	538	(7.9)	-6	(8.1)	569	(8.3)	572	(8.9)	-3	(8.0)
Colombia	477	(5.4)	443	(5.0)	33	(5.9)	537	(6.0)	497	(6.4)	**40**	(7.4)	569	(7.8)	531	(6.9)	**38**	(8.9)
Croatia	543	(6.2)	517	(5.1)	26	(6.5)	600	(6.4)	568	(5.8)	33	(5.9)	631	(6.8)	597	(6.6)	**33**	(7.0)
Cyprus*	516	(3.6)	510	(3.8)	6	(4.8)	576	(3.3)	565	(3.8)	11	(5.2)	613	(4.2)	596	(5.1)	17	(7.5)
Hong Kong-China	609	(5.1)	592	(5.9)	17	(7.2)	661	(4.7)	644	(7.5)	17	(8.8)	690	(4.9)	673	(9.1)	17	(10.5)
Macao-China	602	(2.2)	589	(2.2)	14	(3.0)	647	(3.2)	631	(3.0)	**16**	(4.9)	672	(3.8)	656	(3.2)	**16**	(5.4)
Malaysia	485	(4.8)	474	(4.6)	12	(5.2)	540	(7.0)	524	(5.7)	15	(6.8)	571	(7.9)	551	(5.9)	**20**	(8.0)
Montenegro	469	(3.1)	470	(3.4)	-1	(5.0)	528	(5.6)	524	(3.9)	4	(6.4)	561	(5.8)	552	(5.8)	9	(8.3)
Russian Federation	551	(4.9)	542	(4.7)	9	(4.9)	608	(7.2)	596	(6.1)	12	(7.0)	640	(7.3)	628	(7.0)	12	(6.5)
Serbia	544	(4.5)	528	(3.8)	16	(5.4)	596	(4.0)	576	(4.2)	**20**	(5.3)	626	(4.5)	604	(4.8)	**23**	(6.5)
Shanghai-China	612	(4.4)	585	(5.1)	27	(5.8)	661	(4.2)	633	(6.9)	28	(5.5)	689	(4.6)	661	(6.4)	28	(5.4)
Singapore	639	(2.6)	620	(2.5)	19	(3.5)	692	(3.2)	667	(3.8)	25	(4.6)	720	(3.8)	697	(4.7)	24	(6.3)
Chinese Taipei	610	(4.5)	590	(5.3)	21	(7.6)	657	(4.7)	634	(6.0)	23	(8.8)	683	(4.7)	661	(7.1)	22	(9.8)
United Arab Emirates	476	(6.1)	486	(3.9)	-10	(7.6)	548	(5.9)	545	(4.6)	4	(8.4)	589	(6.1)	580	(4.8)	9	(8.5)
Uruguay	481	(5.0)	461	(4.8)	20	(5.8)	543	(5.0)	519	(4.9)	24	(5.3)	580	(5.5)	552	(6.7)	28	(6.6)

Note: Values that are statistically significant are indicated in bold (see Annex A3).
* See notes at the beginning of this Annex.
StatLink ⟨⟩ http://dx.doi.org/10.1787/888933003706

[Part 1/3]

Table V.4.8   **Differences in problem-solving, mathematics, reading and science performance related to gender**

| | Gender gap: Mean score difference between boys and girls | | | | | | | | | | | |
| | Problem solving (B - G) | | Mathematics (B - G) | | Reading (B - G) | | Science (B - G) | | Computer-based mathematics (B - G) | | Digital reading (B - G) | |
	Score dif.	S.E.	Score dif.	S.E.	Score dif.	S.E.	Score dif.	S.E.	Score dif.	S.E.	Score dif.	S.E.
OECD												
Australia	2	(2.6)	12	(3.1)	-34	(2.9)	5	(3.0)	9	(2.8)	-31	(2.9)
Austria	12	(4.8)	22	(4.9)	-37	(5.0)	9	(5.0)	21	(4.9)	-27	(6.1)
Belgium	8	(3.7)	11	(3.4)	-32	(3.5)	4	(3.6)	14	(3.1)	-25	(4.0)
Canada	5	(2.2)	10	(2.0)	-35	(2.1)	3	(2.1)	17	(1.9)	-21	(1.8)
Chile	13	(3.8)	25	(3.6)	-23	(3.3)	7	(3.3)	19	(3.9)	-9	(4.4)
Czech Republic	8	(4.1)	12	(4.6)	-39	(3.7)	1	(4.0)	m	m	m	m
Denmark	10	(3.1)	14	(2.3)	-31	(2.8)	10	(2.7)	20	(2.5)	-23	(2.4)
Estonia	5	(3.1)	5	(2.6)	-44	(2.4)	-2	(2.7)	9	(2.5)	-37	(2.8)
Finland	-6	(3.0)	-3	(2.9)	-62	(3.1)	-16	(3.0)	m	m	m	m
France	5	(3.1)	9	(3.4)	-44	(4.2)	-2	(3.7)	15	(3.0)	-22	(3.6)
Germany	7	(2.9)	14	(2.8)	-44	(2.5)	-1	(3.0)	10	(2.7)	-30	(3.0)
Hungary	3	(4.8)	9	(3.7)	-40	(3.6)	3	(3.3)	12	(3.8)	-33	(4.9)
Ireland	5	(5.0)	15	(3.8)	-29	(4.2)	4	(4.4)	19	(3.7)	-25	(4.3)
Israel	6	(8.5)	12	(7.6)	-44	(7.9)	-1	(7.6)	3	(8.9)	-27	(6.4)
Italy	18	(5.7)	10	(4.8)	-45	(5.4)	-7	(5.5)	18	(5.0)	-21	(6.0)
Japan	19	(3.7)	18	(4.3)	-24	(4.1)	11	(4.3)	15	(3.8)	-16	(3.8)
Korea	13	(5.5)	18	(6.2)	-23	(5.4)	3	(5.1)	18	(6.7)	-7	(5.1)
Netherlands	5	(3.3)	10	(2.8)	-26	(3.1)	3	(2.9)	m	m	m	m
Norway	-3	(3.6)	2	(3.0)	-46	(3.3)	-4	(3.2)	3	(2.8)	-46	(3.1)
Poland	0	(3.3)	4	(3.4)	-42	(2.9)	-3	(3.0)	11	(3.2)	-34	(3.4)
Portugal	16	(2.6)	11	(2.5)	-39	(2.7)	-2	(2.6)	20	(2.3)	-17	(2.8)
Slovak Republic	22	(4.4)	9	(4.5)	-39	(4.6)	7	(4.5)	11	(3.9)	-19	(4.3)
Slovenia	-4	(3.0)	3	(3.1)	-56	(2.7)	-9	(2.8)	3	(3.0)	-39	(2.7)
Spain	2	(3.4)	13	(2.9)	-32	(2.7)	3	(2.7)	12	(2.5)	-27	(3.1)
Sweden	-4	(3.6)	-3	(3.0)	-51	(3.6)	-7	(3.3)	13	(2.8)	-33	(3.3)
Turkey	15	(4.0)	8	(4.7)	-46	(4.0)	-10	(4.2)	m	m	m	m
England (United Kingdom)	6	(5.5)	13	(5.5)	-24	(5.4)	14	(5.5)	m	m	m	m
United States	3	(3.1)	5	(2.8)	-31	(2.6)	-2	(2.7)	0	(3.0)	-28	(2.6)
OECD average	7	(0.8)	10	(0.7)	-38	(0.7)	1	(0.7)	13	(0.8)	-26	(0.8)
Partners												
Brazil	22	(3.3)	21	(2.4)	-27	(2.9)	2	(2.9)	22	(2.4)	-19	(3.2)
Bulgaria	-17	(4.9)	-2	(4.1)	-70	(5.2)	-20	(4.5)	m	m	m	m
Colombia	31	(3.8)	25	(3.2)	-19	(3.5)	18	(3.4)	12	(3.3)	-4	(4.3)
Croatia	15	(4.4)	12	(4.1)	-48	(4.0)	-2	(3.8)	m	m	m	m
Cyprus*	-9	(2.5)	0	(2.2)	-64	(3.0)	-13	(2.5)	m	m	m	m
Hong Kong-China	13	(5.2)	15	(5.7)	-25	(4.7)	7	(4.2)	17	(4.3)	-19	(5.0)
Macao-China	10	(2.0)	3	(1.9)	-36	(1.7)	-1	(1.7)	13	(2.0)	-18	(1.7)
Malaysia	8	(3.7)	-8	(3.8)	-40	(3.1)	-11	(3.5)	m	m	m	m
Montenegro	-6	(2.8)	0	(2.4)	-62	(3.1)	-17	(2.4)	m	m	m	m
Russian Federation	8	(3.1)	-2	(3.0)	-40	(3.0)	-6	(2.9)	14	(2.8)	-18	(3.0)
Serbia	15	(3.5)	9	(3.9)	-46	(3.8)	-4	(3.9)	m	m	m	m
Shanghai-China	25	(2.9)	6	(3.3)	-24	(2.5)	5	(2.7)	18	(2.9)	-10	(2.8)
Singapore	9	(2.5)	-3	(2.5)	-32	(2.6)	-1	(2.6)	1	(2.3)	-18	(2.2)
Chinese Taipei	12	(6.3)	5	(8.9)	-32	(6.4)	1	(6.4)	15	(6.7)	-17	(5.3)
United Arab Emirates	-26	(5.6)	-5	(4.7)	-55	(4.8)	-28	(5.1)	-13	(4.4)	-50	(6.5)
Uruguay	11	(3.4)	11	(3.1)	-35	(3.5)	-1	(3.4)	m	m	m	m

Note: Values that are statistically significant are indicated in bold (see Annex A3).

* See notes at the beginning of this Annex.

StatLink ⌷ⁱˢ⌷ http://dx.doi.org/10.1787/888933003706

[Part 2/3]

Table V.4.8 **Differences in problem-solving, mathematics, reading and science performance related to gender**

		Gender effect size: Gender difference divided by the variation in scores within each country/economy (standard deviation)										
		Problem solving (B - G)		Mathematics (B - G)		Reading (B - G)		Science (B - G)		Computer-based mathematics (B - G)		Digital reading (B - G)	
		Effect size	S.E.	Effect size	S.E.	Effect size	S.E.	Effect size	S.E.	Effect size	S.E.	Effect size	S.E.
OECD	Australia	0.03	(0.03)	**0.13**	(0.03)	**-0.35**	(0.03)	0.05	(0.03)	**0.10**	(0.03)	**-0.32**	(0.03)
	Austria	**0.13**	(0.05)	**0.24**	(0.05)	**-0.40**	(0.05)	0.09	(0.05)	**0.23**	(0.06)	**-0.26**	(0.06)
	Belgium	**0.07**	(0.03)	**0.11**	(0.03)	**-0.31**	(0.03)	0.04	(0.04)	**0.15**	(0.03)	**-0.26**	(0.04)
	Canada	**0.05**	(0.02)	**0.11**	(0.02)	**-0.38**	(0.02)	0.03	(0.02)	**0.19**	(0.02)	**-0.24**	(0.02)
	Chile	**0.16**	(0.04)	**0.31**	(0.04)	**-0.29**	(0.04)	**0.08**	(0.04)	**0.24**	(0.05)	**-0.11**	(0.05)
	Czech Republic	0.08	(0.04)	**0.12**	(0.05)	**-0.44**	(0.04)	0.01	(0.04)	m	m	m	m
	Denmark	**0.11**	(0.03)	**0.17**	(0.03)	**-0.36**	(0.03)	**0.11**	(0.03)	**0.23**	(0.03)	**-0.27**	(0.03)
	Estonia	0.06	(0.04)	**0.07**	(0.03)	**-0.54**	(0.03)	-0.03	(0.03)	**0.11**	(0.03)	**-0.39**	(0.03)
	Finland	**-0.07**	(0.03)	-0.03	(0.03)	**-0.65**	(0.03)	**-0.18**	(0.03)	m	m	m	m
	France	0.05	(0.03)	**0.09**	(0.03)	**-0.40**	(0.04)	-0.02	(0.04)	**0.16**	(0.03)	**-0.23**	(0.04)
	Germany	**0.07**	(0.03)	**0.14**	(0.03)	**-0.48**	(0.03)	-0.01	(0.03)	**0.10**	(0.03)	**-0.30**	(0.03)
	Hungary	0.03	(0.05)	**0.10**	(0.04)	**-0.43**	(0.04)	0.03	(0.04)	**0.13**	(0.04)	**-0.29**	(0.04)
	Ireland	0.06	(0.05)	**0.18**	(0.05)	**-0.33**	(0.05)	0.04	(0.05)	**0.23**	(0.05)	**-0.31**	(0.05)
	Israel	0.05	(0.07)	0.11	(0.07)	**-0.38**	(0.07)	-0.01	(0.07)	0.02	(0.08)	**-0.24**	(0.05)
	Italy	**0.20**	(0.07)	**0.11**	(0.05)	**-0.46**	(0.05)	-0.08	(0.06)	**0.22**	(0.06)	**-0.22**	(0.06)
	Japan	**0.22**	(0.04)	**0.19**	(0.05)	**-0.24**	(0.04)	**0.12**	(0.04)	**0.17**	(0.04)	**-0.20**	(0.05)
	Korea	**0.14**	(0.06)	**0.18**	(0.06)	**-0.27**	(0.06)	0.04	(0.06)	**0.20**	(0.07)	-0.09	(0.06)
	Netherlands	0.05	(0.03)	**0.11**	(0.03)	**-0.28**	(0.03)	0.03	(0.03)	m	m	m	m
	Norway	-0.03	(0.03)	0.02	(0.03)	**-0.46**	(0.03)	-0.04	(0.03)	0.03	(0.03)	**-0.46**	(0.03)
	Poland	0.00	(0.03)	0.04	(0.04)	**-0.48**	(0.03)	-0.03	(0.03)	**0.13**	(0.04)	**-0.35**	(0.04)
	Portugal	**0.18**	(0.03)	**0.12**	(0.03)	**-0.42**	(0.03)	-0.02	(0.03)	**0.24**	(0.03)	**-0.19**	(0.03)
	Slovak Republic	**0.22**	(0.04)	**0.09**	(0.04)	**-0.38**	(0.05)	0.07	(0.04)	**0.13**	(0.05)	**-0.20**	(0.05)
	Slovenia	-0.04	(0.03)	0.04	(0.03)	**-0.61**	(0.03)	**-0.10**	(0.03)	0.03	(0.03)	**-0.40**	(0.03)
	Spain	0.01	(0.03)	**0.15**	(0.03)	**-0.34**	(0.03)	0.04	(0.03)	**0.15**	(0.03)	**-0.28**	(0.03)
	Sweden	-0.04	(0.04)	-0.03	(0.03)	**-0.48**	(0.03)	**-0.07**	(0.03)	**0.16**	(0.03)	**-0.35**	(0.03)
	Turkey	**0.19**	(0.05)	0.09	(0.05)	**-0.53**	(0.04)	**-0.13**	(0.05)	m	m	m	m
	England (United Kingdom)	0.06	(0.06)	**0.13**	(0.06)	**-0.25**	(0.05)	**0.14**	(0.05)	m	m	m	m
	United States	0.03	(0.03)	0.05	(0.03)	**-0.33**	(0.03)	-0.02	(0.03)	0.00	(0.03)	**-0.32**	(0.03)
	OECD average	**0.07**	**(0.01)**	**0.11**	**(0.01)**	**-0.40**	**(0.01)**	0.01	(0.01)	**0.15**	**(0.01)**	**-0.27**	**(0.01)**
Partners	Brazil	**0.24**	(0.04)	**0.27**	(0.03)	**-0.32**	(0.03)	0.02	(0.04)	**0.26**	(0.03)	**-0.21**	(0.03)
	Bulgaria	**-0.16**	(0.05)	-0.03	(0.04)	**-0.59**	(0.04)	**-0.20**	(0.04)	m	m	m	m
	Colombia	**0.33**	(0.04)	**0.34**	(0.04)	**-0.22**	(0.04)	**0.23**	(0.05)	**0.16**	(0.04)	-0.05	(0.05)
	Croatia	**0.16**	(0.05)	**0.13**	(0.05)	**-0.56**	(0.04)	-0.03	(0.04)	m	m	m	m
	Cyprus*	**-0.09**	(0.02)	0.00	(0.02)	**-0.57**	(0.02)	**-0.13**	(0.03)	m	m	m	m
	Hong Kong-China	**0.15**	(0.06)	**0.16**	(0.06)	**-0.30**	(0.05)	0.08	(0.05)	**0.20**	(0.05)	**-0.20**	(0.05)
	Macao-China	**0.13**	(0.02)	0.03	(0.02)	**-0.43**	(0.02)	-0.02	(0.02)	**0.15**	(0.02)	**-0.26**	(0.02)
	Malaysia	**0.09**	(0.04)	**-0.10**	(0.05)	**-0.48**	(0.04)	**-0.14**	(0.05)	m	m	m	m
	Montenegro	-0.06	(0.03)	0.00	(0.03)	**-0.67**	(0.03)	**-0.20**	(0.03)	m	m	m	m
	Russian Federation	**0.09**	(0.04)	-0.02	(0.04)	**-0.44**	(0.03)	-0.07	(0.03)	**0.18**	(0.03)	**-0.21**	(0.04)
	Serbia	**0.17**	(0.04)	**0.10**	(0.04)	**-0.50**	(0.04)	-0.05	(0.04)	m	m	m	m
	Shanghai-China	**0.28**	(0.03)	0.06	(0.03)	**-0.30**	(0.03)	0.06	(0.03)	**0.20**	(0.03)	**-0.12**	(0.03)
	Singapore	**0.10**	(0.03)	-0.03	(0.02)	**-0.32**	(0.03)	-0.01	(0.02)	0.01	(0.02)	**-0.20**	(0.02)
	Chinese Taipei	0.13	(0.07)	0.05	(0.08)	**-0.35**	(0.07)	0.01	(0.08)	**0.17**	(0.07)	**-0.19**	(0.06)
	United Arab Emirates	**-0.25**	(0.05)	-0.05	(0.05)	**-0.58**	(0.05)	**-0.30**	(0.05)	**-0.15**	(0.05)	**-0.45**	(0.06)
	Uruguay	**0.12**	(0.03)	**0.13**	(0.04)	**-0.37**	(0.03)	-0.01	(0.04)	m	m	m	m

Note: Values that are statistically significant are indicated in bold (see Annex A3).
* See notes at the beginning of this Annex.
StatLink ᠁ http://dx.doi.org/10.1787/888933003706

[Part 3/3]
Table V.4.8 **Differences in problem-solving, mathematics, reading and science performance related to gender**

		\.\.\. Mathematics (PS - M)		\.\.\. Reading (PS - R)		\.\.\. Science (PS - S)		\.\.\. Computer-based mathematics (PS - CBM)		\.\.\. Digital reading (PS - DR)	
		Effect size dif.	S.E.	Effect size dif.	S.E.	Effect size dif.	S.E.	Effect size dif.	S.E.	Effect size dif.	S.E.
OECD	Australia	**-0.10**	(0.02)	**0.38**	(0.02)	-0.02	(0.02)	**-0.07**	(0.02)	**0.34**	(0.02)
	Austria	**-0.11**	(0.03)	**0.53**	(0.03)	0.03	(0.03)	**-0.11**	(0.04)	**0.38**	(0.05)
	Belgium	-0.03	(0.02)	**0.39**	(0.02)	0.04	(0.02)	**-0.07**	(0.02)	**0.33**	(0.03)
	Canada	**-0.06**	(0.02)	**0.44**	(0.02)	0.02	(0.02)	**-0.13**	(0.02)	**0.29**	(0.02)
	Chile	**-0.15**	(0.03)	**0.45**	(0.03)	**0.07**	(0.03)	**-0.08**	(0.04)	**0.27**	(0.04)
	Czech Republic	-0.04	(0.03)	**0.52**	(0.03)	**0.07**	(0.03)	m	m	m	m
	Denmark	**-0.06**	(0.02)	**0.47**	(0.03)	0.00	(0.03)	**-0.12**	(0.02)	**0.38**	(0.03)
	Estonia	-0.01	(0.02)	**0.60**	(0.02)	**0.09**	(0.03)	**-0.05**	(0.02)	**0.45**	(0.03)
	Finland	**-0.03**	(0.02)	**0.58**	(0.02)	**0.11**	(0.02)	m	m	m	m
	France	-0.04	(0.03)	**0.45**	(0.03)	**0.07**	(0.03)	**-0.12**	(0.02)	**0.28**	(0.03)
	Germany	**-0.07**	(0.02)	**0.55**	(0.02)	**0.07**	(0.02)	-0.03	(0.02)	**0.37**	(0.02)
	Hungary	**-0.06**	(0.03)	**0.46**	(0.03)	0.00	(0.03)	**-0.09**	(0.03)	**0.32**	(0.03)
	Ireland	**-0.12**	(0.04)	**0.39**	(0.05)	0.01	(0.04)	**-0.17**	(0.05)	**0.36**	(0.05)
	Israel	**-0.06**	(0.03)	**0.43**	(0.03)	0.06	(0.03)	0.03	(0.03)	**0.28**	(0.04)
	Italy	0.08	(0.05)	**0.65**	(0.05)	**0.27**	(0.05)	-0.03	(0.05)	**0.42**	(0.05)
	Japan	0.03	(0.03)	**0.47**	(0.03)	**0.11**	(0.03)	0.06	(0.03)	**0.43**	(0.03)
	Korea	-0.04	(0.04)	**0.41**	(0.04)	**0.10**	(0.04)	-0.05	(0.05)	**0.23**	(0.05)
	Netherlands	**-0.06**	(0.02)	**0.34**	(0.02)	0.02	(0.02)	m	m	m	m
	Norway	**-0.05**	(0.02)	**0.43**	(0.03)	0.00	(0.02)	**-0.07**	(0.02)	**0.43**	(0.02)
	Poland	-0.04	(0.02)	**0.48**	(0.02)	0.03	(0.02)	**-0.12**	(0.02)	**0.35**	(0.02)
	Portugal	**0.06**	(0.02)	**0.60**	(0.03)	**0.20**	(0.02)	**-0.06**	(0.02)	**0.37**	(0.03)
	Slovak Republic	0.13	(0.03)	**0.60**	(0.03)	**0.15**	(0.03)	0.09	(0.03)	**0.42**	(0.03)
	Slovenia	**-0.08**	(0.02)	**0.56**	(0.02)	**0.06**	(0.02)	**-0.07**	(0.02)	**0.36**	(0.02)
	Spain	**-0.13**	(0.02)	**0.36**	(0.03)	-0.02	(0.02)	**-0.14**	(0.03)	**0.29**	(0.02)
	Sweden	-0.01	(0.02)	**0.44**	(0.03)	0.04	(0.03)	**-0.19**	(0.02)	**0.31**	(0.02)
	Turkey	0.10	(0.03)	**0.72**	(0.03)	**0.32**	(0.04)	m	m	m	m
	England (United Kingdom)	**-0.07**	(0.03)	**0.31**	(0.04)	**-0.08**	(0.03)	m	m	m	m
	United States	-0.02	(0.02)	**0.37**	(0.02)	0.05	(0.02)	0.03	(0.02)	**0.35**	(0.02)
	OECD average	**-0.04**	(0.01)	**0.48**	(0.01)	**0.07**	(0.01)	**-0.07**	(0.01)	**0.35**	(0.01)
Partners	Brazil	-0.03	(0.03)	**0.55**	(0.03)	**0.22**	(0.03)	-0.02	(0.03)	**0.45**	(0.03)
	Bulgaria	**-0.13**	(0.03)	**0.43**	(0.03)	0.04	(0.03)	m	m	m	m
	Colombia	-0.01	(0.03)	**0.56**	(0.03)	**0.10**	(0.03)	**0.17**	(0.04)	**0.38**	(0.04)
	Croatia	0.03	(0.03)	**0.72**	(0.03)	**0.19**	(0.03)	m	m	m	m
	Cyprus*	**-0.09**	(0.02)	**0.48**	(0.02)	0.04	(0.02)	m	m	m	m
	Hong Kong-China	-0.01	(0.03)	**0.45**	(0.04)	0.07	(0.04)	-0.05	(0.04)	**0.35**	(0.04)
	Macao-China	**0.10**	(0.02)	**0.57**	(0.02)	**0.15**	(0.02)	-0.02	(0.02)	**0.39**	(0.02)
	Malaysia	0.19	(0.02)	**0.57**	(0.03)	**0.24**	(0.02)	m	m	m	m
	Montenegro	**-0.06**	(0.02)	**0.61**	(0.02)	**0.14**	(0.02)	m	m	m	m
	Russian Federation	0.11	(0.02)	**0.53**	(0.03)	**0.16**	(0.04)	**-0.08**	(0.02)	**0.30**	(0.02)
	Serbia	0.07	(0.03)	**0.67**	(0.03)	**0.22**	(0.03)	m	m	m	m
	Shanghai-China	**0.22**	(0.02)	**0.58**	(0.03)	**0.22**	(0.03)	0.08	(0.02)	**0.40**	(0.03)
	Singapore	0.13	(0.01)	**0.42**	(0.02)	**0.11**	(0.02)	0.09	(0.02)	**0.30**	(0.02)
	Chinese Taipei	0.09	(0.02)	**0.49**	(0.03)	**0.12**	(0.03)	-0.04	(0.03)	**0.32**	(0.03)
	United Arab Emirates	**-0.19**	(0.04)	**0.33**	(0.04)	0.05	(0.04)	**-0.10**	(0.04)	**0.20**	(0.04)
	Uruguay	-0.01	(0.02)	**0.49**	(0.02)	**0.13**	(0.02)	m	m	m	m

Note: Values that are statistically significant are indicated in bold (see Annex A3).
* See notes at the beginning of this Annex.
StatLink 🔗 http://dx.doi.org/10.1787/888933003706

[Part 1/2]

Table V.4.9 **Relative variation in performance in problem solving, mathematics, reading and science, by gender**

		Variation ratio: Variation in performance among boys as a proportion of the variation in performance among girls											
		Problem solving (B/G)		Mathematics (B/G)		Reading (B/G)		Science (B/G)		Computer-based mathematics (B/G)		Digital reading (B/G)	
		Ratio	S.E.	Ratio	S.E.	Ratio	S.E.	Ratio	S.E.	Ratio	S.E.	Ratio	S.E.
OECD	Australia	**1.12**	(0.04)	**1.12**	(0.05)	**1.20**	(0.05)	**1.12**	(0.04)	**1.12**	(0.05)	**1.14**	(0.04)
	Austria	**1.18**	(0.08)	**1.12**	(0.07)	**1.22**	(0.07)	**1.18**	(0.07)	**1.23**	(0.08)	1.07	(0.09)
	Belgium	**1.16**	(0.06)	**1.14**	(0.05)	**1.22**	(0.06)	**1.22**	(0.06)	**1.16**	(0.05)	**1.21**	(0.05)
	Canada	**1.17**	(0.06)	**1.15**	(0.04)	**1.21**	(0.04)	**1.17**	(0.04)	**1.15**	(0.04)	**1.13**	(0.05)
	Chile	**1.18**	(0.06)	**1.11**	(0.05)	**1.16**	(0.06)	**1.14**	(0.05)	**1.11**	(0.05)	**1.14**	(0.06)
	Czech Republic	**1.14**	(0.07)	1.08	(0.06)	**1.13**	(0.06)	1.12	(0.07)	m	m	m	m
	Denmark	**1.11**	(0.05)	1.05	(0.05)	**1.17**	(0.06)	**1.16**	(0.06)	**1.08**	(0.04)	**1.15**	(0.04)
	Estonia	**1.15**	(0.06)	**1.14**	(0.05)	**1.19**	(0.06)	**1.15**	(0.05)	**1.19**	(0.05)	**1.14**	(0.06)
	Finland	**1.16**	(0.05)	**1.23**	(0.05)	**1.23**	(0.06)	**1.20**	(0.05)	m	m	m	m
	France	**1.16**	(0.08)	**1.21**	(0.06)	**1.28**	(0.07)	**1.25**	(0.07)	**1.18**	(0.09)	**1.16**	(0.08)
	Germany	**1.20**	(0.05)	**1.10**	(0.05)	**1.14**	(0.04)	**1.11**	(0.05)	**1.12**	(0.05)	**1.13**	(0.05)
	Hungary	**1.25**	(0.09)	**1.18**	(0.06)	**1.21**	(0.07)	**1.12**	(0.06)	**1.28**	(0.09)	**1.21**	(0.07)
	Ireland	**1.21**	(0.09)	1.09	(0.06)	**1.19**	(0.07)	**1.13**	(0.07)	**1.14**	(0.06)	**1.16**	(0.07)
	Israel	**1.44**	(0.07)	**1.43**	(0.06)	**1.56**	(0.09)	**1.45**	(0.06)	**1.43**	(0.09)	**1.28**	(0.08)
	Italy	**1.41**	(0.10)	**1.25**	(0.06)	**1.34**	(0.08)	**1.22**	(0.07)	**1.10**	(0.07)	**1.32**	(0.10)
	Japan	**1.25**	(0.07)	**1.22**	(0.08)	**1.31**	(0.08)	**1.23**	(0.07)	**1.27**	(0.08)	**1.24**	(0.10)
	Korea	**1.20**	(0.08)	**1.27**	(0.08)	**1.37**	(0.10)	**1.25**	(0.08)	**1.19**	(0.10)	**1.32**	(0.10)
	Netherlands	**1.11**	(0.07)	1.05	(0.05)	**1.18**	(0.09)	1.06	(0.06)	m	m	m	m
	Norway	**1.14**	(0.06)	**1.10**	(0.06)	**1.22**	(0.07)	**1.12**	(0.06)	1.08	(0.06)	**1.20**	(0.07)
	Poland	**1.33**	(0.07)	**1.19**	(0.06)	**1.33**	(0.08)	**1.17**	(0.05)	**1.27**	(0.06)	**1.26**	(0.07)
	Portugal	**1.18**	(0.05)	**1.17**	(0.04)	**1.25**	(0.06)	**1.17**	(0.06)	**1.24**	(0.05)	**1.25**	(0.06)
	Slovak Republic	**1.13**	(0.07)	**1.13**	(0.06)	1.08	(0.06)	1.10	(0.06)	**1.13**	(0.06)	1.06	(0.07)
	Slovenia	**1.25**	(0.07)	1.07	(0.05)	**1.23**	(0.05)	**1.14**	(0.05)	**1.14**	(0.05)	**1.25**	(0.05)
	Spain	**1.22**	(0.06)	**1.18**	(0.05)	**1.24**	(0.06)	**1.18**	(0.05)	**1.12**	(0.05)	**1.23**	(0.05)
	Sweden	**1.22**	(0.06)	**1.19**	(0.06)	**1.30**	(0.07)	**1.26**	(0.07)	**1.20**	(0.06)	**1.33**	(0.07)
	Turkey	**1.11**	(0.06)	**1.11**	(0.06)	**1.20**	(0.07)	**1.18**	(0.07)	m	m	m	m
	England (United Kingdom)	1.08	(0.08)	1.00	(0.06)	1.04	(0.08)	1.02	(0.07)	m	m	m	m
	United States	**1.22**	(0.06)	**1.13**	(0.05)	**1.23**	(0.06)	**1.20**	(0.06)	**1.26**	(0.06)	**1.29**	(0.07)
	OECD average	**1.20**	(0.01)	**1.15**	(0.01)	**1.23**	(0.01)	**1.17**	(0.01)	**1.18**	(0.01)	**1.20**	(0.02)
Partners	Brazil	**1.19**	(0.06)	**1.14**	(0.05)	**1.13**	(0.06)	**1.16**	(0.06)	**1.13**	(0.05)	**1.13**	(0.06)
	Bulgaria	**1.16**	(0.07)	**1.17**	(0.05)	**1.21**	(0.06)	**1.16**	(0.06)	m	m	m	m
	Colombia	1.08	(0.06)	**1.20**	(0.08)	**1.19**	(0.06)	**1.16**	(0.06)	**1.18**	(0.09)	1.13	(0.09)
	Croatia	**1.33**	(0.07)	**1.19**	(0.06)	**1.30**	(0.07)	**1.25**	(0.06)	m	m	m	m
	Cyprus*	**1.41**	(0.06)	**1.52**	(0.06)	**1.56**	(0.07)	**1.48**	(0.06)	m	m	m	m
	Hong Kong-China	1.08	(0.07)	**1.23**	(0.06)	**1.25**	(0.06)	**1.22**	(0.07)	**1.27**	(0.07)	**1.21**	(0.06)
	Macao-China	1.10	(0.06)	**1.12**	(0.05)	**1.27**	(0.05)	**1.20**	(0.04)	**1.23**	(0.05)	**1.22**	(0.05)
	Malaysia	**1.14**	(0.06)	1.08	(0.07)	**1.18**	(0.06)	**1.13**	(0.07)	m	m	m	m
	Montenegro	**1.16**	(0.06)	**1.13**	(0.05)	**1.23**	(0.07)	**1.16**	(0.06)	m	m	m	m
	Russian Federation	1.06	(0.06)	1.04	(0.04)	**1.12**	(0.04)	**1.14**	(0.04)	1.10	(0.05)	1.06	(0.06)
	Serbia	1.05	(0.06)	1.05	(0.05)	**1.16**	(0.07)	1.09	(0.06)	m	m	m	m
	Shanghai-China	1.06	(0.05)	**1.14**	(0.04)	**1.21**	(0.05)	**1.16**	(0.05)	**1.17**	(0.05)	**1.12**	(0.05)
	Singapore	**1.27**	(0.05)	**1.24**	(0.04)	**1.20**	(0.05)	**1.25**	(0.05)	**1.25**	(0.05)	**1.20**	(0.05)
	Chinese Taipei	**1.28**	(0.09)	**1.21**	(0.09)	**1.27**	(0.09)	**1.22**	(0.10)	**1.35**	(0.10)	**1.29**	(0.07)
	United Arab Emirates	**1.46**	(0.11)	**1.31**	(0.07)	**1.42**	(0.07)	**1.30**	(0.07)	**1.42**	(0.09)	**1.41**	(0.08)
	Uruguay	**1.21**	(0.05)	**1.21**	(0.05)	**1.26**	(0.06)	**1.22**	(0.05)	m	m	m	m

Note: Values that are statistically significant are indicated in bold (see Annex A3).
* See notes at the beginning of this Annex.
StatLink http://dx.doi.org/10.1787/888933003706

[Part 2/2]

Table V.4.9 **Relative variation in performance in problem solving, mathematics, reading and science, by gender**

| | Relative variation ratio: Variation ratio in problem solving (PS), as a proportion of the variation ratio in... | | | | | | | | | |
| | ... Mathematics (PS/M) | | ... Reading (PS/R) | | ... Science (PS/S) | | ... Computer-based mathematics (PS/CBM) | | ... Digital reading (PS/DR) | |
	Ratio	S.E.	Ratio	S.E.	Ratio	S.E.	Ratio	S.E.	Ratio	S.E.
Australia	1.00	(0.04)	0.93	(0.04)	1.00	(0.04)	1.00	(0.04)	0.99	(0.04)
Austria	1.06	(0.06)	0.97	(0.05)	1.00	(0.06)	0.97	(0.06)	1.11	(0.11)
Belgium	1.02	(0.04)	0.96	(0.04)	0.96	(0.04)	1.00	(0.04)	0.96	(0.06)
Canada	1.01	(0.04)	0.97	(0.04)	0.99	(0.04)	1.01	(0.04)	1.03	(0.04)
Chile	1.07	(0.05)	1.02	(0.06)	1.04	(0.05)	1.06	(0.07)	1.04	(0.06)
Czech Republic	1.06	(0.04)	1.01	(0.04)	1.02	(0.04)	m	m	m	m
Denmark	1.05	(0.06)	0.95	(0.05)	0.96	(0.05)	1.03	(0.05)	0.96	(0.05)
Estonia	1.01	(0.03)	0.96	(0.05)	1.00	(0.04)	0.96	(0.05)	1.01	(0.05)
Finland	0.95	(0.04)	0.94	(0.04)	0.97	(0.04)	m	m	m	m
France	0.96	(0.05)	0.91	(0.05)	0.93	(0.05)	0.99	(0.04)	1.00	(0.05)
Germany	**1.09**	(0.04)	1.06	(0.04)	**1.08**	(0.04)	1.07	(0.04)	1.06	(0.05)
Hungary	1.06	(0.05)	1.04	(0.06)	**1.12**	(0.06)	0.98	(0.06)	1.04	(0.06)
Ireland	1.11	(0.07)	1.02	(0.07)	1.07	(0.07)	1.06	(0.08)	1.04	(0.08)
Israel	1.00	(0.05)	0.92	(0.06)	0.99	(0.05)	1.00	(0.06)	**1.12**	(0.06)
Italy	**1.13**	(0.06)	1.05	(0.07)	**1.16**	(0.07)	**1.28**	(0.10)	1.07	(0.08)
Japan	1.03	(0.06)	0.96	(0.07)	1.02	(0.06)	0.99	(0.05)	1.01	(0.06)
Korea	0.94	(0.05)	**0.87**	(0.04)	0.96	(0.05)	1.01	(0.07)	0.90	(0.05)
Netherlands	1.06	(0.06)	0.94	(0.05)	1.05	(0.05)	m	m	m	m
Norway	1.04	(0.05)	0.94	(0.05)	1.02	(0.05)	1.06	(0.05)	0.95	(0.04)
Poland	1.11	(0.07)	1.00	(0.04)	**1.13**	(0.06)	1.04	(0.05)	1.06	(0.04)
Portugal	1.00	(0.04)	0.94	(0.05)	1.01	(0.05)	0.95	(0.04)	0.94	(0.04)
Slovak Republic	1.00	(0.05)	1.04	(0.05)	1.02	(0.05)	1.00	(0.05)	1.07	(0.07)
Slovenia	**1.16**	(0.06)	1.01	(0.05)	1.10	(0.05)	**1.10**	(0.05)	0.99	(0.04)
Spain	1.03	(0.05)	0.98	(0.05)	1.04	(0.05)	1.09	(0.05)	0.99	(0.04)
Sweden	1.02	(0.04)	0.94	(0.05)	0.97	(0.04)	1.02	(0.05)	0.92	(0.05)
Turkey	1.00	(0.04)	0.93	(0.04)	0.94	(0.05)	m	m	m	m
England (United Kingdom)	1.07	(0.07)	1.04	(0.07)	1.06	(0.07)	m	m	m	m
United States	**1.08**	(0.04)	0.99	(0.04)	1.01	(0.04)	0.97	(0.04)	0.94	(0.04)
OECD average	**1.04**	(0.01)	**0.97**	(0.01)	**1.02**	(0.01)	**1.03**	(0.01)	1.01	(0.01)
Brazil	1.04	(0.06)	1.05	(0.07)	1.02	(0.06)	1.05	(0.05)	1.05	(0.06)
Bulgaria	1.00	(0.05)	0.96	(0.05)	1.00	(0.06)	m	m	m	m
Colombia	0.91	(0.05)	0.91	(0.05)	0.94	(0.04)	0.92	(0.06)	0.96	(0.07)
Croatia	**1.12**	(0.04)	1.03	(0.05)	1.07	(0.06)	m	m	m	m
Cyprus*	**0.93**	(0.03)	**0.90**	(0.04)	0.95	(0.04)	m	m	m	m
Hong Kong-China	**0.87**	(0.05)	**0.86**	(0.06)	0.88	(0.06)	**0.85**	(0.05)	0.89	(0.06)
Macao-China	0.98	(0.04)	**0.87**	(0.04)	0.91	(0.05)	**0.90**	(0.04)	**0.90**	(0.04)
Malaysia	1.05	(0.04)	0.97	(0.05)	1.01	(0.04)	m	m	m	m
Montenegro	1.03	(0.04)	0.95	(0.05)	1.00	(0.05)	m	m	m	m
Russian Federation	1.02	(0.07)	0.94	(0.05)	0.93	(0.06)	0.97	(0.05)	1.00	(0.06)
Serbia	1.00	(0.05)	0.91	(0.05)	0.97	(0.06)	m	m	m	m
Shanghai-China	**0.93**	(0.03)	**0.88**	(0.03)	**0.92**	(0.04)	**0.91**	(0.04)	0.95	(0.05)
Singapore	1.02	(0.03)	1.06	(0.04)	1.02	(0.04)	1.02	(0.04)	1.06	(0.04)
Chinese Taipei	1.06	(0.05)	1.01	(0.05)	1.05	(0.05)	0.95	(0.05)	0.99	(0.05)
United Arab Emirates	**1.12**	(0.07)	1.03	(0.06)	**1.12**	(0.08)	1.03	(0.07)	1.03	(0.07)
Uruguay	1.01	(0.04)	0.96	(0.05)	0.99	(0.05)	m	m	m	m

Note: Values that are statistically significant are indicated in bold (see Annex A3).
* See notes at the beginning of this Annex.
StatLink http://dx.doi.org/10.1787/888933003706

[Part 1/1]

Table V.4.10 Relative performance in problem solving, by gender

Girls' performance in problem solving, compared to boys with similar performance in mathematics, reading and science

	Average difference in problem solving compared with boys with similar performance in mathematics[1]		Percentage of girls who outperform boys with similar performance in mathematics[2]		Average difference in problem solving compared with boys with similar performance in reading[1]		Percentage of girls who outperform boys with similar performance in reading[2]		Average difference in problem solving compared with boys with similar performance in science[1]		Percentage of girls who outperform boys with similar performance in science[2]		Average difference in problem solving compared with boys with similar performance in mathematics, reading and science[3]		Percentage of girls who outperform boys with similar performance in mathematics, reading and science[2]	
	Score dif.	S.E.	%	S.E.	Score dif.	S.E.	%	S.E.	Score dif.	S.E.	%	S.E.	Score dif.	S.E.	%	S.E.
OECD																
Australia	8	(1.4)	56.8	(1.3)	-30	(1.8)	30.6	(1.4)	1	(1.7)	51.5	(1.5)	7	(2.2)	56.0	(1.9)
Austria	7	(2.9)	55.1	(2.5)	-42	(2.9)	20.4	(2.1)	-5	(2.8)	46.7	(2.4)	-20	(4.7)	34.1	(3.5)
Belgium	1	(2.2)	50.9	(1.7)	-34	(2.0)	29.1	(1.3)	-4	(2.2)	47.5	(1.5)	-5	(2.5)	46.5	(1.8)
Canada	3	(1.4)	52.4	(1.3)	-34	(1.5)	30.4	(0.9)	-3	(1.4)	48.4	(0.9)	-5	(1.8)	47.0	(1.5)
Chile	9	(2.3)	57.5	(2.1)	-32	(2.1)	28.5	(1.7)	-8	(2.4)	44.6	(2.1)	1	(2.6)	51.1	(2.5)
Czech Republic	3	(2.4)	53.0	(2.5)	-43	(2.3)	20.6	(1.9)	-7	(2.4)	44.7	(2.0)	-8	(3.7)	42.8	(3.2)
Denmark	2	(2.4)	52.0	(1.9)	-34	(2.1)	28.9	(1.4)	-2	(2.4)	48.3	(1.7)	-2	(5.4)	48.7	(3.7)
Estonia	0	(1.8)	50.9	(1.8)	-45	(2.0)	18.4	(1.4)	-7	(2.5)	44.7	(2.3)	-14	(4.2)	37.7	(3.9)
Finland	4	(1.4)	53.6	(1.4)	-44	(2.0)	22.2	(1.2)	-7	(1.6)	45.2	(1.3)	-6	(2.9)	45.5	(2.7)
France	2	(2.3)	54.4	(2.4)	-35	(2.2)	26.4	(2.1)	-6	(2.3)	47.5	(2.2)	-3	(3.9)	49.5	(4.2)
Germany	5	(2.0)	54.3	(1.7)	-47	(2.0)	19.5	(1.5)	-7	(2.0)	44.5	(2.0)	-8	(3.6)	43.9	(2.9)
Hungary	5	(2.8)	53.4	(2.3)	-41	(3.1)	23.0	(1.6)	0	(3.2)	50.2	(2.3)	-10	(4.3)	42.4	(3.6)
Ireland	9	(3.9)	57.0	(3.2)	-29	(4.3)	31.1	(2.6)	-2	(4.0)	49.5	(3.2)	2	(5.3)	51.8	(4.7)
Israel	6	(3.3)	54.2	(2.5)	-46	(3.2)	24.9	(1.8)	-6	(3.4)	46.3	(2.4)	-7	(3.8)	45.2	(3.0)
Italy	-10	(4.4)	42.1	(3.4)	-49	(4.0)	19.3	(2.2)	-23	(4.1)	34.2	(3.0)	-21	(5.4)	34.3	(4.0)
Japan	-7	(2.6)	45.7	(2.0)	-34	(2.4)	28.0	(1.7)	-12	(2.6)	42.0	(2.0)	-9	(3.0)	43.8	(2.7)
Korea	-1	(3.1)	49.9	(2.7)	-32	(3.2)	27.4	(2.3)	-11	(3.3)	43.0	(2.5)	-10	(3.7)	42.7	(3.3)
Netherlands	4	(2.1)	54.7	(2.0)	-28	(1.9)	31.3	(1.8)	-2	(2.0)	48.9	(1.8)	-3	(2.3)	47.6	(2.4)
Norway	5	(2.3)	53.4	(1.7)	-33	(2.7)	30.7	(1.6)	1	(2.3)	50.8	(1.6)	-1	(3.2)	49.3	(2.2)
Poland	3	(2.2)	52.9	(1.8)	-38	(1.9)	25.4	(1.7)	-3	(1.9)	48.7	(2.0)	-21	(3.5)	35.6	(2.7)
Portugal	-7	(1.8)	44.7	(1.8)	-44	(2.1)	20.8	(1.6)	-17	(1.7)	37.6	(1.5)	-17	(2.8)	36.7	(2.9)
Slovak Republic	-14	(2.6)	38.6	(2.4)	-54	(2.6)	15.4	(1.5)	-16	(2.8)	38.4	(2.2)	-29	(3.5)	26.4	(2.6)
Slovenia	7	(2.0)	54.9	(2.0)	-44	(2.3)	22.5	(1.9)	-4	(2.1)	48.3	(2.5)	-7	(4.3)	45.2	(3.2)
Spain	10	(2.2)	57.4	(1.9)	-27	(2.5)	36.3	(1.7)	2	(2.2)	51.7	(1.8)	4	(3.3)	54.2	(2.4)
Sweden	1	(2.3)	50.9	(2.3)	-31	(2.4)	31.1	(1.5)	-1	(2.5)	49.2	(2.1)	2	(3.4)	51.3	(2.8)
Turkey	-9	(2.4)	41.2	(2.4)	-49	(2.2)	15.6	(1.4)	-23	(2.6)	32.6	(2.2)	-24	(2.4)	27.9	(2.1)
England (United Kingdom)	5	(3.0)	55.1	(2.7)	-26	(3.2)	32.4	(2.1)	5	(3.4)	54.5	(2.7)	7	(4.0)	56.4	(3.6)
United States	1	(1.6)	51.4	(1.9)	-29	(1.9)	28.9	(1.7)	-5	(1.6)	46.6	(2.1)	-5	(2.2)	46.5	(2.4)
OECD average	**2**	(0.5)	**51.7**	(0.4)	**-38**	(0.5)	**25.7**	(0.3)	**-6**	(0.5)	**45.9**	(0.4)	**-8**	(0.7)	**44.3**	(0.6)
Partners																
Brazil	-1	(2.6)	49.4	(2.3)	-44	(2.3)	23.3	(1.4)	-20	(2.7)	37.8	(2.0)	-10	(3.5)	42.1	(2.7)
Bulgaria	14	(2.9)	60.4	(2.2)	-34	(3.2)	31.4	(2.4)	0	(3.1)	51.9	(2.1)	2	(3.8)	53.0	(2.7)
Colombia	-8	(2.5)	44.8	(2.0)	-44	(2.6)	23.6	(1.7)	-16	(2.7)	39.7	(2.0)	-18	(3.3)	37.6	(2.4)
Croatia	-5	(2.5)	46.4	(2.4)	-59	(2.6)	12.7	(1.3)	-16	(2.8)	38.2	(2.2)	-18	(3.1)	34.4	(2.8)
Cyprus*	9	(1.8)	56.6	(1.5)	-36	(2.1)	29.0	(1.3)	-1	(2.1)	49.8	(1.5)	-1	(2.5)	48.7	(1.9)
Hong Kong-China	-3	(2.9)	48.9	(2.2)	-33	(3.3)	29.5	(2.2)	-9	(3.3)	44.8	(2.1)	-12	(3.8)	42.2	(2.8)
Macao-China	-9	(1.4)	43.7	(1.6)	-35	(2.4)	25.5	(1.5)	-11	(1.5)	42.5	(1.4)	-13	(2.1)	39.6	(1.8)
Malaysia	-15	(1.7)	37.3	(1.6)	-39	(2.7)	24.9	(1.6)	-17	(1.8)	37.3	(1.8)	-19	(2.1)	33.5	(2.0)
Montenegro	6	(1.6)	54.3	(1.5)	-42	(2.2)	24.8	(1.3)	-8	(1.9)	45.1	(1.8)	-1	(2.8)	49.0	(2.7)
Russian Federation	-9	(2.0)	44.0	(1.5)	-35	(2.7)	27.8	(1.8)	-11	(2.8)	43.3	(1.8)	-18	(2.8)	37.0	(2.2)
Serbia	-8	(2.3)	44.1	(2.0)	-50	(2.3)	19.2	(1.5)	-18	(2.6)	37.5	(2.3)	-18	(2.8)	35.1	(2.4)
Shanghai-China	-21	(1.9)	33.0	(1.9)	-47	(2.0)	16.9	(1.5)	-21	(2.1)	34.7	(1.8)	-32	(2.6)	24.3	(2.2)
Singapore	-13	(1.3)	40.2	(1.2)	-33	(1.8)	29.4	(1.4)	-11	(1.5)	43.2	(1.4)	-9	(1.8)	42.8	(1.6)
Chinese Taipei	-9	(1.9)	42.1	(1.9)	-40	(2.3)	20.2	(1.8)	-12	(2.2)	41.1	(2.4)	-19	(2.5)	33.0	(2.5)
United Arab Emirates	22	(3.7)	64.5	(2.5)	-23	(3.9)	36.5	(2.5)	1	(3.7)	51.6	(2.6)	13	(4.6)	59.5	(3.2)
Uruguay	-1	(2.3)	50.9	(1.8)	-39	(2.1)	27.3	(1.4)	-12	(2.0)	43.3	(1.7)	-13	(2.7)	42.0	(2.0)

Note: Values that are statistically significant are indicated in bold (see Annex A3).
1. This column reports the difference between actual performance and the fitted value from a regression using a cubic polynomial as regression function.
2. This column reports the percentage of students for whom the difference between actual performance and the fitted value from a regression is positive. Values that are indicated in bold are significantly larger or smaller than 50%.
3. This column reports the difference between actual performance and the fitted value from a regression using a second-degree polynomial as regression function (math, math sq., read, read sq., scie, scie sq., math×read, math×scie, read×scie).
* See notes at the beginning of this Annex.
StatLink ⬛ http://dx.doi.org/10.1787/888933003706

[Part 1/1]

Table V.4.11a Performance on problem-solving tasks, by nature of problem and by gender

	Items referring to a static problem situation										Items referring to an interactive problem situation										
	Average proportion of full-credit responses						Relative likelihood of success, in favour of girls (boys = 1.00)				Average proportion of full-credit responses						Relative likelihood of success, in favour of girls (boys = 1.00)			
	Boys		Girls		Gender difference (B - G)		Accounting for booklet effects[1]		Based on success on remaining test items[2]		Boys		Girls		Gender difference (B - G)		Accounting for booklet effects[1]		Based on success on remaining test items[2]	
	%	S.E.	%	S.E.	% dif.	S.E.	Odds ratio	S.E.	Odds ratio	S.E.	%	S.E.	%	S.E.	% dif.	S.E.	Odds ratio	S.E.	Odds ratio	S.E.
OECD																				
Australia	53.5	(0.8)	52.1	(0.6)	-1.4	(1.1)	0.93	(0.04)	0.97	(0.03)	50.2	(0.7)	49.5	(0.6)	-0.6	(0.9)	0.96	(0.03)	1.03	(0.04)
Austria	49.0	(1.4)	47.7	(1.4)	-1.4	(1.1)	0.95	(0.07)	1.02	(0.07)	43.9	(1.1)	42.3	(1.1)	-1.6	(1.6)	0.93	(0.06)	0.98	(0.07)
Belgium	50.0	(1.0)	46.6	(1.0)	-3.4	(1.5)	0.86	(0.05)	0.94	(0.05)	46.4	(0.9)	44.4	(0.8)	-2.0	(1.3)	0.91	(0.05)	1.06	(0.06)
Canada	54.4	(1.1)	51.0	(0.8)	-3.4	(1.4)	0.87	(0.05)	0.89	(0.05)	50.8	(0.8)	50.2	(0.8)	-0.6	(0.8)	0.98	(0.04)	1.12	(0.07)
Chile	35.2	(1.3)	34.7	(1.1)	-0.4	(1.7)	0.97	(0.07)	1.28	(0.09)	34.7	(1.2)	29.0	(0.9)	-5.7	(1.5)	0.75	(0.05)	0.78	(0.06)
Czech Republic	46.8	(1.0)	45.5	(0.9)	-1.3	(1.3)	0.95	(0.05)	1.00	(0.04)	45.0	(1.0)	43.8	(0.9)	-1.2	(1.1)	0.96	(0.04)	1.00	(0.04)
Denmark	48.0	(1.6)	47.9	(1.1)	0.0	(2.1)	1.01	(0.08)	1.16	(0.10)	44.3	(1.2)	40.5	(1.0)	-3.7	(1.6)	0.87	(0.06)	0.87	(0.08)
Estonia	48.9	(1.5)	50.6	(1.0)	1.7	(2.1)	1.08	(0.09)	1.17	(0.10)	46.7	(1.1)	44.6	(1.2)	-2.2	(1.6)	0.92	(0.06)	0.85	(0.07)
Finland	50.1	(0.8)	54.3	(0.9)	4.2	(1.2)	1.18	(0.06)	1.11	(0.05)	47.0	(0.8)	48.5	(0.8)	1.5	(1.1)	1.06	(0.04)	0.90	(0.04)
France	51.6	(1.1)	49.0	(1.4)	-2.6	(1.9)	0.91	(0.07)	0.98	(0.08)	48.8	(1.1)	46.4	(1.0)	-2.5	(1.6)	0.93	(0.06)	1.02	(0.09)
Germany	50.5	(1.2)	48.3	(1.1)	-2.2	(1.7)	0.93	(0.06)	0.97	(0.06)	46.7	(1.1)	45.8	(1.1)	-1.0	(1.4)	0.96	(0.05)	1.03	(0.07)
Hungary	36.8	(1.5)	39.6	(1.5)	2.8	(2.0)	1.13	(0.09)	1.20	(0.10)	34.5	(1.5)	33.2	(1.1)	-1.3	(1.9)	0.94	(0.08)	0.83	(0.07)
Ireland	45.4	(1.5)	43.5	(1.1)	-1.8	(1.9)	0.91	(0.07)	0.98	(0.07)	45.3	(1.5)	44.0	(1.0)	-1.2	(1.8)	0.93	(0.07)	1.02	(0.07)
Israel	40.2	(2.5)	39.2	(1.3)	-0.9	(2.7)	0.95	(0.11)	1.10	(0.08)	37.1	(2.4)	34.2	(1.1)	-2.9	(2.6)	0.86	(0.10)	0.91	(0.07)
Italy	51.1	(1.5)	47.5	(1.5)	-3.6	(2.2)	0.88	(0.07)	1.02	(0.09)	48.6	(1.3)	44.7	(1.2)	-3.9	(1.8)	0.86	(0.06)	0.98	(0.08)
Japan	60.1	(1.1)	57.1	(0.9)	-3.1	(1.3)	0.87	(0.05)	1.05	(0.06)	57.9	(1.0)	53.8	(0.7)	-4.1	(1.2)	0.83	(0.04)	0.96	(0.05)
Korea	60.9	(1.2)	56.6	(1.5)	-4.3	(1.8)	0.83	(0.06)	0.95	(0.07)	59.1	(1.2)	56.1	(1.4)	-3.0	(1.8)	0.87	(0.06)	1.05	(0.08)
Netherlands	51.4	(1.5)	49.4	(1.2)	-2.0	(1.3)	0.92	(0.05)	0.93	(0.06)	46.6	(1.3)	46.4	(1.4)	-0.2	(1.4)	0.99	(0.05)	1.07	(0.07)
Norway	49.6	(1.5)	49.2	(1.3)	-0.4	(2.0)	0.95	(0.08)	1.01	(0.09)	44.9	(1.3)	44.1	(1.4)	-0.8	(1.9)	0.93	(0.07)	0.99	(0.09)
Poland	46.3	(1.5)	41.8	(1.2)	-4.4	(1.7)	0.88	(0.06)	0.96	(0.08)	41.3	(1.5)	38.0	(1.3)	-3.2	(1.7)	0.91	(0.07)	1.04	(0.08)
Portugal	46.8	(1.4)	41.1	(1.3)	-5.8	(2.0)	0.79	(0.06)	0.85	(0.07)	43.0	(1.3)	41.0	(1.1)	-2.0	(1.3)	0.92	(0.05)	1.17	(0.10)
Slovak Republic	46.7	(1.2)	41.3	(1.4)	-5.4	(1.9)	0.80	(0.06)	1.00	(0.08)	41.1	(1.2)	36.0	(1.3)	-5.1	(1.9)	0.80	(0.06)	1.00	(0.08)
Slovenia	42.1	(1.4)	43.8	(1.3)	1.7	(2.2)	1.08	(0.09)	1.12	(0.12)	37.2	(1.1)	36.2	(1.2)	-1.0	(1.6)	0.96	(0.07)	0.89	(0.09)
Spain	44.9	(1.4)	39.7	(1.0)	-5.2	(1.8)	0.82	(0.06)	0.88	(0.06)	40.8	(1.0)	38.8	(1.0)	-1.9	(1.4)	0.93	(0.05)	1.14	(0.08)
Sweden	46.7	(1.5)	48.6	(1.2)	1.9	(2.1)	1.06	(0.08)	0.98	(0.08)	40.5	(1.1)	42.7	(0.9)	2.2	(1.4)	1.08	(0.06)	1.02	(0.08)
Turkey	37.5	(1.1)	33.9	(1.1)	-3.6	(1.4)	0.86	(0.05)	0.98	(0.04)	34.1	(1.1)	31.2	(1.1)	-2.9	(1.1)	0.88	(0.05)	1.03	(0.04)
England (United Kingdom)	50.4	(1.2)	48.6	(1.3)	-1.8	(1.7)	0.93	(0.06)	0.98	(0.06)	48.6	(1.4)	47.4	(1.4)	-1.2	(1.6)	0.95	(0.06)	1.03	(0.05)
United States	48.3	(1.5)	44.9	(1.4)	-3.4	(1.9)	0.86	(0.06)	0.86	(0.07)	45.9	(1.1)	46.0	(1.3)	0.1	(1.3)	1.00	(0.05)	1.16	(0.10)
OECD average	48.0	(0.3)	46.2	(0.2)	-1.8	(0.3)	0.93	(0.01)	1.01	(0.01)	44.7	(0.2)	42.8	(0.2)	-1.9	(0.3)	0.92	(0.01)	0.99	(0.01)
Partners																				
Brazil	31.8	(1.4)	27.9	(1.5)	-3.8	(2.1)	0.84	(0.09)	1.02	(0.12)	31.1	(1.3)	27.2	(1.2)	-3.8	(1.6)	0.83	(0.06)	0.98	(0.12)
Bulgaria	27.1	(1.1)	29.7	(1.1)	2.6	(1.2)	1.14	(0.07)	0.97	(0.05)	21.0	(0.9)	23.8	(1.1)	2.7	(1.1)	1.17	(0.08)	1.03	(0.06)
Colombia	28.8	(1.4)	24.0	(1.0)	-4.8	(1.7)	0.78	(0.07)	1.08	(0.09)	26.8	(1.2)	20.9	(0.8)	-5.9	(1.4)	0.72	(0.05)	0.92	(0.07)
Croatia	39.9	(1.3)	38.7	(1.1)	-1.2	(1.4)	0.95	(0.05)	1.12	(0.06)	37.5	(1.1)	33.8	(1.0)	-3.7	(1.3)	0.85	(0.05)	0.90	(0.05)
Cyprus*	36.8	(0.8)	37.2	(0.7)	0.4	(1.1)	1.02	(0.05)	1.00	(0.06)	31.2	(0.6)	31.6	(0.6)	0.4	(0.8)	1.02	(0.04)	1.00	(0.06)
Hong Kong-China	58.2	(1.2)	53.9	(1.4)	-4.3	(1.8)	0.81	(0.06)	0.98	(0.07)	53.9	(1.0)	50.1	(1.3)	-3.9	(1.7)	0.83	(0.05)	1.02	(0.07)
Macao-China	59.2	(0.9)	54.7	(1.1)	-4.5	(1.6)	0.84	(0.05)	0.95	(0.07)	53.3	(1.0)	50.1	(0.9)	-3.2	(1.4)	0.88	(0.05)	1.06	(0.08)
Malaysia	31.2	(1.1)	29.1	(1.0)	-2.1	(1.1)	0.91	(0.05)	0.97	(0.06)	28.1	(1.0)	26.8	(0.9)	-1.3	(1.1)	0.94	(0.05)	1.03	(0.07)
Montenegro	30.7	(0.9)	29.9	(0.9)	-0.8	(1.2)	0.98	(0.06)	0.83	(0.05)	23.6	(0.7)	26.4	(0.5)	2.9	(0.9)	1.19	(0.06)	1.21	(0.07)
Russian Federation	44.4	(1.1)	43.1	(1.4)	-1.3	(1.7)	0.95	(0.07)	0.94	(0.06)	39.7	(0.9)	39.8	(1.2)	0.2	(1.5)	1.01	(0.06)	1.06	(0.07)
Serbia	42.1	(1.2)	38.6	(0.9)	-3.6	(1.4)	0.85	(0.05)	1.05	(0.04)	39.1	(1.1)	34.5	(0.8)	-4.6	(1.1)	0.81	(0.04)	0.95	(0.04)
Shanghai-China	60.2	(1.3)	53.5	(1.4)	-6.8	(1.8)	0.74	(0.05)	0.98	(0.07)	53.7	(1.0)	47.1	(1.3)	-6.6	(1.7)	0.75	(0.04)	1.02	(0.07)
Singapore	61.6	(1.1)	58.0	(1.1)	-3.6	(1.6)	0.85	(0.06)	0.88	(0.06)	57.8	(0.9)	57.1	(1.0)	-0.7	(1.4)	0.96	(0.06)	1.14	(0.07)
Chinese Taipei	57.5	(1.4)	55.0	(1.3)	-2.5	(2.0)	0.91	(0.08)	1.10	(0.08)	52.5	(1.6)	47.7	(1.2)	-4.8	(2.2)	0.83	(0.07)	0.91	(0.06)
United Arab Emirates	28.4	(1.1)	31.3	(0.9)	3.0	(1.6)	1.16	(0.09)	0.91	(0.06)	24.8	(0.9)	29.2	(0.8)	4.5	(1.3)	1.27	(0.08)	1.09	(0.07)
Uruguay	27.8	(0.9)	27.2	(0.8)	-0.6	(1.0)	0.97	(0.05)	1.07	(0.06)	25.8	(0.8)	23.9	(0.7)	-1.8	(0.9)	0.91	(0.04)	0.94	(0.05)

Note: Values that are statistically significant are indicated in bold (see Annex A3).

1. Generalised odds ratios estimated with logistic regression on national PISA samples. A success indicator for each item is regressed on an item type dummy, a female dummy, and an interaction term (female × item type). Booklet dummies are added to the estimation. This column presents the difference between the logit coefficient on the interaction term and the logit coefficient on the item type dummy in exponentiated form.

2. Generalised odds ratios estimated with logistic regression on national PISA samples. A success indicator for each item is regressed on an item type dummy, a female dummy, and an interaction term (female × item type). Booklet dummies are added to the estimation. This column presents the logit coefficient on the interaction term in exponentiated form.

* See notes at the beginning of this Annex.

StatLink ᵐˢᵖ http://dx.doi.org/10.1787/888933003706

[Part 1/2]

Table V.4.11b **Performance on problem-solving tasks, by process and by gender**

	Items assessing the process of "exploring and understanding"												Items assessing the process of "representing and formulating"											
	Average proportion of full-credit responses						Relative likelihood of success, in favour of girls (boys = 1.00)					Average proportion of full-credit responses						Relative likelihood of success, in favour of girls (boys = 1.00)				
	Boys		Girls		Gender difference (B - G)		Accounting for booklet effects[1]		Based on success on remaining test items[2]			Boys		Girls		Gender difference (B - G)		Accounting for booklet effects[1]		Based on success on remaining test items[2]	
	%	S.E.	%	S.E.	% dif.	S.E.	Odds ratio	S.E.	Odds ratio	S.E.		%	S.E.	%	S.E.	% dif.	S.E.	Odds ratio	S.E.	Odds ratio	S.E.
Australia	56.0	(0.9)	53.9	(0.7)	-2.1	(1.1)	**0.91**	(0.04)	0.94	(0.03)		51.1	(0.9)	47.5	(0.8)	**-3.6**	(1.2)	**0.85**	(0.04)	**0.87**	(0.03)
Austria	49.6	(1.6)	48.8	(1.5)	-0.9	(2.2)	0.97	(0.09)	1.03	(0.07)		43.6	(1.4)	40.0	(1.5)	-3.7	(2.0)	**0.85**	(0.07)	0.88	(0.06)
Belgium	49.8	(1.1)	48.2	(1.1)	-1.6	(1.8)	0.93	(0.07)	1.05	(0.06)		47.4	(1.2)	42.1	(1.1)	**-5.3**	(1.7)	**0.80**	(0.06)	**0.86**	(0.05)
Canada	54.1	(1.0)	54.0	(1.0)	-0.2	(1.3)	0.99	(0.06)	1.08	(0.06)		52.7	(1.2)	48.9	(1.0)	**-3.8**	(1.4)	**0.86**	(0.05)	**0.90**	(0.05)
Chile	34.4	(1.5)	30.6	(1.2)	**-3.8**	(1.8)	**0.83**	(0.07)	1.00	(0.07)		32.3	(1.6)	26.3	(1.2)	**-6.1**	(2.1)	**0.73**	(0.07)	**0.86**	(0.07)
Czech Republic	47.4	(1.0)	46.4	(1.2)	-1.0	(1.8)	0.96	(0.05)	1.01	(0.04)		44.5	(1.2)	41.3	(1.0)	**-3.2**	(1.3)	**0.88**	(0.05)	**0.90**	(0.03)
Denmark	47.7	(1.4)	44.6	(1.3)	-3.0	(1.8)	0.90	(0.06)	0.98	(0.06)		45.0	(1.6)	39.4	(1.4)	**-5.5**	(2.0)	**0.82**	(0.06)	**0.86**	(0.06)
Estonia	48.0	(1.5)	49.7	(1.4)	1.7	(2.2)	1.08	(0.10)	1.14	(0.08)		46.5	(1.4)	42.5	(1.4)	**-4.0**	(1.9)	**0.86**	(0.07)	**0.85**	(0.06)
Finland	52.8	(0.9)	54.7	(1.0)	1.9	(1.4)	1.08	(0.06)	0.97	(0.04)		46.0	(1.0)	46.6	(1.0)	0.6	(1.4)	1.02	(0.06)	0.91	(0.04)
France	53.9	(1.3)	50.5	(1.4)	-3.4	(2.0)	0.88	(0.07)	0.94	(0.07)		48.6	(1.4)	45.4	(1.2)	-3.2	(1.9)	0.90	(0.07)	0.97	(0.05)
Germany	51.7	(1.4)	49.5	(1.5)	-2.2	(1.8)	0.91	(0.07)	0.96	(0.06)		45.3	(1.4)	42.8	(1.4)	-2.5	(1.8)	0.89	(0.07)	0.92	(0.06)
Hungary	36.8	(1.5)	38.6	(1.4)	1.8	(1.8)	1.08	(0.08)	1.09	(0.08)		33.8	(1.7)	31.0	(1.4)	-2.8	(2.3)	0.87	(0.09)	**0.84**	(0.06)
Ireland	48.2	(2.1)	46.9	(1.3)	-1.3	(2.5)	0.93	(0.10)	1.01	(0.08)		42.8	(1.5)	40.1	(1.2)	-2.7	(2.0)	0.87	(0.08)	0.92	(0.06)
Israel	43.1	(2.7)	40.9	(1.1)	-2.2	(2.8)	0.90	(0.10)	1.01	(0.07)		37.5	(2.6)	33.0	(1.6)	-4.5	(3.0)	0.80	(0.10)	0.87	(0.07)
Italy	53.4	(1.7)	49.2	(1.5)	-4.2	(2.2)	0.85	(0.07)	0.98	(0.07)		49.4	(1.7)	44.6	(1.5)	**-4.8**	(2.1)	**0.83**	(0.07)	0.95	(0.06)
Japan	64.3	(1.3)	59.9	(1.1)	**-4.4**	(1.5)	**0.81**	(0.05)	0.95	(0.05)		58.9	(1.2)	52.3	(1.0)	**-6.6**	(1.4)	**0.75**	(0.04)	**0.85**	(0.03)
Korea	67.4	(1.4)	61.6	(1.5)	**-5.8**	(1.9)	**0.76**	(0.06)	**0.86**	(0.06)		64.7	(1.6)	56.0	(1.9)	**-8.6**	(2.3)	**0.67**	(0.06)	**0.74**	(0.05)
Netherlands	52.5	(1.4)	51.0	(1.4)	-1.5	(1.4)	0.94	(0.05)	0.97	(0.05)		44.8	(1.6)	43.6	(1.6)	-1.2	(1.7)	0.95	(0.06)	0.98	(0.04)
Norway	51.4	(1.4)	51.2	(1.5)	-0.3	(2.0)	0.95	(0.08)	1.02	(0.07)		44.9	(1.5)	42.2	(1.7)	-2.7	(2.2)	0.86	(0.08)	0.90	(0.07)
Poland	44.7	(1.7)	42.8	(1.4)	-1.9	(1.8)	0.97	(0.08)	1.10	(0.08)		42.2	(1.8)	34.8	(1.6)	**-7.3**	(2.2)	**0.76**	(0.07)	**0.81**	(0.06)
Portugal	46.4	(1.6)	40.5	(1.4)	**-5.9**	(1.6)	**0.78**	(0.06)	**0.87**	(0.07)		42.3	(1.8)	36.4	(1.4)	**-5.9**	(1.8)	**0.78**	(0.06)	**0.87**	(0.06)
Slovak Republic	46.0	(1.5)	40.6	(1.5)	**-5.4**	(2.1)	**0.80**	(0.07)	1.00	(0.07)		40.9	(1.4)	32.5	(1.6)	**-8.4**	(2.2)	**0.69**	(0.07)	**0.83**	(0.05)
Slovenia	39.2	(1.3)	40.1	(1.6)	0.9	(2.0)	1.04	(0.09)	1.06	(0.09)		36.5	(1.5)	35.0	(1.3)	-1.5	(2.0)	0.94	(0.08)	0.92	(0.06)
Spain	45.7	(1.4)	39.2	(1.4)	**-6.5**	(1.9)	**0.77**	(0.06)	**0.83**	(0.06)		39.2	(1.4)	35.4	(1.2)	-3.8	(1.9)	0.85	(0.07)	0.95	(0.06)
Sweden	47.9	(1.6)	48.6	(1.3)	0.7	(2.0)	1.01	(0.08)	0.92	(0.07)		41.7	(1.4)	42.0	(1.4)	0.3	(1.9)	0.99	(0.08)	0.90	(0.06)
Turkey	35.4	(1.0)	31.6	(1.3)	-3.7	(1.3)	**0.85**	(0.05)	0.96	(0.04)		33.7	(1.4)	29.9	(1.3)	**-3.8**	(1.5)	**0.84**	(0.06)	0.96	(0.04)
England (United Kingdom)	53.0	(1.5)	49.8	(1.7)	-3.1	(2.1)	0.88	(0.07)	0.91	(0.06)		49.9	(1.6)	45.7	(1.6)	-4.2	(1.8)	**0.85**	(0.06)	**0.87**	(0.04)
United States	49.4	(1.5)	48.5	(1.3)	-0.9	(1.6)	0.96	(0.07)	1.02	(0.07)		45.4	(1.5)	42.4	(1.7)	-3.1	(1.9)	0.88	(0.07)	0.91	(0.07)
OECD average	48.9	(0.3)	46.9	(0.3)	**-2.1**	(0.4)	**0.91**	(0.01)	0.99	(0.01)		44.7	(0.3)	40.7	(0.3)	**-4.0**	(0.4)	**0.84**	(0.01)	**0.89**	(0.01)
Brazil	33.0	(1.6)	27.6	(1.4)	**-5.3**	(1.8)	**0.77**	(0.07)	0.91	(0.08)		28.5	(1.5)	22.5	(1.5)	**-5.9**	(1.8)	**0.73**	(0.07)	**0.85**	(0.06)
Bulgaria	26.7	(1.2)	29.0	(1.1)	2.3	(1.3)	1.13	(0.07)	0.96	(0.04)		18.3	(1.1)	20.0	(1.1)	1.7	(1.2)	1.12	(0.09)	0.96	(0.05)
Colombia	28.5	(1.5)	21.4	(1.1)	**-7.1**	(1.8)	**0.68**	(0.07)	0.89	(0.09)		23.0	(1.4)	14.8	(0.8)	**-8.2**	(1.6)	**0.57**	(0.06)	**0.74**	(0.06)
Croatia	38.8	(1.2)	35.7	(1.1)	-3.1	(1.4)	**0.88**	(0.05)	0.98	(0.04)		35.1	(1.6)	30.9	(1.3)	-4.1	(1.7)	**0.83**	(0.06)	0.92	(0.04)
Cyprus*	35.8	(0.8)	36.5	(0.7)	0.7	(0.9)	1.03	(0.04)	1.02	(0.04)		31.5	(0.8)	29.9	(0.8)	-1.6	(1.1)	0.93	(0.05)	**0.89**	(0.04)
Hong Kong-China	63.5	(1.6)	56.4	(1.5)	**-7.0**	(1.9)	**0.72**	(0.06)	**0.84**	(0.06)		58.8	(1.3)	50.2	(1.5)	**-8.7**	(2.0)	**0.68**	(0.05)	**0.78**	(0.05)
Macao-China	62.4	(1.3)	56.4	(1.0)	**-6.0**	(1.5)	**0.78**	(0.06)	**0.87**	(0.06)		60.1	(1.2)	54.2	(1.2)	**-5.9**	(1.7)	**0.78**	(0.05)	**0.88**	(0.05)
Malaysia	30.8	(1.1)	29.3	(1.0)	-1.5	(1.2)	0.93	(0.05)	1.01	(0.05)		29.7	(1.4)	26.2	(1.2)	-3.5	(1.5)	0.84	(0.06)	0.88	(0.05)
Montenegro	26.9	(0.9)	27.7	(0.8)	0.8	(1.3)	1.07	(0.07)	0.95	(0.06)		22.6	(0.9)	24.5	(0.7)	1.9	(1.2)	1.13	(0.07)	1.03	(0.06)
Russian Federation	42.5	(1.3)	41.6	(1.6)	-0.9	(2.1)	0.97	(0.08)	0.97	(0.07)		39.5	(1.4)	37.6	(1.6)	-1.9	(2.1)	0.93	(0.08)	0.92	(0.06)
Serbia	41.1	(1.4)	37.9	(0.9)	-3.2	(1.8)	**0.87**	(0.05)	1.07	(0.05)		39.6	(1.3)	31.8	(0.9)	**-7.9**	(1.4)	**0.70**	(0.04)	**0.81**	(0.04)
Shanghai-China	60.2	(1.3)	56.6	(1.6)	-3.6	(1.9)	**0.84**	(0.07)	1.17	(0.10)		61.8	(1.4)	49.3	(1.6)	**-12.5**	(1.7)	**0.58**	(0.04)	**0.73**	(0.05)
Singapore	65.5	(1.3)	62.5	(1.2)	-3.0	(1.6)	**0.87**	(0.05)	0.92	(0.06)		62.2	(1.3)	57.1	(1.2)	**-5.1**	(1.9)	**0.80**	(0.06)	**0.83**	(0.06)
Chinese Taipei	61.1	(1.6)	55.3	(1.4)	**-5.9**	(2.2)	**0.79**	(0.08)	0.90	(0.06)		59.1	(2.1)	52.1	(1.6)	-7.0	(2.8)	**0.75**	(0.09)	**0.84**	(0.06)
United Arab Emirates	28.0	(1.0)	31.8	(0.9)	3.9	(1.4)	**1.21**	(0.08)	0.99	(0.05)		24.8	(1.1)	28.2	(1.0)	3.5	(1.5)	**1.20**	(0.10)	0.98	(0.06)
Uruguay	27.7	(1.1)	26.6	(0.8)	-1.1	(1.2)	0.95	(0.06)	1.02	(0.06)		23.9	(1.0)	20.6	(0.9)	-3.2	(1.1)	**0.83**	(0.05)	0.87	(0.05)

Note: Values that are statistically significant are indicated in bold (see Annex A3).

1. Generalised odds ratios estimated with logistic regression on national PISA samples. A success indicator for each item is regressed on an item type dummy, a female dummy, and an interaction term (female × item type). Booklet dummies are added to the estimation. This column presents the difference between the logit coefficient on the interaction term and the logit coefficient on the item type dummy in exponentiated form.

2. Generalised odds ratios estimated with logistic regression on national PISA samples. A success indicator for each item is regressed on an item type dummy, a female dummy, and an interaction term (female × item type). Booklet dummies are added to the estimation. This column presents the logit coefficient on the interaction term in exponentiated form.

* See notes at the beginning of this Annex.

StatLink ᴍᴪᴸ http://dx.doi.org/10.1787/888933003706

[Part 2/2]
Table V.4.11b **Performance on problem-solving tasks, by process and by gender**

	Items assessing the process of "planning and executing"										Items assessing the process of "monitoring and reflecting"									
	Average proportion of full-credit responses				Relative likelihood of success, in favour of girls (boys = 1.00)						Average proportion of full-credit responses				Relative likelihood of success, in favour of girls (boys = 1.00)					
	Boys		Girls		Gender difference (B - G)		Accounting for booklet effects[1]		Based on success on remaining test items[2]		Boys		Girls		Gender difference (B - G)		Accounting for booklet effects[1]		Based on success on remaining test items[2]	
	%	S.E.	%	S.E.	% dif.	S.E.	Odds ratio	S.E.	Odds ratio	S.E.	%	S.E.	%	S.E.	% dif.	S.E.	Odds ratio	S.E.	Odds ratio	S.E.
OECD																				
Australia	51.3	(0.7)	51.7	(0.6)	0.4	(0.9)	1.01	(0.04)	**1.10**	(0.03)	45.5	(0.7)	46.4	(0.7)	0.9	(1.0)	1.03	(0.04)	**1.09**	(0.04)
Austria	47.8	(1.2)	47.1	(1.2)	-0.8	(1.5)	0.98	(0.06)	1.07	(0.06)	38.0	(1.3)	36.5	(1.2)	-1.5	(1.8)	0.94	(0.07)	1.00	(0.07)
Belgium	48.5	(0.8)	46.6	(0.9)	-1.9	(1.2)	0.92	(0.05)	1.04	(0.04)	43.2	(1.0)	41.6	(1.0)	-1.6	(1.4)	0.93	(0.06)	1.05	(0.06)
Canada	53.1	(0.8)	51.1	(0.8)	-2.0	(1.1)	0.92	(0.04)	0.97	(0.04)	46.0	(1.0)	46.1	(1.0)	0.1	(1.3)	1.01	(0.05)	1.09	(0.05)
Chile	37.2	(1.1)	33.3	(0.9)	**-4.0**	(1.4)	**0.82**	(0.05)	0.99	(0.05)	33.6	(1.3)	32.8	(1.0)	-0.8	(1.7)	0.95	(0.07)	**1.19**	(0.09)
Czech Republic	47.1	(0.9)	46.7	(0.8)	-0.5	(1.1)	0.98	(0.04)	1.05	(0.03)	41.0	(1.0)	40.4	(0.9)	-0.6	(1.2)	0.98	(0.05)	1.03	(0.04)
Denmark	49.1	(1.4)	47.1	(1.1)	-2.0	(1.8)	0.93	(0.06)	1.02	(0.06)	35.3	(1.6)	36.8	(1.2)	1.5	(2.0)	1.08	(0.10)	**1.21**	(0.10)
Estonia	50.2	(1.3)	48.9	(1.0)	-1.3	(1.7)	0.96	(0.07)	0.97	(0.06)	42.0	(1.2)	42.9	(1.3)	0.9	(1.9)	1.05	(0.09)	1.09	(0.08)
Finland	49.3	(0.7)	52.9	(0.7)	3.6	(1.0)	**1.15**	(0.04)	**1.08**	(0.04)	41.2	(0.8)	44.2	(0.8)	3.0	(1.1)	**1.13**	(0.05)	1.03	(0.04)
France	50.2	(1.1)	48.6	(1.1)	-1.6	(1.5)	0.95	(0.06)	1.06	(0.05)	44.9	(1.1)	42.7	(1.3)	-2.2	(1.7)	0.94	(0.07)	1.02	(0.07)
Germany	49.9	(1.1)	49.1	(1.0)	-0.8	(1.4)	0.98	(0.06)	1.06	(0.06)	42.6	(1.2)	41.9	(1.2)	-0.6	(1.6)	0.98	(0.06)	1.04	(0.07)
Hungary	36.8	(1.5)	38.4	(1.2)	1.6	(1.9)	1.07	(0.09)	1.11	(0.06)	31.6	(1.7)	30.2	(1.4)	-1.4	(2.2)	0.93	(0.09)	0.91	(0.07)
Ireland	46.2	(1.4)	44.8	(1.0)	-1.3	(1.9)	0.94	(0.07)	1.02	(0.06)	42.4	(1.6)	42.1	(1.3)	-0.3	(2.0)	0.97	(0.08)	1.06	(0.08)
Israel	37.5	(2.4)	36.4	(1.3)	-1.1	(2.8)	0.94	(0.11)	1.09	(0.07)	33.8	(2.1)	31.7	(1.4)	-2.2	(2.4)	0.89	(0.10)	1.00	(0.07)
Italy	49.7	(1.4)	45.8	(1.3)	-3.9	(2.0)	0.86	(0.06)	1.00	(0.07)	43.7	(1.4)	41.7	(1.4)	-1.9	(2.2)	0.93	(0.09)	1.09	(0.10)
Japan	57.1	(1.0)	55.5	(0.8)	-1.6	(1.1)	0.93	(0.04)	**1.16**	(0.05)	54.0	(1.1)	50.1	(0.8)	-3.9	(1.3)	**0.84**	(0.04)	1.00	(0.05)
Korea	54.7	(1.2)	54.2	(1.3)	-0.5	(1.7)	0.98	(0.07)	**1.24**	(0.07)	53.8	(1.4)	53.5	(1.5)	-0.3	(1.9)	0.99	(0.08)	**1.19**	(0.07)
Netherlands	50.1	(1.3)	49.3	(1.2)	-0.9	(1.1)	0.97	(0.04)	1.00	(0.04)	42.5	(1.5)	43.1	(1.3)	0.6	(1.6)	1.02	(0.07)	1.07	(0.06)
Norway	48.1	(1.4)	48.1	(1.2)	0.0	(1.8)	0.96	(0.07)	1.04	(0.06)	38.5	(1.5)	38.3	(1.6)	-0.2	(2.2)	0.96	(0.09)	1.03	(0.07)
Poland	45.1	(1.4)	42.2	(1.2)	-2.9	(1.7)	0.93	(0.06)	1.06	(0.06)	37.1	(1.4)	34.0	(1.3)	-3.1	(1.8)	0.92	(0.07)	1.02	(0.07)
Portugal	46.3	(1.3)	45.1	(1.3)	-1.3	(1.6)	0.95	(0.06)	**1.15**	(0.08)	39.6	(1.6)	38.4	(1.3)	-1.3	(1.9)	0.96	(0.08)	1.12	(0.08)
Slovak Republic	45.2	(1.1)	40.8	(1.2)	**-4.3**	(1.7)	**0.84**	(0.06)	1.08	(0.05)	37.1	(1.1)	33.9	(1.4)	-3.2	(1.8)	0.86	(0.07)	1.09	(0.06)
Slovenia	41.7	(0.9)	42.9	(1.1)	1.1	(1.4)	1.05	(0.06)	1.09	(0.06)	35.3	(1.1)	33.0	(1.4)	-2.3	(1.9)	0.90	(0.08)	0.88	(0.06)
Spain	43.0	(1.4)	41.5	(1.0)	-1.5	(1.6)	0.96	(0.06)	1.13	(0.07)	39.5	(1.1)	38.5	(1.3)	-1.0	(1.4)	0.99	(0.06)	1.13	(0.08)
Sweden	42.9	(1.2)	46.2	(0.9)	3.3	(1.5)	**1.13**	(0.07)	1.08	(0.06)	35.8	(1.4)	40.0	(1.2)	4.2	(1.9)	**1.19**	(0.09)	1.13	(0.07)
Turkey	37.3	(1.0)	34.6	(1.0)	-2.7	(1.2)	**0.89**	(0.05)	1.04	(0.05)	32.6	(1.1)	30.2	(1.2)	-2.5	(1.3)	0.89	(0.06)	1.03	(0.05)
England (United Kingdom)	49.1	(1.4)	49.2	(1.3)	0.1	(1.5)	1.00	(0.06)	**1.10**	(0.04)	43.5	(1.3)	44.5	(1.3)	1.1	(1.7)	1.05	(0.07)	**1.13**	(0.05)
United States	47.7	(1.2)	46.6	(1.3)	-1.1	(1.6)	0.95	(0.06)	1.00	(0.06)	42.7	(1.3)	43.4	(1.5)	0.7	(1.5)	1.02	(0.06)	1.09	(0.07)
OECD average	46.9	(0.2)	45.9	(0.2)	**-1.0**	(0.3)	**0.96**	(0.01)	**1.06**	(0.01)	40.6	(0.2)	40.0	(0.2)	-0.6	(0.3)	**0.97**	(0.01)	**1.06**	(0.01)
Partners																				
Brazil	33.0	(1.2)	31.1	(1.3)	-2.0	(1.5)	0.92	(0.07)	**1.19**	(0.07)	28.8	(1.2)	25.6	(1.4)	-3.3	(1.9)	0.85	(0.08)	1.02	(0.09)
Bulgaria	25.1	(0.9)	28.4	(1.1)	3.3	(1.2)	**1.19**	(0.07)	1.04	(0.05)	20.2	(1.0)	23.2	(1.2)	3.0	(1.2)	**1.20**	(0.09)	1.04	(0.05)
Colombia	30.2	(1.2)	25.6	(1.1)	**-4.6**	(1.7)	**0.79**	(0.07)	1.12	(0.09)	25.7	(1.2)	24.1	(1.1)	-1.5	(1.6)	0.92	(0.08)	**1.31**	(0.10)
Croatia	41.5	(1.1)	39.5	(1.0)	-1.9	(1.2)	0.92	(0.05)	1.07	(0.04)	34.9	(1.2)	32.2	(0.9)	-2.7	(1.2)	**0.89**	(0.05)	1.00	(0.04)
Cyprus*	34.7	(0.6)	34.9	(0.7)	0.2	(0.9)	1.01	(0.04)	0.98	(0.03)	28.3	(0.7)	31.3	(0.7)	3.0	(1.0)	**1.15**	(0.05)	**1.16**	(0.05)
Hong Kong-China	51.2	(1.0)	51.0	(1.3)	-0.2	(1.7)	0.96	(0.06)	**1.28**	(0.07)	48.9	(1.3)	47.3	(1.7)	-1.6	(2.1)	0.91	(0.08)	1.13	(0.08)
Macao-China	52.2	(0.8)	50.4	(0.9)	-1.8	(1.4)	0.94	(0.05)	**1.14**	(0.06)	46.5	(1.1)	44.9	(1.1)	-1.7	(1.5)	0.94	(0.06)	1.11	(0.06)
Malaysia	30.1	(0.9)	28.5	(0.9)	-1.6	(1.0)	0.93	(0.04)	1.00	(0.04)	24.2	(0.9)	24.9	(1.0)	0.7	(1.1)	1.04	(0.06)	**1.15**	(0.06)
Montenegro	29.3	(0.9)	30.6	(0.7)	1.3	(1.0)	1.09	(0.05)	0.97	(0.05)	22.1	(0.9)	24.9	(0.6)	2.8	(1.1)	**1.19**	(0.08)	1.10	(0.05)
Russian Federation	44.0	(0.9)	43.6	(1.2)	-0.4	(1.5)	0.99	(0.05)	1.00	(0.06)	36.2	(1.0)	38.5	(1.5)	2.3	(1.7)	1.12	(0.08)	1.15	(0.09)
Serbia	42.4	(1.1)	39.1	(1.0)	-3.3	(1.2)	**0.87**	(0.04)	1.08	(0.04)	34.9	(1.2)	31.3	(1.1)	-3.5	(1.3)	**0.84**	(0.05)	1.02	(0.04)
Shanghai-China	53.4	(1.0)	46.5	(1.3)	-6.9	(1.7)	**0.74**	(0.04)	0.98	(0.06)	48.6	(1.5)	45.8	(1.5)	-2.9	(2.0)	0.88	(0.08)	**1.22**	(0.09)
Singapore	55.2	(1.0)	55.5	(1.2)	0.3	(1.6)	1.01	(0.06)	**1.15**	(0.07)	55.3	(1.3)	55.1	(1.1)	-0.3	(1.6)	0.99	(0.07)	1.08	(0.07)
Chinese Taipei	50.7	(1.3)	49.5	(1.1)	-1.2	(1.9)	0.96	(0.07)	**1.21**	(0.07)	46.7	(1.6)	42.8	(1.4)	-3.9	(2.3)	0.86	(0.08)	1.01	(0.07)
United Arab Emirates	26.4	(1.0)	31.4	(0.9)	5.0	(1.5)	**1.28**	(0.09)	1.08	(0.05)	24.2	(1.1)	26.4	(0.9)	2.2	(1.5)	**1.13**	(0.09)	0.91	(0.05)
Uruguay	28.4	(0.8)	27.4	(0.7)	-1.0	(0.8)	0.95	(0.04)	1.04	(0.04)	23.9	(0.8)	23.5	(0.9)	-0.4	(0.9)	0.98	(0.05)	1.06	(0.04)

Note: Values that are statistically significant are indicated in bold (see Annex A3).

1. Generalised odds ratios estimated with logistic regression on national PISA samples. A success indicator for each item is regressed on an item type dummy, a female dummy, and an interaction term (female × item type). Booklet dummies are added to the estimation. This column presents the difference between the logit coefficient on the interaction term and the logit coefficient on the item type dummy in exponentiated form.

2. Generalised odds ratios estimated with logistic regression on national PISA samples. A success indicator for each item is regressed on an item type dummy, a female dummy, and an interaction term (female × item type). Booklet dummies are added to the estimation. This column presents the logit coefficient on the interaction term in exponentiated form.

* See notes at the beginning of this Annex.

StatLink ⧉ http://dx.doi.org/10.1787/888933003706

[Part 1/2]
Performance in problem solving, by socio-economic status
Table V.4.12   *Results based on students' self-reports*

	PISA index of economic, social and cultural status (ESCS)									
	All students		Bottom quarter		Second quarter		Third quarter		Top quarter	
	Mean index	S.E.	Mean index	S.E.	Mean index	S.E.	Mean index	S.E.	Mean index	S.E.
OECD										
Australia	0.25	(0.01)	-0.84	(0.02)	0.05	(0.02)	0.61	(0.01)	1.18	(0.01)
Austria	0.08	(0.02)	-0.97	(0.03)	-0.25	(0.02)	0.33	(0.03)	1.19	(0.03)
Belgium	0.15	(0.02)	-1.05	(0.03)	-0.19	(0.03)	0.55	(0.02)	1.44	(0.02)
Canada	0.41	(0.02)	-0.75	(0.02)	0.16	(0.02)	0.79	(0.02)	1.44	(0.01)
Chile	-0.58	(0.04)	-1.97	(0.05)	-1.02	(0.04)	-0.27	(0.05)	0.95	(0.03)
Czech Republic	-0.07	(0.02)	-0.98	(0.02)	-0.37	(0.02)	0.16	(0.02)	0.93	(0.02)
Denmark	0.43	(0.02)	-0.70	(0.03)	0.16	(0.04)	0.81	(0.03)	1.44	(0.02)
Estonia	0.11	(0.01)	-0.92	(0.02)	-0.23	(0.02)	0.44	(0.02)	1.16	(0.01)
Finland	0.36	(0.02)	-0.68	(0.02)	0.13	(0.02)	0.73	(0.02)	1.28	(0.01)
France	-0.04	(0.02)	-1.10	(0.02)	-0.30	(0.02)	0.29	(0.02)	0.95	(0.01)
Germany	0.19	(0.02)	-0.99	(0.03)	-0.16	(0.03)	0.52	(0.04)	1.42	(0.02)
Hungary	-0.25	(0.03)	-1.46	(0.04)	-0.65	(0.03)	0.09	(0.04)	1.01	(0.03)
Ireland	0.13	(0.02)	-0.97	(0.02)	-0.19	(0.03)	0.48	(0.03)	1.20	(0.02)
Israel	0.17	(0.03)	-0.98	(0.04)	-0.03	(0.04)	0.58	(0.03)	1.12	(0.02)
Italy	-0.03	(0.03)	-1.24	(0.03)	-0.37	(0.03)	0.26	(0.03)	1.25	(0.04)
Japan	-0.07	(0.02)	-0.99	(0.02)	-0.35	(0.02)	0.20	(0.02)	0.85	(0.02)
Korea	0.01	(0.03)	-0.97	(0.03)	-0.23	(0.03)	0.33	(0.03)	0.92	(0.02)
Netherlands	0.23	(0.02)	-0.82	(0.03)	0.02	(0.03)	0.58	(0.02)	1.15	(0.02)
Norway	0.46	(0.02)	-0.56	(0.02)	0.27	(0.02)	0.79	(0.02)	1.35	(0.02)
Poland	-0.21	(0.03)	-1.22	(0.02)	-0.69	(0.02)	-0.01	(0.05)	1.08	(0.03)
Portugal	-0.48	(0.05)	-1.85	(0.03)	-1.06	(0.04)	-0.23	(0.07)	1.21	(0.07)
Slovak Republic	-0.18	(0.03)	-1.25	(0.04)	-0.57	(0.02)	0.02	(0.04)	1.06	(0.03)
Slovenia	0.07	(0.01)	-1.03	(0.01)	-0.31	(0.02)	0.39	(0.02)	1.22	(0.02)
Spain	-0.18	(0.03)	-1.49	(0.03)	-0.59	(0.03)	0.18	(0.05)	1.17	(0.03)
Sweden	0.28	(0.02)	-0.82	(0.02)	0.02	(0.02)	0.65	(0.02)	1.25	(0.01)
Turkey	-1.46	(0.04)	-2.74	(0.03)	-1.96	(0.03)	-1.21	(0.05)	0.07	(0.06)
England (United Kingdom)	0.29	(0.02)	-0.76	(0.03)	0.02	(0.04)	0.62	(0.03)	1.27	(0.02)
United States	0.17	(0.04)	-1.14	(0.05)	-0.11	(0.04)	0.60	(0.04)	1.35	(0.04)
OECD average	0.01	(0.00)	-1.11	(0.01)	-0.31	(0.01)	0.33	(0.01)	1.13	(0.01)
Partners										
Brazil	-1.11	(0.04)	-2.60	(0.04)	-1.56	(0.04)	-0.74	(0.05)	0.47	(0.06)
Bulgaria	-0.28	(0.04)	-1.59	(0.06)	-0.67	(0.03)	0.10	(0.04)	1.06	(0.03)
Colombia	-1.26	(0.04)	-2.82	(0.04)	-1.65	(0.05)	-0.83	(0.04)	0.24	(0.05)
Croatia	-0.34	(0.02)	-1.35	(0.02)	-0.70	(0.02)	-0.14	(0.03)	0.84	(0.02)
Cyprus*	0.09	(0.01)	-1.06	(0.02)	-0.28	(0.01)	0.43	(0.02)	1.25	(0.02)
Hong Kong-China	-0.79	(0.05)	-2.00	(0.03)	-1.20	(0.05)	-0.46	(0.07)	0.50	(0.06)
Macao-China	-0.89	(0.01)	-1.91	(0.01)	-1.23	(0.01)	-0.68	(0.01)	0.28	(0.02)
Malaysia	-0.72	(0.03)	-1.99	(0.04)	-1.07	(0.03)	-0.38	(0.05)	0.54	(0.04)
Montenegro	-0.25	(0.01)	-1.40	(0.02)	-0.57	(0.02)	0.09	(0.02)	0.89	(0.02)
Russian Federation	-0.11	(0.02)	-1.10	(0.03)	-0.37	(0.03)	0.22	(0.03)	0.95	(0.03)
Serbia	-0.30	(0.02)	-1.37	(0.02)	-0.70	(0.03)	0.06	(0.04)	0.83	(0.03)
Shanghai-China	-0.36	(0.04)	-1.63	(0.05)	-0.54	(0.02)	0.09	(0.02)	0.88	(0.02)
Singapore	-0.26	(0.01)	-1.46	(0.02)	-0.70	(0.03)	-0.11	(0.03)	0.68	(0.03)
Chinese Taipei	-0.40	(0.02)	-1.47	(0.03)	-0.70	(0.02)	0.67	(0.01)	1.26	(0.01)
United Arab Emirates	0.32	(0.02)	-0.82	(0.03)	0.19	(0.02)	0.67	(0.01)	1.26	(0.01)
Uruguay	-0.88	(0.03)	-2.23	(0.02)	-1.40	(0.03)	-0.59	(0.04)	0.69	(0.05)

Note: Values that are statistically significant are indicated in bold (see Annex A3).
1. Single-level bivariate regression of performance on the *PISA index of economic, social and cultural status* (ESCS). The slope of the gradient is the regression coefficient for ESCS; the strength of the relationship is the R-squared.
* See notes at the beginning of this Annex.
StatLink http://dx.doi.org/10.1787/888933003706

[Part 2/2]
Table V.4.12 Performance in problem solving, by socio-economic status
Results based on students' self-reports

		Performance in problem solving, by national quarters of this index: Bottom quarter – Mean score	S.E.	Second quarter – Mean score	S.E.	Third quarter – Mean score	S.E.	Top quarter – Mean score	S.E.	Increased likelihood of students in the bottom quarter of the ESCS index scoring in the bottom quarter of the problem-solving performance distribution – Relative risk	S.E.	Slope of the socio-economic gradient[1]: Score-point difference in problem solving associated with one-unit increase in the ESCS	S.E.	Strength of the relationship between student performance and ESCS[1]: Percentage of explained variation in student performance (R-squared x 100)	S.E.
OECD	Australia	**487**	(2.6)	512	(2.4)	538	(3.1)	**560**	(2.5)	**1.88**	(0.07)	**36**	(1.3)	8.5	(0.6)
	Austria	**467**	(4.7)	495	(5.4)	518	(4.8)	**547**	(4.9)	**1.98**	(0.13)	**36**	(2.6)	10.7	(1.4)
	Belgium	**458**	(4.3)	495	(4.0)	529	(3.3)	**557**	(3.5)	**2.22**	(0.13)	**43**	(2.3)	14.0	(1.5)
	Canada	**503**	(3.4)	518	(2.8)	534	(3.3)	**555**	(3.2)	**1.52**	(0.07)	**23**	(1.7)	4.0	(0.6)
	Chile	**405**	(5.9)	439	(4.6)	454	(4.0)	**493**	(4.8)	**2.12**	(0.17)	**30**	(1.9)	15.8	(1.8)
	Czech Republic	**460**	(4.9)	500	(5.0)	519	(4.1)	**557**	(4.2)	**2.25**	(0.17)	**49**	(2.8)	14.9	(1.5)
	Denmark	**465**	(5.2)	488	(4.0)	511	(3.7)	**529**	(3.5)	**1.89**	(0.14)	**31**	(2.3)	7.9	(1.2)
	Estonia	**495**	(3.8)	503	(3.8)	516	(4.1)	**547**	(3.4)	**1.39**	(0.11)	**25**	(2.0)	5.4	(0.8)
	Finland	**495**	(3.7)	513	(3.0)	531	(3.7)	**556**	(3.0)	**1.67**	(0.10)	**30**	(2.2)	6.5	(0.9)
	France	**472**	(6.0)	497	(4.1)	521	(4.4)	**559**	(4.1)	**2.01**	(0.15)	**43**	(2.8)	12.7	(1.2)
	Germany	**469**	(5.6)	500	(4.5)	539	(4.4)	**555**	(4.2)	**2.17**	(0.15)	**37**	(2.4)	12.7	(1.4)
	Hungary	**397**	(7.2)	445	(4.8)	474	(5.2)	**520**	(6.4)	**2.74**	(0.20)	**49**	(3.3)	20.5	(2.3)
	Ireland	**460**	(4.7)	489	(4.2)	510	(3.5)	**538**	(4.8)	**1.93**	(0.14)	**35**	(2.2)	10.2	(1.1)
	Israel	**393**	(5.7)	437	(6.9)	477	(7.1)	**513**	(7.1)	**2.14**	(0.14)	**53**	(3.0)	13.2	(1.4)
	Italy	**481**	(5.6)	500	(4.4)	524	(5.3)	**535**	(5.6)	**1.68**	(0.15)	**23**	(2.5)	5.9	(1.2)
	Japan	**526**	(5.3)	547	(3.6)	562	(4.0)	**576**	(4.2)	**1.73**	(0.13)	**27**	(3.1)	5.2	(1.1)
	Korea	**534**	(5.3)	552	(5.1)	571	(5.2)	**588**	(5.5)	**1.60**	(0.13)	**28**	(3.0)	5.4	(1.1)
	Netherlands	**473**	(6.7)	502	(5.3)	523	(5.3)	**549**	(6.3)	**1.84**	(0.18)	**38**	(3.8)	9.1	(1.6)
	Norway	**473**	(4.5)	495	(4.1)	518	(4.7)	**533**	(5.0)	**1.66**	(0.12)	**31**	(2.7)	5.2	(0.9)
	Poland	**441**	(5.5)	467	(5.2)	491	(5.8)	**526**	(6.3)	**1.95**	(0.18)	**36**	(2.7)	11.6	(1.7)
	Portugal	**449**	(4.7)	485	(4.5)	504	(4.7)	**543**	(5.8)	**2.27**	(0.15)	**30**	(1.9)	16.1	(2.0)
	Slovak Republic	**424**	(7.5)	477	(4.2)	495	(4.2)	**541**	(5.5)	**2.83**	(0.27)	**49**	(3.3)	21.3	(2.0)
	Slovenia	**434**	(2.6)	463	(3.4)	488	(3.4)	**522**	(2.8)	**1.91**	(0.12)	**40**	(1.6)	12.6	(1.0)
	Spain	**437**	(7.2)	469	(4.3)	485	(4.9)	**517**	(6.6)	**1.84**	(0.13)	**29**	(3.0)	7.9	(1.5)
	Sweden	**460**	(3.7)	482	(4.1)	507	(4.7)	**521**	(4.5)	**1.62**	(0.11)	**29**	(2.3)	6.2	(1.0)
	Turkey	**419**	(4.3)	443	(4.0)	459	(5.1)	**497**	(6.2)	**1.95**	(0.15)	**28**	(1.9)	15.1	(1.8)
	England (United Kingdom)	**486**	(5.4)	505	(5.5)	531	(5.0)	**555**	(4.6)	**1.74**	(0.13)	**33**	(2.8)	7.8	(1.1)
	United States	**473**	(5.7)	493	(4.7)	518	(5.1)	**549**	(4.7)	**1.87**	(0.17)	**30**	(2.0)	10.1	(1.2)
	OECD average	**462**	(1.0)	490	(0.8)	512	(0.9)	**541**	(0.9)	**1.94**	(0.03)	**35**	(0.5)	10.6	(0.3)
Partners	Brazil	**385**	(6.2)	420	(6.8)	436	(6.8)	**477**	(7.0)	**2.13**	(0.19)	**30**	(2.5)	14.6	(2.4)
	Bulgaria	**343**	(8.3)	387	(5.9)	416	(6.6)	**465**	(6.8)	**2.33**	(0.19)	**45**	(3.6)	20.0	(2.5)
	Colombia	**359**	(4.5)	388	(4.5)	406	(4.3)	**442**	(5.9)	**1.97**	(0.14)	**27**	(1.9)	12.6	(1.6)
	Croatia	**434**	(5.1)	458	(4.4)	469	(4.9)	**504**	(5.5)	**1.70**	(0.12)	**32**	(2.6)	8.6	(1.2)
	Cyprus*	**406**	(3.1)	438	(3.3)	450	(3.0)	**488**	(3.0)	**1.84**	(0.11)	**34**	(1.6)	9.5	(0.9)
	Hong Kong-China	**517**	(5.5)	533	(5.0)	546	(4.1)	**567**	(6.9)	**1.58**	(0.12)	**21**	(2.9)	4.9	(1.3)
	Macao-China	**530**	(2.4)	540	(2.3)	545	(2.0)	**548**	(2.3)	**1.27**	(0.07)	**9**	(1.3)	1.0	(0.3)
	Malaysia	**385**	(4.2)	409	(3.8)	427	(4.8)	**469**	(5.4)	**1.99**	(0.14)	**33**	(2.1)	14.9	(1.7)
	Montenegro	**371**	(2.5)	400	(3.0)	410	(3.2)	**447**	(3.1)	**1.92**	(0.13)	**32**	(1.6)	9.8	(1.0)
	Russian Federation	**450**	(3.9)	472	(4.3)	502	(4.2)	**531**	(6.0)	**1.96**	(0.16)	**41**	(3.1)	12.3	(1.5)
	Serbia	**437**	(5.0)	461	(4.1)	476	(4.5)	**519**	(3.5)	**1.90**	(0.13)	**35**	(1.9)	12.8	(1.3)
	Shanghai-China	**492**	(6.5)	528	(3.8)	548	(3.6)	**578**	(5.1)	**2.24**	(0.17)	**35**	(2.6)	14.1	(1.9)
	Singapore	**522**	(2.6)	552	(2.9)	575	(2.8)	**602**	(2.5)	**2.04**	(0.13)	**35**	(1.3)	11.1	(0.9)
	Chinese Taipei	**498**	(4.9)	528	(4.0)	542	(3.2)	**570**	(3.8)	**1.98**	(0.13)	**33**	(2.3)	9.4	(1.2)
	United Arab Emirates	**367**	(4.2)	403	(2.9)	432	(3.6)	**445**	(4.2)	**1.90**	(0.11)	**35**	(1.9)	7.7	(0.8)
	Uruguay	**358**	(4.6)	384	(4.8)	410	(5.2)	**463**	(5.2)	**2.07**	(0.17)	**36**	(1.9)	17.8	(1.6)

Note: Values that are statistically significant are indicated in bold (see Annex A3).
1. Single-level bivariate regression of performance on the *PISA index of economic, social and cultural status* (ESCS). The slope of the gradient is the regression coefficient for ESCS; the strength of the relationship is the R-squared.
* See notes at the beginning of this Annex.
StatLink http://dx.doi.org/10.1787/888933003706

[Part 1/3]

Strength of the relationship between socio-economic status and performance in problem solving, mathematics, reading and science

Table V.4.13   *Results based on students' self-reports*

	Slope of the socio-economic gradient:[1] Score-point difference associated with a one-unit increase in ESCS											
	Problem solving		Mathematics		Reading		Science		Computer-based mathematics		Digital reading	
	Score dif.	S.E.	Score dif.	S.E.	Score dif.	S.E.	Score dif.	S.E.	Score dif.	S.E.	Score dif.	S.E.
Australia	36	(1.3)	42	(1.3)	42	(1.3)	43	(1.3)	35	(1.5)	39	(1.4)
Austria	36	(2.6)	43	(2.2)	42	(2.3)	46	(2.2)	36	(2.5)	44	(3.1)
Belgium	43	(2.3)	49	(1.7)	47	(1.8)	48	(1.7)	43	(1.9)	41	(2.1)
Canada	23	(1.7)	31	(1.2)	30	(1.3)	29	(1.4)	26	(1.5)	25	(1.7)
Chile	30	(1.9)	34	(1.6)	31	(1.5)	32	(1.7)	28	(1.8)	31	(1.9)
Czech Republic	49	(2.8)	51	(2.7)	46	(2.7)	46	(3.1)	m	m	m	m
Denmark	31	(2.3)	39	(1.7)	39	(1.9)	43	(2.2)	32	(1.8)	34	(1.6)
Estonia	25	(2.0)	29	(1.7)	26	(1.9)	27	(1.9)	28	(1.9)	26	(2.4)
Finland	30	(2.2)	33	(1.8)	33	(2.2)	33	(2.1)	m	m	m	m
France	43	(2.8)	57	(2.2)	58	(2.9)	58	(2.4)	47	(2.1)	50	(2.9)
Germany	37	(2.4)	43	(2.0)	37	(2.0)	42	(2.2)	40	(2.3)	33	(2.5)
Hungary	49	(3.3)	47	(2.8)	42	(2.3)	44	(2.3)	41	(2.8)	52	(3.3)
Ireland	35	(2.2)	38	(1.8)	39	(1.9)	41	(2.0)	33	(2.0)	32	(1.8)
Israel	53	(3.0)	51	(2.6)	44	(2.9)	48	(2.9)	46	(2.9)	51	(2.8)
Italy	23	(2.5)	30	(2.3)	31	(2.5)	30	(2.3)	24	(2.3)	23	(2.5)
Japan	27	(3.1)	41	(3.9)	38	(3.9)	36	(3.9)	34	(4.0)	29	(2.7)
Korea	28	(3.0)	42	(3.3)	33	(2.8)	29	(2.6)	40	(3.0)	32	(2.4)
Netherlands	38	(3.8)	40	(3.1)	39	(3.2)	43	(3.1)	m	m	m	m
Norway	31	(2.7)	32	(2.4)	33	(2.7)	34	(2.8)	28	(2.4)	34	(2.6)
Poland	36	(2.7)	41	(2.4)	36	(2.2)	36	(2.4)	35	(2.4)	40	(2.6)
Portugal	30	(1.9)	35	(1.6)	31	(1.8)	32	(1.6)	28	(1.7)	31	(1.9)
Slovak Republic	49	(3.3)	54	(2.9)	56	(3.3)	56	(2.9)	47	(2.7)	50	(2.7)
Slovenia	40	(1.6)	42	(1.5)	40	(1.6)	39	(1.5)	35	(1.3)	39	(1.7)
Spain	29	(3.0)	33	(1.7)	31	(1.9)	30	(1.9)	28	(1.8)	31	(2.6)
Sweden	29	(2.3)	36	(1.9)	38	(2.5)	38	(2.4)	25	(2.1)	28	(2.2)
Turkey	28	(1.9)	32	(2.4)	30	(2.1)	24	(1.8)	m	m	m	m
England (United Kingdom)	33	(2.8)	41	(2.8)	41	(2.8)	46	(2.8)	m	m	m	m
United States	30	(2.0)	35	(1.7)	33	(1.8)	36	(1.8)	31	(2.1)	33	(1.8)
OECD average	**35**	**(0.5)**	**40**	**(0.4)**	**38**	**(0.4)**	**39**	**(0.4)**	**34**	**(0.5)**	**36**	**(0.5)**
Brazil	30	(2.5)	26	(2.7)	23	(2.4)	24	(2.4)	30	(2.7)	28	(2.6)
Bulgaria	45	(3.6)	42	(2.7)	53	(2.9)	47	(2.8)	m	m	m	m
Colombia	27	(1.9)	25	(1.7)	28	(1.9)	23	(1.8)	18	(1.7)	29	(2.0)
Croatia	32	(2.6)	36	(2.6)	34	(2.5)	31	(2.3)	m	m	m	m
Cyprus*	34	(1.6)	38	(1.6)	35	(1.9)	39	(1.7)	m	m	m	m
Hong Kong-China	21	(2.9)	27	(2.6)	20	(2.5)	21	(2.3)	19	(2.8)	19	(2.6)
Macao-China	9	(1.3)	17	(1.5)	11	(1.4)	13	(1.8)	13	(1.3)	13	(1.1)
Malaysia	33	(2.1)	30	(2.1)	23	(2.2)	25	(1.9)	m	m	m	m
Montenegro	32	(1.6)	33	(1.3)	34	(1.5)	32	(1.4)	m	m	m	m
Russian Federation	41	(3.1)	38	(3.2)	43	(3.2)	43	(3.1)	33	(2.5)	37	(2.7)
Serbia	35	(1.9)	34	(2.4)	30	(2.3)	29	(2.2)	m	m	m	m
Shanghai-China	35	(2.6)	41	(2.7)	33	(2.0)	33	(2.1)	39	(2.4)	37	(2.7)
Singapore	35	(1.3)	44	(1.4)	43	(1.4)	46	(1.6)	39	(1.4)	34	(1.2)
Chinese Taipei	33	(2.3)	58	(2.5)	42	(2.2)	40	(1.8)	42	(1.9)	38	(2.4)
United Arab Emirates	35	(1.9)	33	(1.9)	30	(1.9)	33	(2.1)	30	(1.8)	44	(2.5)
Uruguay	36	(1.9)	37	(1.8)	35	(2.0)	37	(1.9)	m	m	m	m

Note: Values that are statistically significant are indicated in bold (see Annex A3).
1. Single-level bivariate regression of performance on the *PISA index of economic, social and cultural status* (ESCS); the slope is the regression coefficient for ESCS.
2. R-squared from the regression coefficient of performance on the *PISA index of economic, social and cultural status* (ESCS).
* See notes at the beginning of this Annex.
StatLink ꡔꡲꡐ http://dx.doi.org/10.1787/888933003706

[Part 2/3]
Strength of the relationship between socio-economic status and performance in problem solving, mathematics, reading and science

Table V.4.13   *Results based on students' self-reports*

		Problem solving		Mathematics		Reading		Science		Computer-based mathematics		Digital reading	
		%	S.E.	%	S.E.	%	S.E.	%	S.E.	%	S.E.	%	S.E.
OECD	Australia	**8.5**	(0.6)	**12.3**	(0.8)	**12.0**	(0.8)	**11.9**	(0.7)	**9.6**	(0.8)	**10.2**	(0.7)
	Austria	**10.7**	(1.4)	**15.8**	(1.5)	**15.3**	(1.6)	**18.3**	(1.7)	**12.2**	(1.6)	**13.4**	(1.5)
	Belgium	**14.0**	(1.5)	**19.6**	(1.4)	**18.2**	(1.4)	**19.2**	(1.4)	**15.8**	(1.3)	**14.4**	(1.4)
	Canada	**4.0**	(0.6)	**9.4**	(0.7)	**8.1**	(0.7)	**7.8**	(0.7)	**6.1**	(0.7)	**6.0**	(0.8)
	Chile	**15.8**	(1.8)	**23.1**	(1.9)	**20.4**	(1.8)	**20.2**	(1.9)	**15.4**	(1.9)	**17.9**	(2.0)
	Czech Republic	**14.9**	(1.5)	**16.2**	(1.5)	**14.8**	(1.5)	**14.3**	(1.7)	m	m	m	m
	Denmark	**7.9**	(1.2)	**16.5**	(1.4)	**15.3**	(1.3)	**15.7**	(1.5)	**9.7**	(1.1)	**11.9**	(1.2)
	Estonia	**5.4**	(0.8)	**8.6**	(0.9)	**6.8**	(1.0)	**7.4**	(0.9)	**7.8**	(1.0)	**5.2**	(0.9)
	Finland	**6.5**	(0.9)	**9.4**	(0.9)	**7.5**	(0.9)	**7.9**	(0.9)	m	m	m	m
	France	**12.7**	(1.2)	**22.5**	(1.3)	**18.7**	(1.5)	**21.5**	(1.3)	**16.9**	(1.8)	**17.2**	(1.8)
	Germany	**12.7**	(1.4)	**16.9**	(1.4)	**15.0**	(1.4)	**17.1**	(1.4)	**15.4**	(1.4)	**9.8**	(1.2)
	Hungary	**20.5**	(2.3)	**23.1**	(2.3)	**20.0**	(2.1)	**22.4**	(2.2)	**18.3**	(2.1)	**19.8**	(1.8)
	Ireland	**10.2**	(1.1)	**14.6**	(1.2)	**15.1**	(1.2)	**14.5**	(1.2)	**11.9**	(1.3)	**10.9**	(1.1)
	Israel	**13.2**	(1.4)	**17.2**	(1.5)	**11.2**	(1.4)	**14.7**	(1.4)	**12.6**	(1.5)	**13.8**	(1.5)
	Italy	**5.9**	(1.2)	**9.4**	(1.2)	**9.3**	(1.3)	**9.2**	(1.3)	**7.9**	(1.3)	**5.6**	(1.1)
	Japan	**5.2**	(1.1)	**9.8**	(1.6)	**7.9**	(1.5)	**7.3**	(1.4)	**7.8**	(1.5)	**6.9**	(1.1)
	Korea	**5.4**	(1.1)	**10.1**	(1.4)	**7.9**	(1.2)	**6.7**	(1.1)	**10.6**	(1.3)	**8.6**	(1.2)
	Netherlands	**9.1**	(1.6)	**11.5**	(1.7)	**10.8**	(1.7)	**12.5**	(1.8)	m	m	m	m
	Norway	**5.2**	(0.9)	**7.4**	(1.0)	**6.3**	(1.0)	**6.9**	(1.0)	**6.0**	(1.0)	**6.8**	(0.9)
	Poland	**11.6**	(1.7)	**16.6**	(1.7)	**13.4**	(1.6)	**14.4**	(1.7)	**13.8**	(1.7)	**14.2**	(1.7)
	Portugal	**16.1**	(2.0)	**19.6**	(1.8)	**16.5**	(1.7)	**18.7**	(1.7)	**14.9**	(1.8)	**17.6**	(1.8)
	Slovak Republic	**21.3**	(2.0)	**24.6**	(2.1)	**24.1**	(2.1)	**26.4**	(2.0)	**24.9**	(2.1)	**23.8**	(1.9)
	Slovenia	**12.6**	(1.0)	**15.6**	(1.0)	**14.2**	(1.1)	**14.1**	(1.0)	**11.9**	(0.8)	**11.9**	(1.0)
	Spain	**7.9**	(1.5)	**15.7**	(1.6)	**12.0**	(1.5)	**13.2**	(1.6)	**11.8**	(1.4)	**10.6**	(1.6)
	Sweden	**6.2**	(1.0)	**10.6**	(1.1)	**9.1**	(1.1)	**10.4**	(1.2)	**5.8**	(0.9)	**5.8**	(0.9)
	Turkey	**15.1**	(1.8)	**14.5**	(1.8)	**14.5**	(1.8)	**11.0**	(1.6)	m	m	m	m
	England (United Kingdom)	**7.8**	(1.1)	**12.4**	(1.4)	**11.8**	(1.3)	**13.7**	(1.4)	m	m	m	m
	United States	**10.1**	(1.2)	**14.8**	(1.3)	**12.6**	(1.3)	**14.2**	(1.4)	**11.9**	(1.5)	**13.5**	(1.4)
	OECD average	**10.6**	(0.3)	**14.9**	(0.3)	**13.2**	(0.3)	**14.0**	(0.3)	**12.1**	(0.3)	**12.0**	(0.3)
Partners	Brazil	**14.6**	(2.4)	**15.5**	(2.9)	**10.3**	(2.0)	**13.2**	(2.3)	**17.6**	(2.9)	**12.9**	(2.4)
	Bulgaria	**20.0**	(2.5)	**22.3**	(2.3)	**21.9**	(2.2)	**23.8**	(2.3)	m	m	m	m
	Colombia	**12.6**	(1.6)	**15.4**	(1.8)	**15.6**	(1.9)	**12.7**	(1.8)	**8.3**	(1.5)	**14.3**	(1.8)
	Croatia	**8.6**	(1.2)	**12.0**	(1.4)	**11.2**	(1.4)	**9.8**	(1.2)	m	m	m	m
	Cyprus*	**9.5**	(0.9)	**14.1**	(1.1)	**8.2**	(0.8)	**13.7**	(1.0)	m	m	m	m
	Hong Kong-China	**4.9**	(1.3)	**7.5**	(1.5)	**5.2**	(1.2)	**6.0**	(1.3)	**4.5**	(1.3)	**3.9**	(1.1)
	Macao-China	**1.0**	(0.3)	**2.6**	(0.4)	**1.5**	(0.4)	**2.1**	(0.6)	**1.7**	(0.4)	**2.4**	(0.4)
	Malaysia	**14.9**	(1.7)	**13.4**	(1.6)	**7.7**	(1.4)	**10.3**	(1.4)	m	m	m	m
	Montenegro	**9.8**	(1.0)	**12.7**	(0.9)	**10.9**	(1.0)	**11.6**	(0.9)	m	m	m	m
	Russian Federation	**12.3**	(1.5)	**11.4**	(1.7)	**13.1**	(1.6)	**14.6**	(1.9)	**9.9**	(1.4)	**10.7**	(1.4)
	Serbia	**12.8**	(1.3)	**11.7**	(1.4)	**8.7**	(1.2)	**8.8**	(1.2)	m	m	m	m
	Shanghai-China	**14.1**	(1.9)	**15.1**	(1.9)	**15.6**	(1.8)	**15.3**	(2.0)	**15.9**	(1.9)	**17.6**	(2.3)
	Singapore	**11.1**	(0.9)	**14.4**	(0.9)	**15.2**	(0.9)	**16.5**	(1.0)	**13.0**	(0.9)	**12.2**	(0.9)
	Chinese Taipei	**9.4**	(1.2)	**17.9**	(1.4)	**15.1**	(1.4)	**16.7**	(1.4)	**15.7**	(1.3)	**13.0**	(1.4)
	United Arab Emirates	**7.7**	(0.8)	**9.8**	(1.0)	**7.1**	(0.9)	**8.9**	(1.0)	**8.8**	(1.0)	**11.6**	(1.1)
	Uruguay	**17.8**	(1.6)	**22.8**	(1.9)	**17.5**	(1.8)	**19.8**	(1.8)	m	m	m	m

Note: Values that are statistically significant are indicated in bold (see Annex A3).
1. Single-level bivariate regression of performance on the *PISA index of economic, social and cultural status* (ESCS); the slope is the regression coefficient for ESCS.
2. R-squared from the regression coefficient of performance on the *PISA index of economic, social and cultural status* (ESCS).
* See notes at the beginning of this Annex.
StatLink 🔗 http://dx.doi.org/10.1787/888933003706

[Part 3/3]
Strength of the relationship between socio-economic status and performance in problem solving, mathematics, reading and science

Table V.4.13 · *Results based on students' self-reports*

	Strength of the relationship between performance in problem solving (PS) and ESCS,[2] compared to...									
	... Mathematics (PS - M)		... Reading (PS - R)		... Science (PS - S)		... Computer-based mathematics (PS - CBM)		... Digital reading (PS - DR)	
	% dif.	S.E.	% dif.	S.E.	% dif.	S.E.	% dif.	S.E.	% dif.	S.E.
Australia	-3.9	(0.6)	-3.5	(0.6)	-3.4	(0.5)	-1.1	(0.6)	-1.7	(0.5)
Austria	-5.1	(1.2)	-4.6	(1.2)	-7.5	(1.3)	-1.5	(1.2)	-2.7	(1.4)
Belgium	-5.7	(0.8)	-4.2	(1.0)	-5.3	(1.0)	-1.8	(0.9)	-0.4	(1.0)
Canada	-5.4	(0.5)	-4.1	(0.5)	-3.8	(0.5)	-2.0	(0.5)	-1.9	(0.6)
Chile	-7.2	(1.4)	-4.6	(1.4)	-4.3	(1.5)	0.4	(1.9)	-2.1	(1.7)
Czech Republic	-1.3	(0.7)	0.1	(1.0)	0.6	(0.9)	m	m	m	m
Denmark	-8.6	(1.2)	-7.4	(1.4)	-7.8	(1.2)	-1.7	(0.9)	-3.9	(1.1)
Estonia	-3.2	(0.6)	-1.4	(0.8)	-1.9	(0.8)	-2.4	(0.8)	0.2	(0.8)
Finland	-2.9	(0.6)	-1.0	(0.7)	-1.4	(0.6)	m	m	m	m
France	-9.8	(1.0)	-6.0	(1.2)	-8.9	(1.0)	-4.3	(1.5)	-4.6	(1.4)
Germany	-4.2	(1.0)	-2.3	(1.2)	-4.4	(1.1)	-2.7	(1.3)	2.9	(1.2)
Hungary	-2.5	(1.1)	0.6	(1.2)	-1.9	(1.0)	2.2	(1.2)	0.7	(1.5)
Ireland	-4.5	(1.0)	-4.9	(1.1)	-4.3	(1.0)	-1.7	(1.1)	-0.7	(1.1)
Israel	-3.9	(0.8)	2.0	(0.8)	-1.5	(0.8)	0.7	(0.8)	-0.5	(0.9)
Italy	-3.5	(0.9)	-3.4	(1.0)	-3.3	(1.0)	-2.0	(1.2)	0.3	(0.8)
Japan	-4.6	(1.0)	-2.7	(0.8)	-2.2	(0.9)	-2.7	(0.8)	-1.8	(0.6)
Korea	-4.7	(0.7)	-2.5	(0.8)	-1.4	(0.7)	-5.2	(0.9)	-3.3	(0.9)
Netherlands	-2.4	(1.0)	-1.6	(1.1)	-3.4	(1.1)	m	m	m	m
Norway	-2.2	(0.7)	-1.1	(0.8)	-1.6	(0.7)	-0.8	(0.6)	-1.6	(0.6)
Poland	-5.1	(1.2)	-1.8	(1.3)	-2.8	(1.4)	-2.2	(1.2)	-2.6	(1.1)
Portugal	-3.6	(1.0)	-0.4	(1.2)	-2.7	(1.2)	1.1	(1.3)	-1.5	(1.4)
Slovak Republic	-3.3	(1.6)	-2.8	(1.6)	-5.1	(1.7)	-3.6	(1.7)	-2.5	(1.5)
Slovenia	-3.0	(0.9)	-1.6	(1.1)	-1.5	(0.7)	0.7	(0.7)	0.7	(0.8)
Spain	-7.8	(1.0)	-4.1	(1.0)	-5.3	(1.0)	-3.9	(1.2)	-2.7	(1.0)
Sweden	-4.5	(0.7)	-2.9	(0.9)	-4.3	(0.9)	0.3	(0.8)	0.4	(0.8)
Turkey	0.6	(0.8)	0.6	(1.1)	4.1	(0.9)	m	m	m	m
England (United Kingdom)	-4.6	(0.9)	-4.0	(1.0)	-5.8	(0.9)	m	m	m	m
United States	-4.7	(0.9)	-2.6	(1.0)	-4.2	(1.0)	-1.9	(1.1)	-3.4	(1.0)
OECD average	**-4.3**	(0.2)	**-2.6**	(0.2)	**-3.4**	(0.2)	**-1.6**	(0.2)	**-1.4**	(0.2)
Brazil	-0.9	(1.4)	4.3	(1.4)	1.4	(1.5)	-3.0	(1.6)	1.6	(1.3)
Bulgaria	-2.3	(1.2)	-1.9	(1.4)	-3.7	(1.4)	m	m	m	m
Colombia	-2.8	(1.2)	-3.0	(1.5)	0.0	(1.4)	4.4	(1.1)	-1.7	(1.3)
Croatia	-3.4	(0.7)	-2.6	(0.9)	-1.2	(0.8)	m	m	m	m
Cyprus*	-4.7	(0.7)	1.3	(0.7)	-4.3	(0.7)	m	m	m	m
Hong Kong-China	-2.6	(0.9)	-0.3	(0.9)	-1.1	(0.9)	0.4	(1.1)	0.9	(0.9)
Macao-China	-1.6	(0.3)	-0.5	(0.3)	-1.1	(0.5)	-0.7	(0.2)	-1.4	(0.4)
Malaysia	1.5	(1.0)	7.2	(1.1)	4.6	(1.1)	m	m	m	m
Montenegro	-3.0	(0.6)	-1.1	(0.9)	-1.8	(0.9)	m	m	m	m
Russian Federation	0.9	(1.4)	-0.8	(1.2)	-2.3	(1.4)	2.4	(1.0)	1.6	(1.2)
Serbia	1.1	(0.8)	4.2	(0.9)	4.0	(1.0)	m	m	m	m
Shanghai-China	-1.0	(0.9)	-1.6	(1.0)	-1.2	(1.1)	-1.9	(1.2)	-3.5	(1.2)
Singapore	-3.3	(0.6)	-4.1	(0.7)	-5.4	(0.8)	-1.8	(0.6)	-1.1	(0.6)
Chinese Taipei	-8.5	(0.6)	-5.6	(0.7)	-7.3	(0.7)	-6.3	(0.7)	-3.6	(0.8)
United Arab Emirates	-2.1	(0.7)	0.6	(0.6)	-1.1	(0.8)	-1.1	(0.6)	-3.9	(0.7)
Uruguay	-5.0	(1.6)	0.4	(1.7)	-2.0	(1.6)	m	m	m	m

Note: Values that are statistically significant are indicated in bold (see Annex A3).
1. Single-level bivariate regression of performance on the *PISA index of economic, social and cultural status* (ESCS); the slope is the regression coefficient for ESCS.
2. R-squared from the regression coefficient of performance on the *PISA index of economic, social and cultural status* (ESCS).
* See notes at the beginning of this Annex.
StatLink ᴍˢᴾ http://dx.doi.org/10.1787/888933003706

[Part 1/1]

Strength of the relationship between socio-economic status and performance in problem solving, between and within schools[1]

Table V.4.14 *Results based on students' self-reports*

	Variation components expressed as a percentage of total variation in student performance in problem solving[2]							
	Variation in problem solving		Variation in problem solving accounted for by the socio-economic status of students and schools[3]		Variation unique to problem solving[4]		Variation unique to problem solving accounted for by the socio-economic status of students and schools[5]	
	Between schools	Within schools	Between schools	Within schools	Between schools	Within schools	Between schools	Within schools
	%	%	%	%	%	%	%	%
OECD								
Australia	27.1	73.3	10.9	2.4	12.1	18.1	0.3	0.6
Austria	47.5	51.2	18.8	1.2	13.4	20.9	0.0	0.4
Belgium	47.8	51.3	24.3	1.7	12.4	21.7	0.0	0.2
Canada	22.6	76.4	5.3	3.6	14.8	27.6	0.4	1.9
Chile	42.7	55.9	23.6	0.1	12.9	22.7	0.1	0.0
Czech Republic	48.2	49.4	31.8	1.1	7.6	14.6	0.3	0.2
Denmark	28.6	71.0	6.0	4.3	20.3	20.4	0.0	0.8
Estonia	23.8	76.6	8.0	1.4	12.2	18.8	0.2	0.5
Finland	10.2	89.5	1.9	5.5	7.2	22.7	0.1	0.7
France	w	w	w	w	w	w	w	w
Germany	54.9	44.7	31.6	0.0	14.4	15.7	1.6	0.0
Hungary	59.1	38.9	41.4	0.8	10.1	19.9	0.3	1.1
Ireland	24.4	74.8	10.0	4.7	13.0	23.2	0.1	0.5
Israel	50.9	48.8	25.9	1.0	9.0	16.5	0.1	0.8
Italy	42.1	54.7	13.9	0.0	14.4	27.9	0.1	0.5
Japan	33.9	65.8	17.6	0.1	7.2	35.5	0.0	0.4
Korea	31.3	67.1	13.1	0.5	7.7	27.4	0.0	0.2
Netherlands	57.7	42.4	27.8	0.5	12.3	16.4	0.0	0.1
Norway	21.4	78.0	4.6	3.1	16.1	20.5	0.5	0.0
Poland	36.1	63.7	10.3	4.8	20.6	22.4	0.2	0.7
Portugal	30.0	70.3	14.9	4.7	11.2	23.9	0.7	0.5
Slovak Republic	49.6	48.2	31.2	2.0	11.4	15.0	0.2	0.1
Slovenia	54.2	45.3	30.5	0.5	14.3	18.7	0.0	0.2
Spain	28.7	71.4	5.9	3.0	19.2	25.2	0.3	0.6
Sweden	18.6	80.7	2.6	4.4	11.9	22.6	0.0	0.8
Turkey	51.9	48.0	30.8	1.0	8.6	21.3	0.7	0.4
England (United Kingdom)	29.3	70.7	12.9	2.4	10.0	16.4	0.2	0.4
United States	28.9	70.9	10.2	3.0	11.6	14.8	0.1	0.4
OECD average	37.8	61.5	17.6	2.1	12.6	20.9	0.2	0.5
Partners								
Brazil	47.4	52.7	21.5	1.2	14.8	16.7	0.3	0.0
Bulgaria	55.5	44.0	36.2	0.9	12.6	21.2	0.9	0.1
Colombia	36.8	62.7	15.8	2.8	15.4	29.5	0.3	1.7
Croatia	40.4	59.5	20.6	0.4	8.6	19.5	0.1	0.5
Cyprus*	35.3	67.9	17.1	1.7	10.3	25.8	0.1	0.6
Hong Kong-China	36.1	63.7	12.1	0.0	10.5	32.4	0.2	0.0
Macao-China	17.2	80.4	2.2	0.2	2.4	33.3	0.0	1.4
Malaysia	37.4	62.5	20.4	2.9	10.0	20.2	0.7	0.6
Montenegro	38.3	61.7	27.1	0.7	6.5	27.0	0.1	0.1
Russian Federation	37.0	63.1	15.2	3.0	21.1	23.9	2.7	0.3
Serbia	37.0	62.3	24.2	1.7	8.4	22.3	0.9	0.6
Shanghai-China	41.2	58.4	26.9	0.7	9.5	20.1	1.1	0.1
Singapore	33.9	66.1	16.2	2.3	11.4	19.2	0.2	0.0
Chinese Taipei	38.9	60.6	23.0	0.7	6.8	18.6	0.0	0.5
United Arab Emirates	50.4	49.4	18.2	1.1	14.5	21.1	0.3	0.4
Uruguay	42.3	57.6	23.8	1.8	14.2	22.7	0.4	0.1

1. In some countries/economies, sub-units within schools were sampled instead of schools; this may affect the estimation of between-school variance components (see Annex A3).
2. Due to the unbalanced clustered nature of the data, the sum of the between- and within-school variation components, as an estimate from a sample, does not necessarily add up to the total. All models were estimated on samples excluding students with missing information on the *PISA index of economic, social and cultural status* (ESCS).
3. Based on the residual variation in a model with student ESCS and school average ESCS. Negative estimates of explained variance values are reported as 0.0.
4. Based on the residual variation in a model with student performance in mathematics and school average performance in mathematics.
5. Based on the residual variation in a model with student performance in mathematics, student ESCS, school average performance in mathematics, and school average ESCS. Negative estimates of explained variance values are reported as 0.0.

* See notes at the beginning of this Annex.

StatLink http://dx.doi.org/10.1787/888933003706

[Part 1/1]
Performance in problem solving and parents' highest occupational status
Table V.4.15 *Results based on students' self-reports*

	Percentage of students by parents' highest occupation						Performance in problem solving by parents' highest occupation						Difference in problem-solving performance: Skilled minus semi-skilled or elementary occupations		Increased likelihood of students with at least one parent working in a skilled occupation scoring below Level 2 (less than 423.42 score points)		Increased likelihood of students with at least one parent working in a skilled occupation scoring at Level 5 or above (above 618.21 score points)	
	Skilled (ISCO 1 to 3)		Semi-skilled or elementary (ISCO 4 to 9)		Missing data on father's and mother's occupation		Skilled (ISCO 1 to 3)		Semi-skilled or elementary (ISCO 4 to 9)		Missing data on father's and mother's occupation							
	%	S.E.	%	S.E.	%	S.E.	Mean score	S.E.	Mean score	S.E.	Mean score	S.E.	Score dif.	S.E.	Relative risk	S.E.	Relative risk	S.E.
OECD																		
Australia	64.5	(0.6)	30.7	(0.5)	4.8	(0.2)	539	(2.0)	499	(2.5)	462	(4.8)	40	(2.1)	**0.53**	(0.03)	**1.92**	(0.12)
Austria	48.7	(1.0)	47.2	(1.0)	4.1	(0.4)	532	(4.1)	482	(4.0)	488	(9.6)	50	(4.0)	**0.48**	(0.05)	**2.60**	(0.34)
Belgium	53.1	(0.9)	41.3	(0.9)	5.6	(0.4)	537	(2.7)	479	(3.3)	438	(9.3)	58	(3.6)	**0.42**	(0.03)	**2.33**	(0.23)
Canada	60.6	(0.7)	32.5	(0.6)	6.9	(0.3)	541	(2.5)	508	(2.6)	478	(8.5)	32	(2.4)	**0.59**	(0.03)	**1.66**	(0.10)
Chile	33.1	(1.2)	60.9	(1.1)	5.9	(0.4)	481	(4.2)	432	(3.9)	421	(7.7)	49	(4.5)	**0.53**	(0.04)	**5.39**	(2.38)
Czech Republic	43.6	(1.0)	52.2	(1.0)	4.3	(0.4)	542	(3.0)	486	(3.8)	446	(14.5)	56	(3.6)	**0.37**	(0.04)	**2.83**	(0.32)
Denmark	58.6	(1.3)	37.4	(1.1)	4.0	(0.4)	516	(2.9)	475	(3.6)	431	(13.8)	40	(3.8)	**0.52**	(0.04)	**2.32**	(0.37)
Estonia	54.2	(0.9)	42.9	(0.8)	2.9	(0.3)	531	(2.8)	497	(3.2)	471	(9.1)	34	(3.3)	**0.53**	(0.05)	**1.95**	(0.26)
Finland	64.1	(0.8)	33.5	(0.8)	2.4	(0.2)	536	(2.4)	503	(3.3)	457	(9.4)	33	(3.5)	**0.55**	(0.05)	**1.88**	(0.21)
France	55.0	(1.0)	38.9	(1.0)	6.1	(0.4)	535	(3.4)	488	(4.5)	442	(8.9)	47	(4.1)	**0.44**	(0.04)	**2.42**	(0.27)
Germany	43.0	(0.9)	37.5	(1.0)	19.5	(0.9)	542	(3.7)	488	(4.2)	476	(7.8)	54	(4.3)	**0.40**	(0.04)	**2.47**	(0.28)
Hungary	40.9	(1.2)	51.8	(1.2)	7.3	(0.6)	502	(4.8)	433	(4.6)	403	(10.5)	68	(6.0)	**0.44**	(0.04)	**4.44**	(0.81)
Ireland	55.7	(0.9)	40.8	(0.9)	3.5	(0.3)	520	(3.4)	476	(3.6)	416	(8.2)	44	(3.3)	**0.52**	(0.04)	**2.64**	(0.38)
Israel	63.3	(1.5)	26.5	(1.1)	10.2	(0.9)	485	(6.0)	407	(5.9)	387	(10.2)	78	(6.8)	**0.52**	(0.04)	**4.49**	(0.93)
Italy	40.7	(1.3)	54.8	(1.3)	4.4	(0.6)	533	(4.7)	496	(4.4)	462	(9.3)	37	(4.3)	**0.48**	(0.06)	**1.83**	(0.24)
Japan	45.6	(0.7)	44.7	(0.8)	9.7	(0.6)	565	(3.5)	545	(3.5)	522	(5.7)	20	(3.5)	**0.57**	(0.08)	**1.34**	(0.10)
Korea	55.7	(1.2)	42.5	(1.2)	1.8	(0.2)	572	(4.4)	548	(4.4)	514	(13.9)	24	(3.2)	**0.66**	(0.08)	**1.41**	(0.09)
Netherlands	66.0	(1.1)	29.0	(1.0)	5.0	(0.5)	530	(4.3)	481	(6.2)	422	(11.4)	49	(5.6)	**0.48**	(0.04)	**2.72**	(0.53)
Norway	68.0	(0.8)	27.1	(0.8)	4.9	(0.4)	517	(3.4)	479	(4.1)	450	(9.4)	37	(3.4)	**0.63**	(0.04)	**1.87**	(0.22)
Poland	42.5	(1.4)	53.7	(1.3)	3.8	(0.3)	512	(4.9)	458	(4.6)	452	(9.7)	54	(4.5)	**0.45**	(0.05)	**3.43**	(0.67)
Portugal	34.3	(1.7)	61.0	(1.6)	4.6	(0.5)	529	(4.1)	478	(3.6)	457	(7.9)	51	(4.3)	**0.43**	(0.05)	**2.83**	(0.41)
Slovak Republic	32.8	(1.1)	59.3	(1.1)	7.9	(0.7)	532	(4.4)	468	(3.6)	396	(8.5)	63	(5.2)	**0.33**	(0.03)	**3.37**	(0.62)
Slovenia	53.9	(0.8)	42.4	(0.8)	3.7	(0.3)	501	(2.1)	450	(2.3)	413	(9.2)	51	(3.1)	**0.52**	(0.03)	**3.24**	(0.80)
Spain	42.2	(1.3)	55.9	(1.3)	1.8	(0.3)	503	(4.6)	458	(4.5)	437	(12.9)	45	(4.6)	**0.54**	(0.04)	**2.07**	(0.30)
Sweden	60.7	(0.9)	34.3	(0.8)	5.0	(0.5)	510	(3.3)	468	(3.2)	416	(10.7)	42	(3.4)	**0.57**	(0.04)	**3.02**	(0.45)
Turkey	18.6	(0.9)	69.2	(1.0)	12.2	(0.7)	488	(6.4)	448	(3.6)	438	(6.0)	40	(5.0)	**0.62**	(0.06)	**4.31**	(1.39)
England (United Kingdom)	61.8	(1.4)	31.8	(1.1)	6.4	(0.6)	536	(3.8)	496	(4.8)	432	(10.8)	40	(4.6)	**0.55**	(0.06)	**2.22**	(0.32)
United States	60.9	(1.4)	33.4	(1.2)	5.7	(0.5)	526	(3.8)	484	(4.2)	457	(8.2)	42	(3.9)	**0.52**	(0.05)	**2.69**	(0.34)
OECD average	50.8	(0.2)	43.3	(0.2)	5.9	(0.1)	525	(0.7)	479	(0.8)	446	(1.8)	46	(0.8)	**0.51**	(0.01)	**2.70**	(0.13)
Partners																		
Brazil	32.9	(1.4)	58.9	(1.4)	8.3	(0.6)	462	(5.5)	416	(5.4)	380	(7.2)	46	(5.9)	**0.61**	(0.05)	**4.69**	(2.02)
Bulgaria	41.1	(1.4)	49.2	(1.2)	9.7	(0.7)	448	(5.3)	378	(5.3)	328	(11.5)	70	(6.5)	**0.58**	(0.03)	**9.42**	(5.55)
Colombia	23.0	(1.0)	70.9	(0.9)	6.1	(0.5)	435	(5.6)	389	(5.5)	383	(6.8)	47	(5.0)	**0.68**	(0.04)	**3.37**	(1.32)
Croatia	39.2	(1.0)	56.0	(1.0)	4.8	(0.3)	498	(4.6)	448	(4.0)	428	(8.4)	50	(4.6)	**0.52**	(0.04)	**3.43**	(0.61)
Cyprus*	40.0	(0.8)	53.6	(0.8)	6.4	(0.4)	477	(2.2)	427	(2.1)	392	(5.0)	49	(3.1)	**0.60**	(0.03)	**4.07**	(0.92)
Hong Kong-China	39.5	(1.9)	52.5	(1.8)	7.9	(0.6)	559	(5.0)	532	(4.0)	492	(6.7)	27	(5.3)	**0.61**	(0.09)	**1.58**	(0.16)
Macao-China	27.1	(0.6)	70.3	(0.6)	2.6	(0.2)	551	(2.2)	538	(1.2)	496	(9.3)	13	(2.6)	**0.68**	(0.09)	1.19	(0.11)
Malaysia	37.5	(1.3)	56.3	(1.3)	6.2	(0.5)	455	(4.6)	405	(3.1)	381	(7.2)	50	(4.3)	**0.60**	(0.04)	**14.21**	(12.86)
Montenegro	37.9	(0.7)	45.9	(0.8)	16.2	(0.6)	441	(2.3)	394	(1.8)	362	(3.6)	48	(3.2)	**0.64**	(0.03)	**4.23**	(3.01)
Russian Federation	53.7	(1.1)	42.2	(1.1)	4.1	(0.4)	512	(3.9)	462	(3.3)	477	(8.4)	50	(3.4)	**0.47**	(0.04)	**4.01**	(0.68)
Serbia	40.5	(1.1)	55.9	(1.1)	3.6	(0.3)	507	(2.9)	451	(3.5)	449	(10.0)	56	(3.7)	**0.44**	(0.03)	**4.43**	(0.88)
Shanghai-China	56.5	(1.3)	41.9	(1.3)	1.6	(0.2)	555	(3.3)	514	(4.0)	461	(13.7)	41	(4.1)	**0.46**	(0.05)	**2.09**	(0.22)
Singapore	67.5	(0.6)	29.8	(0.6)	2.7	(0.2)	579	(1.6)	532	(2.5)	477	(8.1)	47	(3.2)	**0.43**	(0.06)	**1.93**	(0.16)
Chinese Taipei	41.6	(1.2)	53.4	(1.1)	4.9	(0.3)	561	(2.9)	521	(3.1)	448	(8.5)	40	(3.4)	**0.39**	(0.05)	**1.82**	(0.13)
United Arab Emirates	70.0	(0.8)	15.0	(0.5)	15.0	(0.6)	432	(2.6)	369	(4.3)	355	(5.0)	63	(3.7)	**0.65**	(0.02)	**5.56**	(2.45)
Uruguay	26.2	(0.9)	68.8	(0.9)	5.0	(0.3)	460	(4.4)	386	(3.6)	349	(7.5)	74	(5.0)	**0.52**	(0.03)	**8.06**	(3.05)

Note: Values that are statistically significant are indicated in bold (see Annex A3).
1. Increased likelihood relative to students with parents in semi-skilled or elementary occupations. Students who did not report their parents' occupation are excluded from this calculation.
* See notes at the beginning of this Annex.
StatLink http://dx.doi.org/10.1787/888933003706

[Part 1/3]
Differences in problem-solving, mathematics, reading and science performance related to parents' occupational status

Table V.4.16   *Results based on students' self-reports*

	Difference in performance related to parents' highest occupation: Skilled (ISCO 1 to 3) minus semi-skilled or elementary (ISCO 4 to 9)											
	Problem solving		Mathematics		Reading		Science		Computer-based mathematics		Digital reading	
	Score dif.	S.E.	Score dif.	S.E.	Score dif.	S.E.	Score dif.	S.E.	Score dif.	S.E.	Score dif.	S.E.
Australia	**40**	(2.1)	**46**	(2.2)	**45**	(2.3)	**48**	(2.3)	**38**	(2.2)	**43**	(2.2)
Austria	**50**	(4.0)	**54**	(3.6)	**55**	(3.6)	**58**	(3.6)	**47**	(4.0)	**54**	(4.8)
Belgium	**58**	(3.6)	**70**	(3.3)	**69**	(3.2)	**68**	(3.1)	**60**	(3.4)	**61**	(3.6)
Canada	**32**	(2.4)	**41**	(2.0)	**37**	(2.2)	**36**	(2.1)	**33**	(2.2)	**29**	(2.6)
Chile	**49**	(4.5)	**59**	(4.6)	**53**	(4.2)	**55**	(4.4)	**51**	(4.8)	**52**	(4.5)
Czech Republic	**56**	(3.6)	**61**	(3.8)	**54**	(3.4)	**55**	(3.5)	m	m	m	m
Denmark	**40**	(3.8)	**48**	(3.1)	**49**	(3.2)	**52**	(3.7)	**40**	(3.4)	**46**	(3.2)
Estonia	**34**	(3.3)	**40**	(3.0)	**40**	(3.3)	**40**	(3.2)	**38**	(3.3)	**40**	(3.8)
Finland	**33**	(3.5)	**37**	(2.8)	**37**	(3.3)	**38**	(3.1)	m	m	m	m
France	**47**	(4.1)	**67**	(3.5)	**71**	(4.6)	**66**	(3.7)	**53**	(3.0)	**59**	(4.0)
Germany	**54**	(4.3)	**62**	(4.3)	**58**	(4.1)	**60**	(4.5)	**57**	(4.1)	**51**	(4.5)
Hungary	**68**	(6.0)	**65**	(5.2)	**60**	(4.5)	**62**	(4.2)	**60**	(5.1)	**73**	(6.0)
Ireland	**44**	(3.3)	**43**	(2.9)	**46**	(3.3)	**47**	(3.0)	**35**	(3.2)	**33**	(3.3)
Israel	**78**	(6.8)	**73**	(5.9)	**66**	(6.5)	**70**	(6.2)	**62**	(6.4)	**75**	(6.6)
Italy	**37**	(4.3)	**42**	(4.3)	**47**	(4.6)	**48**	(4.4)	**37**	(4.2)	**40**	(4.7)
Japan	**20**	(3.5)	**32**	(3.9)	**30**	(4.0)	**28**	(3.9)	**25**	(4.0)	**22**	(2.8)
Korea	**24**	(3.2)	**34**	(3.8)	**26**	(3.0)	**24**	(3.1)	**35**	(3.5)	**30**	(3.0)
Netherlands	**49**	(5.6)	**52**	(4.2)	**53**	(4.4)	**54**	(4.7)	m	m	m	m
Norway	**37**	(4.0)	**37**	(3.7)	**38**	(4.1)	**39**	(4.1)	**34**	(3.3)	**40**	(3.8)
Poland	**54**	(4.5)	**58**	(4.6)	**54**	(3.9)	**53**	(4.3)	**51**	(4.3)	**60**	(4.4)
Portugal	**51**	(4.3)	**64**	(4.2)	**58**	(4.6)	**58**	(4.3)	**48**	(4.3)	**59**	(4.7)
Slovak Republic	**63**	(5.2)	**71**	(5.1)	**71**	(5.3)	**71**	(5.2)	**58**	(4.6)	**62**	(4.7)
Slovenia	**51**	(3.1)	**53**	(3.2)	**54**	(3.2)	**53**	(2.9)	**46**	(2.9)	**54**	(3.2)
Spain	**45**	(4.6)	**54**	(3.2)	**50**	(3.3)	**47**	(3.3)	**45**	(3.7)	**50**	(4.1)
Sweden	**42**	(3.4)	**50**	(3.3)	**52**	(3.9)	**53**	(3.9)	**34**	(3.5)	**43**	(3.6)
Turkey	**40**	(5.0)	**51**	(6.1)	**50**	(5.6)	**40**	(4.9)	m	m	m	m
England (United Kingdom)	**40**	(4.6)	**49**	(4.3)	**51**	(4.4)	**55**	(4.3)	m	m	m	m
United States	**42**	(3.9)	**50**	(3.1)	**49**	(3.2)	**51**	(3.1)	**45**	(3.4)	**49**	(3.1)
OECD average	**46**	(0.8)	**52**	(0.7)	**51**	(0.8)	**51**	(0.7)	**45**	(0.8)	**49**	(0.9)
Brazil	**46**	(5.9)	**47**	(6.6)	**39**	(6.1)	**44**	(5.9)	**49**	(6.3)	**41**	(6.7)
Bulgaria	**70**	(6.5)	**71**	(5.1)	**86**	(6.2)	**76**	(5.5)	m	m	m	m
Colombia	**47**	(5.0)	**44**	(4.3)	**50**	(4.4)	**43**	(4.0)	**35**	(4.4)	**53**	(5.2)
Croatia	**50**	(4.6)	**56**	(4.8)	**52**	(4.6)	**49**	(4.2)	m	m	m	m
Cyprus*	**49**	(3.1)	**58**	(2.8)	**51**	(3.4)	**60**	(3.2)	m	m	m	m
Hong Kong-China	**27**	(5.3)	**36**	(4.9)	**24**	(4.3)	**27**	(4.2)	**24**	(4.5)	**25**	(4.2)
Macao-China	**13**	(2.6)	**22**	(2.9)	**14**	(2.7)	**19**	(3.1)	**16**	(2.7)	**16**	(2.2)
Malaysia	**50**	(4.3)	**46**	(4.1)	**37**	(4.0)	**38**	(3.8)	m	m	m	m
Montenegro	**48**	(3.2)	**48**	(2.9)	**51**	(3.1)	**48**	(2.8)	m	m	m	m
Russian Federation	**50**	(3.4)	**46**	(4.2)	**52**	(4.3)	**50**	(4.2)	**38**	(3.4)	**39**	(3.5)
Serbia	**56**	(3.7)	**58**	(4.5)	**53**	(4.3)	**50**	(4.1)	m	m	m	m
Shanghai-China	**41**	(4.1)	**49**	(4.5)	**40**	(3.5)	**39**	(3.8)	**44**	(3.9)	**44**	(4.5)
Singapore	**47**	(3.2)	**60**	(3.3)	**57**	(3.3)	**62**	(3.5)	**53**	(3.3)	**45**	(3.1)
Chinese Taipei	**40**	(3.4)	**71**	(4.3)	**50**	(3.6)	**48**	(3.0)	**48**	(3.0)	**46**	(3.5)
United Arab Emirates	**63**	(3.7)	**53**	(3.1)	**49**	(3.4)	**51**	(3.4)	**48**	(2.9)	**69**	(4.4)
Uruguay	**74**	(5.0)	**76**	(5.0)	**73**	(5.2)	**75**	(5.1)	m	m	m	m

Note: Values that are statistically significant are indicated in bold (see Annex A3).
* See notes at the beginning of this Annex.
StatLink ⌗ http://dx.doi.org/10.1787/888933003706

[Part 2/3]
Differences in problem-solving, mathematics, reading and science performance related to parents' occupational status

Table V.4.16 *Results based on students' self-reports*

	Occupational status effect size: Difference in performance related to parents' highest occupation divided by the variation in scores within each country/economy (standard deviation)											
	Problem solving		Mathematics		Reading		Science		Computer-based mathematics		Digital reading	
	Effect size	S.E.	Effect size	S.E.	Effect size	S.E.	Effect size	S.E.	Effect size	S.E.	Effect size	S.E.
Australia	0.42	(0.02)	0.49	(0.02)	0.48	(0.02)	0.49	(0.02)	0.43	(0.02)	0.46	(0.02)
Austria	0.53	(0.04)	0.59	(0.04)	0.61	(0.03)	0.64	(0.04)	0.53	(0.04)	0.54	(0.05)
Belgium	0.55	(0.03)	0.70	(0.03)	0.70	(0.03)	0.70	(0.03)	0.62	(0.03)	0.62	(0.03)
Canada	0.33	(0.02)	0.48	(0.02)	0.42	(0.02)	0.41	(0.02)	0.37	(0.02)	0.34	(0.03)
Chile	0.58	(0.05)	0.73	(0.05)	0.69	(0.05)	0.69	(0.05)	0.63	(0.05)	0.64	(0.05)
Czech Republic	0.60	(0.03)	0.65	(0.03)	0.63	(0.03)	0.62	(0.03)	m	m	m	m
Denmark	0.44	(0.04)	0.60	(0.04)	0.59	(0.04)	0.57	(0.04)	0.47	(0.04)	0.57	(0.04)
Estonia	0.39	(0.04)	0.50	(0.03)	0.50	(0.04)	0.51	(0.04)	0.46	(0.04)	0.44	(0.04)
Finland	0.36	(0.04)	0.44	(0.03)	0.40	(0.03)	0.42	(0.03)	m	m	m	m
France	0.50	(0.04)	0.70	(0.03)	0.66	(0.04)	0.67	(0.03)	0.59	(0.04)	0.62	(0.04)
Germany	0.56	(0.04)	0.65	(0.04)	0.65	(0.04)	0.71	(0.04)	0.66	(0.04)	0.67	(0.04)
Hungary	0.67	(0.05)	0.71	(0.04)	0.68	(0.04)	0.53	(0.03)	0.44	(0.04)	0.41	(0.04)
Ireland	0.48	(0.03)	0.51	(0.03)	0.54	(0.03)	0.53	(0.03)	0.56	(0.06)	0.67	(0.06)
Israel	0.64	(0.05)	0.72	(0.05)	0.60	(0.06)	0.67	(0.05)	0.56	(0.06)	0.67	(0.06)
Italy	0.41	(0.05)	0.46	(0.04)	0.50	(0.04)	0.51	(0.04)	0.45	(0.04)	0.42	(0.04)
Japan	0.24	(0.04)	0.35	(0.04)	0.32	(0.04)	0.30	(0.04)	0.29	(0.04)	0.29	(0.03)
Korea	0.27	(0.03)	0.35	(0.04)	0.30	(0.03)	0.29	(0.04)	0.38	(0.03)	0.37	(0.03)
Netherlands	0.51	(0.05)	0.58	(0.04)	0.59	(0.04)	0.59	(0.05)	m	m	m	m
Norway	0.37	(0.04)	0.41	(0.04)	0.40	(0.04)	0.41	(0.04)	0.40	(0.04)	0.42	(0.04)
Poland	0.56	(0.04)	0.65	(0.04)	0.62	(0.04)	0.62	(0.04)	0.59	(0.04)	0.62	(0.04)
Portugal	0.58	(0.05)	0.69	(0.04)	0.63	(0.04)	0.67	(0.04)	0.57	(0.05)	0.66	(0.04)
Slovak Republic	0.67	(0.04)	0.72	(0.04)	0.72	(0.04)	0.74	(0.04)	0.71	(0.04)	0.70	(0.04)
Slovenia	0.53	(0.03)	0.58	(0.03)	0.59	(0.03)	0.59	(0.03)	0.53	(0.03)	0.55	(0.03)
Spain	0.43	(0.04)	0.62	(0.04)	0.55	(0.03)	0.56	(0.04)	0.55	(0.04)	0.52	(0.04)
Sweden	0.45	(0.04)	0.56	(0.03)	0.51	(0.04)	0.55	(0.04)	0.41	(0.04)	0.45	(0.04)
Turkey	0.50	(0.06)	0.56	(0.06)	0.59	(0.06)	0.51	(0.06)	m	m	m	m
England (United Kingdom)	0.43	(0.05)	0.53	(0.04)	0.54	(0.04)	0.57	(0.04)	m	m	m	m
United States	0.46	(0.04)	0.56	(0.03)	0.54	(0.03)	0.55	(0.03)	0.52	(0.04)	0.56	(0.03)
OECD average	0.48	(0.01)	0.57	(0.01)	0.56	(0.01)	0.56	(0.01)	0.51	(0.01)	0.52	(0.01)
Brazil	0.51	(0.06)	0.60	(0.07)	0.47	(0.06)	0.56	(0.06)	0.59	(0.07)	0.46	(0.07)
Bulgaria	0.68	(0.05)	0.77	(0.04)	0.76	(0.04)	0.77	(0.04)	m	m	m	m
Colombia	0.51	(0.05)	0.59	(0.05)	0.60	(0.05)	0.56	(0.05)	0.47	(0.06)	0.58	(0.05)
Croatia	0.55	(0.04)	0.64	(0.04)	0.62	(0.04)	0.57	(0.04)	m	m	m	m
Cyprus*	0.51	(0.03)	0.63	(0.03)	0.48	(0.03)	0.64	(0.03)	m	m	m	m
Hong Kong-China	0.29	(0.06)	0.38	(0.05)	0.29	(0.05)	0.33	(0.05)	0.29	(0.05)	0.27	(0.04)
Macao-China	0.17	(0.03)	0.24	(0.03)	0.18	(0.03)	0.24	(0.04)	0.19	(0.03)	0.23	(0.03)
Malaysia	0.60	(0.04)	0.57	(0.04)	0.45	(0.04)	0.49	(0.04)	m	m	m	m
Montenegro	0.53	(0.04)	0.59	(0.03)	0.56	(0.03)	0.58	(0.03)	m	m	m	m
Russian Federation	0.57	(0.03)	0.53	(0.05)	0.58	(0.04)	0.59	(0.05)	0.48	(0.04)	0.46	(0.04)
Serbia	0.63	(0.03)	0.64	(0.04)	0.58	(0.04)	0.58	(0.04)	m	m	m	m
Shanghai-China	0.46	(0.04)	0.49	(0.04)	0.51	(0.04)	0.48	(0.04)	0.47	(0.04)	0.53	(0.04)
Singapore	0.50	(0.03)	0.58	(0.03)	0.57	(0.03)	0.60	(0.03)	0.55	(0.03)	0.51	(0.03)
Chinese Taipei	0.46	(0.03)	0.63	(0.03)	0.57	(0.03)	0.60	(0.03)	0.56	(0.03)	0.54	(0.03)
United Arab Emirates	0.61	(0.03)	0.60	(0.03)	0.53	(0.03)	0.55	(0.03)	0.58	(0.03)	0.64	(0.04)
Uruguay	0.76	(0.04)	0.86	(0.04)	0.77	(0.04)	0.80	(0.04)	m	m	m	m

Note: Values that are statistically significant are indicated in bold (see Annex A3).
* See notes at the beginning of this Annex.
StatLink http://dx.doi.org/10.1787/888933003706

[Part 3/3]
Differences in problem-solving, mathematics, reading and science performance related to parents' occupational status

Table V.4.16 *Results based on students' self-reports*

		Difference in occupational status effect sizes between problem solving (PS) and...								
		... Mathematics (PS - M)		... Reading (PS - R)		... Science (PS - S)		... Computer-based mathematics (PS - CBM)		... Digital reading (PS - DR)	
		Effect size dif.	S.E.	Effect size dif.	S.E.	Effect size dif.	S.E.	Effect size dif.	S.E.	Effect size dif.	S.E.
OECD	Australia	-0.07	(0.02)	-0.06	(0.02)	-0.08	(0.02)	-0.01	(0.02)	-0.04	(0.02)
	Austria	-0.06	(0.03)	-0.07	(0.03)	-0.10	(0.03)	0.00	(0.03)	-0.01	(0.05)
	Belgium	-0.15	(0.02)	-0.15	(0.02)	-0.14	(0.02)	-0.07	(0.02)	-0.07	(0.02)
	Canada	-0.15	(0.02)	-0.09	(0.02)	-0.08	(0.02)	-0.04	(0.02)	-0.01	(0.02)
	Chile	-0.16	(0.02)	-0.11	(0.03)	-0.12	(0.03)	-0.05	(0.04)	-0.06	(0.03)
	Czech Republic	-0.05	(0.02)	-0.03	(0.03)	-0.02	(0.02)	m	m	m	m
	Denmark	-0.15	(0.03)	-0.15	(0.04)	-0.13	(0.03)	-0.02	(0.03)	-0.12	(0.04)
	Estonia	-0.11	(0.02)	-0.11	(0.03)	-0.12	(0.03)	-0.07	(0.03)	-0.05	(0.03)
	Finland	-0.09	(0.02)	-0.04	(0.03)	-0.06	(0.02)	m	m	m	m
	France	-0.20	(0.03)	-0.17	(0.03)	-0.17	(0.03)	-0.10	(0.03)	-0.12	(0.03)
	Germany	-0.09	(0.02)	-0.09	(0.03)	-0.07	(0.02)	-0.04	(0.03)	0.03	(0.03)
	Hungary	-0.04	(0.03)	-0.01	(0.03)	-0.04	(0.03)	0.01	(0.02)	0.00	(0.03)
	Ireland	-0.03	(0.02)	-0.06	(0.03)	-0.05	(0.02)	0.04	(0.03)	0.07	(0.03)
	Israel	-0.08	(0.02)	0.04	(0.03)	-0.03	(0.02)	0.08	(0.02)	-0.02	(0.03)
	Italy	-0.05	(0.03)	-0.09	(0.03)	-0.10	(0.03)	-0.04	(0.04)	-0.02	(0.03)
	Japan	-0.11	(0.03)	-0.08	(0.03)	-0.06	(0.03)	-0.04	(0.03)	-0.05	(0.03)
	Korea	-0.08	(0.02)	-0.04	(0.02)	-0.02	(0.02)	-0.12	(0.03)	-0.10	(0.03)
	Netherlands	-0.07	(0.03)	-0.07	(0.03)	-0.08	(0.03)	m	m	m	m
	Norway	-0.04	(0.03)	-0.03	(0.03)	-0.04	(0.03)	-0.03	(0.03)	-0.05	(0.03)
	Poland	-0.08	(0.03)	-0.06	(0.03)	-0.05	(0.04)	-0.03	(0.03)	-0.06	(0.03)
	Portugal	-0.10	(0.02)	-0.05	(0.03)	-0.09	(0.03)	0.01	(0.03)	-0.08	(0.03)
	Slovak Republic	-0.05	(0.03)	-0.04	(0.02)	-0.07	(0.02)	-0.04	(0.03)	-0.02	(0.03)
	Slovenia	-0.05	(0.02)	-0.06	(0.03)	-0.06	(0.02)	0.00	(0.02)	-0.02	(0.02)
	Spain	-0.19	(0.03)	-0.12	(0.03)	-0.12	(0.03)	-0.12	(0.03)	-0.08	(0.03)
	Sweden	-0.11	(0.03)	-0.07	(0.03)	-0.11	(0.03)	0.04	(0.03)	0.00	(0.03)
	Turkey	-0.06	(0.03)	-0.09	(0.04)	0.00	(0.03)	m	m	m	m
	England (United Kingdom)	-0.10	(0.03)	-0.12	(0.03)	-0.15	(0.03)	m	m	m	m
	United States	-0.10	(0.03)	-0.08	(0.03)	-0.09	(0.03)	-0.06	(0.03)	-0.10	(0.03)
	OECD average	-0.09	(0.00)	-0.07	(0.01)	-0.08	(0.01)	-0.03	(0.01)	-0.04	(0.01)
Partners	Brazil	-0.09	(0.03)	0.04	(0.04)	-0.05	(0.03)	-0.08	(0.04)	0.05	(0.03)
	Bulgaria	-0.09	(0.02)	-0.07	(0.03)	-0.08	(0.03)	m	m	m	m
	Colombia	-0.08	(0.03)	-0.09	(0.04)	-0.05	(0.04)	0.04	(0.04)	-0.07	(0.04)
	Croatia	-0.09	(0.02)	-0.07	(0.03)	-0.03	(0.03)	m	m	m	m
	Cyprus*	-0.13	(0.03)	0.03	(0.03)	-0.14	(0.03)	m	m	m	m
	Hong Kong-China	-0.08	(0.03)	0.00	(0.04)	-0.03	(0.04)	0.01	(0.04)	0.03	(0.04)
	Macao-China	-0.08	(0.03)	-0.01	(0.04)	-0.07	(0.04)	-0.02	(0.03)	-0.06	(0.03)
	Malaysia	0.03	(0.03)	0.15	(0.03)	0.11	(0.03)	m	m	m	m
	Montenegro	-0.06	(0.03)	-0.04	(0.03)	-0.05	(0.03)	m	m	m	m
	Russian Federation	0.04	(0.03)	0.00	(0.03)	-0.02	(0.03)	0.09	(0.03)	0.11	(0.03)
	Serbia	-0.01	(0.02)	0.06	(0.02)	0.06	(0.03)	m	m	m	m
	Shanghai-China	-0.03	(0.02)	-0.06	(0.02)	-0.02	(0.03)	-0.02	(0.03)	-0.08	(0.03)
	Singapore	-0.07	(0.02)	-0.06	(0.02)	-0.10	(0.02)	-0.05	(0.02)	0.00	(0.02)
	Chinese Taipei	-0.17	(0.02)	-0.11	(0.02)	-0.14	(0.02)	-0.10	(0.02)	-0.08	(0.03)
	United Arab Emirates	0.01	(0.03)	0.08	(0.03)	0.06	(0.03)	0.03	(0.03)	-0.03	(0.03)
	Uruguay	-0.10	(0.03)	-0.01	(0.04)	-0.04	(0.04)	m	m	m	m

Note: Values that are statistically significant are indicated in bold (see Annex A3).
* See notes at the beginning of this Annex.
StatLink http://dx.doi.org/10.1787/888933003706

[Part 1/1]
Relative performance in problem solving, by parents' occupational status

Table V.4.17 *Results based on students' self-reports*

Problem-solving performance of students whose parents' highest occupation is semi-skilled or elementary (ISCO 4 to 9), compared to students with similar performance in mathematics, reading and science with at least one parent working in a skilled occupation (ISCO 1 to 3)

	Average difference in problem solving compared with students from high-status families with similar performance in mathematics[1]		Percentage of students from low-status families who outperform students from high-status families with similar performance in mathematics[2]		Average difference in problem solving compared with students from high-status families with similar performance in reading[1]		Percentage of students from low-status families who outperform students from high-status families with similar performance in reading[2]		Average difference in problem solving compared with students from high-status families with similar performance in science[1]		Percentage of students from low-status families who outperform students from high-status families with similar performance in science[2]		Average difference in problem solving compared with students from high-status families with similar performance in mathematics, reading and science[3]		Percentage of students from low-status families who outperform students from high-status families with similar performance in mathematics, reading and science[2]	
	Score dif.	S.E.	%	S.E.	Score dif.	S.E.	%	S.E.	Score dif.	S.E.	%	S.E.	Score dif.	S.E.	%	S.E.
Australia	-1	(1.5)	50.4	(1.3)	-5	(1.7)	47.7	(1.3)	-2	(1.5)	49.5	(1.2)	1	(1.5)	51.5	(1.3)
Austria	-4	(3.1)	46.7	(2.6)	-6	(3.1)	46.0	(2.3)	-2	(3.9)	48.6	(3.1)	-1	(3.3)	49.5	(3.1)
Belgium	0	(2.4)	50.3	(1.7)	-4	(2.6)	48.3	(1.7)	-1	(2.3)	49.8	(1.5)	3	(2.2)	51.9	(1.7)
Canada	3	(1.7)	**53.0**	(1.2)	-3	(1.9)	48.4	(1.5)	-2	(1.8)	49.0	(1.3)	4	(1.6)	**53.2**	(1.3)
Chile	0	(2.6)	51.4	(2.0)	-5	(3.0)	46.9	(2.1)	-5	(3.0)	47.6	(2.2)	3	(2.7)	53.1	(2.2)
Czech Republic	-3	(2.7)	48.2	(2.7)	**-12**	(2.9)	**42.2**	(2.0)	**-8**	(3.1)	**44.4**	(2.3)	-2	(2.5)	49.2	(2.5)
Denmark	1	(2.7)	51.0	(2.3)	-3	(3.0)	48.2	(2.1)	-2	(2.8)	47.6	(2.2)	2	(2.6)	51.4	(2.2)
Estonia	2	(2.2)	54.2	(2.2)	-1	(2.4)	50.0	(2.3)	1	(2.3)	51.7	(2.1)	5	(2.1)	**55.6**	(2.3)
Finland	1	(2.1)	51.4	(2.1)	**-6**	(2.4)	**46.0**	(1.8)	-3	(2.3)	47.9	(2.0)	2	(2.0)	51.8	(2.0)
France	9	(2.7)	**59.6**	(2.2)	1	(2.9)	52.8	(2.2)	5	(2.5)	**55.7**	(2.0)	10	(2.6)	**60.8**	(2.2)
Germany	-2	(2.5)	50.5	(2.0)	-5	(2.8)	48.3	(2.1)	-3	(2.5)	48.1	(2.0)	1	(2.3)	51.4	(1.7)
Hungary	**-9**	(3.8)	**43.4**	(2.7)	**-14**	(3.9)	**39.9**	(2.7)	**-9**	(3.7)	**43.6**	(2.8)	-6	(3.7)	45.2	(2.7)
Ireland	**-6**	(2.3)	**44.4**	(2.0)	**-7**	(2.7)	**44.6**	(2.3)	**-6**	(2.5)	**46.0**	(1.9)	-2	(2.4)	49.2	(2.0)
Israel	-2	(3.0)	50.0	(2.2)	**-20**	(3.3)	**39.0**	(2.3)	**-9**	(3.3)	**44.0**	(2.1)	-2	(2.8)	49.2	(2.2)
Italy	**-7**	(3.1)	47.0	(2.2)	-7	(3.1)	46.6	(2.1)	-5	(3.2)	49.0	(2.3)	-4	(3.0)	48.9	(2.2)
Japan	1	(2.5)	51.8	(1.6)	-3	(2.7)	48.3	(1.7)	-3	(2.5)	48.9	(1.7)	1	(2.5)	51.6	(1.5)
Korea	0	(1.7)	51.2	(1.5)	-3	(2.1)	47.9	(1.8)	**-4**	(2.1)	47.2	(1.7)	0	(1.8)	50.8	(1.6)
Netherlands	-3	(3.4)	50.3	(2.8)	-5	(3.2)	48.9	(2.5)	-2	(3.5)	50.0	(2.8)	0	(3.3)	51.9	(2.8)
Norway	-4	(2.7)	47.7	(2.3)	**-9**	(3.1)	**45.8**	(1.9)	**-7**	(3.0)	47.1	(2.1)	-3	(2.6)	47.9	(2.1)
Poland	**-8**	(3.5)	46.4	(2.3)	**-10**	(3.3)	**44.8**	(2.4)	**-10**	(3.7)	**44.5**	(2.7)	-4	(3.3)	48.2	(2.5)
Portugal	-3	(2.4)	48.0	(2.2)	**-12**	(2.9)	**41.8**	(2.1)	**-8**	(2.9)	**44.7**	(2.6)	-2	(2.3)	48.8	(2.1)
Slovak Republic	**-9**	(2.9)	**43.6**	(2.4)	**-16**	(3.0)	**39.7**	(2.1)	**-12**	(3.0)	**42.6**	(2.3)	-7	(3.0)	**44.9**	(2.6)
Slovenia	**-6**	(2.4)	46.8	(1.6)	**-10**	(2.7)	**44.4**	(1.8)	**-7**	(2.4)	46.9	(1.8)	-4	(2.5)	48.8	(2.0)
Spain	4	(3.2)	**54.0**	(2.0)	**-6**	(2.9)	47.3	(1.6)	-3	(3.4)	49.6	(2.2)	4	(3.3)	**54.1**	(2.2)
Sweden	1	(2.8)	50.8	(2.2)	**-8**	(2.7)	**46.2**	(1.9)	-2	(2.7)	48.9	(2.2)	2	(2.6)	51.7	(2.2)
Turkey	-3	(2.4)	47.4	(2.5)	-4	(3.6)	47.1	(2.9)	**-7**	(2.5)	**44.7**	(2.0)	-1	(2.5)	48.6	(2.5)
England (United Kingdom)	2	(3.0)	52.6	(2.6)	0	(3.4)	51.3	(2.7)	5	(2.8)	**54.6**	(2.4)	4	(2.9)	54.6	(2.6)
United States	3	(2.3)	52.8	(2.6)	-2	(2.5)	48.1	(2.2)	0	(2.4)	50.5	(2.4)	4	(2.3)	53.7	(2.4)
OECD average	**-2**	(0.5)	49.8	(0.4)	**-7**	(0.5)	**46.3**	(0.4)	**-4**	(0.5)	**48.0**	(0.4)	0	(0.5)	**50.9**	(0.4)
Brazil	-3	(2.8)	48.1	(2.3)	**-16**	(3.5)	**39.9**	(2.2)	**-8**	(3.1)	45.4	(2.3)	-3	(2.8)	48.2	(2.2)
Bulgaria	**-9**	(3.3)	46.4	(2.2)	**-15**	(3.6)	**42.6**	(2.0)	**-11**	(3.6)	**45.1**	(2.2)	-5	(3.2)	48.7	(2.0)
Colombia	-5	(3.5)	47.5	(2.5)	**-9**	(3.8)	**44.9**	(2.4)	**-11**	(4.1)	**43.5**	(2.6)	-3	(3.7)	48.5	(2.6)
Croatia	-2	(2.4)	50.2	(2.2)	**-9**	(2.8)	**43.8**	(1.8)	**-9**	(2.9)	**44.1**	(2.1)	-1	(2.3)	50.4	(2.1)
Cyprus*	0	(3.2)	49.9	(2.4)	**-17**	(2.8)	**40.5**	(1.9)	-2	(2.8)	49.0	(1.9)	1	(3.0)	50.5	(2.3)
Hong Kong-China	-1	(3.1)	50.7	(2.5)	-7	(3.5)	46.2	(2.3)	-5	(3.7)	47.0	(2.3)	-1	(3.1)	50.0	(2.5)
Macao-China	1	(2.0)	51.8	(1.7)	-5	(2.4)	47.7	(2.0)	-1	(2.3)	50.6	(2.1)	1	(2.1)	52.0	(1.7)
Malaysia	**-11**	(2.3)	**41.7**	(2.4)	**-24**	(2.6)	**34.6**	(1.9)	**-19**	(2.3)	**36.5**	(1.9)	-11	(2.2)	**41.2**	(2.2)
Montenegro	-5	(2.7)	46.2	(2.4)	**-13**	(2.8)	**41.9**	(2.2)	**-9**	(3.0)	**44.2**	(2.0)	-4	(2.8)	46.6	(2.4)
Russian Federation	**-16**	(2.5)	**39.5**	(1.8)	**-18**	(2.4)	**38.9**	(1.5)	**-17**	(2.7)	**40.1**	(1.6)	-15	(2.6)	**40.4**	(1.9)
Serbia	**-10**	(2.3)	**42.9**	(2.1)	**-20**	(2.4)	**37.8**	(1.6)	**-18**	(2.5)	**38.3**	(1.8)	-9	(2.3)	**42.8**	(2.0)
Shanghai-China	-5	(2.1)	47.1	(2.0)	-5	(2.2)	47.4	(1.7)	-7	(2.4)	**45.4**	(2.0)	-3	(2.1)	48.4	(1.9)
Singapore	-3	(2.0)	48.3	(1.9)	**-8**	(2.4)	**45.4**	(1.7)	-3	(2.1)	48.6	(2.4)	-2	(2.0)	48.8	(1.8)
Chinese Taipei	7	(1.8)	**57.1**	(2.1)	-1	(2.2)	49.0	(1.8)	3	(2.0)	52.5	(2.0)	7	(1.9)	**56.9**	(1.9)
United Arab Emirates	**-15**	(3.2)	**42.4**	(2.2)	**-23**	(3.2)	**36.9**	(1.9)	**-20**	(3.0)	**38.2**	(2.1)	-14	(3.0)	**41.6**	(2.1)
Uruguay	-8	(4.3)	46.4	(2.9)	**-23**	(4.2)	**37.2**	(2.3)	**-18**	(3.8)	**39.9**	(2.3)	-5	(3.7)	47.8	(2.7)

OECD (Australia through OECD average); *Partners* (Brazil through Uruguay)

Note: Values that are statistically significant are indicated in bold (see Annex A3).

1. This column reports the difference between actual performance and the fitted value from a regression using a cubic polynomial as regression function.

2. This column reports the percentage of students for whom the difference between actual performance and the fitted value from a regression is positive. Values that are indicated in bold are significantly larger or smaller than 50%.

3. This column reports the difference between actual performance and the fitted value from a regression using a second-degree polynomial as regression function (math, math sq., read, read sq., scie, scie sq., math×read, math×scie, read×scie).

* See notes at the beginning of this Annex.

StatLink http://dx.doi.org/10.1787/888933003706

[Part 1/1]

Performance on problem-solving tasks, by nature of problem and by parents' occupational status

Table V.4.18a *Results based on students' self-reports*

	Items referring to a static problem situation					Items referring to an interactive problem situation				
	Average proportion of full-credit responses, by parents' highest occupation			Relative likelihood of success, in favour of students with at least one parent working in a skilled occupation (semi-skilled or elementary = 1.00)		Average proportion of full-credit responses, by parents' highest occupation			Relative likelihood of success, in favour of students with at least one parent working in a skilled occupation (semi-skilled or elementary = 1.00)	
	Semi-skilled or elementary (ISCO 4 to 9)	Skilled (ISCO 1 to 3)	Difference related to parents' occupational status (skilled - semi-skilled or elementary)	Accounting for booklet effects[1]	Based on success on remaining test items[2]	Semi-skilled or elementary (ISCO 4 to 9)	Skilled (ISCO 1 to 3)	Difference related to parents' occupational status (skilled - semi-skilled or elementary)	Accounting for booklet effects[1]	Based on success on remaining test items[2]
	% | S.E.	% | S.E.	% dif. | S.E.	Odds ratio | S.E.	Odds ratio | S.E.	% | S.E.	% | S.E.	% dif. | S.E.	Odds ratio | S.E.	Odds ratio | S.E.
OECD										
Australia	47.1 (0.8)	55.9 (0.5)	8.8 (0.9)	1.41 (0.05)	1.00 (0.04)	44.3 (0.8)	53.1 (0.5)	8.8 (0.8)	1.41 (0.04)	1.00 (0.04)
Austria	44.3 (1.5)	53.2 (1.2)	8.9 (1.7)	1.47 (0.10)	0.94 (0.08)	38.1 (1.2)	48.4 (1.1)	10.3 (1.5)	1.57 (0.10)	1.07 (0.09)
Belgium	41.0 (1.2)	56.3 (0.9)	15.3 (1.6)	1.84 (0.12)	1.14 (0.07)	40.0 (0.9)	51.9 (0.8)	11.9 (1.3)	1.60 (0.08)	0.87 (0.05)
Canada	49.2 (1.0)	55.2 (0.9)	6.0 (1.4)	1.31 (0.07)	0.92 (0.06)	45.8 (0.9)	53.9 (0.8)	8.0 (1.2)	1.42 (0.07)	1.08 (0.07)
Chile	31.5 (1.0)	41.7 (1.7)	10.2 (2.0)	1.55 (0.14)	0.91 (0.08)	27.8 (0.9)	39.8 (1.3)	12.0 (1.6)	1.70 (0.12)	1.10 (0.09)
Czech Republic	41.3 (0.9)	53.8 (0.8)	12.5 (1.2)	1.66 (0.08)	0.98 (0.05)	39.5 (0.9)	52.5 (0.8)	13.0 (1.1)	1.70 (0.08)	1.02 (0.05)
Denmark	43.1 (1.6)	52.0 (1.1)	8.9 (2.0)	1.46 (0.11)	0.96 (0.07)	37.2 (1.3)	46.8 (0.8)	9.6 (1.5)	1.52 (0.10)	1.04 (0.08)
Estonia	46.0 (1.3)	53.8 (1.3)	7.8 (2.1)	1.36 (0.11)	1.04 (0.09)	42.4 (1.1)	49.0 (1.3)	6.6 (1.7)	1.31 (0.09)	0.96 (0.08)
Finland	47.1 (1.0)	55.0 (0.8)	7.9 (1.2)	1.38 (0.07)	1.05 (0.05)	43.6 (1.0)	50.2 (0.7)	6.6 (1.1)	1.31 (0.06)	0.95 (0.04)
France	45.1 (1.4)	55.1 (1.1)	10.0 (1.9)	1.52 (0.11)	0.92 (0.08)	41.5 (1.2)	53.2 (0.9)	11.7 (1.5)	1.65 (0.10)	1.08 (0.09)
Germany	45.1 (1.6)	56.6 (1.1)	11.5 (2.1)	1.59 (0.12)	0.96 (0.08)	41.0 (1.4)	53.4 (1.0)	12.3 (1.5)	1.66 (0.11)	1.04 (0.08)
Hungary	32.0 (1.3)	48.5 (1.6)	16.6 (1.9)	2.09 (0.18)	1.03 (0.08)	28.1 (1.1)	43.1 (1.4)	14.9 (1.8)	2.02 (0.17)	0.97 (0.07)
Ireland	39.6 (1.7)	49.4 (1.1)	9.8 (2.1)	1.47 (0.12)	0.95 (0.08)	39.2 (1.3)	49.9 (1.1)	10.8 (1.7)	1.55 (0.11)	1.05 (0.09)
Israel	30.6 (1.6)	46.5 (1.7)	15.9 (2.2)	2.06 (0.20)	0.88 (0.07)	24.8 (1.3)	42.5 (1.6)	17.6 (1.7)	2.34 (0.19)	1.13 (0.09)
Italy	48.5 (1.4)	52.0 (1.4)	3.5 (2.0)	1.21 (0.09)	0.98 (0.08)	45.6 (1.3)	49.9 (1.3)	4.3 (1.8)	1.24 (0.09)	1.02 (0.09)
Japan	57.4 (1.1)	60.7 (1.0)	3.3 (1.4)	1.14 (0.06)	0.94 (0.05)	53.9 (0.9)	58.9 (0.9)	5.0 (1.2)	1.21 (0.06)	1.06 (0.06)
Korea	56.0 (1.3)	61.4 (1.3)	5.5 (1.7)	1.31 (0.10)	1.10 (0.08)	56.1 (1.4)	59.1 (1.3)	3.1 (1.8)	1.18 (0.08)	0.91 (0.07)
Netherlands	42.2 (1.5)	54.9 (1.2)	12.7 (1.6)	1.67 (0.11)	0.97 (0.06)	38.0 (1.6)	51.3 (1.2)	13.3 (1.8)	1.73 (0.13)	1.06 (0.06)
Norway	44.2 (1.8)	52.4 (1.1)	8.2 (2.0)	1.44 (0.12)	0.98 (0.09)	38.8 (1.6)	47.4 (1.1)	8.6 (1.9)	1.47 (0.12)	1.02 (0.09)
Poland	39.5 (1.4)	50.9 (1.4)	11.4 (2.1)	1.60 (0.13)	0.95 (0.08)	34.8 (1.2)	47.1 (1.6)	12.3 (1.8)	1.69 (0.13)	1.05 (0.09)
Portugal	41.6 (1.3)	50.2 (1.6)	8.6 (2.2)	1.52 (0.14)	0.86 (0.06)	38.0 (1.1)	50.6 (1.3)	12.5 (1.5)	1.77 (0.11)	1.16 (0.09)
Slovak Republic	41.1 (1.2)	54.0 (1.3)	12.9 (1.6)	1.71 (0.11)	1.11 (0.08)	36.9 (1.1)	47.0 (1.3)	10.1 (1.9)	1.53 (0.12)	0.90 (0.07)
Slovenia	36.2 (1.2)	49.8 (1.2)	13.6 (1.9)	1.81 (0.14)	1.06 (0.10)	31.0 (1.1)	42.5 (1.2)	11.5 (1.6)	1.72 (0.13)	0.95 (0.07)
Spain	38.4 (1.1)	47.7 (1.2)	9.4 (1.7)	1.47 (0.10)	1.01 (0.07)	36.1 (0.9)	45.1 (1.1)	9.0 (1.3)	1.46 (0.08)	0.99 (0.07)
Sweden	43.1 (1.5)	51.7 (1.2)	8.6 (2.2)	1.44 (0.12)	0.96 (0.09)	36.5 (1.2)	45.7 (0.9)	9.2 (1.5)	1.51 (0.09)	1.05 (0.10)
Turkey	34.5 (0.9)	42.4 (1.7)	7.9 (1.6)	1.41 (0.09)	0.93 (0.08)	31.3 (0.8)	40.5 (1.7)	9.2 (1.4)	1.51 (0.09)	1.08 (0.07)
England (United Kingdom)	45.9 (1.0)	52.9 (1.2)	7.0 (1.4)	1.32 (0.07)	1.00 (0.07)	44.7 (1.3)	51.7 (1.2)	7.0 (1.6)	1.31 (0.09)	1.00 (0.07)
United States	39.3 (1.5)	51.2 (1.2)	11.8 (1.9)	1.67 (0.13)	1.08 (0.08)	40.0 (1.3)	50.2 (1.2)	10.1 (1.7)	1.55 (0.11)	0.93 (0.07)
OECD average	42.5 (0.2)	52.3 (0.2)	9.8 (0.3)	1.52 (0.02)	0.98 (0.01)	39.1 (0.2)	49.1 (0.2)	10.0 (0.3)	1.54 (0.02)	1.02 (0.01)
Partners										
Brazil	27.8 (1.5)	35.3 (1.8)	7.4 (2.6)	1.45 (0.17)	0.92 (0.11)	26.3 (1.2)	35.5 (1.6)	9.2 (1.9)	1.57 (0.14)	1.08 (0.12)
Bulgaria	24.4 (1.0)	37.0 (1.3)	12.5 (1.6)	1.82 (0.13)	0.89 (0.05)	18.1 (0.7)	31.1 (1.1)	13.0 (1.2)	2.04 (0.14)	1.12 (0.07)
Colombia	24.2 (1.0)	33.0 (2.0)	8.8 (2.2)	1.55 (0.16)	0.99 (0.08)	21.9 (0.7)	30.4 (1.4)	8.5 (1.5)	1.57 (0.12)	1.01 (0.08)
Croatia	35.4 (1.0)	45.7 (1.3)	10.2 (1.4)	1.53 (0.09)	1.01 (0.06)	32.1 (0.9)	41.8 (1.2)	9.7 (1.3)	1.52 (0.08)	0.99 (0.06)
Cyprus*	33.3 (0.7)	43.7 (0.9)	10.3 (1.2)	1.55 (0.08)	0.97 (0.05)	27.9 (0.6)	38.2 (0.8)	10.3 (1.0)	1.60 (0.07)	1.03 (0.05)
Hong Kong-China	56.4 (1.2)	58.0 (1.4)	1.6 (1.9)	1.06 (0.08)	0.83 (0.07)	50.7 (0.9)	56.7 (1.5)	6.0 (1.8)	1.28 (0.09)	1.21 (0.10)
Macao-China	56.6 (0.7)	59.4 (1.4)	2.8 (1.6)	1.13 (0.08)	1.00 (0.08)	51.0 (0.8)	54.0 (1.0)	3.0 (1.4)	1.13 (0.07)	1.00 (0.08)
Malaysia	26.8 (0.7)	36.0 (1.4)	9.2 (1.5)	1.54 (0.10)	0.86 (0.05)	23.0 (0.7)	34.9 (1.2)	11.9 (1.2)	1.79 (0.10)	1.16 (0.07)
Montenegro	28.3 (0.8)	34.8 (1.0)	6.6 (1.2)	1.35 (0.08)	0.94 (0.05)	23.1 (0.7)	30.2 (0.8)	7.1 (1.1)	1.44 (0.08)	1.07 (0.04)
Russian Federation	38.6 (1.3)	48.4 (1.3)	9.8 (2.0)	1.51 (0.13)	0.99 (0.07)	34.3 (1.0)	43.9 (1.1)	9.6 (1.4)	1.53 (0.09)	1.01 (0.07)
Serbia	34.3 (1.0)	48.6 (1.0)	14.2 (1.4)	1.80 (0.11)	1.08 (0.06)	31.9 (0.9)	43.8 (1.0)	11.9 (1.4)	1.66 (0.10)	0.92 (0.05)
Shanghai-China	51.1 (1.4)	60.6 (1.3)	9.5 (1.6)	1.45 (0.10)	0.99 (0.07)	44.7 (1.3)	54.5 (1.0)	9.8 (1.4)	1.46 (0.09)	1.01 (0.07)
Singapore	53.7 (1.5)	63.4 (0.9)	9.7 (1.8)	1.53 (0.11)	1.12 (0.09)	53.2 (1.4)	60.2 (1.0)	7.0 (1.9)	1.36 (0.10)	0.89 (0.07)
Chinese Taipei	52.7 (1.3)	63.3 (1.3)	10.6 (1.9)	1.58 (0.13)	1.05 (0.07)	46.6 (1.2)	56.5 (1.1)	9.8 (1.7)	1.50 (0.09)	0.95 (0.07)
United Arab Emirates	22.9 (1.6)	33.1 (0.7)	10.1 (1.8)	1.74 (0.17)	0.87 (0.10)	18.9 (1.2)	31.1 (0.6)	12.2 (1.3)	2.00 (0.16)	1.15 (0.14)
Uruguay	24.4 (0.7)	37.3 (1.5)	12.9 (1.7)	1.84 (0.14)	0.97 (0.05)	21.8 (0.6)	34.7 (1.4)	12.9 (1.4)	1.91 (0.13)	1.03 (0.06)

Note: Values that are statistically significant are indicated in bold (see Annex A3).

1. Generalised odds ratios estimated with logistic regression on national PISA samples. A success indicator for each item is regressed on an item type dummy, an occupational status dummy, and an interaction term (occupational status × item type). Booklet dummies are added to the estimation. This column presents the difference between the logit coefficient on the interaction term and the logit coefficient on the item type dummy in exponentiated form.

2. Generalised odds ratios estimated with logistic regression on national PISA samples. A success indicator for each item is regressed on an item type dummy, an occupational status dummy, and an interaction term (occupational status × item type). Booklet dummies are added to the estimation. This column presents the logit coefficient on the interaction term in exponentiated form.

* See notes at the beginning of this Annex.

StatLink ᴍᴤᴘ http://dx.doi.org/10.1787/888933003706

[Part 1/2]

Table V.4.18b **Performance on problem-solving tasks, by process and by parents' occupational status**

Results based on students' self-reports

		Items assessing the process of "exploring and understanding"										Items assessing the process of "representing and formulating"									
		Average proportion of full-credit responses, by parents' highest occupation						Relative likelihood of success, in favour of students with at least one parent working in a skilled occupation (semi-skilled or elementary = 1.00)				Average proportion of full-credit responses, by parents' highest occupation						Relative likelihood of success, in favour of students with at least one parent working in a skilled occupation (semi-skilled or elementary = 1.00)			
		Semi-skilled or elementary (ISCO 4 to 9)		Skilled (ISCO 1 to 3)		Difference related to parents' occupational status (skilled - semi-skilled or elementary)		Accounting for booklet effects[1]		Based on success on remaining test items[2]		Semi-skilled or elementary (ISCO 4 to 9)		Skilled (ISCO 1 to 3)		Difference related to parents' occupational status (skilled - semi-skilled or elementary)		Accounting for booklet effects[1]		Based on success on remaining test items[2]	
		%	S.E.	%	S.E.	% dif.	S.E.	Odds ratio	S.E.	Odds ratio	S.E.	%	S.E.	%	S.E.	% dif.	S.E.	Odds ratio	S.E.	Odds ratio	S.E.
OECD	Australia	48.8	(1.0)	58.5	(0.6)	**9.7**	(1.0)	**1.47**	(0.06)	1.05	(0.04)	43.9	(1.0)	52.5	(0.7)	**8.6**	(1.1)	**1.40**	(0.06)	0.99	(0.04)
	Austria	42.4	(1.3)	56.8	(1.5)	**14.4**	(1.8)	**1.85**	(0.15)	**1.28**	(0.09)	36.0	(1.4)	47.7	(1.5)	**11.7**	(1.9)	**1.68**	(0.14)	1.12	(0.08)
	Belgium	41.7	(1.2)	57.3	(1.0)	**15.6**	(1.6)	**1.87**	(0.13)	**1.15**	(0.07)	38.5	(1.2)	52.3	(0.9)	**13.7**	(1.4)	**1.74**	(0.10)	1.05	(0.06)
	Canada	47.7	(1.2)	58.6	(0.8)	**10.8**	(1.4)	**1.61**	(0.10)	**1.22**	(0.06)	45.6	(1.1)	54.4	(1.1)	**8.8**	(1.4)	**1.48**	(0.08)	1.09	(0.05)
	Chile	28.8	(1.1)	39.8	(1.8)	**11.1**	(2.0)	**1.62**	(0.15)	0.98	(0.07)	24.0	(1.1)	39.9	(1.7)	**15.9**	(2.1)	**2.08**	(0.21)	**1.35**	(0.10)
	Czech Republic	41.3	(1.0)	55.9	(0.9)	**14.7**	(1.1)	**1.81**	(0.08)	**1.10**	(0.04)	37.9	(1.0)	50.9	(1.0)	**12.9**	(1.3)	**1.70**	(0.09)	1.01	(0.04)
	Denmark	40.9	(1.3)	50.5	(1.3)	**9.6**	(1.9)	**1.51**	(0.11)	1.01	(0.06)	36.1	(1.8)	47.2	(1.3)	**11.1**	(2.0)	**1.63**	(0.14)	1.11	(0.07)
	Estonia	44.5	(1.6)	52.9	(1.7)	**8.5**	(2.5)	**1.41**	(0.15)	1.08	(0.09)	42.1	(1.4)	47.0	(1.5)	**4.9**	(2.1)	**1.23**	(0.10)	0.91	(0.05)
	Finland	47.2	(1.1)	57.4	(0.8)	**10.2**	(1.3)	**1.52**	(0.08)	**1.18**	(0.05)	41.7	(1.3)	49.0	(0.9)	**7.3**	(1.7)	**1.35**	(0.09)	1.01	(0.05)
	France	46.1	(1.5)	57.9	(1.3)	**11.8**	(2.0)	**1.64**	(0.13)	1.03	(0.07)	40.8	(1.4)	52.9	(1.2)	**12.1**	(1.9)	**1.67**	(0.13)	1.06	(0.07)
	Germany	44.7	(1.9)	59.7	(1.2)	**15.0**	(2.2)	**1.86**	(0.16)	**1.18**	(0.08)	38.0	(1.6)	52.3	(1.4)	**14.3**	(2.2)	**1.80**	(0.17)	1.13	(0.08)
	Hungary	31.1	(1.3)	48.1	(1.8)	**17.0**	(2.2)	**2.17**	(0.21)	1.08	(0.08)	26.3	(1.3)	42.1	(1.7)	**15.9**	(2.2)	**2.16**	(0.23)	1.07	(0.08)
	Ireland	41.4	(2.0)	53.8	(1.2)	**12.4**	(2.2)	**1.66**	(0.16)	1.12	(0.09)	36.2	(1.5)	46.8	(1.3)	**10.6**	(2.0)	**1.57**	(0.13)	1.04	(0.08)
	Israel	30.5	(1.8)	49.6	(1.7)	**19.1**	(2.2)	**2.35**	(0.24)	1.08	(0.09)	25.0	(1.7)	42.0	(1.9)	**17.1**	(2.3)	**2.30**	(0.26)	1.04	(0.09)
	Italy	48.7	(1.6)	57.3	(1.8)	**8.6**	(2.3)	**1.49**	(0.13)	**1.29**	(0.10)	46.3	(1.4)	49.8	(1.6)	3.5	(1.8)	**1.20**	(0.10)	0.97	(0.07)
	Japan	60.1	(1.2)	65.2	(1.1)	**5.1**	(1.3)	**1.23**	(0.07)	1.05	(0.05)	53.8	(1.1)	58.6	(1.0)	**4.8**	(1.3)	**1.20**	(0.07)	1.02	(0.04)
	Korea	61.5	(1.4)	67.6	(1.4)	**6.1**	(1.8)	**1.38**	(0.11)	**1.16**	(0.07)	58.1	(1.9)	62.8	(1.5)	**4.7**	(2.1)	**1.28**	(0.11)	1.06	(0.07)
	Netherlands	42.6	(1.8)	56.8	(1.2)	**14.2**	(1.8)	**1.79**	(0.13)	1.06	(0.04)	34.2	(1.6)	49.7	(1.4)	**15.4**	(1.8)	**1.91**	(0.15)	**1.15**	(0.06)
	Norway	45.5	(2.1)	54.5	(1.1)	**8.9**	(2.3)	**1.49**	(0.15)	1.03	(0.08)	37.4	(1.8)	46.7	(1.4)	**9.3**	(2.2)	**1.52**	(0.15)	1.06	(0.09)
	Poland	38.9	(1.4)	51.3	(1.8)	**12.4**	(2.2)	**1.67**	(0.15)	1.01	(0.07)	32.6	(1.4)	47.4	(1.8)	**14.9**	(2.0)	**1.90**	(0.15)	**1.19**	(0.08)
	Portugal	39.8	(1.6)	51.9	(1.7)	**12.2**	(2.3)	**1.74**	(0.18)	1.05	(0.10)	35.1	(1.6)	48.6	(1.8)	**13.5**	(2.4)	**1.85**	(0.19)	1.13	(0.11)
	Slovak Republic	41.7	(1.4)	51.9	(1.9)	**10.1**	(2.2)	**1.51**	(0.14)	0.93	(0.07)	34.2	(1.3)	47.3	(1.6)	**13.0**	(2.0)	**1.75**	(0.15)	1.12	(0.07)
	Slovenia	32.4	(1.4)	46.7	(1.5)	**14.4**	(2.2)	**1.91**	(0.19)	1.12	(0.10)	29.1	(1.4)	42.3	(1.3)	**13.2**	(1.9)	**1.87**	(0.15)	1.09	(0.08)
	Spain	38.2	(1.0)	48.3	(1.5)	**10.1**	(1.6)	**1.52**	(0.11)	1.05	(0.06)	32.6	(1.1)	43.6	(1.4)	**11.1**	(1.8)	**1.61**	(0.13)	1.13	(0.08)
	Sweden	42.8	(1.6)	52.9	(1.2)	**10.1**	(1.9)	**1.55**	(0.12)	1.06	(0.08)	34.4	(1.5)	47.5	(1.3)	**13.2**	(2.0)	**1.80**	(0.15)	**1.28**	(0.09)
	Turkey	31.7	(0.8)	43.5	(2.2)	**11.7**	(2.1)	**1.67**	(0.14)	**1.18**	(0.07)	30.2	(1.0)	40.3	(2.0)	**10.1**	(1.8)	**1.58**	(0.12)	1.09	(0.06)
	England (United Kingdom)	48.7	(1.4)	54.6	(1.4)	**5.8**	(1.8)	**1.26**	(0.09)	0.94	(0.05)	42.6	(1.4)	52.4	(1.4)	**9.8**	(1.8)	**1.48**	(0.11)	**1.16**	(0.06)
	United States	40.5	(1.6)	54.6	(1.2)	**14.1**	(1.9)	**1.83**	(0.16)	**1.20**	(0.08)	39.1	(1.8)	47.6	(1.6)	**8.5**	(2.3)	**1.45**	(0.14)	0.89	(0.06)
	OECD average	42.5	(0.3)	54.1	(0.3)	**11.6**	(0.4)	**1.64**	(0.03)	**1.09**	(0.01)	37.6	(0.3)	48.6	(0.3)	**11.1**	(0.4)	**1.63**	(0.03)	**1.08**	(0.01)
Partners	Brazil	28.3	(1.5)	35.6	(1.8)	**7.2**	(2.1)	**1.41**	(0.14)	0.90	(0.07)	21.4	(1.3)	33.7	(2.4)	**12.3**	(2.7)	**1.88**	(0.25)	**1.30**	(0.12)
	Bulgaria	23.5	(1.0)	37.2	(1.4)	**13.7**	(1.7)	**1.94**	(0.15)	0.99	(0.05)	14.9	(0.9)	27.8	(1.3)	**12.9**	(1.5)	**2.20**	(0.20)	**1.16**	(0.08)
	Colombia	22.3	(1.0)	32.9	(2.2)	**10.6**	(2.4)	**1.71**	(0.20)	1.13	(0.12)	16.5	(0.9)	26.3	(2.0)	**9.7**	(2.1)	**1.81**	(0.21)	**1.20**	(0.11)
	Croatia	32.9	(1.0)	44.6	(1.4)	**11.8**	(1.5)	**1.65**	(0.10)	**1.11**	(0.05)	29.1	(1.1)	39.8	(1.7)	**10.8**	(1.6)	**1.61**	(0.12)	1.08	(0.06)
	Cyprus*	32.9	(0.8)	42.3	(0.9)	**9.4**	(1.2)	**1.50**	(0.08)	0.93	(0.04)	26.6	(0.7)	38.3	(1.0)	**11.7**	(1.2)	**1.72**	(0.09)	**1.11**	(0.04)
	Hong Kong-China	58.8	(1.3)	65.0	(1.7)	**6.2**	(1.9)	**1.31**	(0.11)	1.12	(0.07)	53.7	(1.2)	59.2	(1.7)	**5.5**	(2.0)	**1.27**	(0.10)	1.08	(0.08)
	Macao-China	58.2	(1.0)	63.6	(1.4)	**5.4**	(1.6)	**1.28**	(0.10)	**1.17**	(0.08)	56.9	(1.1)	58.6	(1.3)	1.7	(1.7)	1.08	(0.08)	0.94	(0.06)
	Malaysia	26.2	(0.8)	37.0	(1.5)	**10.7**	(1.6)	**1.65**	(0.12)	0.96	(0.05)	23.4	(0.9)	35.9	(1.5)	**12.5**	(1.5)	**1.83**	(0.13)	**1.11**	(0.05)
	Montenegro	24.6	(0.9)	32.6	(1.0)	**8.0**	(1.4)	**1.47**	(0.10)	1.07	(0.06)	21.6	(0.7)	28.8	(1.1)	**7.3**	(1.4)	**1.47**	(0.11)	1.06	(0.06)
	Russian Federation	35.5	(1.4)	47.6	(1.6)	**12.1**	(2.1)	**1.68**	(0.16)	1.14	(0.09)	32.3	(1.7)	43.2	(1.3)	**11.0**	(2.1)	**1.62**	(0.15)	1.09	(0.09)
	Serbia	33.5	(1.2)	47.8	(1.2)	**14.3**	(1.7)	**1.81**	(0.13)	1.08	(0.06)	30.1	(1.0)	43.5	(1.3)	**13.4**	(1.7)	**1.79**	(0.13)	1.06	(0.07)
	Shanghai-China	53.1	(1.6)	62.2	(1.4)	**9.1**	(2.0)	**1.43**	(0.12)	0.98	(0.08)	48.3	(1.9)	60.7	(1.5)	**12.4**	(2.2)	**1.63**	(0.15)	1.15	(0.10)
	Singapore	56.6	(1.7)	68.6	(1.1)	**12.0**	(2.0)	**1.72**	(0.15)	**1.29**	(0.10)	54.9	(1.7)	62.6	(1.2)	**7.7**	(2.3)	**1.41**	(0.13)	0.99	(0.08)
	Chinese Taipei	54.5	(1.4)	65.6	(1.4)	**11.1**	(1.9)	**1.61**	(0.13)	1.07	(0.07)	51.7	(1.6)	62.1	(1.5)	**10.4**	(2.1)	**1.54**	(0.13)	1.01	(0.06)
	United Arab Emirates	21.5	(1.5)	33.6	(0.8)	**12.1**	(1.7)	**1.91**	(0.19)	1.01	(0.09)	17.4	(1.5)	30.3	(0.8)	**13.0**	(1.5)	**2.11**	(0.21)	1.14	(0.12)
	Uruguay	23.8	(0.6)	37.9	(1.6)	**14.1**	(1.7)	**1.95**	(0.14)	1.05	(0.05)	18.4	(0.8)	34.1	(1.7)	**15.7**	(1.8)	**2.30**	(0.20)	**1.28**	(0.07)

Note: Values that are statistically significant are indicated in bold (see Annex A3).

1. Generalised odds ratios estimated with logistic regression on national PISA samples. A success indicator for each item is regressed on an item type dummy, an occupational status dummy, and an interaction term (occupational status × item type). Booklet dummies are added to the estimation. This column presents the difference between the logit coefficient on the interaction term and the logit coefficient on the item type dummy in exponentiated form.

2. Generalised odds ratios estimated with logistic regression on national PISA samples. A success indicator for each item is regressed on an item type dummy, an occupational status dummy, and an interaction term (occupational status × item type). Booklet dummies are added to the estimation. This column presents the logit coefficient on the interaction term in exponentiated form.

* See notes at the beginning of this Annex.

StatLink http://dx.doi.org/10.1787/888933003706

[Part 2/2]

Performance on problem-solving tasks, by process and by parents' occupational status

Table V.4.18b *Results based on students' self-reports*

	Items assessing the process of "planning and executing"										Items assessing the process of "monitoring and reflecting"									
	Average proportion of full-credit responses, by parents' highest occupation						Relative likelihood of success, in favour of students with at least one parent working in a skilled occupation (semi-skilled or elementary = 1.00)				Average proportion of full-credit responses, by parents' highest occupation						Relative likelihood of success, in favour of students with at least one parent working in a skilled occupation (semi-skilled or elementary = 1.00)			
	Semi-skilled or elementary (ISCO 4 to 9)		Skilled (ISCO 1 to 3)		Difference related to parents' occupational status (skilled - semi-skilled or elementary)		Accounting for booklet effects[1]		Based on success on remaining test items[2]		Semi-skilled or elementary (ISCO 4 to 9)		Skilled (ISCO 1 to 3)		Difference related to parents' occupational status (skilled - semi-skilled or elementary)		Accounting for booklet effects[1]		Based on success on remaining test items[2]	
	%	S.E.	%	S.E.	% dif.	S.E.	Odds ratio	S.E.	Odds ratio	S.E.	%	S.E.	%	S.E.	% dif.	S.E.	Odds ratio	S.E.	Odds ratio	S.E.
Australia	46.3	(0.8)	54.4	(0.5)	8.2	(0.9)	**1.37**	(0.05)	0.96	(0.03)	39.9	(0.8)	49.3	(0.5)	9.4	(0.9)	**1.46**	(0.06)	1.04	(0.04)
Austria	43.9	(1.4)	51.5	(1.0)	7.5	(1.6)	**1.39**	(0.09)	**0.85**	(0.05)	34.5	(1.6)	40.4	(1.0)	5.9	(1.8)	**1.32**	(0.11)	**0.83**	(0.07)
Belgium	41.7	(0.9)	53.9	(0.9)	**12.2**	(1.5)	**1.61**	(0.09)	0.93	(0.05)	37.6	(1.0)	.48.3	(1.1)	10.8	(1.6)	**1.54**	(0.10)	0.90	(0.05)
Canada	49.3	(0.9)	54.3	(0.8)	5.0	(1.2)	**1.25**	(0.06)	**0.85**	(0.04)	42.7	(1.1)	48.3	(1.0)	5.6	(1.4)	**1.28**	(0.08)	0.91	(0.06)
Chile	31.9	(0.9)	41.5	(1.2)	9.6	(1.4)	**1.50**	(0.10)	0.87	(0.05)	29.6	(1.0)	39.5	(1.4)	9.9	(1.9)	**1.54**	(0.13)	0.92	(0.06)
Czech Republic	42.3	(0.8)	54.3	(0.8)	**12.0**	(1.1)	**1.62**	(0.07)	0.94	(0.03)	36.3	(1.0)	48.2	(0.9)	**12.0**	(1.2)	**1.64**	(0.09)	0.97	(0.03)
Denmark	42.8	(1.5)	52.5	(0.9)	9.6	(1.7)	**1.51**	(0.10)	1.01	(0.06)	32.9	(1.5)	39.0	(1.2)	6.1	(1.9)	**1.33**	(0.11)	0.87	(0.08)
Estonia	45.9	(1.1)	53.5	(1.2)	7.6	(1.7)	**1.35**	(0.09)	1.03	(0.07)	39.6	(1.2)	45.7	(1.2)	6.2	(1.7)	**1.29**	(0.10)	0.97	(0.07)
Finland	47.3	(0.9)	53.4	(0.7)	6.1	(1.1)	**1.28**	(0.06)	0.94	(0.04)	40.0	(1.0)	44.4	(0.7)	4.4	(1.2)	**1.20**	(0.06)	**0.88**	(0.04)
France	43.7	(1.4)	54.3	(0.9)	10.6	(1.7)	**1.57**	(0.10)	0.96	(0.06)	38.7	(1.2)	49.0	(1.2)	10.3	(1.7)	**1.56**	(0.12)	0.96	(0.07)
Germany	45.4	(1.3)	55.7	(1.0)	10.3	(1.6)	**1.52**	(0.10)	**0.89**	(0.05)	38.4	(1.4)	47.3	(1.2)	8.8	(1.6)	**1.44**	(0.10)	**0.86**	(0.06)
Hungary	31.6	(1.1)	47.6	(1.4)	**16.1**	(1.8)	**2.05**	(0.16)	1.00	(0.06)	26.6	(1.3)	38.3	(1.8)	11.7	(2.0)	**1.76**	(0.17)	0.84	(0.06)
Ireland	40.8	(1.3)	50.1	(1.0)	9.3	(1.7)	**1.44**	(0.10)	0.92	(0.05)	37.2	(1.7)	46.8	(1.4)	9.6	(2.1)	**1.47**	(0.13)	0.96	(0.08)
Israel	27.5	(1.5)	43.8	(1.7)	**16.3**	(1.9)	**2.14**	(0.19)	0.94	(0.07)	22.9	(1.3)	38.4	(1.5)	15.5	(1.7)	**2.19**	(0.19)	0.98	(0.07)
Italy	47.7	(1.2)	49.4	(1.4)	1.7	(1.8)	1.12	(0.08)	**0.86**	(0.05)	41.9	(1.3)	44.9	(1.4)	2.9	(2.0)	1.17	(0.10)	0.94	(0.07)
Japan	54.8	(1.0)	58.5	(0.9)	3.7	(1.3)	**1.15**	(0.06)	0.96	(0.04)	50.6	(0.9)	54.8	(1.1)	4.2	(1.5)	**1.18**	(0.07)	0.99	(0.05)
Korea	53.1	(1.2)	55.7	(1.3)	2.6	(1.8)	**1.15**	(0.08)	0.90	(0.05)	52.2	(1.6)	55.1	(1.4)	2.9	(2.1)	1.16	(0.10)	0.93	(0.07)
Netherlands	42.2	(1.6)	54.2	(1.2)	**12.0**	(1.8)	**1.63**	(0.12)	0.92	(0.04)	35.7	(1.6)	46.8	(1.3)	11.1	(1.8)	**1.59**	(0.12)	0.92	(0.05)
Norway	42.4	(1.7)	51.1	(1.1)	8.6	(1.9)	**1.47**	(0.12)	1.01	(0.07)	34.6	(1.5)	40.4	(1.4)	5.8	(1.9)	**1.32**	(0.12)	0.89	(0.06)
Poland	39.4	(1.3)	50.2	(1.4)	10.8	(1.9)	**1.56**	(0.12)	0.91	(0.06)	31.4	(1.3)	41.9	(1.6)	10.5	(2.1)	**1.59**	(0.15)	0.95	(0.07)
Portugal	42.5	(1.0)	53.3	(1.6)	10.7	(1.8)	**1.64**	(0.12)	0.97	(0.07)	36.5	(1.3)	44.4	(1.9)	7.9	(2.2)	**1.47**	(0.14)	0.86	(0.07)
Slovak Republic	40.4	(1.1)	52.6	(1.3)	**12.2**	(1.7)	**1.65**	(0.11)	1.06	(0.06)	34.4	(1.2)	42.1	(1.4)	7.8	(2.0)	**1.41**	(0.13)	0.87	(0.07)
Slovenia	36.6	(1.0)	48.2	(1.1)	11.6	(1.5)	**1.66**	(0.11)	0.92	(0.05)	29.6	(1.2)	39.4	(1.0)	9.9	(1.6)	**1.60**	(0.12)	0.90	(0.07)
Spain	39.1	(1.1)	46.9	(1.0)	7.8	(1.4)	**1.38**	(0.08)	0.91	(0.06)	35.7	(1.2)	43.8	(1.4)	8.1	(1.8)	**1.40**	(0.11)	0.95	(0.07)
Sweden	40.8	(1.2)	48.0	(0.9)	7.2	(1.6)	**1.36**	(0.08)	**0.88**	(0.05)	34.5	(1.2)	40.8	(1.3)	6.2	(1.8)	**1.33**	(0.10)	**0.86**	(0.06)
Turkey	35.0	(0.8)	41.5	(1.3)	6.5	(1.2)	**1.33**	(0.07)	**0.84**	(0.04)	30.5	(0.9)	38.4	(2.0)	7.9	(2.0)	**1.43**	(0.12)	0.97	(0.07)
England (United Kingdom)	45.1	(1.2)	53.0	(1.1)	7.9	(1.4)	**1.37**	(0.08)	1.06	(0.05)	43.4	(1.5)	46.3	(1.1)	2.9	(1.7)	1.12	(0.08)	**0.82**	(0.05)
United States	40.8	(1.4)	51.3	(1.1)	10.4	(1.6)	**1.56**	(0.10)	0.98	(0.05)	37.4	(1.8)	46.9	(1.3)	9.6	(2.1)	**1.51**	(0.13)	0.94	(0.07)
OECD average	42.2	(0.2)	51.2	(0.2)	**9.1**	(0.3)	**1.47**	(0.02)	**0.94**	(0.01)	36.6	(0.2)	44.6	(0.2)	**8.0**	(0.3)	**1.42**	(0.02)	**0.92**	(0.01)
Brazil	29.9	(1.4)	37.7	(1.6)	7.8	(2.1)	**1.45**	(0.14)	0.92	(0.07)	24.5	(1.1)	32.4	(1.6)	8.0	(2.0)	**1.52**	(0.16)	0.99	(0.09)
Bulgaria	22.7	(0.8)	35.2	(1.1)	**12.5**	(1.2)	**1.85**	(0.11)	0.92	(0.04)	17.8	(0.8)	29.8	(1.3)	**12.1**	(1.4)	**1.97**	(0.15)	1.02	(0.05)
Colombia	26.1	(1.0)	34.2	(1.6)	8.1	(1.9)	**1.48**	(0.13)	0.92	(0.06)	23.7	(1.0)	28.8	(1.5)	5.2	(1.7)	**1.32**	(0.11)	**0.82**	(0.08)
Croatia	37.5	(0.9)	46.0	(1.2)	8.5	(1.3)	**1.42**	(0.07)	**0.89**	(0.04)	29.9	(0.9)	39.0	(1.2)	9.1	(1.2)	**1.50**	(0.08)	0.98	(0.05)
Cyprus*	31.3	(0.6)	41.3	(0.9)	9.9	(1.0)	**1.54**	(0.07)	0.96	(0.03)	26.2	(0.6)	36.8	(0.9)	10.6	(1.1)	**1.64**	(0.09)	1.05	(0.05)
Hong Kong-China	51.0	(1.0)	53.1	(1.5)	2.2	(1.9)	1.08	(0.08)	**0.85**	(0.05)	47.2	(1.2)	52.4	(1.8)	5.2	(2.2)	**1.24**	(0.11)	1.04	(0.08)
Macao-China	50.8	(0.6)	53.4	(1.3)	2.5	(1.4)	**1.11**	(0.06)	0.98	(0.06)	45.8	(1.0)	47.1	(1.3)	1.2	(1.7)	1.05	(0.08)	0.91	(0.06)
Malaysia	25.4	(0.7)	35.7	(1.1)	10.3	(1.1)	**1.63**	(0.08)	0.94	(0.05)	20.5	(0.6)	31.1	(1.2)	10.6	(1.3)	**1.75**	(0.11)	1.04	(0.05)
Montenegro	28.1	(0.8)	35.0	(0.8)	6.8	(1.2)	**1.37**	(0.08)	0.96	(0.05)	22.4	(0.8)	27.7	(1.0)	5.2	(1.2)	**1.32**	(0.09)	0.93	(0.05)
Russian Federation	39.5	(1.0)	47.5	(1.0)	8.0	(1.5)	**1.40**	(0.09)	**0.87**	(0.05)	32.5	(1.1)	41.2	(1.4)	8.6	(1.6)	**1.48**	(0.10)	0.97	(0.06)
Serbia	35.7	(0.9)	47.8	(0.9)	**12.1**	(1.2)	**1.65**	(0.09)	0.94	(0.04)	28.4	(1.2)	39.6	(1.1)	11.2	(1.7)	**1.65**	(0.13)	0.96	(0.05)
Shanghai-China	45.6	(1.2)	52.8	(1.0)	7.2	(1.4)	**1.31**	(0.08)	**0.84**	(0.06)	39.7	(1.6)	52.6	(1.3)	13.0	(1.8)	**1.67**	(0.13)	**1.18**	(0.08)
Singapore	51.7	(1.4)	57.6	(1.0)	5.9	(1.8)	**1.29**	(0.09)	**0.86**	(0.05)	50.6	(1.6)	58.1	(1.1)	7.5	(2.1)	**1.38**	(0.11)	0.97	(0.07)
Chinese Taipei	47.2	(1.2)	55.8	(1.1)	8.6	(1.8)	**1.43**	(0.10)	0.90	(0.05)	40.4	(1.3)	52.4	(1.5)	11.9	(2.0)	**1.64**	(0.13)	1.09	(0.08)
United Arab Emirates	21.8	(1.3)	32.7	(0.7)	10.9	(1.3)	**1.83**	(0.13)	0.94	(0.06)	19.2	(1.2)	29.0	(0.8)	9.8	(1.5)	**1.80**	(0.17)	0.94	(0.08)
Uruguay	25.0	(0.7)	37.1	(1.3)	**12.1**	(1.5)	**1.77**	(0.12)	**0.90**	(0.04)	21.5	(0.7)	31.0	(1.5)	9.5	(1.5)	**1.64**	(0.12)	**0.85**	(0.04)

Note: Values that are statistically significant are indicated in bold (see Annex A3).

1. Generalised odds ratios estimated with logistic regression on national PISA samples. A success indicator for each item is regressed on an item type dummy, an occupational status dummy, and an interaction term (occupational status × item type). Booklet dummies are added to the estimation. This column presents the difference between the logit coefficient on the interaction term and the logit coefficient on the item type dummy in exponentiated form.

2. Generalised odds ratios estimated with logistic regression on national PISA samples. A success indicator for each item is regressed on an item type dummy, an occupational status dummy, and an interaction term (occupational status × item type). Booklet dummies are added to the estimation. This column presents the logit coefficient on the interaction term in exponentiated form.

* See notes at the beginning of this Annex.

StatLink http://dx.doi.org/10.1787/888933003706

[Part 1/2]
Performance in problem solving and immigrant background
Table V.4.19   *Results based on students' self-reports*

	Non-immigrant students				Second-generation immigrant students				First-generation immigrant students				Students with an immigrant background (first- or second-generation immigrant students)			
	Percentage of students		Performance in problem solving		Percentage of students		Performance in problem solving		Percentage of students		Performance in problem solving		Percentage of students		Performance in problem solving	
	%	S.E.	Mean score	S.E.	%	S.E.	Mean score	S.E.	%	S.E.	Mean score	S.E.	%	S.E.	Mean score	S.E.
OECD																
Australia	77.3	(0.7)	524	(1.9)	12.4	(0.6)	537	(4.8)	10.3	(0.4)	524	(4.0)	22.7	(0.7)	531	(3.4)
Austria	83.5	(1.1)	516	(3.6)	10.9	(0.7)	465	(6.0)	5.6	(0.6)	454	(8.6)	16.5	(1.1)	461	(5.7)
Belgium	84.7	(0.9)	522	(2.5)	8.0	(0.6)	438	(7.0)	7.3	(0.6)	455	(7.7)	15.3	(0.9)	446	(6.0)
Canada	70.4	(1.3)	532	(2.2)	16.6	(0.8)	519	(5.6)	13.0	(0.7)	521	(5.9)	29.6	(1.3)	520	(5.0)
Chile	99.1	(0.2)	448	(3.7)	0.2	(0.1)	c	c	0.7	(0.1)	454	(15.7)	0.9	(0.2)	448	(15.5)
Czech Republic	96.7	(0.4)	510	(3.2)	1.4	(0.3)	477	(20.6)	1.9	(0.2)	482	(11.5)	3.3	(0.4)	480	(11.4)
Denmark	90.8	(0.6)	505	(2.9)	6.1	(0.5)	436	(7.6)	3.0	(0.2)	424	(7.6)	9.2	(0.6)	432	(6.0)
Estonia	91.9	(0.5)	519	(2.5)	7.5	(0.5)	489	(7.3)	0.7	(0.2)	c	c	8.1	(0.5)	486	(7.3)
Finland	96.6	(0.2)	526	(2.3)	1.5	(0.1)	461	(5.7)	1.9	(0.2)	426	(8.2)	3.4	(0.2)	442	(5.2)
France	85.0	(1.1)	523	(3.5)	10.0	(0.8)	464	(8.7)	5.0	(0.5)	432	(10.3)	15.0	(1.1)	454	(7.1)
Germany	86.6	(0.8)	523	(3.4)	10.6	(0.7)	475	(6.8)	2.8	(0.3)	463	(10.6)	13.4	(0.8)	473	(6.1)
Hungary	98.3	(0.2)	459	(4.0)	1.0	(0.2)	482	(14.7)	0.8	(0.2)	c	c	1.7	(0.2)	479	(14.0)
Ireland	89.8	(0.7)	501	(3.4)	1.7	(0.2)	493	(14.1)	8.5	(0.7)	487	(5.6)	10.2	(0.7)	488	(5.1)
Israel	81.7	(1.2)	452	(5.7)	12.7	(0.8)	481	(9.4)	5.6	(0.6)	460	(10.7)	18.3	(1.2)	474	(8.4)
Italy	92.7	(0.6)	514	(4.1)	1.9	(0.3)	493	(10.1)	5.4	(0.5)	451	(10.5)	7.3	(0.6)	462	(9.2)
Japan	99.7	(0.1)	553	(3.1)	0.2	(0.1)	c	c	0.1	(0.0)	c	c	0.3	(0.1)	c	c
Korea	100.0	(0.0)	562	(4.3)	0.0	(0.0)	c	c	0.0	(0.0)	c	c	0.0	(0.0)	c	c
Netherlands	89.1	(1.0)	520	(4.0)	8.1	(0.9)	450	(9.7)	2.7	(0.4)	440	(15.8)	10.9	(1.0)	448	(9.5)
Norway	90.5	(0.9)	510	(3.0)	4.7	(0.6)	467	(17.1)	4.8	(0.5)	446	(8.7)	9.5	(0.9)	457	(10.5)
Poland	99.8	(0.1)	482	(4.4)	0.2	(0.1)	c	c	0.0	(0.0)	c	c	0.2	(0.1)	c	c
Portugal	93.1	(0.6)	498	(3.6)	3.3	(0.4)	459	(10.5)	3.6	(0.5)	475	(8.0)	6.9	(0.6)	468	(7.7)
Slovak Republic	99.3	(0.2)	485	(3.5)	0.4	(0.1)	c	c	0.3	(0.1)	c	c	0.7	(0.2)	512	(29.8)
Slovenia	91.3	(0.5)	481	(1.4)	6.5	(0.4)	453	(5.5)	2.2	(0.2)	383	(13.9)	8.7	(0.5)	435	(6.0)
Spain	89.6	(0.8)	482	(4.0)	1.4	(0.2)	458	(15.2)	9.0	(0.7)	440	(6.9)	10.4	(0.8)	443	(7.1)
Sweden	85.1	(0.9)	501	(3.2)	8.7	(0.6)	461	(5.8)	6.2	(0.5)	417	(9.1)	14.9	(0.9)	443	(5.1)
Turkey	99.1	(0.2)	455	(4.0)	0.7	(0.2)	489	(28.6)	0.2	(0.1)	c	c	0.9	(0.2)	466	(25.1)
England (United Kingdom)	85.7	(1.3)	523	(4.0)	6.4	(0.6)	474	(8.5)	7.9	(1.0)	503	(10.3)	14.3	(1.3)	490	(7.8)
United States	78.4	(2.0)	512	(3.8)	14.8	(1.4)	503	(6.9)	6.8	(0.8)	487	(11.4)	21.6	(2.0)	498	(7.1)
OECD average	90.2	(0.2)	505	(0.7)	5.6	(0.1)	475	(2.4)	4.2	(0.1)	458	(2.2)	9.8	(0.2)	469	(2.2)
Partners																
Brazil	99.3	(0.2)	431	(4.7)	0.4	(0.2)	c	c	0.3	(0.1)	c	c	0.7	(0.2)	409	(18.7)
Bulgaria	99.5	(0.2)	405	(5.0)	0.4	(0.2)	c	c	0.2	(0.1)	c	c	0.5	(0.2)	c	c
Colombia	99.7	(0.1)	400	(3.5)	0.2	(0.0)	c	c	0.1	(0.1)	c	c	0.3	(0.1)	322	(24.3)
Croatia	87.9	(0.8)	467	(4.0)	8.4	(0.5)	458	(6.0)	3.7	(0.4)	469	(8.5)	12.1	(0.8)	461	(5.4)
Cyprus*	91.5	(0.4)	447	(1.5)	1.8	(0.3)	457	(10.4)	6.7	(0.3)	429	(6.2)	8.5	(0.4)	435	(5.2)
Hong Kong-China	65.3	(1.5)	545	(4.7)	20.5	(0.8)	544	(3.7)	14.2	(1.0)	519	(5.1)	34.7	(1.5)	534	(3.7)
Macao-China	34.9	(0.6)	538	(1.8)	49.7	(0.7)	545	(1.7)	15.4	(0.4)	535	(3.0)	65.1	(0.6)	543	(1.4)
Malaysia	98.3	(0.3)	424	(3.5)	1.7	(0.3)	417	(8.6)	0.1	(0.0)	c	c	1.7	(0.3)	415	(8.4)
Montenegro	94.2	(0.4)	406	(1.2)	2.7	(0.2)	439	(9.6)	3.1	(0.3)	412	(8.7)	5.8	(0.4)	425	(6.9)
Russian Federation	89.1	(0.8)	490	(3.6)	7.7	(0.6)	485	(5.9)	3.2	(0.4)	476	(8.7)	10.9	(0.8)	482	(5.5)
Serbia	91.5	(0.8)	474	(3.2)	6.6	(0.6)	480	(7.1)	1.9	(0.3)	473	(14.5)	8.5	(0.8)	478	(7.1)
Shanghai-China	99.1	(0.2)	538	(3.2)	0.3	(0.1)	c	c	0.6	(0.1)	437	(13.8)	0.9	(0.2)	428	(12.7)
Singapore	81.7	(0.8)	561	(1.4)	5.9	(0.3)	592	(5.4)	12.4	(0.7)	567	(4.3)	18.3	(0.8)	575	(3.2)
Chinese Taipei	99.5	(0.1)	535	(2.9)	0.4	(0.1)	c	c	0.1	(0.0)	c	c	0.5	(0.1)	534	(15.4)
United Arab Emirates	45.2	(1.4)	376	(3.4)	23.2	(0.7)	424	(3.8)	31.6	(1.0)	459	(3.7)	54.8	(1.4)	444	(3.2)
Uruguay	99.5	(0.1)	405	(3.4)	0.2	(0.1)	c	c	0.3	(0.1)	c	c	0.5	(0.1)	c	c

Notes: Values that are statistically significant are indicated in bold (see Annex A3).
This table was calculated considering all students with information on their immigrant status (students with missing data on the *PISA index of economic, social and cultural status* included).
* See notes at the beginning of this Annex.
StatLink ⬛ᵍᵉᴸ http://dx.doi.org/10.1787/888933003706

[Part 2/2]
Performance in problem solving and immigrant background
Table V.4.19   *Results based on students' self-reports*

	Difference in problem-solving performance										Increased likelihood of students with an immigrant background scoring below Level 2 (less than 423.42 score points)		Increased likelihood of students with an immigrant background scoring at or above Level 5 (above 618.21 score points)	
	Second-generation immigrant students minus non-immigrant students		First-generation immigrant students minus non-immigrant students		First-generation immigrant students minus second-generation immigrant students		Students with an immigrant background minus non-immigrant students		Students with an immigrant background minus non-immigrant students, after accounting for students' socio-economic status					
	Score dif.	S.E.	Score dif.	S.E.	Score dif.	S.E.	Score dif.	S.E.	Score dif.	S.E.	Relative risk	S.E.	Relative risk	S.E.
Australia	13	(4.6)	0	(3.9)	-14	(5.9)	7	(3.1)	10	(3.0)	0.99	(0.07)	1.20	(0.09)
Austria	-51	(5.6)	-62	(9.2)	-12	(8.6)	-55	(5.8)	-32	(5.1)	2.24	(0.26)	0.30	(0.09)
Belgium	-84	(6.9)	-67	(7.5)	17	(8.7)	-76	(5.8)	-56	(4.9)	2.50	(0.20)	0.30	(0.05)
Canada	-13	(5.7)	-11	(5.9)	2	(5.6)	-12	(5.1)	-9	(4.8)	1.32	(0.12)	0.93	(0.09)
Chile	c	c	6	(15.2)	c	c	0	(14.6)	-9	(13.7)	1.00	(0.21)	1.31	(0.62)
Czech Republic	-34	(20.3)	-28	(12.0)	6	(22.7)	-30	(11.5)	-22	(11.0)	1.51	(0.27)	0.70	(0.21)
Denmark	-69	(8.5)	-80	(7.5)	-12	(9.7)	-72	(6.7)	-51	(5.8)	2.66	(0.24)	0.30	(0.07)
Estonia	-30	(7.2)	c	c	c	c	-33	(7.1)	-33	(6.8)	1.77	(0.22)	0.61	(0.15)
Finland	-65	(6.1)	-100	(7.9)	-35	(10.4)	-85	(5.1)	-65	(4.4)	3.28	(0.24)	0.30	(0.07)
France	-59	(8.6)	-91	(10.5)	-32	(12.7)	-69	(7.2)	-48	(6.8)	2.81	(0.35)	0.27	(0.08)
Germany	-48	(6.7)	-60	(10.4)	-12	(11.9)	-50	(5.9)	-24	(5.4)	2.09	(0.21)	0.39	(0.08)
Hungary	23	(14.4)	c	c	c	c	19	(13.7)	0	(14.4)	0.73	(0.22)	1.24	(0.50)
Ireland	-8	(14.2)	-14	(6.0)	-7	(15.5)	-13	(5.5)	-15	(5.2)	1.18	(0.13)	0.69	(0.16)
Israel	28	(8.3)	8	(11.4)	-20	(10.8)	22	(7.8)	32	(6.9)	0.79	(0.08)	1.12	(0.17)
Italy	-21	(9.5)	-63	(9.8)	-42	(12.3)	-52	(8.4)	-42	(8.4)	2.51	(0.31)	0.69	(0.16)
Japan	c	c	c	c	c	c	c	c	c	c	c	c	c	c
Korea	c	c	c	c	c	c	c	c	c	c	c	c	c	c
Netherlands	-70	(9.1)	-80	(14.7)	-10	(15.9)	-73	(8.4)	-52	(9.1)	2.62	(0.29)	0.31	(0.09)
Norway	-43	(16.7)	-63	(8.7)	-20	(16.2)	-53	(10.1)	-37	(10.1)	2.02	(0.22)	0.59	(0.16)
Poland	c	c	c	c	c	c	c	c	c	c	c	c	c	c
Portugal	-38	(10.4)	-23	(7.8)	16	(11.0)	-30	(7.5)	-25	(8.5)	1.62	(0.20)	0.71	(0.22)
Slovak Republic	c	c	c	c	c	c	27	(29.7)	26	(24.0)	1.03	(0.37)	2.57	(1.16)
Slovenia	-28	(5.6)	-98	(13.9)	-69	(14.1)	-46	(6.1)	-21	(5.7)	1.75	(0.13)	0.60	(0.19)
Spain	-24	(14.7)	-41	(6.3)	-17	(13.6)	-39	(6.4)	-25	(6.2)	1.59	(0.13)	0.58	(0.15)
Sweden	-40	(5.8)	-84	(9.6)	-44	(11.0)	-58	(5.4)	-43	(5.4)	2.09	(0.18)	0.29	(0.08)
Turkey	34	(28.6)	c	c	c	c	11	(25.2)	4	(22.0)	1.06	(0.27)	4.28	(3.09)
England (United Kingdom)	-49	(8.4)	-20	(9.8)	29	(11.7)	-33	(7.5)	-28	(6.2)	1.80	(0.23)	0.63	(0.14)
United States	-9	(6.6)	-25	(11.2)	-16	(10.8)	-14	(6.7)	9	(5.9)	1.32	(0.18)	0.86	(0.15)
OECD average	-30	(2.4)	-47	(2.2)	-15	(2.8)	-32	(2.2)	-22	(2.0)	1.77	(0.05)	0.87	(0.14)
Brazil	c	c	c	c	c	c	-22	(18.1)	-39	(19.1)	1.29	(0.23)	1.13	(2.50)
Bulgaria	c	c	c	c	c	c	c	c	c	c	c	c	c	c
Colombia	c	c	c	c	c	c	-78	(24.2)	-75	(22.1)	1.33	(0.18)	0.00	c
Croatia	-9	(6.0)	2	(8.2)	11	(9.3)	-6	(5.2)	3	(4.9)	1.04	(0.11)	0.56	(0.17)
Cyprus*	10	(10.6)	-18	(6.1)	-28	(12.3)	-12	(5.3)	-6	(5.0)	1.18	(0.08)	1.20	(0.32)
Hong Kong-China	-1	(4.2)	-26	(5.7)	-25	(4.7)	-11	(4.3)	3	(3.8)	1.10	(0.15)	0.81	(0.07)
Macao-China	7	(2.7)	-2	(3.6)	-9	(3.5)	5	(2.5)	8	(2.6)	0.79	(0.09)	1.03	(0.08)
Malaysia	-7	(8.6)	c	c	c	c	-9	(8.4)	11	(8.9)	1.11	(0.14)	0.24	(0.81)
Montenegro	33	(9.7)	6	(8.9)	-28	(11.8)	18	(7.1)	14	(6.7)	0.83	(0.08)	0.97	(1.11)
Russian Federation	-5	(5.3)	-14	(8.6)	-9	(9.1)	-8	(5.0)	-5	(4.5)	1.16	(0.13)	0.93	(0.18)
Serbia	6	(7.0)	-1	(14.1)	-7	(14.4)	5	(6.9)	4	(6.3)	0.93	(0.11)	1.53	(0.31)
Shanghai-China	c	c	-101	(13.6)	c	c	-110	(12.7)	-86	(13.4)	4.12	(0.92)	0.06	(0.13)
Singapore	31	(5.8)	6	(4.6)	-25	(7.4)	14	(3.7)	-1	(3.9)	0.68	(0.11)	1.20	(0.08)
Chinese Taipei	c	c	c	c	c	c	-1	(14.9)	16	(14.0)	0.80	(0.66)	0.66	(0.46)
United Arab Emirates	48	(4.3)	84	(4.4)	36	(4.0)	69	(3.9)	65	(3.8)	0.60	(0.02)	9.30	(3.05)
Uruguay	c	c	c	c	c	c	c	c	c	c	c	c	c	c

Notes: Values that are statistically significant are indicated in bold (see Annex A3).
This table was calculated considering all students with information on their immigrant status (students with missing data on the *PISA index of economic, social and cultural status* included).
* See notes at the beginning of this Annex.
StatLink 🔗 http://dx.doi.org/10.1787/888933003706

[Part 1/3]
Differences in problem-solving, mathematics, reading and science performance related to immigrant background

Table V.4.20 *Results based on students' self-reports*

		Score-point difference related to immigrant background: Immigrant minus non-immigrant students										
		Problem solving		Mathematics		Reading		Science		Computer-based mathematics		Digital reading	
		Score dif.	S.E.	Score dif.	S.E.	Score dif.	S.E.	Score dif.	S.E.	Score dif.	S.E.	Score dif.	S.E.
OECD	Australia	7	(3.1)	26	(3.5)	19	(3.0)	11	(3.5)	22	(3.5)	18	(3.4)
	Austria	-55	(5.8)	-60	(5.2)	-51	(5.8)	-70	(5.0)	-48	(5.9)	-62	(6.8)
	Belgium	-76	(5.8)	-76	(5.1)	-66	(4.2)	-10	(4.7)	7	(5.5)	1	(4.0)
	Canada	-12	(5.1)	-2	(4.5)	3	(4.2)	-10	(4.7)	7	(5.5)	1	(4.0)
	Chile	0	(14.6)	-1	(13.3)	9	(14.2)	2	(13.1)	17	(13.5)	32	(15.5)
	Czech Republic	-30	(11.5)	-28	(11.5)	-20	(10.4)	-38	(10.7)	m	m	m	m
	Denmark	-72	(6.7)	-67	(3.5)	-59	(3.5)	-80	(3.8)	-62	(5.3)	-61	(3.6)
	Estonia	-33	(7.1)	-30	(5.8)	-35	(5.2)	-32	(5.9)	-41	(5.5)	-45	(7.4)
	Finland	-85	(5.1)	-86	(4.9)	-93	(5.1)	-106	(5.4)	m	m	m	m
	France	-69	(7.2)	-67	(6.9)	-67	(8.5)	-77	(8.6)	-58	(7.1)	-54	(8.4)
	Germany	-50	(5.9)	-56	(5.9)	-49	(5.7)	-66	(6.1)	-40	(6.2)	-44	(6.0)
	Hungary	19	(13.7)	32	(13.1)	16	(14.0)	24	(11.5)	4	(13.1)	16	(16.9)
	Ireland	-13	(5.5)	-3	(4.7)	-11	(4.9)	-2	(5.0)	1	(5.1)	-11	(5.8)
	Israel	22	(7.8)	7	(5.7)	8	(6.2)	10	(6.4)	7	(6.4)	14	(6.7)
	Italy	-52	(8.4)	-49	(7.4)	-64	(8.9)	-52	(7.6)	-53	(5.9)	-42	(8.4)
	Japan	c	c	c	c	c	c	c	c	c	c	c	c
	Korea	c	c	c	c	c	c	c	c	c	c	c	c
	Netherlands	-73	(8.4)	-58	(7.0)	-56	(7.8)	-68	(6.8)	m	m	m	m
	Norway	-53	(10.1)	-47	(6.7)	-50	(6.5)	-69	(7.4)	-35	(6.9)	-65	(8.6)
	Poland	c	c	c	c	c	c	c	c	c	c	c	c
	Portugal	-30	(7.5)	-44	(7.1)	-38	(7.8)	-44	(7.5)	-35	(6.0)	-45	(6.4)
	Slovak Republic	27	(29.7)	6	(21.1)	7	(20.3)	-10	(21.5)	31	(19.0)	2	(25.4)
	Slovenia	-46	(6.1)	-52	(5.2)	-46	(4.8)	-58	(4.6)	-40	(4.9)	-43	(5.5)
	Spain	-39	(6.4)	-57	(5.1)	-53	(4.9)	-52	(5.7)	-64	(4.8)	-57	(6.7)
	Sweden	-58	(5.4)	-60	(5.1)	-63	(5.8)	-72	(5.4)	-41	(4.3)	-54	(5.6)
	Turkey	11	(25.2)	3	(31.1)	-12	(26.9)	-17	(27.5)	m	m	m	m
	England (United Kingdom)	-33	(7.5)	-15	(8.4)	-13	(8.1)	-26	(8.0)	m	m	m	m
	United States	-14	(6.7)	-13	(5.8)	-7	(5.2)	-26	(5.8)	-16	(6.2)	-19	(6.6)
	OECD average	**-32**	(2.2)	**-32**	(2.0)	**-32**	(2.0)	**-40**	(1.9)	**-25**	(1.8)	**-30**	(2.2)
Partners	Brazil	-22	(18.1)	-78	(16.1)	-84	(22.8)	-78	(17.4)	-99	(23.7)	-86	(20.9)
	Bulgaria	c	c	c	c	c	c	c	c	m	m	m	m
	Colombia	-78	(24.2)	-69	(13.0)	-92	(21.7)	-81	(16.2)	-89	(13.9)	-122	(25.8)
	Croatia	-6	(5.2)	-19	(5.2)	-19	(6.4)	-23	(5.7)	m	m	m	m
	Cyprus*	-12	(5.3)	-21	(5.0)	-10	(5.3)	-16	(5.2)	m	m	m	m
	Hong Kong-China	-11	(4.3)	-7	(4.4)	0	(4.3)	-6	(3.8)	-7	(4.0)	-6	(4.4)
	Macao-China	5	(2.5)	16	(2.8)	22	(2.2)	16	(2.3)	14	(2.8)	15	(2.1)
	Malaysia	-9	(8.4)	-21	(8.9)	2	(11.8)	-15	(9.6)	m	m	m	m
	Montenegro	18	(7.1)	21	(6.5)	3	(7.1)	24	(6.2)	m	m	m	m
	Russian Federation	-8	(5.0)	-22	(4.5)	-29	(4.7)	-30	(4.8)	-20	(3.9)	-8	(5.5)
	Serbia	5	(6.9)	15	(6.2)	24	(6.8)	13	(6.7)	m	m	m	m
	Shanghai-China	-110	(12.7)	-126	(14.6)	-90	(13.8)	-109	(12.7)	-92	(11.1)	-123	(14.4)
	Singapore	14	(3.7)	26	(4.3)	18	(4.1)	22	(3.9)	21	(4.3)	-3	(3.2)
	Chinese Taipei	-1	(14.9)	-32	(23.1)	-17	(15.3)	-14	(14.6)	-56	(15.3)	-27	(17.1)
	United Arab Emirates	69	(3.9)	66	(3.1)	63	(3.1)	66	(3.2)	54	(3.3)	79	(4.4)
	Uruguay	c	c	c	c	c	c	c	c	m	m	m	m

Note: Values that are statistically significant are indicated in bold (see Annex A3).
* See notes at the beginning of this Annex.
StatLink ᵐˢˡ http://dx.doi.org/10.1787/888933003706

[Part 2/3]
Differences in problem-solving, mathematics, reading and science performance related to immigrant background
Table V.4.20   *Results based on students' self-reports*

	Immigrant effect size: Performance difference related to immigrant background divided by the variation in scores within each country/economy (standard deviation)											
	Problem solving		Mathematics		Reading		Science		Computer-based mathematics		Digital reading	
	Effect size	S.E.	Effect size	S.E.	Effect size	S.E.	Effect size	S.E.	Effect size	S.E.	Effect size	S.E.
Australia	**0.07**	(0.03)	**0.27**	(0.04)	**0.20**	(0.03)	**0.11**	(0.03)	**0.24**	(0.04)	**0.19**	(0.03)
Austria	**-0.59**	(0.06)	**-0.65**	(0.05)	**-0.55**	(0.06)	**-0.76**	(0.05)	**-0.55**	(0.06)	**-0.60**	(0.06)
Belgium	**-0.72**	(0.05)	**-0.75**	(0.05)	**-0.66**	(0.06)	**-0.77**	(0.05)	**-0.59**	(0.05)	**-0.72**	(0.06)
Canada	**-0.12**	(0.05)	-0.03	(0.05)	0.03	(0.05)	**-0.11**	(0.05)	0.08	(0.06)	0.02	(0.05)
Chile	0.00	(0.17)	-0.02	(0.16)	0.11	(0.18)	0.03	(0.16)	0.21	(0.16)	**0.39**	(0.19)
Czech Republic	**-0.32**	(0.12)	**-0.30**	(0.12)	-0.23	(0.12)	**-0.42**	(0.12)	m	m	m	m
Denmark	**-0.79**	(0.07)	**-0.83**	(0.04)	**-0.70**	(0.05)	**-0.88**	(0.04)	**-0.72**	(0.06)	**-0.74**	(0.05)
Estonia	**-0.38**	(0.08)	**-0.37**	(0.07)	**-0.44**	(0.07)	**-0.41**	(0.07)	**-0.50**	(0.07)	**-0.49**	(0.08)
Finland	**-0.91**	(0.05)	**-1.02**	(0.06)	**-1.00**	(0.06)	**-1.16**	(0.06)	m	m	m	m
France	**-0.72**	(0.08)	**-0.70**	(0.07)	**-0.62**	(0.08)	**-0.77**	(0.08)	**-0.63**	(0.07)	**-0.56**	(0.09)
Germany	**-0.52**	(0.06)	**-0.58**	(0.06)	**-0.54**	(0.06)	**-0.69**	(0.06)	**-0.42**	(0.06)	**-0.45**	(0.06)
Hungary	0.19	(0.13)	**0.34**	(0.14)	0.17	(0.15)	**0.27**	(0.13)	0.04	(0.14)	0.14	(0.15)
Ireland	**-0.14**	(0.06)	-0.04	(0.06)	**-0.13**	(0.06)	-0.03	(0.06)	0.01	(0.06)	-0.14	(0.07)
Israel	**0.18**	(0.06)	0.07	(0.05)	0.07	(0.06)	0.09	(0.06)	0.07	(0.06)	**0.12**	(0.06)
Italy	**-0.57**	(0.09)	**-0.54**	(0.08)	**-0.67**	(0.09)	**-0.55**	(0.08)	**-0.64**	(0.07)	**-0.44**	(0.09)
Japan	c	c	c	c	c	c	c	c	c	c	c	c
Korea	c	c	c	c	c	c	c	c	c	c	c	c
Netherlands	**-0.74**	(0.08)	**-0.64**	(0.07)	**-0.61**	(0.08)	**-0.73**	(0.07)	m	m	m	m
Norway	**-0.52**	(0.10)	**-0.53**	(0.07)	**-0.51**	(0.07)	**-0.71**	(0.07)	**-0.41**	(0.08)	**-0.66**	(0.08)
Poland	c	c	c	c	c	c	c	c	c	c	c	c
Portugal	**-0.35**	(0.08)	**-0.48**	(0.08)	**-0.42**	(0.09)	**-0.50**	(0.08)	**-0.42**	(0.07)	**-0.51**	(0.07)
Slovak Republic	0.27	(0.31)	0.06	(0.21)	0.07	(0.20)	-0.10	(0.21)	0.36	(0.22)	0.02	(0.27)
Slovenia	**-0.47**	(0.06)	**-0.57**	(0.06)	**-0.51**	(0.05)	**-0.64**	(0.05)	**-0.46**	(0.06)	**-0.44**	(0.06)
Spain	**-0.37**	(0.06)	**-0.66**	(0.06)	**-0.59**	(0.05)	**-0.62**	(0.06)	**-0.78**	(0.06)	**-0.58**	(0.07)
Sweden	**-0.61**	(0.06)	**-0.66**	(0.06)	**-0.61**	(0.06)	**-0.74**	(0.06)	**-0.48**	(0.05)	**-0.56**	(0.06)
Turkey	0.14	(0.32)	0.04	(0.34)	-0.14	(0.31)	-0.21	(0.35)	m	m	m	m
England (United Kingdom)	**-0.34**	(0.08)	-0.16	(0.09)	-0.14	(0.08)	**-0.27**	(0.08)	m	m	m	m
United States	**-0.15**	(0.07)	**-0.15**	(0.06)	-0.08	(0.06)	**-0.27**	(0.06)	**-0.19**	(0.07)	**-0.21**	(0.08)
OECD average	**-0.34**	(0.02)	**-0.36**	(0.02)	**-0.34**	(0.02)	**-0.43**	(0.02)	**-0.29**	(0.02)	**-0.31**	(0.02)
Brazil	-0.24	(0.20)	**-0.98**	(0.20)	**-0.99**	(0.26)	**-1.00**	(0.22)	**-1.18**	(0.27)	**-0.94**	(0.22)
Bulgaria	c	c	c	c	c	c	c	c	m	m	m	m
Colombia	**-0.86**	(0.26)	**-0.93**	(0.17)	**-1.10**	(0.26)	**-1.06**	(0.21)	**-1.22**	(0.19)	**-1.34**	(0.28)
Croatia	-0.06	(0.06)	**-0.21**	(0.06)	**-0.22**	(0.07)	**-0.27**	(0.07)	m	m	m	m
Cyprus*	**-0.12**	(0.05)	**-0.23**	(0.05)	-0.09	(0.05)	**-0.17**	(0.05)	m	m	m	m
Hong Kong-China	**-0.12**	(0.05)	-0.08	(0.05)	-0.01	(0.05)	-0.07	(0.05)	-0.09	(0.05)	-0.07	(0.05)
Macao-China	**0.06**	(0.03)	**0.17**	(0.03)	**0.27**	(0.03)	**0.21**	(0.03)	**0.17**	(0.03)	**0.21**	(0.03)
Malaysia	-0.11	(0.10)	**-0.26**	(0.11)	0.03	(0.14)	-0.19	(0.12)	m	m	m	m
Montenegro	**0.20**	(0.08)	**0.26**	(0.08)	0.03	(0.08)	**0.29**	(0.07)	m	m	m	m
Russian Federation	-0.09	(0.06)	**-0.25**	(0.05)	**-0.32**	(0.05)	**-0.36**	(0.06)	**-0.26**	(0.05)	-0.09	(0.06)
Serbia	0.05	(0.08)	**0.16**	(0.07)	**0.26**	(0.07)	0.15	(0.08)	m	m	m	m
Shanghai-China	**-1.23**	(0.14)	**-1.25**	(0.14)	**-1.13**	(0.17)	**-1.34**	(0.15)	**-0.99**	(0.12)	**-1.48**	(0.16)
Singapore	**0.15**	(0.04)	**0.25**	(0.04)	**0.18**	(0.04)	**0.22**	(0.04)	**0.22**	(0.04)	-0.03	(0.04)
Chinese Taipei	-0.01	(0.16)	-0.28	(0.20)	-0.19	(0.17)	-0.17	(0.18)	**-0.64**	(0.17)	-0.31	(0.19)
United Arab Emirates	**0.66**	(0.03)	**0.74**	(0.03)	**0.67**	(0.03)	**0.71**	(0.03)	**0.65**	(0.03)	**0.72**	(0.04)
Uruguay	c	c	c	c	c	c	c	c	m	m	m	m

Note: Values that are statistically significant are indicated in bold (see Annex A3).
* See notes at the beginning of this Annex.

StatLink ⫘⫙ http://dx.doi.org/10.1787/888933003706

[Part 3/3]
Differences in problem-solving, mathematics, reading and science performance related to immigrant background

Table V.4.20   *Results based on students' self-reports*

| | Difference in immigrant effect sizes between problem solving (PS) and... | | | | | | | | | |
| | ... Mathematics (PS - M) | | ... Reading (PS - R) | | ... Science (PS - S) | | ... Computer-based mathematics (PS - CBM) | | ... Digital reading (PS - DR) | |
	Effect size dif.	S.E.	Effect size dif.	S.E.	Effect size dif.	S.E.	Effect size dif.	S.E.	Effect size dif.	S.E.
Australia	-0.20	(0.02)	-0.12	(0.02)	-0.04	(0.02)	-0.16	(0.02)	-0.11	(0.02)
Austria	0.06	(0.04)	-0.03	(0.05)	0.18	(0.04)	-0.04	(0.05)	0.01	(0.06)
Belgium	0.03	(0.03)	-0.06	(0.04)	0.05	(0.04)	-0.14	(0.04)	0.00	(0.04)
Canada	-0.09	(0.03)	-0.15	(0.03)	-0.01	(0.03)	-0.20	(0.04)	-0.14	(0.04)
Chile	0.02	(0.11)	-0.11	(0.11)	-0.03	(0.13)	-0.21	(0.13)	-0.39	(0.19)
Czech Republic	-0.02	(0.05)	-0.09	(0.08)	0.10	(0.06)	m	m	m	m
Denmark	0.04	(0.05)	-0.09	(0.08)	0.09	(0.06)	-0.07	(0.04)	-0.04	(0.06)
Estonia	0.00	(0.05)	0.07	(0.06)	0.03	(0.06)	0.12	(0.06)	0.11	(0.07)
Finland	0.10	(0.04)	0.08	(0.04)	0.25	(0.04)	m	m	m	m
France	-0.03	(0.05)	-0.10	(0.06)	0.05	(0.06)	-0.10	(0.04)	-0.17	(0.05)
Germany	0.07	(0.04)	0.02	(0.04)	0.18	(0.04)	-0.10	(0.04)	-0.07	(0.04)
Hungary	-0.15	(0.09)	0.01	(0.12)	-0.08	(0.09)	0.14	(0.14)	0.05	(0.11)
Ireland	-0.11	(0.04)	-0.01	(0.05)	-0.12	(0.04)	-0.15	(0.05)	-0.01	(0.05)
Israel	0.12	(0.04)	0.11	(0.04)	0.09	(0.04)	0.12	(0.05)	0.06	(0.05)
Italy	-0.04	(0.06)	0.10	(0.07)	-0.02	(0.05)	0.06	(0.06)	-0.13	(0.07)
Japan	c	c	c	c	c	c	c	c	c	c
Korea	c	c	c	c	c	c	c	c	c	c
Netherlands	-0.11	(0.08)	-0.13	(0.09)	-0.01	(0.07)	m	m	m	m
Norway	0.01	(0.05)	-0.01	(0.07)	0.19	(0.06)	-0.11	(0.08)	0.14	(0.07)
Poland	c	c	c	c	c	c	c	c	c	c
Portugal	0.13	(0.05)	0.08	(0.06)	0.16	(0.07)	0.07	(0.05)	0.17	(0.07)
Slovak Republic	0.22	(0.28)	0.21	(0.24)	0.38	(0.28)	-0.08	(0.20)	0.26	(0.16)
Slovenia	0.09	(0.05)	0.03	(0.05)	0.16	(0.04)	-0.02	(0.04)	-0.03	(0.04)
Spain	0.29	(0.05)	0.22	(0.06)	0.25	(0.05)	0.40	(0.07)	0.21	(0.06)
Sweden	0.05	(0.05)	0.00	(0.05)	0.13	(0.05)	-0.13	(0.05)	-0.05	(0.05)
Turkey	0.10	(0.09)	0.28	(0.14)	0.35	(0.14)	m	m	m	m
England (United Kingdom)	-0.18	(0.05)	-0.21	(0.05)	-0.08	(0.05)	m	m	m	m
United States	-0.01	(0.04)	-0.07	(0.05)	0.12	(0.05)	0.03	(0.05)	0.06	(0.06)
OECD average	0.02	(0.02)	0.00	(0.02)	0.09	(0.02)	-0.03	(0.02)	0.00	(0.02)
Brazil	0.74	(0.15)	0.75	(0.20)	0.75	(0.15)	0.94	(0.23)	0.70	(0.22)
Bulgaria	c	c	c	c	c	c	m	m	m	m
Colombia	0.08	(0.26)	0.24	(0.29)	0.20	(0.26)	0.36	(0.27)	0.48	(0.28)
Croatia	0.15	(0.04)	0.16	(0.05)	0.21	(0.04)	m	m	m	m
Cyprus*	0.10	(0.04)	-0.03	(0.04)	0.05	(0.04)	m	m	m	m
Hong Kong-China	-0.04	(0.03)	-0.11	(0.03)	-0.05	(0.03)	-0.03	(0.03)	-0.05	(0.04)
Macao-China	-0.10	(0.03)	-0.21	(0.02)	-0.14	(0.03)	-0.11	(0.03)	-0.15	(0.03)
Malaysia	0.15	(0.09)	-0.14	(0.12)	0.08	(0.11)	m	m	m	m
Montenegro	-0.06	(0.04)	0.17	(0.06)	-0.09	(0.06)	m	m	m	m
Russian Federation	0.16	(0.05)	0.23	(0.05)	0.26	(0.06)	0.16	(0.04)	0.00	(0.04)
Serbia	-0.11	(0.04)	-0.21	(0.05)	-0.10	(0.05)	m	m	m	m
Shanghai-China	0.02	(0.12)	-0.10	(0.16)	0.10	(0.13)	-0.25	(0.11)	0.24	(0.16)
Singapore	-0.10	(0.02)	-0.02	(0.03)	-0.07	(0.02)	-0.07	(0.03)	0.18	(0.03)
Chinese Taipei	0.26	(0.13)	0.18	(0.13)	0.15	(0.14)	0.63	(0.11)	0.29	(0.14)
United Arab Emirates	-0.08	(0.03)	-0.01	(0.03)	-0.05	(0.03)	0.01	(0.02)	-0.06	(0.03)
Uruguay	c	c	c	c	c	c	m	m	m	m

Note: Values that are statistically significant are indicated in bold (see Annex A3).
* See notes at the beginning of this Annex.
StatLink ᵐˢᵖ http://dx.doi.org/10.1787/888933003706

[Part 1/1]
Relative performance in problem solving, by immigrant background

Table V.4.21 — *Results based on students' self-reports*

Problem-solving performance among immigrant students, compared to that of non-immigrant students with similar performance in mathematics, reading and science

	Average difference in problem solving compared with non-immigrant students with similar performance in mathematics[1]		Percentage of immigrant students who outperform non-immigrant students with similar performance in mathematics[2]		Average difference in problem solving compared with non-immigrant students with similar performance in reading[1]		Percentage of immigrant students who outperform non-immigrant students with similar performance in reading[2]		Average difference in problem solving compared with non-immigrant students with similar performance in science[1]		Percentage of immigrant students who outperform non-immigrant students with similar performance in science[2]		Average difference in problem solving compared with non-immigrant students with similar performance in mathematics, reading and science[3]		Percentage of immigrant students who outperform non-immigrant students with similar performance in mathematics, reading and science[2]	
	Score dif.	S.E.	%	S.E.	Score dif.	S.E.	%	S.E.	Score dif.	S.E.	%	S.E.	Score dif.	S.E.	%	S.E.
OECD																
Australia	**-14**	(2.0)	**40.1**	(1.8)	**-8**	(2.2)	**45.7**	(1.7)	-1	(2.2)	49.7	(1.8)	**-12**	(2.0)	**41.7**	(1.7)
Austria	-7	(3.9)	44.3	(3.2)	**-16**	(4.3)	**38.9**	(3.3)	0	(4.5)	50.1	(3.4)	-7	(4.0)	43.3	(4.0)
Belgium	**-13**	(4.1)	**42.4**	(2.9)	**-23**	(4.3)	**38.2**	(2.5)	**-13**	(4.2)	**43.3**	(2.6)	**-11**	(4.0)	**43.6**	(2.6)
Canada	**-10**	(2.9)	**44.1**	(2.2)	**-14**	(3.2)	**41.4**	(2.3)	-4	(3.0)	48.1	(2.1)	**-9**	(2.8)	**44.3**	(2.2)
Chile	2	(9.1)	52.0	(10.3)	-7	(8.5)	48.2	(8.1)	-1	(10.3)	49.0	(9.8)	0	(8.5)	52.6	(11.0)
Czech Republic	-4	(4.7)	49.5	(5.6)	-13	(7.1)	43.2	(6.9)	2	(6.0)	51.7	(7.5)	-2	(4.8)	50.1	(7.5)
Denmark	**-15**	(5.5)	**40.2**	(3.6)	**-30**	(7.3)	**33.6**	(3.4)	**-17**	(6.3)	**39.9**	(3.8)	**-14**	(5.9)	**40.9**	(3.9)
Estonia	-6	(4.4)	45.2	(4.0)	-3	(4.9)	48.8	(4.4)	-4	(4.8)	46.8	(4.9)	-2	(4.3)	48.7	(4.6)
Finland	-6	(4.4)	46.8	(4.4)	**-17**	(3.5)	**40.2**	(3.6)	0	(3.9)	51.4	(3.6)	0	(4.1)	51.7	(3.8)
France	**-15**	(5.3)	**42.2**	(4.0)	**-26**	(5.3)	**34.5**	(3.4)	**-11**	(5.6)	45.0	(3.8)	**-11**	(5.5)	44.6	(4.3)
Germany	-3	(3.4)	49.1	(3.2)	**-10**	(3.7)	46.1	(3.0)	5	(3.9)	55.2	(3.6)	1	(3.4)	52.7	(3.5)
Hungary	-10	(8.5)	43.7	(8.1)	5	(10.6)	53.4	(8.1)	-4	(8.8)	46.7	(10.0)	-7	(8.4)	43.7	(9.9)
Ireland	**-11**	(3.7)	**40.5**	(2.9)	-4	(4.2)	47.0	(3.0)	**-11**	(3.9)	**41.3**	(3.3)	**-10**	(3.6)	**41.3**	(3.9)
Israel	**15**	(4.6)	**61.1**	(2.9)	**15**	(4.9)	**59.0**	(3.5)	**12**	(4.9)	**58.4**	(3.5)	**14**	(4.5)	**60.0**	(3.3)
Italy	**-16**	(5.8)	42.7	(3.9)	-12	(6.5)	43.1	(4.4)	**-17**	(5.5)	43.0	(3.9)	**-13**	(5.9)	44.4	(4.3)
Japan	c	c	c	c	c	c	c	c	c	c	c	c	c	c	c	c
Korea	c	c	c	c	c	c	c	c	c	c	c	c	c	c	c	c
Netherlands	**-22**	(8.2)	**38.9**	(4.6)	**-27**	(8.7)	**36.2**	(4.4)	-13	(7.7)	42.8	(5.6)	-15	(7.7)	42.3	(5.0)
Norway	-11	(6.4)	42.5	(4.5)	**-17**	(7.6)	**41.9**	(4.0)	1	(7.2)	51.4	(4.2)	-7	(6.8)	45.3	(4.8)
Poland	c	c	c	c	c	c	c	c	c	c	c	c	c	c	c	c
Portugal	4	(4.0)	55.5	(3.9)	-4	(4.6)	48.5	(4.2)	3	(5.2)	54.4	(4.3)	4	(4.1)	56.6	(4.5)
Slovak Republic	22	(26.7)	52.7	(13.7)	22	(23.6)	59.1	(12.0)	35	(26.4)	62.6	(13.7)	23	(25.8)	52.8	(14.0)
Slovenia	-1	(4.5)	53.6	(3.2)	**-10**	(4.6)	44.2	(4.8)	3	(4.2)	55.8	(3.8)	2	(4.2)	54.7	(3.8)
Spain	**15**	(4.8)	**60.9**	(3.1)	4	(6.0)	54.4	(4.2)	**10**	(4.9)	55.3	(3.3)	**16**	(4.5)	**61.6**	(3.0)
Sweden	-7	(4.7)	44.6	(3.5)	**-18**	(4.6)	**39.5**	(3.2)	-5	(4.7)	46.6	(3.3)	-4	(4.9)	46.0	(3.6)
Turkey	10	(7.1)	63.5	(9.3)	18	(11.5)	59.9	(10.2)	**23**	(10.6)	67.0	(11.0)	13	(7.4)	63.1	(9.1)
England (United Kingdom)	**-19**	(4.0)	**35.6**	(4.8)	**-23**	(4.4)	**35.2**	(3.0)	**-12**	(4.5)	42.0	(4.7)	**-17**	(3.8)	**37.6**	(5.0)
United States	-2	(4.0)	48.4	(3.7)	-8	(4.6)	43.6	(3.5)	7	(4.4)	55.9	(3.7)	-1	(4.2)	49.4	(3.4)
OECD average	**-5**	(1.5)	**47.2**	(1.1)	**-9**	(1.5)	**45.0**	(1.0)	0	(1.6)	50.1	(1.2)	**-3**	(1.5)	48.5	(1.2)
Partners																
Brazil	**55**	(14.4)	**82.4**	(13.9)	**40**	(14.8)	**75.6**	(11.2)	**43**	(11.5)	**80.0**	(10.2)	**59**	(13.3)	**84.7**	(12.4)
Bulgaria	c	c	c	c	c	c	c	c	c	c	c	c	c	c	c	c
Colombia	-17	(22.1)	42.3	(13.6)	-16	(22.1)	42.7	(13.5)	-17	(21.4)	43.0	(13.5)	-10	(22.0)	45.5	(13.5)
Croatia	**11**	(3.1)	**59.4**	(3.2)	**10**	(3.7)	55.9	(3.2)	**15**	(3.0)	**60.7**	(2.7)	**13**	(3.1)	**60.7**	(3.0)
Cyprus*	6	(4.0)	55.2	(3.2)	-6	(3.8)	46.7	(3.3)	1	(3.5)	51.5	(3.7)	4	(3.7)	53.0	(3.0)
Hong Kong-China	**-6**	(2.6)	47.9	(2.2)	**-10**	(2.7)	**44.6**	(1.9)	**-6**	(2.8)	46.8	(2.2)	**-7**	(2.8)	46.8	(2.4)
Macao-China	**-6**	(2.0)	**45.7**	(1.6)	**-10**	(1.9)	**43.6**	(1.5)	**-7**	(2.0)	**45.6**	(1.7)	**-7**	(1.9)	**44.6**	(1.5)
Malaysia	9	(7.0)	57.4	(8.6)	-11	(8.0)	41.0	(7.5)	3	(8.0)	50.5	(8.9)	7	(7.1)	54.9	(7.8)
Montenegro	-1	(3.9)	49.9	(3.9)	**17**	(4.9)	**62.1**	(3.8)	-2	(5.2)	48.8	(5.0)	-1	(4.0)	49.1	(3.8)
Russian Federation	**8**	(4.0)	55.5	(3.3)	**10**	(4.2)	**56.2**	(2.7)	**12**	(4.7)	**58.2**	(3.1)	**9**	(3.9)	56.6	(3.6)
Serbia	-7	(3.8)	43.4	(3.9)	**-12**	(4.2)	43.8	(4.0)	-6	(4.4)	46.7	(4.3)	**-8**	(3.8)	**42.3**	(3.6)
Shanghai-China	-16	(9.9)	39.5	(11.8)	**-30**	(12.6)	**30.6**	(8.8)	-15	(11.0)	40.6	(10.8)	-15	(10.8)	40.0	(10.3)
Singapore	**-5**	(1.9)	**46.0**	(2.0)	2	(2.5)	51.1	(1.8)	-2	(2.3)	48.9	(1.9)	**-6**	(2.0)	**45.6**	(2.1)
Chinese Taipei	20	(10.3)	66.4	(11.8)	13	(10.7)	60.6	(11.1)	11	(11.6)	58.7	(10.8)	18	(10.1)	66.7	(12.4)
United Arab Emirates	**11**	(3.5)	**58.3**	(2.4)	**19**	(3.2)	**61.1**	(2.0)	**13**	(2.8)	**59.3**	(1.9)	**8**	(3.0)	**56.3**	(2.3)
Uruguay	c	c	c	c	c	c	c	c	c	c	c	c	c	c	c	c

Note: Values that are statistically significant are indicated in bold (see Annex A3).
1. This column reports the difference between actual performance and the fitted value from a regression using a cubic polynomial as regression function.
2. This column reports the percentage of students for whom the difference between actual performance and the fitted value from a regression is positive. Values that are indicated in bold are significantly larger or smaller than 50%.
3. This column reports the difference between actual performance and the fitted value from a regression using a second-degree polynomial as regression function (math, math sq., read, read sq., scie, scie sq., math×read, math×scie, read×scie).
* See notes at the beginning of this Annex.

StatLink http://dx.doi.org/10.1787/888933003706

[Part 1/1]
Performance on problem-solving tasks, by nature of problem and by immigrant background
Table V.4.22a   *Results based on students' self-reports*

	Items referring to a static problem situation										Items referring to an interactive problem situation									
	Average proportion of full-credit responses						Relative likelihood of success, in favour of immigrant students (non-immigrant students = 1.00)				Average proportion of full-credit responses						Relative likelihood of success, in favour of immigrant students (non-immigrant students = 1.00)			
	Non-immigrant students		Immigrant students		Difference between immigrant and non-immigrant students		Accounting for booklet effects[1]		Based on success on remaining test items[2]		Non-immigrant students		Immigrant students		Difference between immigrant and non-immigrant students		Accounting for booklet effects[1]		Based on success on remaining test items[2]	
	%	S.E.	%	S.E.	% dif.	S.E.	Odds ratio	S.E.	Odds ratio	S.E.	%	S.E.	%	S.E.	% dif.	S.E.	Odds ratio	S.E.	Odds ratio	S.E.
OECD																				
Australia	53.1	(0.5)	54.1	(1.1)	1.0	(1.2)	1.05	(0.05)	1.00	(0.04)	50.3	(0.5)	51.4	(1.0)	1.0	(1.0)	1.05	(0.04)	1.00	(0.04)
Austria	50.2	(1.0)	41.0	(2.6)	-9.2	(2.7)	**0.66**	(0.07)	1.05	(0.10)	45.0	(0.8)	34.7	(1.8)	-10.3	(1.9)	**0.63**	(0.05)	0.95	(0.09)
Belgium	51.2	(0.8)	35.3	(1.9)	-16.0	(2.3)	**0.51**	(0.05)	1.02	(0.09)	48.3	(0.6)	32.1	(1.7)	-16.1	(1.9)	**0.50**	(0.04)	0.98	(0.09)
Canada	54.6	(0.7)	49.4	(1.8)	-5.3	(2.1)	**0.81**	(0.07)	0.90	(0.06)	51.7	(0.7)	49.1	(1.6)	-2.7	(1.8)	0.90	(0.07)	1.11	(0.08)
Chile	35.0	(0.9)	c	c	c	c	c	c	c	c	31.8	(0.8)	c	c	c	c	c	c	c	c
Czech Republic	46.4	(0.7)	39.2	(4.0)	-7.2	(4.2)	0.74	(0.13)	0.96	(0.14)	44.7	(0.7)	38.6	(2.3)	-6.1	(2.4)	**0.77**	(0.08)	1.04	(0.15)
Denmark	49.0	(1.0)	37.8	(1.9)	-11.2	(2.0)	**0.61**	(0.05)	1.07	(0.09)	43.7	(0.8)	31.3	(1.5)	-12.4	(1.6)	**0.57**	(0.04)	0.93	(0.08)
Estonia	50.4	(0.8)	44.6	(3.2)	-5.8	(3.3)	0.79	(0.10)	0.94	(0.13)	45.9	(0.9)	41.8	(2.9)	-4.1	(3.1)	0.84	(0.10)	1.07	(0.15)
Finland	52.7	(0.6)	37.3	(2.2)	-15.4	(2.3)	**0.54**	(0.05)	1.08	(0.09)	48.3	(0.6)	31.5	(2.3)	-16.8	(2.3)	**0.50**	(0.05)	0.93	(0.08)
France	51.9	(0.8)	41.0	(2.9)	-10.8	(3.0)	**0.63**	(0.08)	1.07	(0.12)	49.6	(0.8)	37.6	(2.3)	-12.1	(2.4)	**0.59**	(0.06)	0.94	(0.11)
Germany	51.8	(0.9)	47.9	(3.1)	-4.0	(3.2)	0.80	(0.10)	**1.32**	(0.17)	49.1	(0.9)	38.2	(2.7)	-10.9	(2.8)	**0.60**	(0.07)	**0.76**	(0.10)
Hungary	38.2	(1.1)	c	c	c	c	c	c	c	c	33.8	(0.9)	c	c	c	c	c	c	c	c
Ireland	44.8	(1.0)	43.2	(2.7)	-1.7	(3.0)	0.93	(0.11)	1.11	(0.15)	45.2	(1.0)	40.8	(2.4)	-4.4	(2.8)	0.84	(0.09)	0.90	(0.12)
Israel	40.3	(1.6)	39.9	(2.2)	-0.4	(2.3)	1.01	(0.10)	0.88	(0.07)	35.6	(1.4)	38.3	(2.3)	2.7	(2.3)	1.15	(0.12)	1.14	(0.09)
Italy	51.0	(1.1)	34.7	(3.1)	-16.3	(3.4)	**0.51**	(0.08)	**0.70**	(0.08)	47.6	(1.0)	39.9	(2.3)	-7.7	(2.3)	**0.72**	(0.08)	**1.43**	(0.16)
Japan	58.8	(0.8)	c	c	c	c	c	c	c	c	56.0	(0.7)	c	c	c	c	c	c	c	c
Korea	59.1	(1.0)	c	c	c	c	c	c	c	c	57.9	(1.0)	c	c	c	c	c	c	c	c
Netherlands	52.2	(1.0)	37.6	(3.2)	-14.6	(2.8)	**0.55**	(0.07)	1.03	(0.10)	48.3	(1.0)	33.5	(3.3)	-14.8	(3.0)	**0.54**	(0.07)	0.98	(0.09)
Norway	50.5	(1.0)	44.9	(3.2)	-5.5	(3.5)	**0.76**	(0.10)	**1.56**	(0.21)	46.2	(1.0)	30.8	(3.2)	-15.4	(3.4)	**0.49**	(0.07)	**0.64**	(0.09)
Poland	44.2	(1.0)	c	c	c	c	c	c	c	c	39.8	(1.1)	c	c	c	c	c	c	c	c
Portugal	44.7	(1.0)	40.6	(3.2)	-4.1	(3.3)	0.82	(0.11)	1.07	(0.16)	42.8	(1.0)	37.5	(2.6)	-5.3	(2.6)	**0.77**	(0.09)	0.94	(0.14)
Slovak Republic	44.7	(1.0)	c	c	c	c	c	c	c	c	39.0	(0.8)	c	c	c	c	c	c	c	c
Slovenia	44.3	(0.9)	29.0	(3.1)	-15.3	(3.6)	**0.55**	(0.09)	0.85	(0.15)	37.9	(0.9)	27.2	(2.0)	-10.7	(2.2)	**0.64**	(0.07)	1.18	(0.21)
Spain	43.9	(0.8)	31.8	(2.8)	-12.1	(2.9)	**0.62**	(0.08)	0.95	(0.10)	41.4	(0.8)	30.9	(2.1)	-10.5	(2.4)	**0.65**	(0.07)	1.06	(0.11)
Sweden	49.4	(1.0)	40.6	(2.0)	-8.8	(2.3)	**0.71**	(0.06)	0.95	(0.10)	43.2	(0.9)	36.0	(1.8)	-7.2	(2.1)	**0.75**	(0.07)	1.05	(0.11)
Turkey	36.0	(0.9)	c	c	c	c	c	c	c	c	32.8	(0.9)	c	c	c	c	c	c	c	c
England (United Kingdom)	50.6	(1.0)	43.5	(3.1)	-7.1	(3.3)	**0.74**	(0.10)	0.98	(0.07)	49.0	(1.1)	42.4	(3.0)	-6.6	(3.1)	**0.76**	(0.10)	1.02	(0.08)
United States	48.3	(1.2)	41.0	(2.4)	-7.3	(2.7)	**0.76**	(0.08)	0.79	(0.10)	46.5	(1.2)	45.2	(2.3)	-1.3	(2.6)	0.96	(0.10)	1.26	(0.15)
OECD average	48.1	(0.2)	40.7	(0.6)	-8.4	(0.6)	**0.70**	(0.02)	1.00	(0.02)	44.7	(0.2)	37.6	(0.5)	-8.2	(0.5)	**0.70**	(0.02)	1.00	(0.02)
Partners																				
Brazil	30.5	(1.0)	c	c	c	c	c	c	c	c	29.7	(1.0)	c	c	c	c	c	c	c	c
Bulgaria	28.8	(0.9)	c	c	c	c	c	c	c	c	22.8	(0.8)	c	c	c	c	c	c	c	c
Colombia	26.5	(0.9)	c	c	c	c	c	c	c	c	23.9	(0.7)	c	c	c	c	c	c	c	c
Croatia	39.3	(1.0)	39.2	(1.9)	-0.1	(1.9)	1.00	(0.08)	1.14	(0.09)	36.1	(0.9)	33.0	(1.4)	-3.1	(1.5)	**0.87**	(0.06)	0.87	(0.07)
Cyprus*	37.5	(0.5)	33.3	(1.5)	-4.3	(1.6)	**0.83**	(0.06)	0.89	(0.06)	31.9	(0.5)	30.3	(1.5)	-1.6	(1.6)	0.93	(0.07)	1.12	(0.07)
Hong Kong-China	56.8	(1.3)	56.0	(1.3)	-0.8	(2.0)	0.96	(0.08)	1.04	(0.10)	53.3	(1.1)	51.7	(1.0)	-1.6	(1.6)	0.92	(0.06)	0.96	(0.09)
Macao-China	57.9	(1.3)	56.7	(0.9)	-1.2	(1.8)	0.95	(0.07)	0.94	(0.07)	51.4	(1.0)	51.9	(0.8)	0.5	(1.4)	1.01	(0.05)	1.06	(0.07)
Malaysia	30.4	(0.8)	c	c	c	c	c	c	c	c	27.7	(0.8)	c	c	c	c	c	c	c	c
Montenegro	30.2	(0.6)	32.4	(2.6)	2.2	(2.8)	1.11	(0.14)	0.93	(0.11)	25.0	(0.4)	28.5	(2.0)	3.5	(2.1)	1.19	(0.13)	1.08	(0.13)
Russian Federation	44.1	(0.9)	41.2	(2.8)	-2.9	(2.8)	0.91	(0.11)	1.05	(0.13)	40.1	(0.9)	36.2	(1.8)	-3.8	(2.0)	0.87	(0.08)	0.95	(0.12)
Serbia	40.4	(0.8)	41.5	(2.7)	1.1	(2.6)	1.05	(0.11)	1.06	(0.08)	37.0	(0.8)	36.6	(2.2)	-0.4	(2.2)	0.99	(0.09)	0.94	(0.07)
Shanghai-China	56.9	(1.0)	c	c	c	c	c	c	c	c	50.7	(0.9)	c	c	c	c	c	c	c	c
Singapore	59.8	(0.9)	62.8	(2.2)	3.1	(2.6)	1.13	(0.13)	0.97	(0.10)	57.1	(0.8)	60.7	(1.9)	3.7	(2.2)	1.16	(0.10)	1.03	(0.10)
Chinese Taipei	56.6	(0.9)	c	c	c	c	c	c	c	c	50.4	(0.8)	c	c	c	c	c	c	c	c
United Arab Emirates	23.8	(0.8)	35.6	(0.9)	**11.8**	(1.4)	**1.78**	(0.12)	**0.81**	(0.06)	19.0	(0.9)	34.1	(0.7)	**15.1**	(1.1)	**2.21**	(0.14)	**1.24**	(0.09)
Uruguay	27.8	(0.7)	c	c	c	c	c	c	c	c	25.2	(0.6)	c	c	c	c	c	c	c	c

Note: Values that are statistically significant are indicated in bold (see Annex A3).
1. Generalised odds ratios estimated with logistic regression on national PISA samples. A success indicator for each item is regressed on an item type dummy, an immigrant dummy, and an interaction term (immigrant × item type). Booklet dummies are added to the estimation. This column presents the difference between the logit coefficient on the interaction term and the logit coefficient on the item type dummy in exponentiated form.
2. Generalised odds ratios estimated with logistic regression on national PISA samples. A success indicator for each item is regressed on an item type dummy, an immigrant dummy, and an interaction term (immigrant × item type). Booklet dummies are added to the estimation. This column presents the logit coefficient on the interaction term in exponentiated form.
* See notes at the beginning of this Annex.
StatLink ⌐⌐ http://dx.doi.org/10.1787/888933003706

[Part 1/2]
Performance on problem-solving tasks, by process and by immigrant background
Table V.4.22b *Results based on students' self-reports*

	Items assessing the process of "exploring and understanding"										Items assessing the process of "representing and formulating"									
	Average proportion of full-credit responses						Relative likelihood of success, in favour of immigrant students (non-immigrant students = 1.00)				Average proportion of full-credit responses						Relative likelihood of success, in favour of immigrant students (non-immigrant students = 1.00)			
	Non-immigrant students		Immigrant students		Difference between immigrant and non-immigrant students		Accounting for booklet effects[1]		Based on success on remaining test items[2]		Non-immigrant students		Immigrant students		Difference between immigrant and non-immigrant students		Accounting for booklet effects[1]		Based on success on remaining test items[2]	
	%	S.E.	%	S.E.	% dif.	S.E.	Odds ratio	S.E.	Odds ratio	S.E.	%	S.E.	%	S.E.	% dif.	S.E.	Odds ratio	S.E.	Odds ratio	S.E.
Australia	54.9	(0.6)	57.6	(1.2)	2.7	(1.3)	**1.14**	(0.06)	**1.11**	(0.04)	49.9	(0.7)	51.5	(1.2)	1.7	(1.3)	1.09	(0.06)	1.04	(0.04)
Austria	51.1	(1.2)	41.5	(2.6)	-9.6	(2.9)	**0.65**	(0.08)	1.03	(0.09)	44.7	(1.0)	28.7	(2.5)	**-16.0**	(2.5)	**0.48**	(0.06)	**0.69**	(0.07)
Belgium	52.3	(0.8)	34.2	(2.0)	**-18.1**	(2.0)	**0.47**	(0.05)	0.91	(0.06)	48.1	(0.9)	28.8	(1.8)	**-19.3**	(2.1)	**0.43**	(0.04)	**0.82**	(0.06)
Canada	55.6	(0.8)	51.9	(1.8)	-3.6	(2.1)	0.87	(0.08)	0.99	(0.06)	52.5	(1.0)	49.0	(1.8)	-3.5	(2.1)	0.87	(0.08)	1.00	(0.05)
Chile	32.6	(1.0)	c	c	c	c	c	c	c	c	29.3	(0.9)	c	c	c	c	c	c	c	c
Czech Republic	47.3	(0.9)	39.9	(3.8)	-7.3	(4.1)	0.73	(0.13)	0.96	(0.14)	43.2	(0.9)	36.7	(3.4)	-6.4	(3.7)	0.76	(0.12)	0.99	(0.12)
Denmark	47.4	(1.1)	34.3	(1.8)	**-13.1**	(2.1)	**0.56**	(0.05)	0.94	(0.07)	43.4	(1.2)	31.0	(2.1)	**-12.4**	(2.3)	**0.57**	(0.06)	0.96	(0.09)
Estonia	49.7	(1.1)	39.7	(3.6)	-9.9	(3.7)	**0.67**	(0.11)	**0.75**	(0.10)	44.5	(1.1)	44.9	(3.8)	0.5	(4.0)	1.02	(0.16)	**1.31**	(0.16)
Finland	54.4	(0.6)	36.9	(2.4)	**-17.5**	(2.4)	**0.50**	(0.05)	0.96	(0.09)	46.9	(0.7)	29.8	(3.1)	**-17.1**	(3.2)	**0.49**	(0.07)	0.93	(0.10)
France	54.0	(1.0)	42.0	(2.9)	**-12.0**	(3.1)	**0.60**	(0.08)	0.99	(0.10)	49.1	(0.9)	36.3	(2.9)	**-12.8**	(3.0)	**0.57**	(0.08)	0.93	(0.10)
Germany	54.0	(1.2)	43.5	(3.1)	**-10.5**	(3.2)	**0.61**	(0.08)	0.89	(0.09)	46.7	(1.2)	36.9	(3.1)	-9.8	(3.4)	**0.63**	(0.09)	0.93	(0.11)
Hungary	37.7	(1.1)	c	c	c	c	c	c	c	c	32.5	(1.1)	c	c	c	c	c	c	c	c
Ireland	48.5	(1.4)	41.1	(3.2)	-7.5	(3.7)	0.73	(0.12)	0.80	(0.10)	41.4	(1.1)	42.9	(2.9)	1.5	(3.3)	1.08	(0.14)	**1.31**	(0.17)
Israel	42.1	(1.7)	43.9	(2.4)	1.8	(2.7)	1.11	(0.13)	1.02	(0.08)	35.4	(1.5)	37.0	(3.1)	1.5	(3.0)	1.10	(0.15)	1.00	(0.10)
Italy	52.9	(1.3)	38.4	(3.8)	**-14.5**	(3.9)	**0.54**	(0.10)	0.81	(0.13)	48.0	(1.3)	39.4	(3.4)	-8.6	(3.3)	**0.70**	(0.11)	1.12	(0.15)
Japan	62.3	(0.9)	c	c	c	c	c	c	c	c	55.9	(0.9)	c	c	c	c	c	c	c	c
Korea	64.9	(1.1)	c	c	c	c	c	c	c	c	60.9	(1.3)	c	c	c	c	c	c	c	c
Netherlands	53.5	(1.1)	38.7	(3.6)	**-14.8**	(3.2)	**0.55**	(0.08)	1.01	(0.09)	46.2	(1.2)	29.2	(3.8)	**-17.1**	(3.5)	**0.48**	(0.08)	0.85	(0.08)
Norway	53.1	(1.2)	38.8	(3.2)	**-14.3**	(3.7)	**0.52**	(0.08)	0.88	(0.12)	45.0	(1.3)	31.8	(3.8)	**-13.3**	(4.0)	**0.53**	(0.10)	0.90	(0.13)
Poland	43.9	(1.2)	c	c	c	c	c	c	c	c	38.7	(1.3)	c	c	c	c	c	c	c	c
Portugal	44.5	(1.4)	39.8	(3.2)	-4.6	(3.5)	0.80	(0.13)	1.02	(0.19)	40.3	(1.3)	35.6	(4.0)	-4.7	(4.0)	0.78	(0.13)	0.98	(0.16)
Slovak Republic	44.1	(1.1)	c	c	c	c	c	c	c	c	37.3	(1.1)	c	c	c	c	c	c	c	c
Slovenia	41.1	(1.1)	26.9	(2.7)	**-14.1**	(3.1)	**0.55**	(0.09)	0.89	(0.14)	37.2	(1.0)	23.5	(2.7)	**-13.8**	(2.9)	**0.54**	(0.09)	0.85	(0.13)
Spain	44.1	(1.1)	30.5	(3.1)	**-13.6**	(3.2)	**0.57**	(0.09)	0.86	(0.11)	38.8	(1.0)	28.3	(2.5)	**-10.4**	(2.7)	**0.64**	(0.08)	0.99	(0.11)
Sweden	49.9	(1.1)	42.2	(2.5)	-7.7	(2.7)	**0.75**	(0.09)	1.02	(0.12)	44.1	(1.2)	33.1	(2.4)	**-10.9**	(2.7)	**0.63**	(0.08)	**0.83**	(0.08)
Turkey	33.7	(1.0)	c	c	c	c	c	c	c	c	32.0	(1.1)	c	c	c	c	c	c	c	c
England (United Kingdom)	52.5	(1.3)	45.1	(3.4)	-7.3	(3.5)	**0.73**	(0.10)	0.97	(0.06)	48.7	(1.3)	41.5	(3.5)	-7.2	(3.5)	**0.74**	(0.11)	0.97	(0.07)
United States	50.6	(1.2)	44.0	(3.2)	-6.6	(3.4)	0.77	(0.10)	0.84	(0.10)	44.1	(1.6)	44.9	(2.4)	0.8	(2.9)	1.03	(0.12)	**1.22**	(0.09)
OECD average	49.0	(0.2)	40.5	(0.6)	**-9.6**	(0.7)	**0.67**	(0.02)	**0.93**	(0.02)	43.7	(0.2)	36.2	(0.6)	**-8.4**	(0.7)	**0.69**	(0.02)	0.97	(0.02)
Brazil	31.0	(1.1)	c	c	c	c	c	c	c	c	26.2	(1.2)	c	c	c	c	c	c	c	c
Bulgaria	28.3	(0.9)	c	c	c	c	c	c	c	c	19.6	(0.9)	c	c	c	c	c	c	c	c
Colombia	24.9	(0.9)	c	c	c	c	c	c	c	c	18.8	(0.8)	c	c	c	c	c	c	c	c
Croatia	37.6	(1.0)	35.4	(1.8)	-2.2	(1.8)	0.91	(0.07)	0.99	(0.07)	33.6	(1.2)	29.1	(1.8)	**-4.5**	(1.6)	**0.81**	(0.06)	**0.86**	(0.06)
Cyprus*	36.7	(0.5)	34.3	(1.9)	-2.4	(1.9)	0.91	(0.08)	1.02	(0.06)	31.2	(0.6)	28.2	(1.9)	-3.0	(2.0)	0.87	(0.09)	0.96	(0.07)
Hong Kong-China	61.9	(1.6)	58.7	(1.3)	-3.2	(2.0)	0.86	(0.08)	0.89	(0.07)	56.1	(1.3)	54.2	(1.5)	-1.9	(2.0)	0.91	(0.08)	0.96	(0.07)
Macao-China	59.0	(1.3)	59.9	(1.2)	0.9	(1.8)	1.03	(0.07)	1.06	(0.07)	56.5	(1.5)	57.9	(1.1)	1.4	(1.9)	1.06	(0.08)	1.09	(0.07)
Malaysia	30.4	(0.9)	c	c	c	c	c	c	c	c	28.2	(1.0)	c	c	c	c	c	c	c	c
Montenegro	27.2	(0.6)	30.5	(2.7)	3.3	(2.8)	1.18	(0.16)	1.02	(0.11)	23.7	(0.6)	24.2	(2.4)	0.5	(2.5)	1.03	(0.14)	0.86	(0.08)
Russian Federation	42.3	(1.1)	39.1	(2.7)	-3.2	(3.0)	0.90	(0.13)	1.02	(0.15)	38.6	(1.2)	37.0	(2.7)	-1.5	(2.7)	0.95	(0.12)	1.10	(0.12)
Serbia	39.5	(1.0)	41.5	(2.4)	2.0	(2.5)	1.09	(0.11)	1.11	(0.08)	35.9	(0.9)	35.9	(2.6)	0.0	(2.5)	1.00	(0.11)	1.00	(0.07)
Shanghai-China	58.5	(1.1)	c	c	c	c	c	c	c	c	55.8	(1.2)	c	c	c	c	c	c	c	c
Singapore	64.2	(1.1)	66.7	(2.3)	2.6	(2.5)	1.11	(0.13)	0.95	(0.08)	58.8	(1.0)	65.5	(2.3)	6.7	(2.6)	**1.33**	(0.15)	**1.20**	(0.10)
Chinese Taipei	58.6	(1.0)	c	c	c	c	c	c	c	c	55.7	(1.2)	c	c	c	c	c	c	c	c
United Arab Emirates	22.4	(0.9)	36.7	(1.0)	14.2	(1.4)	**2.02**	(0.15)	0.99	(0.06)	20.1	(1.1)	32.6	(1.0)	12.5	(1.4)	**1.94**	(0.15)	0.94	(0.06)
Uruguay	27.4	(0.7)	c	c	c	c	c	c	c	c	22.5	(0.8)	c	c	c	c	c	c	c	c

Note: Values that are statistically significant are indicated in bold (see Annex A3).

1. Generalised odds ratios estimated with logistic regression on national PISA samples. A success indicator for each item is regressed on an item type dummy, an immigrant dummy, and an interaction term (immigrant × item type). Booklet dummies are added to the estimation. This column presents the difference between the logit coefficient on the interaction term and the logit coefficient on the item type dummy in exponentiated form.

2. Generalised odds ratios estimated with logistic regression on national PISA samples. A success indicator for each item is regressed on an item type dummy, an immigrant dummy, and an interaction term (immigrant × item type). Booklet dummies are added to the estimation. This column presents the logit coefficient on the interaction term in exponentiated form.

* See notes at the beginning of this Annex.

StatLink ᴍᔕᒪ http://dx.doi.org/10.1787/888933003706

[Part 2/2]
Performance on problem-solving tasks, by process and by immigrant background

Table V.4.22b *Results based on students' self-reports*

	Items assessing the process of "planning and executing"										Items assessing the process of "monitoring and reflecting"									
	Average proportion of full-credit responses						Relative likelihood of success, in favour of immigrant students (non-immigrant students = 1.00)				Average proportion of full-credit responses						Relative likelihood of success, in favour of immigrant students (non-immigrant students = 1.00)			
	Non-immigrant students		Immigrant students		Difference between immigrant and non-immigrant students		Accounting for booklet effects[1]		Based on success on remaining test items[2]		Non-immigrant students		Immigrant students		Difference between immigrant and non-immigrant students		Accounting for booklet effects[1]		Based on success on remaining test items[2]	
	%	S.E.	%	S.E.	% dif.	S.E.	Odds ratio	S.E.	Odds ratio	S.E.	%	S.E.	%	S.E.	% dif.	S.E.	Odds ratio	S.E.	Odds ratio	S.E.
OECD																				
Australia	52.1	(0.5)	51.7	(1.0)	-0.4	(1.0)	**1.00**	(0.04)	**0.91**	(0.03)	46.3	(0.5)	46.9	(1.1)	0.6	(1.2)	1.03	(0.05)	0.97	(0.04)
Austria	49.2	(0.9)	40.1	(2.1)	**-9.1**	(2.3)	**0.66**	(0.06)	1.06	(0.09)	38.2	(0.9)	33.9	(2.4)	-4.3	(2.4)	**0.80**	(0.09)	**1.31**	(0.16)
Belgium	50.2	(0.6)	36.1	(1.8)	**-14.1**	(2.0)	**0.55**	(0.05)	**1.17**	(0.07)	44.9	(0.8)	31.1	(1.8)	**-13.8**	(2.0)	**0.54**	(0.05)	1.10	(0.09)
Canada	54.0	(0.6)	49.0	(1.7)	**-5.0**	(1.8)	**0.82**	(0.06)	0.91	(0.05)	46.5	(0.8)	46.0	(1.9)	-0.5	(2.1)	0.99	(0.08)	**1.17**	(0.07)
Chile	35.2	(0.8)	c	c	c	c	c	c	c	c	33.0	(0.8)	c	c	c	c	c	c	c	c
Czech Republic	47.2	(0.7)	39.7	(2.8)	-7.5	(2.9)	**0.73**	(0.09)	0.94	(0.09)	40.8	(0.7)	37.9	(3.7)	-2.9	(3.8)	0.88	(0.14)	1.19	(0.19)
Denmark	49.5	(0.9)	36.4	(1.5)	**-13.1**	(1.6)	**0.56**	(0.04)	0.94	(0.06)	36.9	(1.0)	29.9	(1.6)	**-7.0**	(1.9)	**0.71**	(0.07)	**1.27**	(0.11)
Estonia	49.9	(0.9)	46.2	(2.4)	-3.7	(2.6)	0.86	(0.07)	1.07	(0.07)	43.0	(0.9)	36.8	(3.0)	-6.2	(3.2)	**0.77**	(0.10)	0.92	(0.10)
Finland	51.7	(0.6)	35.9	(2.0)	**-15.8**	(2.0)	**0.53**	(0.04)	1.05	(0.07)	43.2	(0.6)	28.4	(2.9)	**-14.7**	(2.9)	**0.53**	(0.07)	1.04	(0.10)
France	51.1	(0.8)	39.8	(2.4)	**-11.3**	(2.6)	**0.62**	(0.06)	1.03	(0.08)	45.6	(0.9)	35.1	(2.4)	**-10.5**	(2.6)	**0.63**	(0.07)	1.05	(0.10)
Germany	52.2	(0.8)	44.5	(2.9)	-7.6	(3.0)	**0.69**	(0.09)	1.04	(0.11)	44.0	(1.1)	38.8	(2.3)	-5.3	(2.4)	**0.75**	(0.07)	1.16	(0.12)
Hungary	37.6	(0.9)	c	c	c	c	c	c	c	c	30.9	(1.1)	c	c	c	c	c	c	c	c
Ireland	46.0	(0.9)	43.1	(2.5)	-2.9	(2.7)	0.89	(0.09)	1.03	(0.11)	42.8	(1.1)	37.6	(2.8)	-5.2	(3.1)	0.81	(0.11)	0.92	(0.13)
Israel	37.4	(1.5)	38.5	(2.2)	1.1	(2.2)	1.07	(0.10)	0.96	(0.07)	32.5	(1.4)	34.9	(2.3)	2.4	(2.5)	1.13	(0.13)	1.04	(0.09)
Italy	49.3	(1.0)	35.1	(2.7)	**-14.2**	(2.9)	**0.55**	(0.07)	0.80	(0.10)	43.0	(1.0)	42.3	(3.7)	-0.6	(3.9)	0.98	(0.17)	**1.68**	(0.28)
Japan	56.4	(0.7)	c	c	c	c	c	c	c	c	52.1	(0.7)	c	c	c	c	c	c	c	c
Korea	54.6	(0.9)	c	c	c	c	c	c	c	c	53.9	(1.1)	c	c	c	c	c	c	c	c
Netherlands	51.6	(1.0)	36.7	(2.8)	**-14.9**	(2.5)	**0.54**	(0.06)	1.00	(0.09)	44.2	(1.0)	33.0	(3.6)	**-11.2**	(3.3)	**0.62**	(0.09)	1.17	(0.10)
Norway	49.5	(1.0)	39.3	(3.3)	**-10.1**	(3.4)	**0.62**	(0.09)	1.13	(0.12)	39.5	(1.2)	29.7	(3.6)	**-9.8**	(3.7)	**0.61**	(0.11)	1.07	(0.13)
Poland	43.8	(1.0)	c	c	c	c	c	c	c	c	35.6	(1.1)	c	c	c	c	c	c	c	c
Portugal	46.4	(1.0)	40.3	(3.3)	-6.2	(3.3)	**0.75**	(0.09)	0.93	(0.12)	39.4	(1.1)	36.9	(3.7)	-2.5	(3.7)	0.88	(0.15)	1.13	(0.18)
Slovak Republic	43.5	(0.9)	c	c	c	c	c	c	c	c	36.0	(0.9)	c	c	c	c	c	c	c	c
Slovenia	43.4	(0.8)	32.2	(2.2)	**-11.2**	(2.5)	**0.66**	(0.07)	1.15	(0.12)	35.3	(0.8)	25.4	(2.4)	**-9.9**	(2.6)	**0.66**	(0.09)	1.11	(0.11)
Spain	43.8	(0.9)	33.9	(2.4)	**-9.9**	(2.6)	**0.68**	(0.08)	1.11	(0.09)	40.6	(1.0)	30.0	(3.1)	**-10.6**	(3.3)	**0.65**	(0.10)	1.03	(0.12)
Sweden	46.4	(0.8)	37.5	(1.6)	**-9.0**	(1.9)	**0.70**	(0.07)	0.93	(0.08)	38.5	(1.0)	37.1	(2.4)	-1.3	(2.8)	0.96	(0.12)	**1.38**	(0.14)
Turkey	36.1	(0.9)	c	c	c	c	c	c	c	c	31.6	(1.0)	c	c	c	c	c	c	c	c
England (United Kingdom)	50.3	(1.1)	42.8	(2.8)	-7.5	(2.9)	**0.73**	(0.09)	0.95	(0.06)	44.8	(0.9)	41.3	(3.4)	-3.5	(3.5)	0.85	(0.12)	1.17	(0.11)
United States	48.3	(1.2)	43.7	(1.8)	**-4.6**	(2.1)	**0.85**	(0.07)	0.94	(0.07)	43.6	(1.3)	41.9	(2.4)	-1.7	(2.5)	0.95	(0.10)	1.10	(0.08)
OECD average	47.4	(0.2)	40.1	(0.5)	**-8.4**	(0.5)	**0.70**	(0.02)	1.00	(0.02)	40.9	(0.2)	35.9	(0.6)	**-5.6**	(0.6)	**0.78**	(0.02)	**1.13**	(0.03)
Partners																				
Brazil	32.6	(1.1)	c	c	c	c	c	c	c	c	27.5	(0.9)	c	c	c	c	c	c	c	c
Bulgaria	27.1	(0.8)	c	c	c	c	c	c	c	c	22.1	(0.9)	c	c	c	c	c	c	c	c
Colombia	28.0	(0.8)	c	c	c	c	c	c	c	c	25.1	(0.8)	c	c	c	c	c	c	c	c
Croatia	40.5	(0.9)	40.3	(1.7)	-0.2	(1.6)	0.99	(0.07)	**1.14**	(0.05)	33.8	(0.9)	31.2	(1.6)	-2.6	(1.8)	0.89	(0.07)	0.96	(0.06)
Cyprus*	35.2	(0.6)	33.3	(1.4)	-1.9	(1.5)	0.93	(0.06)	1.06	(0.06)	30.3	(0.6)	26.6	(1.4)	**-3.7**	(1.6)	**0.84**	(0.07)	0.93	(0.05)
Hong Kong-China	51.7	(1.1)	51.4	(1.0)	-0.3	(1.5)	0.98	(0.06)	1.08	(0.06)	48.7	(1.4)	48.5	(1.4)	-0.2	(1.9)	0.98	(0.08)	1.06	(0.08)
Macao-China	52.2	(1.1)	50.9	(0.7)	-1.3	(1.4)	0.95	(0.05)	0.93	(0.05)	46.4	(1.3)	45.5	(1.2)	-1.0	(1.9)	0.95	(0.07)	0.95	(0.06)
Malaysia	29.6	(0.8)	c	c	c	c	c	c	c	c	24.9	(0.8)	c	c	c	c	c	c	c	c
Montenegro	29.9	(0.6)	33.4	(2.1)	3.4	(2.2)	1.17	(0.12)	1.02	(0.09)	23.4	(0.6)	28.2	(2.5)	4.8	(2.6)	1.29	(0.17)	1.13	(0.13)
Russian Federation	44.3	(0.8)	40.4	(2.5)	-3.9	(2.4)	0.87	(0.09)	0.98	(0.11)	37.8	(1.1)	32.2	(2.6)	-5.6	(3.0)	0.80	(0.11)	0.89	(0.11)
Serbia	41.0	(0.8)	40.4	(2.4)	-0.6	(2.3)	0.98	(0.09)	0.96	(0.06)	33.2	(0.9)	31.9	(2.7)	-1.3	(2.7)	0.95	(0.12)	0.93	(0.08)
Shanghai-China	50.1	(0.7)	c	c	c	c	c	c	c	c	47.6	(1.1)	c	c	c	c	c	c	c	c
Singapore	55.1	(0.9)	57.9	(1.9)	2.8	(2.3)	1.12	(0.10)	0.95	(0.07)	55.2	(0.9)	57.4	(2.3)	2.3	(2.5)	1.10	(0.12)	0.95	(0.09)
Chinese Taipei	50.5	(0.8)	c	c	c	c	c	c	c	c	45.1	(1.0)	c	c	c	c	c	c	c	c
United Arab Emirates	21.3	(0.8)	35.6	(0.8)	**14.3**	(1.1)	**2.04**	(0.12)	1.01	(0.05)	18.1	(0.9)	32.2	(1.0)	**14.1**	(1.5)	**2.16**	(0.19)	1.08	(0.07)
Uruguay	28.2	(0.7)	c	c	c	c	c	c	c	c	24.1	(0.7)	c	c	c	c	c	c	c	c

Note: Values that are statistically significant are indicated in bold (see Annex A3).
1. Generalised odds ratios estimated with logistic regression on national PISA samples. A success indicator for each item is regressed on an item type dummy, an immigrant dummy, and an interaction term (immigrant × item type). Booklet dummies are added to the estimation. This column presents the difference between the logit coefficient on the interaction term and the logit coefficient on the item type dummy in exponentiated form.
2. Generalised odds ratios estimated with logistic regression on national PISA samples. A success indicator for each item is regressed on an item type dummy, an immigrant dummy, and an interaction term (immigrant × item type). Booklet dummies are added to the estimation. This column presents the logit coefficient on the interaction term in exponentiated form.
* See notes at the beginning of this Annex.
StatLink ⬛⬛ http://dx.doi.org/10.1787/888933003706

[Part 1/1]

Association between problem-solving performance and perseverance/openness to problem solving

Table V.4.23 *Results based on students' self-reports*

| | Score-point difference that is associated with students' perseverance, by performance decile in problem solving | | | | | | Score-point difference that is associated with students' openness to problem solving, by performance decile in problem solving | | | | | |
| | Mean | | 10th percentile[1] | | 90th percentile[1] | | Mean | | 10th percentile[2] | | 90th percentile[2] | |
	Score dif.	S.E.	Score dif.	S.E.	Score dif.	S.E.	Score dif.	S.E.	Score dif.	S.E.	Score dif.	S.E.
Australia	**23**	(1.4)	**20**	(2.4)	**22**	(2.9)	**31**	(1.3)	**25**	(3.1)	**37**	(2.3)
Austria	**10**	(2.2)	9	(6.3)	9	(4.5)	**26**	(1.9)	**19**	(4.2)	**30**	(3.7)
Belgium	**13**	(2.1)	9	(4.7)	**17**	(3.2)	**26**	(2.0)	**19**	(4.6)	**31**	(2.4)
Canada	**20**	(1.3)	**20**	(2.5)	**18**	(2.4)	**33**	(1.2)	**29**	(2.9)	**34**	(2.6)
Chile	**14**	(1.7)	**15**	(3.1)	**13**	(3.6)	**19**	(1.7)	**13**	(3.5)	**24**	(3.2)
Czech Republic	**9**	(2.4)	8	(5.8)	9	(4.4)	**31**	(2.2)	**23**	(6.1)	**36**	(5.3)
Denmark	**17**	(2.0)	**13**	(4.5)	**18**	(4.5)	**26**	(2.5)	**20**	(4.3)	**29**	(4.0)
Estonia	1	(2.0)	0	(4.2)	0	(3.6)	**27**	(2.0)	**17**	(4.7)	**34**	(2.9)
Finland	**30**	(1.6)	**28**	(3.1)	**31**	(3.2)	**37**	(1.6)	**32**	(3.4)	**41**	(3.0)
France	**18**	(2.0)	**11**	(4.6)	**22**	(2.3)	**22**	(1.9)	**12**	(4.5)	**29**	(2.8)
Germany	**13**	(2.5)	4	(4.4)	**16**	(4.3)	**19**	(2.1)	9	(5.0)	**24**	(4.5)
Hungary	**14**	(2.7)	11	(7.8)	**15**	(4.2)	**24**	(3.3)	**17**	(7.7)	**22**	(4.8)
Ireland	**23**	(2.1)	**21**	(4.4)	**27**	(3.6)	**30**	(1.7)	**20**	(4.0)	**38**	(3.6)
Israel	1	(1.8)	8	(4.1)	0	(4.2)	**12**	(2.5)	5	(5.7)	**24**	(4.2)
Italy	0	(2.1)	0	(5.3)	1	(3.7)	**13**	(2.7)	8	(5.9)	**18**	(3.9)
Japan	**14**	(2.5)	**13**	(3.7)	**16**	(3.2)	**23**	(2.3)	**22**	(3.9)	**23**	(2.6)
Korea	**20**	(2.9)	**21**	(5.1)	**19**	(5.4)	**37**	(2.3)	**39**	(4.0)	**29**	(4.1)
Netherlands	**6**	(2.5)	6	(4.2)	10	(5.6)	**19**	(2.3)	**13**	(4.5)	**29**	(5.7)
Norway	**22**	(1.9)	**21**	(4.7)	**23**	(2.8)	**26**	(1.8)	**21**	(3.1)	**29**	(3.0)
Poland	**20**	(2.0)	**19**	(3.7)	**19**	(4.3)	**20**	(1.9)	**18**	(4.3)	**20**	(4.4)
Portugal	**21**	(1.9)	**20**	(2.9)	**20**	(3.2)	**25**	(2.0)	**15**	(3.6)	**33**	(3.9)
Slovak Republic	**12**	(2.0)	1	(6.9)	**16**	(4.3)	**19**	(2.4)	9	(5.0)	**26**	(4.7)
Slovenia	**7**	(2.3)	7	(4.9)	7	(5.5)	**25**	(2.4)	**18**	(3.7)	**35**	(5.3)
Spain	**16**	(2.3)	**15**	(5.3)	**19**	(2.9)	**25**	(2.0)	**19**	(5.0)	**34**	(4.3)
Sweden	**25**	(2.1)	**20**	(5.3)	**28**	(3.5)	**27**	(1.9)	**15**	(4.2)	**33**	(2.9)
Turkey	**10**	(1.7)	9	(2.7)	**11**	(3.5)	**14**	(2.0)	9	(3.4)	**25**	(3.3)
England (United Kingdom)	**20**	(2.0)	**19**	(4.8)	**19**	(3.8)	**34**	(2.2)	**30**	(4.9)	**39**	(4.0)
United States	**19**	(1.8)	**15**	(3.3)	**23**	(4.6)	**26**	(1.7)	**15**	(3.4)	**35**	(3.3)
OECD average	**15**	(0.4)	**13**	(0.9)	**16**	(0.7)	**25**	(0.4)	**18**	(0.9)	**30**	(0.7)
Brazil	**18**	(1.9)	**16**	(3.9)	**17**	(5.1)	**16**	(2.7)	5	(4.1)	**22**	(5.3)
Bulgaria	**17**	(2.1)	**19**	(3.4)	**12**	(3.7)	**8**	(2.3)	2	(4.2)	**14**	(4.3)
Colombia	**9**	(1.8)	7	(3.9)	**11**	(4.2)	**8**	(2.1)	3	(4.3)	**17**	(3.9)
Croatia	**6**	(1.6)	**10**	(2.7)	2	(2.9)	**16**	(2.2)	6	(4.1)	**29**	(5.0)
Cyprus*	**20**	(2.3)	**20**	(4.9)	**20**	(3.5)	**23**	(1.9)	**17**	(3.8)	**28**	(3.3)
Hong Kong-China	**7**	(2.6)	**12**	(4.4)	3	(4.7)	**22**	(2.1)	**21**	(4.0)	**23**	(4.5)
Macao-China	**13**	(1.9)	**14**	(4.6)	**11**	(3.7)	**22**	(1.5)	**23**	(3.3)	**19**	(3.2)
Malaysia	**13**	(2.0)	**12**	(3.5)	**14**	(3.2)	**8**	(1.8)	-1	(3.4)	**19**	(4.6)
Montenegro	**13**	(1.7)	**13**	(2.9)	**14**	(2.8)	1	(2.0)	-5	(3.7)	**8**	(4.0)
Russian Federation	**6**	(1.7)	6	(3.7)	6	(3.2)	**20**	(2.1)	**12**	(3.2)	**28**	(4.2)
Serbia	**10**	(1.7)	**11**	(3.3)	6	(3.4)	**12**	(2.0)	5	(4.1)	**20**	(3.8)
Shanghai-China	**9**	(2.1)	8	(3.7)	7	(3.9)	**26**	(2.0)	**26**	(2.9)	**23**	(3.3)
Singapore	**13**	(2.1)	**13**	(3.6)	11	(4.4)	**18**	(2.0)	**12**	(4.4)	**20**	(3.3)
Chinese Taipei	**13**	(1.7)	**10**	(4.4)	**11**	(3.6)	**21**	(1.7)	**17**	(3.3)	**22**	(3.7)
United Arab Emirates	**26**	(1.5)	**29**	(2.4)	**22**	(3.6)	**10**	(1.8)	2	(3.3)	**19**	(3.6)
Uruguay	**13**	(2.3)	**10**	(4.7)	**16**	(2.7)	**14**	(2.1)	2	(2.9)	**28**	(3.6)

Note: Values that are statistically significant are indicated in bold (see Annex A3).
1. Results based on quantile regression of problem-solving performance on the *index of perseverance*.
2. Results based on quantile regression of problem-solving performance on the *index of openness to problem solving*.
* See notes at the beginning of this Annex.
StatLink ⌐ŝ┐ http://dx.doi.org/10.1787/888933003706

[Part 1/1]
Performance in problem solving and access to a computer at home
Table V.4.24   *Results based on students' self-reports*

	Students who have at least one computer at home to use for school work																	
	Percentage of students													Difference in problem-solving performance				
	All students		Boys		Girls		Gender difference (B - G)		Parents' highest occupation: Skilled (ISCO 1 to 3)		Parents' highest occupation: Semi-skilled or elementary (ISCO 4 to 9)		Difference related to parents' highest occupation: Skilled - semi-skilled or elementary		Observed		After accounting for socio-demographic characteristics of students[1]	
	%	S.E.	%	S.E.	%	S.E.	% dif.	S.E.	%	S.E.	%	S.E.	% dif.	S.E.	Score dif.	S.E.	Score dif.	S.E.
OECD																		
Australia	97.8	(0.1)	97.3	(0.1)	98.2	(0.1)	-0.9	(0.1)	98.6	(0.1)	97.0	(0.1)	1.5	(0.2)	72	(7.2)	36	(6.7)
Austria	98.6	(0.2)	98.6	(0.3)	98.5	(0.2)	0.1	(0.3)	99.3	(0.1)	97.8	(0.3)	1.5	(0.3)	47	(13.3)	24	(13.9)
Belgium	97.0	(0.1)	96.7	(0.2)	97.2	(0.1)	-0.5	(0.3)	98.2	(0.1)	96.3	(0.2)	1.9	(0.3)	86	(8.6)	46	(6.5)
Canada	97.2	(0.1)	97.1	(0.1)	97.4	(0.1)	-0.4	(0.2)	98.3	(0.1)	95.9	(0.2)	2.4	(0.2)	48	(7.0)	26	(7.6)
Chile	86.3	(0.5)	86.2	(0.6)	86.3	(0.5)	-0.1	(0.4)	95.5	(0.3)	81.3	(0.6)	14.2	(0.6)	59	(5.9)	24	(4.4)
Czech Republic	97.3	(0.1)	96.9	(0.2)	97.8	(0.1)	-0.9	(0.3)	99.4	(0.1)	96.5	(0.2)	2.8	(0.2)	89	(13.5)	31	(12.9)
Denmark	99.0	(0.1)	98.8	(0.1)	99.2	(0.1)	-0.4	(0.1)	99.5	(0.1)	98.6	(0.2)	0.9	(0.1)	43	(16.8)	12	(18.8)
Estonia	89.3	(0.3)	91.9	(0.3)	86.8	(0.4)	5.0	(0.4)	90.2	(0.3)	88.5	(0.4)	1.7	(0.4)	-9	(5.0)	-16	(4.9)
Finland	98.9	(0.1)	98.6	(0.1)	99.2	(0.1)	-0.6	(0.1)	99.3	(0.1)	98.2	(0.2)	1.1	(0.2)	48	(11.4)	25	(11.1)
France	96.8	(0.1)	96.6	(0.2)	97.0	(0.2)	-0.4	(0.3)	98.2	(0.1)	95.2	(0.3)	3.0	(0.3)	64	(9.7)	33	(9.8)
Germany	98.2	(0.1)	97.8	(0.2)	98.7	(0.1)	-0.8	(0.2)	99.2	(0.1)	97.6	(0.2)	1.7	(0.3)	97	(13.7)	70	(16.1)
Hungary	94.1	(0.3)	94.6	(0.3)	93.7	(0.4)	0.9	(0.4)	96.7	(0.2)	93.6	(0.3)	3.0	(0.4)	90	(11.6)	36	(11.4)
Ireland	95.2	(0.2)	93.5	(0.2)	97.0	(0.2)	-3.5	(0.3)	96.0	(0.2)	94.6	(0.3)	1.4	(0.3)	34	(8.5)	18	(8.1)
Israel	94.3	(0.3)	96.5	(0.3)	92.3	(0.4)	4.2	(0.5)	96.1	(0.3)	92.1	(0.5)	4.1	(0.6)	61	(9.5)	7	(8.5)
Italy	96.6	(0.1)	96.0	(0.2)	97.4	(0.2)	-1.4	(0.3)	97.5	(0.2)	96.3	(0.2)	1.2	(0.3)	26	(8.3)	12	(8.3)
Japan	70.1	(0.4)	67.1	(0.5)	73.4	(0.5)	-6.3	(0.6)	74.6	(0.5)	66.5	(0.5)	8.1	(0.6)	27	(3.9)	17	(3.4)
Korea	94.6	(0.2)	93.9	(0.3)	95.5	(0.3)	-1.6	(0.4)	95.2	(0.2)	93.9	(0.3)	1.3	(0.3)	31	(7.8)	17	(6.9)
Netherlands	98.3	(0.1)	98.1	(0.2)	98.5	(0.1)	-0.4	(0.2)	98.7	(0.1)	97.5	(0.2)	1.2	(0.2)	74	(19.0)	55	(15.6)
Norway	98.6	(0.1)	98.2	(0.1)	99.0	(0.1)	-0.7	(0.1)	99.2	(0.1)	97.6	(0.2)	1.6	(0.2)	71	(15.1)	24	(13.5)
Poland	97.4	(0.2)	97.5	(0.3)	97.3	(0.2)	0.2	(0.3)	98.8	(0.1)	96.6	(0.3)	2.2	(0.4)	67	(7.3)	27	(8.1)
Portugal	96.7	(0.2)	96.2	(0.2)	97.3	(0.2)	-1.1	(0.3)	98.6	(0.2)	96.0	(0.3)	2.6	(0.3)	64	(9.8)	30	(9.5)
Slovak Republic	91.9	(0.3)	91.8	(0.4)	91.9	(0.4)	-0.1	(0.5)	98.5	(0.2)	91.6	(0.4)	6.9	(0.4)	119	(8.1)	61	(7.0)
Slovenia	98.6	(0.1)	98.3	(0.1)	98.9	(0.2)	-0.6	(0.2)	98.9	(0.1)	98.6	(0.2)	0.3	(0.2)	70	(12.7)	40	(14.2)
Spain	96.1	(0.2)	96.2	(0.3)	96.0	(0.2)	0.2	(0.3)	97.9	(0.1)	94.9	(0.3)	3.0	(0.3)	60	(8.6)	31	(8.1)
Sweden	98.7	(0.1)	98.6	(0.1)	98.7	(0.1)	-0.1	(0.2)	99.1	(0.1)	98.2	(0.1)	0.9	(0.2)	59	(17.0)	34	(16.6)
Turkey	68.3	(0.5)	68.5	(0.7)	68.0	(0.6)	0.5	(0.8)	86.7	(0.7)	65.7	(0.5)	21.0	(0.7)	53	(4.3)	28	(3.8)
England (United Kingdom)	96.8	(0.2)	96.6	(0.4)	97.0	(0.2)	-0.4	(0.4)	97.9	(0.2)	96.1	(0.3)	1.8	(0.3)	65	(10.0)	30	(10.8)
United States	91.1	(0.3)	89.8	(0.4)	92.5	(0.3)	-2.8	(0.4)	95.0	(0.3)	85.6	(0.4)	9.4	(0.5)	42	(6.3)	9	(5.9)
OECD average	94.1	(0.0)	93.8	(0.1)	94.3	(0.1)	-0.5	(0.1)	96.5	(0.0)	92.8	(0.1)	3.7	(0.1)	59	(2.0)	28	(2.0)
Partners																		
Brazil	73.2	(0.6)	74.9	(0.8)	71.6	(0.7)	3.4	(0.8)	90.7	(0.4)	64.9	(0.8)	25.8	(0.7)	66	(5.1)	37	(4.6)
Bulgaria	93.0	(0.3)	92.7	(0.4)	93.2	(0.6)	-0.5	(0.9)	99.0	(0.1)	90.9	(0.3)	8.1	(0.4)	110	(11.6)	42	(10.3)
Colombia	62.9	(0.7)	62.9	(0.7)	62.9	(0.9)	0.0	(0.9)	84.5	(0.8)	56.5	(0.7)	28.0	(1.0)	53	(4.6)	27	(3.8)
Croatia	94.2	(0.2)	94.9	(0.2)	93.5	(0.3)	1.4	(0.4)	95.5	(0.2)	93.6	(0.2)	1.9	(0.3)	40	(6.5)	26	(6.1)
Cyprus*	96.7	(0.1)	95.2	(0.2)	98.2	(0.1)	-3.0	(0.2)	98.4	(0.1)	96.1	(0.2)	2.3	(0.2)	73	(8.5)	39	(9.3)
Hong Kong-China	98.8	(0.1)	98.7	(0.1)	98.9	(0.1)	-0.2	(0.2)	98.9	(0.1)	98.8	(0.1)	0.1	(0.2)	33	(15.4)	20	(14.6)
Macao-China	97.1	(0.1)	96.5	(0.2)	97.9	(0.1)	-1.4	(0.2)	97.7	(0.2)	97.2	(0.1)	0.6	(0.3)	36	(6.3)	32	(6.4)
Malaysia	69.6	(0.9)	68.8	(1.0)	70.4	(1.0)	-1.6	(0.7)	84.6	(0.8)	59.8	(1.0)	24.8	(0.7)	50	(3.9)	24	(3.7)
Montenegro	91.8	(0.2)	92.6	(0.3)	91.0	(0.3)	1.6	(0.4)	96.5	(0.2)	89.4	(0.3)	7.0	(0.4)	46	(5.0)	14	(5.5)
Russian Federation	93.0	(0.3)	92.9	(0.4)	93.2	(0.4)	-0.3	(0.5)	96.9	(0.3)	89.0	(0.4)	7.9	(0.4)	44	(5.9)	7	(7.1)
Serbia	95.4	(0.2)	95.9	(0.2)	94.9	(0.3)	1.0	(0.3)	98.8	(0.1)	93.2	(0.3)	5.6	(0.3)	74	(7.4)	39	(6.7)
Shanghai-China	83.3	(0.5)	81.2	(0.7)	85.3	(0.5)	-4.0	(0.7)	87.4	(0.3)	78.0	(1.1)	9.5	(1.2)	42	(6.6)	17	(4.1)
Singapore	94.6	(0.2)	94.2	(0.2)	95.1	(0.2)	-0.9	(0.3)	96.1	(0.2)	91.6	(0.4)	4.5	(0.4)	61	(6.2)	32	(6.4)
Chinese Taipei	90.6	(0.2)	89.3	(0.4)	91.9	(0.3)	-2.5	(0.6)	93.5	(0.2)	89.2	(0.4)	4.3	(0.5)	45	(6.4)	26	(5.9)
United Arab Emirates	92.9	(0.2)	91.7	(0.2)	94.1	(0.2)	-2.5	(0.3)	94.5	(0.2)	91.2	(0.3)	3.4	(0.3)	59	(4.7)	28	(5.1)
Uruguay	88.9	(0.2)	89.8	(0.4)	88.2	(0.4)	1.6	(0.6)	97.2	(0.2)	86.3	(0.3)	10.9	(0.4)	51	(5.1)	12	(4.7)

Note: Values that are statistically significant are indicated in bold (see Annex A3).
1. The difference in problem-solving performance after accounting for socio-demographic characteristics of students corresponds to the coefficient from a regression where the *PISA index of economic, social and cultural status* (ESCS), ESCS squared, boy, and an immigrant (first generation) dummy are introduced as further independent variables.
* See notes at the beginning of this Annex.
StatLink ⌗⌗⌗ http://dx.doi.org/10.1787/888933003706

[Part 1/1]
Performance in problem solving and use of a computer at home
Table V.4.25 *Results based on students' self-reports*

	Students who use a desktop, laptop or tablet computer at home													Difference in problem-solving performance			
	Percentage of students															After accounting for socio-demographic characteristics of students[1]	
	All students		Boys		Girls		Gender difference (B - G)		Parents' highest occupation: Skilled (ISCO 1 to 3)		Parents' highest occupation: Semi-skilled or elementary (ISCO 4 to 9)		Difference related to parents' highest occupation: Skilled - semi-skilled or elementary		Observed			
	%	S.E.	%	S.E.	%	S.E.	% dif.	S.E.	%	S.E.	%	S.E.	% dif.	S.E.	Score dif.	S.E.	Score dif.	S.E.
Australia	97.1	(0.1)	96.7	(0.1)	97.5	(0.1)	-0.8	(0.2)	98.2	(0.1)	95.6	(0.2)	2.6	(0.2)	75	(5.9)	50	(6.4)
Austria	98.7	(0.1)	98.7	(0.2)	98.8	(0.1)	-0.1	(0.2)	99.3	(0.1)	98.2	(0.2)	1.1	(0.2)	72	(18.8)	50	(20.0)
Belgium	98.2	(0.1)	98.1	(0.2)	98.4	(0.1)	-0.3	(0.2)	98.9	(0.1)	97.6	(0.2)	1.2	(0.2)	85	(11.3)	60	(10.2)
Canada	m	m	m	m	m	m	m	m	m	m	m	m	m	m	m	m	m	m
Chile	87.0	(0.5)	86.8	(0.5)	87.2	(0.6)	-0.4	(0.5)	96.1	(0.3)	82.1	(0.6)	14.1	(0.6)	55	(5.8)	21	(4.3)
Czech Republic	97.4	(0.2)	97.3	(0.2)	97.5	(0.2)	-0.2	(0.2)	99.5	(0.1)	96.3	(0.2)	3.2	(0.2)	115	(12.6)	59	(13.1)
Denmark	99.2	(0.1)	99.0	(0.1)	99.4	(0.1)	-0.4	(0.1)	99.5	(0.1)	98.9	(0.1)	0.6	(0.1)	71	(18.2)	44	(17.2)
Estonia	98.6	(0.1)	98.6	(0.1)	98.6	(0.1)	0.0	(0.2)	99.2	(0.1)	97.9	(0.2)	1.3	(0.2)	47	(11.3)	33	(12.0)
Finland	99.1	(0.1)	99.0	(0.1)	99.2	(0.1)	-0.2	(0.1)	99.3	(0.1)	98.9	(0.1)	0.5	(0.1)	43	(16.4)	24	(14.6)
France	m	m	m	m	m	m	m	m	m	m	m	m	m	m	m	m	m	m
Germany	99.1	(0.1)	99.0	(0.1)	99.2	(0.1)	-0.2	(0.2)	99.4	(0.1)	99.1	(0.1)	0.2	(0.2)	59	(18.0)	32	(20.1)
Hungary	94.7	(0.2)	95.1	(0.3)	94.3	(0.4)	0.8	(0.6)	97.5	(0.2)	94.4	(0.3)	3.1	(0.4)	99	(10.7)	40	(10.0)
Ireland	97.0	(0.1)	96.7	(0.2)	97.3	(0.2)	-0.6	(0.2)	97.8	(0.1)	96.2	(0.2)	1.6	(0.3)	31	(10.3)	11	(10.3)
Israel	96.1	(0.1)	96.4	(0.2)	95.7	(0.2)	0.7	(0.4)	97.9	(0.1)	93.7	(0.5)	4.2	(0.5)	94	(11.8)	47	(11.7)
Italy	97.4	(0.2)	96.9	(0.3)	98.0	(0.2)	-1.2	(0.3)	98.6	(0.1)	96.9	(0.3)	1.7	(0.4)	52	(18.9)	30	(20.0)
Japan	81.4	(0.4)	81.1	(0.4)	81.6	(0.5)	-0.5	(0.5)	85.6	(0.5)	78.0	(0.4)	7.7	(0.5)	35	(4.3)	24	(3.9)
Korea	83.5	(0.5)	83.0	(0.5)	84.1	(0.7)	-1.1	(0.8)	87.1	(0.4)	79.6	(0.7)	7.5	(0.6)	45	(4.6)	33	(4.2)
Netherlands	98.9	(0.1)	98.7	(0.1)	99.0	(0.1)	-0.3	(0.2)	99.1	(0.1)	98.5	(0.2)	0.6	(0.2)	92	(14.7)	77	(13.0)
Norway	98.7	(0.1)	98.2	(0.1)	99.1	(0.1)	-0.9	(0.1)	99.0	(0.1)	98.5	(0.2)	0.5	(0.2)	87	(15.6)	58	(15.6)
Poland	96.1	(0.2)	96.5	(0.2)	95.6	(0.3)	0.9	(0.3)	98.5	(0.2)	94.5	(0.4)	4.0	(0.6)	74	(8.5)	38	(8.6)
Portugal	96.0	(0.2)	95.6	(0.2)	96.4	(0.3)	-0.8	(0.3)	98.4	(0.2)	94.7	(0.3)	3.7	(0.3)	63	(8.6)	31	(8.2)
Slovak Republic	94.3	(0.2)	94.4	(0.3)	94.1	(0.3)	0.4	(0.4)	98.3	(0.2)	94.1	(0.2)	4.2	(0.3)	107	(9.1)	51	(7.3)
Slovenia	96.2	(0.2)	95.2	(0.3)	97.4	(0.2)	-2.2	(0.3)	97.0	(0.2)	95.9	(0.2)	1.1	(0.3)	37	(8.6)	22	(7.9)
Spain	96.6	(0.2)	96.6	(0.3)	96.5	(0.2)	0.2	(0.4)	98.3	(0.1)	95.5	(0.4)	2.8	(0.4)	63	(9.3)	37	(8.3)
Sweden	98.5	(0.1)	98.4	(0.1)	98.7	(0.1)	-0.3	(0.2)	98.9	(0.1)	98.4	(0.1)	0.4	(0.2)	65	(15.5)	47	(14.7)
Turkey	68.3	(0.5)	69.9	(0.6)	66.7	(0.6)	3.1	(0.8)	85.9	(0.6)	65.7	(0.5)	20.2	(0.7)	48	(3.9)	24	(3.4)
England (United Kingdom)	m	m	m	m	m	m	m	m	m	m	m	m	m	m	m	m	m	m
United States	m	m	m	m	m	m	m	m	m	m	m	m	m	m	m	m	m	m
OECD average	94.5	(0.0)	94.4	(0.1)	94.6	(0.1)	-0.2	(0.1)	97.0	(0.0)	93.3	(0.1)	3.7	(0.1)	67	(2.5)	39	(2.5)
Brazil	m	m	m	m	m	m	m	m	m	m	m	m	m	m	m	m	m	m
Bulgaria	m	m	m	m	m	m	m	m	m	m	m	m	m	m	m	m	m	m
Colombia	m	m	m	m	m	m	m	m	m	m	m	m	m	m	m	m	m	m
Croatia	97.0	(0.1)	97.0	(0.1)	97.0	(0.2)	0.0	(0.2)	98.4	(0.1)	96.4	(0.2)	2.0	(0.2)	73	(11.3)	53	(11.1)
Cyprus*	m	m	m	m	m	m	m	m	m	m	m	m	m	m	m	m	m	m
Hong Kong-China	97.5	(0.1)	97.6	(0.2)	97.3	(0.2)	0.2	(0.3)	98.2	(0.2)	97.2	(0.1)	1.0	(0.2)	59	(9.9)	42	(10.8)
Macao-China	97.2	(0.1)	96.4	(0.2)	97.9	(0.1)	-1.5	(0.2)	98.9	(0.1)	96.9	(0.1)	2.0	(0.2)	36	(7.7)	33	(8.0)
Malaysia	m	m	m	m	m	m	m	m	m	m	m	m	m	m	m	m	m	m
Montenegro	m	m	m	m	m	m	m	m	m	m	m	m	m	m	m	m	m	m
Russian Federation	91.6	(0.4)	91.2	(0.4)	92.0	(0.6)	-0.8	(0.7)	95.9	(0.3)	87.4	(0.5)	8.5	(0.4)	52	(4.7)	19	(4.3)
Serbia	91.1	(0.3)	92.8	(0.4)	89.4	(0.3)	3.4	(0.5)	96.2	(0.2)	87.8	(0.4)	8.4	(0.5)	79	(5.2)	56	(5.8)
Shanghai-China	85.5	(0.5)	84.0	(0.6)	87.0	(0.6)	-3.0	(0.5)	90.7	(0.3)	79.0	(0.9)	11.7	(0.9)	56	(6.7)	28	(5.1)
Singapore	95.4	(0.1)	95.6	(0.2)	95.1	(0.2)	0.5	(0.3)	96.7	(0.1)	92.7	(0.3)	4.0	(0.3)	50	(6.3)	24	(5.7)
Chinese Taipei	94.7	(0.1)	94.6	(0.3)	94.8	(0.2)	-0.2	(0.4)	96.9	(0.2)	93.5	(0.2)	3.4	(0.3)	50	(8.1)	25	(7.9)
United Arab Emirates	m	m	m	m	m	m	m	m	m	m	m	m	m	m	m	m	m	m
Uruguay	84.4	(0.4)	85.9	(0.5)	83.2	(0.4)	2.7	(0.6)	96.3	(0.3)	80.6	(0.5)	15.8	(0.7)	59	(5.2)	21	(5.3)

Note: Values that are statistically significant are indicated in bold (see Annex A3).
1. The difference in problem-solving performance after accounting for socio-demographic characteristics of students corresponds to the coefficient from a regression where the *PISA index of economic, social and cultural status* (ESCS), ESCS squared, boy, and an immigrant (first generation) dummy are introduced as further independent variables.
* See notes at the beginning of this Annex.
StatLink ᵐᵃˢᵖ http://dx.doi.org/10.1787/888933003706

[Part 1/1]
Performance in problem solving and use of computers at school
Table V.4.26   *Results based on students' self-reports*

	Students who use a desktop, laptop or tablet computer at school														Difference in problem-solving performance			
	Percentage of students																	
	All students		Boys		Girls		Gender difference (B - G)		Parents' highest occupation: Skilled (ISCO 1 to 3)		Parents' highest occupation: Semi-skilled or elementary (ISCO 4 to 9)		Difference related to parents' highest occupation: Skilled - semi-skilled or elementary		Observed		After accounting for socio-demographic characteristics of students[1]	
	%	S.E.	%	S.E.	%	S.E.	% dif.	S.E.	%	S.E.	%	S.E.	% dif.	S.E.	Score dif.	S.E.	Score dif.	S.E.
Australia	93.7	(0.1)	93.5	(0.1)	93.8	(0.2)	-0.4	(0.2)	94.5	(0.1)	92.6	(0.2)	**1.8**	(0.2)	**34**	(4.3)	**25**	(4.0)
Austria	81.6	(0.5)	81.3	(0.6)	81.9	(0.6)	-0.6	(0.8)	78.9	(0.6)	84.7	(0.6)	**-5.8**	(0.6)	-3	(5.2)	1	(4.7)
Belgium	65.3	(0.4)	65.6	(0.5)	65.1	(0.5)	0.4	(0.7)	65.0	(0.4)	65.7	(0.6)	-0.8	(0.7)	**13**	(4.2)	**10**	(3.9)
Canada	m	m	m	m	m	m	m	m	m	m	m	m	m	m	m	m	m	m
Chile	61.3	(0.7)	59.8	(1.0)	62.8	(0.8)	**-3.0**	(1.2)	61.6	(1.2)	60.9	(0.7)	0.7	(1.1)	1	(4.0)	-3	(3.5)
Czech Republic	84.0	(0.6)	82.8	(0.9)	85.2	(0.7)	**-2.4**	(0.8)	82.6	(0.8)	85.2	(0.6)	**-2.6**	(0.7)	**-11**	(5.8)	-7	(5.1)
Denmark	86.9	(0.4)	86.4	(0.4)	87.4	(0.5)	**-1.1**	(0.4)	85.6	(0.5)	89.3	(0.5)	**-3.6**	(0.6)	**-16**	(5.4)	**-14**	(5.4)
Estonia	61.3	(0.5)	59.4	(0.7)	63.2	(0.7)	**-3.8**	(0.9)	60.2	(0.6)	62.7	(0.6)	**-2.5**	(0.7)	**-8**	(3.2)	**-8**	(3.0)
Finland	89.4	(0.4)	87.5	(0.4)	91.5	(0.5)	**-4.0**	(0.4)	89.4	(0.4)	89.8	(0.4)	-0.5	(0.4)	-5	(4.1)	-7	(4.3)
France	m	m	m	m	m	m	m	m	m	m	m	m	m	m	m	m	m	m
Germany	68.2	(0.6)	69.1	(0.7)	67.4	(0.6)	**1.7**	(0.6)	66.3	(0.9)	71.8	(0.7)	**-5.6**	(0.8)	**-9**	(4.1)	-7	(3.8)
Hungary	75.4	(0.6)	75.8	(0.8)	74.9	(0.6)	0.9	(0.7)	74.2	(0.7)	76.7	(0.8)	**-2.5**	(0.7)	-4	(4.2)	-4	(3.8)
Ireland	63.4	(0.6)	62.0	(0.8)	64.9	(0.7)	**-2.8**	(0.9)	62.8	(0.7)	64.0	(0.8)	-1.2	(0.8)	0	(3.8)	1	(3.7)
Israel	55.2	(0.7)	56.3	(0.9)	53.9	(0.8)	**2.4**	(1.1)	53.8	(0.8)	56.8	(1.0)	**-2.9**	(1.2)	**-25**	(5.1)	**-24**	(4.5)
Italy	66.5	(0.6)	70.6	(1.0)	61.9	(1.0)	**8.7**	(1.7)	60.6	(0.7)	70.3	(0.7)	**-9.6**	(0.8)	**-10**	(5.0)	-6	(4.6)
Japan	59.7	(0.9)	56.7	(0.9)	63.1	(1.2)	**-6.4**	(1.0)	59.7	(1.0)	59.8	(0.9)	-0.1	(0.8)	-4	(3.8)	-4	(3.5)
Korea	42.7	(0.9)	40.9	(1.0)	44.8	(1.2)	**-3.9**	(1.2)	43.0	(0.9)	42.5	(1.2)	0.4	(1.0)	0	(3.8)	0	(4.7)
Netherlands	93.9	(0.3)	93.6	(0.4)	94.1	(0.3)	-0.4	(0.4)	94.0	(0.4)	93.6	(0.4)	0.4	(0.4)	**30**	(9.9)	**28**	(9.0)
Norway	91.9	(0.3)	90.7	(0.4)	93.1	(0.3)	**-2.5**	(0.4)	92.1	(0.4)	92.3	(0.5)	-0.2	(0.6)	**28**	(7.8)	**22**	(7.5)
Poland	61.0	(0.7)	60.8	(0.7)	61.1	(0.9)	-0.4	(0.8)	58.2	(0.8)	63.3	(0.8)	**-5.1**	(0.7)	-1	(3.9)	1	(3.6)
Portugal	69.4	(0.6)	71.5	(0.8)	67.3	(0.6)	**4.2**	(0.8)	66.8	(1.0)	71.3	(0.6)	**-4.5**	(1.0)	**-21**	(4.3)	**-16**	(4.0)
Slovak Republic	80.0	(0.4)	77.5	(0.5)	82.8	(0.6)	**-5.2**	(0.6)	79.6	(0.6)	81.5	(0.5)	**-1.9**	(0.5)	**26**	(5.3)	**21**	(4.4)
Slovenia	57.1	(0.4)	58.0	(0.5)	56.2	(0.6)	**1.8**	(0.8)	55.7	(0.5)	58.7	(0.6)	**-3.0**	(0.8)	6	(3.4)	5	(3.1)
Spain	75.3	(0.6)	75.8	(0.6)	74.7	(0.8)	1.1	(0.6)	75.0	(0.8)	75.5	(0.7)	-0.5	(0.7)	**12**	(5.1)	**11**	(4.8)
Sweden	87.8	(0.7)	87.0	(0.7)	88.6	(0.8)	**-1.6**	(0.5)	88.7	(0.8)	86.8	(0.6)	**1.9**	(0.7)	**21**	(6.5)	**17**	(5.4)
Turkey	49.2	(0.8)	50.7	(0.9)	47.8	(0.9)	**3.0**	(0.7)	48.5	(1.2)	50.1	(0.8)	-1.7	(1.1)	8	(3.7)	4	(3.3)
England (United Kingdom)	m	m	m	m	m	m	m	m	m	m	m	m	m	m	m	m	m	m
United States	m	m	m	m	m	m	m	m	m	m	m	m	m	m	m	m	m	m
OECD average	71.7	(0.1)	71.4	(0.1)	72.0	(0.1)	**-0.6**	(0.2)	70.7	(0.2)	72.7	(0.1)	**-2.0**	(0.2)	**3**	(1.0)	**2**	(1.0)
Brazil	m	m	m	m	m	m	m	m	m	m	m	m	m	m	m	m	m	m
Bulgaria	m	m	m	m	m	m	m	m	m	m	m	m	m	m	m	m	m	m
Colombia	m	m	m	m	m	m	m	m	m	m	m	m	m	m	m	m	m	m
Croatia	78.5	(0.5)	80.3	(0.5)	76.5	(0.7)	**3.8**	(0.7)	76.2	(0.9)	80.5	(0.5)	**-4.3**	(0.8)	-9	(5.2)	-8	(4.5)
Cyprus*	m	m	m	m	m	m	m	m	m	m	m	m	m	m	m	m	m	m
Hong Kong-China	83.5	(0.4)	80.9	(0.5)	86.5	(0.4)	**-5.6**	(0.5)	82.1	(0.8)	85.0	(0.4)	**-2.9**	(0.9)	7	(6.4)	9	(5.9)
Macao-China	87.9	(0.3)	86.2	(0.4)	89.6	(0.3)	**-3.4**	(0.4)	88.9	(0.5)	87.9	(0.3)	**1.1**	(0.5)	**11**	(4.3)	**11**	(4.1)
Malaysia	m	m	m	m	m	m	m	m	m	m	m	m	m	m	m	m	m	m
Montenegro	m	m	m	m	m	m	m	m	m	m	m	m	m	m	m	m	m	m
Russian Federation	80.4	(0.4)	79.5	(0.5)	81.3	(0.5)	**-1.8**	(0.6)	80.2	(0.4)	80.6	(0.6)	-0.4	(0.6)	4	(5.1)	2	(4.5)
Serbia	82.4	(0.5)	82.5	(0.4)	82.4	(0.7)	0.2	(0.7)	83.8	(0.7)	82.0	(0.5)	**1.8**	(0.7)	**20**	(5.2)	**15**	(4.5)
Shanghai-China	38.7	(0.6)	38.1	(0.6)	39.3	(0.7)	**-1.3**	(0.6)	39.6	(0.7)	37.9	(0.8)	1.7	(0.9)	**16**	(4.0)	**12**	(3.5)
Singapore	69.7	(0.3)	67.2	(0.4)	72.2	(0.4)	**-5.0**	(0.6)	69.0	(0.4)	70.9	(0.5)	**-2.0**	(0.6)	**-18**	(3.2)	**-16**	(2.9)
Chinese Taipei	78.8	(0.4)	75.6	(0.6)	82.0	(0.4)	**-6.3**	(0.6)	80.2	(0.6)	78.4	(0.5)	**1.9**	(0.7)	**13**	(4.1)	**11**	(3.7)
United Arab Emirates	m	m	m	m	m	m	m	m	m	m	m	m	m	m	m	m	m	m
Uruguay	49.7	(0.6)	55.4	(0.8)	44.8	(0.7)	**10.5**	(0.8)	51.7	(1.5)	48.9	(0.6)	2.8	(1.5)	**-16**	(5.4)	**-23**	(4.3)

Note: Values that are statistically significant are indicated in bold (see Annex A3).
1. The difference in problem-solving performance after accounting for socio-demographic characteristics of students corresponds to the coefficient from a regression where the *PISA index of economic, social and cultural status* (ESCS), ESCS squared, boy, and an immigrant (first-generation) dummy are introduced as further independent variables.
* See notes at the beginning of this Annex.
StatLink ᠁᠍᠍᠍ http://dx.doi.org/10.1787/888933003706

[Part 1/3]

Differences in problem-solving, mathematics, reading and science performance related to computer use

Table V.4.27 *Results based on students' self-reports*

	Difference in performance associated with the use of computers at home, after accounting for socio-demographic characteristics of students[1]											
	Problem solving (use - no use)		Mathematics (use - no use)		Reading (use - no use)		Science (use - no use)		Computer-based mathematics (use - no use)		Digital reading (use - no use)	
	Score dif.	S.E.	Score dif.	S.E.	Score dif.	S.E.	Score dif.	S.E.	Score dif.	S.E.	Score dif.	S.E.
Australia	50	(6.4)	51	(5.7)	53	(6.5)	52	(6.4)	52	(4.7)	56	(6.6)
Austria	50	(20.0)	39	(15.6)	45	(16.2)	36	(14.7)	36	(13.8)	36	(13.3)
Belgium	60	(10.2)	43	(9.0)	48	(8.8)	42	(8.0)	51	(9.7)	67	(10.8)
Canada	m	m	m	m	m	m	m	m	m	m	m	m
Chile	21	(4.3)	16	(3.5)	20	(4.3)	18	(4.1)	14	(4.0)	20	(4.2)
Czech Republic	59	(13.1)	45	(11.4)	50	(11.5)	51	(12.3)	m	m	m	m
Denmark	44	(17.2)	45	(12.6)	60	(15.7)	54	(15.8)	53	(15.8)	58	(13.7)
Estonia	33	(12.0)	32	(10.8)	38	(12.3)	32	(12.6)	17	(12.1)	33	(13.8)
Finland	24	(14.6)	1	(12.0)	15	(13.2)	10	(11.9)	m	m	m	m
France	m	m	m	m	m	m	m	m	m	m	m	m
Germany	32	(20.1)	34	(16.0)	28	(15.1)	44	(17.1)	37	(15.0)	50	(20.2)
Hungary	40	(10.0)	30	(6.7)	41	(8.5)	36	(7.8)	23	(7.8)	32	(9.8)
Ireland	11	(10.3)	5	(7.9)	4	(7.7)	3	(7.9)	7	(7.1)	3	(7.3)
Israel	47	(11.7)	42	(8.6)	49	(9.4)	50	(8.0)	44	(9.9)	56	(10.4)
Italy	30	(20.0)	35	(14.7)	44	(14.7)	32	(13.8)	29	(11.8)	40	(14.6)
Japan	24	(3.9)	24	(3.6)	23	(3.8)	24	(3.6)	26	(3.8)	23	(3.5)
Korea	33	(4.2)	45	(4.3)	39	(4.0)	36	(3.6)	35	(4.1)	29	(3.5)
Netherlands	77	(13.0)	78	(12.4)	88	(13.1)	76	(13.2)	m	m	m	m
Norway	58	(15.6)	55	(12.3)	70	(14.8)	58	(13.2)	42	(13.0)	81	(17.6)
Poland	38	(8.6)	24	(8.3)	27	(7.9)	26	(8.0)	32	(7.5)	38	(9.0)
Portugal	31	(8.2)	39	(8.0)	42	(8.3)	36	(8.7)	25	(6.6)	40	(8.1)
Slovak Republic	51	(7.3)	44	(7.3)	49	(7.0)	45	(7.0)	35	(6.1)	56	(8.0)
Slovenia	22	(7.9)	12	(7.0)	24	(7.4)	23	(6.7)	14	(6.7)	32	(7.6)
Spain	37	(8.3)	30	(6.3)	35	(7.0)	30	(7.0)	37	(6.9)	29	(8.1)
Sweden	47	(14.7)	37	(12.6)	61	(14.7)	51	(14.5)	45	(11.9)	34	(14.5)
Turkey	24	(3.4)	19	(3.6)	18	(3.1)	17	(3.2)	m	m	m	m
England (United Kingdom)	m	m	m	m	m	m	m	m	m	m	m	m
United States	m	m	m	m	m	m	m	m	m	m	m	m
OECD average	39	(2.5)	34	(2.0)	40	(2.2)	37	(2.1)	33	(2.2)	41	(2.5)
Brazil	m	m	m	m	m	m	m	m	m	m	m	m
Bulgaria	m	m	m	m	m	m	m	m	m	m	m	m
Colombia	m	m	m	m	m	m	m	m	m	m	m	m
Croatia	53	(11.1)	46	(7.6)	42	(7.8)	44	(7.1)	m	m	m	m
Cyprus*	m	m	m	m	m	m	m	m	m	m	m	m
Hong Kong-China	42	(10.8)	44	(10.1)	36	(9.9)	41	(9.8)	44	(11.2)	37	(11.6)
Macao-China	33	(8.0)	35	(8.1)	31	(7.1)	31	(7.2)	31	(7.8)	26	(6.5)
Malaysia	m	m	m	m	m	m	m	m	m	m	m	m
Montenegro	m	m	m	m	m	m	m	m	m	m	m	m
Russian Federation	19	(4.3)	24	(6.2)	25	(5.2)	20	(6.1)	18	(4.9)	36	(6.5)
Serbia	56	(5.8)	52	(4.8)	53	(5.4)	45	(5.8)	m	m	m	m
Shanghai-China	28	(5.1)	13	(4.5)	13	(3.2)	10	(3.8)	18	(5.1)	25	(4.1)
Singapore	24	(5.7)	35	(6.2)	36	(5.6)	34	(6.1)	29	(5.6)	28	(4.9)
Chinese Taipei	25	(7.9)	26	(8.0)	21	(5.6)	19	(5.2)	23	(5.7)	32	(5.8)
United Arab Emirates	m	m	m	m	m	m	m	m	m	m	m	m
Uruguay	21	(5.3)	23	(4.7)	26	(4.6)	21	(4.1)	m	m	m	m

Note: Values that are statistically significant are indicated in bold (see Annex A3).
1. The adjusted effects correspond to the coefficient from a regression where the *PISA index of economic, social and cultural status* (ESCS), ESCS squared, boy, and an immigrant (first generation) dummy are introduced as further independent variables.
* See notes at the beginning of this Annex.
StatLink http://dx.doi.org/10.1787/888933003706

[Part 2/3]
Differences in problem-solving, mathematics, reading and science performance related to computer use
Table V.4.27   *Results based on students' self-reports*

	Computer use effect size: Difference in performance related to computer use, after accounting for socio-demographic characteristics of students,[1] divided by the variation in scores within each country/economy (standard deviation)											
	Problem solving (use - no use)		**Mathematics** (use - no use)		**Reading** (use - no use)		**Science** (use - no use)		**Computer-based mathematics** (use - no use)		**Digital reading** (use - no use)	
	Effect size	S.E.	Effect size	S.E.	Effect size	S.E.	Effect size	S.E.	Effect size	S.E.	Effect size	S.E.
Australia	**0.51**	(0.07)	**0.54**	(0.06)	**0.56**	(0.07)	**0.53**	(0.06)	**0.58**	(0.05)	**0.58**	(0.07)
Austria	**0.53**	(0.21)	**0.43**	(0.17)	**0.50**	(0.18)	**0.40**	(0.16)	**0.41**	(0.16)	**0.40**	(0.15)
Belgium	**0.59**	(0.10)	**0.43**	(0.09)	**0.51**	(0.09)	**0.44**	(0.08)	**0.54**	(0.10)	**0.70**	(0.11)
Canada	m	m	m	m	m	m	m	m	m	m	m	m
Chile	**0.24**	(0.05)	**0.19**	(0.04)	**0.25**	(0.05)	**0.22**	(0.05)	**0.18**	(0.05)	**0.24**	(0.05)
Czech Republic	**0.63**	(0.14)	**0.47**	(0.12)	**0.57**	(0.13)	**0.57**	(0.14)	m	m	m	m
Denmark	**0.48**	(0.19)	**0.56**	(0.15)	**0.74**	(0.19)	**0.61**	(0.18)	**0.62**	(0.18)	**0.71**	(0.17)
Estonia	**0.37**	(0.14)	**0.40**	(0.13)	**0.48**	(0.15)	**0.40**	(0.16)	0.21	(0.15)	**0.36**	(0.15)
Finland	0.26	(0.16)	0.02	(0.15)	0.17	(0.15)	0.11	(0.13)	m	m	m	m
France	m	m	m	m	m	m	m	m	m	m	m	m
Germany	0.34	(0.21)	**0.36**	(0.17)	0.33	(0.17)	**0.49**	(0.19)	**0.40**	(0.16)	**0.52**	(0.21)
Hungary	**0.39**	(0.09)	**0.33**	(0.07)	**0.46**	(0.09)	**0.41**	(0.09)	**0.25**	(0.08)	**0.29**	(0.09)
Ireland	0.12	(0.11)	0.06	(0.09)	0.05	(0.09)	0.03	(0.09)	0.08	(0.09)	0.04	(0.09)
Israel	**0.38**	(0.09)	**0.41**	(0.08)	**0.45**	(0.09)	**0.48**	(0.08)	**0.40**	(0.09)	**0.48**	(0.09)
Italy	0.34	(0.22)	**0.39**	(0.16)	**0.46**	(0.15)	**0.34**	(0.14)	**0.35**	(0.14)	**0.42**	(0.15)
Japan	**0.28**	(0.04)	**0.26**	(0.04)	**0.23**	(0.04)	**0.26**	(0.04)	**0.30**	(0.04)	**0.30**	(0.04)
Korea	**0.36**	(0.04)	**0.46**	(0.04)	**0.45**	(0.04)	**0.44**	(0.04)	**0.38**	(0.04)	**0.36**	(0.04)
Netherlands	**0.82**	(0.14)	**0.88**	(0.14)	**1.01**	(0.15)	**0.85**	(0.14)	m	m	m	m
Norway	**0.56**	(0.15)	**0.61**	(0.14)	**0.72**	(0.15)	**0.59**	(0.14)	**0.49**	(0.15)	**0.82**	(0.18)
Poland	**0.40**	(0.09)	**0.27**	(0.09)	**0.31**	(0.09)	**0.30**	(0.09)	**0.37**	(0.09)	**0.39**	(0.09)
Portugal	**0.35**	(0.09)	**0.42**	(0.09)	**0.46**	(0.09)	**0.41**	(0.10)	**0.29**	(0.08)	**0.45**	(0.09)
Slovak Republic	**0.53**	(0.07)	**0.44**	(0.07)	**0.48**	(0.07)	**0.46**	(0.07)	**0.42**	(0.07)	**0.60**	(0.08)
Slovenia	**0.23**	(0.08)	0.13	(0.08)	**0.27**	(0.08)	**0.26**	(0.08)	**0.16**	(0.08)	**0.32**	(0.08)
Spain	**0.36**	(0.08)	**0.35**	(0.07)	**0.39**	(0.08)	**0.36**	(0.08)	**0.45**	(0.08)	**0.30**	(0.08)
Sweden	**0.49**	(0.15)	**0.42**	(0.14)	**0.60**	(0.14)	**0.53**	(0.15)	**0.53**	(0.14)	**0.35**	(0.15)
Turkey	**0.30**	(0.04)	**0.21**	(0.04)	**0.21**	(0.04)	**0.22**	(0.04)	m	m	m	m
England (United Kingdom)	m	m	m	m	m	m	m	m	m	m	m	m
United States	m	m	m	m	m	m	m	m	m	m	m	m
OECD average	**0.41**	(0.03)	**0.38**	(0.02)	**0.44**	(0.02)	**0.40**	(0.02)	**0.37**	(0.02)	**0.43**	(0.03)
Brazil	m	m	m	m	m	m	m	m	m	m	m	m
Bulgaria	m	m	m	m	m	m	m	m	m	m	m	m
Colombia	m	m	m	m	m	m	m	m	m	m	m	m
Croatia	**0.57**	(0.12)	**0.52**	(0.09)	**0.49**	(0.09)	**0.51**	(0.08)	m	m	m	m
Cyprus*	m	m	m	m	m	m	m	m	m	m	m	m
Hong Kong-China	**0.46**	(0.12)	**0.46**	(0.10)	**0.42**	(0.11)	**0.49**	(0.12)	**0.51**	(0.13)	**0.39**	(0.12)
Macao-China	**0.41**	(0.10)	**0.38**	(0.09)	**0.37**	(0.09)	**0.40**	(0.09)	**0.38**	(0.09)	**0.38**	(0.09)
Malaysia	m	m	m	m	m	m	m	m	m	m	m	m
Montenegro	m	m	m	m	m	m	m	m	m	m	m	m
Russian Federation	**0.22**	(0.05)	**0.28**	(0.07)	**0.28**	(0.06)	**0.24**	(0.07)	**0.22**	(0.06)	**0.42**	(0.07)
Serbia	**0.63**	(0.06)	**0.58**	(0.05)	**0.58**	(0.06)	**0.52**	(0.06)	m	m	m	m
Shanghai-China	**0.31**	(0.05)	**0.13**	(0.04)	**0.16**	(0.04)	**0.12**	(0.05)	**0.19**	(0.05)	**0.30**	(0.05)
Singapore	**0.25**	(0.06)	**0.33**	(0.06)	**0.36**	(0.06)	**0.33**	(0.06)	**0.30**	(0.06)	**0.31**	(0.05)
Chinese Taipei	**0.27**	(0.08)	**0.22**	(0.07)	**0.23**	(0.06)	**0.22**	(0.06)	**0.26**	(0.06)	**0.36**	(0.06)
United Arab Emirates	m	m	m	m	m	m	m	m	m	m	m	m
Uruguay	**0.21**	(0.05)	**0.27**	(0.05)	**0.28**	(0.05)	**0.23**	(0.04)	m	m	m	m

Note: Values that are statistically significant are indicated in bold (see Annex A3).
1. The adjusted effects correspond to the coefficient from a regression where the *PISA index of economic, social and cultural status* (ESCS), ESCS squared, boy, and an immigrant (first generation) dummy are introduced as further independent variables.
* See notes at the beginning of this Annex.
StatLink ᴍ�sᴘ http://dx.doi.org/10.1787/888933003706

[Part 3/3]
Differences in problem-solving, mathematics, reading and science performance related to computer use
Table V.4.27   *Results based on students' self-reports*

	Difference in computer use effect sizes between problem solving (PS) and...									
	... Mathematics (PS - M)		... Reading (PS - R)		... Science (PS - S)		... Computer-based mathematics (PS - CBM)		... Digital reading (PS - DR)	
	Effect size dif.	S.E.	Effect size dif.	S.E.	Effect size dif.	S.E.	Effect size dif.	S.E.	Effect size dif.	S.E.
Australia	-0.02	(0.04)	-0.05	(0.05)	-0.02	(0.04)	-0.06	(0.05)	-0.07	(0.06)
Austria	0.10	(0.09)	0.03	(0.09)	0.14	(0.09)	0.12	(0.12)	0.13	(0.14)
Belgium	0.15	(0.08)	0.08	(0.09)	0.15	(0.08)	0.05	(0.08)	-0.12	(0.08)
Canada	m	m	m	m	m	m	m	m	m	m
Chile	0.05	(0.04)	-0.01	(0.05)	0.02	(0.04)	0.07	(0.05)	0.00	(0.04)
Czech Republic	0.15	(0.08)	0.05	(0.10)	0.06	(0.09)	m	m	m	m
Denmark	-0.09	(0.15)	-0.26	(0.20)	-0.13	(0.14)	-0.14	(0.18)	-0.23	(0.18)
Estonia	-0.03	(0.10)	-0.11	(0.10)	-0.03	(0.11)	0.17	(0.10)	0.01	(0.10)
Finland	**0.24**	(0.08)	0.09	(0.11)	0.14	(0.10)	m	m	m	m
France	m	m	m	m	m	m	m	m	m	m
Germany	-0.03	(0.13)	0.01	(0.13)	-0.16	(0.13)	-0.07	(0.15)	-0.18	(0.16)
Hungary	0.06	(0.06)	-0.07	(0.07)	-0.03	(0.07)	0.13	(0.09)	0.09	(0.07)
Ireland	0.06	(0.08)	0.08	(0.08)	0.09	(0.08)	0.04	(0.09)	0.08	(0.08)
Israel	-0.03	(0.06)	-0.08	(0.06)	-0.11	(0.06)	-0.02	(0.07)	-0.10	(0.07)
Italy	-0.05	(0.11)	-0.12	(0.14)	0.00	(0.17)	-0.01	(0.13)	-0.09	(0.15)
Japan	0.02	(0.04)	0.05	(0.04)	0.03	(0.04)	-0.02	(0.04)	-0.02	(0.03)
Korea	**-0.10**	(0.03)	**-0.09**	(0.03)	**-0.08**	(0.03)	-0.02	(0.03)	0.00	(0.04)
Netherlands	-0.06	(0.14)	-0.19	(0.13)	-0.03	(0.11)	m	m	m	m
Norway	-0.05	(0.11)	-0.16	(0.12)	-0.03	(0.12)	0.07	(0.10)	**-0.26**	(0.11)
Poland	0.13	(0.07)	0.09	(0.06)	0.10	(0.06)	0.03	(0.06)	0.01	(0.07)
Portugal	-0.07	(0.05)	-0.10	(0.06)	-0.06	(0.07)	0.06	(0.07)	-0.10	(0.07)
Slovak Republic	0.09	(0.06)	0.05	(0.06)	0.07	(0.06)	0.10	(0.06)	-0.07	(0.07)
Slovenia	0.10	(0.07)	-0.04	(0.07)	-0.03	(0.06)	0.06	(0.07)	-0.10	(0.05)
Spain	0.00	(0.07)	-0.03	(0.09)	0.00	(0.07)	-0.09	(0.08)	0.06	(0.08)
Sweden	0.07	(0.09)	-0.11	(0.11)	-0.04	(0.09)	-0.04	(0.12)	0.13	(0.11)
Turkey	**0.09**	(0.03)	**0.09**	(0.03)	**0.08**	(0.03)	m	m	m	m
England (United Kingdom)	m	m	m	m	m	m	m	m	m	m
United States	m	m	m	m	m	m	m	m	m	m
OECD average	0.03	(0.02)	-0.03	(0.02)	0.01	(0.02)	0.02	(0.02)	-0.04	(0.02)
Brazil	m	m	m	m	m	m	m	m	m	m
Bulgaria	m	m	m	m	m	m	m	m	m	m
Colombia	m	m	m	m	m	m	m	m	m	m
Croatia	0.05	(0.07)	0.08	(0.07)	0.06	(0.10)	m	m	m	m
Cyprus*	m	m	m	m	m	m	m	m	m	m
Hong Kong-China	0.00	(0.10)	0.04	(0.10)	-0.04	(0.11)	-0.05	(0.10)	0.06	(0.09)
Macao-China	0.03	(0.07)	0.04	(0.07)	0.01	(0.07)	0.03	(0.09)	0.04	(0.07)
Malaysia	m	m	m	m	m	m	m	m	m	m
Montenegro	m	m	m	m	m	m	m	m	m	m
Russian Federation	-0.06	(0.07)	-0.06	(0.06)	-0.02	(0.07)	0.00	(0.05)	**-0.20**	(0.07)
Serbia	0.05	(0.04)	0.05	(0.05)	**0.12**	(0.05)	m	m	m	m
Shanghai-China	**0.18**	(0.04)	**0.15**	(0.04)	**0.19**	(0.05)	**0.12**	(0.04)	0.01	(0.05)
Singapore	**-0.08**	(0.04)	**-0.11**	(0.05)	**-0.08**	(0.04)	-0.05	(0.04)	-0.06	(0.05)
Chinese Taipei	0.05	(0.04)	0.04	(0.05)	0.05	(0.05)	0.01	(0.06)	-0.09	(0.06)
United Arab Emirates	m	m	m	m	m	m	m	m	m	m
Uruguay	-0.05	(0.04)	-0.06	(0.05)	-0.01	(0.04)	m	m	m	m

Note: Values that are statistically significant are indicated in bold (see Annex A3).
1. The adjusted effects correspond to the coefficient from a regression where the *PISA index of economic, social and cultural status* (ESCS), ESCS squared, boy, and an immigrant (first generation) dummy are introduced as further independent variables.
* See notes at the beginning of this Annex.
StatLink ⬛ http://dx.doi.org/10.1787/888933003706

ANNEX B2
RESULTS FOR REGIONS WITHIN COUNTRIES

[Part 1/2]

Table B2.V.1 **Percentage of students at each proficiency level in problem solving, by region**

	Below Level 1 (below 358.49 score points)		Level 1 (from 358.49 to less than 423.42 score points)		Level 2 (from 423.42 to less than 488.35 score points)		Level 3 (from 488.35 to less than 553.28 score points)		Level 4 (from 553.28 to less than 618.21 score points)		Level 5 (from 618.21 to less than 683.14 score points)		Level 6 (above 683.14 score points)	
	%	S.E.	%	S.E.	%	S.E.	%	S.E.	%	S.E.	%	S.E.	%	S.E.
Australia														
Australian Capital Territory	6.4	(1.2)	9.5	(1.2)	17.6	(1.5)	24.1	(2.2)	24.0	(2.1)	13.5	(1.8)	4.8	(1.1)
New South Wales	5.2	(0.6)	10.3	(0.8)	18.9	(0.9)	25.6	(1.0)	22.1	(0.9)	12.7	(0.9)	5.2	(0.7)
Northern Territory	9.1	(1.5)	12.4	(2.3)	18.1	(2.5)	21.7	(3.2)	21.5	(3.0)	12.2	(3.2)	5.0	(2.7)
Queensland	4.9	(0.7)	10.7	(1.0)	19.8	(1.1)	25.8	(1.1)	22.8	(0.9)	11.7	(0.9)	4.3	(0.6)
South Australia	4.4	(0.7)	10.7	(1.0)	20.6	(1.4)	27.2	(1.3)	22.0	(1.4)	11.8	(1.2)	3.3	(0.6)
Tasmania	10.2	(1.0)	16.5	(1.9)	22.8	(1.7)	22.8	(1.5)	16.0	(1.5)	8.5	(1.1)	3.2	(0.7)
Victoria	4.6	(0.8)	10.5	(1.3)	19.5	(1.2)	26.3	(1.4)	22.9	(1.2)	12.4	(1.1)	3.9	(0.6)
Western Australia	4.5	(0.9)	9.3	(1.1)	18.5	(1.2)	25.9	(1.7)	24.7	(1.4)	12.8	(1.2)	4.4	(0.9)
Belgium														
Flemish Community*	6.7	(0.7)	9.5	(0.9)	16.8	(0.9)	24.9	(1.0)	24.2	(1.0)	13.9	(1.0)	4.1	(0.5)
French Community	12.6	(1.1)	14.4	(0.8)	20.3	(1.2)	24.0	(1.1)	19.1	(1.1)	8.1	(0.9)	1.5	(0.4)
German-speaking Community	5.8	(0.9)	9.1	(1.1)	19.5	(1.7)	26.3	(2.1)	24.7	(1.5)	11.1	(1.2)	3.6	(0.6)
Canada														
Alberta	4.6	(0.6)	9.6	(1.0)	16.8	(1.4)	26.2	(1.6)	23.9	(1.6)	13.6	(1.2)	5.3	(0.8)
British Columbia	3.1	(0.7)	9.4	(1.0)	18.2	(1.3)	26.1	(1.4)	24.0	(1.4)	13.8	(1.3)	5.3	(0.7)
Manitoba	7.3	(1.0)	13.2	(1.2)	21.6	(1.1)	24.8	(1.6)	21.2	(1.4)	9.2	(1.2)	2.7	(0.5)
New Brunswick	5.4	(0.7)	10.3	(1.2)	20.8	(1.6)	28.0	(2.4)	23.4	(1.7)	9.3	(1.2)	2.8	(0.6)
Newfoundland and Labrador	7.6	(2.1)	11.3	(1.6)	21.6	(1.5)	26.9	(1.7)	21.0	(1.6)	9.3	(1.1)	2.3	(0.6)
Nova Scotia	5.1	(1.4)	10.8	(1.6)	22.6	(3.2)	27.3	(2.8)	22.6	(2.4)	9.2	(1.1)	2.5	(0.8)
Ontario	5.1	(0.7)	9.4	(1.0)	19.4	(1.1)	24.9	(1.2)	22.5	(1.3)	12.6	(1.0)	6.0	(1.0)
Prince Edward Island	7.0	(0.7)	14.2	(1.2)	25.7	(1.5)	28.2	(2.1)	17.7	(1.2)	5.6	(0.9)	1.6	(0.5)
Quebec	5.8	(0.8)	8.9	(0.7)	18.0	(1.0)	26.5	(1.2)	23.4	(0.9)	12.6	(1.1)	4.7	(0.8)
Saskatchewan	5.2	(0.7)	11.1	(1.0)	21.1	(1.6)	28.0	(1.6)	20.7	(1.3)	10.9	(1.1)	2.9	(0.6)
Italy														
Centre	6.2	(1.6)	9.8	(2.7)	18.3	(2.4)	30.3	(3.6)	23.9	(2.2)	9.6	(2.2)	1.9	(1.0)
North East	4.2	(1.1)	8.1	(1.6)	19.3	(2.1)	27.5	(1.7)	25.9	(2.2)	11.9	(1.4)	3.1	(0.8)
North West	2.5	(0.8)	6.8	(1.8)	18.8	(2.1)	29.2	(3.1)	28.3	(3.2)	12.1	(2.5)	2.3	(0.8)
South	6.6	(1.9)	17.7	(2.8)	31.6	(2.9)	27.5	(2.2)	14.0	(2.6)	2.4	(0.8)	0.1	(0.2)
South Islands	7.4	(2.0)	16.2	(2.5)	27.7	(2.0)	25.3	(2.3)	15.9	(2.1)	6.1	(1.6)	1.2	(0.6)
Portugal														
Alentejo	6.0	(2.0)	11.2	(2.1)	23.4	(2.4)	28.1	(2.7)	21.2	(2.7)	8.4	(2.6)	1.8	(1.3)
Spain														
Basque Country*	8.0	(0.8)	13.2	(0.8)	23.2	(0.9)	27.3	(0.9)	18.7	(1.1)	7.6	(0.6)	2.1	(0.3)
Catalonia*	11.2	(2.4)	12.4	(1.5)	24.0	(1.9)	25.3	(1.9)	18.0	(1.7)	7.3	(1.1)	1.9	(0.6)
Madrid	6.8	(2.0)	13.5	(2.6)	19.6	(3.0)	26.0	(2.2)	21.7	(3.0)	9.8	(3.0)	2.6	(1.2)
Brazil														
Central-West Region	16.3	(4.5)	25.3	(3.5)	29.3	(2.7)	19.6	(4.0)	7.3	(2.1)	1.8	(0.9)	0.5	(0.4)
Northeast Region	37.8	(4.1)	25.1	(2.9)	20.0	(3.0)	10.7	(2.4)	3.9	(1.4)	1.6	(0.8)	0.8	(0.5)
North Region	40.2	(5.6)	30.3	(3.6)	17.8	(3.5)	9.0	(2.8)	2.6	(1.2)	0.2	(0.2)	0.0	(0.0)
Southeast Region	14.4	(1.9)	24.5	(2.1)	29.8	(2.0)	21.2	(2.3)	8.4	(1.3)	1.5	(0.4)	0.3	(0.2)
South Region	17.5	(3.1)	27.1	(2.7)	30.4	(2.8)	17.3	(2.9)	6.1	(1.3)	1.6	(0.7)	0.1	(0.1)
Colombia														
Bogotá	27.1	(2.4)	28.3	(1.6)	27.2	(1.8)	13.2	(1.5)	3.4	(0.8)	0.8	(0.3)	0.1	(0.1)
Cali	31.6	(4.1)	28.1	(2.0)	24.6	(2.1)	12.4	(1.7)	2.9	(0.9)	0.4	(0.2)	0.1	(0.1)
Manizales	21.9	(2.1)	27.0	(1.7)	28.9	(2.0)	15.6	(1.7)	5.3	(0.9)	1.0	(0.4)	0.4	(0.2)
Medellín	24.8	(2.6)	26.9	(2.8)	23.8	(2.7)	15.0	(1.7)	6.8	(1.4)	2.2	(0.9)	0.5	(0.3)
United Arab Emirates														
Abu Dhabi*	37.7	(2.2)	23.0	(1.4)	20.5	(1.1)	12.2	(1.0)	4.9	(0.6)	1.5	(0.4)	0.2	(0.1)
Ajman	42.6	(4.5)	29.1	(2.8)	19.5	(2.5)	8.1	(2.5)	0.7	(0.6)	0.0	c	0.0	c
Dubai*	18.1	(0.6)	19.6	(1.1)	22.6	(1.3)	20.6	(0.9)	12.7	(0.7)	5.1	(0.5)	1.4	(0.2)
Fujairah	32.4	(2.8)	32.6	(2.8)	22.4	(2.7)	9.6	(1.0)	2.6	(0.8)	0.3	(0.3)	0.0	c
Ras al-Khaimah	40.6	(4.6)	31.4	(3.0)	18.3	(2.4)	7.3	(1.2)	1.9	(0.7)	0.5	(0.2)	0.0	c
Sharjah	24.2	(4.0)	29.4	(3.2)	26.1	(3.0)	14.8	(2.2)	4.8	(1.5)	0.6	(0.5)	0.1	(0.2)
Umm al-Quwain	44.8	(3.5)	28.8	(3.3)	18.5	(2.4)	6.2	(1.6)	1.5	(0.7)	0.1	(0.2)	0.0	c

* PISA adjudicated region.

Notes: Italian administrative regions are grouped into larger geographical units: Centre (*Lazio, Marche, Toscana, Umbria*), North East (*Bolzano, Emilia Romagna, Friuli Venezia Giulia, Trento, Veneto*), North West (*Liguria, Lombardia, Piemonte, Valle d'Aosta*), South (*Abruzzo, Campania, Molise, Puglia*), South Islands (*Basilicata, Calabria, Sardegna, Sicilia*).
Brazilian states are grouped into larger geographical units: Central-West Region (*Federal District, Goiás, Mato Grosso, Mato Grosso do Sul*), Northeast Region (*Alagoas, Bahia, Ceará, Maranhão, Paraíba, Pernambuco, Piauí, Rio Grande do Norte, Sergipe*), North Region (*Acre, Amapá, Amazonas, Pará, Rondônia, Roraima, Tocantins*), Southeast Region (*Espírito Santo, Minas Gerais, Rio de Janeiro, São Paulo*), South Region (*Paraná, Rio Grande do Sul, Santa Catarina*).
See Table V.2.1 for national data.
StatLink ᴹᔆᴾ http://dx.doi.org/10.1787/888933003763

[Part 2/2]
Table B2.V.1 **Percentage of students at each proficiency level in problem solving, by region**

| | Percentage of students at or above each proficiency level | | | | | | | | | | | |
| | Level 1 or above (above 358.49 score points) | | Level 2 or above (above 423.42 score points) | | Level 3 or above (above 488.35 score points) | | Level 4 or above (above 553.28 score points) | | Level 5 or above (above 618.21 score points) | | Level 6 (above 683.14 score points) | |
	%	S.E.	%	S.E.	%	S.E.	%	S.E.	%	S.E.	%	S.E.
Australia												
Australian Capital Territory	93.6	(1.2)	84.1	(1.4)	66.5	(1.8)	42.4	(2.0)	18.4	(1.8)	4.8	(1.1)
New South Wales	94.8	(0.6)	84.5	(1.1)	65.5	(1.4)	40.0	(1.5)	17.9	(1.3)	5.2	(0.7)
Northern Territory	90.9	(1.5)	78.5	(2.4)	60.4	(3.0)	38.7	(4.1)	17.2	(3.9)	5.0	(2.7)
Queensland	95.1	(0.7)	84.4	(1.3)	64.6	(1.6)	38.8	(1.4)	16.0	(1.0)	4.3	(0.6)
South Australia	95.6	(0.7)	84.9	(1.3)	64.3	(1.8)	37.2	(2.0)	15.2	(1.5)	3.3	(0.6)
Tasmania	89.8	(1.0)	73.2	(1.9)	50.5	(1.8)	27.7	(1.6)	11.7	(1.4)	3.2	(0.7)
Victoria	95.4	(0.8)	85.0	(1.4)	65.4	(1.9)	39.2	(2.0)	16.3	(1.3)	3.9	(0.6)
Western Australia	95.5	(0.9)	86.2	(1.4)	67.7	(1.7)	41.8	(2.0)	17.2	(1.5)	4.4	(0.9)
Belgium												
Flemish Community•	93.3	(0.7)	83.8	(1.2)	67.0	(1.4)	42.2	(1.5)	18.0	(1.2)	4.1	(0.5)
French Community	87.4	(1.1)	73.0	(1.5)	52.6	(1.9)	28.7	(1.6)	9.6	(1.0)	1.5	(0.4)
German-speaking Community	94.2	(0.9)	85.1	(1.2)	65.6	(1.8)	39.3	(1.6)	14.7	(1.2)	3.6	(0.6)
Canada												
Alberta	95.4	(0.6)	85.8	(1.3)	69.1	(2.1)	42.9	(2.4)	19.0	(1.6)	5.3	(0.8)
British Columbia	96.9	(0.7)	87.5	(1.2)	69.3	(1.6)	43.2	(1.7)	19.1	(1.4)	5.3	(0.7)
Manitoba	92.7	(1.0)	79.5	(1.3)	57.9	(1.6)	33.1	(1.5)	11.9	(1.2)	2.7	(0.5)
New Brunswick	94.6	(0.7)	84.3	(1.3)	63.5	(1.7)	35.5	(2.0)	12.1	(1.3)	2.8	(0.6)
Newfoundland and Labrador	92.4	(2.1)	81.1	(2.8)	59.5	(2.6)	32.6	(2.0)	11.6	(1.2)	2.3	(0.6)
Nova Scotia	94.9	(1.4)	84.1	(2.1)	61.5	(3.8)	34.2	(2.8)	11.6	(1.5)	2.5	(0.8)
Ontario	94.9	(0.7)	85.5	(1.5)	66.1	(2.1)	41.2	(2.3)	18.7	(1.7)	6.0	(1.0)
Prince Edward Island	93.0	(0.7)	78.8	(1.4)	53.2	(1.7)	25.0	(1.4)	7.3	(0.8)	1.6	(0.5)
Quebec	94.2	(0.8)	85.3	(1.1)	67.2	(1.6)	40.8	(1.8)	17.3	(1.5)	4.7	(0.8)
Saskatchewan	94.8	(0.7)	83.7	(1.1)	62.6	(1.6)	34.5	(1.7)	13.8	(1.1)	2.9	(0.6)
Italy												
Centre	93.8	(1.6)	84.0	(3.9)	65.8	(5.7)	35.5	(4.2)	11.6	(2.6)	1.9	(1.0)
North East	95.8	(1.1)	87.7	(2.1)	68.4	(2.9)	40.9	(3.2)	15.0	(1.9)	3.1	(0.8)
North West	97.5	(0.8)	90.7	(2.2)	71.9	(3.7)	42.7	(4.9)	14.4	(2.9)	2.3	(0.8)
South	93.4	(1.9)	75.7	(4.1)	44.1	(4.2)	16.5	(3.0)	2.6	(0.8)	0.1	(0.2)
South Islands	92.6	(2.0)	76.4	(3.5)	48.6	(3.9)	23.3	(3.0)	7.3	(2.0)	1.2	(0.6)
Portugal												
Alentejo	94.0	(2.0)	82.8	(3.9)	59.5	(5.5)	31.4	(5.3)	10.3	(3.9)	1.8	(1.3)
Spain												
Basque Country•	92.0	(0.8)	78.8	(1.3)	55.6	(1.7)	28.4	(1.5)	9.6	(0.8)	2.1	(0.3)
Catalonia•	88.8	(2.4)	76.4	(3.1)	52.4	(3.4)	27.1	(2.6)	9.2	(1.5)	1.9	(0.6)
Madrid	93.2	(2.0)	79.7	(4.0)	60.1	(5.3)	34.1	(5.8)	12.4	(3.9)	2.6	(1.2)
Brazil												
Central-West Region	83.7	(4.5)	58.4	(5.7)	29.1	(5.1)	9.6	(2.8)	2.3	(1.0)	0.5	(0.4)
Northeast Region	62.2	(4.1)	37.1	(5.2)	17.0	(3.7)	6.3	(2.3)	2.4	(1.3)	0.8	(0.5)
North Region	59.8	(5.6)	29.5	(4.7)	11.8	(3.3)	2.8	(1.3)	0.2	(0.2)	0.0	(0.0)
Southeast Region	85.6	(1.9)	61.1	(3.2)	31.3	(3.4)	10.2	(1.6)	1.7	(0.5)	0.3	(0.2)
South Region	82.5	(3.1)	55.4	(4.3)	25.0	(3.5)	7.7	(1.4)	1.6	(0.7)	0.1	(0.1)
Colombia												
Bogotá	72.9	(2.4)	44.7	(3.0)	17.5	(2.0)	4.3	(1.0)	0.9	(0.3)	0.1	(0.1)
Cali	68.4	(4.1)	40.3	(3.6)	15.7	(2.2)	3.4	(0.9)	0.5	(0.2)	0.1	(0.1)
Manizales	78.1	(2.1)	51.1	(2.6)	22.2	(1.9)	6.6	(1.1)	1.3	(0.4)	0.4	(0.2)
Medellín	75.2	(2.6)	48.3	(3.9)	24.6	(3.3)	9.5	(2.2)	2.7	(1.1)	0.5	(0.3)
United Arab Emirates												
Abu Dhabi•	62.3	(2.2)	39.3	(2.0)	18.8	(1.6)	6.6	(0.9)	1.7	(0.4)	0.2	(0.1)
Ajman	57.4	(4.5)	28.3	(4.2)	8.8	(2.5)	0.7	(0.6)	0.0	c	0.0	c
Dubai•	81.9	(0.6)	62.3	(1.1)	39.6	(0.9)	19.1	(0.6)	6.4	(0.5)	1.4	(0.2)
Fujairah	67.6	(2.8)	35.0	(2.7)	12.6	(1.4)	3.0	(0.9)	0.3	(0.3)	0.0	c
Ras al-Khaimah	59.4	(4.6)	28.0	(3.4)	9.6	(1.6)	2.4	(0.7)	0.5	(0.2)	0.0	c
Sharjah	75.8	(4.0)	46.4	(4.0)	20.3	(3.0)	5.5	(1.8)	0.7	(0.4)	0.1	(0.2)
Umm al-Quwain	55.2	(3.5)	26.4	(2.4)	7.9	(1.6)	1.7	(0.6)	0.1	(0.2)	0.0	c

• PISA adjudicated region.
Notes: Italian administrative regions are grouped into larger geographical units: Centre (*Lazio, Marche, Toscana, Umbria*), North East (*Bolzano, Emilia Romagna, Friuli Venezia Giulia, Trento, Veneto*), North West (*Liguria, Lombardia, Piemonte, Valle d'Aosta*), South (*Abruzzo, Campania, Molise, Puglia*), South Islands (*Basilicata, Calabria, Sardegna, Sicilia*).
Brazilian states are grouped into larger geographical units: Central-West Region (*Federal District, Goiás, Mato Grosso, Mato Grosso do Sul*), Northeast Region (*Alagoas, Bahia, Ceará, Maranhão, Paraíba, Pernambuco, Piauí, Rio Grande do Norte, Sergípe*), North Region (*Acre, Amapá, Amazonas, Pará, Rondônia, Roraima, Tocantins*), Southeast Region (*Espírito Santo, Minas Gerais, Rio de Janeiro, São Paulo*), South Region (*Paraná, Rio Grande do Sul, Santa Catarina*).
See Table V.2.1 for national data.
StatLink ⟨ᴍᴤ⅃ http://dx.doi.org/10.1787/888933003763

[Part 1/2]
Table B2.V.2 Mean score and variation in student performance in problem solving, by region

	Mean score		Standard deviation		Percentiles												
					5th		10th		25th		50th (median)		75th		90th		95th	
	Mean	S.E.	S.D.	S.E.	Score	S.E.	Score	S.E.	Score	S.E.	Score	S.E.	Score	S.E.	Score	S.E.	Score	S.E.
Australia																		
Australian Capital Territory	526	(3.7)	103	(3.3)	344	(13.8)	388	(10.6)	461	(6.2)	534	(4.7)	597	(5.0)	650	(6.2)	682	(8.4)
New South Wales	525	(3.5)	99	(2.1)	356	(6.0)	394	(5.2)	459	(4.6)	527	(4.0)	593	(4.7)	652	(5.1)	684	(5.3)
Northern Territory	513	(7.9)	112	(6.1)	313	(15.3)	364	(15.2)	438	(11.5)	524	(10.0)	593	(13.2)	653	(22.3)	676	(27.0)
Queensland	522	(3.4)	97	(2.3)	359	(7.2)	396	(6.2)	457	(5.3)	525	(3.5)	589	(4.0)	644	(4.2)	677	(6.1)
South Australia	520	(4.1)	93	(2.2)	364	(8.8)	400	(7.6)	458	(4.8)	522	(5.1)	584	(6.2)	639	(6.0)	669	(6.4)
Tasmania	490	(4.0)	105	(2.6)	317	(7.5)	356	(6.9)	418	(6.7)	489	(5.7)	561	(5.5)	628	(8.5)	666	(9.7)
Victoria	523	(4.1)	95	(2.1)	363	(9.1)	398	(6.0)	460	(5.5)	526	(4.7)	590	(4.9)	643	(4.9)	673	(5.7)
Western Australia	528	(4.0)	96	(2.9)	363	(9.7)	402	(8.0)	465	(5.1)	533	(4.8)	595	(4.9)	647	(5.3)	677	(9.2)
Belgium																		
Flemish Community*	525	(3.3)	102	(2.3)	341	(7.4)	385	(6.1)	461	(5.2)	534	(4.0)	597	(3.5)	648	(3.5)	676	(4.4)
French Community	485	(4.4)	108	(2.8)	288	(10.3)	340	(8.5)	415	(5.7)	495	(5.4)	564	(4.5)	616	(4.9)	645	(5.7)
German-speaking Community	520	(2.6)	97	(2.4)	348	(11.9)	392	(7.5)	459	(6.9)	529	(4.4)	586	(4.3)	638	(5.7)	668	(7.1)
Canada																		
Alberta	531	(5.1)	98	(2.3)	362	(7.1)	400	(7.8)	467	(8.1)	536	(6.3)	600	(5.6)	652	(6.5)	685	(6.4)
British Columbia	535	(3.5)	94	(2.3)	379	(8.3)	409	(5.7)	471	(4.8)	538	(4.3)	599	(5.1)	653	(4.8)	685	(6.2)
Manitoba	504	(3.6)	102	(3.3)	332	(13.2)	375	(6.2)	440	(5.1)	507	(3.9)	576	(3.9)	627	(5.6)	659	(5.0)
New Brunswick	515	(3.1)	92	(2.2)	353	(8.3)	395	(6.2)	456	(5.0)	520	(3.7)	579	(5.4)	627	(6.0)	656	(10.9)
Newfoundland and Labrador	504	(7.3)	100	(6.2)	329	(17.9)	376	(19.2)	445	(9.2)	511	(6.5)	572	(4.5)	626	(5.9)	655	(7.2)
Nova Scotia	512	(5.7)	92	(3.0)	359	(8.7)	392	(9.7)	452	(10.7)	515	(8.0)	575	(6.0)	625	(6.4)	656	(8.6)
Ontario	528	(5.7)	103	(3.1)	356	(7.9)	399	(8.4)	461	(6.3)	530	(6.0)	597	(5.8)	656	(7.5)	691	(8.3)
Prince Edward Island	493	(2.6)	90	(2.1)	342	(6.9)	376	(5.6)	435	(4.5)	495	(3.8)	553	(4.3)	605	(4.4)	636	(4.9)
Quebec	525	(4.5)	102	(3.8)	349	(11.1)	397	(7.2)	465	(4.9)	531	(4.3)	593	(5.0)	648	(5.8)	680	(7.5)
Saskatchewan	515	(2.8)	93	(1.9)	357	(8.2)	393	(5.9)	453	(4.2)	517	(4.0)	579	(5.2)	635	(5.1)	665	(5.5)
Italy																		
Centre	514	(10.8)	93	(5.5)	345	(17.4)	389	(16.3)	459	(18.0)	524	(11.2)	577	(9.1)	625	(11.6)	653	(12.9)
North East	527	(6.4)	91	(3.7)	367	(17.3)	409	(12.9)	470	(8.7)	533	(7.9)	589	(6.7)	636	(7.5)	665	(9.1)
North West	533	(8.6)	83	(3.4)	392	(13.0)	428	(11.4)	480	(10.3)	539	(9.3)	590	(9.1)	634	(9.6)	661	(9.4)
South	474	(8.4)	82	(4.5)	344	(23.2)	377	(13.3)	424	(9.7)	476	(8.2)	529	(8.6)	574	(10.6)	599	(8.6)
South Islands	486	(8.5)	90	(4.0)	339	(14.3)	374	(11.5)	428	(10.2)	485	(9.3)	548	(8.7)	600	(12.1)	634	(12.2)
Portugal																		
Alentejo	506	(13.4)	90	(5.2)	348	(18.3)	388	(17.9)	447	(14.9)	511	(13.0)	569	(14.8)	619	(16.4)	645	(21.5)
Spain																		
Basque Country*	496	(3.9)	97	(2.5)	330	(7.7)	371	(5.6)	436	(4.6)	501	(4.1)	562	(4.1)	616	(4.3)	648	(4.2)
Catalonia*	488	(8.4)	103	(5.4)	302	(18.3)	350	(16.8)	428	(10.7)	495	(9.0)	559	(6.7)	614	(8.8)	645	(9.9)
Madrid	507	(13.0)	97	(4.8)	345	(14.3)	378	(15.9)	439	(15.0)	513	(14.9)	575	(15.1)	627	(16.5)	660	(17.9)
Brazil																		
Central-West Region	441	(11.9)	87	(5.2)	297	(19.6)	331	(17.8)	384	(15.6)	441	(13.2)	498	(13.1)	552	(12.2)	582	(16.2)
Northeast Region	393	(11.0)	105	(8.2)	227	(18.0)	262	(13.9)	324	(11.2)	390	(12.3)	460	(15.3)	524	(18.7)	569	(25.9)
North Region	383	(10.9)	83	(5.0)	253	(19.6)	284	(12.5)	327	(11.1)	377	(13.2)	437	(14.9)	495	(14.7)	528	(16.1)
Southeast Region	447	(6.3)	83	(2.4)	309	(8.1)	341	(6.7)	390	(6.9)	447	(6.9)	504	(8.4)	554	(8.5)	578	(7.5)
South Region	435	(7.8)	82	(2.6)	301	(9.9)	330	(13.0)	379	(9.3)	435	(8.9)	488	(8.9)	541	(9.6)	573	(11.8)
Colombia																		
Bogotá	411	(5.7)	84	(2.6)	272	(7.4)	302	(7.0)	352	(6.5)	411	(6.5)	467	(6.3)	518	(7.3)	549	(7.2)
Cali	398	(9.0)	90	(4.4)	245	(20.2)	278	(16.0)	339	(12.1)	402	(9.2)	460	(8.4)	512	(7.0)	537	(8.0)
Manizales	425	(4.3)	86	(2.6)	284	(7.6)	314	(7.3)	367	(6.5)	426	(5.9)	481	(5.3)	535	(6.5)	564	(8.1)
Medellín	424	(7.6)	95	(5.1)	274	(9.8)	305	(7.4)	359	(7.8)	419	(9.7)	487	(11.9)	550	(13.9)	589	(18.7)
United Arab Emirates																		
Abu Dhabi*	391	(5.3)	109	(2.8)	212	(8.1)	250	(6.8)	319	(6.8)	394	(6.0)	466	(6.1)	529	(5.7)	568	(6.9)
Ajman	375	(8.0)	80	(3.6)	242	(11.8)	273	(8.5)	320	(9.0)	373	(10.0)	431	(10.2)	481	(12.1)	507	(14.4)
Dubai*	457	(1.3)	108	(1.1)	274	(4.0)	316	(3.0)	383	(2.8)	458	(2.7)	533	(2.9)	595	(3.2)	630	(4.5)
Fujairah	395	(4.0)	81	(2.6)	262	(8.1)	290	(6.2)	340	(6.5)	394	(5.6)	448	(6.6)	501	(6.5)	531	(9.6)
Ras al-Khaimah	373	(11.9)	95	(11.3)	205	(51.0)	253	(28.4)	318	(15.5)	379	(9.3)	433	(9.9)	486	(8.6)	516	(11.4)
Sharjah	416	(8.6)	85	(6.2)	273	(19.7)	305	(16.0)	361	(11.2)	416	(8.8)	474	(9.2)	526	(11.0)	557	(12.5)
Umm al-Quwain	372	(3.5)	81	(2.9)	241	(11.1)	270	(9.6)	315	(5.7)	369	(6.9)	427	(7.9)	476	(10.0)	506	(12.0)

* PISA adjudicated region.

Notes: Italian administrative regions are grouped into larger geographical units: Centre (*Lazio, Marche, Toscana, Umbria*), North East (*Bolzano, Emilia Romagna, Friuli Venezia Giulia, Trento, Veneto*), North West (*Liguria, Lombardia, Piemonte, Valle d'Aosta*), South (*Abruzzo, Campania, Molise, Puglia*), South Islands (*Basilicata, Calabria, Sardegna, Sicilia*).
Brazilian states are grouped into larger geographical units: Central-West Region (*Federal District, Goiás, Mato Grosso, Mato Grosso do Sul*), Northeast Region (*Alagoas, Bahia, Ceará, Maranhão, Paraíba, Pernambuco, Piauí, Rio Grande do Norte, Sergipe*), North Region (*Acre, Amapá, Amazonas, Pará, Rondônia, Roraima, Tocantins*), Southeast Region (*Espírito Santo, Minas Gerais, Rio de Janeiro, São Paulo*), South Region (*Paraná, Rio Grande do Sul, Santa Catarina*).

See Table V.2.2 for national data.

StatLink ⏵ http://dx.doi.org/10.1787/888933003763

[Part 2/2]
Table B2.V.2 **Mean score and variation in student performance in problem solving, by region**

		Range of performance							
		Inter-quartile range (75th minus 25th percentile)		Inter-decile range (90th minus 10th percentile)		Top range (90th minus 50th percentile)		Bottom range (50th minus 10th percentile)	
		Range	S.E.	Range	S.E.	Range	S.E.	Range	S.E.
OECD	**Australia**								
	Australian Capital Territory	136	(7.2)	262	(12.9)	116	(7.2)	146	(10.6)
	New South Wales	134	(4.5)	258	(6.7)	126	(4.2)	133	(4.9)
	Northern Territory	155	(12.3)	289	(26.9)	129	(21.2)	160	(16.4)
	Queensland	132	(5.8)	248	(6.6)	120	(4.5)	128	(6.0)
	South Australia	126	(5.8)	239	(8.4)	116	(4.9)	123	(6.9)
	Tasmania	143	(7.4)	272	(10.7)	139	(8.8)	133	(7.8)
	Victoria	130	(4.8)	245	(6.5)	118	(4.5)	127	(5.5)
	Western Australia	129	(5.7)	245	(8.8)	114	(5.4)	131	(7.2)
	Belgium								
	Flemish Community•	136	(5.2)	262	(6.8)	114	(3.2)	148	(5.5)
	French Community	148	(5.0)	276	(8.8)	121	(4.8)	155	(8.0)
	German-speaking Community	126	(8.9)	245	(9.6)	108	(6.7)	137	(8.5)
	Canada								
	Alberta	133	(7.2)	252	(7.6)	116	(6.4)	136	(7.0)
	British Columbia	128	(5.1)	244	(7.1)	115	(5.1)	128	(5.2)
	Manitoba	136	(4.8)	252	(8.0)	120	(5.1)	132	(6.2)
	New Brunswick	123	(7.2)	232	(8.4)	107	(6.0)	125	(6.0)
	Newfoundland and Labrador	127	(8.3)	250	(19.1)	115	(6.4)	134	(15.6)
	Nova Scotia	123	(8.9)	233	(10.6)	110	(8.9)	123	(7.5)
	Ontario	136	(4.8)	257	(8.5)	125	(5.2)	131	(6.8)
	Prince Edward Island	118	(5.3)	228	(7.1)	110	(5.3)	119	(6.6)
	Quebec	128	(4.3)	251	(8.3)	117	(4.5)	135	(6.6)
	Saskatchewan	126	(6.2)	242	(8.5)	117	(5.1)	125	(7.1)
	Italy								
	Centre	118	(14.5)	235	(17.9)	100	(10.0)	135	(12.2)
	North East	119	(7.4)	228	(14.2)	103	(7.2)	125	(12.8)
	North West	110	(7.6)	206	(10.9)	95	(6.4)	111	(8.7)
	South	106	(7.5)	197	(12.1)	98	(7.7)	99	(9.7)
	South Islands	121	(8.0)	226	(13.6)	115	(10.2)	111	(8.7)
	Portugal								
	Alentejo	122	(10.4)	231	(15.8)	108	(10.1)	123	(10.3)
	Spain								
	Basque Country•	125	(3.7)	245	(5.8)	115	(3.8)	130	(4.4)
	Catalonia•	131	(8.2)	263	(16.1)	119	(7.4)	144	(13.3)
	Madrid	136	(13.2)	249	(17.2)	114	(11.0)	135	(14.6)
Partners	**Brazil**								
	Central-West Region	115	(12.9)	221	(18.5)	111	(12.8)	110	(13.0)
	Northeast Region	137	(12.9)	263	(22.8)	134	(14.9)	128	(16.6)
	North Region	110	(10.6)	211	(16.7)	118	(13.9)	92	(10.9)
	Southeast Region	114	(5.9)	214	(8.0)	107	(6.3)	106	(5.7)
	South Region	108	(6.5)	211	(11.9)	107	(9.5)	105	(12.2)
	Colombia								
	Bogotá	115	(5.7)	216	(7.9)	106	(6.0)	110	(6.0)
	Cali	121	(7.4)	234	(14.6)	110	(7.2)	123	(12.2)
	Manizales	113	(6.2)	221	(8.6)	109	(6.5)	112	(6.7)
	Medellín	128	(9.8)	244	(14.8)	131	(12.8)	114	(9.0)
	United Arab Emirates								
	Abu Dhabi•	147	(5.5)	279	(7.4)	136	(5.3)	143	(5.6)
	Ajman	111	(8.7)	208	(12.4)	108	(9.0)	100	(9.5)
	Dubai•	150	(3.4)	279	(4.6)	137	(4.1)	142	(4.1)
	Fujairah	108	(7.3)	210	(9.1)	107	(8.6)	103	(7.7)
	Ras al-Khaimah	115	(12.9)	233	(27.5)	108	(8.0)	125	(24.0)
	Sharjah	113	(12.4)	220	(19.0)	110	(10.3)	110	(12.9)
	Umm al-Quwain	112	(9.0)	206	(13.6)	107	(11.1)	99	(10.6)

• PISA adjudicated region.
Notes: Italian administrative regions are grouped into larger geographical units: Centre (*Lazio, Marche, Toscana, Umbria*), North East (*Bolzano, Emilia Romagna, Friuli Venezia Giulia, Trento, Veneto*), North West (*Liguria, Lombardia, Piemonte, Valle d'Aosta*), South (*Abruzzo, Campania, Molise, Puglia*), South Islands (*Basilicata, Calabria, Sardegna, Sicilia*).
Brazilian states are grouped into larger geographical units: Central-West Region (*Federal District, Goiás, Mato Grosso, Mato Grosso do Sul*), Northeast Region (*Alagoas, Bahia, Ceará, Maranhão, Paraíba, Pernambuco, Piauí, Rio Grande do Norte, Sergipe*), North Region (*Acre, Amapá, Amazonas, Pará, Rondônia, Roraima, Tocantins*), Southeast Region (*Espírito Santo, Minas Gerais, Rio de Janeiro, São Paulo*), South Region (*Paraná, Rio Grande do Sul, Santa Catarina*).
See Table V.2.2 for national data.
StatLink http://dx.doi.org/10.1787/888933003763

[Part 1/3]

Table B2.V.3 **Relative performance in problem solving compared with performance in mathematics, reading and science, by region**

	Relative performance in problem solving compared with students around the world[1] with similar scores in...											
	... Mathematics, reading and science (expected performance)				... Mathematics							
	Relative performance across all students[2] (actual minus expected score)		Percentage of students who perform above their expected score[3]		Relative performance across all students[4]		Relative performance among strong and top performers in mathematics (at or above Level 4)[4]		Relative performance among moderate and low performers in mathematics (at or below Level 3)[4]		Difference in relative performance: strong and top performers minus moderate and low performers	
	Score dif.	S.E.	%	S.E.	Score dif.	S.E.	Score dif.	S.E.	Score dif.	S.E.	Score dif.	S.E.
Australia												
Australian Capital Territory	-2	(2.2)	51.1	(1.7)	2	(2.2)	8	(4.6)	-3	(3.5)	11	(6.8)
New South Wales	6	(2.6)	**54.6**	(2.1)	8	(2.5)	13	(2.9)	6	(3.1)	7	(3.3)
Northern Territory	40	(6.4)	**75.0**	(4.5)	44	(6.0)	48	(13.8)	43	(6.3)	4	(14.0)
Queensland	7	(3.1)	**56.5**	(2.3)	9	(3.1)	13	(3.5)	7	(3.4)	5	(3.0)
South Australia	15	(3.0)	**61.9**	(2.6)	18	(3.2)	20	(4.4)	18	(3.6)	2	(4.5)
Tasmania	-5	(2.2)	46.0	(2.1)	-2	(2.3)	12	(4.2)	-6	(2.8)	19	(5.2)
Victoria	9	(3.2)	**57.9**	(2.7)	12	(3.2)	19	(4.0)	10	(3.5)	9	(3.7)
Western Australia	2	(3.9)	52.5	(3.0)	5	(3.9)	7	(4.9)	4	(4.6)	3	(5.3)
Belgium												
Flemish Community•	-5	(2.4)	**45.9**	(1.9)	-9	(2.4)	-7	(2.7)	-11	(3.2)	4	(3.7)
French Community	-16	(3.9)	**39.0**	(2.4)	-19	(3.9)	-15	(4.8)	-21	(4.5)	5	(5.3)
German-speaking Community	5	(2.2)	50.0	(2.1)	1	(2.2)	0	(3.2)	2	(3.1)	-2	(4.8)
Canada												
Alberta	2	(3.7)	51.4	(2.9)	7	(3.6)	14	(4.7)	2	(4.0)	12	(4.5)
British Columbia	1	(3.5)	50.1	(2.9)	6	(3.6)	13	(4.6)	2	(4.0)	12	(4.4)
Manitoba	-1	(2.6)	50.9	(1.9)	-1	(2.7)	5	(2.8)	-3	(3.4)	8	(4.1)
New Brunswick	4	(1.9)	**54.8**	(2.1)	2	(1.9)	10	(3.4)	-1	(2.3)	11	(4.2)
Newfoundland and Labrador	-3	(4.9)	49.4	(3.5)	1	(4.8)	8	(3.3)	-1	(6.3)	9	(6.9)
Nova Scotia	1	(4.1)	52.0	(3.6)	3	(3.8)	8	(6.0)	2	(4.7)	6	(7.9)
Ontario	3	(3.9)	53.0	(2.3)	6	(4.1)	12	(4.2)	2	(4.6)	10	(3.8)
Prince Edward Island	-1	(2.8)	48.5	(1.9)	-1	(2.8)	-45	(5.0)	12	(3.4)	-57	(6.4)
Quebec	-8	(3.7)	**45.8**	(2.2)	-15	(3.8)	-13	(4.3)	-16	(4.6)	3	(4.6)
Saskatchewan	-1	(2.5)	48.5	(2.2)	-1	(2.6)	7	(3.9)	-5	(2.9)	12	(4.0)
Italy												
Centre	11	(7.2)	57.0	(5.1)	10	(7.2)	4	(5.6)	12	(8.9)	-8	(7.8)
North East	4	(4.9)	53.3	(4.1)	3	(5.1)	-1	(7.3)	6	(6.2)	-8	(8.7)
North West	15	(8.4)	**61.3**	(5.5)	16	(8.5)	4	(9.7)	21	(9.0)	-17	(7.8)
South	10	(7.5)	55.8	(5.4)	7	(7.3)	-16	(10.1)	11	(7.7)	-27	(11.1)
South Islands	9	(8.2)	55.5	(5.3)	7	(8.3)	-3	(10.1)	10	(9.1)	-12	(11.1)
Portugal												
Alentejo	7	(10.0)	55.7	(7.0)	5	(10.0)	3	(14.6)	6	(9.4)	-3	(10.5)
Spain												
Basque Country•	-17	(3.0)	**39.8**	(1.9)	-20	(3.0)	-13	(3.2)	-23	(3.5)	9	(3.2)
Catalonia•	-15	(7.6)	43.9	(4.0)	-17	(7.8)	-16	(8.6)	-17	(8.4)	2	(7.2)
Madrid	-3	(9.1)	48.3	(6.9)	-2	(8.9)	5	(12.8)	-5	(7.9)	9	(9.0)
Brazil												
Central-West Region	20	(8.9)	**68.8**	(7.8)	19	(9.8)	32	(13.9)	18	(10.0)	14	(14.2)
Northeast Region	-9	(8.0)	43.7	(6.5)	-10	(7.8)	38	(20.6)	-11	(7.6)	49	(19.6)
North Region	-7	(11.1)	44.3	(9.4)	-7	(10.7)	-16	(29.2)	-7	(10.7)	-9	(25.8)
Southeast Region	15	(4.5)	**63.1**	(3.5)	15	(4.7)	17	(9.1)	15	(4.8)	2	(8.6)
South Region	3	(6.8)	51.2	(6.1)	1	(7.3)	0	(21.4)	1	(7.3)	-1	(20.6)
Colombia												
Bogotá	-10	(5.7)	43.9	(4.1)	-9	(5.8)	21	(18.3)	-9	(5.8)	30	(17.3)
Cali	-11	(7.4)	45.5	(4.2)	-9	(7.4)	16	(22.4)	-10	(7.4)	26	(21.2)
Manizales	-6	(4.8)	45.0	(4.2)	-4	(4.8)	-15	(23.4)	-3	(4.4)	-11	(21.1)
Medellín	3	(5.2)	53.4	(4.7)	5	(5.3)	23	(5.8)	4	(5.5)	19	(6.7)
United Arab Emirates												
Abu Dhabi•	-53	(3.5)	**20.5**	(1.7)	-52	(3.6)	-43	(7.0)	-53	(3.7)	11	(7.0)
Ajman	-54	(5.7)	**16.4**	(3.4)	-54	(6.1)	-72	(15.8)	-53	(6.1)	-19	(15.4)
Dubai•	-23	(1.2)	**35.1**	(1.0)	-23	(1.2)	-5	(2.6)	-28	(1.4)	22	(2.9)
Fujairah	-39	(6.5)	**26.2**	(4.4)	-40	(6.3)	-56	(11.7)	-39	(6.2)	-17	(10.8)
Ras al-Khaimah	-65	(8.7)	**12.9**	(2.4)	-67	(9.0)	-49	(11.4)	-68	(9.3)	18	(12.9)
Sharjah	-43	(6.9)	**22.0**	(3.7)	-43	(7.3)	-51	(11.2)	-42	(7.9)	-9	(12.5)
Umm al-Quwain	-51	(2.8)	**15.7**	(2.2)	-52	(3.0)	-64	(23.5)	-52	(3.1)	-12	(24.2)

OECD

Partners

• PISA adjudicated region.

Notes: Values that are statistically significant are indicated in bold (see Annex A3).

Italian administrative regions are grouped into larger geographical units: Centre (*Lazio, Marche, Toscana, Umbria*), North East (*Bolzano, Emilia Romagna, Friuli Venezia Giulia, Trento, Veneto*), North West (*Liguria, Lombardia, Piemonte, Valle d'Aosta*), South (*Abruzzo, Campania, Molise, Puglia*), South Islands (*Basilicata, Calabria, Sardegna, Sicilia*).

Brazilian states are grouped into larger geographical units: Central-West Region (*Federal District, Goiás, Mato Grosso, Mato Grosso do Sul*), Northeast Region (*Alagoas, Bahia, Ceará, Maranhão, Paraíba, Pernambuco, Piauí, Rio Grande do Norte, Sergipe*), North Region (*Acre, Amapá, Amazonas, Pará, Rondônia, Roraima, Tocantins*), Southeast Region (*Espírito Santo, Minas Gerais, Rio de Janeiro, São Paulo*), South Region (*Paraná, Rio Grande do Sul, Santa Catarina*).

See Table V.2.6 for national data.

1. "Students around the world" refers to 15-year-old students in countries that participated in the PISA 2012 assessment of problem solving. National samples are weighted according to the size of the target population using final student weights.

2. This column reports the difference between actual performance and the fitted value from a regression using a second-degree polynomial as regression function (math, math sq., read, read sq., scie, scie sq., math×read, math×scie, read×scie).

3. This column reports the percentage of students for whom the difference between actual performance and the fitted value from a regression is positive. Values that are indicated in bold are significantly larger or smaller than 50%.

4. This column reports the difference between actual performance and the fitted value from a regression using a cubic polynomial as regression function.

StatLink ⌐┌┐╜ http://dx.doi.org/10.1787/888933003763

[Part 2/3]
Table B2.V.3 **Relative performance in problem solving compared with performance in mathematics, reading and science, by region**

Relative performance in problem solving compared with students around the world[1] with similar scores in...

		... Reading								... Science							
		Relative performance across all students[4]		Relative performance among strong and top performers in reading (at or above Level 4)[4]		Relative performance among moderate and low performers in reading (at or below Level 3)[4]		Difference in relative performance: strong and top performers minus moderate and low performers		Relative performance across all students[4]		Relative performance among strong and top performers in science (at or above Level 4)[4]		Relative performance among moderate and low performers in science (at or below Level 3)[4]		Difference in relative performance: strong and top performers minus moderate and low performers	
		Score dif.	S.E.	Score dif.	S.E.	Score dif.	S.E.	Score dif.	S.E.	Score dif.	S.E.	Score dif.	S.E.	Score dif.	S.E.	Score dif.	S.E.
OECD	**Australia**																
	Australian Capital Territory	2	(2.7)	6	(5.5)	-1	(3.0)	7	(6.6)	-4	(2.3)	-5	(4.6)	-2	(3.3)	-2	(6.4)
	New South Wales	**12**	(2.8)	**13**	(3.3)	**11**	(3.4)	3	(4.0)	3	(2.8)	1	(3.4)	4	(3.3)	-3	(3.7)
	Northern Territory	**34**	(6.4)	**32**	(12.9)	**34**	(6.3)	-2	(12.8)	**24**	(6.7)	16	(13.3)	**27**	(6.0)	-11	(12.6)
	Queensland	**12**	(3.3)	**9**	(4.1)	**14**	(3.7)	-5	(4.0)	5	(3.1)	4	(3.7)	6	(3.3)	-2	(3.3)
	South Australia	**16**	(3.2)	**18**	(4.8)	**15**	(3.3)	2	(4.5)	**8**	(3.3)	1	(4.4)	**11**	(3.7)	**-10**	(4.8)
	Tasmania	-1	(2.3)	4	(8.0)	-4	(2.8)	8	(9.5)	**-12**	(2.4)	-10	(5.2)	**-12**	(2.7)	3	(5.9)
	Victoria	7	(3.6)	7	(4.7)	6	(3.8)	1	(4.3)	**7**	(3.5)	4	(4.3)	**9**	(3.9)	-4	(4.3)
	Western Australia	**10**	(4.1)	8	(5.7)	**11**	(4.7)	-3	(6.3)	-1	(3.8)	-5	(4.2)	2	(4.8)	-7	(5.1)
	Belgium																
	Flemish Community•	**7**	(2.6)	**12**	(3.1)	4	(3.2)	7	(3.8)	**8**	(2.5)	**9**	(2.9)	**8**	(3.0)	1	(3.3)
	French Community	**-16**	(4.1)	**-23**	(5.2)	**-13**	(4.6)	-10	(5.7)	-6	(4.1)	-2	(4.8)	-8	(4.8)	6	(5.5)
	German-speaking Community	**17**	(2.2)	-2	(4.5)	**26**	(3.0)	**-28**	(5.9)	**12**	(2.3)	**11**	(4.6)	**13**	(2.9)	-2	(5.9)
	Canada																
	Alberta	8	(4.3)	10	(5.3)	6	(4.8)	4	(5.3)	-3	(4.2)	-2	(4.9)	-3	(4.9)	1	(5.2)
	British Columbia	4	(3.9)	3	(4.4)	4	(5.0)	-1	(5.5)	-3	(3.5)	-2	(4.3)	-3	(4.2)	1	(4.8)
	Manitoba	4	(2.6)	**7**	(2.9)	2	(3.4)	5	(4.1)	0	(2.8)	1	(3.1)	-1	(3.5)	2	(4.1)
	New Brunswick	**15**	(2.5)	7	(4.1)	**18**	(2.8)	**-11**	(4.5)	**8**	(2.3)	4	(5.2)	**10**	(2.7)	-6	(6.2)
	Newfoundland and Labrador	-2	(5.4)	-9	(5.0)	1	(7.4)	-10	(8.6)	-10	(5.8)	**-11**	(3.5)	-9	(8.0)	-2	(8.2)
	Nova Scotia	2	(5.1)	-4	(5.0)	4	(6.3)	-8	(6.4)	-3	(5.5)	-8	(5.8)	-1	(7.1)	-7	(8.1)
	Ontario	2	(4.1)	2	(5.3)	2	(4.4)	0	(4.9)	5	(3.7)	6	(4.8)	4	(3.9)	2	(4.1)
	Prince Edward Island	-2	(2.8)	**-48**	(5.4)	**14**	(3.4)	**-62**	(6.6)	-1	(2.8)	**-45**	(5.6)	**12**	(3.3)	**-57**	(6.9)
	Quebec	6	(3.5)	-1	(4.4)	**10**	(4.3)	**-11**	(5.2)	**10**	(3.8)	**13**	(4.3)	**9**	(4.4)	4	(4.4)
	Saskatchewan	**8**	(2.7)	5	(4.0)	**9**	(3.1)	-4	(4.8)	0	(2.5)	-1	(4.2)	0	(2.8)	-2	(4.7)
	Italy																
	Centre	**19**	(8.6)	4	(7.7)	**25**	(10.8)	-22	(11.3)	10	(7.6)	1	(7.3)	13	(9.4)	-12	(9.2)
	North East	**15**	(5.5)	-3	(5.3)	**25**	(6.8)	**-28**	(6.5)	4	(5.2)	-3	(6.1)	8	(6.6)	-11	(8.0)
	North West	**25**	(8.4)	6	(8.6)	**34**	(9.7)	**-29**	(8.3)	15	(8.3)	-2	(8.9)	**24**	(9.1)	**-26**	(8.1)
	South	7	(8.3)	**-31**	(12.6)	13	(8.3)	**-44**	(13.8)	13	(7.7)	-20	(11.4)	**17**	(7.6)	**-38**	(11.4)
	South Islands	9	(7.6)	-5	(10.8)	12	(8.5)	-17	(12.1)	11	(8.2)	-8	(12.3)	15	(8.2)	**-23**	(10.9)
	Portugal																
	Alentejo	11	(9.4)	8	(16.8)	12	(8.7)	-5	(14.0)	10	(11.0)	9	(17.6)	10	(10.4)	-1	(13.4)
	Spain																
	Basque Country•	**-6**	(3.2)	-6	(3.6)	-6	(3.6)	0	(3.8)	**-11**	(3.1)	**-10**	(3.4)	**-11**	(3.5)	1	(3.6)
	Catalonia•	**-16**	(7.8)	**-25**	(8.4)	-12	(8.5)	-12	(7.5)	-7	(7.2)	-2	(7.0)	-8	(7.8)	7	(6.7)
	Madrid	0	(8.7)	2	(11.6)	-1	(8.3)	3	(7.9)	-5	(10.4)	2	(13.4)	-9	(9.9)	11	(9.2)
Partners	**Brazil**																
	Central-West Region	6	(7.9)	9	(14.4)	6	(8.0)	3	(13.7)	**15**	(7.0)	**38**	(14.5)	**14**	(7.0)	24	(14.9)
	Northeast Region	**-25**	(9.8)	3	(21.5)	**-26**	(9.9)	29	(20.6)	**-18**	(8.4)	24	(22.7)	**-20**	(8.3)	**44**	(21.4)
	North Region	**-29**	(12.9)	-34	(21.5)	**-29**	(13.0)	-5	(21.7)	-18	(10.8)	-7	(20.0)	-18	(10.8)	11	(23.3)
	Southeast Region	3	(4.6)	-10	(10.9)	4	(4.7)	-14	(11.3)	**11**	(4.2)	7	(9.9)	**11**	(4.2)	-4	(9.5)
	South Region	-9	(5.8)	-13	(14.9)	-9	(5.8)	-5	(14.4)	3	(6.7)	-2	(20.9)	3	(6.6)	-5	(20.0)
	Colombia																
	Bogotá	**-31**	(5.3)	-18	(14.0)	**-32**	(5.3)	14	(13.1)	**-17**	(6.1)	-3	(21.4)	**-18**	(6.1)	15	(20.0)
	Cali	**-34**	(7.1)	**-33**	(10.9)	**-34**	(7.3)	1	(12.0)	**-23**	(7.9)	-23	(16.5)	**-23**	(8.0)	0	(16.8)
	Manizales	**-25**	(5.1)	**-39**	(11.9)	**-24**	(5.0)	-15	(10.8)	**-17**	(5.1)	-25	(17.6)	**-16**	(4.9)	-9	(16.5)
	Medellín	**-19**	(6.1)	-1	(13.3)	**-20**	(6.3)	19	(13.2)	**-10**	(4.8)	**21**	(8.8)	**-11**	(5.0)	**32**	(9.2)
	United Arab Emirates																
	Abu Dhabi•	**-58**	(3.9)	**-47**	(7.7)	**-60**	(4.0)	13	(7.9)	**-61**	(3.4)	**-53**	(6.3)	**-62**	(3.6)	9	(6.3)
	Ajman	**-62**	(4.9)	**-90**	(10.5)	**-60**	(5.1)	**-30**	(10.7)	**-62**	(5.2)	**-86**	(13.4)	**-60**	(5.1)	**-26**	(12.2)
	Dubai•	**-22**	(1.4)	**-9**	(2.8)	**-26**	(1.6)	**16**	(3.1)	**-24**	(1.2)	**-11**	(2.8)	**-27**	(1.5)	**16**	(3.4)
	Fujairah	**-43**	(6.2)	**-76**	(15.4)	**-42**	(6.2)	-34	(17.6)	**-46**	(4.6)	**-53**	(9.6)	**-45**	(4.7)	-8	(10.4)
	Ras al-Khaimah	**-64**	(9.2)	**-63**	(21.4)	**-64**	(9.4)	1	(22.1)	**-72**	(8.9)	**-59**	(14.4)	**-72**	(9.1)	14	(15.0)
	Sharjah	**-49**	(5.5)	**-53**	(12.8)	**-48**	(5.6)	-5	(12.5)	**-44**	(7.8)	**-60**	(9.8)	**-42**	(8.0)	-17	(9.6)
	Umm al-Quwain	**-54**	(3.2)	**-65**	(15.4)	**-54**	(3.4)	-11	(16.1)	**-60**	(2.6)	**-68**	(15.1)	**-60**	(2.8)	-8	(15.9)

• PISA adjudicated region.
Notes: Values that are statistically significant are indicated in bold (see Annex A3).
Italian administrative regions are grouped into larger geographical units: Centre (*Lazio, Marche, Toscana, Umbria*), North East (*Bolzano, Emilia Romagna, Friuli Venezia Giulia, Trento, Veneto*), North West (*Liguria, Lombardia, Piemonte, Valle d'Aosta*), South (*Abruzzo, Campania, Molise, Puglia*), South Islands (*Basilicata, Calabria, Sardegna, Sicilia*).
Brazilian states are grouped into larger geographical units: Central-West Region (*Federal District, Goiás, Mato Grosso, Mato Grosso do Sul*), Northeast Region (*Alagoas, Bahia, Ceará, Maranhão, Paraíba, Pernambuco, Piauí, Rio Grande do Norte, Sergipe*), North Region (*Acre, Amapá, Amazonas, Pará, Rondônia, Roraima, Tocantins*), Southeast Region (*Espírito Santo, Minas Gerais, Rio de Janeiro, São Paulo*), South Region (*Paraná, Rio Grande do Sul, Santa Catarina*).
See Table V.2.6 for national data.

1. "Students around the world" refers to 15-year-old students in countries that participated in the PISA 2012 assessment of problem solving. National samples are weighted according to the size of the target population using final student weights.
2. This column reports the difference between actual performance and the fitted value from a regression using a second-degree polynomial as regression function (math, math sq., read, read sq., scie, scie sq., math×read, math×scie, read×scie).
3. This column reports the percentage of students for whom the difference between actual performance and the fitted value from a regression is positive. Values that are indicated in bold are significantly larger or smaller than 50%.
4. This column reports the difference between actual performance and the fitted value from a regression using a cubic polynomial as regression function.

StatLink http://dx.doi.org/10.1787/888933003763

[Part 3/3]

Table B2.V.3 **Relative performance in problem solving compared with performance in mathematics, reading and science, by region**

	Relative performance in problem solving compared with students in countries that also assessed mathematics on computers who have similar scores in…					
	...Paper-based mathematics (A)		...Computer-based mathematics (B)		Mode effects: Score-point difference attributed to computer delivery (A - B)	
	Relative performance across all students[4]		Relative performance across all students[4]			
	Score dif.	S.E.	Score dif.	S.E.	Score dif.	S.E.
Australia						
Australian Capital Territory	0	(2.3)	**11**	(2.4)	**-11**	(1.4)
New South Wales	**7**	(2.6)	**15**	(2.8)	**-8**	(1.9)
Northern Territory	**43**	(6.1)	**34**	(5.5)	**9**	(3.3)
Queensland	**8**	(3.1)	**13**	(3.4)	-5	(2.5)
South Australia	**17**	(3.2)	**17**	(3.4)	0	(3.5)
Tasmania	-3	(2.3)	4	(2.3)	**-7**	(1.6)
Victoria	**11**	(3.3)	**9**	(3.4)	2	(2.2)
Western Australia	4	(4.0)	**12**	(4.1)	**-8**	(3.5)
Belgium						
Flemish Community•	**-11**	(2.4)	-4	(2.7)	**-7**	(2.1)
French Community	**-21**	(4.0)	**-11**	(4.0)	**-10**	(2.7)
German-speaking Community	0	(2.2)	**6**	(2.5)	**-6**	(1.8)
Canada						
Alberta	5	(3.7)	**13**	(5.0)	**-8**	(3.2)
British Columbia	5	(3.6)	4	(4.2)	1	(3.0)
Manitoba	-2	(2.7)	5	(3.1)	**-7**	(1.6)
New Brunswick	1	(2.0)	**14**	(2.6)	**-13**	(1.9)
Newfoundland and Labrador	-1	(4.8)	-10	(5.1)	**10**	(1.4)
Nova Scotia	2	(3.8)	5	(3.2)	-3	(2.5)
Ontario	4	(4.1)	-2	(3.9)	6	(3.2)
Prince Edward Island	-3	(2.8)	-3	(3.5)	0	(2.8)
Quebec	**-16**	(3.8)	0	(4.4)	**-16**	(2.5)
Saskatchewan	-2	(2.7)	**11**	(3.1)	**-13**	(2.1)
Italy						
Centre	8	(7.2)	10	(8.3)	-2	(5.3)
North East	2	(5.2)	12	(7.0)	-11	(5.4)
North West	14	(8.5)	8	(7.3)	6	(5.3)
South	6	(7.3)	-11	(7.5)	**16**	(7.4)
South Islands	6	(8.3)	8	(6.5)	-3	(5.8)
Portugal						
Alentejo	4	(10.1)	15	(9.2)	-12	(6.2)
Spain						
Basque Country•	**-21**	(3.0)	0	(3.2)	**-21**	(2.1)
Catalonia•	**-19**	(7.7)	-1	(8.3)	**-17**	(5.2)
Madrid	-3	(9.0)	9	(9.6)	**-13**	(3.5)
Brazil						
Central-West Region	17	(9.8)	8	(7.7)	9	(6.2)
Northeast Region	-11	(7.7)	**-22**	(6.6)	11	(6.0)
North Region	-9	(10.7)	**-35**	(12.5)	**26**	(5.7)
Southeast Region	13	(4.6)	0	(4.9)	**13**	(3.9)
South Region	-1	(7.2)	-6	(6.3)	5	(7.5)
Colombia						
Bogotá	-11	(5.9)	**-16**	(6.2)	5	(3.4)
Cali	-11	(7.5)	-17	(7.9)	6	(8.1)
Manizales	-6	(4.8)	1	(5.0)	**-7**	(2.4)
Medellín	3	(5.3)	-4	(4.5)	7	(4.2)
United Arab Emirates						
Abu Dhabi•	**-54**	(3.6)	**-46**	(3.4)	**-8**	(3.0)
Ajman•	**-56**	(6.1)	**-34**	(3.3)	**-22**	(4.9)
Dubai•	**-25**	(1.3)	**-13**	(1.3)	**-12**	(1.0)
Fujairah	**-42**	(6.4)	**-45**	(4.4)	3	(4.9)
Ras al-Khaimah	**-69**	(9.0)	**-58**	(10.9)	**-11**	(4.8)
Sharjah	**-45**	(7.3)	**-37**	(5.3)	-8	(5.7)
Umm al-Quwain	**-54**	(3.1)	**-37**	(3.5)	**-17**	(2.8)

• PISA adjudicated region.
Notes: Values that are statistically significant are indicated in bold (see Annex A3).
Italian administrative regions are grouped into larger geographical units: Centre (*Lazio, Marche, Toscana, Umbria*), North East (*Bolzano, Emilia Romagna, Friuli Venezia Giulia, Trento, Veneto*), North West (*Liguria, Lombardia, Piemonte, Valle d'Aosta*), South (*Abruzzo, Campania, Molise, Puglia*), South Islands (*Basilicata, Calabria, Sardegna, Sicilia*).
Brazilian states are grouped into larger geographical units: Central-West Region (*Federal District, Goiás, Mato Grosso, Mato Grosso do Sul*), Northeast Region (*Alagoas, Bahia, Ceará, Maranhão, Paraíba, Pernambuco, Piauí, Rio Grande do Norte, Sergipe*), North Region (*Acre, Amapá, Amazonas, Pará, Rondônia, Roraima, Tocantins*), Southeast Region (*Espírito Santo, Minas Gerais, Rio de Janeiro, São Paulo*), South Region (*Paraná, Rio Grande do Sul, Santa Catarina*).
See Table V.2.6 for national data.
1. "Students around the world" refers to 15-year-old students in countries that participated in the PISA 2012 assessment of problem solving. National samples are weighted according to the size of the target population using final student weights.
2. This column reports the difference between actual performance and the fitted value from a regression using a second-degree polynomial as regression function (math, math sq., read, read sq., scie, scie sq., math×read, math×scie, read×scie).
3. This column reports the percentage of students for whom the difference between actual performance and the fitted value from a regression is positive. Values that are indicated in bold are significantly larger or smaller than 50%.
4. This column reports the difference between actual performance and the fitted value from a regression using a cubic polynomial as regression function.
StatLink ⟲ᵐˢᴸ http://dx.doi.org/10.1787/888933003763

[Part 1/2]

Table B2.V.4 **Percentage of students at each proficiency level in problem solving, by gender and by region**

	Below Level 1 (below 358.49 score points)		Level 1 (from 358.49 to less than 423.42 score points)		Level 2 (from 423.42 to less than 488.35 score points)		Level 3 (from 488.35 to less than 553.28 score points)		Level 4 (from 553.28 to less than 618.21 score points)		Level 5 (from 618.21 to less than 683.14 score points)		Level 6 (above 683.14 score points)	
	%	S.E.	%	S.E.	%	S.E.	%	S.E.	%	S.E.	%	S.E.	%	S.E.
Australia														
Australian Capital Territory	7.7	(1.7)	10.5	(2.3)	17.1	(1.9)	23.8	(2.8)	21.7	(3.4)	13.8	(2.9)	5.5	(1.3)
New South Wales	6.0	(0.8)	10.8	(1.2)	18.6	(1.5)	24.3	(1.4)	21.2	(1.3)	12.7	(1.3)	6.5	(1.2)
Northern Territory	10.3	(2.2)	12.9	(3.3)	16.5	(3.7)	17.2	(3.8)	21.1	(4.3)	14.3	(3.8)	7.8	(4.3)
Queensland	4.9	(0.8)	11.4	(1.1)	19.4	(1.4)	24.6	(1.6)	23.3	(1.4)	11.6	(1.2)	4.9	(1.0)
South Australia	5.1	(0.9)	11.1	(1.5)	20.5	(2.2)	25.8	(2.1)	22.0	(2.1)	11.6	(1.7)	3.8	(0.8)
Tasmania	12.1	(1.6)	16.8	(2.5)	20.9	(2.9)	20.9	(2.2)	17.1	(2.2)	8.4	(1.6)	3.9	(1.1)
Victoria	4.6	(1.1)	10.7	(1.7)	18.9	(1.4)	26.5	(2.0)	22.4	(1.5)	12.8	(1.3)	4.1	(0.8)
Western Australia	3.8	(0.9)	8.8	(1.3)	16.8	(1.6)	24.8	(2.0)	26.3	(2.1)	14.5	(1.6)	5.0	(1.5)
Belgium														
Flemish Community●	6.3	(0.8)	9.3	(1.2)	16.0	(1.2)	24.0	(1.1)	24.2	(1.4)	15.2	(1.2)	5.0	(0.6)
French Community	13.7	(1.5)	14.6	(1.1)	18.2	(1.3)	22.2	(1.5)	19.7	(1.3)	9.4	(1.1)	2.2	(0.6)
German-speaking Community	5.5	(1.2)	8.8	(1.6)	16.5	(2.4)	22.4	(2.7)	26.6	(2.9)	14.9	(1.9)	5.3	(1.2)
Canada														
Alberta	4.5	(0.8)	9.2	(1.3)	15.9	(1.5)	26.3	(2.0)	25.0	(2.1)	13.4	(1.5)	5.7	(1.1)
British Columbia	2.9	(0.7)	9.1	(1.1)	17.5	(1.5)	26.3	(1.9)	23.1	(1.7)	14.7	(1.9)	6.5	(1.1)
Manitoba	7.4	(1.4)	12.7	(1.6)	21.7	(2.4)	24.5	(2.6)	21.6	(1.9)	9.2	(1.6)	2.9	(0.7)
New Brunswick	6.4	(1.3)	11.0	(1.6)	21.8	(2.1)	26.9	(3.3)	21.6	(1.9)	9.3	(2.1)	3.0	(0.8)
Newfoundland and Labrador	9.9	(2.8)	12.2	(1.8)	19.8	(1.9)	25.5	(2.6)	21.5	(2.4)	9.0	(1.4)	2.1	(0.8)
Nova Scotia	6.5	(2.1)	10.6	(1.8)	21.0	(3.2)	27.4	(3.8)	21.7	(2.6)	10.2	(1.8)	2.6	(1.2)
Ontario	5.0	(1.1)	9.2	(1.3)	18.9	(1.7)	23.6	(1.4)	22.3	(1.6)	13.7	(1.3)	7.3	(1.3)
Prince Edward Island	7.6	(1.2)	13.8	(1.6)	24.9	(2.5)	29.1	(3.2)	17.3	(2.2)	6.0	(1.0)	1.2	(0.5)
Quebec	6.5	(1.2)	9.3	(1.0)	16.0	(1.4)	25.4	(1.4)	24.2	(1.3)	13.2	(1.4)	5.4	(1.0)
Saskatchewan	6.2	(1.2)	11.7	(1.6)	21.4	(2.1)	27.2	(2.2)	21.0	(1.8)	10.1	(1.7)	2.5	(0.7)
Italy														
Centre	6.9	(2.4)	9.7	(3.6)	14.3	(2.3)	30.0	(4.9)	24.8	(2.8)	11.8	(2.6)	2.6	(1.4)
North East	5.4	(1.8)	7.2	(2.4)	13.3	(2.3)	22.1	(2.5)	29.0	(2.4)	17.7	(2.1)	5.3	(1.5)
North West	2.9	(1.1)	6.9	(2.4)	18.1	(2.4)	25.9	(2.9)	28.2	(3.9)	14.7	(2.6)	3.2	(1.0)
South	5.9	(2.0)	17.4	(3.9)	28.2	(3.6)	27.7	(3.2)	16.7	(3.7)	3.8	(1.2)	0.2	(0.3)
South Islands	7.7	(2.2)	14.5	(3.4)	25.1	(3.2)	22.9	(3.5)	18.9	(2.9)	9.3	(2.9)	1.6	(1.1)
Portugal														
Alentejo	5.6	(2.0)	9.8	(2.4)	21.0	(3.4)	26.8	(4.0)	22.8	(3.0)	10.8	(3.3)	3.2	(2.2)
Spain														
Basque Country●	8.3	(1.0)	13.1	(1.0)	22.2	(1.1)	26.1	(1.3)	19.5	(1.2)	8.5	(0.8)	2.4	(0.5)
Catalonia●	13.3	(2.7)	12.2	(1.7)	21.8	(2.1)	24.0	(2.4)	17.7	(2.2)	8.4	(1.5)	2.6	(1.1)
Madrid	6.9	(2.0)	14.1	(2.9)	18.0	(3.6)	25.4	(3.2)	22.0	(3.8)	10.3	(3.2)	3.2	(1.5)
Brazil														
Central-West Region	13.4	(5.2)	20.7	(5.5)	30.5	(5.0)	21.9	(4.6)	9.9	(3.1)	3.0	(1.4)	0.6	(0.8)
Northeast Region	32.8	(4.8)	25.3	(3.7)	20.3	(3.2)	12.1	(3.0)	5.7	(2.1)	2.2	(1.0)	1.5	(1.0)
North Region	37.0	(7.4)	29.8	(4.7)	20.0	(4.8)	10.0	(4.4)	2.8	(1.5)	0.4	(0.3)	0.0	(0.0)
Southeast Region	12.4	(2.4)	22.5	(2.2)	28.7	(2.4)	22.7	(3.0)	11.2	(2.2)	2.1	(0.7)	0.5	(0.3)
South Region	16.6	(3.2)	23.3	(3.5)	30.6	(4.1)	19.5	(4.1)	7.8	(1.8)	2.1	(1.1)	0.1	(0.2)
Colombia														
Bogotá	21.1	(2.7)	26.0	(2.6)	29.5	(2.3)	16.8	(2.3)	5.2	(1.6)	1.2	(0.7)	0.2	(0.2)
Cali	28.8	(3.6)	27.6	(2.3)	24.2	(2.3)	14.8	(2.2)	3.9	(1.5)	0.6	(0.4)	0.2	(0.2)
Manizales	14.7	(1.8)	23.6	(2.4)	30.8	(2.3)	20.4	(2.6)	8.3	(1.6)	1.6	(0.9)	0.7	(0.5)
Medellín	19.5	(2.9)	26.5	(3.2)	24.4	(3.2)	17.3	(2.4)	9.1	(2.2)	2.5	(1.3)	0.6	(0.5)
United Arab Emirates														
Abu Dhabi●	46.3	(3.1)	19.7	(1.9)	16.8	(1.5)	10.8	(1.3)	4.9	(1.0)	1.5	(0.5)	0.2	(0.2)
Ajman	56.4	(4.5)	26.6	(4.5)	12.9	(3.4)	3.6	(1.7)	0.4	(0.6)	0.0	c	0.0	c
Dubai●	21.7	(1.0)	18.5	(1.2)	20.8	(1.7)	19.0	(1.3)	13.3	(1.1)	5.1	(0.7)	1.5	(0.4)
Fujairah	32.7	(3.6)	31.4	(3.4)	20.1	(3.4)	10.8	(1.7)	4.3	(1.3)	0.7	(0.7)	0.0	c
Ras al-Khaimah	47.5	(7.1)	28.6	(4.8)	15.2	(3.1)	7.0	(1.7)	1.3	(0.7)	0.4	(0.3)	0.0	c
Sharjah	31.8	(8.1)	29.1	(5.6)	21.4	(4.5)	12.1	(3.8)	4.6	(2.2)	0.8	(0.8)	0.2	(0.4)
Umm al-Quwain	61.3	(5.1)	25.1	(4.4)	10.6	(3.9)	1.9	(1.9)	0.9	(0.5)	0.3	(0.4)	0.0	c

● PISA adjudicated region.
Notes: Values that are statistically significant are indicated in bold (see Annex A3).
Italian administrative regions are grouped into larger geographical units: Centre (*Lazio, Marche, Toscana, Umbria*), North East (*Bolzano, Emilia Romagna, Friuli Venezia Giulia, Trento, Veneto*), North West (*Liguria, Lombardia, Piemonte, Valle d'Aosta*), South (*Abruzzo, Campania, Molise, Puglia*), South Islands (*Basilicata, Calabria, Sardegna, Sicilia*).
Brazilian states are grouped into larger geographical units: Central-West Region (*Federal District, Goiás, Mato Grosso, Mato Grosso do Sul*), Northeast Region (*Alagoas, Bahia, Ceará, Maranhão, Paraíba, Pernambuco, Piauí, Rio Grande do Norte, Sergipe*), North Region (*Acre, Amapá, Amazonas, Pará, Rondônia, Roraima, Tocantins*), Southeast Region (*Espírito Santo, Minas Gerais, Rio de Janeiro, São Paulo*), South Region (*Paraná, Rio Grande do Sul, Santa Catarina*).
See Table V.4.6 for national data.
StatLink ⊗ http://dx.doi.org/10.1787/888933003763

[Part 2/2]

Table B2.V.4 **Percentage of students at each proficiency level in problem solving, by gender and by region**

| | Girls | | | | | | | | | | | | | | Increased likelihood of boys scoring below Level 2 (less than 423.42 score points) | | Increased likelihood of boys scoring at or above Level 5 (above 618.21 score points) | |
| | Below Level 1 (below 358.49 score points) | | Level 1 (from 358.49 to less than 423.42 score points) | | Level 2 (from 423.42 to less than 488.35 score points) | | Level 3 (from 488.35 to less than 553.28 score points) | | Level 4 (from 553.28 to less than 618.21 score points) | | Level 5 (from 618.21 to less than 683.14 score points) | | Level 6 (above 683.14 score points) | | | | | |
	%	S.E.	%	S.E.	%	S.E.	%	S.E.	%	S.E.	%	S.E.	%	S.E.	Relative risk	S.E.	Relative risk	S.E.
Australia																		
Australian Capital Territory	5.0	(1.5)	8.6	(1.6)	18.2	(2.3)	24.4	(3.1)	26.4	(3.3)	13.2	(2.2)	4.2	(1.7)	1.35	(0.31)	1.11	(0.23)
New South Wales	4.5	(0.8)	9.8	(1.0)	19.3	(1.6)	26.9	(1.3)	22.9	(1.3)	12.6	(1.2)	4.0	(0.6)	1.18	(0.15)	1.15	(0.14)
Northern Territory	8.0	(1.8)	11.9	(3.0)	19.6	(4.2)	26.0	(5.1)	22.0	(3.6)	10.2	(4.8)	2.3	(2.1)	1.17	(0.33)	1.81	(0.89)
Queensland	4.9	(0.9)	10.1	(1.3)	20.2	(2.0)	27.1	(1.8)	22.2	(1.7)	11.9	(1.4)	3.7	(0.7)	1.09	(0.10)	1.06	(0.15)
South Australia	3.8	(0.9)	10.3	(1.4)	20.6	(2.2)	28.6	(2.1)	22.0	(2.2)	12.0	(2.0)	2.8	(0.9)	1.16	(0.18)	1.04	(0.18)
Tasmania	8.2	(1.4)	16.2	(1.9)	24.8	(2.4)	24.8	(2.8)	14.8	(2.7)	8.5	(2.2)	2.6	(0.8)	1.18	(0.12)	1.13	(0.31)
Victoria	4.6	(0.8)	10.2	(1.4)	20.2	(1.7)	26.0	(2.2)	23.5	(2.1)	11.9	(1.4)	3.6	(0.8)	1.04	(0.12)	1.10	(0.15)
Western Australia	5.2	(1.3)	9.9	(1.6)	20.4	(1.8)	27.0	(2.4)	22.9	(1.9)	10.9	(1.7)	3.7	(1.0)	0.83	(0.11)	1.34	(0.24)
Belgium																		
Flemish Community •	7.1	(1.1)	9.7	(1.1)	17.5	(1.2)	25.7	(1.5)	24.2	(1.3)	12.6	(1.3)	3.2	(0.5)	0.93	(0.13)	**1.28**	(0.12)
French Community	11.5	(1.1)	14.2	(1.1)	22.5	(2.0)	25.8	(1.3)	18.5	(1.5)	6.7	(1.0)	0.9	(0.4)	1.10	(0.08)	**1.55**	(0.22)
German-speaking Community	6.1	(1.3)	9.4	(1.7)	22.6	(3.0)	30.5	(3.8)	22.6	(2.8)	6.9	(1.6)	1.8	(0.7)	0.92	(0.17)	**2.36**	(0.61)
Canada																		
Alberta	4.7	(0.8)	9.9	(1.3)	17.7	(2.0)	26.0	(2.7)	22.8	(2.3)	13.9	(1.5)	4.9	(1.0)	0.94	(0.11)	1.01	(0.11)
British Columbia	3.4	(1.0)	9.7	(1.6)	18.9	(1.8)	25.9	(2.3)	25.0	(2.5)	12.9	(1.5)	4.2	(0.9)	0.91	(0.13)	1.24	(0.16)
Manitoba	7.2	(1.4)	13.7	(1.8)	21.5	(1.8)	25.2	(2.3)	20.8	(2.0)	9.1	(1.1)	2.5	(0.6)	0.97	(0.13)	1.04	(0.15)
New Brunswick	4.4	(0.9)	9.6	(1.4)	19.8	(2.1)	29.1	(2.6)	25.2	(2.5)	9.4	(1.7)	2.5	(1.0)	1.25	(0.20)	1.04	(0.25)
Newfoundland and Labrador	5.3	(2.1)	10.4	(2.1)	23.3	(2.0)	28.3	(2.1)	20.0	(2.0)	9.7	(1.5)	2.5	(0.9)	**1.41**	(0.22)	0.91	(0.16)
Nova Scotia	3.6	(1.4)	11.1	(2.7)	24.2	(4.4)	27.2	(2.4)	23.5	(4.0)	8.1	(1.3)	2.3	(1.0)	1.18	(0.23)	1.24	(0.27)
Ontario	5.2	(0.9)	9.6	(1.3)	19.9	(1.7)	26.2	(1.7)	22.6	(1.6)	11.7	(1.3)	4.8	(0.9)	0.96	(0.10)	**1.27**	(0.11)
Prince Edward Island	6.4	(1.0)	14.6	(1.7)	26.4	(1.9)	27.2	(2.5)	18.1	(1.7)	5.2	(1.4)	2.0	(0.7)	1.02	(0.11)	1.01	(0.26)
Quebec	5.2	(0.8)	8.5	(0.9)	20.1	(1.6)	27.5	(1.5)	22.7	(1.3)	11.9	(1.2)	4.1	(0.8)	1.15	(0.12)	1.17	(0.12)
Saskatchewan	4.1	(1.0)	10.5	(1.4)	20.8	(1.9)	29.0	(2.1)	20.5	(1.8)	11.8	(1.6)	3.3	(0.8)	1.23	(0.18)	0.83	(0.11)
Italy																		
Centre	5.2	(1.7)	9.9	(2.7)	23.7	(4.3)	30.7	(3.4)	22.7	(4.4)	6.7	(2.4)	1.1	(0.7)	1.10	(0.40)	**1.87**	(0.50)
North East	2.8	(1.2)	9.1	(2.6)	25.8	(4.0)	33.5	(2.4)	22.6	(4.1)	5.6	(1.4)	0.6	(0.4)	1.06	(0.44)	**3.75**	(0.84)
North West	2.1	(0.8)	6.7	(2.1)	19.4	(3.4)	32.7	(4.2)	28.4	(4.1)	9.3	(3.1)	1.3	(1.1)	1.13	(0.41)	1.69	(0.56)
South	7.6	(3.0)	18.2	(3.9)	36.3	(3.5)	27.4	(3.0)	10.1	(2.4)	0.5	(0.6)	0.0	c	0.91	(0.25)	13.30	(22.50)
South Islands	7.2	(2.3)	18.0	(2.6)	30.5	(2.9)	27.8	(2.8)	12.8	(2.4)	2.9	(1.0)	0.8	(0.3)	0.88	(0.14)	**2.97**	(1.09)
Portugal																		
Alentejo	6.4	(2.2)	12.6	(2.8)	25.8	(2.7)	29.3	(2.8)	19.5	(3.9)	6.0	(2.2)	0.5	(0.6)	0.82	(0.14)	**2.18**	(0.52)
Spain																		
Basque Country •	7.7	(0.9)	13.3	(1.1)	24.1	(1.3)	28.5	(1.1)	18.0	(1.3)	6.6	(0.7)	1.8	(0.4)	1.02	(0.07)	**1.30**	(0.14)
Catalonia •	8.9	(2.4)	12.7	(2.1)	26.3	(3.2)	26.7	(2.2)	18.2	(2.3)	6.1	(1.3)	1.1	(0.5)	1.19	(0.16)	1.54	(0.38)
Madrid	6.6	(2.5)	12.9	(3.1)	21.3	(3.2)	26.5	(3.9)	21.4	(3.6)	9.3	(3.4)	1.9	(1.3)	1.07	(0.17)	1.22	(0.31)
Brazil																		
Central-West Region	18.8	(5.1)	29.2	(4.1)	28.3	(3.9)	17.5	(5.0)	5.0	(2.0)	0.9	(0.6)	0.3	(0.3)	**0.71**	(0.12)	3.27	(2.46)
Northeast Region	42.2	(4.4)	25.0	(2.9)	19.8	(3.8)	9.5	(2.3)	2.3	(1.0)	1.0	(0.7)	0.2	(0.3)	**0.87**	(0.05)	**3.15**	(1.15)
North Region	42.9	(6.0)	30.7	(4.5)	15.9	(3.7)	8.1	(2.9)	2.3	(1.5)	0.1	(0.2)	0.0	c	0.91	(0.09)	4.91	(10.69)
Southeast Region	16.3	(2.1)	26.4	(2.6)	30.8	(2.3)	19.7	(2.9)	5.8	(1.0)	0.9	(0.4)	0.1	(0.1)	**0.82**	(0.05)	2.54	(1.35)
South Region	18.3	(3.8)	30.8	(3.8)	30.3	(3.6)	15.1	(3.3)	4.4	(1.4)	1.1	(0.6)	0.0	c	0.81	(0.09)	2.08	(1.92)
Colombia																		
Bogotá	32.5	(3.0)	30.3	(2.4)	25.0	(2.5)	10.0	(1.6)	1.8	(0.6)	0.3	(0.3)	0.0	c	**0.75**	(0.05)	4.72	(6.92)
Cali	33.8	(5.2)	28.4	(3.3)	24.8	(2.9)	10.6	(2.0)	2.1	(0.8)	0.3	(0.2)	0.0	c	0.91	(0.05)	2.38	(2.58)
Manizales	28.7	(3.2)	30.1	(2.3)	27.1	(3.2)	11.1	(2.1)	2.5	(0.9)	0.4	(0.3)	0.1	(0.1)	**0.65**	(0.05)	6.08	(8.66)
Medellín	29.8	(3.4)	27.3	(3.1)	23.1	(3.4)	12.8	(2.1)	4.5	(1.3)	2.0	(0.8)	0.4	(0.2)	**0.81**	(0.07)	1.29	(0.65)
United Arab Emirates																		
Abu Dhabi •	29.3	(2.8)	26.2	(2.0)	24.1	(1.6)	13.6	(1.5)	5.0	(0.9)	1.6	(0.6)	0.1	(0.1)	**1.19**	(0.07)	0.97	(0.40)
Ajman	29.7	(6.5)	31.4	(3.2)	25.7	(3.6)	12.3	(3.7)	0.9	(0.9)	0.0	c	0.0	c	**1.36**	(0.14)	c	c
Dubai •	14.4	(0.6)	20.7	(1.4)	24.6	(1.4)	22.1	(1.3)	12.0	(1.0)	5.0	(0.7)	1.2	(0.3)	**1.15**	(0.04)	1.08	(0.15)
Fujairah	32.1	(4.3)	33.8	(4.2)	24.7	(4.0)	8.4	(1.8)	1.0	(0.8)	0.0	c	0.0	c	0.97	(0.08)	c	c
Ras al-Khaimah	34.0	(5.6)	34.2	(3.1)	21.2	(3.6)	7.5	(2.1)	2.6	(1.3)	0.5	(0.5)	0.0	c	1.12	(0.10)	1.20	(3.28)
Sharjah	18.1	(3.6)	29.6	(4.4)	29.8	(3.1)	17.0	(3.1)	4.9	(2.4)	0.5	(0.5)	0.1	(0.2)	1.28	(0.22)	2.32	(5.44)
Umm al-Quwain	28.9	(3.9)	32.4	(4.8)	26.2	(3.5)	10.5	(2.6)	2.1	(1.2)	0.0	c	0.0	c	**1.41**	(0.11)	c	c

• PISA adjudicated region.
Notes: Values that are statistically significant are indicated in bold (see Annex A3).
Italian administrative regions are grouped into larger geographical units: Centre (*Lazio, Marche, Toscana, Umbria*), North East (*Bolzano, Emilia Romagna, Friuli Venezia Giulia, Trento, Veneto*), North West (*Liguria, Lombardia, Piemonte, Valle d'Aosta*), South (*Abruzzo, Campania, Molise, Puglia*), South Islands (*Basilicata, Calabria, Sardegna, Sicilia*).
Brazilian states are grouped into larger geographical units: Central-West Region (*Federal District, Goiás, Mato Grosso, Mato Grosso do Sul*), Northeast Region (*Alagoas, Bahia, Ceará, Maranhão, Paraíba, Pernambuco, Piauí, Rio Grande do Norte, Sergipe*), North Region (*Acre, Amapá, Amazonas, Pará, Rondônia, Roraima, Tocantins*), Southeast Region (*Espírito Santo, Minas Gerais, Rio de Janeiro, São Paulo*), South Region (*Paraná, Rio Grande do Sul, Santa Catarina*).
See Table V.4.6 for national data.
StatLink ᴍᴤᴾ http://dx.doi.org/10.1787/888933003763

[Part 1/3]
Table B2.V.5 **Mean score and variation in student performance in problem solving, by gender and by region**

	Mean score						Standard deviation						5th percentile					
	Boys		Girls		Difference (B - G)		Boys		Girls		Difference (B - G)		Boys		Girls		Difference (B - G)	
	Mean	S.E.	Mean	S.E.	Score dif.	S.E.	S.D.	S.E.	S.D.	S.E.	Dif.	S.E.	Score	S.E.	Score	S.E.	Score dif.	S.E.
Australia																		
Australian Capital Territory	522	(5.9)	529	(4.9)	-7	(8.0)	109	(4.6)	96	(5.0)	13.4	(7.0)	336	(15.9)	359	(21.7)	-23	(27.0)
New South Wales	525	(5.1)	525	(4.1)	0	(6.0)	104	(2.8)	95	(2.6)	**9.2**	(3.5)	349	(7.9)	364	(9.1)	-14	(11.2)
Northern Territory	519	(10.1)	507	(11.1)	12	(14.0)	121	(7.5)	101	(6.5)	**20.2**	(7.2)	304	(19.8)	323	(17.1)	-18	(26.8)
Queensland	523	(4.1)	521	(4.2)	1	(4.7)	99	(3.0)	95	(2.8)	4.3	(3.5)	359	(9.0)	359	(10.2)	0	(11.6)
South Australia	519	(4.7)	521	(4.8)	-2	(5.0)	96	(2.9)	90	(2.9)	5.9	(3.8)	358	(9.2)	376	(12.1)	-18	(13.6)
Tasmania	489	(5.4)	491	(5.5)	-3	(7.5)	110	(3.6)	100	(3.4)	**10.5**	(4.8)	311	(14.5)	326	(16.3)	-14	(23.9)
Victoria	524	(4.9)	522	(4.5)	2	(4.6)	95	(2.4)	94	(3.0)	1.3	(3.4)	362	(9.9)	365	(11.4)	-3	(11.4)
Western Australia	537	(5.5)	519	(5.6)	**17**	(7.6)	96	(3.5)	95	(3.5)	1.2	(4.1)	373	(10.7)	356	(11.0)	17	(13.4)
Belgium																		
Flemish Community•	530	(4.0)	519	(4.6)	11	(5.5)	103	(2.7)	100	(3.4)	3.1	(3.9)	342	(9.7)	338	(9.9)	4	(12.9)
French Community	487	(5.2)	483	(4.9)	4	(4.8)	114	(3.8)	101	(2.6)	**13.1**	(3.3)	282	(11.4)	296	(13.9)	-14	(15.1)
German-speaking Community	533	(4.3)	507	(3.8)	**26**	(6.2)	101	(3.6)	89	(3.8)	**11.9**	(5.7)	352	(20.8)	345	(14.4)	6	(23.9)
Canada																		
Alberta	533	(5.1)	529	(5.6)	5	(3.7)	99	(3.3)	97	(2.5)	2.2	(3.7)	363	(10.1)	361	(8.1)	2	(11.6)
British Columbia	540	(4.0)	530	(5.1)	9	(5.9)	96	(2.8)	92	(2.9)	3.9	(3.3)	381	(8.3)	378	(11.3)	3	(10.9)
Manitoba	504	(4.5)	503	(5.1)	1	(6.3)	103	(3.9)	100	(4.6)	3.1	(5.4)	325	(21.2)	336	(16.0)	-11	(27.4)
New Brunswick	511	(4.7)	520	(4.0)	-9	(6.1)	94	(3.1)	89	(3.3)	4.9	(4.7)	344	(12.8)	366	(12.6)	-22	(17.7)
Newfoundland and Labrador	496	(10.6)	512	(5.4)	-16	(8.3)	109	(9.3)	90	(3.7)	**19.4**	(8.2)	290	(35.3)	355	(19.1)	-66	(36.9)
Nova Scotia	512	(5.5)	512	(8.0)	-1	(7.4)	96	(3.9)	88	(3.8)	8.7	(4.9)	348	(18.0)	371	(14.7)	-23	(23.9)
Ontario	533	(6.8)	523	(5.2)	**9**	(4.1)	107	(5.1)	98	(2.5)	9.2	(5.1)	358	(10.9)	355	(11.3)	2	(14.3)
Prince Edward Island	492	(3.3)	494	(3.5)	-2	(4.5)	90	(3.0)	90	(3.0)	0.7	(4.2)	337	(8.9)	347	(7.8)	-9	(11.0)
Quebec	526	(5.5)	523	(4.7)	4	(4.8)	107	(5.6)	97	(3.0)	**9.7**	(4.6)	340	(15.4)	357	(9.7)	-16	(15.4)
Saskatchewan	510	(3.7)	520	(3.9)	-10	(5.1)	94	(2.9)	91	(2.6)	3.4	(3.9)	347	(10.0)	369	(10.0)	-22	(15.0)
Italy																		
Centre	520	(13.2)	506	(11.4)	14	(13.2)	99	(8.5)	84	(5.4)	15.0	(9.0)	332	(35.5)	354	(20.8)	-22	(42.1)
North East	543	(10.2)	509	(8.7)	**35**	(13.5)	100	(6.0)	75	(3.8)	**25.3**	(7.3)	350	(32.0)	383	(18.2)	-32	(39.5)
North West	537	(9.1)	528	(11.8)	9	(12.1)	87	(4.7)	78	(4.1)	9.8	(5.4)	387	(18.3)	397	(14.7)	-10	(20.8)
South	481	(10.3)	464	(9.2)	17	(10.8)	87	(5.8)	73	(4.7)	**14.5**	(6.0)	346	(27.4)	339	(28.1)	7	(33.8)
South Islands	496	(10.8)	476	(7.5)	**20**	(8.5)	96	(4.6)	81	(4.5)	**14.8**	(4.8)	337	(12.8)	342	(19.2)	-5	(18.5)
Portugal																		
Alentejo	518	(15.4)	495	(12.3)	**23**	(8.2)	95	(6.8)	84	(4.6)	**10.6**	(5.0)	351	(23.4)	347	(16.3)	4	(16.5)
Spain																		
Basque Country•	498	(4.4)	494	(4.1)	4	(3.6)	100	(3.4)	94	(2.4)	6.0	(3.1)	326	(9.5)	334	(8.1)	-7	(8.1)
Catalonia•	487	(9.7)	489	(8.2)	-2	(6.5)	110	(5.8)	94	(6.4)	**16.2**	(5.6)	284	(20.7)	321	(23.5)	**-37**	(18.0)
Madrid	509	(13.5)	506	(13.9)	4	(8.3)	99	(5.3)	94	(6.4)	5.4	(6.5)	346	(20.0)	346	(16.3)	0	(21.3)
Brazil																		
Central-West Region	457	(12.3)	429	(12.3)	**28**	(8.2)	89	(6.8)	83	(5.5)	6.0	(6.3)	305	(28.6)	291	(18.6)	14	(31.1)
Northeast Region	407	(13.2)	380	(10.0)	**27**	(7.6)	111	(10.2)	97	(6.7)	**14.2**	(5.4)	231	(24.7)	225	(16.5)	6	(19.5)
North Region	387	(15.5)	380	(10.8)	6	(14.8)	89	(7.5)	78	(6.3)	11.4	(9.6)	233	(51.2)	268	(16.0)	-35	(53.6)
Southeast Region	457	(7.2)	437	(6.0)	**20**	(4.2)	85	(3.3)	79	(2.6)	5.5	(3.5)	316	(10.3)	303	(9.0)	13	(11.1)
South Region	444	(9.1)	426	(8.2)	**18**	(6.9)	85	(3.2)	77	(4.0)	7.8	(4.8)	303	(13.1)	299	(12.8)	4	(15.0)
Colombia																		
Bogotá	428	(7.1)	395	(5.7)	**33**	(6.0)	85	(3.8)	81	(2.2)	4.3	(3.9)	290	(10.3)	261	(9.4)	**29**	(11.5)
Cali	407	(8.2)	391	(10.4)	**16**	(6.3)	90	(4.5)	89	(5.0)	1.1	(4.0)	255	(16.7)	235	(30.5)	19	(24.5)
Manizales	447	(5.6)	404	(5.5)	**43**	(6.5)	85	(3.9)	81	(2.5)	4.8	(4.4)	305	(9.1)	268	(10.9)	**37**	(12.8)
Medellín	438	(9.6)	410	(8.6)	**28**	(9.9)	93	(6.2)	94	(5.5)	-1.4	(6.3)	293	(10.9)	262	(10.0)	**31**	(13.2)
United Arab Emirates																		
Abu Dhabi•	374	(7.7)	408	(6.4)	**-35**	(9.6)	116	(4.2)	98	(3.5)	**18.3**	(5.6)	192	(11.2)	243	(11.2)	**-51**	(15.5)
Ajman	348	(8.1)	399	(11.2)	**-50**	(13.8)	77	(5.6)	75	(4.3)	1.9	(6.9)	225	(19.3)	271	(22.1)	-46	(28.6)
Dubai•	450	(2.2)	463	(1.8)	**-13**	(3.2)	116	(1.6)	99	(1.5)	**16.8**	(2.1)	254	(4.4)	302	(5.1)	**-48**	(6.6)
Fujairah	398	(4.5)	391	(6.7)	8	(7.5)	86	(4.8)	76	(2.7)	10.0	(5.6)	263	(13.8)	260	(13.2)	3	(17.5)
Ras al-Khaimah	356	(19.9)	388	(12.5)	-32	(22.4)	103	(17.5)	84	(7.0)	19.0	(18.4)	165	(92.3)	244	(26.4)	-80	(96.5)
Sharjah	400	(18.2)	430	(9.2)	-30	(20.9)	94	(10.7)	75	(4.9)	19.4	(12.1)	239	(29.2)	312	(10.3)	**-72**	(30.6)
Umm al-Quwain	340	(5.8)	402	(4.9)	**-62**	(8.1)	78	(4.8)	72	(3.9)	5.0	(6.4)	212	(15.7)	283	(10.6)	**-70**	(19.0)

• PISA adjudicated region.
Notes: Values that are statistically significant are indicated in bold (see Annex A3).
Italian administrative regions are grouped into larger geographical units: Centre (*Lazio, Marche, Toscana, Umbria*), North East (*Bolzano, Emilia Romagna, Friuli Venezia Giulia, Trento, Veneto*), North West (*Liguria, Lombardia, Piemonte, Valle d'Aosta*), South (*Abruzzo, Campania, Molise, Puglia*), South Islands (*Basilicata, Calabria, Sardegna, Sicilia*).
Brazilian states are grouped into larger geographical units: Central-West Region (*Federal District, Goiás, Mato Grosso, Mato Grosso do Sul*), Northeast Region (*Alagoas, Bahia, Ceará, Maranhão, Paraíba, Pernambuco, Piauí, Rio Grande do Norte, Sergipe*), North Region (*Acre, Amapá, Amazonas, Pará, Rondônia, Roraima, Tocantins*), Southeast Region (*Espírito Santo, Minas Gerais, Rio de Janeiro, São Paulo*), South Region (*Paraná, Rio Grande do Sul, Santa Catarina*).
See Table V.4.7 for national data.
StatLink ⬛⬛ http://dx.doi.org/10.1787/888933003763

[Part 2/3]

Table B2.V.5   **Mean score and variation in student performance in problem solving, by gender and by region**

	10th percentile						25th percentile						50th percentile (median)					
	Boys		Girls		Difference (B - G)		Boys		Girls		Difference (B - G)		Boys		Girls		Difference (B - G)	
	Score	S.E.	Score	S.E.	Score dif.	S.E.	Score	S.E.	Score	S.E.	Score dif.	S.E.	Score	S.E.	Score	S.E.	Score dif.	S.E.
Australia																		
Australian Capital Territory	376	(14.6)	403	(13.4)	-27	(22.0)	451	(10.7)	468	(7.1)	-17	(13.3)	530	(9.2)	536	(7.1)	-6	(12.9)
New South Wales	388	(7.0)	402	(6.7)	-15	(9.2)	456	(6.5)	463	(5.2)	-7	(7.4)	527	(5.5)	527	(5.1)	1	(7.0)
Northern Territory	357	(20.0)	372	(14.1)	-16	(21.8)	432	(15.7)	443	(14.8)	-11	(20.0)	532	(15.6)	519	(13.8)	13	(20.2)
Queensland	394	(6.8)	399	(8.1)	-5	(7.9)	455	(7.0)	460	(5.5)	-5	(6.9)	526	(5.3)	524	(4.4)	2	(6.8)
South Australia	391	(9.6)	408	(7.1)	-17	(10.8)	454	(6.3)	462	(6.0)	-8	(6.9)	522	(6.0)	523	(6.4)	-1	(7.7)
Tasmania	344	(10.6)	371	(9.2)	-26	(14.9)	410	(8.8)	425	(7.5)	-15	(9.7)	488	(8.5)	490	(8.1)	-2	(12.5)
Victoria	397	(6.9)	401	(7.6)	-5	(7.7)	461	(6.5)	460	(6.2)	1	(7.2)	526	(5.9)	525	(4.9)	1	(5.6)
Western Australia	410	(9.2)	396	(9.6)	14	(11.2)	474	(7.2)	458	(6.8)	16	(8.7)	542	(6.2)	522	(6.4)	**20**	(8.7)
Belgium																		
Flemish Community*	390	(8.5)	382	(8.7)	8	(11.9)	465	(7.4)	458	(6.4)	7	(8.9)	539	(4.5)	528	(5.5)	11	(6.3)
French Community	332	(10.5)	347	(7.0)	-15	(9.5)	411	(7.1)	421	(6.3)	-9	(7.2)	498	(5.7)	493	(6.3)	5	(6.2)
German-speaking Community	391	(14.4)	392	(12.3)	-2	(20.5)	469	(9.9)	453	(7.0)	16	(11.7)	546	(6.3)	512	(5.2)	**34**	(8.4)
Canada																		
Alberta	400	(9.7)	400	(9.4)	0	(10.2)	472	(9.0)	461	(8.0)	11	(7.7)	540	(6.2)	532	(6.7)	8	(5.9)
British Columbia	412	(5.5)	407	(8.2)	5	(8.1)	474	(5.7)	468	(6.7)	6	(7.7)	540	(5.2)	535	(6.4)	5	(7.3)
Manitoba	376	(8.5)	375	(9.1)	1	(11.6)	441	(5.9)	439	(7.9)	2	(9.5)	507	(5.3)	506	(5.9)	1	(7.6)
New Brunswick	386	(10.6)	406	(7.3)	-19	(14.6)	452	(6.6)	460	(5.7)	-9	(8.2)	512	(6.9)	527	(5.5)	-14	(8.2)
Newfoundland and Labrador	358	(29.1)	394	(17.0)	-36	(25.5)	434	(15.3)	453	(9.1)	-18	(13.5)	508	(9.2)	513	(6.9)	-5	(9.4)
Nova Scotia	381	(17.5)	401	(11.7)	-20	(17.4)	451	(9.0)	453	(14.8)	-1	(14.8)	518	(7.7)	514	(11.1)	4	(12.2)
Ontario	400	(9.0)	399	(10.4)	2	(10.3)	464	(7.2)	459	(7.3)	5	(7.2)	535	(7.6)	526	(5.9)	9	(5.5)
Prince Edward Island	373	(8.8)	378	(6.9)	-5	(10.9)	435	(7.0)	435	(6.0)	0	(8.8)	496	(6.3)	493	(4.7)	3	(7.4)
Quebec	392	(11.0)	401	(7.6)	-9	(10.8)	465	(6.6)	465	(5.0)	0	(6.4)	536	(5.5)	527	(4.9)	9	(5.7)
Saskatchewan	385	(10.4)	402	(8.8)	-17	(13.0)	446	(6.5)	459	(6.1)	-13	(9.0)	514	(5.2)	521	(5.1)	-6	(6.6)
Italy																		
Centre	385	(21.5)	398	(18.9)	-13	(27.2)	466	(31.3)	454	(13.8)	12	(31.4)	533	(9.2)	510	(13.3)	23	(12.6)
North East	402	(24.4)	414	(13.1)	-12	(29.3)	484	(19.9)	463	(11.5)	21	(24.5)	558	(9.6)	513	(12.0)	**45**	(14.8)
North West	425	(16.0)	430	(13.4)	-5	(18.7)	478	(13.5)	481	(12.2)	-2	(15.6)	545	(11.8)	534	(11.7)	11	(14.7)
South	381	(14.9)	373	(18.8)	8	(20.5)	427	(15.0)	422	(9.9)	5	(16.0)	484	(12.0)	467	(8.5)	17	(13.1)
South Islands	376	(15.9)	373	(11.2)	2	(14.9)	432	(12.5)	423	(10.2)	8	(11.1)	495	(14.7)	477	(8.5)	18	(12.4)
Portugal																		
Alentejo	393	(17.5)	381	(22.6)	12	(15.5)	459	(18.3)	439	(13.0)	20	(15.3)	524	(13.3)	500	(12.8)	**24**	(10.6)
Spain																		
Basque Country*	370	(6.1)	374	(7.0)	-4	(7.0)	435	(5.2)	437	(5.3)	-1	(5.3)	503	(5.1)	498	(4.4)	5	(4.9)
Catalonia*	337	(19.7)	367	(18.9)	**-30**	(15.1)	421	(14.9)	434	(9.9)	-13	(12.1)	495	(10.3)	494	(10.1)	2	(9.8)
Madrid	377	(14.4)	384	(20.3)	-7	(20.1)	436	(16.7)	440	(15.7)	-4	(13.7)	516	(16.0)	510	(15.5)	6	(12.9)
Brazil																		
Central-West Region	343	(24.9)	323	(20.6)	20	(25.9)	398	(16.3)	374	(14.2)	24	(14.4)	455	(13.2)	428	(15.3)	27	(14.0)
Northeast Region	268	(21.2)	257	(11.0)	11	(15.8)	337	(13.3)	314	(11.0)	23	(12.5)	404	(12.7)	379	(13.0)	25	(11.6)
North Region	274	(26.2)	288	(11.3)	-14	(27.1)	329	(23.2)	326	(9.6)	3	(21.7)	388	(18.1)	371	(13.1)	17	(17.8)
Southeast Region	349	(9.1)	334	(7.4)	14	(8.9)	396	(8.2)	383	(7.5)	**14**	(6.8)	457	(9.6)	438	(6.6)	19	(6.8)
South Region	333	(13.5)	327	(16.8)	6	(12.5)	385	(10.8)	374	(11.1)	11	(8.9)	444	(11.5)	426	(10.4)	18	(10.0)
Colombia																		
Bogotá	314	(12.3)	287	(11.4)	**27**	(13.7)	369	(8.6)	341	(7.3)	**28**	(8.6)	429	(7.2)	396	(8.3)	**33**	(8.0)
Cali	286	(20.3)	274	(16.3)	12	(17.1)	346	(9.9)	331	(14.7)	15	(10.3)	408	(9.5)	397	(11.5)	11	(8.2)
Manizales	338	(10.0)	299	(6.5)	**39**	(9.9)	392	(6.6)	349	(7.7)	**43**	(8.9)	446	(6.0)	406	(7.7)	**41**	(8.3)
Medellín	324	(10.8)	292	(11.3)	**32**	(13.3)	373	(8.3)	346	(8.9)	27	(9.3)	433	(11.7)	407	(10.0)	**27**	(11.6)
United Arab Emirates																		
Abu Dhabi*	229	(9.1)	282	(10.1)	**-53**	(13.7)	294	(8.9)	346	(8.4)	**-52**	(12.5)	369	(9.8)	410	(6.0)	**-41**	(11.4)
Ajman	255	(14.9)	304	(15.0)	**-49**	(22.3)	296	(10.9)	348	(14.0)	**-52**	(17.8)	346	(8.5)	399	(14.6)	**-53**	(17.0)
Dubai*	296	(5.0)	337	(4.0)	**-41**	(7.2)	372	(4.3)	394	(3.3)	**-22**	(5.7)	452	(3.7)	464	(3.6)	**-12**	(5.5)
Fujairah	292	(10.8)	289	(8.7)	3	(14.3)	340	(10.3)	340	(9.7)	0	(15.4)	393	(7.3)	394	(9.4)	-2	(12.4)
Ras al-Khaimah	228	(65.1)	282	(27.6)	-54	(67.5)	298	(25.5)	337	(13.9)	-39	(27.7)	363	(16.2)	390	(11.8)	-27	(18.9)
Sharjah	275	(27.9)	336	(10.9)	**-61**	(28.9)	339	(27.9)	376	(9.3)	-37	(28.7)	400	(16.5)	428	(11.0)	-27	(19.8)
Umm al-Quwain	244	(12.3)	308	(14.4)	**-64**	(20.3)	290	(7.8)	351	(7.1)	**-61**	(11.0)	336	(10.4)	398	(8.7)	**-62**	(14.2)

* PISA adjudicated region.

Notes: Values that are statistically significant are indicated in bold (see Annex A3).
Italian administrative regions are grouped into larger geographical units: Centre (*Lazio, Marche, Toscana, Umbria*), North East (*Bolzano, Emilia Romagna, Friuli Venezia Giulia, Trento, Veneto*), North West (*Liguria, Lombardia, Piemonte, Valle d'Aosta*), South (*Abruzzo, Campania, Molise, Puglia*), South Islands (*Basilicata, Calabria, Sardegna, Sicilia*).
Brazilian states are grouped into larger geographical units: Central-West Region (*Federal District, Goiás, Mato Grosso, Mato Grosso do Sul*), Northeast Region (*Alagoas, Bahia, Ceará, Maranhão, Paraíba, Pernambuco, Piauí, Rio Grande do Norte, Sergipe*), North Region (*Acre, Amapá, Amazonas, Pará, Rondônia, Roraima, Tocantins*), Southeast Region (*Espírito Santo, Minas Gerais, Rio de Janeiro, São Paulo*), South Region (*Paraná, Rio Grande do Sul, Santa Catarina*).
See Table V.4.7 for national data.
StatLink ᛗᑭ⅃ http://dx.doi.org/10.1787/888933003763

[Part 3/3]

Table B2.V.5 **Mean score and variation in student performance in problem solving, by gender and by region**

	75th percentile Boys Score	S.E.	Girls Score	S.E.	Difference (B - G) Score dif.	S.E.	90th percentile Boys Score	S.E.	Girls Score	S.E.	Difference (B - G) Score dif.	S.E.	95th percentile Boys Score	S.E.	Girls Score	S.E.	Difference (B - G) Score dif.	S.E.
Australia																		
Australian Capital Territory	599	(8.9)	596	(5.5)	2	(10.3)	657	(8.9)	644	(8.1)	13	(11.6)	687	(12.5)	677	(15.6)	10	(20.2)
New South Wales	597	(7.3)	591	(5.2)	6	(8.4)	659	(8.8)	646	(5.3)	14	(9.8)	693	(8.6)	675	(5.8)	18	(10.0)
Northern Territory	608	(15.8)	578	(17.7)	30	(22.6)	667	(23.1)	629	(20.6)	38	(26.0)	699	(37.6)	660	(34.1)	39	(43.9)
Queensland	591	(5.4)	587	(5.7)	4	(7.8)	647	(6.7)	641	(5.6)	6	(8.4)	682	(8.7)	672	(6.7)	10	(11.7)
South Australia	586	(7.8)	583	(8.4)	3	(10.6)	641	(8.8)	636	(7.6)	5	(10.0)	673	(8.7)	666	(6.8)	7	(11.3)
Tasmania	565	(8.8)	555	(8.6)	10	(12.3)	630	(11.4)	624	(11.4)	6	(15.2)	671	(14.1)	659	(13.4)	12	(19.9)
Victoria	592	(6.5)	589	(5.7)	3	(7.6)	645	(6.0)	640	(7.2)	5	(7.7)	677	(6.5)	669	(7.2)	8	(9.6)
Western Australia	605	(7.0)	584	(7.5)	20	(10.4)	654	(9.3)	636	(9.6)	18	(14.9)	683	(12.7)	669	(11.2)	14	(16.7)
Belgium																		
Flemish Community *	604	(4.5)	590	(4.6)	**14**	(5.0)	655	(4.1)	641	(4.8)	**14**	(5.3)	684	(4.9)	669	(4.4)	**15**	(5.3)
French Community	572	(6.3)	556	(6.3)	**16**	(6.9)	624	(5.9)	605	(5.8)	**19**	(5.3)	653	(6.8)	633	(7.6)	**20**	(8.4)
German-speaking Community	602	(6.8)	567	(6.8)	**36**	(9.7)	655	(8.2)	612	(8.6)	**43**	(12.5)	684	(10.4)	642	(12.1)	**42**	(17.5)
Canada																		
Alberta	601	(5.9)	598	(6.9)	3	(6.9)	655	(8.0)	651	(8.1)	4	(9.4)	686	(7.6)	681	(8.7)	5	(11.2)
British Columbia	605	(6.3)	594	(5.9)	10	(8.2)	661	(6.6)	644	(8.0)	17	(10.5)	695	(12.1)	673	(10.4)	22	(16.1)
Manitoba	578	(5.6)	573	(5.1)	5	(7.7)	627	(9.2)	627	(6.3)	0	(10.2)	662	(8.5)	658	(6.8)	5	(11.7)
New Brunswick	576	(7.9)	581	(6.5)	-5	(9.9)	628	(9.2)	626	(8.5)	1	(12.8)	661	(12.1)	654	(14.1)	7	(19.1)
Newfoundland and Labrador	572	(6.3)	573	(5.2)	-1	(7.0)	622	(8.1)	629	(8.0)	-6	(11.4)	651	(9.5)	660	(8.8)	-10	(11.5)
Nova Scotia	577	(7.6)	573	(7.7)	4	(9.5)	630	(10.9)	620	(7.1)	9	(13.4)	659	(10.7)	653	(13.6)	5	(14.9)
Ontario	605	(7.7)	590	(5.8)	16	(6.3)	664	(8.2)	645	(7.5)	19	(7.6)	701	(10.0)	681	(10.2)	20	(11.5)
Prince Edward Island	553	(5.5)	554	(6.2)	-1	(8.1)	604	(8.4)	605	(5.8)	-1	(10.3)	635	(6.0)	638	(12.6)	-3	(14.2)
Quebec	598	(5.9)	588	(6.3)	10	(6.3)	653	(7.3)	644	(6.4)	8	(7.4)	686	(7.8)	673	(8.2)	13	(9.0)
Saskatchewan	576	(6.5)	583	(7.0)	-6	(8.6)	629	(8.5)	640	(6.8)	-11	(10.8)	661	(8.4)	669	(8.2)	-8	(12.1)
Italy																		
Centre	587	(10.0)	564	(11.1)	**23**	(9.4)	634	(12.5)	607	(13.5)	**27**	(12.1)	660	(17.2)	638	(15.1)	22	(14.9)
North East	614	(7.8)	560	(8.1)	**54**	(10.9)	657	(8.9)	599	(7.7)	**58**	(10.9)	686	(11.7)	624	(6.8)	**62**	(11.7)
North West	600	(10.0)	581	(12.9)	20	(13.6)	644	(7.7)	619	(13.2)	24	(12.8)	667	(7.5)	646	(20.0)	22	(19.4)
South	541	(11.4)	514	(11.4)	**27**	(12.8)	589	(12.0)	553	(9.2)	**35**	(12.6)	613	(10.7)	574	(10.8)	**39**	(14.8)
South Islands	565	(11.7)	531	(7.8)	**35**	(11.2)	621	(13.5)	576	(9.6)	**45**	(13.8)	647	(15.8)	606	(12.9)	**41**	(16.3)
Portugal																		
Alentejo	583	(18.0)	557	(16.8)	26	(14.9)	635	(24.5)	602	(14.6)	33	(17.0)	663	(25.7)	625	(14.9)	**38**	(19.2)
Spain																		
Basque Country *	567	(4.9)	556	(4.1)	**11**	(4.3)	622	(4.9)	609	(5.6)	**13**	(5.4)	654	(5.0)	641	(4.7)	**12**	(5.9)
Catalonia *	564	(8.7)	554	(7.7)	10	(8.5)	624	(11.1)	601	(9.4)	23	(13.6)	655	(14.4)	631	(10.1)	24	(17.9)
Madrid	579	(18.7)	572	(14.5)	7	(15.1)	633	(18.4)	622	(17.8)	11	(16.8)	665	(18.1)	654	(24.6)	10	(23.8)
Brazil																		
Central-West Region	515	(16.5)	485	(13.4)	31	(16.8)	568	(15.3)	533	(12.2)	**34**	(13.2)	604	(24.3)	561	(18.6)	**43**	(21.0)
Northeast Region	476	(18.0)	445	(16.8)	31	(11.6)	549	(26.7)	505	(16.0)	**44**	(21.2)	599	(32.3)	537	(16.1)	**61**	(26.2)
North Region	447	(18.7)	428	(20.3)	18	(24.4)	498	(14.0)	490	(23.7)	9	(22.4)	529	(19.3)	528	(21.2)	1	(20.9)
Southeast Region	518	(9.3)	491	(7.8)	26	(8.5)	565	(6.9)	539	(6.9)	**26**	(7.5)	588	(7.6)	565	(7.2)	23	(8.2)
South Region	500	(11.4)	477	(10.7)	23	(12.8)	552	(10.2)	526	(12.0)	**26**	(13.1)	588	(15.8)	557	(13.2)	31	(20.3)
Colombia																		
Bogotá	484	(8.2)	452	(6.2)	33	(7.8)	538	(11.4)	496	(8.1)	**42**	(12.8)	566	(16.3)	524	(8.9)	**42**	(17.8)
Cali	471	(9.5)	451	(9.3)	20	(10.0)	522	(7.3)	501	(10.3)	20	(10.7)	550	(13.4)	529	(9.8)	21	(13.3)
Manizales	504	(9.1)	457	(6.6)	47	(10.3)	556	(9.4)	505	(9.5)	**52**	(13.5)	582	(12.0)	538	(9.7)	**45**	(16.9)
Medellín	501	(12.5)	470	(10.6)	31	(13.3)	562	(15.4)	532	(16.8)	30	(18.2)	600	(19.3)	573	(21.5)	26	(22.9)
United Arab Emirates																		
Abu Dhabi *	455	(10.1)	474	(7.0)	-19	(11.8)	527	(8.7)	532	(7.5)	-4	(11.0)	568	(12.8)	568	(7.8)	0	(14.6)
Ajman	398	(11.7)	451	(11.9)	**-53**	(15.6)	450	(16.8)	498	(12.6)	**-48**	(20.2)	480	(14.1)	520	(12.4)	**-40**	(19.1)
Dubai *	534	(3.8)	531	(4.6)	3	(6.3)	598	(4.7)	590	(5.7)	8	(7.6)	631	(6.5)	627	(6.6)	4	(10.0)
Fujairah	455	(8.8)	442	(10.0)	13	(13.1)	512	(10.3)	485	(9.1)	**28**	(12.6)	553	(16.8)	515	(11.6)	**38**	(18.8)
Ras al-Khaimah	419	(11.3)	441	(13.0)	-22	(17.0)	481	(10.4)	490	(13.7)	-9	(17.1)	508	(10.4)	529	(21.4)	-22	(24.1)
Sharjah	462	(22.8)	482	(12.9)	-20	(28.2)	521	(24.0)	528	(14.8)	-6	(30.7)	559	(27.2)	556	(14.6)	2	(31.8)
Umm al-Quwain	388	(10.2)	452	(12.2)	**-64**	(16.8)	436	(14.2)	497	(9.7)	**-61**	(16.8)	470	(25.3)	519	(10.7)	**-49**	(27.3)

* PISA adjudicated region.
Notes: Values that are statistically significant are indicated in bold (see Annex A3).
Italian administrative regions are grouped into larger geographical units: Centre (*Lazio, Marche, Toscana, Umbria*), North East (*Bolzano, Emilia Romagna, Friuli Venezia Giulia, Trento, Veneto*), North West (*Liguria, Lombardia, Piemonte, Valle d'Aosta*), South (*Abruzzo, Campania, Molise, Puglia*), South Islands (*Basilicata, Calabria, Sardegna, Sicilia*).
Brazilian states are grouped into larger geographical units: Central-West Region (*Federal District, Goiás, Mato Grosso, Mato Grosso do Sul*), Northeast Region (*Alagoas, Bahia, Ceará, Maranhão, Paraíba, Pernambuco, Piauí, Rio Grande do Norte, Sergipe*), North Region (*Acre, Amapá, Amazonas, Pará, Rondônia, Roraima, Tocantins*), Southeast Region (*Espírito Santo, Minas Gerais, Rio de Janeiro, São Paulo*), South Region (*Paraná, Rio Grande do Sul, Santa Catarina*).
See Table V.4.7 for national data.
StatLink ⌘🔗 http://dx.doi.org/10.1787/888933003763

[Part 1/2]
Performance in problem solving, by socio-economic status and by region
Table B2.V.6   *Results based on students' self-reports*

	PISA index of economic, social and cultural status (ESCS)									
	All students		Bottom quarter		Second quarter		Third quarter		Top quarter	
	Mean index	S.E.	Mean index	S.E.	Mean index	S.E.	Mean index	S.E.	Mean index	S.E.
Australia										
Australian Capital Territory	0.62	(0.02)	-0.23	(0.05)	0.49	(0.02)	0.87	(0.02)	1.33	(0.03)
New South Wales	0.25	(0.02)	-0.86	(0.03)	0.04	(0.03)	0.62	(0.02)	1.19	(0.02)
Northern Territory	0.14	(0.06)	-0.95	(0.09)	-0.04	(0.07)	0.51	(0.06)	1.06	(0.07)
Queensland	0.20	(0.02)	-0.86	(0.03)	-0.02	(0.04)	0.53	(0.03)	1.14	(0.02)
South Australia	0.19	(0.02)	-0.90	(0.05)	0.00	(0.03)	0.54	(0.02)	1.11	(0.03)
Tasmania	0.02	(0.03)	-1.05	(0.03)	-0.25	(0.04)	0.35	(0.04)	1.05	(0.03)
Victoria	0.30	(0.02)	-0.76	(0.03)	0.11	(0.04)	0.66	(0.03)	1.20	(0.02)
Western Australia	0.26	(0.03)	-0.82	(0.04)	0.04	(0.04)	0.62	(0.03)	1.19	(0.03)
Belgium										
Flemish Community*	0.16	(0.02)	-1.04	(0.04)	-0.18	(0.03)	0.58	(0.03)	1.28	(0.02)
French Community	0.12	(0.03)	-1.05	(0.04)	-0.21	(0.04)	0.51	(0.04)	1.25	(0.03)
German-speaking Community	0.29	(0.03)	-0.81	(0.04)	-0.05	(0.04)	0.66	(0.04)	1.35	(0.03)
Canada										
Alberta	0.51	(0.03)	-0.58	(0.04)	0.27	(0.04)	0.87	(0.04)	1.51	(0.02)
British Columbia	0.46	(0.04)	-0.67	(0.04)	0.19	(0.05)	0.84	(0.04)	1.48	(0.03)
Manitoba	0.26	(0.03)	-0.94	(0.05)	0.00	(0.04)	0.66	(0.03)	1.34	(0.03)
New Brunswick	0.37	(0.02)	-0.72	(0.03)	0.10	(0.04)	0.73	(0.03)	1.37	(0.03)
Newfoundland and Labrador	0.28	(0.04)	-0.89	(0.06)	-0.04	(0.05)	0.65	(0.05)	1.41	(0.04)
Nova Scotia	0.31	(0.03)	-0.78	(0.03)	0.04	(0.04)	0.63	(0.05)	1.33	(0.03)
Ontario	0.44	(0.04)	-0.76	(0.05)	0.20	(0.05)	0.83	(0.04)	1.49	(0.03)
Prince Edward Island	0.33	(0.02)	-0.77	(0.04)	0.09	(0.03)	0.72	(0.03)	1.31	(0.02)
Quebec	0.34	(0.03)	-0.80	(0.03)	0.09	(0.04)	0.73	(0.03)	1.34	(0.02)
Saskatchewan	0.40	(0.02)	-0.65	(0.03)	0.09	(0.03)	0.72	(0.03)	1.45	(0.03)
Italy										
Centre	0.17	(0.06)	-1.00	(0.06)	-0.15	(0.06)	0.47	(0.09)	1.35	(0.06)
North East	0.00	(0.05)	-1.16	(0.04)	-0.32	(0.03)	0.24	(0.06)	1.24	(0.10)
North West	0.00	(0.06)	-1.16	(0.07)	-0.32	(0.07)	0.28	(0.06)	1.20	(0.07)
South	-0.10	(0.07)	-1.36	(0.05)	-0.53	(0.08)	0.21	(0.09)	1.29	(0.09)
South Islands	-0.20	(0.07)	-1.44	(0.05)	-0.60	(0.08)	0.09	(0.09)	1.15	(0.08)
Portugal										
Alentejo	-0.35	(0.14)	-1.72	(0.07)	-0.87	(0.15)	-0.05	(0.19)	1.25	(0.16)
Spain										
Basque Country*	0.03	(0.03)	-1.21	(0.03)	-0.30	(0.03)	0.46	(0.04)	1.18	(0.02)
Catalonia*	-0.14	(0.08)	-1.45	(0.07)	-0.53	(0.09)	0.27	(0.12)	1.15	(0.06)
Madrid	0.03	(0.15)	-1.28	(0.10)	-0.36	(0.16)	0.43	(0.21)	1.36	(0.15)
Brazil										
Central-West Region	-1.03	(0.11)	-2.46	(0.13)	-1.47	(0.11)	-0.73	(0.14)	0.58	(0.17)
Northeast Region	-1.26	(0.11)	-2.84	(0.13)	-1.75	(0.14)	-0.86	(0.12)	0.40	(0.12)
North Region	-0.91	(0.10)	-2.28	(0.12)	-1.26	(0.12)	-0.58	(0.10)	0.48	(0.07)
Southeast Region	-1.01	(0.06)	-2.49	(0.04)	-1.46	(0.05)	-0.64	(0.09)	0.54	(0.09)
South Region	-1.32	(0.09)	-2.70	(0.07)	-1.76	(0.10)	-1.01	(0.11)	0.22	(0.16)
Colombia										
Bogotá	-1.09	(0.05)	-2.34	(0.04)	-1.42	(0.06)	-0.75	(0.06)	0.14	(0.07)
Cali	-0.81	(0.08)	-2.09	(0.07)	-1.12	(0.09)	-0.49	(0.08)	0.46	(0.10)
Manizales	-0.77	(0.07)	-2.25	(0.09)	-1.03	(0.10)	-0.36	(0.07)	0.57	(0.05)
Medellín	-0.94	(0.10)	-2.43	(0.10)	-1.31	(0.09)	-0.57	(0.11)	0.56	(0.15)
United Arab Emirates										
Abu Dhabi*	0.29	(0.03)	-0.91	(0.06)	0.14	(0.04)	0.65	(0.03)	1.28	(0.02)
Ajman	-0.09	(0.06)	-1.30	(0.12)	-0.26	(0.06)	0.25	(0.06)	0.96	(0.06)
Dubai*	0.50	(0.01)	-0.46	(0.02)	0.37	(0.01)	0.77	(0.01)	1.32	(0.01)
Fujairah	0.01	(0.03)	-1.17	(0.06)	-0.19	(0.04)	0.36	(0.04)	1.03	(0.03)
Ras al-Khaimah	0.06	(0.08)	-1.19	(0.14)	-0.12	(0.09)	0.43	(0.07)	1.11	(0.06)
Sharjah	0.44	(0.04)	-0.59	(0.09)	0.34	(0.05)	0.76	(0.03)	1.25	(0.03)
Umm al-Quwain	-0.10	(0.04)	-1.33	(0.09)	-0.25	(0.05)	0.27	(0.05)	0.93	(0.05)

OECD (left margin for Australia through Spain block)
Partners (left margin for Brazil through United Arab Emirates block)

* PISA adjudicated region.
Notes: Values that are statistically significant are indicated in bold (see Annex A3).
Italian administrative regions are grouped into larger geographical units: Centre (*Lazio, Marche, Toscana, Umbria*), North East (*Bolzano, Emilia Romagna, Friuli Venezia Giulia, Trento, Veneto*), North West (*Liguria, Lombardia, Piemonte, Valle d'Aosta*), South (*Abruzzo, Campania, Molise, Puglia*), South Islands (*Basilicata, Calabria, Sardegna, Sicilia*).
Brazilian states are grouped into larger geographical units: Central-West Region (*Federal District, Goiás, Mato Grosso, Mato Grosso do Sul*), Northeast Region (*Alagoas, Bahia, Ceará, Maranhão, Paraíba, Pernambuco, Piauí, Rio Grande do Norte, Sergipe*), North Region (*Acre, Amapá, Amazonas, Pará, Rondônia, Roraima, Tocantins*), Southeast Region (*Espírito Santo, Minas Gerais, Rio de Janeiro, São Paulo*), South Region (*Paraná, Rio Grande do Sul, Santa Catarina*).
See Table V.4.12 for national data.
1. Single-level bivariate regression of performance on ESCS. The slope of the gradient is the regression coefficient for ESCS; the strength of the relationship is the R-squared.
StatLink ᐃᔕ᠋ http://dx.doi.org/10.1787/888933003763

[Part 2/2]
Performance in problem solving, by socio-economic status and by region
Table B2.V.6   *Results based on students' self-reports*

	Performance in problem solving, by national quarters of this index								Increased likelihood of students in the bottom quarter of the ESCS index scoring in the bottom quarter of the problem-solving performance distribution		Slope of the socio-economic gradient[1] Score-point difference in problem solving associated with one-unit increase in the ESCS		Strength of the relationship between student performance and ESCS[1] Percentage of explained variation in student performance (R-squared × 100)	
	Bottom quarter		Second quarter		Third quarter		Top quarter							
	Mean score	S.E.	Mean score	S.E.	Mean score	S.E.	Mean score	S.E.	Relative risk	S.E.		S.E.		S.E.
OECD														
Australia														
Australian Capital Territory	**482**	(8.5)	523	(8.8)	554	(7.4)	**554**	(8.1)	**2.19**	(0.45)	46	(6.6)	8.4	(2.5)
New South Wales	**487**	(5.4)	515	(4.5)	537	(5.3)	**569**	(5.0)	**1.92**	(0.16)	38	(2.8)	10.0	(1.4)
Northern Territory	**469**	(16.5)	512	(14.9)	530	(15.3)	**554**	(17.8)	**1.90**	(0.43)	48	(9.0)	11.6	(4.0)
Queensland	**485**	(5.7)	507	(4.3)	534	(5.8)	**563**	(5.1)	**1.90**	(0.18)	39	(3.1)	10.0	(1.5)
South Australia	**487**	(7.8)	514	(7.4)	529	(5.9)	**551**	(6.7)	**1.79**	(0.25)	28	(4.2)	5.9	(1.7)
Tasmania	**447**	(7.7)	478	(7.0)	504	(7.9)	**536**	(8.7)	**2.13**	(0.37)	43	(4.4)	10.9	(2.1)
Victoria	**493**	(5.9)	508	(6.1)	544	(5.9)	**552**	(5.4)	**1.73**	(0.15)	31	(2.5)	6.6	(1.0)
Western Australia	**498**	(6.2)	519	(7.2)	541	(6.9)	**559**	(5.8)	**1.66**	(0.18)	30	(3.3)	6.2	(1.2)
Belgium														
Flemish Community•	**473**	(5.6)	511	(5.7)	548	(4.5)	**574**	(4.6)	**2.42**	(0.19)	44	(2.8)	16.1	(2.1)
French Community	**437**	(6.7)	474	(6.8)	506	(6.3)	**531**	(6.1)	**2.25**	(0.21)	41	(3.6)	12.2	(1.9)
German-speaking Community	**495**	(7.7)	514	(8.5)	530	(7.2)	**541**	(8.3)	**1.57**	(0.25)	21	(4.7)	3.4	(1.5)
Canada														
Alberta	**503**	(6.2)	521	(8.1)	535	(7.1)	**566**	(6.7)	**1.60**	(0.20)	30	(3.1)	6.0	(1.2)
British Columbia	**507**	(5.6)	521	(5.5)	547	(5.9)	**567**	(6.0)	**1.74**	(0.22)	27	(2.9)	6.2	(1.3)
Manitoba	**477**	(6.6)	499	(6.4)	511	(6.0)	**535**	(6.0)	**1.57**	(0.18)	25	(3.4)	5.1	(1.2)
New Brunswick	**491**	(6.7)	516	(5.2)	521	(6.6)	**536**	(7.2)	**1.55**	(0.20)	19	(4.7)	3.0	(1.5)
Newfoundland and Labrador	**461**	(21.1)	477	(7.5)	520	(7.8)	**557**	(5.3)	**2.02**	(0.47)	41	(9.0)	13.1	(4.8)
Nova Scotia	**497**	(7.0)	500	(13.2)	522	(6.4)	**538**	(6.4)	**1.23**	(0.23)	19	(3.5)	2.9	(1.0)
Ontario	**510**	(7.5)	521	(6.7)	536	(7.8)	**554**	(7.2)	**1.43**	(0.14)	19	(3.1)	2.8	(0.9)
Prince Edward Island	**463**	(6.4)	483	(5.2)	493	(5.9)	**529**	(4.8)	**1.66**	(0.24)	31	(3.7)	7.8	(1.8)
Quebec	**500**	(5.8)	522	(6.0)	536	(5.5)	**551**	(6.1)	**1.56**	(0.14)	23	(3.2)	3.6	(0.9)
Saskatchewan	**493**	(5.7)	506	(5.4)	519	(6.0)	**544**	(4.8)	**1.45**	(0.19)	25	(2.8)	4.9	(1.1)
Italy														
Centre	**488**	(14.4)	508	(13.9)	534	(11.9)	**527**	(17.9)	**1.52**	(0.29)	20	(4.9)	3.8	(2.0)
North East	**489**	(10.2)	520	(7.3)	546	(7.6)	**555**	(13.3)	**1.93**	(0.37)	30	(6.2)	9.3	(3.4)
North West	**518**	(11.3)	518	(10.6)	544	(11.3)	**551**	(7.7)	**1.32**	(0.22)	14	(4.8)	2.5	(1.6)
South	**453**	(12.0)	461	(12.0)	481	(13.2)	**503**	(8.6)	**1.57**	(0.45)	21	(3.6)	6.7	(2.2)
South Islands	**460**	(13.4)	476	(10.7)	492	(10.1)	**517**	(12.3)	**1.75**	(0.39)	24	(4.9)	7.0	(2.7)
Portugal														
Alentejo	**459**	(15.8)	492	(17.9)	520	(11.6)	**554**	(18.0)	**2.45**	(0.53)	31	(4.9)	15.2	(3.8)
Spain														
Basque Country•	**464**	(6.5)	491	(5.2)	505	(5.0)	**527**	(4.5)	**1.67**	(0.14)	26	(2.9)	6.1	(1.2)
Catalonia•	**459**	(10.8)	474	(11.8)	497	(10.5)	**522**	(11.8)	**1.54**	(0.23)	24	(5.0)	5.7	(2.2)
Madrid	**468**	(16.9)	500	(9.0)	511	(17.3)	**553**	(26.9)	**1.97**	(0.56)	31	(10.1)	10.9	(6.9)
Partners														
Brazil														
Central-West Region	**391**	(16.2)	427	(19.0)	451	(15.7)	**503**	(17.3)	**2.88**	(1.09)	37	(4.4)	25.3	(6.0)
Northeast Region	**340**	(10.6)	369	(15.6)	400	(15.9)	**465**	(21.4)	**2.28**	(0.50)	39	(7.1)	21.3	(5.3)
North Region	**350**	(11.6)	386	(15.9)	383	(13.4)	**416**	(16.9)	**1.76**	(0.59)	23	(5.7)	8.7	(4.1)
Southeast Region	**415**	(7.2)	439	(10.3)	455	(8.8)	**482**	(8.8)	**1.83**	(0.21)	23	(3.3)	10.5	(3.2)
South Region	**394**	(8.7)	418	(13.4)	450	(9.4)	**477**	(11.0)	**2.17**	(0.39)	30	(3.5)	16.7	(4.4)
Colombia														
Bogotá	**390**	(6.6)	405	(6.8)	415	(7.1)	**434**	(9.8)	**1.56**	(0.20)	19	(4.0)	4.9	(2.0)
Cali	**360**	(12.7)	386	(11.3)	404	(10.3)	**441**	(10.2)	**1.90**	(0.34)	30	(4.7)	10.9	(2.9)
Manizales	**383**	(9.9)	419	(6.5)	436	(9.4)	**454**	(9.2)	**2.11**	(0.40)	26	(4.2)	11.6	(3.4)
Medellín	**381**	(7.2)	401	(9.4)	422	(8.9)	**495**	(21.7)	**1.86**	(0.37)	39	(5.2)	22.0	(5.3)
United Arab Emirates														
Abu Dhabi•	**355**	(6.4)	381	(6.7)	412	(7.4)	**424**	(8.2)	**1.65**	(0.16)	28	(3.6)	5.5	(1.3)
Ajman	**353**	(11.2)	366	(8.6)	383	(13.2)	**397**	(9.8)	**1.64**	(0.36)	19	(4.2)	4.5	(2.1)
Dubai•	**406**	(3.5)	447	(3.5)	480	(3.7)	**495**	(3.1)	**2.10**	(0.14)	48	(2.3)	10.5	(0.9)
Fujairah	**371**	(5.4)	384	(6.8)	403	(6.3)	**420**	(10.0)	**1.56**	(0.25)	23	(4.3)	6.5	(2.4)
Ras al-Khaimah	**350**	(11.0)	346	(19.2)	389	(14.0)	**405**	(10.2)	1.31	(0.31)	25	(3.0)	6.1	(2.4)
Sharjah	**389**	(12.1)	415	(7.6)	440	(13.1)	**421**	(12.5)	**1.48**	(0.29)	18	(5.4)	2.7	(1.4)
Umm al-Quwain	**349**	(9.3)	377	(10.2)	370	(9.8)	**395**	(9.5)	**1.81**	(0.45)	22	(4.3)	5.9	(2.4)

• PISA adjudicated region.
Notes: Values that are statistically significant are indicated in bold (see Annex A3).
Italian administrative regions are grouped into larger geographical units: Centre (*Lazio, Marche, Toscana, Umbria*), North East (*Bolzano, Emilia Romagna,· Friuli Venezia Giulia, Trento, Veneto*), North West (*Liguria, Lombardia, Piemonte, Valle d'Aosta*), South (*Abruzzo, Campania, Molise, Puglia*), South Islands (*Basilicata, Calabria, Sardegna, Sicilia*).
Brazilian states are grouped into larger geographical units: Central-West Region (*Federal District, Goiás, Mato Grosso, Mato Grosso do Sul*), Northeast Region (*Alagoas, Bahia, Ceará, Maranhão, Paraíba, Pernambuco, Piauí, Rio Grande do Norte, Sergipe*), North Region (*Acre, Amapá, Amazonas, Pará, Rondônia, Roraima, Tocantins*), Southeast Region (*Espírito Santo, Minas Gerais, Rio de Janeiro, São Paulo*), South Region (*Paraná, Rio Grande do Sul, Santa Catarina*).
See Table V.4.12 for national data.
1. Single-level bivariate regression of performance on ESCS. The slope of the gradient is the regression coefficient for ESCS; the strength of the relationship is the R-squared.
StatLink ᴍ⬤ http://dx.doi.org/10.1787/888933003763

[Part 1/3]
Strength of the relationship between socio-economic status and performance in problem solving, mathematics, reading and science, by region

Table B2.V.7   *Results based on students' self-reports*

| | Slope of the socio-economic gradient:[1] Score-point difference associated with a one-unit increase in ESCS | | | | | | | | | | | |
| | Problem solving | | Mathematics | | Reading | | Science | | Computer-based mathematics | | Digital reading | |
	Score dif.	S.E.	Score dif.	S.E.	Score dif.	S.E.	Score dif.	S.E.	Score dif.	S.E.	Score dif.	S.E.
Australia												
Australian Capital Territory	46	(6.6)	52	(5.3)	54	(6.0)	53	(5.4)	48	(5.0)	50	(5.5)
New South Wales	38	(2.8)	44	(3.0)	45	(2.5)	46	(2.9)	37	(2.9)	41	(2.8)
Northern Territory	48	(9.0)	62	(7.8)	66	(8.7)	70	(6.6)	56	(5.5)	71	(8.6)
Queensland	39	(3.1)	46	(2.7)	45	(3.2)	45	(2.8)	38	(2.9)	39	(3.6)
South Australia	28	(4.2)	38	(3.7)	35	(3.8)	41	(3.7)	33	(4.6)	35	(4.5)
Tasmania	43	(4.4)	46	(3.9)	44	(4.1)	51	(4.5)	44	(3.0)	49	(4.5)
Victoria	31	(2.5)	35	(2.5)	34	(2.7)	36	(2.6)	28	(3.0)	31	(2.7)
Western Australia	30	(3.3)	43	(3.1)	41	(3.0)	43	(3.0)	39	(3.9)	41	(3.7)
Belgium												
Flemish Community*	44	(2.8)	50	(2.3)	44	(2.1)	48	(2.1)	44	(2.3)	42	(2.5)
French Community	41	(3.6)	48	(2.6)	50	(3.4)	47	(2.9)	41	(2.7)	39	(3.3)
German-speaking Community	21	(4.7)	22	(4.0)	24	(4.3)	26	(4.0)	9	(3.6)	9	(4.9)
Canada												
Alberta	30	(3.1)	33	(2.4)	32	(2.8)	32	(3.0)	32	(4.1)	28	(3.1)
British Columbia	27	(2.9)	26	(2.6)	24	(3.2)	24	(3.0)	23	(3.0)	25	(2.5)
Manitoba	25	(3.4)	37	(3.0)	35	(3.1)	34	(3.1)	29	(3.1)	25	(3.0)
New Brunswick	19	(4.7)	26	(4.2)	24	(4.1)	23	(4.6)	23	(4.3)	26	(3.8)
Newfoundland and Labrador	41	(9.0)	40	(4.6)	36	(4.3)	36	(3.8)	37	(4.3)	37	(5.2)
Nova Scotia	19	(3.5)	29	(2.9)	23	(3.8)	22	(3.2)	29	(2.6)	20	(5.0)
Ontario	19	(3.1)	30	(2.4)	28	(2.4)	28	(2.5)	24	(3.0)	23	(3.3)
Prince Edward Island	31	(3.7)	29	(3.0)	28	(3.4)	29	(3.3)	15	(3.7)	39	(4.1)
Quebec	23	(3.2)	36	(2.7)	33	(2.7)	29	(2.5)	26	(2.7)	23	(2.7)
Saskatchewan	25	(2.8)	25	(2.2)	24	(3.0)	26	(2.6)	27	(2.6)	21	(2.7)
Italy												
Centre	20	(4.9)	25	(4.1)	30	(5.5)	27	(4.6)	19	(4.9)	24	(5.9)
North East	30	(6.2)	37	(5.5)	40	(5.1)	35	(4.9)	29	(6.9)	27	(6.7)
North West	14	(4.8)	21	(4.5)	20	(4.7)	22	(4.9)	19	(4.6)	16	(4.7)
South	21	(3.6)	27	(3.8)	31	(4.3)	29	(4.1)	19	(5.1)	20	(4.9)
South Islands	24	(4.9)	30	(6.3)	31	(6.5)	30	(5.9)	27	(4.7)	23	(4.5)
Portugal												
Alentejo	31	(4.9)	33	(3.6)	27	(4.1)	27	(3.1)	28	(4.2)	27	(5.1)
Spain												
Basque Country*	26	(2.9)	28	(1.8)	28	(2.2)	26	(2.0)	25	(2.2)	27	(2.6)
Catalonia*	24	(5.0)	35	(3.1)	31	(3.0)	31	(2.9)	24	(3.5)	31	(4.7)
Madrid	31	(10.1)	35	(7.5)	28	(7.7)	27	(6.3)	26	(6.0)	31	(7.3)
Brazil												
Central-West Region	37	(4.4)	38	(6.2)	33	(5.5)	36	(5.5)	38	(7.1)	40	(8.5)
Northeast Region	39	(7.1)	32	(4.8)	28	(5.6)	29	(4.9)	31	(4.4)	32	(5.6)
North Region	23	(5.7)	23	(4.7)	21	(6.4)	16	(5.0)	25	(5.5)	26	(6.8)
Southeast Region	23	(3.3)	23	(4.5)	19	(3.7)	21	(3.8)	28	(4.3)	23	(3.9)
South Region	30	(3.5)	25	(7.4)	25	(6.6)	24	(6.8)	28	(6.9)	27	(5.6)
Colombia												
Bogotá	19	(4.0)	19	(3.6)	18	(2.9)	18	(3.6)	17	(4.4)	24	(4.3)
Cali	30	(4.7)	27	(3.5)	29	(4.1)	28	(3.3)	19	(3.6)	32	(5.5)
Manizales	24	(3.7)	28	(3.2)	26	(2.8)	23	(3.5)	15	(3.1)	29	(2.6)
Medellín	39	(5.2)	35	(5.3)	32	(4.9)	31	(4.8)	30	(5.1)	31	(4.4)
United Arab Emirates												
Abu Dhabi*	28	(3.6)	29	(3.2)	24	(3.5)	29	(3.5)	28	(3.8)	38	(4.7)
Ajman	19	(4.2)	21	(3.8)	22	(4.9)	23	(3.8)	13	(3.4)	24	(6.5)
Dubai*	48	(2.3)	43	(2.0)	43	(2.2)	47	(2.1)	43	(1.9)	57	(2.3)
Fujairah	23	(4.3)	20	(7.2)	15	(8.0)	15	(6.0)	12	(5.2)	23	(7.1)
Ras al-Khaimah	25	(3.0)	22	(3.5)	17	(5.0)	19	(4.0)	13	(3.4)	23	(4.3)
Sharjah	18	(5.4)	28	(6.6)	22	(6.6)	27	(7.8)	16	(3.4)	34	(7.3)
Umm al-Quwain	22	(4.3)	22	(5.3)	20	(5.0)	21	(4.6)	17	(4.0)	23	(8.0)

* PISA adjudicated region.

Notes: Values that are statistically significant are indicated in bold (see Annex A3).

Italian administrative regions are grouped into larger geographical units: Centre (*Lazio, Marche, Toscana, Umbria*), North East (*Bolzano, Emilia Romagna, Friuli Venezia Giulia, Trento, Veneto*), North West (*Liguria, Lombardia, Piemonte, Valle d'Aosta*), South (*Abruzzo, Campania, Molise, Puglia*), South Islands (*Basilicata, Calabria, Sardegna, Sicilia*).

Brazilian states are grouped into larger geographical units: Central-West Region (*Federal District, Goiás, Mato Grosso, Mato Grosso do Sul*), Northeast Region (*Alagoas, Bahia, Ceará, Maranhão, Paraíba, Pernambuco, Piauí, Rio Grande do Norte, Sergipe*), North Region (*Acre, Amapá, Amazonas, Pará, Rondônia, Roraima, Tocantins*), Southeast Region (*Espírito Santo, Minas Gerais, Rio de Janeiro, São Paulo*), South Region (*Paraná, Rio Grande do Sul, Santa Catarina*).

See Table V.4.13 for national data.

1. Single-level bivariate regression of performance on the *PISA index of economic, social and cultural status* (ESCS), the slope is the regression coefficient for ESCS.

2. R-squared from the regression coefficient of performance on the *PISA index of economic, social and cultural status* (ESCS).

StatLink ⟐⟐ http://dx.doi.org/10.1787/888933003763

[Part 2/3]
Strength of the relationship between socio-economic status and performance in problem solving, mathematics, reading and science, by region

Table B2.V.7   *Results based on students' self-reports*

	Strength of the relationship between performance and ESCS:[2] Percentage of explained variation in performance											
	Problem solving		Mathematics		Reading		Science		Computer-based mathematics		Digital reading	
	%	S.E.	%	S.E.	%	S.E.	%	S.E.	%	S.E.	%	S.E.
Australia												
Australian Capital Territory	8.4	(2.5)	12.5	(2.7)	12.7	(2.9)	11.5	(2.3)	11.7	(2.5)	11.5	(2.5)
New South Wales	10.0	(1.4)	12.8	(1.6)	13.5	(1.5)	12.8	(1.5)	9.9	(1.4)	11.7	(1.5)
Northern Territory	11.6	(4.0)	20.7	(5.0)	18.9	(4.7)	20.6	(4.5)	18.3	(3.9)	20.0	(4.7)
Queensland	10.0	(1.5)	14.9	(1.6)	13.5	(1.7)	13.6	(1.6)	11.3	(1.6)	10.6	(1.7)
South Australia	5.9	(1.7)	11.1	(2.0)	9.4	(1.8)	11.3	(2.0)	8.7	(2.1)	7.9	(1.9)
Tasmania	10.9	(2.1)	16.0	(2.4)	14.1	(2.3)	15.8	(2.5)	13.8	(2.2)	14.1	(2.3)
Victoria	6.6	(1.0)	9.0	(1.1)	8.4	(1.2)	8.8	(1.1)	6.4	(1.2)	6.8	(1.1)
Western Australia	6.2	(1.2)	13.4	(1.7)	12.0	(1.7)	11.9	(1.6)	10.7	(1.8)	11.1	(1.8)
Belgium												
Flemish Community•	16.1	(2.1)	19.9	(1.9)	17.6	(1.8)	19.5	(1.8)	16.0	(1.8)	15.5	(1.9)
French Community	12.2	(1.9)	20.6	(2.0)	19.4	(2.2)	19.6	(2.0)	16.7	(2.0)	13.6	(1.9)
German-speaking Community	3.4	(1.5)	4.4	(1.6)	4.5	(1.7)	5.9	(1.8)	0.8	(0.6)	0.5	(0.7)
Canada												
Alberta	6.0	(1.2)	8.9	(1.3)	8.8	(1.5)	8.5	(1.5)	7.1	(1.4)	6.6	(1.3)
British Columbia	6.2	(1.3)	7.1	(1.3)	5.7	(1.5)	5.7	(1.3)	4.8	(1.2)	6.6	(1.2)
Manitoba	5.1	(1.2)	14.1	(2.2)	11.6	(1.8)	10.9	(1.8)	8.6	(1.8)	6.8	(1.6)
New Brunswick	3.0	(1.5)	6.7	(2.0)	4.9	(1.6)	4.9	(1.8)	4.9	(1.9)	6.4	(1.8)
Newfoundland and Labrador	13.1	(4.8)	17.6	(4.0)	11.5	(2.9)	12.7	(3.0)	15.8	(4.1)	13.0	(3.6)
Nova Scotia	2.9	(1.0)	8.9	(1.7)	4.5	(1.4)	4.6	(1.3)	7.8	(1.4)	3.7	(1.8)
Ontario	2.8	(0.9)	9.6	(1.3)	7.9	(1.3)	7.2	(1.2)	5.7	(1.5)	5.5	(1.5)
Prince Edward Island	7.8	(1.8)	8.3	(1.6)	6.2	(1.5)	7.1	(1.5)	1.8	(0.9)	8.5	(1.7)
Quebec	3.6	(0.9)	11.6	(1.5)	9.2	(1.3)	8.7	(1.4)	5.9	(1.1)	5.2	(1.0)
Saskatchewan	4.9	(1.1)	6.2	(1.0)	5.1	(1.2)	6.3	(1.1)	5.8	(1.1)	4.3	(1.0)
Italy												
Centre	3.8	(2.0)	6.3	(1.9)	8.7	(3.0)	7.5	(2.5)	4.8	(2.5)	5.9	(3.0)
North East	9.3	(3.4)	14.3	(3.2)	15.5	(3.0)	13.1	(2.9)	9.8	(4.0)	7.1	(2.9)
North West	2.5	(1.6)	5.4	(2.1)	3.6	(1.7)	5.1	(2.2)	4.9	(2.1)	3.0	(1.7)
South	6.7	(2.2)	10.2	(2.6)	11.2	(2.5)	10.2	(3.0)	7.5	(3.2)	5.3	(2.4)
South Islands	7.0	(2.7)	10.7	(3.7)	9.6	(3.4)	10.2	(3.6)	11.4	(3.3)	5.4	(1.8)
Portugal												
Alentejo	15.2	(3.8)	17.9	(3.3)	12.9	(2.9)	14.9	(2.9)	14.0	(2.7)	14.1	(4.3)
Spain												
Basque Country•	6.1	(1.2)	10.4	(1.2)	10.2	(1.5)	9.2	(1.3)	8.2	(1.3)	7.8	(1.3)
Catalonia•	5.7	(2.2)	17.9	(2.9)	12.5	(2.2)	15.1	(2.6)	9.6	(2.3)	9.5	(2.3)
Madrid	10.9	(6.9)	17.0	(6.7)	11.5	(5.9)	11.2	(5.1)	12.6	(6.0)	12.8	(5.8)
Brazil												
Central-West Region	25.3	(6.0)	28.5	(6.7)	22.4	(6.3)	25.7	(5.3)	28.3	(7.8)	26.7	(7.7)
Northeast Region	21.3	(5.3)	22.6	(4.6)	15.0	(4.7)	18.4	(4.6)	19.4	(5.0)	15.0	(3.9)
North Region	8.7	(4.1)	11.9	(4.1)	6.9	(3.3)	6.1	(3.5)	15.3	(4.5)	9.0	(3.8)
Southeast Region	10.5	(3.2)	12.2	(4.3)	7.3	(2.7)	10.3	(3.5)	15.8	(4.3)	10.8	(3.7)
South Region	16.7	(4.4)	13.9	(8.0)	10.6	(5.6)	12.7	(7.0)	15.9	(6.2)	12.3	(5.7)
Colombia												
Bogotá	4.9	(2.0)	7.9	(2.8)	5.5	(1.8)	6.6	(2.5)	5.2	(2.6)	7.8	(2.8)
Cali	10.9	(2.9)	14.4	(3.3)	12.6	(3.3)	13.7	(3.1)	5.6	(2.2)	11.1	(3.0)
Manizales	8.9	(2.6)	16.8	(2.9)	14.1	(2.5)	12.2	(3.1)	5.9	(2.0)	13.4	(2.2)
Medellín	22.0	(5.3)	24.2	(5.8)	19.3	(5.5)	20.4	(5.6)	18.1	(5.6)	16.6	(4.6)
United Arab Emirates												
Abu Dhabi•	5.5	(1.3)	8.4	(1.6)	5.1	(1.4)	7.2	(1.6)	8.5	(2.0)	10.1	(2.2)
Ajman	4.5	(2.1)	6.6	(2.2)	5.3	(2.2)	6.2	(2.0)	3.0	(1.4)	4.6	(2.3)
Dubai•	10.5	(0.9)	11.1	(1.0)	9.8	(0.9)	12.3	(1.0)	12.1	(1.0)	13.8	(1.1)
Fujairah	6.5	(2.4)	4.8	(3.4)	2.2	(2.6)	2.6	(2.3)	1.9	(1.6)	4.6	(2.6)
Ras al-Khaimah	6.1	(2.4)	7.6	(2.4)	3.6	(2.2)	5.3	(2.3)	2.6	(1.3)	5.9	(2.1)
Sharjah	2.7	(1.4)	6.6	(2.6)	4.3	(2.3)	5.9	(3.2)	3.3	(1.2)	6.7	(2.4)
Umm al-Quwain	5.9	(2.4)	6.9	(3.1)	4.2	(2.1)	5.3	(2.3)	4.8	(2.1)	3.2	(2.3)

• PISA adjudicated region.

Notes: Values that are statistically significant are indicated in bold (see Annex A3).

Italian administrative regions are grouped into larger geographical units: Centre (*Lazio, Marche, Toscana, Umbria*), North East (*Bolzano, Emilia Romagna, Friuli Venezia Giulia, Trento, Veneto*), North West (*Liguria, Lombardia, Piemonte, Valle d'Aosta*), South (*Abruzzo, Campania, Molise, Puglia*), South Islands (*Basilicata, Calabria, Sardegna, Sicilia*).
Brazilian states are grouped into larger geographical units: Central-West Region (*Federal District, Goiás, Mato Grosso, Mato Grosso do Sul*), Northeast Region (*Alagoas, Bahia, Ceará, Maranhão, Paraíba, Pernambuco, Piauí, Rio Grande do Norte, Sergipe*), North Region (*Acre, Amapá, Amazonas, Pará, Rondônia, Roraima, Tocantins*), Southeast Region (*Espírito Santo, Minas Gerais, Rio de Janeiro, São Paulo*), South Region (*Paraná, Rio Grande do Sul, Santa Catarina*).

See Table V.4.13 for national data.

1. Single-level bivariate regression of performance on the *PISA index of economic, social and cultural status* (ESCS), the slope is the regression coefficient for ESCS.

2. R-squared from the regression coefficient of performance on the *PISA index of economic, social and cultural status* (ESCS).

StatLink ᵐˢ┗ http://dx.doi.org/10.1787/888933003763

[Part 3/3]
Strength of the relationship between socio-economic status and performance in problem solving, mathematics, reading and science, by region

Table B2.V.7 — *Results based on students' self-reports*

| | Strength of the relationship between performance in problem solving (PS) and ESCS,[2] compared to… | | | | | | | | | |
| | … Mathematics (PS - M) | | … Reading (PS - R) | | … Science (PS - S) | | … Computer-based mathematics (PS - CBM) | | … Digital reading (PS - DR) | |
	% dif.	S.E.	% dif.	S.E.	% dif.	S.E.	% dif.	S.E.	% dif.	S.E.
Australia										
Australian Capital Territory	**-4.1**	(1.7)	**-4.3**	(1.8)	-3.1	(1.8)	**-3.3**	(1.5)	-3.1	(1.9)
New South Wales	**-2.8**	(1.1)	**-3.5**	(1.1)	**-2.8**	(1.0)	0.1	(1.2)	-1.7	(1.2)
Northern Territory	**-9.1**	(4.3)	-7.4	(4.3)	**-9.0**	(3.9)	**-6.7**	(3.0)	**-8.4**	(4.0)
Queensland	**-4.9**	(1.1)	**-3.5**	(1.3)	**-3.7**	(1.1)	-1.4	(1.2)	-0.6	(1.3)
South Australia	**-5.2**	(1.1)	**-3.5**	(1.3)	**-5.3**	(1.4)	**-2.7**	(1.3)	-2.0	(1.3)
Tasmania	**-5.1**	(1.6)	**-3.1**	(1.6)	**-4.9**	(1.7)	**-2.9**	(1.2)	**-3.2**	(1.4)
Victoria	**-2.4**	(1.0)	-1.8	(1.1)	**-2.2**	(1.0)	0.2	(1.1)	-0.2	(1.0)
Western Australia	**-7.2**	(1.5)	**-5.8**	(1.5)	**-5.7**	(1.4)	**-4.5**	(1.6)	**-4.9**	(1.4)
Belgium										
Flemish Community*	**-3.8**	(0.9)	-1.5	(1.1)	**-3.5**	(1.0)	0.0	(1.0)	0.6	(1.1)
French Community	**-8.4**	(1.6)	**-7.2**	(1.9)	**-7.4**	(1.7)	**-4.5**	(1.7)	-1.4	(1.7)
German-speaking Community	-1.0	(1.0)	-1.2	(1.3)	-2.5	(1.3)	**2.6**	(1.3)	**2.8**	(1.2)
Canada										
Alberta	**-2.9**	(0.9)	**-2.8**	(1.1)	**-2.5**	(1.0)	-1.1	(1.2)	-0.5	(1.0)
British Columbia	-0.9	(0.9)	0.4	(1.0)	0.5	(1.0)	1.3	(1.1)	-0.4	(1.1)
Manitoba	**-9.0**	(1.7)	**-6.6**	(1.3)	**-5.8**	(1.2)	**-3.5**	(1.4)	-1.7	(1.4)
New Brunswick	**-3.7**	(1.1)	-1.9	(1.1)	-1.9	(1.0)	-1.9	(1.2)	**-3.5**	(1.1)
Newfoundland and Labrador	**-4.5**	(2.0)	1.6	(2.8)	0.4	(2.7)	-2.7	(1.8)	0.1	(2.3)
Nova Scotia	**-6.0**	(1.5)	-1.6	(1.5)	-1.7	(1.1)	**-4.9**	(1.5)	-0.8	(2.0)
Ontario	**-6.8**	(1.0)	**-5.1**	(1.0)	**-4.4**	(0.8)	**-2.9**	(1.0)	**-2.7**	(1.1)
Prince Edward Island	-0.5	(1.7)	1.6	(1.8)	0.7	(1.6)	**6.0**	(1.9)	-0.7	(2.1)
Quebec	**-8.0**	(1.2)	**-5.6**	(1.0)	**-5.2**	(1.1)	**-2.3**	(1.0)	-1.6	(0.8)
Saskatchewan	-1.3	(0.7)	-0.1	(0.8)	-1.4	(0.8)	-0.9	(1.0)	0.6	(0.8)
Italy										
Centre	**-2.6**	(1.2)	**-4.9**	(1.9)	**-3.7**	(1.6)	-1.0	(3.0)	-2.1	(2.0)
North East	**-5.1**	(1.9)	**-6.2**	(2.3)	-3.8	(2.1)	-0.5	(3.0)	2.1	(1.8)
North West	**-2.9**	(1.4)	-1.0	(1.3)	-2.5	(1.5)	-2.4	(1.4)	-0.4	(1.1)
South	-3.5	(2.3)	-4.6	(2.6)	-3.5	(2.6)	-0.9	(4.1)	1.4	(2.1)
South Islands	-3.7	(2.7)	-2.6	(2.4)	-3.2	(2.7)	-4.4	(2.8)	1.6	(1.8)
Portugal										
Alentejo	-2.7	(3.1)	2.2	(3.8)	0.3	(2.5)	1.2	(3.7)	1.1	(3.2)
Spain										
Basque Country*	**-4.3**	(0.9)	**-4.1**	(1.2)	**-3.1**	(0.9)	**-2.1**	(0.9)	-1.7	(1.0)
Catalonia*	**-12.2**	(2.1)	**-6.8**	(1.9)	**-9.4**	(1.7)	**-3.9**	(1.8)	**-3.8**	(1.9)
Madrid	-6.1	(3.8)	-0.7	(3.8)	-0.4	(3.6)	-1.8	(3.9)	-1.9	(4.9)
Brazil										
Central-West Region	-3.2	(3.2)	2.9	(3.4)	-0.4	(3.5)	-3.0	(4.8)	-1.4	(3.7)
Northeast Region	-1.3	(3.2)	6.3	(3.5)	2.8	(4.2)	1.9	(3.1)	6.3	(3.9)
North Region	-3.2	(2.8)	1.8	(3.5)	2.6	(2.6)	-6.6	(4.2)	-0.3	(4.1)
Southeast Region	-1.8	(1.8)	**3.2**	(1.6)	0.2	(1.5)	**-5.3**	(2.4)	-0.3	(1.5)
South Region	2.8	(4.4)	**6.1**	(2.1)	4.0	(3.8)	0.7	(3.4)	4.3	(2.3)
Colombia										
Bogotá	**-2.9**	(1.5)	-0.5	(1.4)	-1.6	(1.2)	-0.3	(1.2)	-2.9	(1.7)
Cali	-3.5	(2.5)	-1.7	(2.3)	-2.8	(2.1)	**5.3**	(2.2)	-0.2	(2.2)
Manizales	**-7.8**	(3.0)	-5.2	(2.9)	-3.2	(3.5)	3.0	(2.7)	-4.4	(2.8)
Medellín	-2.2	(2.2)	2.8	(3.2)	1.6	(2.3)	4.0	(2.2)	5.5	(4.2)
United Arab Emirates										
Abu Dhabi*	**-2.9**	(1.1)	0.4	(1.0)	-1.7	(1.0)	**-3.0**	(1.3)	**-4.6**	(1.5)
Ajman	-2.0	(2.0)	-0.8	(2.0)	-1.7	(1.6)	1.6	(1.5)	0.0	(2.3)
Dubai*	-0.5	(0.6)	0.7	(0.7)	**-1.8**	(0.6)	**-1.6**	(0.6)	**-3.3**	(0.6)
Fujairah	1.7	(2.2)	**4.3**	(2.0)	**3.8**	(1.6)	**4.6**	(2.0)	1.9	(2.1)
Ras al-Khaimah	-1.5	(2.1)	2.5	(2.0)	0.9	(1.9)	3.5	(2.1)	0.2	(2.8)
Sharjah	-3.9	(2.1)	-1.6	(1.5)	-3.2	(2.5)	-0.6	(0.9)	**-4.0**	(1.8)
Umm al-Quwain	-1.0	(2.5)	1.7	(2.1)	0.7	(2.1)	1.2	(2.6)	2.7	(2.1)

* PISA adjudicated region.

Notes: Values that are statistically significant are indicated in bold (see Annex A3).
Italian administrative regions are grouped into larger geographical units: Centre (*Lazio, Marche, Toscana, Umbria*), North East (*Bolzano, Emilia Romagna, Friuli Venezia Giulia, Trento, Veneto*), North West (*Liguria, Lombardia, Piemonte, Valle d'Aosta*), South (*Abruzzo, Campania, Molise, Puglia*), South Islands (*Basilicata, Calabria, Sardegna, Sicilia*).
Brazilian states are grouped into larger geographical units: Central-West Region (*Federal District, Goiás, Mato Grosso, Mato Grosso do Sul*), Northeast Region (*Alagoas, Bahia, Ceará, Maranhão, Paraíba, Pernambuco, Piauí, Rio Grande do Norte, Sergipe*), North Region (*Acre, Amapá, Amazonas, Pará, Rondônia, Roraima, Tocantins*), Southeast Region (*Espírito Santo, Minas Gerais, Rio de Janeiro, São Paulo*), South Region (*Paraná, Rio Grande do Sul, Santa Catarina*).

See Table V.4.13 for national data.

1. Single-level bivariate regression of performance on the *PISA index of economic, social and cultural status* (ESCS), the slope is the regression coefficient for ESCS.
2. R-squared from the regression coefficient of performance on the *PISA index of economic, social and cultural status* (ESCS).

StatLink ⟨ms⟩ http://dx.doi.org/10.1787/888933003763

[Part 1/1]

Performance in problem solving and use of a computer at home, by region

Table B2.V.8 *Results based on students' self-reports*

	Students who use a desktop, laptop or tablet computer at home														Difference in problem-solving performance			
	Percentage of students																	
	All students		Boys		Girls		Gender difference (B - G)		Parents' highest occupation: Skilled (ISCO 1 to 3)		Parents' highest occupation: Semi-skilled or elementary (ISCO 4 to 9)		Difference related to parents' highest occupation: Skilled - semi-skilled or elementary		Observed		After accounting for socio-demographic characteristics of students[1]	
	%	S.E.	%	S.E.	%	S.E.	% dif.	S.E.	%	S.E.	%	S.E.	% dif.	S.E.	Score dif.	S.E.	Score dif.	S.E.
Australia																		
Australian Capital Territory	99.0	(0.2)	98.7	(0.3)	99.3	(0.3)	-0.6	(0.5)	99.7	(0.2)	95.7	(0.8)	**3.9**	(0.8)	c	c	c	c
New South Wales	96.8	(0.2)	96.6	(0.2)	97.1	(0.2)	**-0.6**	(0.3)	98.3	(0.1)	94.6	(0.4)	**3.7**	(0.4)	77	(7.7)	48	(7.6)
Northern Territory	92.8	(0.9)	91.2	(1.6)	94.3	(0.6)	-3.2	(1.7)	95.5	(1.1)	91.1	(1.4)	**4.4**	(1.8)	104	(33.1)	70	(30.7)
Queensland	95.9	(0.2)	95.1	(0.4)	96.7	(0.2)	**-1.6**	(0.5)	97.2	(0.2)	93.6	(0.5)	**3.7**	(0.4)	79	(13.1)	55	(14.9)
South Australia	97.9	(0.2)	97.8	(0.3)	98.0	(0.4)	-0.2	(0.5)	98.5	(0.2)	96.9	(0.4)	**1.6**	(0.4)	46	(18.2)	35	(18.0)
Tasmania	93.5	(0.4)	92.9	(0.6)	94.2	(0.5)	-1.3	(0.8)	95.3	(0.5)	93.8	(0.6)	1.5	(0.7)	68	(16.3)	24	(14.6)
Victoria	98.8	(0.1)	98.6	(0.2)	99.0	(0.1)	-0.4	(0.3)	99.2	(0.1)	98.6	(0.2)	0.6	(0.2)	77	(17.5)	m	m
Western Australia	96.6	(0.3)	95.8	(0.4)	97.6	(0.5)	**-1.8**	(0.7)	97.6	(0.3)	95.5	(0.5)	2.2	(0.5)	61	(14.7)	33	(14.2)
Belgium																		
Flemish Community•	98.9	(0.1)	98.8	(0.2)	99.0	(0.1)	-0.3	(0.2)	99.3	(0.1)	98.4	(0.2)	**1.0**	(0.2)	96	(12.6)	69	(14.7)
French Community	97.3	(0.2)	97.1	(0.2)	97.5	(0.2)	-0.4	(0.3)	98.2	(0.1)	96.7	(0.3)	**1.5**	(0.3)	65	(15.3)	42	(13.5)
German-speaking Community	98.4	(0.2)	97.3	(0.3)	99.5	(0.2)	**-2.2**	(0.4)	99.2	(0.2)	98.0	(0.5)	1.2	(0.6)	c	c	c	c
Canada																		
Alberta	m	m	m	m	m	m	m	m	m	m	m	m	m	m	m	m	m	m
British Columbia	m	m	m	m	m	m	m	m	m	m	m	m	m	m	m	m	m	m
Manitoba	m	m	m	m	m	m	m	m	m	m	m	m	m	m	m	m	m	m
New Brunswick	m	m	m	m	m	m	m	m	m	m	m	m	m	m	m	m	m	m
Newfoundland and Labrador	m	m	m	m	m	m	m	m	m	m	m	m	m	m	m	m	m	m
Nova Scotia	m	m	m	m	m	m	m	m	m	m	m	m	m	m	m	m	m	m
Ontario	m	m	m	m	m	m	m	m	m	m	m	m	m	m	m	m	m	m
Prince Edward Island	m	m	m	m	m	m	m	m	m	m	m	m	m	m	m	m	m	m
Quebec	m	m	m	m	m	m	m	m	m	m	m	m	m	m	m	m	m	m
Saskatchewan	m	m	m	m	m	m	m	m	m	m	m	m	m	m	m	m	m	m
Italy																		
Centre	96.5	(0.7)	94.9	(1.1)	98.5	(0.3)	**-3.6**	(1.1)	98.9	(0.2)	94.4	(1.2)	**4.5**	(1.3)	c	c	c	c
North East	97.3	(0.3)	96.7	(0.5)	98.0	(0.4)	-1.3	(0.7)	98.6	(0.3)	96.9	(0.3)	**1.7**	(0.3)	69	(28.8)	20	(25.8)
North West	97.8	(0.3)	97.4	(0.4)	98.2	(0.3)	**-0.9**	(0.4)	97.7	(0.4)	98.2	(0.5)	-0.5	(0.7)	c	c	c	c
South	97.4	(0.3)	97.5	(0.4)	97.3	(0.4)	0.2	(0.6)	98.3	(0.5)	96.8	(0.5)	1.5	(0.8)	c	c	c	c
South Islands	98.0	(0.3)	98.0	(0.4)	98.0	(0.6)	0.0	(0.8)	99.8	(0.1)	97.4	(0.4)	**2.4**	(0.4)	c	c	c	c
Portugal																		
Alentejo	97.8	(0.3)	97.8	(0.5)	97.9	(0.4)	-0.1	(0.6)	99.5	(0.2)	97.4	(0.4)	**2.1**	(0.4)	c	c	c	c
Spain																		
Basque Country•	96.3	(0.2)	95.6	(0.3)	96.9	(0.2)	**-1.3**	(0.4)	97.2	(0.2)	95.7	(0.3)	**1.6**	(0.3)	58	(17.5)	46	(13.5)
Catalonia•	98.7	(0.2)	98.9	(0.2)	98.5	(0.4)	0.4	(0.4)	99.2	(0.2)	98.5	(0.2)	**0.7**	(0.2)	c	c	c	c
Madrid	98.2	(0.7)	97.7	(0.8)	98.6	(0.6)	-0.9	(0.7)	98.8	(0.4)	97.5	(0.9)	1.3	(0.7)	c	c	c	c
Brazil																		
Central-West Region	m	m	m	m	m	m	m	m	m	m	m	m	m	m	m	m	m	m
Northeast Region	m	m	m	m	m	m	m	m	m	m	m	m	m	m	m	m	m	m
North Region	m	m	m	m	m	m	m	m	m	m	m	m	m	m	m	m	m	m
Southeast Region	m	m	m	m	m	m	m	m	m	m	m	m	m	m	m	m	m	m
South Region	m	m	m	m	m	m	m	m	m	m	m	m	m	m	m	m	m	m
Colombia																		
Bogotá	m	m	m	m	m	m	m	m	m	m	m	m	m	m	m	m	m	m
Cali	m	m	m	m	m	m	m	m	m	m	m	m	m	m	m	m	m	m
Manizales	m	m	m	m	m	m	m	m	m	m	m	m	m	m	m	m	m	m
Medellín	m	m	m	m	m	m	m	m	m	m	m	m	m	m	m	m	m	m
United Arab Emirates																		
Abu Dhabi•	m	m	m	m	m	m	m	m	m	m	m	m	m	m	m	m	m	m
Ajman	m	m	m	m	m	m	m	m	m	m	m	m	m	m	m	m	m	m
Dubai•	m	m	m	m	m	m	m	m	m	m	m	m	m	m	m	m	m	m
Fujairah	m	m	m	m	m	m	m	m	m	m	m	m	m	m	m	m	m	m
Ras al-Khaimah	m	m	m	m	m	m	m	m	m	m	m	m	m	m	m	m	m	m
Sharjah	m	m	m	m	m	m	m	m	m	m	m	m	m	m	m	m	m	m
Umm al-Quwain	m	m	m	m	m	m	m	m	m	m	m	m	m	m	m	m	m	m

• PISA adjudicated region.

Notes: Values that are statistically significant are indicated in bold (see Annex A3).

Italian administrative regions are grouped into larger geographical units: Centre (*Lazio, Marche, Toscana, Umbria*), North East (*Bolzano, Emilia Romagna, Friuli Venezia Giulia, Trento, Veneto*), North West (*Liguria, Lombardia, Piemonte, Valle d'Aosta*), South (*Abruzzo, Campania, Molise, Puglia*), South Islands (*Basilicata, Calabria, Sardegna, Sicilia*).

Brazilian states are grouped into larger geographical units: Central-West Region (*Federal District, Goiás, Mato Grosso, Mato Grosso do Sul*), Northeast Region (*Alagoas, Bahia, Ceará, Maranhão, Paraíba, Pernambuco, Piauí, Rio Grande do Norte, Sergipe*), North Region (*Acre, Amapá, Amazonas, Pará, Rondônia, Roraima, Tocantins*), Southeast Region (*Espírito Santo, Minas Gerais, Rio de Janeiro, São Paulo*), South Region (*Paraná, Rio Grande do Sul, Santa Catarina*).

See Table V.4.25 for national data.

1. The adjusted result corresponds to the coefficient from a regression where the *PISA index of economic, social and cultural status* (ESCS), ESCS squared, boy, and an immigrant (first generation) dummy are introduced as further independent variables.

StatLink ⬛ http://dx.doi.org/10.1787/888933003763

[Part 1/1]
Performance in problem solving and use of computers at school, by region

Table B2.V.9 *Results based on students' self-reports*

	Students who use a desktop, laptop or tablet computer at school														Difference in problem-solving performance			
	Percentage of students																	
	All students		Boys		Girls		Gender difference (B - G)		Parents' highest occupation: Skilled (ISCO 1 to 3)		Parents' highest occupation: Semi-skilled or elementary (ISCO 4 to 9)		Difference related to parents' highest occupation: Skilled - semi-skilled or elementary		Observed		After accounting for socio-demographic characteristics of students[1]	
	%	S.E.	%	S.E.	%	S.E.	% dif.	S.E.	%	S.E.	%	S.E.	% dif.	S.E.	Score dif.	S.E.	Score dif.	S.E.
Australia																		
Australian Capital Territory	93.5	(0.4)	93.1	(0.6)	93.9	(0.7)	-0.8	(0.9)	94.2	(0.5)	93.7	(1.1)	0.5	(1.2)	**40**	(17.3)	32	(16.3)
New South Wales	89.8	(0.3)	89.8	(0.4)	89.7	(0.4)	0.1	(0.5)	90.9	(0.4)	88.6	(0.5)	**2.3**	(0.5)	**35**	(6.1)	**23**	(6.3)
Northern Territory	89.3	(1.5)	92.9	(1.5)	86.1	(1.8)	**6.8**	(1.6)	87.6	(2.1)	93.2	(1.1)	**-5.6**	(2.1)	4	(29.2)	-4	(22.2)
Queensland	94.4	(0.2)	92.6	(0.5)	96.2	(0.3)	**-3.6**	(0.6)	95.5	(0.3)	93.0	(0.5)	**2.4**	(0.5)	**69**	(11.1)	**59**	(11.0)
South Australia	97.5	(0.3)	97.9	(0.5)	97.2	(0.3)	0.7	(0.6)	97.9	(0.3)	97.1	(0.5)	0.8	(0.5)	**56**	(18.8)	**45**	(16.8)
Tasmania	97.4	(0.3)	96.4	(0.5)	98.4	(0.3)	**-2.0**	(0.6)	97.7	(0.4)	97.0	(0.5)	0.7	(0.7)	51	(26.6)	28	(20.6)
Victoria	96.5	(0.2)	96.5	(0.3)	96.4	(0.3)	0.1	(0.5)	96.8	(0.2)	95.7	(0.4)	**1.1**	(0.4)	**25**	(11.6)	20	(10.9)
Western Australia	94.2	(0.3)	95.1	(0.4)	93.2	(0.6)	1.9	(0.8)	95.0	(0.4)	92.9	(0.6)	**2.1**	(0.7)	0	(12.7)	-8	(11.5)
Belgium																		
Flemish Community•	86.2	(0.4)	84.9	(0.5)	87.5	(0.5)	**-2.6**	(0.5)	86.6	(0.5)	85.8	(0.8)	0.8	(1.0)	**16**	(5.7)	**12**	(4.5)
French Community	37.2	(0.7)	39.0	(0.9)	35.4	(0.8)	**3.6**	(1.0)	35.6	(0.9)	39.1	(1.1)	**-3.5**	(1.4)	**-27**	(5.3)	**-25**	(4.9)
German-speaking Community	60.6	(0.6)	60.3	(0.9)	61.0	(1.0)	-0.7	(1.5)	58.7	(1.0)	62.8	(1.4)	**-4.0**	(1.9)	-7	(7.1)	-6	(7.1)
Canada																		
Alberta	m	m	m	m	m	m	m	m	m	m	m	m	m	m	m	m	m	m
British Columbia	m	m	m	m	m	m	m	m	m	m	m	m	m	m	m	m	m	m
Manitoba	m	m	m	m	m	m	m	m	m	m	m	m	m	m	m	m	m	m
New Brunswick	m	m	m	m	m	m	m	m	m	m	m	m	m	m	m	m	m	m
Newfoundland and Labrador	m	m	m	m	m	m	m	m	m	m	m	m	m	m	m	m	m	m
Nova Scotia	m	m	m	m	m	m	m	m	m	m	m	m	m	m	m	m	m	m
Ontario	m	m	m	m	m	m	m	m	m	m	m	m	m	m	m	m	m	m
Prince Edward Island	m	m	m	m	m	m	m	m	m	m	m	m	m	m	m	m	m	m
Quebec	m	m	m	m	m	m	m	m	m	m	m	m	m	m	m	m	m	m
Saskatchewan	m	m	m	m	m	m	m	m	m	m	m	m	m	m	m	m	m	m
Italy																		
Centre	61.4	(1.5)	67.9	(2.4)	53.5	(2.1)	**14.4**	(3.4)	56.6	(1.7)	65.6	(2.0)	**-9.0**	(2.2)	-1	(12.6)	1	(11.6)
North East	74.6	(1.2)	74.7	(1.6)	74.5	(1.2)	0.1	(1.6)	70.7	(1.5)	77.5	(1.3)	**-6.8**	(1.6)	-5	(9.2)	-2	(9.3)
North West	64.7	(1.3)	69.1	(1.6)	59.9	(1.8)	**9.2**	(1.9)	57.7	(1.7)	70.1	(1.2)	**-12.4**	(0.9)	**-16**	(6.8)	-12	(6.4)
South	68.4	(1.8)	70.6	(2.3)	65.6	(2.8)	5.0	(3.5)	62.2	(2.8)	71.4	(2.0)	**-9.1**	(2.4)	-3	(11.7)	2	(10.3)
South Islands	63.8	(1.5)	71.1	(1.9)	56.3	(2.4)	**14.8**	(3.1)	57.1	(1.9)	66.5	(1.5)	**-9.4**	(1.5)	**-24**	(11.7)	**-22**	(10.6)
Portugal																		
Alentejo	76.5	(0.9)	74.7	(1.1)	78.2	(1.0)	**-3.5**	(1.0)	76.9	(2.0)	76.8	(1.0)	0.2	(2.2)	**-20**	(8.1)	-15	(9.7)
Spain																		
Basque Country•	74.6	(0.8)	74.1	(0.9)	75.1	(0.8)	-1.1	(0.6)	71.9	(0.9)	77.8	(0.8)	**-5.9**	(0.6)	-2	(4.2)	1	(3.8)
Catalonia•	85.3	(1.2)	85.0	(1.2)	85.6	(1.4)	-0.6	(1.1)	84.5	(1.7)	86.3	(0.9)	-1.9	(1.5)	**26**	(11.2)	**26**	(10.1)
Madrid	77.0	(1.3)	79.5	(1.4)	74.6	(1.7)	**4.9**	(1.5)	75.8	(2.2)	78.2	(1.5)	-2.4	(2.5)	11	(19.8)	4	(15.4)
Brazil																		
Central-West Region	m	m	m	m	m	m	m	m	m	m	m	m	m	m	m	m	m	m
Northeast Region	m	m	m	m	m	m	m	m	m	m	m	m	m	m	m	m	m	m
North Region	m	m	m	m	m	m	m	m	m	m	m	m	m	m	m	m	m	m
Southeast Region	m	m	m	m	m	m	m	m	m	m	m	m	m	m	m	m	m	m
South Region	m	m	m	m	m	m	m	m	m	m	m	m	m	m	m	m	m	m
Colombia																		
Bogotá	m	m	m	m	m	m	m	m	m	m	m	m	m	m	m	m	m	m
Cali	m	m	m	m	m	m	m	m	m	m	m	m	m	m	m	m	m	m
Manizales	m	m	m	m	m	m	m	m	m	m	m	m	m	m	m	m	m	m
Medellín	m	m	m	m	m	m	m	m	m	m	m	m	m	m	m	m	m	m
United Arab Emirates																		
Abu Dhabi•	m	m	m	m	m	m	m	m	m	m	m	m	m	m	m	m	m	m
Ajman	m	m	m	m	m	m	m	m	m	m	m	m	m	m	m	m	m	m
Dubai•	m	m	m	m	m	m	m	m	m	m	m	m	m	m	m	m	m	m
Fujairah	m	m	m	m	m	m	m	m	m	m	m	m	m	m	m	m	m	m
Ras al-Khaimah	m	m	m	m	m	m	m	m	m	m	m	m	m	m	m	m	m	m
Sharjah	m	m	m	m	m	m	m	m	m	m	m	m	m	m	m	m	m	m
Umm al-Quwain	m	m	m	m	m	m	m	m	m	m	m	m	m	m	m	m	m	m

• PISA adjudicated region.
Notes: Values that are statistically significant are indicated in bold (see Annex A3).
Italian administrative regions are grouped into larger geographical units: Centre (*Lazio, Marche, Toscana, Umbria*), North East (*Bolzano, Emilia Romagna, Friuli Venezia Giulia, Trento, Veneto*), North West (*Liguria, Lombardia, Piemonte, Valle d'Aosta*), South (*Abruzzo, Campania, Molise, Puglia*), South Islands (*Basilicata, Calabria, Sardegna, Sicilia*).
Brazilian states are grouped into larger geographical units: Central-West Region (*Federal District, Goiás, Mato Grosso, Mato Grosso do Sul*), Northeast Region (*Alagoas, Bahia, Ceará, Maranhão, Paraíba, Pernambuco, Piauí, Rio Grande do Norte, Sergipe*), North Region (*Acre, Amapá, Amazonas, Pará, Rondônia, Roraima, Tocantins*), Southeast Region (*Espírito Santo, Minas Gerais, Rio de Janeiro, São Paulo*), South Region (*Paraná, Rio Grande do Sul, Santa Catarina*).
See Table V.4.26 for national data.
1. The adjusted result corresponds to the coefficient from a regression where the *PISA index of economic, social and cultural status* (ESCS), ESCS squared, boy, and an immigrant (first-generation) dummy are introduced as further independent variables.
StatLink ⌸⌸ http://dx.doi.org/10.1787/888933003763

ANNEX B3

LIST OF TABLES AVAILABLE ON LINE

The following tables are available in electronic form only.

Chapter 4 How problem-solving performance varies within countries

http://dx.doi.org/10.1787/888933003706

WEB	Table V.4.5	Differences in problem-solving, mathematics, reading and science performance related to education tracks
WEB	Table V.4.11c	Performance on problem-solving tasks, by technology setting and by gender
WEB	Table V.4.11d	Performance on problem-solving tasks, by social focus and by gender
WEB	Table V.4.11e	Performance on problem-solving tasks, by response format and by gender
WEB	Table V.4.18c	Performance on problem-solving tasks, by technology setting and by parents' occupational status
WEB	Table V.4.18d	Performance on problem-solving tasks, by social focus and by parents' occupational status
WEB	Table V.4.18e	Performance on problem-solving tasks, by response format and by parents' occupational status
WEB	Table V.4.22c	Performance on problem-solving tasks, by technology setting and by immigrant background
WEB	Table V.4.22d	Performance on problem-solving tasks, by social focus and by immigrant background
WEB	Table V.4.22e	Performance on problem-solving tasks, by response format and by immigrant background

Annex B2 Results for regions within countries

http://dx.doi.org/10.1787/888933003763

WEB	Table B2.V.10	Performance in problem solving, by nature of the problem situation and by region
WEB	Table B2.V.11	Performance in problem solving, by process and by region
WEB	Table B2.V.12	Relative performance on knowledge-acquisition and knowledge-utilisation tasks, by region

These tables, as well as additional material, may be found at: *www.pisa.oecd.org*.

Annex C

THE DEVELOPMENT AND IMPLEMENTATION OF PISA –
A COLLABORATIVE EFFORT

PISA is a collaborative effort, bringing together experts from the participating countries, steered jointly by their governments on the basis of shared, policy-driven interests.

A PISA Governing Board, on which each country is represented, determines the policy priorities for PISA, in the context of OECD objectives, and oversees adherence to these priorities during the implementation of the programme. This includes setting priorities for the development of indicators, for establishing the assessment instruments, and for reporting the results.

Experts from participating countries also serve on working groups that are charged with linking policy objectives with the best internationally available technical expertise. By participating in these expert groups, countries ensure that the instruments are internationally valid and take into account the cultural and educational contexts in OECD member and partner countries and economies, that the assessment materials have strong measurement properties, and that the instruments place emphasise authenticity and educational validity.

Through National Project Managers, participating countries and economies implement PISA at the national level subject to the agreed administration procedures. National Project Managers play a vital role in ensuring that the implementation of the survey is of high quality, and verify and evaluate the survey results, analyses, reports and publications.

The design and implementation of the surveys, within the framework established by the PISA Governing Board, is the responsibility of external contractors. For PISA 2012, the development and implementation of the cognitive assessment and questionnaires, and of the international options, was carried out by a consortium led by the Australian Council for Educational Research (ACER). Other partners in this Consortium include cApStAn Linguistic Quality Control in Belgium, the Centre de Recherche Public Henri Tudor (CRP-HT) in Luxembourg, the Department of Teacher Education and School Research (ILS) at the University of Oslo in Norway, the Deutsches Institut für Internationale Pädagogische Forschung (DIPF) in Germany, the Educational Testing Service (ETS) in the United States, the Leibniz Institute for Science and Mathematics Education (IPN) in Germany, the National Institute for Educational Policy Research in Japan (NIER), the Unité d'analyse des systèmes et des pratiques d'enseignement (aSPe) at the University of Liège in Belgium, and WESTAT in the United States, as well as individual consultants from several countries. ACER also collaborated with Achieve, Inc. in the United States to develop the mathematics framework for PISA 2012.

The OECD Secretariat has overall managerial responsibility for the programme, monitors its implementation daily, acts as the secretariat for the PISA Governing Board, builds consensus among countries and serves as the interlocutor between the PISA Governing Board and the international Consortium charged with implementing the activities. The OECD Secretariat also produces the indicators and analyses and prepares the international reports and publications in co-operation with the PISA Consortium and in close consultation with member and partner countries and economies both at the policy level (PISA Governing Board) and at the level of implementation (National Project Managers).

PISA Governing Board

Chair of the PISA Governing Board: Lorna Bertrand

OECD countries

Australia: Tony Zanderigo

Austria: Mark Német

Belgium: Christiane Blondin and Isabelle Erauw

Canada: Pierre Brochu, Patrick Bussiere and Tomasz Gluszynski

Chile: Leonor Cariola Huerta

Czech Republic: Jana Paleckova

Denmark: Tine Bak and Elsebeth Aller

Estonia: Maie Kitsing

Finland: Tommi Karjalainen

France: Bruno Trosseille

Germany: Elfriede Ohrnberger and Susanne von Below

Greece: Vassilia Hatzinikita and Chryssa Sofianopoulou

Hungary: Benõ Csapó

Iceland: Júlíus Björnsson

Ireland: Jude Cosgrove and Gerry Shiel

Israel: Michal Beller and Hagit Glickman

Italy: Paolo Sestito

Japan: Ryo Watanabe

Korea: Sungsook Kim and Keunwoo Lee

Luxembourg: Amina Kafai

Mexico: Francisco Ciscomani and Eduardo Backhoff Escudero

Netherlands: Paul van Oijen

New Zealand: Lynne Whitney

Norway : Anne-Berit Kavli and Alette Schreiner

Poland: Stanislaw Drzazdzewski and Hania Bouacid

Portugal: Luisa Canto and Castro Loura

Slovak Republic: Romana Kanovska and Paulina Korsnakova

Slovenia: Andreja Barle Lakota

Spain: Ismael Sanz Labrador

Sweden: Anita Wester

Switzerland: Vera Husfeldt and Claudia Zahner Rossier

Turkey: Nurcan Devici and Mustafa Nadir Çalis

United Kingdom: Lorna Bertrand and Jonathan Wright

United States: Jack Buckley, Dana Kelly and Daniel McGrath

Observers

Albania: Ermal Elezi

Argentina: Liliana Pascual

Brazil: Luiz Claudio Costa

Bulgaria: Neda Kristanova

Chinese Taipei: Gwo-Dong Chen and Chih-Wei Hue

Colombia: Adriana Molina

Costa Rica: Leonardo Garnier Rimolo

Croatia: Michelle Bras Roth

Hong Kong-China: Esther Sui-chu Ho

Indonesia: Khairil Anwar Notodiputro

Jordan: Khattab Mohammad Abulibdeh

Kazakhstan: Almagul Kultumanova

Latvia: Andris Kangro, Ennata Kivrina and Dita Traidas

Lithuania: Rita Dukynaite

Macao-China: Leong Lai

Montenegro: Zeljko Jacimovic

Panama: Arturo Rivera

Peru: Liliana Miranda Molina

Qatar: Hamda Al Sulaiti

Romania: Roxana Mihail

Russian Federation: Isak Froumin and Galina Kovaleva

Serbia: Dragica Pavlovic-Babic

Shanghai-China: Minxuan Zhang

Singapore: Khah Gek Low

Thailand: Precharn Dechsri

United Arab Emirates: Moza al Ghufly and Ayesha G. Khalfan Almerri

Uruguay: Andrés Peri and Maria Helvecia Sanchez Nunez

Viet Nam: Le Thi My Ha

PISA 2012 National Project Managers

Albania: Alfonso Harizaj

Argentina: Liliana Pascual

Australia: Sue Thomson

Austria: Ursula Schwantner

Belgium: Inge De Meyer and Ariane Baye

Brazil: João Galvão Bacchetto

Bulgaria: Svetla Petrova

Canada: Pierre Brochu and Tamara Knighton

Chile: Ema Lagos Campos

Colombia: Francisco Reyes

Costa Rica: Lilliam Mora

Croatia: Michelle Bras Roth

Czech Republic: Jana Paleckova

Denmark: Niels Egelund

Estonia: Gunda Tire

Finland: Jouni Välijärvi

France: Ginette Bourny

Germany: Christine Sälzer and Manfred Prenzel

Greece: Vassilia Hatzinikita

Hong Kong-China: Esther Sui-chu Ho

Hungary: Ildikó Balazsi

Iceland: Almar Midvik Halldorsson

Indonesia: Yulia Wardhani Nugaan and Hari Setiadi

Ireland: Gerry Shiel and Rachel Perkins

Israel: Joel Rapp and Inbal Ron-Kaplan

Italy: Carlo Di Chiacchio

Japan: Ryo Watanabe

Jordan: Khattab Mohammad Abulibdeh

Kazakhstan: Gulmira Berdibayeva and Zhannur Azmagambetova

Korea: Ji-Min Cho and Mi-Young Song

Latvia: Andris Kangro

Liechtenstein: Christian Nidegger

Lithuania: Mindaugas Stundza

Luxembourg: Bettina Boehm

Macao-China: Kwok Cheung Cheung

Malaysia: Ihsan Ismail and Muhamad Zaini Md Zain

Mexico: María Antonieta Díaz Gutierrez

Montenegro: Divna Paljevic Sturm

Netherlands: Jesse Koops

New Zealand: Kate Lang and Steven May

Norway: Marit Kjaernsli

Peru: Liliana Miranda Molina

Poland: Michal Federowicz

Portugal: Ana Sousa Ferreira

Qatar: Aysha Al-Hashemi and Assad Tounakti

Romania: Silviu Cristian Mirescu

Russian Federation: Galina Kovaleva

Scotland: Rebecca Wheater

Serbia: Dragica Pavlovic-Babic

Shanghai-China: Jing Lu and Minxuan Zhang

Singapore: Chew Leng Poon and Sean Tan

Slovak Republic: Julia Miklovicova and Jana Ferencova

Slovenia: Mojca Straus

Spain: Lis Cercadillo Pérez

Sweden: Magnus Oskarsson

Switzerland: Christian Nidegger

Chinese Taipei: Pi-Hsia Hung

Thailand: Sunee Klainin

Tunisia: Mohamed Kamel Essid

Turkey: Serdar Aztekin

United Arab Emirates: Moza al Ghufly

United Kingdom: Rebecca Wheater

United States: Dana Kelly and Holly Xie

Uruguay: Maria Helvecia Sánchez Nunez

Viet Nam: Thi My Ha Le

OECD Secretariat

Andreas Schleicher (Strategic development)

Marilyn Achiron (Editorial support)

Francesco Avvisati (Analytic services)

Brigitte Beyeler (Administrative support)

Simone Bloem (Analytic services)

Marika Boiron (Translation support)

Francesca Borgonovi (Analytic services)

Jenny Bradshaw (Project management)

Célia Braga-Schich (Production support)

Claire Chetcuti (Administrative support)

Michael Davidson (Project management and analytic services)

Cassandra Davis (Dissemination co-ordination)

Elizabeth Del Bourgo (Production support)

Juliet Evans (Administration and partner country/economy relations)

Tue Halgreen (Project management)

Miyako Ikeda (Analytic services)

Tadakazu Miki (Analytic services)

Guillermo Montt (Analytic services)

Giannina Rech (Analytic services)

Diana Tramontano (Administration)

Sophie Vayssettes (Analytic services)

Elisabeth Villoutreix (Production co-ordination)

Pablo Zoido (Analytic services)

PISA 2012 mathematics expert group

Kaye Stacey (Chair) (University of Melbourne, Australia)

Caroline Bardini (University of Melbourne, Australia)

Werner Blum (University of Kassel, Germany)

Joan Ferrini-Mundy (Michigan State University, United States)

Solomon Garfunkel (COMAP, United States)

Toshikazu Ikeda (Yokohama National University, Japan)

Zbigniew Marciniak (Warsaw University, Poland)

Mogens Niss (Roskilde University, Denmark)

Martin Ripley (World Class Arena Limited, United Kingdom)

William Schmidt (Michigan State University, United States)

PISA 2012 problem solving expert group

Joachim Funke (Chair) (University of Heidelberg, Germany)

Benő Csapó (University of Szeged, Hungary)

John Dossey (Illinois State University, United States)

Arthur Graesser (The University of Memphis United States)

Detlev Leutner (Duisburg-Essen University, Germany)

Romain Martin (Université de Luxembourg FLSHASE, Luxembourg)

Richard Mayer (University of California, United States)

Ming Ming Tan (Ministry of Education, Singapore)

PISA 2012 financial literacy expert group

Annamaria Lusardi (Chair) (The George Washington University School of Business, United States)

Jean-Pierre Boisivon (Université de Paris II Panthéon-Assas, France)

Diana Crossan (Commission for Financial Literacy and Retirement Income, New Zealand)

Peter Cuzner (Australian Securities and Investments Commission, Australia)

Jeanne Hogarth (Federal Reserve System, United States)

Dušan Hradil (Ministry of Finance, Czech Republic)

Stan Jones (Consultant, Canada)

Sue Lewis (Consultant, United Kingdom)

PISA 2012 questionnaire expert group

Eckhard Klieme (Chair) (Deutsches Institut für Internationale Pädagogische Forschung (DIPF), Germany)

Eduardo Backhoff (University of Baja California at the Institute of Educational Research and Development, Mexico)

Ying-yi Hong (Nanyang Business School of Nanyang Technological University, Singapore)

David Kaplan (University of Wisconsin – Madison, United States)

Henry Levin (Columbia University, United States)

Jaap Scheerens (University of Twente, Netherlands)

William Schmidt (Michigan State University, United States)

Fons van de Vijver (Tilburg University, Netherlands)

Technical advisory group

Keith Rust (Chair) (Westat, United States)

Ray Adams (ACER, Australia)

Cees Glas (University of Twente, Netherlands)

John de Jong (Language Testing Services, Netherlands)

David Kaplan (University of Wisconsin – Madison, United States)

Christian Monseur (University of Liège, Belgium)

Sophia Rabe-Hesketh (University of California – Berkeley, United States)

Thierry Rocher (Ministry of Education, France)

Norman Verhelst (CITO, Netherlands)

Kentaro Yamamoto (ETS, United States)

Rebecca Zwick (University of California, United States)

PISA 2012 Consortium

Australian Council for Educational Research

Ray Adams (International Project Director)

Susan Bates (Project administration)

Alla Berezner (Data management and analysis)

Yan Bibby (Data processing and analysis)

Phillipe Bickham (IT services)

Esther Brakey (Administrative support)

Robin Buckley (IT services)

Mark Butler (Financial literacy instruments and test development)

Wei Buttress (Project administration and quality monitoring)

Renee Chow (Data processing and analysis)

John Cresswell (Reporting and dissemination)

Alex Daraganov (Data processing and analysis)

Jorge Fallas (Data processing and analysis)

Kate Fitzgerald (Data processing and sampling)

Kim Fitzgerald (IT Services)

Paul Golden (IT and helpdesk support)

Jennifer Hong (Data processing and sampling)

Nora Kovarcikova (Survey operations)

Winson Lam (IT services)

Petra Lietz (Questionnaire development)

Tom Lumley (Reading instruments and test development)

Greg Macaskill (Data management and processing and sampling)

Ron Martin (Science instruments and test development)

Barry McCrae (Problem solving and science instruments and test development)

Louise McDonald (Graphic design)

Juliette Mendelovits (Reading and financial literacy instruments and test development)

Martin Murphy (Field operations and sampling)

Thoa Nguyen (Data processing and analysis)

Stephen Oakes (IT management and support)

Elizabeth O'Grady (Questionnaire development and project support)

Penny Pearson (Administrative support)

Ray Peck (Mathematics and financial literacy instruments and test development)

Fei Peng (Quality monitoring and project support)

Ray Philpot (Problem Solving instruments and test development)

Anna Plotka (Graphic design)

Dara Ramalingam (Reading instruments and test development)

Sima Rodrigues (Data processing and analysis)

Alla Routitsky (Data management and processing)

James Spithill (Mathematics instruments and test development)

Rachel Stanyon (Project support)

Naoko Tabata (Survey operations)

Stephanie Templeton (Project administration and support)

Mollie Tobin (Questionnaire development and project support)

David Tout (Mathematics instruments and test development)

Ross Turner (Management, mathematics instruments and test development)

Maryanne Van Grunsven (Project support)

Charlotte Waters (Project administration, data processing and analysis)

Maurice Walker (Management, computer-based assessment)

Louise Wenn (Data processing and analysis)

Yan Wiwecka (IT services)

cApStAn Linguistic Quality Control (BELGIUM)

Raphael Choppinet (Computer-based verification management)

Steve Dept (Translation and verification operations)

Andrea Ferrari (Linguistic quality assurance and quality control designs)

Musab Hayatli (Right-to-left scripts, cultural adaptations)

Elica Krajceva (Questionnaire verification co-ordinator)

Shinoh Lee (Cognitive test verification co-ordinator)

Irene Liberati (Manuals verification co-ordinator)

Laura Wayrynen (Verifier training and verification procedures)

Educational Testing Service (ETS)

Jonas Bertling (Questionnaire instruments and test development)

Irwin Kirsch (Reading Components)

Patricia Klag (Problem-solving instruments and test development)

Patrick Kyllonen (Questionnaire instruments and test development)

Marylou Lennon (Questionnaire instruments and test development)

Richard Roberts (Questionnaire instruments and test development)

Matthias von Davier (Questionnaire instruments and test development)

Kentaro Yamamoto (Member TAG, problem-solving instruments and test development)

Deutches Institut für Internationale Pädagogische Forschung (DIPF, GERMANY)

Frank Goldhammer (Test developer, problem solving)

Eckhard Klieme (Chair of Questionnaire Expert Group)

Silke Hertel (Questionnaire development)

Jean-Paul Reeff (International Consultant)

Heiko Rolke (Software Design & Software Development Management [Delivery System, Translation System])

Brigitte Steinert (Questionnaire development)

Svenja Vieluf (Questionnaire development)

Institutt for Lærerutdanning Og Skoleutvikling (ILS, NORWAY)

Bjornar Alseth (Mathematics instruments and test development)

Ole Kristian Bergem (Mathematics instruments and test development)

Knut Skrindo (Mathematics instruments and test development)

Rolf V. Olsen (Mathematics instruments and test development)

Arne Hole (Mathematics instruments and test development)

Therese Hopfenbeck (Problem-solving instruments and test development)

Leibniz Institute for Science and Mathematics Education (IPN, GERMANY)

Christoph Duchhardt (Mathematics instruments and test development)

Aiso Heinze (Mathematics instruments and test development)

Eva Knopp (Mathematics instruments and test development)

Martin Senkbeil (Mathematics instruments and test development)

National Institute for Educational Policy Research (NIER, JAPAN)

Keiichi Nishimura (Mathematics instruments and test development)

Yuji Surata (Mathematics instruments and test development)

The TAO Initiative: Henry Tudor Public Research Centre, University of Luxembourg (LUXEMBOURG)

Joel Billard (Software Engineer, School Questionnaire)

Marilyn Binkley (Project Consultant, Assessment Expert)

Jerome Bogaerts (Software Engineer, TAO Platform)

Gilbert Busana (Electronic Instruments, Usability)

Christophe Henry (System Engineer, School Questionnaire and Hosting)

Raynald Jadoul (Technical Lead, School Questionnaire and Electronic Instruments)

Isabelle Jars (Project Manager)

Vincent Koenig (Electronic Instruments, Usability)

Thibaud Latour (Project Leader, TAO Platform)

Lionel Lecaque (Software Engineer, Quality)

Primael Lorbat (Software Engineer, Electronic Instruments)

Romain Martin (Problem Solving Expert Group Member)

Matteo Melis (Software Engineer, School Questionnaire)

Patrick Plichart (Software Architect, TAO Platform)

Vincent Porro (Software Engineer, Electronic Instruments)

Igor Ribassin (Software Engineer, Electronic Instruments)

Somsack Sipasseuth (Software Engineer, Electronic Instruments)

Unité d'analyse des Systèmes et des Pratiques d'enseignement (ASPE, BELGIUM)

Isabelle Demonty (Mathematics instruments and test development)

Annick Fagnant (Mathematics instruments and test development)

Anne Matoul (French source development)

Christian Monseur (Member of Technical Advisory Group)

WESTAT

Susan Fuss (Sampling and weighting)

Amita Gopinath (Weighting)

Jing Kang (Sampling and weighting)

Sheila Krawchuk (Sampling, weighting and quality monitoring)

Thanh Le (Sampling, weighting and quality monitoring)

John Lopdell (Sampling and weighting)

Keith Rust (Director of the PISA Consortium for sampling and weighting)

Erin Willey (Sampling and weighting)

Shawn Lu (Weighting)

Teresa Strickler (Weighting)

Yumiko Sugawara (Weighting)

Joel Wakesberg (Sampling and weighting)

Sergey Yagodin (Weighting)

Achieve Inc.

Michael Cohen (Mathematics framework development)

Kaye Forgione (Mathematics framework development)

Morgan Saxby (Mathematics framework development)

Laura Slover (Mathematics framework development)

Bonnie Verrico (Project support)

HallStat SPRL

Beatrice Halleux (Consultant, translation/verification referee, French source development)

University of Heidelberg

Joachim Funke (Chair, Problem Solving Expert Group)

Samuel Greiff (Problem-solving instruments and test development)

University of Melbourne

Caroline Bardini (Member Mathematics Expert Group)

John Dowsey (Mathematics instruments and test development)

Derek Holton (Mathematics instruments and test development)

Kaye Stacey (Chair Mathematics Expert Group)

Other experts

Michael Besser (Mathematics instruments and test development, University of Kassel, Germany)

Khurrem Jehangir (Data analysis for TAG, University of Twente, Netherlands)

Kees Lagerwaard (Mathematics instruments and test development, Institute for Educational Measurement of Netherlands, Netherlands)

Dominik Leiss (Mathematics instruments and test development, University of Kassel, Germany)

Anne-Laure Monnier (Consultant French source development, France)

Hanako Senuma (Mathematics instruments and test development, Tamagawa University, Japan)

Publication layout

Fung Kwan Tam

ORGANISATION FOR ECONOMIC CO-OPERATION AND DEVELOPMENT

The OECD is a unique forum where governments work together to address the economic, social and environmental challenges of globalisation. The OECD is also at the forefront of efforts to understand and to help governments respond to new developments and concerns, such as corporate governance, the information economy and the challenges of an ageing population. The Organisation provides a setting where governments can compare policy experiences, seek answers to common problems, identify good practice and work to co-ordinate domestic and international policies.

The OECD member countries are: Australia, Austria, Belgium, Canada, Chile, the Czech Republic, Denmark, Estonia, Finland, France, Germany, Greece, Hungary, Iceland, Ireland, Israel, Italy, Japan, Korea, Luxembourg, Mexico, the Netherlands, New Zealand, Norway, Poland, Portugal, the Slovak Republic, Slovenia, Spain, Sweden, Switzerland, Turkey, the United Kingdom and the United States. The European Union takes part in the work of the OECD.

OECD Publishing disseminates widely the results of the Organisation's statistics gathering and research on economic, social and environmental issues, as well as the conventions, guidelines and standards agreed by its members.

OECD PUBLISHING, 2, rue André-Pascal, 75775 PARIS CEDEX 16
(98 2014 01 1P) ISBN 978-92-64 20806-3 – 2014-04